*Harold K. Faye*

# PRESIDENTIAL TRAVELS
## in the NORTH, 1789 and 1790

- - - - *Washington's Inaugural Journey, 1789*

———— *Washington's New England Tour, 1790*

· · · · · · *Washington's Visit to Rhode Island, 1790*

Statute Miles

0 10    50    100    150

DELAWARE

Wilmington
New Castle

MARYLAND

Hagerstown
Frederick
Harpers Ferry
Havre de Grace
Baltimore
Annapolis
Alexandria
Mount Vernon

*Potomac*
*Shenandoah River*

Chesapeake Bay

*Potomac River*

VIRGINIA

Richmond
*James River*
Petersburg

NORTH CAROLINA

# GEORGE WASHINGTON

A GREAT MAN'S LIKENESS CREATED BY ANOTHER GREAT MAN

Not only the finest marble, but also the finest sculptor was approved by Congress for fashioning a statue of George Washington. In October 1785, Jean Antoine Houdon came to America to model and to measure his renowned subject from life. Both men were immortalized by the magnificent statue that resulted to grace the Virginia State Capitol. This clay bust, the sculptor's original work, has remained at Mount Vernon through the years as its most cherished treasure.

# GEORGE
# WASHINGTON

## *A BIOGRAPHY*

By

Douglas Southall Freeman

VOLUME SIX

PATRIOT AND PRESIDENT

*With a Foreword*
BY
DUMAS MALONE

*NEW YORK*
CHARLES SCRIBNER'S SONS

Library of Congress Catalogue No. 48-8880

# CONTENTS

## APPENDICES

# ILLUSTRATIONS

## MAPS

# THE PEN
## OF DOUGLAS SOUTHALL FREEMAN

*by* DUMAS MALONE

# THE PEN OF DOUGLAS SOUTHALL FREEMAN

## By Dumas Malone

WHEN DEATH came to Douglas Southall Freeman in Richmond on the thirteenth day of June, 1953, he was sixty-seven years old. He delivered his regular radio broadcast on the morning of the day he died, speaking like a father to his fellow Virginians in his familiar drawl, and, almost at the end, he finished the last chapter in this volume. Lying on his desk in his third-floor study at "Westbourne" was a framed quotation from Tennyson's "Ulysses" which included these words:

> Something ere the end,
> Some work of noble note may yet be done,
> Not unbecoming men that strove with gods.

This quiet man, whose tireless pen had traced the marches and described the battles of so many great Captains, did not have quite time enough to finish his own last work of noble note. He lacked several months of living as long as George Washington did, and his own labors ended before he could carry that hero through his second term as President and bring him home to Mount Vernon for the rest and peace he so richly deserved and had so vainly sought. Douglas Freeman himself had long ago found the peace of an ordered life, but rest was the last thing on earth he wanted. Almost certainly he would have finished another and final volume and attained another major goal had he been permitted to fill out the biblical span of three-score years and ten. To his friends it is an even more important consideration that he would have been deeply happy in these continued labors.

Yet, if we disregard the mere tale of years and apply the measure of labor and achievement, he had lived several lives already. He himself gave no sign of a split personality, but for purposes of description we will say that he lived at least two lives—as an editor and as a historian. Either one of these would have been far too full for most mortals, but this incredibly effective man serenely proceeded from task to task with unhurried step. No one can fully explain how he did all that he did, for inner springs of power are invisible to the observer, but unquestionably he pursued clear-purposed goals through the tangles and perplexities of daily existence, and by mastering himself made himself the master of his destiny. He revealed a quality that he assigned to young George Washington: "the quenchless ambition of an ordered mind." Also, he was a living illustration of certain truths that Thomas Jefferson proclaimed to his young daughter: "No person will have occasion to complain of the want of time who never loses any," said that incessantly active Virginian. "It is wonderful how much may be done if we are always doing."

The major clue to his extraordinary accomplishments must be sought in the man himself, not in environmental influences that he shared with others; but his remarkable career cannot be understood or even viewed outside of its distinctive setting. Theodore Roosevelt in his AUTOBIOGRAPHY quoted a bit of homely exhortation from a rural Virginian which is pertinent in this connection, for Lee's biographer found the same philosophy in the General and was himself an exemplar of it: "Do what you can, with what you've got, where you are." Douglas Freeman liked to speak of himself as a "tramp newspaperman," but actually his career as an editor was wholly confined to Richmond. He was never a foreign correspondent, and only as a lecturer or consultant did he ply the journalistic trade in other cities. No one would think of describing this author of vast military volumes as provincial, but the fact is that he dealt first and primarily with the great chieftains of his own State. He stayed where he was and started with what was there. This exhaustive investigator eventually sought materials from everywhere, but, because of the physical necessities of his professional life, he had these materials brought to him as a rule—in books and photostats and microfilm—and he surveyed them in his own study. Long before his career ended he was traveling many thousands of miles every year, but there never was a time when his life did not center in Richmond, and neither in spirit nor manner did he ever cease to be a Virginian.

Virginians are not all alike, to be sure, and some of them did not lay the emphasis on the same things that he did. He did not romanticize the past and the first families. Once in private conversation I remarked to him that he was the most efficient Virginian since Jefferson—a charge that he smilingly denied. I still regard this particular parallel as close, but I doubt if this Richmonder got his major inspiration from Jefferson, even in matters of industry and order. If he consciously modeled himself on anyone it was on Robert E. Lee, whose statue he saluted every day as he drove to and from his office. Also, by right of his own surpassing knowledge, this man of the pen who never drew sword became the literary embodiment of the historic tradition which Lee personified and which George Washington had symbolized before him.

## I

Douglas Freeman was born in Lynchburg, but his family moved to Richmond when he was only a little boy, and he grew up in the former seat of the Confederacy. In stories he often referred to the "Jeems" River, which flowed by both these small cities. Even Richmond was small in his boyhood, and his own talk always retained the flavor and humor of the countryside. His father, Walker B. Freeman, was a Confederate veteran who had served in the ranks throughout the War and was at Appomattox at the surrender. In later years he was known as "General" Freeman but he gained this title as an officer of the United Confederate Veterans, not as an officer in Lee's army. In Virginia very little notice seems to have been taken of the fact that the "General" came of *Mayflower* stock, and it made little difference in those days that he was not conspicuously prosperous in his insurance business. Hardly anybody in that locality at that time was prosperous in any business. It was more significant in his son's life that he came of a long line of devout Baptists. Douglas Freeman was a deeply religious man, and in his youth he gave serious thought to becoming a minister. It was highly significant, also, that the boy heard stories of the Army of Northern Virginia at his father's knee. He himself attended Confederate reunions, where he saw gnarled and wounded men, and from an early age he cherished the ambition to tell their full story. He was born and bred a Confederate, though there is no sign that he was ever a bitter one.

In the old Confederate capital above the James the boy received all of his formal education through the college stage. He attended the University of Richmond, a Baptist institution, and was always loyal to it, serving it afterwards for many years as head of the Board of

Trustees. At all stages he was a good student and his interest in history may almost be described as innate, but this was quickened by Professor Samuel Chiles Mitchell, an inspiring teacher, who encouraged him to pursue the subject further. While an undergraduate he began to be a newspaper correspondent, besides contributing to the college literary magazine, and once having got printer's ink into his veins he never could get it out. For the moment, however, history had the priority. He gained a fellowship at the Johns Hopkins University, where he studied history and economics, and at the unusually early age of twenty-two received the Ph.D. degree. Throughout the rest of his life the title "Doctor" was fastened on him. Incidentally, he picked up a good deal of medical knowledge in Baltimore—from medical students he associated with and from his elder brother, Allen, who became a doctor in the more usual meaning of the term. The only copy of the young graduate student's dissertation—on the Virginia Secession Convention—was destroyed by fire before ever it was published, but his CALENDAR OF CONFEDERATE STATE PAPERS appeared in the same year (1908) that he took his degree.

Leaving Baltimore, where the atmosphere may have seemed Southern but was not quite Confederate, he returned to Richmond. There, before embarking irrevocably upon a newspaper career, he served as secretary of the Tax Commission of the state and drafted its report. For a time he was on the staff of the *Times Dispatch,* but his enduring connection was with the afternoon paper, the *News Leader.* This began when he was twenty-five. At the age of twenty-nine (1915) he became the editor, and he held this post until he was sixty-three. It was also when he was twenty-nine that his edition of LEE's DISPATCHES appeared in print and that he signed a contract for a biography of the great Captain, but nearly a score of years were to pass before he could publish that.

Of Dr. Freeman's journalistic career I can speak with no special competence and I make no pretense of describing it with any adequacy. Being the editor of a paper with a small staff was no sinecure. One of his associates on the *News Leader* estimated at the time of his death that during his service of more than a third of a century he wrote at least 600,000 words every year—that is, the equivalent of about three books the size of this one and perhaps a hundred altogether. Yet his associates remembered him as one who always emphasized the virtue of brevity in a newspaperman. With this went an emphasis on restraint. "Don't gush, and don't twitter," he told his juniors. "Play it straight." In the course of his career he championed many changes which may be described as "reforms" while opposing others which he regarded as backward steps, but the predominant impression he gave was not that of a crusading editor. He was too judicious for that, and, while liberal in spirit, he could hardly have embodied the Lee tradition without being conservative in the true sense of that much abused term. He sought to safeguard old and enduring values and was wholly unsympathetic with demagoguery of any brand.

He was fully aware of the ephemeral nature of his own writing for a newspaper—"writing in sand" he called it—and as an editor he was relatively a local figure. During the first World War he won his spurs as a daily commentator on military events. He himself never served in the armed forces, since he was incapacitated by hernia, but long before he achieved national fame he was recognized in Virginia and the South as an authority on military matters and on the Confederacy. Some wag remarked that the Confederate flag might as well be flown from the masthead of the *News Leader,* and during the second World War he vivified his comments on terrain and movements by drawing analogies from the Virginia scene and Lee's battles.

Most of the stories about him as a newspaperman that are still current relate to his later years, when he had become a legend. He worked behind an uncluttered desk and under a sign which read: "Time alone is irreplaceable . . . Waste it not." He answered his letters immediately, wasting no words in his replies, but during his office hours he gave his visitors no impression of being hurried. His junior colleagues spoke of his daily editorial conferences as "pow-wows" and described themselves as "carrying wampum to the great white father." No pipe of peace was circulated, however; nobody smoked at these conferences because he did not, and in his presence everybody guarded himself against profanity, which he did not use because of his respect for the English language. Perhaps the publisher, John Stewart Bryan, sometimes called him "Douglas" in private but he did not do so in public; and Dr. Freeman never called his long-time friend anything but "Mr. Bryan." Both of them antedated the first-name era, and were heirs of a tradition of politeness which avoided excess of familiarity. Like Mr. Bryan, however, Dr. Freeman was characteristically genial; he told a good story, and there was plenty of laughter at his staff conferences.

No small part of his local and regional reputation before the appearance of his great historical works was owing to his frequent appearances as a speaker. Besides considering the ministry as a calling, he had flirted in his youth with the idea of becoming an actor, and he soon made himself at home on the public platform. In later years he often described speaking as a waste of time, but until the end of his days he engaged in it, and it might almost be described as his third life and third career.

The first time I ever saw the versatile and indefatigable young editor was when he was making a speech. It was at a convocation at the University of Virginia, whither I recently had come to teach American history, and as I remember, he delivered a challenging and inspirational address, such as everybody expected. He was about thirty-seven at the time, and stories were current about the incredible number and variety of things he did. Obviously he was a well-informed, a high-minded and a public-spirited man—just the sort of person one would turn to for a challenging speech in behalf of a good cause, such as the advancement of Southern education. But I wondered at the time if he were not spending himself too freely, if he were not scattering his fire too widely; and no external observer could have anticipated at this stage that, while still performing his manifold editorial tasks and making his innumerable public appearances, he would gain enduring fame as a writer of history. Nor could one who listened to his spoken words have anticipated the quality of his formal writings. Rarely did he write out his speeches and rarely did they represent him at his best; he simply took them in his stride. He had to take an enormous number of them before he was through: in the year 1937, when he seems to have been at the peak, he spoke eighty-three times to various audiences, besides delivering ninety lectures on journalism in Columbia University.

Long before then his radio talks had made his name a household word in the Old Dominion. Beginning in 1925 he was a daily commentator, and on Sunday he delivered what amounted to a lay sermon. I speak of these programs chiefly from hearsay, for I had no radio during the years that I was a resident of his State and I never had much chance to hear them. Those that I did hear were just what I had expected from the common account of them. His radio performances were highly distinctive, if not unique. He made no special preparation for them, except such as he had already made in going over the news of the day and writing his editorials, and he spoke from the briefest of notes. On a local station, without a nation-wide hookup, he talked to his fellow Virginians, and he was just as relaxed as he was in his weekly current-events class or in his office at the *News Leader*. This was homely fare every day, and on Sundays it was inspirational. Everybody knew who Dr. Freeman was. Even before his great books came out he was the local authority on the Confederacy, on Richmond's past and present, and on everything military; and until the end he was to his own people a combination of lay pastor and family physician.

## II

The local celebrity became a national literary figure and gained a sure place in American historiography with the publication of R. E. LEE in 1934–1935, when he was forty-eight. The one-volume work he had contracted for in 1915 had grown to four large volumes, and the calendar showed that it had been a score of years in preparation. To those who were unfamiliar with the slow processes of research and writing this seemed a long time, no doubt, but to the initiated who were also aware of this author's other tasks it was a notable performance by any reckoning. Probably it would have been impossible if he had not firmly regularized his own procedure and advanced with steady and unflagging step toward the distant goal of his high ambition.

It was in 1926, when he was forty, that he began to follow his now-famous schedule. It is now impossible to believe that he was ever unsystematic; and while soaking up Confederate lore as a young editor he must have done a vast amount of work on the life and campaigns of the great Confederate chieftain. But as his original plan expanded and his canvas lengthened, he became convinced that he must make a second vocation out of the historical research and writing which was his first love anyway. This necessitated a careful apportionment of his precious hours, and as rigid an observance of his historical as of his editorial schedule. At first he set himself a program of fourteen hours a week, and to make sure that he would attain it he began to keep books on himself. He did more than maintain a balance. He amassed credits—"s.c.o." or "special carry over" of hours he called them—and he made up for lost time before he lost it. From the day in 1926 when he began to keep these records until December 10, 1933, when he finished R. E. LEE, he spent 6100 hours on that work.

This impressive total could not have been attained in that period unless he had exceeded his original weekly allowance. This grew from fourteen hours to twenty-four, and his working day was lengthened by making it start sooner. Sometimes his doctor intervened—he was dangerously ill in 1929—but as a rule his day dawned at 2:30. He always regarded these undisturbed morning hours, when the world was still asleep, as the best ones, but actually he did his newspaper work first. Through with that, by the time that most people are only at the halfway point, he went home for luncheon, rested briefly, worked in the garden for a bit, and then turned to history in the afternoon—as he always did on Sundays. He rigidly restricted his social engagements, and in the evening, after listening to some music, he retired very early. He gave no impression of being hurried and he made light of the rigors of his schedule, but he was doing more than time and a half by ordinary human standards and was wasting no moment of it.

Eventually the story of his working habits became widely known and helped make him a legendary character on the national as well as the local scene, but when his first major work was published reviewers and readers judged him by results without much knowledge of processes. I shall never forget the impression his R. E. LEE made on me at the very first reading. By that time, although I had no such acquaintance with the man as I gained later, I had first-hand knowledge of his scholarship, for I had seen the articles on Lee, Stonewall Jackson, and others that he had prepared for the DICTIONARY OF AMERICAN BIOGRAPHY. He afterwards told me that he found the writing of these sketches, under sharp restrictions of space, a cruel task. These were miniatures, and to paint them he had to turn aside from the vast canvas on which he was then working and to which he had become accustomed. But they left no doubt of his historical craftsmanship and his skill in portraiture, whatever the scale might be, and I awaited with confidence the appearance of his long-heralded life of

Lee. Great as my personal expectations were, the realization far surpassed them, and never did I devour a major historical work with such insatiable appetite and more unalloyed satisfaction. The book reached the full stature of the man, in my opinion, and to say this was praise enough for Douglas Southall Freeman, who had so often saluted the greatest of Southern soldiers and so long lived in spiritual companionship with that supremely great gentleman.

Having grown up in the shadow of the Lost Cause, I could not wholly divest myself of sentiment when I read this book, and, besides having an honored place on my shelves, it has retained a special place in my affections. For that reason I may be giving it greater relative emphasis than the author himself would like. As he perfected his craftsmanship in later years, he saw faults in his earlier work which he regretted. That often happens with good workmen, however, and if there were any accusing voices when R. E. LEE appeared these were drowned in the chorus of praise which rose spontaneously. Northern and Southern accents were undistinguishable, and the public response showed unmistakably that Lee was a national and not merely a Southern hero. He had long been that, to be sure, but to everybody it seemed fitting that he had been most fully described and most adequately portrayed by a son of the Confederacy who lived in Richmond.

This work, like all the major works of Freeman, is a blend of biography and military history, and it has the qualities of exhaustiveness and judiciousness which became his hallmark. The author himself never expected that all of his military judgments would be accepted without question, and some of them may be disputed, no doubt, after the lapse of a score of years. In the interval the style of writing about what he called the War Between the States has taken on a somewhat more Northern tinge and General Ulysses S. Grant, for one, has gained new admirers. To this Lee's biographer would raise no objection whatsoever. He would say now as he did then: "Circumstance is incommensurable: . . . why invoke comparatives?" Recognizing that Lee, like every other leader, must be judged "by what he accomplished, where he was, with what he had at his command," he indulged in no extravagant utterance and purposely avoided historical controversy. He gave the record of deeds and events with unexampled fulness and can be safely controverted only by students of comparable diligence, of whom there never can be many. Some have objected to his story on the ground that he always viewed the scene through the eyes of Lee and kept the reader at Confederate G.H.Q. That, however, was a matter of method, and a wise method it was, for this was intended as no history of the War Between the States. It is a biography of the Confederate Commander and a story of the war as he waged it. Gettysburg was a Federal victory as well as a Confederate defeat, but Freeman sought to show, in terms of military circumstances and personalities, why Lee lost it, leaving to others the task of describing it from Meade's headquarters.

As military history this story requires supplementation, and nobody realized that more than its author, but as the biography of a great soldier it approximated completeness so nearly as to be virtually unchallengeable. By comparison, other accounts of Lee—neglecting important phases of his earlier and later life, and emphasizing battles to the exclusion of problems of management and supply—seem pale and meagre. There is vast leisureliness in this narrative and at times its flow is impeded by detail which may seem unnecessary, but trivial items may assume crucial importance in battle and the texture of this tapestry is provided by its richness of detail. From this carefully wrought and slow-moving story Lee emerges in full glory. This is not to say that he was impeccable in judgment; Freeman describes his mistakes with complete candor at the times he made them and sums them up in a final critique—the chapter entitled "The Sword of Robert E. Lee." Also, he underlines the General's chief temperamental flaw, his excessive amiability at times in dealing with his commanders. But the balance is heavily on the credit side, and fresh and needed emphasis is laid on the intellectual quality of Lee's generalship. In his great ability as an administrator and his genius as a commander there was more of the infinite capacity for taking pains, more of the clear thought of an orderly and penetrating mind, than had been previously supposed. It took the orderly and penetrating mind of a Freeman to discern this.

The man who is shown is essentially the Lee of legend, far more fully pictured and far better explained. He is made more real by being made more human, but in life as in legend he was heroic—a knight *sans peur et sans reproche* and the *beau idéal* of the Christian gentleman. If there be those among us who have repudiated this ideal, or those whose vanity is flattered when human idols are shown to have feet of clay, they will find scant comfort in this book. But as most

Americans rejoiced a score of years ago they can still rejoice that the painstaking labors and fair judgment of scholarship served to provide a firm foundation for one of the noblest of our symbols. Lee may still seem almost too good to be true, but his memory inspires no jealousy— since his life was set on a background of dark tragedy, just as Lincoln's was. It seems safe to predict, therefore, that this classic portrait of him, done in the grand manner by patient and skillful hands, will be cherished as long as the ideals of the Republic shall endure.

While performing his daily task as an editor, Douglas Freeman had produced a major work which was immediately hailed as a classic, and he could have been readily forgiven if he had rested on his laurels. He had had financial success; he had more invitations to make speeches than he could possibly accept; he was serving on more and more boards—business, educational, and philanthropic; and he was drawn into constant consultation about scholarly and journalistic matters. Actually he did not enter upon another major historical undertaking for two or three years, but given the necessary health and strength, he was sure to do so, for he had not yet completed the task he set himself in his youth. This was "to preserve the record of our fathers of the Army of Northern Virginia." In a real sense his R. E. LEE told the story of that army, but in that military biography he had wisely adopted the device of viewing the field from headquarters and thus had been unable to give a full account of the actions of Lee's officers. Fearing that unwittingly he had done them an injustice, he wanted to redress the balance and fill out the story. The result was a second major work, LEE's LIEUTENANTS, which may be regarded as a supplement to its predecessor but turned out to be even more popular. On June 14, 1936, he began work on it. In his Diary that day he made this entry: "Outlined scope on train between N. Y. City and Meriden, Conn., and finished broad outline at Middletown, Conn., this A.M." Almost eight years later he completed the work, having spent on it 7121 hours. It was published in three volumes, 1942–1945.

Before finishing the first volume of LEE's LIEUTENANTS, he turned aside to do a little book which grew out of a series of lectures he delivered in 1939 at Alabama College for Women. This was THE SOUTH TO POSTERITY, and he described it in a subtitle as "An Introduction to the Writing of Confederate History." This readable volume, which he insisted was merely an introduction to a vast body of writing, has proved useful to professional historians and laymen as he hoped it would. It unmistakably reveals his understanding of his Confederate compatriots and his sympathy with them, but it shows him as no special pleader. One of his conclusions was that "Confederate history was most persuasive where authors had the least intention of making it so." Friends were not won to the Lost Cause by "mustered argument and paraded declamation" but by simple tales of actual events and experiences. It was in the spirit of truth-seeking and fair play that he wrote his own books, and that is a major reason why they gained a national and international audience.

The popularity of LEE's LIEUTENANTS was partly owing to the author's established reputation, partly to the fact that these volumes came out while the world was at war and that his findings were very pertinent. More even than R. E. LEE, this work is required reading in military circles. Freeman himself regarded it as the best of his books—chiefly because it imposed on him the most difficult problems of organization. No book plans itself, but there is a degree of simplicity in a biography, for it centers in a single figure and events can be grouped around him. In his desire to do justice to Lee's officers, Freeman began a series of sketches, but he soon saw that these would involve too much repetition in the accounts of battles. He got his clue at length from a letter of Lee to Hood (1863) in which Lee agreed that the Army would be invincible if properly organized and officered. "There never were such men in an Army before," he said. "They will go anywhere and do anything if properly led. But there is the difficulty—proper commanders—where can they be obtained?" Lee's biographer decided, therefore, to write a book about the Command of the Army, the connecting thread of which would be the effort to create and maintain proper senior officers. This is the story of a shifting group of leaders— shown in action. The point of view is not that of headquarters but of these commanders. This is again a combination of biography and military history, but it is group biography, and that is exceedingly difficult to write. The scene has to shift to bring in commander after commander, as it did from Jackson to Early to Wilcox at Chancellorsville, and the sense of unity is sometimes lost. But the plan of organization is admirable and the results received plaudits enough to satisfy anybody. Probably this is the most colorful of all Freeman's works; it has been accepted as a classic in the field of tactics; and it will long live as a penetrating study of military personalities.

## III

Two weeks after his fifty-eighth birthday, Freeman finished LEE's LIEUTENANTS, and he began outlining the first chapter of another major work six months later—on January 7, 1945, to be precise. This was his biography of George Washington, and he was engaged on it the rest of his life, spending 15,693 hours on it according to his own records. In the midst of this period of eight and a half years (June 30, 1949) he retired from the editorship of the *News Leader*. He continued his radio broadcasts and many other public activities, but more nearly than ever before he became a full-time historian. That is, he worked at history fifty-six hours a week as a rule. His labors on R. E. LEE and LEE's LIEUTENANTS were spread over a period of twenty-nine years, and he did not keep exact records during the first of these. It is impossible to make exact mathematical comparisons between the time spent on these two works and on GEORGE WASHINGTON, but, roughly speaking, the third major undertaking may be compared to the two others in bulk and in the hours directly devoted to it. Against the seven volumes of Confederate biography may be set the five volumes on Washington that he published before his death, the sixth that is published here, and the seventh that he never got to. In sum, he embarked at the age of fifty-eight on a literary and historical task which was roughly equivalent to the one he had performed already.

The question naturally arises, why did he do it? He did not then lack for useful and interesting employment. Besides doing his editorial work, he was serving on many boards; he belonged to all the major historical and literary societies, and in them could have consorted even more than he did with his brethren in letters and learning; he was traveling on the average 20,000 miles a year and could have had endless speaking engagements. He had fame enough, being now indisputably recognized as one of the first military historians of the world. Also, it might seem that he had won the right to rest, or at least to modify a schedule that most men would have found intolerable.

He made his decision after some pressure. To many it seemed desirable, even imperative, that his powers be employed in something fully worthy of them. No minor task would do; it had to be a major undertaking. Stephen Vincent Benét summed the matter up when he said that Douglas Freeman ought to be "chained to his desk" and forced to write a life of George Washington. There was logic in this, beyond a doubt. Materials on Washington that were now available had not been fully exploited; an authoritative military estimate of him was needed; and Washington was the fountainhead of the tradition which had been inherited by Lee as a man and soldier. The first great American hero clearly deserved and seemed now to require full-length treatment, and the finger of destiny pointed to America's greatest military biographer. Freeman never considered anything less than a spacious study of the whole man and his whole life. The work he planned was to be more extensive than any that had ever been written on this subject. Indeed, it had no real parallel in American biography, and in sheer bulk the task was enough to deter any but the most indefatigable workman. What was more, it fell within another century, which Dr. Freeman had never explored as a scholar and in which he had not lived in spirit—as he had lived so long in Lee's Virginia and the Southern Confederacy.

His acceptance of this challenge may be attributed, perhaps, to the "quenchless ambition of an ordered mind," which he was soon to perceive in Washington. In Freeman himself this took the form of eagerness to match his talents and skills against an immense task while there was yet time. There were grave risks but these were calculated risks, and he assumed them fully confident of his demonstrated powers and his tested methods. He viewed this gigantic undertaking with the eye of an engineer; he counted the time and concluded that he could perform it, relying on his unequalled craftsmanship. A notable aspect of his treatment of Lee was his emphasis on that General's ability in organization and administration, and this was to be even more notable in his treatment of Washington. Native ability and high character are not enough; industry and system are indispensable to those who would achieve greatly. He counted on them in his own case, and if there have been other American historians who have matched him in industry (which is doubtful), no one of them seems ever to have matched him in system.

His methods can be commented on most appropriately in connection with his last work. They developed through the years and received full systematization in the period when he had most need to realize upon them, because time was running short. It was not until after he had begun to work on Washington that I ever talked with him about the mechanics of research and writing. Like many other people, I knew a good deal about his schedule, but I did not know just how he spent his time in his third-floor study. In the late nineteen-forties he told me and showed me, the net result being that I emerged from these conversations with enhanced humility and a number of excellent ideas. It is a great pity that he did not write an article on the subject of historical method, for it could have been a classic of its kind.

His procedure was systematized to a degree that I have never seen equalled, but no one should say that he was engaged in mass production. He had more help in his last years than when doing his Confederate books, but, considering the scale of his operations, his staff was always small. In his work on Washington he had a regular research assistant who looked up things for him, going to places where he could not conveniently go, and her services were invaluable. But he never saw things through the eyes of anybody else; the fact that an abstract had been made by an assistant never relieved him of the responsibility of looking at an important document, and no scholar whom I have known was more conscientious about a personal examination of source material. He took nothing on secondary authority, and at times he carried almost to the degree of fault his independence of the conclusions of others. He mastered the facts for himself, expressed his own opinions, and wrote his books with his own pen. The last statement is literally true of his final work, for he wrote it in longhand, having concluded that his typewriter by its very speed led him down false trails that had to be retraced and into inaccuracies that had to be painfully corrected. He always remained a master craftsman and the significance of his methods lies chiefly in his skill in making himself effective without loss of motion.

Fortunately, he was in good position to get all the necessary materials that were obtainable, and his collections on the Confederacy and on the age of Washington might have been envied by any scholar and almost any library. This policy with respect to materials was partly a matter of necessity, since he had to remain at home, but he had the advantage of working from the sources themselves and not merely from notes made on them. Thus he was able to reduce note-taking to the minimum. One of the most helpful hints I got from him was not to copy long extracts out of books you have in your own library and can easily refer to; a card, giving date, reference, and some idea of contents is quite enough. He had an advantage over academic scholars in that he collected his materials for use in a particular book. There was no need for him to put something down because of the thought that some time he would use it in a classroom. The form of his notes need not concern us here except to say that he had worked everything out on the basis of experience and that he saved thousands of waste motions by maintaining uniformity and perfect order. He used cards (size 5½ x 4¼) and "long sheets" in ring binders. The former, which were strictly chronological, constituted the master file, to which the latter were a supplement. Each of the latter had a card of a distinctive color. All these were numbered before he began to write, and when he made a chapter outline he referred to them by number. Anyone who has ever tried to write a chapter from a folder of untidy notes on paper of various sizes (as is often the case with beginners and sometimes with the mature) can realize the anguish and frustration which this orderly workman saved himself by care and system. One can also see how he was able to weave into his story countless details about marches and battles, without losing any of them in the process.

His books were always in order, so he wasted no time in finding one of them; he had weights to keep books open at the proper place; he had a place to write standing if he got tired of sitting; he used specially ruled paper and could tell almost at a glance how many words were on it; he could tell what time it was from the clock in the back of his head; he could tell within a page how long a chapter would be before he had finished it, and even before he started. This last he was enabled to do because of his practice of elaborately outlining a chapter in advance, and I have found this one of the most interesting items in his procedure, though I must confess that so far as I am concerned it is quite inimitable. He was convinced that it was a great time-saver. On March 13, 1947, he made this entry in his Diary:

Finished outline of Chapter XVII (Braddock's Defeat). It took about 11 hours and will save 20 at least.

An earlier entry, breaking down into hours Chapter VIII in his first volume (Washington's mission to Fort Le Boeuf), is of even greater interest:

| | |
|---|---|
| Outline | 25:00 |
| Composition | 42:00 |
| Revision | 17:00 |
| Total | 84:00 |

This chapter came to 23,000 words and he estimated that the first writing and revision together came to an average of 325 words per hour. By my own calculation, his first writing was done at the rate of 547½, which by my standard is fast. The scheme of outlining in advance undoubtedly worked well in this instance, for this is an exceptionally good chapter. The method, it seems, is best adapted to a narrative of external events, in which hundreds of details have to be worked into a mosaic. Freeman had to write many chapters of that sort and so far as my memory goes all of them are admirable. I am not sure whether it was because of the method or the nature of the materials themselves that the results were less happy in more static and descriptive chapters, such as the very long one, "Virginia During the Youth of Washington." The author took nineteen days to outline that and unquestionably he put it in good order, but there is a certain rigidity about it, and from the literary point of view it suffers from an excess of factual detail.

By means of organization and system he saved himself hundreds of precious hours, and by rigid adherence to his exacting schedule he kept his record books in balance. In fact, he was always ahead of the game, doing more than his quota of time and accumulating credits which he could draw on when he made business or pleasure trips. He always carried his briefcase along, but he gave himself no credit for the revising or proofreading he did on trains and planes. Every large-scale enterprise of research and writing is an endurance contest, rather than a sprint, and Freeman, relying on regularity and persistence, did not let himself be hurried. He set a gruelling pace, nonetheless, and occasionally he put on a tremendous burst of speed. On one October Sunday in 1948, when the trees outdoors were golden, he wrote 4800 words, noting that this seemed to be his record. He took nearly twelve hours, however, and probably would have denied that he was sprinting. This was while he was still doing full time as an editor and he was taking advantage of the only day in the week that was wholly free. It was at the end of the following June that he retired from the *News Leader* and instituted a fifty-six-hour week in his third-floor study. During the first week of his new freedom, when he was sixty-three years old, he went beyond this and put in sixty-five hours!

A major secret of his success, unquestionably, was his ability to work effectively for a much longer stretch than is possible for most people, but not even he would have been able to maintain such a program if he had not found joy in it. Several years before this, returning to history after a round of commencement speeches, he had written in his Diary: "Rejoiced to get back to my beloved work." His entry at the end of the first week after he became a full-time historian is even more eloquent:

Life is so beautiful now I'm afraid it is a dream from which I shall be awakened by a voice that says: 'Get up and go downtown and write two columns of editorial.'

Sometimes he spoke of himself as "plugging away," but at the end of six years of work on Washington he described it as "joyous labor." It was, he said, "the most delightful intellectual experience" of his life. Before the end, however, he himself admitted that he was overdoing it. In the autumn of 1950 he wrote in his Diary: "I am working too long hours, and for the good of myself and the completion of the work at a high level, I must shorten the week so as to give me time every day for exercise . . . I must not let my interest override my discretion." The remedy, however, was not a drastic one. The new schedule, exclusive of mail and broadcast preparation, was to consist of eight hours daily and seven on music days. He was then taking music lessons twice a week, so the schedule seemed to call for fifty-four hours. He did not always take that hour of exercise in his garden, but music was a solace even during worktime: he often played records while writing. Beethoven accompanied his pen as he traced the career and assayed the personality of George Washington.

Five of the volumes of George Washington, which resulted from the unceasing but joyous labors in the study at "Westbourne," have already been extensively reviewed and the sixth soon will be. It is quite unnecessary, therefore, to review the work here, and any attempt to anticipate the consensus of historical judgment on it would be presumptuous as well as premature. Something may be said, however, about the sort of work this is, and the sum of the matter is that in view of the author's interest, training, and methods, it is just what might have been expected of him.

It is an extraordinarily full story of a man of affairs and action, set on an immediate background which is always meticulously drawn and often elaborately detailed. If Freeman did not know precisely where Washington was and what Washington was doing every day of his adult life, as he did in the case of Lee, he came as near to it as is humanly possible and he carefully reconstructed every important scene. He rode and fought alongside of Washington, maintaining an Olympian detachment all the while and afterwards summing up these actions and operations with unerring skill. Also, he viewed with penetrating eye the man's personality and character as these developed, analyzing them stage by stage as no other writer had ever done. This is biography in the grand manner which gains its texture and color from exact detail but which is unmarred by special pleading. It is as full a story of a planter's life as anybody is likely ever to write, and it is military biography *par excellence*. It is the full record of a public man, and in its portrayal of Washington's relations with the civil authorities, from Governor Dinwiddie to the Continental Congress, the author is an irreproachable narrator and commentator. Finally, it is a thoroughgoing examination and judicious appraisal of a legend.

Yet, while it is all of this, it is not everything; it is not the history of an age and, despite its extraordinary richness of detail, it requires supplementation. The author explored with zest the society of Virginia in the hero's youth and turned up and organized a mass of fresh descriptive material, but he did not write social history in the full sense. He focused attention on the immediate scene rather than the larger setting, and he did not have time to attain the degree of familiarity with the eighteenth-century world that he had gained with the times of Lee and Jackson. For all Washington's nobility of spirit and high intelligence he was not a man of thought in the sense that Franklin, Jefferson, and John Adams were, and his biographer did not venture far into the history of ideas. He did not even write political history in the usual meaning of the term. He did not essay a fresh interpretation of the causes of the American Revolution or of the movement for the Constitution, and in his account of Washington's first term he kept out of the partisan struggle, just as the President himself tried to keep above it. At this point the biographer's unwillingness to accept secondary authority and his determination to hew his own path did him some disservice. He may be criticized for his rather external treatment of Hamilton, Jefferson, and Madison—about all of whom, apparently, he was reserving judgment until he should come to the time when Washington himself was unable to remain above the combat. He stuck to Washington, saw the scene through his eyes, and raised no question which was not voiced by the President himself. In this work as a whole he did not adhere to the formula he had used in his biography of Lee, but he seems to have recurred to it at the last. The result is that his account of Washington as President is only part of the story, just as his account of the battle of Gettysburg is. He speaks with the voice of unimpeachable authority, however, when he describes the President's specific actions and movements and his assumption of his historic role as the Father of a united people.

It will appear, I think, that Douglas Southall Freeman rendered the same sort of service to his countrymen in the case of George Washington that he did in that of Lee. By the slow and painstaking processes of scholarship he examined, verified, and preserved a major legend. With a wave of the hand he dismissed the trivial and false story of the cherry tree, but he placed on a new pedestal of truth the legendary figure of a national hero whose greatness lay chiefly in his unselfish patriotism and unassailable character. The portrait is convincing because it is utterly candid, and the character assumes reality in the mind of the observer because it is shown not as something static but as something that develops. At the end of the first two volumes of this work, when the character of a bold and dashing but ambitious and calculating young man was analyzed with devastating candor, no reader could help wondering if the legend of Washington was not something of a hoax. But as the man and patriot grew before the discerning eye in the successive volumes, as his portrait was painted by a thousand deft but scrupulously honest strokes, he emerged in the lineaments that his countrymen have so long recognized and so long honored. By and large, his latest and greatest biographer enhances his military stature, showing him not as a military genius but as a great commander, within the sharp limits that were set by circumstance. What the American cause most needed in him was "patience and determination, inexhaustible and inextinguishable," and Washington manifested these very qualities while providing in his relations with the civil authorities a model for all time. Some may have wondered then and some may wonder now if the man could have been as irreproachable, as inflexibly just, as dedicated a patriot as he seemed to be. The verdict of the scrupulous historian after years of unremitting inquiry is that, as nearly as can be in human life, the legend and the man were identical.

To say that the biographer merely gave us in elaborate form what we already had is, however, to do much less than justice to the invaluable work of historical conservation. Legends grow shadowy with the passing years and need to be buttressed by freshly established truth; and the finest traditions of a free people, like their liberties, can be maintained only by eternal vigilance and incessant labors. National heroes can be cast from their pedestals by unholy hands and the ideals that patriots lived by can be dishonored. Unlike stones, literary monuments have life within them and they often prove more enduring. The creators of noble books about noble men are public benefactors, and such a creator was Douglas Southall Freeman.

# PREFATORY NOTE

# PREFATORY NOTE

WITHIN THESE PAGES are the last written words of Douglas Southall Freeman.

In 1935, following publication of his *R. E. Lee*, certain scholars and students of history urged Douglas Freeman to do the historical portrait of another great American—to revivify, in fact, the finest figure of our national history—George Washington. Perhaps they recognized that twenty years devoted to the study of the Confederacy and the Life of its leader were perfect preparation for a new biographer of Washington, one whose presentation should be complete, conclusive. The suggestion was a challenging one, but before he committed himself to this tremendous undertaking, Freeman wished to determine whether sufficient material about the more intimate details of Washington's life was available. Experience had convinced him that the indispensable major printed sources were not enough; only through employment of certain minutiae of historical data could a writer make "the countless small strokes that give the semblance of life and blood to a biographical picture." When preliminary investigation proved the existence of such facts in unpublished papers and in Washington's own letters, the challenge was accepted. Now he must withdraw from the regional, well-defined nineteenth-century setting to the wider stage of eighteenth-century America—a stage whose confines, though very real, were more obscured by time and space. He would remain his own captive, as it were, until he won his own release with the deliverance of Washington from the background shadows.

Although he turned readily to this new project, the author soon found he could not yet definitely dismiss from his mind the period of the Confederacy. As General Lee was brought forward into brilliant radiance, had not his fellow officers been paled somewhat—automatically? By the same pen, should not full historical justice also be done those deputies who served their General in the foremost Confederate ranks? The compelling desire to do further homage to Lee's men was to Freeman a command in characteristic accord with Lee's spirit.

First chains, then, must be loosed before he could become bonded as the agent of another great leader. The *Washington* therefore was laid aside and the ensuing several years dedicated to the writing of *Lee's Lieutenants*.

His conscience clear, after completion of this exacting self-assignment, Freeman resumed with heightened vigor his studies for the *Washington*. The narrative was begun January 7, 1945, following the first period of research with the scholarly assistance of Dr. Gertrude R. B. Richards who, under his direction, had begun preparation of the bibliography and the collection of material in October, 1944.

The objective was a definitive biography of George Washington. Douglas Freeman's idea of a definitive work embraced in its code more than the combing of all available sources and sifting of all assembled facts. It represented the measuring and blending of material so that the picture might have proper proportion and perspective. It would make a man and his time, however remote chronologically from the reader, appear logical and understandable; it would bring the subject forward into contemporaneous reality and explanation at the same moment that it transported the audience, quite without awareness, into the life and surroundings of the subject. The writer with the accurate historical lens, who let himself live and think concurrently with his subject and the period, should be able to effect such accommodation without effort on the part of the reader, and without contrivance. Freeman knew innately, and through past historical experience, that the true historian must not let himself be projected into his subject. Rather he must remain neutral while he studied intently, intensively. Presently, his malleable mind would become cognizant of the individual he sought to comprehend; the character, the qualities of intellect and spirit of the man would become perceptible through the things he did not do, as readily as by those he did perform; through his friends, through his enemies; through the letters written to him as well as those penned by him.

Douglas Freeman believed the largest potential service of the historical writer was grounded in the proper presentation of fact, but he believed also that it was the obligation of the historian to make truth dynamic. Why should not the scholar, like the scientist, state his conclusion when, to the best of his capacity, he had measured the facts and weighed the evidence? Out of the irrefutable data would come the picture in black and white; only in the resultant interpretation could it take on color and shading, tint and tone; but it must be a true interpretation, filtered through the light of impartiality. When new light was to be had, new windows must be cut, however tedious and time-consuming the process.

First of all, then, Washington must be portrayed as he was disclosed through a telescopic eye that took into account every phase and every feature of the individual, his background, his behavior, his development in private and in public life, as substantiated by primary documents or proven authorities. Nothing would be presupposed—not even Washington's generally accepted greatness—nothing acknowledged in the way of human frailty—though human he was and must thereby have had imperfections. The "fabric of fact" must first be uncovered where it had been "lost under the embroidery of fancy." If such a portrayal entailed any diminution of glory for the long and blindly reverenced one, then that would be the price of historical verity. If, on the other hand, the crucible of the author's testing disclosed a Washington worthy of more fame even, of greater veneration, then in rediscovery would be the infinite satisfaction of enhanced honor through unbiased and searching scientific scrutiny.

Struck by the "glorious mass of unused material," Douglas Freeman said, after five years of study and much searching of the archives: "There are no great, unknown depositories of Washington or of other papers that are going to flood dark corridors with revelatory light. The stubborn fact stands out: More that is 'unknown' about Washington exists in his papers at the Library of Congress and in printed books and records than in everything else combined. The great 'discoveries' are those of overlooked fact." Consequently, as the enterprise progressed, he came to find his most exacting duty (certainly in the period from 1774 onward) to be that of selectivity in the use of materials. Multitudes of data were sifted but the mass of them and the labyrinth of detail never dismayed him. Be the trail sweet or foul, it must be followed; he might disappoint but he would not knowingly deceive. He was writing for the future—in the hope that this work of his never would need redoing. He gave to every chapter the same exquisite care in the organization of thousands of chronological and topical notes and cross references, extracted and abstracted from countless sources, for the full outline—completed to the last possible particular—that always preceded composition. It was his policy "first to recapture, then to narrate."

He would exact of himself always to discriminate between the probable and the proven in order that there never should be any doubt in the mind of the reader where fact ended and probability began. He would let the story tell itself, unhampered by rhetorical flourishes. Of the biography he himself said: "I may not have told the tale well; I at least know the tale is true." In his mention of the quiet, uncommunicative Houdon, Freeman said: "Houdon let the marble speak for itself. It did." In another medium, might not another enduring monument be built out of carefully hewn words, wrought with infinite patience, also to speak for itself? Then the tragic element in the fame of Washington, long lamented by the author—that the hero was so highly exalted he could not now be seen to pulse and breathe as a human being—might for all time be removed.

In this biography it was important to have Washington *grow* great before our eyes and in our understanding. Only then would the paragon become a person. To Freeman, Washington's emergence was clear ere his narrative of the "Leader of the Revolution" had been set down. The author had marked admiration and respect for Washington as a field commander though, in his opinion, "he probably was not of the first order of military acumen"; but what Washington was able to accomplish as an army administrator was the predominant final factor at this point in the establishment of the General's greatness. Throughout the war, Washington's problems had been more of diplomacy in human relationships than of strategy in military maneuvers. Thus it was and was to be that Washington, the man, the administrator, compelled more attention than did Washington, the soldier. This shift of emphasis from the military to the administrative, Freeman regarded as most significant in his treatment of Washington. It was the crux of his historical approach and interpretation of the man. The pinnacle the hero had occupied, obscured by the mist of tradition, already could be seen to rest on the firm rock of fact, no longer remote from upward looking faces. How better could this happy conclusion have been expressed than in the letter he wrote Raymond B. Fosdick, the friend largely responsible for this biographical enterprise: "What more could I ask for myself than to make the rediscovery that in Washington this nation and the western hemisphere have a man, 'greater than the world

knew, living and dying,' a man dedicated, just and incorruptible, an
example for long centuries of what character and diligence can
achieve?"

As Volume Five came to a close, we saw Washington, the soldier, at
Yorktown in the most shining hour of his military career. We heard
him bid farewell to his faithful lieutenants at Fraunces' Tavern, saw
the tears that brave men shed as they parted. Then, when the last red-
coat was carried out to sea, we witnessed preparations for his homeward
journey. We were with him at Annapolis where, on the 23rd of December, 1783, before "the United States in Congress assembled" the General
read a simple address, returned the commission given him in June,
1775, and received President Mifflin's high tribute. The next day he
alighted at the door of his beloved Mount Vernon.

At the beginning of Volume Six, Washington, with zest and determination, takes up his new farm duties and domestic problems, both
old and new. Major repairs to the house at Mount Vernon are coupled
with an effort at major repairs to the General's financial structure—
even more urgent. Interest in the restoration of his life as a farmer is
second only to interest in restoring the fabric of the country's economy,
the *sine qua non* of a strong union itself. At the same time that he
sought increased income from his western lands, he sought increased
circulation of national commerce by a plan for opening navigation between the Ohio and the Potomac or the James.

Beset by illness, unrelieved in financial stress, he watched with growing concern the disintegration that threatened as the States grew further
and further apart in their activities and in their interests. The selfish
ambitions of individuals were reflected in the narrow jealousies of these
separate States. As he watched and waited, counselled and cautioned,
still he hoped to hold the good will of his contemporaries while he
lived and worked as the peaceful planter there on the "River of Swans."
Yet everywhere, in crisis that followed crisis, his judgment continued
to be sought just as if he even now were in command, but his counsel
from afar held less of power for good than did his presence, even in
silence. Wherever he was, there was strength simply in his nearness.
The imperative call on him for active leadership was not to be denied;
the evolution of peace in a new nation was to become for him as challenging as ever had been the revolution of war. He might be plantation

owner, proprietor even, but no longer could he be both "Planter and Patriot"; he must again be altogether "Patriot." In the minds of the people he was their commander still, as surely as when he led their troops in the war years; he was their civil chief long before he himself acquiesced or admitted that indubitable destiny.

As he left his retreat to give silent strength to public problems, ranging from that of the Society of the Cincinnati to the battle for drafting of a Constitution, and its subsequent ratification, his anxiety for a union of the States was intensified. That 28th of June, 1788, not only brought the gladdening news that the Constitution had been sanctioned by nine States, but also it brought the certain summons, soon to be official, for him to be their head. The fanfare of the inaugural journey and the social demands of the Presidential office he bore with equanimity though, added to his governmental duties, they were at times exceedingly burdensome. Soon came the real testing of the Constitution as a guide and a bond for the people. Amendments there must be but they must not mar or weaken the Constitutional structure. Argument and debate were natural and, to a degree, desirable, but the problem of principles became one of personalities also. Accusation and its concomitant, animosity, surged. Washington still was plagued by financial difficulties, private and public. For the nation, that situation called for sound fiscal reorganization, but the issue of assumption of State debts and the funding bill served only to needle every nerve. Relations abroad were a major concern for which a balanced foreign policy must be conceived, cautiously adapted and applied as conditions varied with European powers. The unyielding persistence of Great Britain in commercial matters and her suspected connivings with the Indians required a delicate touch, a sure hand. Her hold on the northwestern forts and the Spanish hold on the Mississippi threatened to choke the new nation. The French Revolution instilled fear that America might become embroiled through military obligation to France in return for her part in its deliverance. At home, Indian affairs filled the administration with dread and with humiliation, too, of which the dark St. Clair defeat was only a part. Federalists and Anti-Federalists formed their respective ranks; there was the newspaper war—Fenno and his Federal adherents arrayed against Freneau and the emergent "Republicans." Saddest of all, in a personal sense, and of increasing bitterness, was the rivalry between Hamilton and Jefferson, on both of whom Washington leaned heavily. Everything pointed to sharpened suspicion and self-interest, both individual and sectional.

Throughout all this and more in those first years as President, Washington somehow endured, somehow remained apart from the confusion and conflict, somehow kept himself in the calm of the whirlpool, as it were. His was the only voice heeded above the noise of friction in the tension and dissension that prevailed. He had been, as he had said he would be, President of *all* the People, and he alone remained the nucleus of a united effort. The premise and the success of his executive policy was "administration without interference." Many factions, many forebodings there were, but above these the harmonious belief endured that in Washington as their continued leader rested hope for the next crucial years in the establishment of the government. Here was proof that "the faith of Americans in him was undiminished." Unanimity meant security; in him alone now was there unanimity.

That the people at heart approved a union was exemplified in the final, if painful, accomplishment of it. Too much had been achieved, too much now was at stake to let the threatening forces gain advantage by Washington's withdrawal as their Executive. So it was that slowly, cautiously, reluctantly, Washington relinquished once more his dream of retirement, to stay and serve America. He did so in the hope that the nation and its government, as envisaged by him and other like-minded patriots, might be saved.

Just as there had come preparation in the days of his youth for the years of responsibility in early maturity, so the school of the frontier had been for him the almost ideal school for the Revolutionary. In like manner, the school of the Revolutionary furnished further preparation for the years of public service to follow—the years that, all in all, called forth his supreme effort. It was in the Presidential period that Washington met the darkest challenge, the most grievous problems, the most destructive forces. The earlier Revolutionary struggle against ominous physical foes—the literal body blows of man and nature—was succeeded by struggle against even more elusive, more ominous foes and sharper thrusts against the spirit—suspicion and greed.

The narrative stops, as it chances, at the eve of the second administration, March 4, 1793, though the finished volume, as planned, would have continued to February 22, 1794, Washington's sixty-second birthday, when a year of his second term had been spent. Of that period, replete with perplexities and complexities for the Executive, we are not privileged to read here. What disclosures would have been made in the treatment of Washington's policy and proclamation of neutrality, of the French Minister Genet's mission and recall, of the heightened tension in the conflict between Hamilton and Jefferson, we cannot even surmise. The full impact of that unhappy relationship between Secretary of State and Secretary of the Treasury does not appear in this volume. Freeman had not yet treated the climactic point at which Washington himself became wholly aware of it. The President was grieved by the sad realization of the fevered political differences of the two, but was just beginning to sense the serious complication of personal animosity that presaged a grave, irreducible fracture. It was the nature of Washington to "watch and wait," and the reader is conditioned to apprehend with the same deliberateness, the same caution, the same patience. Later in the period of his second administration, the Whiskey Rebellion, the Jay Treaty, and the sad, strange case of Edmund Randolph, controversial still, also flash across our minds. It is a sober reflection when we recall the author's conviction that "Washington, the President, had been almost disregarded in the portrayal of Washington, the Hero."

After the painstaking outline had been made ready, Douglas Freeman began composition of Chapter Sixteen—his final chapter—on June 2, 1953. The closing words were written a few minutes before one o'clock on the day of his death, June 13, 1953. The pages were, as always, in his autograph, neatly numbered and carefully placed in the customary black binder—all except the very last, that is. The concluding paragraph still was on his writing board, secured by the usual rubber band. He would put it with the others when he returned to his study in the early afternoon. The fact that these last written words of his were thoughtfully reworked is both affecting and significant. Usually, the manuscript did not show detailed revision until the whole of a chapter was examined critically later on. That this final paragraph was so thoughtfully revised at the moment of its composition seems in itself prophetic.

He did not come back. Instead, after laughter at the luncheon table and talk of many things, he went to his room for a brief afternoon nap. Suddenly a heaviness and sharp pain filled his chest. In a little while it was over. For him had come "the slanting sun and then the silent sea."

The author who had lived for nearly half his life "in the company of great men," as he so often referred to the hours he spent with Lee and Washington, had, in a sense, predeceased his most recent companion. He had walked with Lee through the whole of a life, knew him as Lee's contemporaries knew the man—Lee who, Freeman was convinced, consciously emulated Washington. In the same way he had come to know the man Washington. Often, to the music of Haydn, or perhaps Beethoven, Freeman would translate himself into the setting of a particular eighteenth-century day and, as he read and studied, would "listen" as Washington spoke or as the great man himself listened to the words of the men about him. In effect, Freeman became one of Washington's contemporaries too—an ever present one.

In anticipation of his narrative of the period 1789-1799, Freeman had set out to examine, with the help of his staff, all the historical literature of Washington's administration, as well as the writings of "every Federal official who was apt to know what Washington said or did." The larger portion of this ground had been covered, but some awaited more intimate study pertaining to the last of the Presidential years that for so long have begged conclusive historical treatment. For example, every known sermon and eulogy of 1799-1800 inspired by Washington's death had been examined, not only for the purpose of ascertaining what the people thought of the Father of their Country, but also on the mere chance that some incident of prime historical interest might be uncovered—long buried and forgotten.

Even had this sixth volume been carried to its planned conclusion, it would not have appeared until completion of Volume Seven and, incidentally, of the biography. The two books were designed for release together as with earlier volumes—One and Two, then Three and Four. Volume Five was published singly to bring the military phase of the Life to a close. Volume Six never would have stood alone to be judged alone: its narrative would have flowed without interruption into that of the final book and the brace of them would have been read continuously as an unbroken treatment of the interim of the returned planter, the Presidential period and the last Mount Vernon years.

Most noteworthy of all expectations for Volume Seven was the plan for the third and final sketch of the character of Washington. Here would have come the full interpretation. Out of the assorted evidence Freeman had catalogued over the years, mentally as well as actually, and distilled through the invariable logic of his thinking, would have evolved an over-all analysis. An elaborate survey and review of all Washington's achievements was to serve as the basis for a final summation of the character of the man—an epitome of the entire work. It would, in effect, have been a short biography within a long one, but it would have blended into the narrative as part of the whole. In Freeman's opinion, it was a far different thing to make analogies and form judgments in the course of a research and to employ them at the end of a study, when all the forces of fact could be marshalled in proper rank to support a stand that was logical, not theoretical. This is borne out in a letter written in late 1952 to a contemporary historian: "If in the end an author expresses his opinion, the reader is gratified if he already has reached that conclusion, and if he has not formed that judgment, he is at least challenged to review his own conclusions."

When asked by a friend what in the course of his prolonged historical study was the most important single thing he had learned, Douglas Freeman answered: "The influence of personality on history." Unfinished though this Life of Washington is—by a matter of six unchronicled years—we can find conclusive comfort and authentic assurance in the words of the author to his editor: "The more I study George Washington, the more am I convinced that the great reputation he enjoyed with his contemporaries and with men of the next generation was entirely justified. He was greater than any of us believed he was."

Douglas Freeman always spoke of his historical work in terms of "we," never "I." Implied in that plural pronoun were, first of all, Mrs. Inez Goddin Freeman, "The Best Loved," and she "Who Never Doubted"; Raymond B. Fosdick, whose inspiration and reassurance gave the author encouragement to embark on this long labor; Dr. Gertrude R. B. Richards, his associate throughout the whole project, whose immensely important contributions have been attested in the progress of the work; his publisher; his editor, Wallace Meyer, with whom he had collaborated in the production of thirteen volumes, exclusive of the present book; the other members of his small staff; the Carnegie Corporation of New York and the John Simon Guggenheim Foundation, whose support made possible the undertaking. Yet his was the single creative force; his the planning and direction, his the only hand at composition. For each of us he could so readily simplify the difficult or clarify the confused. He had the rare ability to elicit the best efforts of those about him, to perfectly coordinate and integrate their relatively small parts into a magnificent whole of his own fashioning.

Without the author's guiding hand, the duties of staff members in preparation of Volume Six for publication were necessarily extended beyond their usual radius. The so-called front matter and end matter, always logically prepared after completion of the body of the book, remained to be compiled. The volume carries, therefore, no Introduction, as only Douglas Southall Freeman could have written it. Final selectivity in the choice of illustrations customarily was made subsequent to completion of the narrative, also. In the case of Volume Six, many of the illuminating pages had been determined and the author's preference for certain others had been clearly indicated. The captions that accompany them were written by J. A. Carroll, for several years the author's full-time associate and researcher in the Library of Congress. The two Appendices also were prepared by him. The one on Mount Vernon was composed from notes and data among material already assembled by Freeman. The Newspaper Appendix stems chiefly from the detailed study of the newspapers of the period done as Mr. Carroll's specific assignment.

The Bibliography of Manuscript Sources is logically the work of Dr. Richards; that of the Printed Sources was prepared most appropriately by Mrs. Geneva B. Snelling, the author's librarian. Each of these contributions carries its own Note and the respective by-line of the associate earlier commissioned by the author for that particular task. No deviation from the usual procedure was necessary for preparation of the Short-Title Index and the General Index to this volume.

MARY WELLS ASHWORTH
Historical Associate to Douglas Southall Freeman

Richmond, Virginia
March 21, 1954

# GEORGE WASHINGTON

# CHAPTER I

## Washington "Cannot Bear a Vacancy"

### (1784)

HOME WAS contrast and content. Instead of the clatter of the restless camp, the returned soldier had the quiet of the slow Potomac. The crowing of the rooster and not the rolling of the drum awakened Washington in the winter's dawn. When he stepped out on the piazza to sniff the morning air, the wind brought him the scent of pine trees and of leaf-covered damp earth in place of the stench of slaughter pits and fetid ditches. If a rider dismounted in the courtyard, he was not a General with a grievance but a neighborhood gentleman with a friendly greeting. At the dinner table, there no longer had to be the restraint of rank and command. Host and guests, friendly equals, could talk of crops and cattle, of the ship that was coming up the river and of the news the midwife brought from the last home she visited on the Occoquan. Peace of nations, peace of mind: not the least blessing of the one was that it brought the other.

Welcome though the quiet was, blessed as Washington found the delights of home, a mind trained for eight years to put above everything else the administration of his country's defence could not abandon overnight its concentration on Army, finance, and the nation's distress. For some weeks after he returned to Mount Vernon as a private citizen, following his resignation as Commander-in-Chief of the American Army, Dec. 23, 1783, his first waking thought in the morning was of public affairs.[1] It seemed incredible and unreal that his time was his own again, to devote to his private business in a world not only narrowed by retirement but dramatically imprisoned, as it chanced, by snow and ice that kept him housebound almost continuously from Christmas, 1783, to the second week in February.[2] During this season

[1] 27 *G. W.*, 340.
[2] *Ibid.*, 312, 315, 319.

I

of impassable roads he prepared few letters [3] and had no visitors. Except for the absence of hunger and cold, Mount Vernon was a Valley Forge on the Potomac.

After a month and a little more, Washington had convinced himself that he was a planter again. "The tranquil walks of domestic life are now beginning to unfold themselves," he cheerfully confided to Rochambeau; [4] and to Lafayette he wrote, "I am retiring within myself, . . . envious of none . . . determined to be pleased with all." [5] In still another letter to a comrade, he spoke of himself as a "wearied traveler" who "after treading many a painful step, with a heavy burden on his shoulders," was eased of his load and was able to look back on the quicksands and mires, "into which none but the All-powerful guide and great disposer of human Events could have prevented his falling." [6] Two days after making this humble confession, he did something that must have puzzled his friends. Briskly he wrote Capt. Daniel McCarty, vestryman of Truro Parish:

"It is not convenient for me to be at Colchester tomorrow, and as I shall no longer act as a vestryman, the sooner my place is filled with another, the better. This letter, or something more formal if required, may evidence my resignation, and authorize a new choice." He added a paragraph on the relief of certain poor concerning whom McCarty had written him; but he said not one word in explanation of his withdrawal from the vestry, [7] which then was undergoing reorganization after years during which it seldom had met. [8] Subsequently, although Washington's recorded appearances at church were rare, [9] he remained on friendly terms with his rector [10] and probably attended Christ

[3] Two only of these had interest. One was a call for a general meeting of the Society of the Cincinnati in May (27 *G. W.*, 340); the other was a request to the Secretary of Congress for the return, if permissible, of the commission Washington had placed in President Mifflin's hands at Annapolis the day before he came home. This document, the General facetiously said, might be of some interest to his grandchildren (*ibid.*, 312). Charles Thomson replied that Congress probably would present the paper to the General in a "gold box" (7 *Burnett*, 437), but nothing was done.

[4] Feb. 1, 1784; 27 *G. W.*, 317.      [5] *Ibid.*, 318.
[6] *Ibid.*, 340–41.      [7] *Ibid.*, 341–42.

[8] Philip Slaughter, *History of Truro Parish in Virginia*, E. L. Goodwin, ed., 94–95. Captain McCarty resigned at the meeting, Feb. 23, 1784, when Washington's resignation was accepted (*ibid.*, 95). George Mason is said (*ibid.*, n) to have ceased attendance after that date.

[9] Oct. 2, 1785, 2 *Diaries*, 419; Oct. 15, 1786, 3 *ibid.*, 125. It will be remembered there is no diary for any part of 1784 except for the month of Washington's "western tour," September 1–October 4.

[10] See 27 *G. W.*, 438, in answer to a letter of June 30, 1784, in which Mr. Massey said he had not called because he thought Washington busy with private affairs and with the entertainment of guests (230 *Papers of G. W.*, 85, LC). The one mention in Washington's diary of Mr. Massey's presence at Mount Vernon after the General's resignation from the vestry was when

Church in Alexandria on occasion when weather and roads permitted. He continued to acknowledge himself "not amongst the number of those who are so much alarmed at the thoughts of making people pay towards the support of that which they profess . . ."[11]

Unwillingness to attend church did not imply any narrowing of interests. On the contrary, he undertook to bring himself down to date on many subjects he had neglected. He hoped, even, for spare moments in which to enlarge his knowledge of history and, perhaps, of the French language, but he found quickly that legs accustomed to the saddle were not altogether at ease when stretched overlong by the fireside. His muscles made him restless; demanding duties began to devour his days, new duties as well as old, duties imposed by fame along with those exacted by ownership. Visitors from the neighborhood on occasion had been uncomfortably numerous before the war. Now they arrived in larger numbers, stayed at their leisure and, in some instances, returned with exacting frequency.[12] He began to think of going to Niagara and into Canada after he had attended a scheduled meeting of the Cincinnati in Philadelphia;[13] but he found that whenever he stirred from the vicinity of Mount Vernon, it became a formal occasion with ceremonies and salutes and addresses. This happened even when he went to Fredericksburg to see his mother.[14] Pleasing as was the cordial-

he came, Apr. 24, 1787, to christen the dying infant of George Augustine and Frances Bassett Washington (3 *Diaries*, 204).

[11] He added: "if of the denomination of Christians, or declare themselves Jews, Mohammedans or othewise and thereby obtain proper relief" (Letter of Oct. 3, 1785, to George Mason; 28 *G. W.*, 285). The statement in the text is all that seems justified regarding this period of Washington's non-attendance at Pohick Church. He owned a pew at Christ Church from April, 1785 (Fairfax Parish Vestry Book, 120). No other reference to Washington occurs in the vestry book. Nor is there particular mention of such journeys to Alexandria made in a diary that usually records all his absences from home in 1785–87. The supposition that Masonry to some extent was a substitute for religion in the mind of Washington at this time must remain mere supposition. Elkanah Watson sent him from Nantes a Masonic apron, "executed in a superior and expensive style" by "nuns in one of the convents" (W. C. Watson, ed., *Men and Times of the Revolution; or Memoirs of Elkanah Watson, Including Journals of Travels in Europe and America from 1777 to 1842*, p. 156; 24 *G. W.*, 497). Washington preserved this apron—it is now in the rooms of his old lodge in Alexandria, Virginia—and he may have worn it on Feb. 13, 1785, at the funeral of William Ramsay, when, as he wrote in his diary, he "walked in a procession as a free mason, Mr. Ramsay in his life being one, and now buried with the ceremonies and honors due to one" (2 *Diaries*, 342). This is the only observed reference to the Masonic Order in Washington's papers of this period.

[12] Cf. *ibid.*, 339, 364. The most frequent visitor, it should be added, was among the most welcome—Dr. James Craik.

[13] 27 *G. W.*, 400.

[14] *Ibid.*, 328, 330, 332, 339. He was welcomed at Fredericksburg, February 12, with a formal address, to which he replied, and on the 14th, he was tendered a dinner. The details, which are not of importance, were printed in the *Va. Gazette* (Richmond), Feb. 21, 1784, p. 3, and reprinted in *Virginia Magazine of History and Biography*, v. 17, p. 436–38. This publication is cited hereafter as V.

ity of the people to a man who still found public approval the greatest of rewards, lengthy receptions and dinners served with the thick sauce of endless speeches were more to be avoided than enjoyed.

Another experience of Washington's after he adjusted himself to renewed home-life was one for which he was in some measure prepared. This was a new reminder from his own books that the Army had not been alone in its suffering from 1775 through 1783. Speculators, manufacturers and perhaps some farmers had made money, but men with capital invested in notes and bonds, and not a few of those planters who lived near the scene of hostilities, had been heavy losers. For Washington, eight years of service with the troops had been eight years of neglect at home. Conditions were worse than he had assumed them to be.[15] Ante-bellum debtors who had made any payment had done so, usually, in depreciated currency.[16] During the British raid of 1781, eighteen slaves had run away;[17] nine had been sold in the most difficult years to provide money for taxes;[18] plantation industries and the ferry had done well on paper for service paid in paper;[19] Lund Washington's preoccupation on the estate and his aversion to travel and to bookkeeping had led to neglect of rent collection from western lands; current and capital accounts had been confused.[20] The pinch of hard times had been felt everywhere except at the dining table. Yet, even when the war had been at its worst, the General had directed and Lund had supervised the continued improvement of the mansion house;[21]

[15] 27 G. W., 309.

[16] *Ibid.*, 345. For Washington's earlier reflections on this device of debtors to cheat their creditors, see 13 *ibid.*, 424; 14 *ibid.*, 148, 432. Although he had been disposed in September, 1779, to decline to accept payment in paper money fast becoming worthless, he had concluded that Lund Washington, in acting for him, should follow the advice of "some sensible Whigs who are known to be men of discernment, and of honor and probity, (that are acquainted with the laws and practices of the State in like cases) . . ." (16 *ibid.*, 291). The most enraging case after the close of hostilities was that of Gilbert Simpson, who paid in depreciated currency the trifle that Washington was able to collect for the gross misuse of his mill and plantation in Fayette County, Pennsylvania. See *infra*, p. 18 and *Ledger B*, f. 138, entry of Sept. 16, 1784, or *post*.

[17] See Vol. V, p. 282–83.

[18] *Ledger B*, f. 156. They brought £2303.

[19] *Ibid.*, f. 142 ff; for the fisheries, see *ibid.*, 162 and for the ferry, *ibid.*, 160.

[20] 26 G. W., 126; 27 *ibid.*, 2; Lund to Washington, Jan. n.d., 1783, *Mount Vernon MSS.*; *Ledger B*, f. 151, 152, 153, 154, 155, 156, 157, 158, 160. The General's share of £300 in a privateer that bore his name had yielded certain domestic supplies and perhaps a small profit in the familiar, tattered currency that had almost no purchasing power. The vessel had not been employed in actual privateering but in two voyages to the West Indies; *ibid.*, f. 150, 158, 160.

[21] Supt. C. C. Wall of Mount Vernon has established the fact that the first work done by Going Lanphire after Washington became Commander-in-Chief, was in the dining room, where William B. Sears carved the chimney-piece. The "new room" on the north end of the house was raised and probably was enclosed about the same time. In 1777, the piazza may have been added, the cupola that year or in 1778. The weather-vane dates from 1787. See 29 G. W.,

and now that he was back home and was expecting many visitors, he was ambitious to have the new room decorated in stucco, expensive though he knew this would be.[22] He undertook, besides, to pave the piazza with flagstones from England,[23] built a greenhouse,[24] made plans for a better way of keeping his ice in summer,[25] paid for and put into use the French plate ordered by Lafayette [26] and replenished his stock of claret.[27] Other drink and day-by-day food represented a continuing expense. Within a short time the immediate household was to consist of Martha, two of her grandchildren, the General, Lund Washington for a good many of his meals, and subsequently George Augustine Washington and Fanny Bassett, a niece of the mistress of the house.[28] Seven or eight white persons consequently had to be fed daily from the main kitchen, but they usually represented only a few more than half of those who sat down for dinner in mid-afternoon. On occasion as many as ten or even fifteen guests, invited or unexpected, joined the family at the meal.[29] In addition, as there was no nearby inn to which considerate visitors could send their servants and their horses, the quarters and the stables were crowded whenever the mansion was.[30] Several of these early guests were distinguished;[31] most of them were welcome, and a few only were impostors, or presumptuous, uncouth persons who came to fill their stomachs or to have an experience of which to boast;[32] but in the aggregate they accounted for numerous young beeves, sheep and roasting pigs, and for a con-

---

250, and Worth Bailey in *Christian Science Monitor*, Feb. 21, 1948, p. 3 ff. The old wooden stable was burned accidentally in the autumn of 1781, with the reported loss of ten horses (23 G. W., 435; *von Closen's Diary*, v. 2, f. 113). No other structural change of importance occurred, except that the shingles and planking on the west side of the roof of the main house had to be replaced (Washington to Lund Washington, Aug. 13, 1783—a new letter not in G. W.— *Mount Vernon Ladies' Asso. Annual Report*, 1950, p. 28–31).

[22] 27 G. W., 298, 388; 28 *ibid.*, 237, 239, 324, 330, 332–33, 369, 458; 29 *ibid.*, 201–02, 279. The account of this work, which was not completed till 1787, is in *Ledger B*, f. 222.

[23] 27 G. W., 434–35; 28 *ibid.*, 317, 426, 453. These flagstones arrived in the spring of 1785.

[24] 27 *ibid.*, 454; 29 *ibid.*, 264, 283.

[25] 27 *ibid.*, 413.          [26] 28 *ibid.*, 16–17.

[27] Burgundy and champagne were to be added if cheap (27 *ibid.*, 396, 397).

[28] George Augustine came back to Mount Vernon, May 14, 1785, as a semi-permanent member of the family (2 *Diaries*, 375). He and Fanny were married October 15 of the same year (*ibid.*, 423).

[29] On the 19th of October, 1785, dinner guests numbered thirteen (*ibid.*, 426); on Nov. 4, 1786, there were at least twelve (3 *ibid.*, 134). The record appears to have been set with fifteen, the 26th of the same month (*ibid.*, 141).

[30] Mazzei in *Chinard*, 83.

[31] Lafayette, for example, in August, 1784 (27 G. W., 459), and Mrs. Catherine Macaulay Graham, a British historical writer, in May, 1785 (cf. 2 *Ballagh, Lee Letters*, 352). For details of these and other visitors, see *infra*, p. 36 ff.

[32] 3 *Diaries*, 30–31, 187, 213.

siderable part of the eight tons of pork sent to the smoke houses in a given year,[33] to say nothing of flour and vegetables, milk and butter, fish from the river and game from the marshes. Claret, Madeira and spirits disappeared in large volume. The cost of candles was not to be laughed off, because a majority of the guests spent the night and by no means all of them left after breakfast the next day. A visiting British artist, Robert Edge Pine, stayed for almost three weeks;[34] a nephew of Washington's, recovering from an illness, was a guest for nearly eight weeks.[35] Always there was someone. From the time he came home in December, 1783, more than a year and a half was to elapse before he was able to write in his diary that he had dined alone with Martha.[36] The financial burden of this entertainment was apparent, of course, to friends and to Congress, whose members endlessly were asked by foreign travelers how arrangements might be made for interviews with the General. A suggestion of the Pennsylvania Executive Council that he accept a gift from Congress was promptly and gratefully disapproved by him in January, 1784.[37] Later a proposal was made for a Federal allowance to him of 500 dollars a month for his extra table expenses, a figure subsequently raised to 10,000 dollars a year, but no action was taken on this.[38]

Washington almost certainly would have declined this money had it been tendered him. Every consideration dictated his adherence to the principle of unpaid public service, the principle that had won applause from the very hour he had told Congress in June, 1775, that he would accept no salary as Commander-in-Chief. Pride and a desire for popularity did not of themselves exclusively shape this pattern of duty. Something deeper within him set upon his lips the seal of quiet acceptance of the price the patriot had to pay for peace. If bounties of land could be given the survivors of the war, let the warrants be drawn liberally and not with a stinting hand. When offices were to be filled, look first for qualified men among those who had spent their most valuable years in defence of their country. This much was due them. Even if it was allowed, it might not restore their earnings or balance

---

[33] Lund Washington's MS account book at Mount Vernon contains numerous references to fresh meat from one of the farms. The figure of approximately 16,000 lbs. of "new meat" for the family is the net of the "hog-killing" of 1785 (2 *ibid.*, 456).

[34] *Ibid.*, 370–71, 377.      [35] *Ibid.*, 383–84.

[36] June 30, 1785; *ibid*, 386.      [37] 9 *Sparks*, 10; 27 *G. W.*, 301.

[38] 7 *Burnett*, 507; 26 *JCC.*, 317, 323; 34 *ibid.*, 625. No reason for the postponement of action appears in the record.

their deserts in comparison with those of men who had escaped the mighty burden of a heavy musket and the day-long misery of an empty stomach. Beyond this scanty compensation, the rewards of the intelligent soldier were those he himself created and paid to himself—the consolation that at least his children might reap where he had sown, the satisfaction of believing that a fortress of freedom would rise on foundations he had laid, the self-respect that strengthened the heart when the tongue refused to whine or to fashion a complaint.

This was the unvoiced philosophy of Washington. It was the valid coin of conscience even if it did not feed his guests or pay his bills. He had predicted that he would come home "with empty pockets" [39] and he almost literally had done so—to find numerous, unexpected calls for money. Because of the shortage of revenue at Mount Vernon, Lund Washington had drawn no pay as steward after April, 1778, but he had said nothing of this to the General, lest he add to the burdens of the returned planter.[40] When the owner came home and found this obligation, he had no ready way of meeting it.[41] Many other unanticipated requirements for money had also to be met. A hundred guineas were found somehow by the General for his nephew, George Augustine Washington, Lafayette's former aide, who needed to go to the West Indies for his health.[42] Later in the year, when "Jack" Washington wanted to borrow £400 to £600, his brother, the General, could not lend the amount but offered to become security for it.[43] In explaining to his nephew, Fielding Lewis, Jr., why he could not make a loan, Washington confessed one of the main reasons for his new financial distress: "My living," he said, "under the best economy I can use must unavoidably be expensive." [44] In spite of all this, he remained optimistic that after he got his neglected affairs in order and received from London the money due on "Patsy" Custis's stock in the Bank of England, his situation would be better.[45] Something, perhaps, could be had

[39] 26 G. W., 127.

[40] In the same fine spirit, he had shown some resentment when he thought Washington believed he might quit the plantation or demand more pay because he could not be replaced easily. See his letter of Mch. 18, 1778, to the General; Mount Vernon MSS.

[41] Lund's balance-sheet of February, 1783, is in Ledger B, f. 170, but his accounts were not settled finally till Mch. 2, 1789, when the General gave him a bond for £1220. Interest on this was still being paid in September, 1792. See ibid., f. 315, 346, 370; Ledger C, f. 1. The last payment of interest was made July 8, 1794, and the account closed.

[42] Entry of Apr. 25, 1784; Ledger B, f. 197.

[43] 28 G. W., 8–9.        [44] 27 ibid., 346.

[45] Ibid., 212, 450; 28 ibid., 326, 491. Patsy's Virginia estate had been settled, July 13, 1778, through George Mason. See Ledger B, f. 153, 216.

meantime from tenants and debtors without too much dunning; [46] and if new discouragement must be faced, he always held to the conviction that the advantageous lease or profitable sale of his western holdings ultimately would reimburse him for his wartime losses and for his expenditures in the improvement of Mount Vernon. During the course of hostilities, he had written his brother John Augustine: "It ever was my opinion, though candor obliges me to confess it is not consistent with national policy, to have my property as much as possible in lands. I have seen no cause to change this opinion; but abundant reason to confirm me in it; being persuaded that a few years peace will inundate these States with emigrants and of course enhance the price of land far above the common interest of money." [47]   To this opinion he adhered.

Four months were spent in varied initial efforts to adjust himself to the position of a landed proprietor who had seen "the whirlwind pass." Then, in May, 1784, he had to answer the first call to renewed public service in a matter that had alarmed him for weeks. The Society of the Cincinnati had become unpopular with a considerable element in America, for reasons none of the founders had anticipated. Benjamin Franklin had ridiculed it; [48] Judge Ædanus Burke of South Carolina [49] had written a furious "address" of warning that a "race of hereditary patricians" was being created; [50] Elbridge Gerry had become suspicious; [51] Delegate Samuel Osgood had pictured a conspiracy against the treasury; [52] Henry Knox had reported that antagonism was widespread and vehement in New England, where the Society was alleged to be the creation of foreign influence, the first step towards a martial oligarchy that would overthrow American democratic institutions. [53] On hearing this outcry, Washington responded as he usually had to

[46] 27 G. W., 328, 333–36, 436, 442.

[47] Letter of June 6–July 6, 1780; 19 ibid., 135.

[48] 9 Smyth's Franklin, 161.

[49] He must not be confused with Thomas Burke, the vehement critic of Gen. John Sullivan (see Vol. IV, p. 492 and 2 Burnett, 496–97, 519–20).

[50] Cf. The Life and Correspondence of Joseph Reed, William B. Reed, ed., cited hereafter as Reed, v. 2, p. 409. Ædanus Burke's Considerations on the Society or Order of Cincinnati . . . was printed by Robert Bell at Philadelphia in 1783 with this on the title page: "By Cassius. Supposed to be written by Ædanus Burke, Esquire, one of the Chief Justices of the State of South-Carolina." The pamphlet was put into French by Mirabeau, and was reprinted in English and later in a German translation of Mirabeau's version. A somewhat detailed bibliography of the various editions will be found in E. E. Hume, "Early Opposition to the Cincinnati," 30 Americana, 597 ff.   See also a brief note in 28 G. W., 327.

[51] 7 Burnett, 522.          [52] Ibid., 416, 434.

[53] 229 Papers of G. W., 47, LC.

complaints in the Army: let the nature and the justice of the protests be determined;[54] then call on the most influential of the senior officers to attend the general meeting of the Society due to be held in Philadelphia;[55] ask these leaders to change promptly the rules in a manner to remove all reasonable objection to it. If antagonism could not be overcome, the men who established the Cincinnati should dissolve it for the country's sake.[56] Did this seem an unreasonable request to make of former officers whose badge of the Cincinnati was perhaps the one shining symbol of a service the indifferent, preoccupied public seemed already to be forgetting? The question was not raised or even implied in a single line from Washington's pen. The true patriot did not renounce his faith when he discarded his uniform. He surrendered his right to order but not his duty to serve. As surely as an officer had learned to combat the shifting tactics of the enemy, so must he adapt himself to the changing temper of the people. He must be tolerant even of intolerance, patient in facing impatience, disciplined in dealing with disdain. His continuing commission, never outdated, never expiring, was that of self-command.

Concerning the involved issues of policy, as distinguished from duty, Washington sought in particular the advice of Thomas Jefferson,[57] who judiciously expressed the hope the General would not become involved in "subordinate altercations."[58] Nathanael Greene, whose counsel Washington also cherished, most vigorously declared himself against yielding to clamor.[59] Other reports and letters strengthened the conclusion of the retired Commander-in-Chief: a drastic reorganization must be effected.[60] As President-General, he reviewed the Society's rules or "Institution," line by line,[61] and probably had his detailed recommendations in order on his departure for Philadelphia, Apr. 26, 1784, the first long journey he had made after his home-coming Christmas Eve.[62]

When he rode into Philadelphia on the 1st of May, the Sons of St.

---

[54] 27 *G. W.*, 365, 370.

[55] *Ibid.*, 343, 366–67, 372–73. See *supra*, p. 3.

[56] 27 *G. W.*, 386; 7 *Burnett*, 516; cf. *ibid.*, 526.

[57] 27 *G. W.*, 388.          [58] 7 *Burnett*, 494.

[59] 9 *Sparks*, 495. Greene subsequently wrote Washington that he was surprised at the magnitude of the opposition and was glad Washington did not heed him (Letter of Aug. 29, 1784; 231 *Papers of G. W.*, 16–17, LC).

[60] 27 *G. W.*, 393 ff.

[61] *Ibid.*, 393–96. See 230 *Papers of G. W.*, 11 ff, LC, for Washington's autographed alterations of the text. See illustration in this volume.

[62] His itinerary is covered by his expense account, 27 *G. W.*, 405–06, which the Society paid.

Tammany were holding their annual celebration on the Schuylkill. Their shout was "General Washington is arrived, huzza," and as this appealed to their mood, they made of it a sort of slogan which was repeated endlessly during the day. Washington went to Robert Morris's for dinner and there he later had the honor of a visit from the "Sons" with their fifes and drums. Thirteen cheers were given him; thirteen cannon were fired [63] in a welcome as warm as ever. Four months at home had not affected in the slightest his place as national hero.

Proceedings of the Cincinnati showed, likewise, that his leadership of his old officers was accepted as readily as if he still were at field headquarters. It was Tuesday, the 4th of May, when a quorum of delegates appeared at the City Tavern,[64] and it was the 15th when the debate-loving members completed their deliberations and approved a circular to be sent the State Societies. Washington had been inclined, when the meetings began, to abandon the whole project but he was restrained by the conciliatory attitude of most of the delegates [65] and by two other considerations: an opportunity was presented through the Society of relieving in a small way the financial distress of unfortunate members, and, second, French officers were taking so seriously the establishment of a new "Order" that disbandment would humiliate them.[66] At the same time, Washington felt that nothing less drastic than the changes he proposed in the rules of the Society would put an end to clamor, even though much of the opposition was without reason.[67]

His prime insistence was that the delegates "strike out every word,

[63] *Penn. Gazette*, May 5, p. 3; *Penn. Packet*, May 4, p. 3, May 6, p. 2; *Penn. Journal*, May 5, p. 3; *Independent Gazetteer*, May 8, p. 2, 3; *Freeman's Journal*, May 5, 1784, p. 3, all of Philadelphia. The last-named of these newspapers published in its issue of May 12, 1784, p. 2, "A Pindarick Ode; or a Panegyrick, on the Success of His Excellencys Arms; and the Present Greatness of the American Empire . . . by a young Gentleman of Kent County, in the State of Delaware," in twenty-two numbered stanzas.

[64] For the meeting place, see *Penn. Journal*, May 5, 1784, p. 3. By the 10th, forty-seven delegates were recognized—only one from New Hampshire and two from Delaware but as many as five from some States. Rhode Island was not represented until the 12th. See John C. Daves, ed., "Proceedings of the General Society of the Cincinnati," cited hereafter as *Proc. Cin.*, v. 1, p. 3, 4, 10. A "fair copy" of the proceedings, sixteen pages, is in 230 *Papers of G. W.*, 7 ff, but the information is of the meagrest. Three additional pages in Washington's hand are appended to this copy.

[65] 27 *G. W.*, 420. Cf. letter of unnamed delegate: ". . . I apprehend that it will be the universal sense of this meeting, to expunge, strictly define, and explain every part which can possibly give, or has given, offence to any honest, candid man." Quoted, without source, in C. B. Alexander, "Assaults on the Society of the Cincinnati and Its Vindication," 18–19.

[66] 28 *G. W.*, 352. Some of the French interest in the Society may be glimpsed in Baron de Contenson, *La Société des Cincinnati de France et la Guerre d'Amérique, 1778–1783* . . . , p. 19 ff.

[67] 28 *G. W.*, 350, 351.

sentence and clause which has a political tendency." Hereditary membership was to be discontinued completely; no more honorary members were to be admitted; donations to the Society were not to be received except from citizens of the United States; funds were to be placed in such status that their misuse, presumably for political purposes, could not even be suspected. Washington urged, further, that all foreign officers meet in France as a self-governing body that would have authority to pass on applications, within the terms of the "Institution." This, needless to say, was proposed to meet the charge that these officers —Frenchmen who had risked their lives in war against a common foe—were seeking to impose alien rule on America. Finally Washington advocated the abandonment of general meetings and perhaps of district gatherings also. Members would assemble formally in their own States only.[68]

In the end, after much debate, the delegates adopted substantially all of Washington's proposals except the one for the abandonment of general meetings.[69] If any compromise lay behind the broad acquiescence in Washington's wishes, it was the decision of the general meeting to recommend the whole of the revised "Institution" to the State Societies for their acceptance, rather than to declare it the governing law of the Society. This point was not covered by the new text of the "Institution" itself but by the language of this opening paragraph of the circular letter to the State Societies: "We the delegates . . . have thought proper to recommend that the enclosed 'Institution of the Society of the Cincinnati, as altered and amended at their first meeting,' should be adopted by your State Society." A long, long sentence near the end of the letter included an appeal "for the ratification of our proceedings . . ."[70] Although elections were conducted and procedure authorized by the General Society as if the revised "Institution" was in operation, the intent of the Delegates undoubtedly was to make the changes contingent on the approval of all the State Societies.[71] Wash-

[68] 27 G. W., 393–96. The original "Institution," printed in John Schuyler, *The Institution of the Society of the Cincinnati*, 13, provided that each State Society should be divided "into such districts as shall be directed by the State Society."

[69] The officers of Louis XVI were authorized under the amended "Institution" to hold meetings and to "form regulations for their police, conformably to the objects of the Institution and to the spirit of their government" (1 *Proc. Cin.*, 12). This was approximately what Washington had advocated, though he perhaps would have preferred to have all the foreign officers in one self-governing European Society.

[70] 1 *Proc. Cin.*, 17.

[71] Proof of this is afforded by the proceedings of nearly all the general meetings of the Society from 1787 to 1800. (See *ibid.*, 28–29, 33, 38, 48, 52, 55). In 1800, disgusted by the

ington said nothing then or thereafter to indicate that he considered reference of the question to the State Societies as a device to prevent change while the storm of opposition blew itself out. The original "Institution" was silent concerning amendment and revision, but congressional usage and the inclination of most men was to defer to the States. Members of the Cincinnati were following the popular pattern when they made the reform of their Society contingent on the affirmative vote of the State branches.[72] Had Washington regarded this procedure as in any way evasive, he would not have accepted, even with the reluctance he displayed, unanimous reelection as President-General for a term of three years.[73]

The length of the general meeting put out of mind the hope he had renewed of visiting Niagara and Canada, though, in reality, even if he had possessed the leisure and the ready funds, he would have been loath to request a British passport.[74] As rapidly as he could, he hurried homeward [75] to take up the burden of entertainment and of farm management, and to pay another of the prices of being a national hero, the price of correspondence that became more nearly intolerable with each post.[76] Veterans sought certificates of their service; [77] historical writers solicited access to his papers; [78] endless, unwarranted requests were

indifference of some of the State Societies to the ratification of the amendments, the general meeting resolved unanimously that the State Societies did not "accede to the proposed reform" and "that the Institution of the Society remains as it was originally proposed and adopted by the officers of the American army at their cantonments on the banks of the Hudson River, in 1783" (*ibid.*, 63).

[72] Perhaps it is significant that when Mirabeau wrote his criticism of the circular letter, he dwelt in detail on almost every possible flaw but did not hint that reference of the new "Institution" to the State Societies was a subterfuge. See his *Considerations on the Order of Cincinnatus*, 132 ff.

[73] 1 *Proc. Cin.*, 18; 29 *G. W.*, 32. Horatio Gates was named Vice President, and Henry Knox Secretary.

[74] 27 *G. W.*, 450.

[75] After delay in crossing the Chesapeake, he arrived home May 23 (*ibid.*, 406, 409).

[76] For his regular dispatch of a messenger to the Alexandria post office in 1786, see 28 *ibid.*, 369, 485. His practice in 1784 probably was the same. At this period, he was sending French letters to Alexandria or to private homes for translation by Dr. David Stuart, who had married the widow of "Jack" Custis. See 229 *Papers of G. W.*, 21, 121, LC.

[77] 27 *G. W.*, 418, 461; 28 *ibid.*, 47, 91, 94-95, 104-05, 105-06, 324-25; 29 *ibid.*, 200, 498; 30 *ibid.*, 31, 154. He had to make it his rule, after a time, to decline to recommend individuals for particular positions (28 *ibid.*, 241), and he had to insist also that subordinate officers who desired certificates should apply through their Colonels or through their commanding Brigadiers (28 *ibid.*, 442; cf. 29 *ibid.*, 363, 371). Instances of tactful declination to give certificates or to aid in reopening the verdicts of military courts will be found in 29 *ibid.*, 482, and 30 *ibid.*, 283.

[78] He met most of these applications with the statement that he did not think it proper for his official records to be opened until those of Congress were. See 27 *ibid.*, 370-71, 398; 28 *ibid.*, 99-100. See also 26 *JCC.*, 427-28, and Thomas Mifflin to Washington, May 31, 1784, 230 *Papers of G. W.*, 38, LC. When David Humphreys exhorted Washington to write his memoirs (*ibid.*, 99; 231 *ibid.*, 32), the General offered all facilities and a place in his household to Humphreys if that 'r isted former aide undertook studies of the Revolution (28 *G. W.*, 203).

made of him; the more he did, the more was he called upon to perform. Later he protested that in eight years of public service, he never had been compelled to write so much in person.[79] He told Humphreys: "What with letters (often of an unmeaning nature) from foreigners, inquiries after Dick, Tom and Harry, who *may have been* in some part, or at *some time* in the Continental service, letters or certificates of service for those who want to go out of their own State, introductions, applications for copies of papers, references of a thousand old matters with which I *ought* not to be troubled more than the Grand Mogul but which must receive an answer of some sort, deprive me of my usual exercise . . ."[80] He daily was hampered because he had not yet been able to find a private secretary [81] or to do more than make a beginning in the rearrangement of his legal papers which had become frightfully mixed and disordered because they had been thrown into chests hurriedly and had been hauled away each time the British had appeared on the Potomac.[82]

The unpleasant crowding of his hours as a national clerk, so to say, as well as a national hero, did not relieve him of calls for every sort of neighborly service. Those who knew him at all understood that he considered it his duty to assist them when they appealed to him—and they seldom hesitated to look to him, though they must have realized how busy he was.[83] The affairs of the Mercer brothers were, if possible, more confused than ever.[84] He needed for his own concerns the time he was giving to others.

---

[79] *Ibid.*, 70; cf. *ibid.*, 83, 100, 149.

[80] *Ibid.*, 65. The following will be found typical of some of Washington's replies to unreasonable requests: a declination to write to vestrymen he did not know, in behalf of a former tutor whom he offered to help in other respects (27 *ibid.*, 447–48); a recommendation of a minister as a trustworthy mortgagee (28 *ibid.*, 400); a refusal to endorse a complete stranger (*ibid.*, 455–56); an appeal for the recovery of a runaway slave (*ibid.*, 407); a repeated and indignant denial of his alleged retention of the non-existent trust estate of a man unknown to him (*ibid.*, 163).

[81] *Ibid.*, 149. For his initial efforts to procure a secretary, see *ibid.*, 23, 65, 70, 149, 157, 158, 177, 179. Matteson indexed this important subject under *Private Secretary*, not under *Secretary*.

[82] *Ibid.*, 84, 148, 149.

[83] Mrs. Savage was dead by this time, though final disposition had not been made of her estate, nor had Washington been repaid the £53 he had sent her in 1772 (3 *G. W.*, 79; 28 *ibid.*, 413); the Colville estate was not settled yet (*ibid.*, 481; 29 *ibid.*, 55–56, 109, 130, 195–96). For later complications see *ibid.*, 391–92, an important entry, and 394; 30 *ibid.*, 25, 121, 213, 275–76; *Ledger B*, f. 358; 3 *Diaries*, 63, 140, 434).

[84] The background of this long controversy was outlined by Washington in 30 *G. W.*, 190 ff, and in *Ledger B*, f. 221. For developments, see 27 *G. W.*, 426–27, 436, 463–64; 28 *ibid.*, 362–63, 515; 29 *ibid.*, 5, 56–58, 81–83, 104, 106–07, 116–18, 150–51, 192–93, 301, 378–79. The details are of no importance in the life of Washington, though they were for years a continuing irritant.

Inquiries were being made about his western lands, inquiries he usually was able to answer after much searching;[85] but it was manifest that part of his properties in the Ohio Valley were occupied by trespassers. Some of these men boldly were offering for sale in Philadelphia, and even in Europe, tracts Washington himself had patented years previously.[86] The mill and plantation which Gilbert Simpson had mismanaged shamefully must be leased, if possible, to someone else.[87] From the time he returned home, Washington had planned to make an early visit to these possessions beyond the mountains,[88] and he now had an added reason, not wholly personal, for doing so. Interest was being revived in the old project of linking the upper waters of the Ohio with the Virginia rivers. Thomas Jefferson had appealed to him to take the lead in this before New York State captured the western trade by opening an easy route to the Hudson.[89] Washington, in answer, had explained how the enterprise had been hampered by public indifference and by the jealousies of rival advocates of the Potomac and the James. He had not altogether rejected Jefferson's appeal that he assume the initiative in an undertaking that always had stirred his imagination.[90] Now that he was going West on his own business he studied available maps and resolved to ascertain, if he could, which was the best line for a road between the navigable upper waters of the Potomac and of some deep flowing tributary of the Ohio. If he found the route, he believed Virginia and Maryland would find the money for it.

He set out on the 1st of September with Dr. James Craik,[91] and made his way westward by the familiar old road with few experiences he had not met before the war. The only difference was that wherever his coming was known in advance, all the gentlemen of the neighborhood assembled to welcome him. This was more acceptable than ordinarily it might have been because there were no formal addresses to be answered and there always were present men who knew, or thought they knew, something about the roads and rivers of the divide between the Potomac and the Youghiogheny and Monongahela. Washington

---

[85] Cf. 27 *ibid.*, 348–56, 361, 364, 453.
[86] *Ibid.*, 443; 2 *Diaries*, 317.
[87] 27 *G. W.*, 439.
[88] *Ibid.*, 433, 437, 440, 441.
[89] 229 *Papers of G. W.*, 70, LC; 4 *LTW.*, 62–66.
[90] 27 *G. W.*, 373–76.
[91] Three servants attended. Dr. Craik's son, William, and the General's nephew, Bushrod, either accompanied Washington from the first or soon joined him (2 *Diaries*, 279).

resumed his diary to record this information, which he wrote down as carefully as he penned the terms of his leases and the condition of those of his farms that he visited.[92]

By the 6th, Washington reached the familiar resort, Berkeley Springs, which now had been laid out as a town and had been named Bath.[93] There he met a storekeeper and builder, James Rumsey, who demonstrated an invention which he claimed would enable boats to ascend easily a swiftly flowing stream. Washington grew enthusiastic as he watched and, later, at Rumsey's instance, he wrote a certificate in which he described what he had seen. He added that in his opinion, "the discovery is of vast importance, may be of the greatest usefulness in our inland navigation, and, if it succeeds, of which I have no doubt, that the value of it is greatly enhanced by the simplicity of the works which, when seen and explained to, might be executed by the most common mechanics."[94] Washington did not stop with this. Ill-circumstanced though he was to assume new financial obligations, he was in such good humor with Bath and so pleased with Rumsey that he authorized the inventor to build him near the springs a two-story dwelling, with a stable and a kitchen as separate buildings,[95] the whole to be ready in July, 1785.

From Bath, the General and his party proceeded to the familiar

[92] As far as is known, he had not kept a diary after the Yorktown campaign ended.

[93] By an act of 1776; 9 H 247.

[94] Certificate of Sept. 7, 1784; 27 G. W., 468. Rumsey said later that he was uncertain at this time whether steam engines "could be reduced to such simplicity and cheapness as to make them of public benefit; not being certain of this, though being perfectly convinced of the power, was my only reason for not mentioning this scheme also to the General at that exhibition . . ." (James Rumsey, A Short Treatise on the Application of Steam, 5). The inventor explained that he soon developed his ideas of the use of steam, and consequently did not perfect his mechanical boats. From what he wrote Washington, it appears that in 1784 he contemplated the use of two boats (ibid., 26 n) which operated together with "paddle board ahead." See Rumsey to Washington, Mch. 10, 1785 (232 Papers of G. W., 32–33, LC), partially printed in Ella May Turner, James Rumsey, Pioneer in Steam Navigation, 18–21. He believed the force of the current could be converted into power that would drive the boat forward and in a letter of Sept. 19, 1786, to Washington (236 Papers of G. W., 82), he described his mechanism in more detail. James Fitch contemptuously called this Rumsey's "Pole Boat," and maintained that Washington's endorsement of it was "one of the most imprudent acts of [the General's] life" (Turner, op. cit., 14). Rumsey lost no time in publishing Washington's certificate in the Va. Gazette (Richmond), Oct. 9, 1784, p. 2, 3.

[95] The agreed size of the house and the number and dimensions of the rooms are given in Washington's entry of Sept. 6, 1784; 2 Diaries, 283–84. A "gallery" seven feet deep and two stories high, was to surround the dwelling, which was to be 36 by 24 feet, with a cellar under half of it. Further unimportant details of the main building and outhouses appear in 231 Papers of G. W., 87; 232 ibid., 34, and 233 ibid., 48. The house proved more expensive than the estimate had indicated (Rumsey to Washington, Sept. 5, 1785, 236 ibid., 71) and was poorly built at that (Lewis to Washington, Aug. 25, 1786, with addendum by J. A. Washington, ibid., 62).

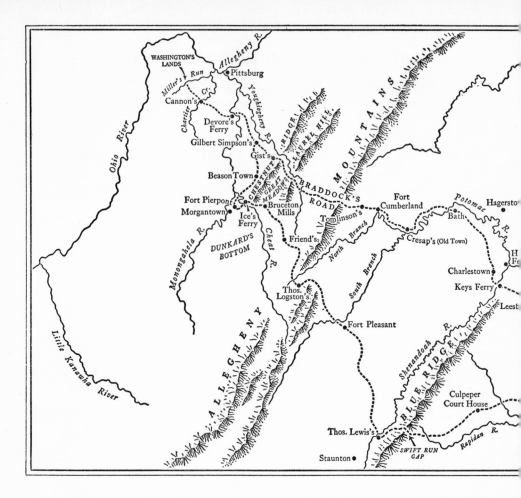

settlement of Col. Thomas Cresap, on the site known as Old Town.[96]
The Colonel was still there, 80 years of age or more, and of feeble eye-
sight but with intellect scarcely impaired.[97] Washington had met
Cresap as long previously as 1748, when as a boy of 16 he had gone out
with one of Lord Fairfax's survey parties, and with Cresap first had
witnessed an Indian dance and had touched the frontier.[98] A long,
long time ago that seemed, but Washington, as usual, had little inclination to dwell on the past; his thought increasingly was of the domain
beyond the mountains. It must continue America's and must be bound
to the Union by the ties of economic self-interest. Nothing so certainly

[96] 2 *Diaries,* 286–87. Old Town has survived as Oldtown, Allegany County, Md.; A. B.
Hulbert, in *Washington and the West,* cited hereafter as *Hulbert,* 132, gave its location as
"opposite Green Spring Station on the Baltimore and Ohio Railway."
[97] K. P. Bailey, in his *Thomas Cresap,* did not mention Washington's visit. Cresap's age was
given variously. A visitor of 1785 was told that "the Colonel" was more than 100 years old
(*Bailey,* op. cit., 163). Bailey seems to have accepted the year of the pioneer's birth as approximately 1694; Wroth in *DAB* gave the year as c. 1702.      [98] Vol. I, p. 217 ff.

WASHINGTON'S WESTERN TOUR, 1784

Adapted principally from A. B. Hulbert, *Washington and the West* (op. p. 32), with certain features traced from a map of The Travels of George Washington, compiled and drawn in the Cartographic Section of the National Geographic Society for "The National Geographic Magazine," Gilbert Grosvenor, ed., and supported with information furnished by Dr. Roy Bird Cook. Bath is now Berkeley Springs, W. Va.; Tomlinson's is Frostburg, Md.; Gist's was at the foot of the range which actually is a continuation of Chestnut Ridge, though South of the Youghiogheny River it also is called "Laurel Hill," as if it were part of the dominant range approximately twelve miles to the East (see Charles B. Trego, *A Geography of Pennsylvania* (1843), p. 29, 243–44, and his frontispiece map). Washington described Gist's as "at the foot of Laurel" (2 Diaries, 288–89). Simpson's is Perryopolis; Devore's Ferry is Monongahela; Cannon's is Canonsburg; Beason Town is Uniontown, Penn.; Ft. Pierpont is Easton, W. Va.; Friend's is Oakland, Md. The road from Ft. Cumberland to Gist's was known in Washington's time as "Braddock's Road."

would assure this adherence as the existence of a profitable market for peltry and furs at the end of a short, easy water route to the seaboard.

The General had many questions for another guest at Cresap's, a man who lived at the mouth of Ten Mile Creek on the Monongahela,[99] and then he started for Gilbert Simpson's in order to be certain to arrive in time for the advertised sale of the mill. The route was through Great Meadows and to the plantation of Thomas Gist,[100] "at the foot of Laurel Mountain"—the very names enough to make Washington shudder with dark memories—but he wrote no other comment than that the whole of the Meadows might be reclaimed, that the site

[99] 2 *Diaries*, 286–87.

[100] Thomas Gist was a younger brother of Christopher Gist and was Gen. Mordecai Gist's father. For Christopher Gist, see Vol. I, p. 282. Mordecai Gist, Maryland Brigadier (see K. W. Blakeslee, *Mordecai Gist*, 7), is not to be confused with Nathaniel Gist, Colonel of the Sixteenth Virginia, remnant of one of the "Additional Regiments of 1776," the man responsible for the court martial of Henry Lee after the Powles Hook affair of August, 1779. See Vol. V, p. 131.

was a good one for a tavern, and that much hay might be cut if grass were planted.[101]

Washington tried to cover the twelve miles of difficult road between Gist's and Simpson's at what he termed his "usual traveling gait of five miles an hour," [102] but when he met travelers proceeding eastward with pack loads of ginseng, he could not resist the temptation to stop and to make inquiry concerning the navigable streams that were familiar, he hoped, to these residents of the frontier. The men gave him some information on the streams up which the produce of the Ohio might be carried on batteaux, but they knew nothing about the country through which it would be necessary to open a portage. Something more personally unpleasant was told Washington by these wayfarers: Indians to the westward were in ugly mood if not actually in arms. It might be dangerous for him to go down the Ohio, as he had planned, to his large holdings on the mouth of the Kanawha. The General thought this probably was good advice but a decision must wait, he told himself, until he procured further information at the sale of the mill on the tract held jointly with Gilbert Simpson.[103]

To that individual's house, Washington came in the late afternoon of September 12,[104] and not with pleasant anticipations, because nearly all his relations with Simpson had been unpleasant and expensive. As long previously as the summer of 1775, amid the woes of the siege of Boston, he had written, "I never hear of the mill under the direction of Simpson, without a degree of warmth and vexation at his extreme stupidity," [105] but stupidity was not the word to apply to a man who had the art of beguiling Washington not once, but time after time. Now, fresh disappointments crowded the hours of his stay at Simpson's. The mill was in disrepair;[106] there was no reservoir; the dam had given way; it was futile to hope for any rent worth collecting from the property,[107] though Washington first and last had spent almost £1200 of hard money on it.[108] The adjacent farm, which Simpson was

101 2 *Diaries*, 288–89. The stage-by-stage ride to Gist's is given in *Hulbert*, 133–34, 140, and on the map, p. 16–17, adapted from Hulbert's.                         102 2 *Diaries*, 289.

103 *Ibid.*, 289–90. A full description of the property was given in Washington's advertisement, *Penn. Packet*, July 29, 1784, p. 4. Simpson's account of affairs on the farm was in a letter of July 31, 1784, to Washington (230 *Papers of G. W.*, 123, LC).

104 2 *Diaries*, 289.                         105 To Lund Washington; 3 *G. W.*, 432.

106 The mill was on a stream, now known as Washington's Run, about three-quarters of a mile from the Youghiogheny. See *Hulbert*, 142. Washington's Run, which flows into the river from the West, is close to the town of Perryopolis, Fayette County, Penn., and is eight miles Northwest of Connellsville. The course of the little stream may be followed in the Connellsville and Brownsville Quadrangles of the United States Geological Survey.

107 2 *Diaries*, 291.                         108 28 *G. W.*, 211.

supposed to be cultivating, was in fair condition but, to Washington's eye, it did not appear to be of as good land as he had thought it was.[109] At the sale, no bid was made for the mill; to encourage a lease of the farm the General had to offer to accept rent in wheat and, in the end, made a new and bad bargain with the wily Simpson for the use of the farm and of the slaves who lived there.[110] Ill luck continued to dog the General as he went from Simpson's to his own property on Miller's Run,[111] where numbers of families were occupying land to which he held title. After a long conference with Washington, they chose to stand suit for ejectment, alleging title of their own, rather than to pay rent.[112]

Visiting dignitaries and an officer of the Pittsburgh garrison by this time had confirmed the roadside report of Indian unrest down the Ohio. Washington's experience and common sense told him he must turn back.[113]

As a man of business, he of course lamented the fruitless, expensive and time-consuming effort to set his western properties in order. Still, he had become so interested in finding the best route to the Ohio that details of leases and of the area of his various tracts commanded less space in his diary than he gave to the meagre and conflicting information he thus far had accumulated on rivers that seemed almost as little known as they were when he first had crossed the mountains. The spirit of the adventurous surveyor asserted itself. What others could not tell him, he would go into the woods and discover. He would leave his baggage for the Craiks to bring home, while he and his nephew Bushrod, with a guide for the first stage, would ride southward to Cheat River, which then seemed the most accessible tributary of the Monongahela.[114] After examining the Cheat, he would proceed eastward to the North Branch of the Potomac.[115] It was an arduous enterprise but inconvenience and hard riding in an unknown country did not weigh against curiosity and a belief that discovery of an easy, safe route would unify and enrich America.

---

[109] 2 *Diaries*, 291.          [110] The details of this are not clear. See 28 *G. W.*, 293–95.
[111] This stream, which fortunately has kept its name, flows from the West into the South-and-North stretch of Chartier's Creek at a point about three miles South of Carnegie, Allegheny County, Penn. The upper waters only of Miller's Run are in Washington County.
[112] 2 *Diaries*, 291–92, 294–98.          [113] *Ibid.*, 292.
[114] *Ibid.*, 300. In terms of present-day geography (see the map, p. 16–17), the route Washington had in mind at this time was from a point about eight miles North of Morgantown, West Virginia, to the vicinity of Kingwood, Preston County, and thence southeastward to the North Branch of the Potomac between Garrett County, Maryland, and Preston County, West Virginia.
[115] *Ibid.*

He set out from the Youghiogheny about noon on the 23rd, on the 24th crossed the Cheat,[116] and proceeded to Fort Pierpont [117] where he vainly searched the records in the surveyor's office for papers that should have been filed in his name for lands on the Little Kanawha.[118] That night he was given the views of several residents of the neighborhood who were supposed to be acquainted with the watercourses and with such roads as existed.[119] The testimony of these men led Washington to believe, for the moment, that the passage of Cheat River through Laurel Hill could not be opened to navigation and that he was throwing time away in examining that route. He consequently decided to start home by a path that led back across the Cheat at Ice's Ferry,[120] and thence southeastward over the mountains to the North Branch of the Potomac.[121]

At the ferry, Andrew Ice talked so convincingly of the ease with which obstacles could be removed from Cheat River that Washington rejected what had been told him the previous evening and concluded, once again, that the best passage to the West would be from the North Branch by portage to Dunkard's Bottom and thence down the Cheat to the Monongahela and on to the Ohio.[122] Convinced of this, he proceeded eastward from Ice's Ferry on September 25th, but he had to pay for acting as if he were living in 1754, as a youth in his early twenties. Bad weather had attended him frequently, and on the evening of the 25th, it overtook him so far from any habitation that he had to sleep on the ground in the rain, with no other covering than his cloak.[123] It was an experience strange in its contrast to the ties of daily life at home but familiar as a link with the past. Before many years, seeking quarters in an unfamiliar place, the General was to write "I am not very nice" [124] and he did not flatter himself in using that synonym of "fastidious." He never had permitted his possessions to possess him. If

---

[116] This crossing was close to Point Marion, Pennsylvania.

[117] The modern Easton, West Virginia.        [118] 2 *Diaries*, 302–03.

[119] *Ibid.*, 303–04; *Hulbert*, 161–62. It was here that Washington saw young Albert Gallatin, who said years afterwards that Washington froze him with a look when he ventured an opinion concerning the geography of the region. Later in the evening Washington is supposed to have said, "You are right, young man." Some sort of an exchange occurred, but the details are so different in several works that the truth cannot be disentangled from the tradition. Hulbert, *op. cit.*, 162 ff, gives the various versions so far as they are known. Gallatin himself left no written account of the incident, though he often was quoted as saying Washington always seemed to him the most "inaccessible" man he ever had known.

[120] The name survives in the crossing of the Cheat Lake on the road Northeast from Morgantown to Cooper's Rock State Forest. Cheat Lake today covers the site of Ice's Ferry, though a marker has been placed as nearly as possible on the site of Adam Ice's house. Details of this part of the journey have been supplied most generously by Roy Bird Cook of Charleston, W. Va.

[121] 2 *Diaries*, 304.                    [122] *Ibid.*, 305.

[123] *Ibid.*, 306.                    [124] See 30 *G. W.*, 255 and *infra*, p. 162, n.138.

circumstance or his country's poverty should measure out to him the soldier's ration of the starving weeks at Morristown—"every kind of horse food but hay" [125]—he could eat it as cheerfully as he would enjoy a festive dinner at Mount Vernon, with a favorite fresh fish from the river. The decanter of Madeira was on a par, in his mind, with the spring by the wayside. Enjoyment never was dependence. So it was now, when the rain sounded its commands on the fallen leaves of the mountain wilderness.

How that word "wilderness" was woven into the story of his life! He had been 21 when he had gone through those same forests with Christopher Gist en route to Fort Le Boeuf. At 22 he had fought his first pathetic little campaign in the confusing fastnesses of the Alleghenies. The site of Fort Necessity was distant about eighteen miles only from this drenching encampment. He could remember when three days' tramp through those woods had not crossed a single trail that led to a white man's cabin. Even more vivid may have been the memory of that terrible night of July 9, 1755, after Braddock's defeat, when young Washington had ridden through devouring darkness on the road to Dunbar's Camp and, for part of the way, had heard the cries and the curses of unseen wounded whom he had to pass by if he was to reach his destination. The forest had been peopled with affliction, then, before he came to the silent places that even the staunchest and most resolute of the wounded from the battlefield had not been able to reach. Now the tragedy was effaced and the ghastly sequence happily reversed. Whenever the rain ceased momentarily to pour on the resounding carpet of golden leaves and pine needles around Washington's bivouac, silence was as intense as it had been almost thirty years previously. The wilderness seemed as bare of habitation; but in the darkness of '84 as in the black night of '55, the woods were peopled with promise and with the echoing shouts of men—not of wounded, retreating redcoats, but of oncoming settlers in hunting shirts. "Help us out of this hell," had been the plea of Braddock's men; "Show us the road to the Ohio, to the Mississippi," was to be the slogan of Washington's veterans.

At the first house their old commander reached the next day, September 26, he could get no feed for his horses, and nothing for himself except boiled corn. [126] Although he was worn by his ordeal to the extent that he had to allow himself a full day's rest after he reached Fort

[125] See Vol. V, p. 143.          [126] 2 *Diaries*, 307.

Pleasant on the 27th,[127] he counted that as nothing. The puzzle had been solved, he thought. By way of the Cheat, batteaux from the Ohio could be brought within ten miles, as he computed the distance, of water that flowed into Chesapeake Bay.[128] The next and last stage of his journey was over the Alleghenies to procure from Thomas Lewis, who resided near Staunton, documents with which to support the action for ejectment of the men who were occupying his land on Miller's Run.[129]

Washington alighted at Mount Vernon before sunset on the 4th of October,[130] three weeks ahead of the expected date of his return, and, if he had little to show in money for a journey of 680 miles and a month and four days of his time,[131] he had a reward of enthusiastic interest he had not displayed in years. Peace had brought to Washington a challenge to peaceful effort as absorbing as that of war. Said he: "The more the navigation of Potomac is investigated and duly considered, the greater the advantages arising from them appear." [132] A bold, broad policy took form in his mind: "Extend the inland navigation of the eastern waters, communicate them as near as possible (by excellent roads) with those which run to the westward. Open these to the Ohio and such others as extend from the Ohio towards Lake Erie; and we shall not only draw the produce of the western settlers, but the fur and peltry trade of the Lakes also, to our ports (being the nearest and easiest of transportation) to the amazing increase of our exports, while we bind those people to us by a chain which never can be broken." [133]

Obstacles existed, the General admitted, but they must be overcome— and could be. If there still was doubt in any mind concerning the best route, let it be resolved by careful surveys made at the instance of the government of Virginia,[134] or on order of Congress.[135] Meantime,

127 *Ibid.*, 312, 313. His route was via present-day Bruceton Mills, then to the vicinity of Cranesville, close to the West Virginia-Maryland line, and on to Oakland. In all likelihood, he struck the North Branch near Gormania. The next day probably was through Greenland Gap to Patterson's Creek and on to Old Fields, the site of Fort Pleasant.
128 *Ibid.*, 308. There is no valid reason for assuming that his informants deliberately had given Washington incorrect data on the navigation of the Cheat. They probably were guided by their hopes, not by their observations.          129 *Ibid.*, 313.
130 Return was via Swift Run Gap, Culpeper Court House, Norman's Ford and Colchester. Dr. Craik had preceded the General and, on the 2nd of October, filed a report on his observations (28 *A.H.R.*, 705). This and other important documents on the development of the Potomac are in the files of the Minnesota Historical Society.
131 2 *Diaries*, 317.
132 *Ibid.*, 318.
133 Letter of Nov. 3, 1784, to Jacob Read; 27 *G. W.*, 489.
134 *Ibid.*, 477.
135 28 *ibid.*, 11.

companies might be organized and made ready to develop the Potomac and the James also if this second enterprise was necessary to remove jealousies and was believed to be profitable.[136] Did the plan seem impracticable to Virginians and to Marylanders because both of the least inaccessible rivers, the Youghiogheny and the Monongahela, ran through Pennsylvania, a State that was agitating for the development of a route of its own from the West to the Schuylkill River? Washington did not think it likely that Pennsylvania would attempt to prevent a movement, via the Potomac, of manifest utility and profit to the thousands of her people who dwelt beyond the mountains,[137] though, of course, no State should be discouraged from pursuing any plan of its own that it considered beneficial.[138] ". . . the more communications are opened to it," said Washington, "the closer we bind that rising world (for indeed it may be so called) to our interests and the greater strength shall we acquire by it . . ." [139]

To enlarge safely that new empire of the Ohio Valley, Congress, in Washington's opinion, should purchase from the Indians sufficient land for one or two States, "fully adequate to all our present purposes" and should sell this land at figures low enough for settlers but too high for speculators. Severest penalties should be imposed on adventurers who surveyed or attempted to settle in the savages' country beyond the limits of the proposed new States.[140]

If, finally, it was maintained that trade would go down the Mississippi as soon as Spain had the wisdom to welcome it, this was an indirect argument for the development of the Potomac. The proceeds of pelts, furs and wheat sent to the Gulf of Mexico would be invested in goods which could be delivered to the Ohio far more cheaply and more quickly via the Potomac than by the long, long voyage back up the Mississippi against the current.[141]

To marshal these arguments and to put them in form for presentation to Congress and to the affected States was a long labor for a man who composed a good letter slowly. Time was scarce, too, because of

---

[136] 27 ibid., 478.
[137] Ibid., 473, 479.
[138] Ibid., 483.
[139] Ibid.
[140] Ibid., 487.
[141] Ibid., 479; 2 Diaries, 327. The second of these references is to a detailed review of his travel observations that Washington entered in his diary soon after his return home. He drew extensively from this in letters to Benjamin Harrison (27 G. W., 471–80), to George Plater (ibid., 482–84) and to Jacob Read (ibid., 485–90). It may be in order to caution the reader who examines these letters that the one to Thomas Johnson (ibid., 481) is dated wrongly Oct. 15, 1784. It appears, with some minor alterations, in its correct place (29 ibid., 60–61) under its proper date, Nov. 12, 1786. Fitzpatrick evidently was led into this error by the misdating of the letter in a secondary authority.

the attention the host at Mount Vernon felt he should give his guests, but Washington had put his hand to his self-appointed task of getting Virginia and Maryland to develop the navigation of the Potomac and, as always, he unflinchingly paid the price in hours for the result he hoped to achieve. In some sense, it was a new adventure. When he had been a Virginia Burgess, with such prestige as he had won in the French and Indian War, he had on occasion sought to muster votes for the passage of bills he thought proper. That had been action from within. In dealing with Congress from without, he usually had been as successful as could have been expected where both power and funds were of the meagrest; but he then had spoken as Commander-in-Chief and could describe with authority the disasters that might attend the rejection of his appeals. Now he was to plead as a private citizen for future development at a time when the cost of war still was being exacted of taxpayers. How far, then, might he expect to be heeded? In what measure had his wartime influence survived the struggle that had created it? He did not know and he did not make the experiment consciously, but the test would be interesting as respected both the extent of his influence and the speed with which it could be exerted.

Circumstance favored him. During a new tour of the East, Lafayette had visited Mount Vernon in August and had left at the time Washington set out for the West.[142] An understanding perhaps had been reached then that the Marquis would return to the estate whence they would proceed to Richmond, Virginia, which Lafayette desired to visit again. An invitation had come also from Gov. Benjamin Harrison, for years a friend of the retired Commander-in-Chief. Washington decided to accept and reasoned, doubtless, that besides doing honor to Lafayette, he could pay his respects to the Governor and, as the General Assembly was in session, he would have an excellent opportunity of discussing with public men the improvement of the Potomac and of the James.[143] The visit may, indeed, have been proposed and the invitation extended primarily with this object in view.

Lafayette decided to change his route to Richmond, but Washington set out on the designated date, reached the new capital of his Commonwealth on the 15th of November, and went through the ceremonials

[142] 27 *G. W.*, 458, 465; Madison to Jefferson, 5 *Madison Papers*, 21, L.C; also in Gaillard Hunt, ed., *Writings of James Madison*, cited hereafter as *Hunt's Madison*, v. 2, p. 77.

[143] 27 *G. W.*, 471. Reservation has to be made here because the reasons for this visit to Richmond nowhere are set forth explicitly.

of addresses and responses.[144] He found the members of the General Assembly divided in support of the James and the Potomac routes to the West but entirely willing to approve either one if the other was included. Washington accepted this as one of the realities of politics and in return he soon had the promise of legislators that they would take action before they adjourned the session. Back at home by the afternoon of November 24, with Lafayette,[145] Washington had the best of reasons for being satisfied with the start he had made but, at the moment, the host let other matters wait while he enjoyed his beloved French guest. When Lafayette started northward again on the 28th, to take ship from New York, Washington went with him to Annapolis and shared the festivities there. Then he continued with the Marquis for some distance on the road to Baltimore, but, regretfully, he had at length to draw rein, to say farewell [146] and to turn back. "I often asked myself," he wrote later, ". . . whether that was the last sight I ever should have of you; and though I wished to say 'No,' my fears answered 'Yes.' " [147]

After that, everything at Mount Vernon was in the usual pattern of work and of entertainment for two weeks and a little more, but not to the exclusion of the great new design that rapidly was shaping itself. Washington pressed his plea for a survey of the mountain streams by engineers Congress employed; he renewed his suggestion for a stock company, whose capital would supplement State appropriations; and, as the legislative sessions were approaching their end both in Maryland and in the Old Dominion, he urged that committees be named to confer on the drafting of identical bills.[148] Virginia still was willing to follow his leadership. On the 19th of December an express from Richmond brought him the text of resolutions the General Assembly of Virginia had passed on the 13th. These set forth that a petition of Virginians and Marylanders had been received for the establishment of a company to develop the navigation of the Potomac and that this seemed reasonable [149] but that acts passed by Virginia and Maryland

---

[144] 9 Sparks, 71–72 n; 27 G. W., 495; W. A. Christian, Richmond Her Past and Present, 23–26; Journal of the House of Delegates of Virginia, 1781–86, cited hereafter as Jour. H.D. Va. (session of October, 1784 to January, 1785), p. 24.

[145] 27 G. W., 496. Departure from Richmond probably had been on the 20th.

[146] Ibid., 505; 28 ibid., 7.          [147] Ibid., heavily repunctuated.

[148] 27 G. W., 504–05; 28 ibid., 11.

[149] The petition had been received by the House of Delegates on December 4 and had been the basis of a bill considered on December 4, 7, 9, and 10 (Jour. H.D. Va., loc. cit., 58, 61, 63, 64, 68), but had been postponed for the reason set forth in the resolution.

without previous consultation might not be similar; wherefore Washington, Gen. Horatio Gates and Thomas Blackburn, any two of them, be named to confer with Maryland authorities and to report their proceedings to the General Assembly.[150] Washington responded as promptly as if this had been an order of Congress in the seventeen-seventies for a forced march: he designated the 23rd as the date of the meeting, sent the express on to Annapolis, notified Blackburn of what was contemplated, and quickly made his own plans for the journey to the Maryland capital, even though this would involve absence from Mount Vernon Christmas Day.[151] By the 22nd, he was in Annapolis with the responsibility of serving as Virginia's sole active representative, because it was impossible for Colonel Blackburn to attend[152] and General Gates had fallen sick almost immediately on arrival.[153] The next day found Washington in close conference with Marylanders on the relative difficulties and advantages of the routes from the Potomac to the Cheat, the Youghiogheny and the Monongahela. He did not record, if indeed he remembered, the fact that the date was the first anniversary of his formal resignation, in that same Annapolis, of his commission as head of the American Army.

The conference progressed without hitch or halt. Unanimous recommendation was made for the careful survey of the various suggested routes from the Potomac to the nearest navigable streams that flowed ultimately into the Ohio. Hope was expressed that the Potomac itself could be opened as far inland as the mouth of Stony Creek, about forty-five miles upstream from Fort Cumberland.[154] It was suggested, further, that Maryland and Virginia each purchase fifty shares of the stock of a private company organized to develop the river and that jointly they assume the responsibility of constructing the portage roads. An initial appropriation of 3333 dollars was advocated for each State. Specific tolls were to be based primarily on the value of the product transported.

In much of this, Washington's direction was apparent, and in the drafting of the report to the Virginia Legislature, his was the pen, with no David Humphreys at hand to draft nor a Tench Tilghman to copy.

---

[150] *Ibid.*, p. 68. No copy of the Journal of the Senate for this session is known to be in existence.    [151] 28 *G. W.*, 14.

[152] See Blackburn to Washington, Dec. 20, 1784; 28 *A.H.R.*, 712.

[153] 28 *G. W.*, 20.

[154] The stream, now called Stony River, enters the Potomac almost on the line between Grant and Mineral Counties, West Virginia.

"It is now near 12 at night," Washington informed Madison on December 28, "and I am writing with an aching head, having been constantly employed in this business since the 22nd, without assistance from my colleagues . . ."[155] This, politely if superfluously, he made into an apology for not being able to send a "fairer" letter.[156]

The result was better than fair. The Maryland Legislature promptly passed a bill that included almost verbatim the recommendations of the Commissioners. This was hurried to Washington who forwarded it immediately to Richmond,[157] where Virginia lawmakers adopted a similar measure on January 4.[158] Bad weather delayed the receipt of official news of this by the General,[159] though he heard earlier rumor of a favorable outcome. At length, on the 16th of January he had the full facts, and the next day he informed Maryland that Virginia's acts and resolutions duplicated those of her nearest neighbor to the northward.

Had Washington turned back his calendar as he wrote that information, he would have observed that his plan had become law within a little more than four months from the time he had set out for the West, and almost exactly three months from the date of his return.[160] His popularity undoubtedly facilitated action. Some lawmakers probably voted for the bills not because they had great faith in the plan but because they wished to show their appreciation of him by doing what he desired. His energy and his experience were almost as influential as his prestige, but the keen eye of James Madison saw something besides this in Washington's exertions: "The earnestness with which he espouses the undertaking is hardly to be described, and shows that a mind like his, capable of grand views, and which has long been occupied with them, cannot bear a vacancy." [161]

[155] 28 G. W., 20.

[156] The report to the General Assembly of Virginia, in his autograph, appears in *ibid.*, 20–22; the proceedings of the Commissioners are printed in Mrs. Corra Bacon-Foster, *Early Chapters in the Development of the Patomac Route to the West*, cited hereafter as *Mrs. Bacon-Foster*, 45 ff.

[157] 28 G. W., 26–27.

[158] *Jour. H.D. Va.*, loc. cit., 101, 103, 105; 11 *H* 510 ff; James Madison to his father, Jan. 7, 1785; 5 *Madison Papers*, 56, LC.

[159] 28 G. W., 31–32.

[160] A bill for making a survey of the James and Potomac "and of the western waters to the head branches" of those rivers also received consideration but did not become a law because the House and Senate could not agree on its provisions (*Jour. H.D. Va.*, loc. cit., 77, 79, 92, 95, 99, 100, 101, 102).

[161] Letter of Jan. 9, 1785, to Jefferson, 5 *Madison Papers*, 59, LC; 2 *Hunt's Madison*, 109; cf. R. H. Lee to William Short, June 13, 1785: "You well know his persevering spirit, and attentive character." 2 *Ballagh, Lee Letters*, 373.

# CHAPTER II

## A Year of Drought and Distraction

## (1785)

THE EMBARRASSMENT of a great gift came to Washington early in January, 1785: Under an act of the General Assembly of Virginia, fifty shares of the stock of the Potomac Company and 100 shares in the James River Company were to be purchased by the Treasurer and were to be vested in Washington, "his heirs and assigns, forever, in as effectual a manner as if the subscriptions had been made by himself or by his attorney." This stock was in addition to that for which the Legislature had subscribed in the people's interest; a graceful preamble expressed the hope that as the public improvements sponsored by Washington would be "durable monuments of his glory," they should be made "monuments also of the gratitude of his country." [1] Washington knew, of course, that his refusal to accept compensation for his service during the Revolutionary War had done as much, probably, as any positive achievement of his career to win for him the respect and admiration of the country. [2] He no more was disposed in 1785 than in 1775 to have it said of him that he served America for monetary reward, or for any other reason than that he loved his country, had a vision of its future, and cherished still his old ambition to deserve and to possess the good will of his fellow-citizens. To accept from the public what he believed to be potentially a very valuable stock was contrary to an unfailing rule of his life.

At the same time, could he refuse the gift without offending the

[1] *Jour. H.D. Va.*, 1781–86; session October 1784–January 1785, p. 105, 106, 107, 110; 11 *H* 525–26. Benjamin Harrison's notification of Washington, Jan. 6, 1785, is in 231 *Papers of G. W.*, 90, LC. Harrison's original letter is incorrectly dated 1784, but Washington's endorsement on the item is properly placed in the *Papers of G. W.* (see letter of Washington to Harrison, Jan. 22, 1785; 28 *G. W.*, 34). For the manner in which some of Washington's friends acquiesced in this as the least objectionable form of a gift the Assembly was determined to make, see William Grayson to Washington, Mch. 10, 1785; 232 *Papers of G. W.*, 37–38, LC.

[2] Cf. James Henry, King and Queen Co., Virginia, to Washington, June 2, 1784: ". . . to retire without reward, perquisite or plunder has stamped a seal of immortality on General Washington's character . . ." 230 *Papers of G. W.*, 39, LC.

people of his own State, who sought to do him unique honor? His impulse was to decline the stock; his caution prompted him to seek the counsel of close friends and of those Virginia leaders who were apt to be critical.[3] Their answers were sympathetic and generally were in favor of his acceptance, but not with warmth or without misgiving.[4] Henry Knox's proposal was the one that most appealed to the General— that Washington suggest to the Legislature the use of the dividends to relieve maimed veterans and to assist the children of slain soldiers of the Virginia Line.[5] After long hesitation, Washington wrote Governor Henry a careful letter in which he asked that so far as the law "has for its object my personal emolument [it] may not have its effect; but if it should please the General Assembly to permit me to turn the destination of the fund vested in me, from my private emolument, to objects of a public nature, it will be my study in selecting these to prove the sincerity of my gratitude for the honor conferred on me, by preferring such as may appear most subservient to the enlightened and patriotic views of the Legislature"[6]—an arrangement the General Assembly at once approved.[7]

The spirit of the entire Potomac project accorded for the greater part of 1785 with this gift and with this decision. His enthusiasm carried him to what some of his friends might have regarded as optimism out of character with his innate caution. "Were I disposed to encounter present inconvenience for a future income," he told Robert Morris, "I would hazard all the money I could raise upon the navigation of the river."[8] Other Virginians and numerous Marylanders believed as fully, even if they were not willing to speculate so deeply, in the development of Potomac navigation. The amount of their subscription appeared for a time in doubt and led Washington to inquire into the possibility of

---

[3] 28 G. W., 34–36, 37–38, 72, 80–81, 85, 90–91, 92–93, 138–39, 146, 167 n, 214–15.

[4] Typical are: William Grayson, 232 *Papers of G. W.*, 37–38, LC; Benjamin Harrison, *ibid.*, 5, and 4 *LTW.*, 89–91; Patrick Henry, 232 *Papers of G. W.*, 41, LC, and 4 *LTW.*, 93; also in 2 *W. W. Henry*, 257; James Madison, 6 *Madison Papers*, 15, LC, and 2 *Hunt's Madison*, 191–92; Lafayette, *LOLTW.*, 298–99.     [5] 232 *Papers of G. W.*, 50, LC.

[6] Letter of Oct. 29, 1785, to Gov. Patrick Henry; 28 G. W., 304; cf. Letter to Madison, *ibid.*, 302–03.

[7] *Ibid.*, 359; 12 *H* 42–44. The legislators took pains to include the full letter of declination in the act that authorized Washington to make such public disposition of the dividends as he pleased.

[8] Letter of Feb. 1, 1785; 28 G. W., 55. Cf. to Lafayette, Feb. 15, 1785: "I give it as my *decided* opinion to you that *both* [the James and the Potomac developments] are practicable beyond all manner of doubt; and that men who can afford to lay a little while out of their money are laying the foundation of the greatest returns of any speculation I know of in the world" (*ibid.*, 75).

procuring foreign capital;[9] but when the first meeting was held after the stockbooks were closed, the minimum legal requirement of the sale of 250 shares as a warrant for incorporation had been met and almost doubled.[10] By that time, too, there was assurance that the navigation of Chesapeake Bay and of the Potomac would be enjoyed by Virginians and Marylanders without any sort of interference with one another. Equal use and equal treatment were guaranteed under a pact between the two, debated and accepted by commissioners who met at Alexandria and then adjourned to Mount Vernon. There was distinct encouragement for the future of good relations in the ease and equity with which, under date of Mch. 28, 1785, this joint use of the waters was established in perpetuum.[11] Care was taken, also, to provide for future annual conferences between representatives of the two States for the review of commercial questions that might arise.[12]

Where an auspicious prospect of Potomac development was opening, through the efforts of Washington, it was natural for stockholders to look to him for continued leadership. Somewhat against his wishes, he was named President of the Potomac Company [13] and was one of the active directors who undertook to find a manager. In the absence of applications by experienced engineers, the choice fell on James Rumsey, inventor of the boat Washington had seen in miniature at Bath.[14] In August, 1785, the retired Commander-in-Chief began periodic inspection tours of the Potomac from Harpers Ferry to the Great Falls above Georgetown.[15] He always encountered some disappointment but usually he found encouragement,[16] especially after the legislatures of Maryland and Virginia agreed to a reduction from four to two feet in

[9] *Ibid.*, 79–80, 135–36. The books were open for subscriptions from Feb. 8 to May 10, 1785, *ibid.*, 65.

[10] *Ibid.*, 145–46; *ibid.*, cf. 278.

[11] The Virginia joint resolution for this conference, adopted June 30, 1784, is in *Jour. H. D. Va.*, op. cit., session May–June, 1784, p. 84, 89. No copy of the printed *Journal of the Senate* for that session, if it was printed, is known to be in existence. The text of the resolution is printed in part in 2 *Rowland, Mason*, 72. Details of the conference, as far as they are known in the absence of minutes, are given in *ibid.*, 81 ff. Virginia's ratification of October, 1785, is in *Jour. H.D. Va.*, op. cit., session October, 1785–January, 1786, p. 118–19; *Journal of the Senate of the Commonwealth of Virginia*, 1785–1790, session October, 1785–January, 1786, cited hereafter as *Jour. Sen. Va.*, 70, 71; 12 *H* 50–55. Washington's participation—the use of his carriage and the entertainment of the commissioners at Mount Vernon—is noted casually in 2 *Diaries*, 352–54. Virginia representatives in attendance were Colonel Mason and Alexander Henderson.

[12] See *infra*, p. 66, 115.

[13] 28 *G. W.*, 219; 2 *Diaries*, 376; 2 *Ballagh, Lee Letters*, 373.

[14] 28 *G. W.*, 189, 211; Ella May Turner, *op. cit.*, Chap. III.

[15] Cf. 28 *G. W.*, 232, 254–55.

[16] *Ibid.*, 232, 234, 245, 265–66; 6 *Madison Papers*, 7, LC; 2 *Hunt's Madison*, 182.

the depth of the canals around the falls of the river.[17] Although the General soon was to confess that clearing the river for batteaux involved questions on which he did not feel he had competence,[18] he did not doubt, as the months passed, that the river could be opened for light-draft navigation at a cost within the subscription.[19] He made it plain, all the while, that development of waterways was no substitute for the maintenance and improvement of Virginia roads.[20] He did decline the presidency of the James River Company, which, in his opinion, had an inauspicious beginning, but he took care to subscribe to its stock and to commend it in terms as warm as those in which he endorsed the Potomac project.[21]

Still another enterprise that demanded a place in Washington's mind during 1785 was the Dismal Swamp Company which he and other "proprietors" had organized in 1763 [22] but never had developed with vigor. First, John Robinson's financial catastrophe [23] and then the Revolution had discouraged the digging of the many small canals required for the drainage of the tangled, black-earth swamp. Management was feeble; records were lost, scattered or forgotten; [24] the few Negroes assigned the Company could do little more than raise a crop and cut shingles; [25] a meeting proposed for May, 1784, and the subject of no little correspondence,[26] was held in October at Richmond.[27]  A

[17] 28 *G. W.*, 329, 337–38, 339–41, 364–65. The agreement is in 12 *H* 69. The preamble sets forth the assumed engineering reasons why two feet would suffice.

[18] 28 *G. W.*, 397.

[19] The most direct approach to the considerable volume of historical writing on the Potomac Canal is through the footnotes in W. S. Sanderlin, *The Great National Project; A History of the Chesapeake and Ohio Canal*, The Johns Hopkins Studies in His. and Pol. Science, Ser. 64, No. 1, 1946. Other basic works are "Chesapeake and Ohio Canal," 19th Cong., 1st Session, House Report No. 228, May 22, 1826; *Washington and the Potomac*, a collection of documents now in the Minnesota Historical Society, carefully edited by Grace L. Nute; John Pickell, *A New Chapter in the Early Life of Washington in Connection with the Narrative History of the Potomac Company*; Mrs. Corra Bacon-Foster, *Early Chapters in the Development of the Patomac Route to the West*.

[20] He asked Governor Henry: ". . . do you not think . . . that the credit, the saving and convenience of this country all require that our great roads leading from one public place to another should be shortened, straightened and established by law; and the power in the county courts to alter them withdrawn?" 28 *G. W.*, 334–35.

[21] *Ibid.*, 146, 219. He left the door open in event of a public demand that he become head of the James River enterprise.

[22] Vol. III, p. 93–95, 101–03.          [23] *Ibid.*, 165–67.

[24] Cf. 28 *G. W.*, 127; David Jamieson's account with the Company, in a role apparently that of Treasurer, Aug. 26, 1774–July 17, 1780, is in Duke Univ. Lib.

[25] Cf. David Jamison [?] to William Nelson, Jan. 4, 1785; *Dismal Swamp Papers*, Duke Univ. Lib.

[26] Thomas Walker to Washington, Jan. 24, 1784, 229 *Papers of G. W.*, 19, LC; 27 *G. W.*, 377 ff, 391–92, 463.

[27] David Jamieson [?] to Dr. Thomas Walker [?] Sept. 29, 1784; Miles Hunter's receipt to Dr. Thomas Walker, Oct. 23, 1784, for advertisement of the meeting; David Jamieson to

further meeting in May, 1785, with Washington in attendance,[28] led to a discussion of the question of obtaining laborers in Baltimore, or of bringing from Germany or Holland as many as 300 "acquainted with drainage and other branches of agriculture." A small loan for a term of seven years was authorized,[29] and inquiries were dispatched concerning the possibility of procuring £4000 or £5000 in Amsterdam,[30] but neither this nor a proposal for constructing a large canal through Dismal Swamp to Albemarle Sound yielded immediate result.[31]

Washington continued to believe that the swamp lands of that region would "in time become the most valuable property in this country" [32] and he declined with regret to participate in a plan Patrick Henry had in hand for the drainage and extensive development of the southern end of the swamp. The reason for abstaining, the General wrote in full candor, was that "it would be most advisable for me, in my situation, not to add to my present expenditures." [33] Had he felt it necessary to go into detail, he could have given at least four reasons why 1785 was of all years of his life as a planter the one in which he should add to income rather than increase outgo. His western lands were yielding little except suits for eviction [34] and troublesome searches for documents with which to prove his titles.[35] In part of this work, he was hampered by meagre knowledge of his own property on the Ohio,[36] and in seeking ejectments he was held back by his reluctance to enjoin those who appealed to him on any ground that raised in his mind a doubt of his own just dealing.[37] He would tell his agents to press hard for overdue rents,[38] and then would acquiesce in almost any plea for leniency.[39] The result was a trifling return from old tenants and no leases with new. "I presume," said Washington, "the terms are thought too high; but as I know the situation and convenience of [the farms], and that the quality of the soil is inferior to none in all the Western

---

unnamed correspondent, Oct. 25, 1784, *Dismal Swamp Papers*, Duke Univ. Lib.; *Va. Gazette* (Richmond), Oct. 2, 1784, p. 1.

[28] 28 *G. W.*, 120–21, 127, 136, 139 n; 2 *Diaries*, 371–72. Washington left home April 29 and returned May 6. He was in the Virginia capital from the evening of May 1 till May 4.

[29] *Dismal Swamp Papers*, LC, resolution of May 1, 1785.

[30] 28 *G. W.*, 258–59.          [31] *Ibid.*, 279, 286, 333.

[32] *Ibid.*, 176.          [33] *Ibid.*

[34] *Ibid.*, 261–62; Thomas Smith to Washington, Feb. 9, 1785; 232 *Papers of G. W.*, 6, LC.

[35] 28 *G. W.*, 110–11, 155–57, 192, 200, 220.

[36] Cf. *ibid.*, 128.

[37] See, for example, his explanation of his reasons for combining action for trespass with ejectment proceedings, *ibid.*, 346–47.

[38] *Ibid.*, 353–55.          [39] *Ibid.*, 375, 390–91.

Territory, I do not incline to make any change in my terms unless I am in a manner compelled to it by taxation . . ." He added that he wished to see taxes imposed heavily in order "that the officers and soldiers, and other public creditors may receive their just dues." [40] He certainly did not receive his own dues. His 32,373 acres of Ohio and Kanawha land, on which he set a price of 30,000 guineas, yielded him scarcely enough to justify him in entering it on his books.[41] From his mill in Fayette County, his most valuable holding in Pennsylvania, he still could not get a farthing of rent.[42]

A second adverse condition—it might almost be termed a calamity —was hostile weather. The long, wet and disagreeable winter of 1784-85 [43] was followed by what Washington described as "the most unfavorable" spring he ever knew,[44] and that an unpropitious planting season gave place to a drought that continued until August 27.[45] The mill on Dogue Run had no water; [46] a new insect pest sapped the corn and ruined much of the grass.[47]

Between the backward spring and the beginning of the drought, a messenger arrived at Mount Vernon with the news that Martha's brother, Bartholomew Dandridge, and their mother, Mrs. Frances Jones Dandridge, had died within a few days of each other. Mrs. Dandridge was 74 years of age and had finished her active life, but Judge Dandridge was 48 and had in his care the tangled estate of "Jack" Custis.[48] The Judge, moreover, had served as guardian of some of "Jack's" children,[49] and had a considerable debt to the General and Mrs. Washington on his own account and because of a loan made in 1758 by Martha's estate to William Dandridge.[50] Washington had dealt often with

[40] *Ibid.*, 199.
[41] For his acreage and valuation, see *ibid.*, 436–37.
[42] *Ibid.*, 211.                    [43] *Ibid.*, 246–47; 2 *Diaries*, 339.
[44] 28 *G. W.*, 134.
[45] *Ibid.*, 246–47, 249; 2 *Diaries*, 404, 408, cf. 409.
[46] 28 *G. W.*, 249.                    [47] 2 *Diaries*, 405.
[48] In 28 *G. W.*, 137. Washington spoke of the "embarrassed affairs of Mr. Custis."
[49] Cf. his letter of Mch. 13, 1784, to Washington: "I have endeavored to arrange the affairs of Mr. Custis's estate in such a manner as I judged most for its interest, but I must own I have not succeeded in it agreeably to my wishes or expectations, but when I have done the best I could, I hope I may not be blamed for consequences that I could not guard against . . ." 229 *Papers of G. W.*, 77.
[50] William Dandridge, Martha's brother, in 1758 secured a loan from the Custis estate for £600 and gave bond for the sum (*Ledger B*, f. 220). In 1761 the bond was assigned to Martha Parke Custis as part of her share of her father's estate (*Ledger A*, f. 110). William Dandridge was drowned in January, 1776, and his brother Bartholomew took over that bond as well as one given by William and Bartholomew Dandridge and William Whitehead Claiborne dated May 15, 1758 (*Ledger B*, f. 220). George Mason, it will be remembered, had reconciled during the war the accounts of the Custis estate with Washington and his wife. For

similar affairs over a period of thirty years and doubtless had concluded
that executorships were the eighth Egyptian plague, but even he must
have admitted that new financial distress would be involved in any
arrangement of Judge Dandridge's affairs. When this had occurred
previously, with other estates, most of the waiting, the inconvenience
and the loss of interest usually had been Washington's. Debtors had
changed to "ye" the pronoun in the scriptural injunction, "we then
that are strong ought to bear the infirmities of the weak . . ."

The last clause of that exhortation of the Apostle might have been
applied by Washington to some of the guests whose steady flow to
Mount Vernon was the fourth reason for the General's increasing financial distress. His home, he wrote later, "may be compared to a well-
resorted tavern, as scarcely any strangers who are going from North
to South, or from South to North, do not spend a day or two at it." [51]
This imposition was becoming worse, not better. Some visitors came
in reverence and departed in awe; an occasional guest felt disappointment because of the General's reticence or weariness or both. A
22-year-old Dutchman, Gijsbert Karel van Hogendorp, a kinsman
of his country's minister to the United States, wrote home that on
reaching Mount Vernon, he was taken "to a chamber where Madame
Washington was seated with two of her friends; with them were two
or three gentlemen." Said Hogendorp: "They greeted my arrival with
dismal silence, regarding me with that careless manner I have met so
often in America. After a brief conversation, carried on almost entirely
by me, I heard the door behind me open and saw Washington himself
enter the room. There is such integrity in his face that he prepossesses
in his favor all those who see him for the first time. They are not
able to understand the great man. I had the desire to appreciate him
but at the outset his mien and his conversation seemed to me so commonplace that I was bewildered by what I observed . . . I became
convinced that he was not a man of genius, that he had no great talents
. . . He is slow of perception; he expresses himself slowly. Transition
from one subject to another is difficult for him; he does not consider
matters profoundly; he shares the indolence common to Americans
who stifle in themselves all inclinations to industry. He possesses so

---

the use of Martha's share in the Custis properties on the Pamunkey and the York, "Jack's"
estate was supposed to pay Washington £525 annually (*Ledger B*, f. 224, 272 and *infra*,
p. 59–60).
    [51] 29 *G. W.*, 160–61.

little vivacity and enthusiasm that he seemed embarrassed by the evidence of these qualities in others . . . I could never be on familiar terms with the General—a man so cold, so cautious, so obsequious, fearing to speak even of his campaigns . . . giving his opinions vaguely or repeating his annoying, 'In truth I know nothing about it . . .' " Hogendorp went on to say that Mrs. Washington "has not a bad opinion of me for not adoring her husband; she has eyes more perceptive than her husband; she has made many piquant remarks to me that reveal to me that she is not irritated by what I say, as she would be if I were wrong."

The complacent Dutchman conceded, at the end, "It is not to be denied that they make the stranger feel at home and entertain him very well"; [52] but apparently he never realized that a man apt to be quoted by some of his visitors naturally was reticent in the presence of a young stranger, well introduced though Hogendorp was.[53]

It is probable that the General was especially cautious and was ill at ease in dealing with men whose native speech he did not understand, but where he knew his words would not be passed on, he now had lost some of his military reserve. One visitor of 1785 wrote, "The General with a few glasses of champagne got quite merry, and being with his intimate friends laughed and talked a good deal. Before strangers, he is generally very reserved and seldom says a word. I was fortunate in being in his company with his particular acquaintances." [54] Some of Washington's friends, marking all this, were of opinion that his reserve gave him advantages. It "hid such imperfections as he possessed," Col. John Allan wrote, "and it saved him from criticism that careless remarks might have provoked." [55] A few years previously, Washington had warned his nephew Bushrod against quick attachments; [56] he never spoke freely before any except those whose discretion and loyalty had long been tested.

Few visitors resented this, few were as caustic as was Hogendorp, and some who might have been expected to be troublesome were easy. The previous year Rev. William Gordon had been an exacting cor-

[52] This visit was late in April, 1784. *Brieven en Gedenkschriften van Gijsbert Karel van Hogendorp* . . . v. 1, p. 349–57.

[53] For his credentials see 7 *Burnett*, 495 n. Jefferson wrote of Hogendorp, "[I] consider him as the best informed man of his age I have ever seen." 229 *Papers of G. W.*, 101, LC.

[54] Wright and Tinling, eds., *Quebec to Carolina in 1785–1786, Being the Travel Diary and Observations of Robert Hunter, Jr., a Young Merchant of London*, 194.

[55] 30 *N. E. His. Gen. Reg.*, 389–90.            [56] See Vol. V, p. 491; 26 *G. W.*, 39.

respondent—the type of man who wishes to know secrets because of the sense of self-importance the possession of them gives. When it finally was arranged that Congress would afford Gordon access to official papers for the preparation of his history of the Revolution,[57] Washington agreed to do the same thing though he was careful to limit the scope of this privilege by underlining a word when he wrote of opening "my *public* papers for your information." [58] Gordon arrived early on the morning of June 2, 1784, and went to work, as soon as politeness permitted, on the manuscript records and transcripts Washington had sent home in 1783. The minister began daily at dawn to read, to copy and to abstract. He stopped for meals only, worked until late at night, with steady declination of all hospitality in the neighborhood, and completed his search on the 19th. Then he considerately went his way, perhaps the least exacting visitor who ever remained so long a time at Mount Vernon.[59]

After Gordon's departure, hot weather and then Washington's absence in the West reduced the number of visitors, except for the always welcome Lafayette. The next year, 1785, brought a long succession of guests, some of them interesting and distinguished, and all of them expensive and time-consuming. Elkanah Watson, merchant adventurer and enthusiastic advocate of canals, came to Mount Vernon in January to explain what he had seen of the waterways of the Low Countries. He was then 27 and already had made a fortune that had been swept away in 1783. His impression of the General was almost the reverse of Hogendorp's: "He soon put me at ease, by unbending, in a

[57] See *supra*, p. 12.     [58] 27 *G. W.*, 398–99; cf. *ibid.*, 52.
[59] This is merely a rephrasing of the account of an incident admirably presented in Merrill Jensen's *The New Nation, a History of the United States during the Confederation, 1781–1789*, p. 97–98. According to a letter of Gordon's to Gen. Horatio Gates, quoted by Jensen, private as well as personal papers were made available to Gordon, but he may have used "private" in the sense of "secret." An informed modern reader of Gordon's narrative will find few evidences of the use of the Washington papers placed at his disposal. The reason may be the incredibly poor choice of method Gordon made in presenting the various episodes of the war in what purported to be a series of contemporary letters written by an observer in America who knew more than anyone possibly could have ascertained at the time. With no responsibility for method or result, Washington obligingly furnished desired information after the minister departed, and in January, 1786, he somewhat reluctantly circulated a subscription list for the work (28 *G. W.*, 344–45, 372, 412, 455). At the last, Washington became cautious in dealing with Gordon, whose finished book, *The History of the Rise, Progress, and Establishment of the Independence of the United States of America . . .*, pleased neither British nor Americans (30 *G. W.*, 168–70, 212). George Otto Trevelyan's exasperation with Gordon (*The American Revolution*, ed. 1905, v. 2, p. 122–26) is as amusing as it is extreme, but the fact seems to be that if Gordon had been as much interested in history as in being considered an historian he might have written an invaluable book. No other resident in America during the revolutionary years had such an opportunity.

free and affable conversation. The cautious reserve, which wisdom and policy dictated, whilst engaged in rearing the glorious fabric of our independence, was evidently the result of consummate prudence, and not characteristic of his nature . . . I observed a peculiarity in his smile, which seemed to illuminate his eye: his whole countenance beamed with intelligence, while it commanded confidence and respect . . . I found him kind and benignant in the domestic circle, revered and beloved by all around him; agreeably sociable, without ostentation; delighting in anecdote and adventures without assumption; his domestic arrangements harmonious and systematic." Watson had arrived with a bad cold and a severe cough, which Washington tried to induce him to treat with remedies the guest declined. That night, kept awake by coughing, Watson heard the door of his room gently opened. "On drawing my bed-curtains, to my utter astonishment, I beheld Washington himself, standing at my bedside, with a bowl of hot tea in his hand. I was mortified and distressed beyond expression. This little incident, occurring in common life with an ordinary man, would not have been noticed; but as a trait of the benevolence and private virtue of Washington, deserves to be recorded. He modestly waived all allusions to the events, in which he had acted so glorious and conspicuous a part. Much of his conversation had reference to the interior country, and to the opening of the navigation of the Potomac . . ." [60]

One story of a different sort, confided to Watson by the General, had to do with a visit by the artist, Joseph Wright, who asked Washington to permit him to make a life mask in plaster. The General went on: "I consented with some reluctance. He oiled my features over, and placing me flat upon my back, upon a cot, proceeded to daub my face with the plaster. Whilst in this ludicrous attitude, Mrs. Washington entered the room, and seeing my face thus overspread with the plaster, involuntarily exclaimed. Her cry excited in me a disposition to smile, which gave my mouth a slight twist or compression of the lips, that is now observable in the busts Wright afterwards made." [61]

As it chanced, the next conspicuous guest at Mount Vernon, after Watson's departure, was another artist, Robert Edge Pine, whose sym-

[60] *Elkanah Watson,* op. cit., 243–44. From the edition of 1856, with punctuation unchanged.
[61] *Ibid.,* 119. This is quoted in Morgan and Fielding, *The Life Portraits of Washington,* 82, opposite a reproduction of an oval wax medallion in relief, by Wright, which shows the twist of the mouth, though the medallion is in profile. Fiske Kimball printed in 15 *Antiques,* 377–82, an authoritative review of "Joseph Wright and His Portraits of Washington," cited in *Morgan and Fielding,* 71 n.

pathy with America had cost him his profitable business as a portraitist in England. An appealing letter of introduction by George William Fairfax [62] was followed in 1785 by one from Francis Hopkinson, a favorite of Washington's. The Philadelphian wrote that he knew the General would rather fight a battle than sit for a portrait, but that Pine, who was the most eminent artist ever to come to America, intended to make pictures of the Revolutionary War and could not do this without portraits of Washington.[63] Washington replied, almost merrily, in what has become one of his own familiar letters: "In for a penny, in for a pound is an old adage. I am so hackneyed to the touches of the painters' pencil that I am now altogether at their beck, and sit like patience on a monument while they are delineating the lines of my face. It is a proof among many others of what habit and custom can effect. At first I was as impatient at the request, and as restive under the operation, as a colt is of the saddle. The next time I submitted very reluctantly, but with less flouncing. Now, no dray moves more readily to the thill [64] than I to the painter's chair. It may easily be conceived therefore that I yielded a ready obedience to your request and to the views of Mr. Pine." [65] The artist remained at Mount Vernon for three weeks.[66] Among the family portraits he painted were Frances Bassett, Nelly, Eliza and George Washington Custis—commonly known as "Mr. Tub"—and perhaps one of Washington also.[67]

About a fortnight after Pine left Mount Vernon, Mrs. Catherine Macaulay Graham and her husband arrived, with Washington's old aide, Col. John Fitzgerald of Alexandria, and George Lux of Baltimore as escort.[68] The lady brought her own credentials—her great reputation as historian and controversialist—and she had, in addition, letters

[62] Dated Aug. 23, 1784; 231 *Papers of G. W.*, 11, LC. If Pine is the subject of any biographical interest, this letter will be found of value.

[63] Letter of Apr. 19, 1785; *Emmet Col.*, NYPL.

[64] This early word for shaft or pole seems to have passed almost completely from American speech. Strangely, Shakespeare never used the word, nor "shaft" in the same sense.

[65] Letter of May 16, 1785; 28 *G. W.*, 140–41.

[66] Apr. 28–May 19, 1785; 2 *Diaries*, 370, 377. During eight days of this time, Washington had to be absent, in attendance on the meeting at Richmond of the Dismal Swamp Company (28 *G. W.*, 151–52).

[67] For the argument whether any of the four surviving portraits of Washington by Pine was from life, see *Morgan and Fielding*, op. cit., 85–86. Pine's portraits of the Mount Vernon household were not received until December, 1785. Washington paid for them Feb. 25, 1786. See *Ledger B*, f. 212 and 28 *G. W.*, 373, 387. The artist, according to Morgan and Fielding, "was highly regarded as a painter by reason of his fine coloring, although he was somewhat careless of detail and as a portraitist does not take high rank" (*Morgan and Fielding*, op. cit., 86). Pine died suddenly in Philadelphia, Nov. 19, 1788.

[68] 2 *Diaries*, 381, entry of June 4, 1785.

of introduction from Richard Henry Lee [69] and from Henry Knox. [70] Washington and the mistress of Mount Vernon of course received her with their usual hospitality and with the delicate attentions due a woman of literary distinction; but they must have been as much puzzled as her friends had been by her taste in personal adornment and in men. When she had been about 44, and a widow of nine years' weeds, with fame as a writer, she suddenly displayed a fondness for gaudy dress and began to apply rouge with a purposeful hand. John Wilkes, who hated her heartily, alleged that she was "painted up to the eyes" and looked "as rotten as an old Catharine pear." Then, in 1778, when she was 47, she stunned her friends by marrying William Graham, aged 21. She consequently had passed her fifty-fourth birthday—was in fact almost a year older than Washington—when she appeared on the Potomac with a husband of 28. [71] If there was gossip over this strange union, no echo of it found its way into the General's correspondence. His references were to the entertainment of the guests and to the honor of having "a visit from a lady so celebrated in the literary world." [72] When she left after about ten days, Washington had satisfaction in her agreement with him that the powers of Congress were inadequate. [73]

Other visitors there were during the summer and autumn, some of them already distinguished and some of them soon to be—Noah Webster, who considered the possibility of becoming secretary and tutor at Mount Vernon, though his larger interest was in schoolbooks; [74] James Fitch, who did not relish Washington's endorsement of James Rumsey's boat; [75] the adventurer Lewis Littlepage, who had served with

[69] 2 *Ballagh, Lee Letters*, 352–53. Lee, it will be remembered, at this time was President of the Continental Congress.

[70] Mch. 29, 1785; 232 *Papers of G. W.*, 62, LC—an amusingly self-conscious and ponderous letter by a man who usually wrote his old chief with pleasant informality, though always with respect.

[71] *DNB*.      [72] 28 *G. W.*, 159, 169.

[73] *Ibid.*, 174. For the later exchange of civilities between the General and Mrs. Macaulay Graham, see *ibid.*, 370–71 and the *Papers of G. W.*, LC, for 1785 and 1786.

[74] See Harry F. Warfel, *Noah Webster, Schoolmaster to America*, 122; E. E. F. Ford,, *Notes on the life of Noah Webster*, v. 1, p. 104 ff; E. C. Shoemaker, *Noah Webster, Pioneer of Learning*, 51–52. Webster's letters to Washington are in 1 Ford, *Notes*, as *supra*, 92, 107–08, 110, 180, 288–89. Other letters are in the *Washington Papers*, LC, originals as well as photostats. These cover the period from July 18, 1785, to Sept. 2, 1790. Washington's letters to Webster will be found in 28 *G. W.*, 216, 358, 409; 29 *ibid.*, 301; 30 *ibid.*, 26; 31 *ibid.*, 105; 33 *ibid.*, 360—July 30, 1785 to May 9, 1794.

[75] Thompson Westcott, *Life of John Fitch, Inventor of the Steamboat*, 139–42; Thomas Boyd, *Poor John Fitch, Inventor of the Steamboat*, 145–47. Fitch wrote of Washington: "I believe that his greatest failure is a too great delicacy of his own honour, which we hardly

John Jay in Spain and temporarily had quit diplomacy for arms;[76] Count Luigi Castiglioni, an Italian botanist,[77] and numerous others.[78]

The guest of 1785 who came on the most conspicuous mission was the French sculptor, Jean Antoine Houdon. By a resolution of June, 1784, the General Assembly of Virginia requested the Governor "to take measures for procuring a statue of General Washington, to be of the finest marble and the best workmanship" and to carry an inscription set forth in the enactment.[79] Under this resolution, Thomas Jefferson, then in France, had been asked to engage an artist. Jefferson's reply was, "There could be no question raised as to the sculptor who should be employed; the reputation of Monsieur Houdon of this city being unrivalled in Europe."[80] Negotiations were concluded readily, if on somewhat expensive terms, and Houdon after a delay occasioned by illness, left for the United States in the company of Benjamin Franklin.[81] The first news Washington had of the artist's arrival was in a letter received about September 25 from Doctor Franklin, who stated that Houdon was in Philadelphia. As soon as the sculptor could replace tools and materials that had not reached him before he sailed, he would come to Mount Vernon.[82] The General replied in a warm letter of acknowledgment[83] and sent a formal welcome to the statuary, in just such language as he had employed in darker years when a French Admiral or General reached port.[84]

---

can suppose can be carried to excess" (*Westcott*, op. cit., 139). Washington declined to explain to Fitch what had been told him by Rumsey concerning propulsion of boats.

[76] "An extraordinary character," Washington wrote of this violent Virginian of 23, who later was a conspicuous figure in Polish wars. The sketch in *DAB* mentions such bibliographical materials as have survived. Washington's reference was in 2 *Diaries*, 433. Littlepage was introduced by Patrick Henry. See 2 *W. W. Henry*, 267.

[77] Although the Count spent four days at Mount Vernon during the Christmas season of 1785, he left but a brief description of Washington in his *Viaggio negli Stati Uniti dell' America Settentrionale . . . 1785, 1786, e 1787*, v. 2, p. 181 ff. A part only of this appears in A. J. Morrison, *Travels in Virginia in Revolutionary Times*, 63.

[78] Joseph Hadfield, a young Manchester merchant, was one of these. His account of his visit (D. S. Robertson, ed., *An Englishman in America, 1785, Being the Diary of Joseph Hadfield*, p. vi, 11–15) is of small interest except for his statement concerning the General's reputation as a planter. See *infra*, p. 44. In 2 *Diaries*, 337 n, Fitzpatrick surmised that "a Mr. Blaine" who spent the evening at Mount Vernon, Jan. 25, 1785, may have been Ephraim Blaine, the former Commissary General. Had this been the man, Washington certainly would have identified him. For Blaine's movements in 1783–84, see *The Blaine Family: James Blaine, Emigrant, and His Children*, 39–42. Rev. Dr. Thomas Coke, Methodist Bishop, was at Alexandria, Mch. 9, 1785, but he did not call at Mount Vernon. See Morrison, *op. cit.*, 72–73, with extracts from Coke's *Five Visits to America*.

[79] Passed the House, June 22, and the Senate, June 24, 1784; 11 *H* 552.

[80] Letter of Jan. 12, 1785, to the Governor of Virginia—Patrick Henry having succeeded Benjamin Harrison—*Executive Papers*, VSL; 2 *W. W. Henry*, 263.

[81] 3 *ibid.*, 305–06; 9 *Smyth's Franklin*, 368–69.

[82] *Ibid.*, 464–65.     [83] 28 *G. W.*, 282.     [84] *Ibid.*, 277.

About 11 o'clock on the night of October 2, after Washington had gone to bed, there was clatter and conversation and the barking of dogs: Monsieur Houdon had arrived by boat from Alexandria, with three assistants and a French resident of the nearby town, who acted as interpreter.[85] Two clergymen and several other guests already were occupying most of the spare beds, but room was made for the five late comers, and household calm was restored. The next morning Houdon delivered letters from Lafayette, Jefferson and David Humphreys[86] and began to prepare for modeling. Jefferson had written that Houdon probably would not spend more than a month at Mount Vernon with the General in making his masks and measurements, though he would require from two to three years to complete the statue;[87] the artist proceeded as if he did not intend to waste a day. Perhaps he saved time, after his interpreter left on the 5th,[88] because he spoke no English and did not linger loquaciously over the Madeira or the tea. Besides, Washington was very busy. In wet weather he had the special duty of preparing a lawn and of seeing that part of the house was reshingled properly.[89] By the 6th, Houdon was ready to begin on the bust of Washington. That day and the next the General sat for him.[90]

Houdon went with Washington and two other guests to attend a funeral in the neighborhood on the 9th,[91] perhaps from a desire to see how the Americans conducted obsequies. He probably was interested, also, in the wedding of George Augustine Washington and Frances Bassett on the evening of the 15th. With Sally Ramsay and Kitty Washington as the bridesmaids, and Rev. Spencer Grayson as the clergyman,[92] the ceremony doubtless was sufficiently beautiful to have pleased an artist. Washington himself must have shared the romance of a union between Mrs. Washington's niece and his nephew. In his Diary he wrote: "After the candles were lighted, George Aug^e. Wash-

---

[85] 2 *Diaries*, 419.
[86] *LOLTW.*, 300; 4 *LTW.*, 107; 28 *G. W.*, 305.
[87] *Executive Papers*, VSL; 2 *W. W. Henry*, 264.
[88] 2 *Diaries*, 419.  [89] *Ibid.*, 419–21.
[90] *Ibid.*, 420. Apparently Houdon made a life-mask and from this fashioned a bust in clay which he forthwith duplicated. The mask and one of the clay busts he took back to France; one of the busts he left at Mount Vernon (see *Morgan and Fielding*, op. cit., 112). See frontispiece, this volume. There is, lamentably, no basis for the tradition that Houdon was at a loss to determine an appropriate pose for Washington until one day he walked out with the General to look at a yoke of oxen a farmer offered to sell. When the man named his price, Washington drew himself up in angry protest against an unreasonable figure. Houdon, according to the story, cried out in satisfaction: he had the pose for which he had been waiting! Actually, neither the posture nor the apparel of the General was determined for the statue until after Houdon was back in France.  [91] 2 *Diaries*, 421.  [92] *Ibid.*, 423.

ington and Frances Bassett were married by Mr. Grayson." Seldom
did Washington permit himself in his matter-of-fact journal so sentimental a phrase as "after the candles were lighted." [93]

Houdon looked, Houdon listened as best he could—and Houdon
worked. "As a man," Jefferson said of him, "he is disinterested, generous and candid, and panting after glory." [94] Doubtless Houdon justified the tribute, but when he completed his work and left, October 17,
on the Mount Vernon barge to take the Philadelphia stage at Alexandria,[95] there remained not one *bon mot,* not one diverting episode to
be mentioned in Washington's letters. There had been some talk of
the costume to be used in the statue; Washington had hinted that
classical garb might not be appropriate; [96] he had observed closely how
Houdon prepared plaster and he set down the process in his diary.[97]
With these incidents, the record was closed. The General wrote David
Humphreys, "I feel great obligations [to Mr. Houdon] for quitting
France and the pressing calls of the Great Ones to make a bust of me
from the life." [98] Doubtless he said as much to Houdon; doubtless the
answer of the artist was urbane; but there was no au revoir, no letter
of thanks from Philadelphia or from Paris, not even "I hope you like
it" when the statue was finished and shipped. Houdon let the marble
speak for itself. It did.[99]

Houdon was the exceptional guest. Some of the others were more
exacting. Washington remained the generous host, but, with all his

[93] Washington had taken pains neither to advocate nor to discourage this match and had
so assured Burwell Bassett (28 *G. W.,* 152). While the General apparently did not think the
impairment of George Augustine's health serious enough to make marriage unwise, he several
times observed that the young Major's sickness had not been overcome completely. Before the
marriage, Washington and his wife assured the young people they would be welcome to live
at Mount Vernon " 'til the squalling and trouble of children might become disagreeable"
(*ibid.,* 318). The prospect of the consummation of marriage was one of the few subjects, perhaps the only one, on which Washington allowed himself to write with a levity that was distinctly broad. When George Augustine went to the Springs, prior to the marriage, the General
remarked that he did so "to obtain a better stock to fit him for the pleasures, and duties, too,
of a matrimonial voyage" (*ibid.,* 181). The same metaphor was used in a letter to Lafayette,
George Augustine's war-time chief: "He is now on a journey to the Sweet Springs, to procure
a stock sufficient to fit him for a matrimonial voyage in the Frigate F. Bassett, on board which
he means to embark at his return in October: how far his case is desperate, I leave you to
judge, if it is so, the remedy however pleasing at first, will certainly be violent" (*ibid.,* 210,
verbatim).
[94] 233 *Papers of G. W.,* 14, LC; 4 *LTW.,* 107.
[95] 2 *Diaries,* 426; 28 *G. W.,* 308.      [96] 28 *G. W.,* 504.
[97] 2 *Diaries,* 421.      [98] Letter of Oct. 30, 1785; 28 *G. W.,* 305.
[99] Houdon's son-in-law, Raoul Rochette, wrote that in later life the visit to Mount Vernon
"always shone with peculiar radiance" in Houdon's mind "for . . . the pleasure of having
been close to Washington left memories he was fond of recurring to when others of various
kinds had long been forgotten" (Hart and Biddle, *Memoirs of the Life and Works of Jean
Antoine Houdon, the Sculptor of Voltaire and of Washington,* 218).

regard for the laws of hospitality, the clock ticked inexorably. The annoyance of uninvited guests might become an affliction to the General who had to find time for his correspondence and for the care of his estate. By the beginning of 1785 he was learning how to entrust to various persons at Mount Vernon part of the entertainment of his guests. Young men interested in agriculture were turned over to the manager, to one of the overseers, or to the Negro major domo, Jack, whom Washington knew to be entirely reliable.[100] Even with this assistance, breakfast at 7 o'clock and the dedication of his mornings to work, Washington often left his guests for two hours between tea and supper, and sometimes he did not appear at the evening meal. Dinner was at 2 p.m.; nine remained his bedtime unless a visitor brought news in which he had special interest.[101] Some relief came after July, when Washington employed William Shaw as his secretary,[102] but Shaw, having acquaintances in nearby towns, soon developed the habit of riding off to a social affair from which he came home tardily. Washington had not prohibited this in his agreement with Shaw and apparently he did not protest, but his diary fairly dripped distress when he wrote down the early hour of the secretary's departure and the late minute of his return.

Inasmuch as Washington, relieved or burdened, had determined to continue his scale of entertainment as long as he could afford it, he made the best of his difficult role as national host and he undoubtedly took pride in having his lands, his house and his table impress visitors. So far as is known, he never said so in plain words, but he was ambitious to have Mount Vernon as elegant as one of the English estates his traveled friends had described to him. In the late winter and early spring of 1785, he began elaborate planting of shade and ornamental trees—only to have most of them destroyed in the drought.[103] His chief

[100] *Robert Hunter, Jr.*, op. cit., 195–96.

[101] *Ibid.*, 192, 194; *Samuel Vaughan's Diary*, Aug. 10, 1787; LC microfilm of the original manuscript.

[102] 2 *Diaries*, 393. Washington's amusing specifications of the paragon he hoped to procure for board, lodging and not more than £75 a year, Virginia currency, are given in 28 *G. W.*, 158, 177. For negotiations with Shaw, see *ibid.*, 179, 190–91.

[103] 28 *G. W.*, 134, 181, 183; 2 *Diaries*, 345, 373, 378, 392; Mount Vernon Ladies' Association of the Union, *A List of Ornamental Trees and Shrubs Noted in the Writings of George Washington*. In 2 *Diaries*, 344 ff, is virtually a day-by-day account of what he planted—dogwood, redbud, sassafras, mulberry, maple, aspen, poplar, black gum, ash, locust, yellow willow, crab, magnolia, elm, cedar, paw paw, honey locust, catalpa, hemlock, walnut, pine, live oak, yew, fringe, weeping willow, linden and even four specimens of a tree found on the plantation and unknown to him by name (*ibid.*, 346). Holly, buckeye, rare varieties of oak, the so-called Kentucky coffee-tree and others he undertook to grow from berries or acorns (*ibid.*, 357, 358, 360–61). He had

regret in that year was that he could not complete the new chamber and adorn it with a fine marble mantelpiece presented by Samuel Vaughan of London. Even though this large room was not yet finished,[104] the improvements made in 1784 and early in 1785 had given added beauty to the entire plantation. "It is impossible," wrote a young Manchester merchant, "to do justice to the order and management of the General's affairs." The guest continued: "His large estates, cultivated in the best manner, furnish him with all the necessaries of life, and his revenues enabled him, as well as the presents he received from all parts, to have all the luxuries of every clime. His gardens and pleasure grounds . . . were very extensive . . . He is allowed to be one of the best informed as well as successful planters in America."[105] More than one visitor got the same impression that Washington's style of living represented great wealth. "I fancy," one young visitor wrote, "he is worth £100,000 sterling, and lives at the rate of three or four thousand a year . . ."[106] In reality, before the end of 1785 the General confessed, "to be plain, my coffers are not overflowing with money,"[107] and he was compelled to buy corn with which to carry his stock through the winter that followed the calamitous drought,[108] but the strange paradox of his domestic economy once again was apparent: While continuing to spend freely for Mount Vernon, he pledged £1000 toward the endowment of a school at Alexandria, and as he could not afford to pay his subscription, he agreed to assume an annual interest charge of £50.[109] He never explained why it was that he scarcely ever curtailed any of his expenditures when his income was reduced or his cash depleted. His well-fed guests, drinking toasts in his champagne, would have been aghast had they known that the cash with which he was to begin 1786 was no more than £86.[110]

Besides his concern over money, Washington had in 1785 continuing and rising anxiety with respect to public affairs from which he could not divorce himself in what he continued to style his "retirement." The Society of the Cincinnati remained one of these cares. Washington

better luck with a deer park concerning which he corresponded at intervals for years (the more interesting of numerous references are: 28 G. W., 86, 221, 314, 468; 29 ibid., 281, 397).

104 See supra, p. 5.
105 Joseph Hadfield, op. cit., 13; cf. supra, p. 40, n.78.
106 Robert Hunter, Jr., op. cit., 197.
107 December 10; 28 G. W., 349.              108 Ibid., 348–49, 363, 366, 378, 381.
109 His purpose previously had been to make this a bequest (ibid., 357).
110 Ledger B, f. 207.

had a little routine correspondence on admissions in the organization[111] and he still was so much *in loco parentis* that Horatio Gates said, "it will take all his support to prop the falling Institution; to act without that is only confirming its ruin."[112] Washington suspected vaguely that opposition to the Society was slumbering, not dead,[113] but he confessed himself surprised by the appearance of Mirabeau's *"Considérations sur l'ordre de Cincinnatus,"* of which an English translation reached Mount Vernon in November, 1785.[114] The General's first inclination was to ignore it,[115] but reflection and a letter from Alexander Hamilton[116] convinced him that the State Societies should act promptly to approve the revised constitution and to remove all ground of reasonable objection. He confided to Hamilton that only the involvement of foreign officers and the charitable features of the organization had kept him from advocating in 1784 that it be abolished.[117] While he did not say so, the most for which he could hope, on so provocative a theme for demagogues, was that no new agitation would be started. He had not a single degree of enthusiasm for the Society.

Another and personal threat of revived controversy came in a letter from the Baltimore printer, William Goddard, the man who had been forced by indignant Marylanders to apologize for circulating one of Charles Lee's attacks on the General.[118] On this occasion Goddard explained that sometime previously Lee had requested him to prepare and publish papers which now had come into his hands from the estate of the dead man. "I have taken care," the printer wrote, "to suppress many passages that might be offensive in the General's pieces and correspondence." Goddard elaborated: "While it was my duty to preserve what was useful in military and political knowledge, I took the liberty to suppress such expressions as appeared to be the ebullitions of a disappointed and irritated mind; so that I flatter myself your Excellency will be convinced of the candor of my intention in the execution of the work." He enclosed a title page and soon would forward the "pro-

---

[111] 28 *G. W.*, 255, 273, 325–26.
[112] Letter of Apr. 19, 1785, to Gen. Peter Muhlenberg; *Gates Papers*, NYHS.
[113] 28 *G. W.*, 240.
[114] See *supra*, p. 8 n and p. 12 n.     [115] 28 *G. W.*, 327.
[116] *Works of Alexander Hamilton*, Henry Cabot Lodge, ed., hereafter cited as *A. Hamilton*, v. 9, p. 412–13.
[117] 28 *G. W.*, 351–52.     [118] See Vol. V., p. 424 n.

posals" for Lee's book. Meantime he wished "to know whether your Excellency has any particular request respecting the said work." [119]

It was of the very nature of Washington, as a cautious man, to avoid trouble if honorably he could, but when a dispute arose he was no less diligent to make his position plain, and, having taken a stand, to hold his ground against all attack. He would use clean weapons cleanly, as a gentleman should, but he would use them as skillfully as he could, and while the fight continued, he would neither ask nor give quarter. Goddard was answered with complete candor: "Your own good judgment must direct you in the publication of the manuscript papers of General Lee. I can have no request to make concerning the work." Washington then stated that he never had any difference with Lee except "on public grounds" and that he acted as he did "on this occasion" —that is, after the Battle of Monmouth—as he thought his duty required. "I . . . can never consider the conduct I pursued, with respect to him, either wrong or improper . . . Should there appear in General Lee's writings anything injurious or unfriendly to me, the impartial and dispassionate world must decide how far I deserved it from the general tenor of my conduct." Washington then added this paragraph which tacitly combined a plea for fair play with notice that he would not aid the circulation of Lee's charges by replying to them: "I am gliding down the stream of life, and wish, as is natural, that my remaining days may be undisturbed and tranquil; and conscious of my integrity I would willingly hope that nothing would occur tending to give me anxiety; but should anything present itself in this or any other publication, I shall never undertake the painful task of recrimination, nor do I know that I should ever enter upon my justification. I consider the communication you have made as a mark of great attention, and the whole of your letter as a proof of your esteem." [120] That was the end of the matter. Goddard never published the Lee papers,[121] and never explained formally his reasons for failing to do so. As his printed

---

[119] Letter of May 30, 1785; 233 *Papers of G. W.*, 12, LC; 4 *LTW.*, 105–06. The title page was in MS (233 *Papers of G. W.*, 13, LC); the three-page printed "proposals" (*ibid.*, 37) were for the publication of Lee's papers in three volumes.

[120] 28 *G. W.*, 162.

[121] Goddard's partner in the enterprise, Edward Langworthy, issued in New York, 1792, a work of 439 pages entitled *Memoirs of the Life of the Late Charles Lee, Esq. Second in Command . . . to which are added his Political and Military Essays . . .* This was reprinted in London and in Dublin the same year. Langworthy wrote the *Memoir* (p. 1–70). All of *The Lee Papers*, needless to say, appeared in the edition printed by *NYHS* and quoted many times in earlier volumes of the present work.

"Proposals" followed the lines of his letter to Washington and were a disclaimer of any intent to discredit the General or to reproduce Lee's most violent utterances, Washington would have been entirely justified in assuming the plan's collapse because of the lack of public interest in what Lee had to say.

Washington's deepest anxiety, in this year of drought and distraction, was for the Union of the States. The appeal of Congress in 1781 for the right to levy a 5 per cent tax on imports had been answered favorably by all the States except Rhode Island, but the refusal of that State to say "Aye" and the action of Virginia in repealing her statute of acquiescence had put an end to all hope of deriving from that measure the money required for paying the interest on the Federal debt.[122] In desperation, Congress in April, 1783, had submitted to the States the amendment of the Articles of Confederation to authorize the levy of specific taxes on certain imported luxuries and a 5 per cent ad valorem tax on all other goods brought into the United States. This was to be imposed for twenty-five years only, and the proceeds were to be used exclusively for the payment of interest and principal on the war debt. A million and a half dollars for the support of government were to be supplied by the States annually, in specified amounts based on population. This measure was crowded with every sort of concession to the pridefully asserted sovereignty of the States,[123] but Rhode Island, New York, Maryland and Georgia were in opposition. To persuade them to ratify the amendment was the task of those who believed the Union would perish unless it had assured revenue. Another measure presented to the States for their approval was one that authorized Congress for a period to prohibit imports from or exports to countries that had no commercial treaties with the United States [124]—a plea for weapons with which to inflict reprisals on Britain for her discrimination against American ships and cargoes. Here again, the compliance of the States was slow and was hedged about with so many whereases and provisos that Congress remained powerless in dealing with Britain. Other pro-

---

[122] See A. C. McLaughlin, *The Confederation and the Constitution*, cited hereafter as *McLaughlin*, 53–54; *Merrill Jensen*, op. cit., 63–65, 408–09. The Virginia act of repeal is in 11 *H* 171 with the preamble: "Whereas the permitting any power, other than the General Assembly of this Commonwealth, to levy duties or taxes upon the citizens of this State within the same, is injurious to its sovereignty, may prove destructive of the rights and liberty of the people, and so far as Congress might exercise the same is contravening the spirit of the Confederation in the eighth article thereof . . ."

[123] Apr. 18, 1783; 24 *JCC.*, 257–61.

[124] Adopted Apr. 30, 1784; 26 *JCC.*, 321–22.

posals were being made for amending the Articles of Confederation but the best of these, largely the work of James Monroe, never were passed and transmitted to the States.[125]

Washington had been too busy and too far from New York to study with care the plans for amending various articles of the Confederation, but by every test of reason and every lesson of experience, he approved the "import tax" and the "navigation act" as the two specific measures were styled.[126] Congress must have more power or the Union would cease to exist. ". . . it is unfortunate for us," he wrote, "that evils which might have been averted, must be first felt, and our national character for wisdom, justice and temperance, suffer in the eyes of the world, before we can guide the political machine as it ought to be." [127] He told Henry Knox: ". . . contracted ideas, local pursuits and absurd jealousy are continually leading us from those great and fundamental principles which are characteristic of wise and powerful nations, and without which we are no more than a rope of sand, and shall as easily be broken." [128] British commercial policy, he thought, in time would force the States to vest Congress with the power necessary to protect common interests,[129] but, at the moment, he maintained, "the Confederation appears to me to be little more than a shadow without the substance." [130] His correspondence and that of many of his old friends resounded with arguments over a stronger union and over the demand, from the other camp, that the States make no additional grant of power to build up New England tyranny over the South.[131] Washington answered with fundamentals: "If we are afraid to trust one another under qualified powers, there is an end of the Union" [132] and again: "We are either a united people, or we are not. If the former, let us in all matters of general concern act as a nation, which have national objects to promote, and a national character to support. If we are not, let us no

[125] 28 *JCC.*, 17 n, 201 and 205 n. This report was read Mch. 28, 1785. A condensed copy, misdated May, 1785, is in 9 *Sparks*, 503–06.

[126] Not infrequently the second of these was termed the measure "to regulate commerce."

[127] Letter of June 22, 1785, to Richard Henry Lee; 28 *G. W.*, 174.

[128] Letter of Feb. 28, 1785; 28 *G. W.*, 93.

[129] 28 *G. W.*, 161, 184, 250. British legislation and orders in council are sketched briefly in *McLaughlin*, 73–74.          [130] 28 *G. W.*, 290.

[131] See as typical of this point of view, McHenry to Washington, Aug. 14, 1785; 8 *Burnett*, 182–83, also in 9 *Sparks*, 501–02; and R. H. Lee to unnamed person, Oct. 10, 1785, 2 *Ballagh*, *Lee Letters*, 387.

[132] To David Stuart, Nov. 30, 1785; 28 *G. W.*, 328.

longer act a farce by pretending to it." [133] This was not, to him, the fruit of political philosophy but the seed-corn of reality. Common sense dictated union.

In that conviction, the General did not hesitate to express himself when he talked with his friends or wrote to them, though never, it would appear, did he have any thought of assuming the leadership in an effort to procure larger powers for Congress. He remained the retired observer, and no more than that, except as his prestige gave weight to his private remarks. Again and again he repeated his dictum that the evils of infirm government had to be felt before they could be seen, and, while he continued to hope for the ratification of the impost and of the navigation act, he saw no financial relief for Congress otherwise than through the sale of the western lands ceded by the States. After tedious debate,[134] Congress on the 20th of May, 1785, had passed an "Ordinance for Ascertaining the mode of Disposing of Lands in the Western Territory," [135] a measure that provided for surveying townships and "lots," one-seventh of which were to be assigned "for the use of the late Continental Army." Subject to various reservations, the six-sevenths were "to be drawn for, in the name of the thirteen States respectively, according to the quotas in the last preceding requisition on all the States." These lands were to be sold for not less than one dollar, specie, per acre, and the proceeds were to be made available to the Board of Treasury through the Commissioners of the Loan Office in the various States.[136] "I confess," Washington wrote, "it does not strike me as a very eligible [mode for disposing of the western lands]," but he added with his usual caution: "however, mine is only an opinion, and I wish to be mistaken in it, as the fund would be very productive and afford great relief to the public creditors if the lands meet with a ready sale." [137]

This, perhaps, was no more than hope, but insofar as the future of the Union was involved, it was by hope that Washington lived. Surely, America would not throw away the Union without which freedom

[133] To Madison, *ibid.*, 336.
[134] Summarized, as to date, in 8 *Burnett*, 97 n.
[135] A remarkably clear measure; 28 *JCC.*, 375–81.
[136] *Ibid.*, 378.
[137] Letter of Sept. 5, 1785, to Luzerne; 28 *G. W.*, 251. Cf. *ibid.*, 173–74. For statements by William Grayson that this was the best ordinance that could be passed, though not the best that could be drawn, see 4 *LTW.*, 102; 233 *Papers of G. W.*, 17, LC.

could not have been won and could not now be retained! In December, he wrote his old comrade, Rochambeau: ". . . our governments are acquiring a better tone. Congress, I am persuaded, will soon be vested with greater powers. The commercial interests throughout the Union are exerting themselves to obtain these, and I have no doubt will effect it." [138] As for his own affairs and his own way of living, he did not permit his financial distress to dampen the delights of his plantation; nor did he complain because "retirement" had brought him less leisure than he had anticipated. He had decided that he would be his own manager, with his nephew, George Augustine Washington, as his assistant to discharge some of the duties previously performed by Lund, whose farm and other interests called for attention. In acting as steward, Lund had made large sacrifice for his kinsman during the war; his long-cherished desire to resign his post could not in decency be disregarded further.[139] Temporarily Lund continued to direct the sale of flour from the mill and he doubtless counselled George Augustine in compliance with the General's hint that his advice to the younger man might "be useful." [140] A new safeguard was thus described by the master of Mount Vernon: "If I should not be able to visit the plantation as often as I could wish (owing to company or other engagements) I am resolved that an account of the stock and every occurrence that happens in the course of the week shall be minutely detailed to me every Saturday. Matters cannot go much out of sorts in that time without a seasonable remedy." [141]

New faces at Mount Vernon, new problems of personal finance and national solvency, new methods of managing the estate—these did not destroy for Washington the old satisfactions of a planter's life. There on the hillock overlooking the slow Potomac was the family, there the faithful servants. At a little distance were the horses, the hounds, the

---

[138] 28 G. W., 339.

[139] 28 G. W., 318–19. Supt. C. C. Wall of Mount Vernon notes: "Lund's property was a tract of land adjoining Mount Vernon to the West, a part at least of which Lund had purchased from his employer some years earlier. Here a site was chosen and construction was begun in 1782; the house, a commodious structure of brick, was completed in July, 1784. This new home, which Lund called 'Hayfield,' was the realization of his ambition to own a modest place where he could 'live and give a neighbor beef and toddy.' Here he passed the remainder of his days in peaceful retirement." The General's fine tribute to him was in this language: "I shall always retain a grateful sense of your endeavors to serve me; for as I have repeatedly intimated to you in my letters from camp, nothing but that entire confidence which I reposed could have made me easy under an absence of almost nine years from my family and estate, or could have enabled me, consequently, to have given not only my time but my whole attention to the public concerns of this country for that space" (28 G. W., 319).

[140] 28 G. W., 364.          [141] Ibid.

kine and the sheep. Pervading all was peace, the peace for the attainment of which he had given his country those bloody, all-demanding years from Cambridge to Newburgh. Peace—"my first wish is . . . to see the whole world in peace, and the inhabitants of it as one band of brothers, striving who should contribute most to the happiness of mankind." [142]

[142] Letter of Oct. 7, 1785, to Charles Armand-Tuffin, Marquis de La Rouerie; *ibid.*, 289. For similar expressions on peace, see *ibid.*, 251–52, 254.

# CHAPTER III

## "Influence Is No Government"
## (1786)

THE SECOND anniversary of Washington's retirement from command of the American Army was spent cheerfully with friends in fox hunting. Christmas, 1785, found numerous guests at Mount Vernon, but as soon as they left and the usual holidays were over, the retired General became a surveyor again on his Dogue Run plantation, "with a view," as he said, "to new model the fields at that place." [1] Now that Washington was his own farm manager, he was determined to reorganize his estate and to make it all it could be. For this long task he had more time because his guests, though numerous, included fewer celebrities whose entertainment ate up his hours. Another gain of the early months of 1786 was a decrease in the troublesome, time-consuming correspondence [2] that had devoured entire days when Washington's records were in the worst of their disorder.[3] He was irked by his mail [4] but was not as heavily burdened, relatively, as he sometimes thought he was.[5] Later in the year, Washington changed private secretaries and procured in Tobias Lear exactly the man he wanted. Lear was 24 years old, a well-born native of New Hampshire and a graduate of Harvard, who had resided for a time in Europe and read French well enough to translate it easily. He was good-natured, sober, industrious and companionable,[6] and he made an excellent impression from the first.[7]

---

[1] 2 *Diaries*, 460–61.     [2] Cf. 28 *G. W.*, 379.
[3] *Ibid.*, 148, 472.     [4] *Ibid.*, 518.
[5] For 1786, only 225 letters are printed in 28 and 29 *G. W.* No more than seven for January of that year are preserved.
[6] A useful bibliography on Lear is appended to the sketch in *DAB*. Washington employed him on the recommendation of Benjamin Lincoln (28 *G. W.*, 379, 405, 409; Lincoln to Washington, Jan. 4, 1786; 234 *Papers of G. W.*, 119). Others who were asked by Washington to be on the alert for a suitable person were Noah Webster and George William Fairfax (28 *G. W.*, 409, 469). Lear's pay was to be 200 dollars a year, and he was to live in the family (3 *Diaries*, 66–67; 28 *G. W.*, 379). For his knowledge of French, see 29 *G. W.*, 228, and Lincoln's letter, *supra*. Lear's account is in *Ledger B*, f. 229, 259; *Ledger C*, f. 4–6.
[7] 28 *G. W.*, 469. Shaw, the previous secretary, left in August, 1786, to go to the West Indies (3 *Diaries*, 105, 108).

Another change by which Washington hoped to improve his management of Mount Vernon was the employment of a type of man he had long desired, "a thorough bred *practical* English farmer." [8] On May 31, through the efforts of George William Fairfax, he made a one-year contract, at sixty guineas, with James Bloxham, "a plain, honest farmer" recently arrived in America, whose appearance and conversation were as "much in his favor" as were his recommendations from the English proprietor for whom Bloxham had worked.[9] The farmer-manager began at once to apply good British usage, but, Washington complained, "he makes no allowances for the ravages of a nine-years' war from which we are just beginning to emerge, nor does he consider that if our system of husbandry had been as perfect as it may be found on your farms, or in some of the best farming Counties in England, that there would have been no occasion for his services." [10]

Bloxham began, unfortunately, in another adverse season. Twenty days of May, 1786, were rainy and were ruinous to spring grain. In some places, half the wheat and three-fourths of the barley moulded or rotted; the ground became so watersoaked that it could not be plowed; Washington feared that his thin young corn would be choked by weeds.[11] This prospect seemed the more calamitous because Mount Vernon bins and cribs still showed the effects of the drought of 1785. The General was feeding his servants and his stock, in part, with purchased maize. By September, this would be exhausted.[12] Bloxham and his employer had to make the best of this condition—the manager with lament and with sighs for old England, the proprietor with determination to re-divide his farms and, as he said, to "go into an entire new course of cropping." [13] For this purpose, large as were his tenures, he leased new land on Dogue Run at the formidable figure of £136 per annum [14] and as soon thereafter as he could, he surveyed his acquisitions [15] and made his holdings into six distinct but cooperating

---

[8] 28 *G. W.*, 185.

[9] *Ibid.*, 445–46, 469, 513; George William Fairfax to Washington, Dec. 12, 1786; 237 *Papers of G. W.*, 25. Bloxham had some distinguished descendants in America, among them William Dunnington Bloxham, twice Governor of Florida. See Ruby Leach Carson in 27 *Fla. His. Quar.*, 207 ff.

[10] Letter of Aug. 5, 1786, to William Peacey, 28 *G. W.*, 509.

[11] 28 *G. W.*, 459–60.     [12] Cf. 3 *Diaries*, 116.     [13] 29 *G. W.*, 17.

[14] The labor of the slaves was included in the rent which was later to be £150. This was "French's farm," the property of Mrs. Penelope Manley French, procured by Washington, Oct. 16, 1786, after long and provoking negotiations. See 3 *Diaries*, 110–11, 114, 119, 126, 29; 29 *G. W.*, 16–21. Cf. Appendix VI-1.

[15] 3 *Diaries*, 142.

plantations—the Mansion House, Dogue, Ferry, River, Muddy Hole and French. Unless company or absence prevented, he visited all of these farms every weekday—a round of about twenty miles [16]—and, after he came home, he wrote in his diary what was being done at each place. In an extension of arrangements that existed before the war, horses, cattle, hogs and sheep were apportioned among the plantations. Implements, tools and equipment were allotted.[17] An overseer had general charge of each property. He might be a white man hired on wages or shares; he might be a slave. When, for example, John Alton died, that old white servant of the French and Indian conflict was succeeded at River Plantation by "Mulatto Davy," who was transferred from Muddy Hole.[18] Under each overseer were a suitable number of the 200 and more slaves that Washington and his wife owned.[19] Old Negroes were assigned light duties; small children of course were left to play; the able-bodied girls and women were daily in the fields. At least two of them drove plows.[20]

The "new course of cropping" that Washington instituted as rapidly as he could in 1786 and afterwards, was substantially the same on all his plantations [21] and was designed to yield food or marketable crops without exhausting the land in the old, "ruinous mode of farming." [22] He believed in all the implications of a statement he later addressed to Arthur Young: "The general custom has been first to raise a crop of Indian corn (maize) which, according to the mode of cultivation, is a good preparation for wheat; then a crop of wheat, after which the ground is respited (except from weeds and every trash that can contribute to its foulness) for about eighteen months; and so on, alternately, without any dressing, till the land is exhausted, when it is turned

[16] *Samuel Vaughan's Diary*, Aug. 13, 1787, LC Photocopy of the original, 55–56.
[17] Cf. 2 *Diaries*, 446–49.
[18] *Ibid.*, 453, 457. Alton died Dec. 3, 1785.
[19] 3 *ibid.*, 15–22. The slow increase in slaves raises a question concerning the mortality among these Africans. In his ledger, Washington frequently entered payment for the delivery of slave women by midwives and he never mentioned deaths among the infants, but a very large percentage of them must have succumbed. Otherwise, it would seem, the number of servants would have risen more rapidly. Another factor that influenced the growth of the slave population at Mount Vernon may have been the steady increase in average age. Where few ever had been sold and replaced by younger females, an undue percentage of the women in 1785–90 may have been past the child-bearing age.
[20] *Ibid.*, 261, 277; cf. 380.
[21] Except for special work done by the "mansion house hands" in the improvement of the grounds.
[22] Cf. letter of Nov. 10, 1785, to George William Fairfax; 28 *G. W.*, 313.

out without being sown with grass seeds, or any method taken to restore it; and another piece is ruined in the same manner." [23]

Arthur Young's publications in England [24] and Washington's own experience on the Potomac indicated that prevention of this ruin depended on three essentials—the return of plowland to grass, the more liberal use of manure, and the prompt stoppage of all flow of ground water that might create gullies.[25] This became the basic pattern of farming at Mount Vernon, followed in good years and in bad, when the owner had money and when he had to borrow. Washington's first difficulty in adhering to his plan of saving and improving his land was represented by lack of good seed, especially clover, delivered early. In spite of this, he had unshakable faith in seed and he would test any that came to the plantation. As his interest in the untried soon was familiar to his friends, seed became a favored gift to him, in quantities from a few grains to overflowing bushels. Washington would plant it and watch it, no matter how alien its habitat. Once, at least, he set out seed when he remembered neither what it was supposed to be nor who had given it to him. A collection of Chinese seed of many sorts was entrusted to the ground, and the transliterated names were recorded carefully, with no other reward for his care than the appearance of a few frail shoots.[26] Somewhat larger experiments with South African and Siberian wheat,[27] with carrots, and with corn from other parts of the Union led to the undramatic conclusion that varieties long raised on the banks of the Potomac usually yielded more satisfactorily than much lauded importations did. "Here," Washington wrote in manifest disappointment with one of his experiments, "the difference against the early or Eastern is found greater than at Muddy Hole, and decidedly in both in favor of the common corn of the country." [28] Later his confession was that he had planted "several kinds of seeds, trees, etc., which are natives of a warmer climate and [had] the mortification

---

[23] Letter of Nov. 1, 1787; 29 *ibid.*, 298.

[24] For Washington's interest in procuring these, see 28 *ibid.*, 429, 459, 484; Henry Lee to Washington, July 3, 1786, 236 *Papers of G. W.*, 22.

[25] In modern agricultural parlance, crop rotation, the regular use of proper fertilizer, and the prevention of soil erosion.

[26] 2 *Diaries*, 388–89, 404.

[27] Cf. 28 *G. W.*, 306–07; 30 *ibid.*, 48; 3 *Diaries*, 4, 40 ff.

[28] *Ibid.*, 138. Few subjects were more extensively treated in Washington's correspondence than were exotic seed, roots, bulbs and shoots, few of which prospered at Mount Vernon. See, as typical, 2 *Diaries*, 404; 3 *ibid.*, 80, 344, 347, 411; 27 *G. W.*, 493–94; 28 *ibid.*, 38, 46, 55–56, 134, 141–42, 181, 182, 198, 306–07, 406—and almost endlessly on.

to find them destroyed by the severity of our winters," [29] and, he might have added, by ignorance or carelessness on the part of overseers or slaves. Frequently when he came home from his daily ride over the farms he would record mistakes in planting and in cultivation, mistakes from which he owned himself not free.[30]

Another obstacle to the success of Washington's "new course of cropping" was the relatively small amount of animal manure available to him. Although he and Mrs. Washington had on the Mount Vernon estate an average of about 130 horses, 350 cattle and 350 sheep,[31] most of these animals were in pasture for the greater part of the year. They increased slowly the general fertility of the soil but they did not supply stable manure in sufficient quantity for the large crops Washington undertook to raise.[32] The General used an avid figure of speech in describing to George William Fairfax the ideal farmer for Mount Vernon —"above all, Midas like, one who can convert everything he touches into manure, as the first transmutation towards gold." [33] Washington continued to get additional "gold," as he thought, from the mud on the bottom of the Potomac, and as he kept spreading this, season after season, on his ground, he evidently satisfied himself that it had value.[34] His maxim was, "The profit of every farm is greater or less, in proportion to the quantity of the manure which is made thereon, or can be obtained, and by keeping the fields in good condition." [35]

The worst of Washington's difficulties in making his worn plantations better was one he was slow to understand or, at least, to admit. This was the nature and thinness of most of his land around Mount Vernon. Successive crops of tobacco had devoured the limited natural fertility of the soil. The hardpan was so close to the surface that plowed ground remained wet after heavy rains and then formed clogs that could not be broken otherwise than by cross-plowing or by harrowing and hoeing. Washington may have erred by failing to train plow-

---

[29] 30 G. W., 165.

[30] For example: wet plowing (3 *Diaries*, 68), shattered buckwheat (*ibid.*, 247; cf. 254), potatoes left too long in the ground (*ibid.*, 271), and poor planting of artichokes (*ibid.*, 357).

[31] Cf. 2 *Diaries*, 449–50.

[32] In 3 *ibid.*, 369 ff, will be found an interesting review by Washington of the results he attained by growing the same products on the ground that had and had not been fertilized.

[33] 28 G. W., 186.

[34] 2 *Diaries*, 431; 3 *ibid.*, 442; 28 G. W., 271, 306; 30 *ibid.*, 256. Good results attended the use of fish-heads and intestines as manure (3 *Diaries*, 239, 330–34, 371).

[35] 30 G. W., 256. This quotation is from a letter of Mch. 31, 1789, to his nephew, George Augustine Washington, perhaps the best brief summary of his general methods of farm management.

men in sufficient number to put quickly in order all the fields he intended for wheat and corn. If downpours were frequent at the approach of the planting season, he became fearful that the farms might not be in condition for seeding at the proper time. He yielded again and again to the temptation to turn the ground while it still was too wet, and thereby he made it uneven and sometimes unproductive for the entire growing season. By the end of 1786, Washington understood some of the limitations set inexorably by the "hard clay or (if it had as much the properties as the appearance, might be denominated) marl, from eighteen inches to three feet below the surface."[36] Later he decided that it was better to plow "in such squares as are proportioned to the size of the farms and strength of the teams than to break the whole up first, unless *repeated* plowings is intended and can be given."[37]

Progress towards a crop system that would feed this poor land was not easy, but Washington persisted in his tests and finally developed a six-year rotation.[38] Although he was not entirely satisfied with this slowly developed system, it probably represented the most useful experiment Washington conducted after he returned home. Next in practical value was his determination of the wheat that gave the most satisfactory yield on his plantations. Few of his other experiments with cereals

---

[36] *Ibid.*, 65.                                    [37] 3 *Diaries*, 358.

[38] He thus described it to John Beale Bordley: "By the usual mode (it is scarcely necessary to observe) we have *three* fields—viz—one in corn, one in wheat, and one in hay. By my plan these three fields are divided into *six*. In 1788 for instance, one of them (say No. 1) is planted with corn 8 feet by 2, single stalks, with Irish potatoes or carrots, or partly both, between. That corn planted in this manner will yield as much to the acre as in any other. That the quantity of potatoes will at least quadruple the quantity of corn, and that the potatoes do not exhaust the soil, are facts well established in my mind. In April, 1789, it is sown with buckwheat for manure, which is plowed in before harvest when the seed begins to ripen and there is a sufficiency of it to seed the ground a second time. In July it is again plowed; which gives two dressings to the land at the expense of a bushel of buckwheat and the plowings which would otherwise be essential for a summer fallow. In August, after the putrefaction and fermentation is over, wheat is sown, and in 1790 harvested. In 1791 the best and earliest kind of Indian Pease are sown broadcast, to be mowed when generally ripe. Since the adoption of this course, and progress that has been made to carry it into effect, I have had too much cause to be convinced, that pease harvested in this manner is a considerable exhaustion of the soil. I have some thoughts therefore of substituting a medley of pease, buckwheat for seed, turnips, pompions [i.e. large pumpkins] in such parts of the field as best suit them, they will be useful and serve as preparatives. In 1792, spring barley or oats, or equal quantities of each, will be sown with red clover, the latter to be fed with light stock the first year after harvest. In 1793, the field remains in clover for hay, or grazing according to circumstances, and in 1794 comes into corn again, and goes on as before" (30 *G. W.*, 49–50, with spelling and capitalization drastically revised). Elaboration of this program for the crop year 1800 will be found in 37 *G. W.*, 463 ff; but neither there nor anywhere else, as far as is known, did Washington describe the particular "Indian Pease" that caused, he thought, a "considerable exhaustion of the soil."

and vegetables produced material results, but they did not cost much, they were interesting to him, and they were continued.[39]

His luck in breeding animals was better. Invaluable as horses had been to him during the war, he did not believe them the most economical beast of burden on the farm. From what he had learned of mules, he had concluded that they would do more and consume less, and he decided that he would import a jackass to breed them. When this plan of his became known, the King of Spain presented him two of these animals. One died on the voyage but the other reached Mount Vernon in December, 1785, and received the name "Royal Gift." [40] This lordling of the pasture threatened to prove costly. He was sluggish and indifferent [41] and refused to bestir himself until July, 1786.[42] Thereafter he improved steadily and by the autumn of 1787, he won Washington's proud tribute, "He never fails." [43] Meantime, Lafayette had sent from Malta a jack and two she-asses, which arrived in November, 1786.[44] Washington dubbed the jack "Knight of Malta" and studied with some care the virtues of the Mediterranean islander in comparison with the boasted excellences of "Royal Gift." [45] With his usual zeal for experimentation, the master of Mount Vernon decided in February, 1786, to test the qualities of South American asses, and he accordingly sent a consignment of flour to Surinam, Dutch Guiana, to be traded for a jenny, which in due time was delivered to him.[46] Washington already was standing the young Arabian stallion, Magnolio, which he had taken over [47] at £500 from the estate of "Jack" Custis. The General owned, also, a work-horse stallion and, with the accession of the two asses, he had a four-animal stud. The service of Magnolio was at £4 "for the season"; Royal Gift or Knight of Malta covered at five

---

[39] Among his undertakings were the use of plaster of Paris to improve grass (2 *Diaries*, 368–70, 373–74); the insulation of an ice-house with straw (*ibid.*, 434); a test of the cost of spermaceti compared with tallow candles (*ibid.*, 452); the "drilling" of oats (3 *ibid.*, 99); a comparison of the yield of carrots and potatoes (*ibid.*, 157, 158, 201); numerous inquiries into the most profitable thickness of seeding, with varying amounts of manure (e.g., *ibid.*, 178, 186–87). Different varieties of barley, oats, beans, etc., were under almost constant, comparative test, but seldom with any important discoveries.

[40] 234 *Papers of G. W.*, 112, LC; 2 *Diaries*, 454; 28 *G. W.*, 74, 147, 160–61, 209, 244, 296 ff, 331, 359 ff.

[41] *Ibid.*, 409, 423, 426–27, 454, 479; *LOLTW.*, 320.

[42] 28 *G. W.*, 479.     [43] 29 *ibid.*, 281.

[44] *LOLTW.*, 315, 320; 29 *G. W.*, 59, 74; 3 *Diaries*, 136, 138, 139 n.

[45] 29 *G. W.*, 432. Apparently, Lafayette intended the Maltese asses, which Washington valued at 200 guineas, as a present to his old Commander (*ibid.*, 260) but the gift had a tragic aftermath, recorded Jan. 29, 1793, in *Ledger B*, f. 233 and in 32 *G. W.*, 322, to be described in a later volume.

[46] 28 *ibid.*, 380–81, 382; 29 *ibid.*, 79–80.     [47] 30 *ibid.*, 181.

guineas.[48] Financially the arrangement was not profitable.[49] Washington was glad, a little later, to sell Magnolio to Henry Lee for 5000 acres of Kentucky land, the patent of which did not satisfy the General on first examination.[50] Royal Gift and Knight of Malta remained at Mount Vernon, except for appearance occasionally at some public event.[51] The General continued to stand them and, by breeding mules only,[52] he felt that he was improving his live stock and that of his neighbors.[53]

Most of his outlays had ultimate utility and in time would make Mount Vernon more valuable as well as more attractive, but throughout 1786 they drained a strongbox into which he seldom could put cash. He did a fair business at the mill with some profit [54] and he continued his fishery,[55] but the main sources of income were the notes and bonds of kinsfolk whom it was exceedingly embarrassing to press. Under almost any other system of economy, in fact, caution would have prevented the building up of one family loan on another, lest the fall of one branch might involve the collapse of all. As it was, family itself had been regarded as security; the wealth of one was the resource of every kinsman. The estate of Martha's first husband owed her—and therefore owed the General—£1119 balance and back payments for six years on the "rent or annuity" of £525 annually due from the yield of the properties on the Pamunkey and York; [56] Bartholomew Dandridge on his own account and as "Jack" Custis's executor, had died with unsettled obligations of approximately £2500 to General and Mrs. Washington; [57] the owner of Mount Vernon still had claim to £500

---

[48] 29 *G. W.*, 178 n.  [49] *Ibid.*, 390.

[50] 30 *ibid.*, 144, 156, 181, 203; 3 *Diaries*, 452–53. The whole subject of animal breeding at Mount Vernon is diverting because Washington himself was amusingly interested in it. In commenting on the indifference of Royal Gift to the Virginia mares, he came as close as ever he did to humorous writing.

[51] See, as typical, 3 *Diaries*, 321.  [52] 30 *G. W.*, 144; cf. 156.

[53] *Ibid.*, 152: "I am convinced from the little experiments I have made with the ordinary mules (which perform as much labor, with vastly less feeding than horses) that those of a superior quality will be the best cattle we can employ for the harness. And, indeed, in a few years, I intend to drive no other in my carriage, having appropriated for the sole purpose of breeding them, upwards of twenty of my best mares."

[54] See 28 *G. W.*, 404, 443–44.

[55] Cf. *ibid.*, 389. The light haul of 1786 yielded little for the market. 3 *Diaries*, 46, 47, 49, 54, 55, 56.

[56] See *supra*, p. 33, n. 50 and *Ledger B*, f. 4, 224, 226. Washington allowed a credit of £4168 in 1786 for interest on stock of the Bank of England, though he maintained (*ibid.*, 224, 226) that this use of the interest was not intended. Loss of most of the papers of the Custis estate makes it difficult to untangle this transaction, which involved "Patsy" Custis's holding of bank stock.

[57] There were £2888 in February, 1788, but that total probably included interest. See *Ledger B*, f. 280.

sterling of Bank of England stock from Patsy's estate but he had not been able to compel his London agents to sell it;[58] the General probably did not know precisely how his dead brother Samuel's account with him stood.[59] Where kinsmen were not involved, old friends were,[60] and if the friends were not close, then business associations had been, and the debts sometimes had been in proportion.[61] The most alarming and enraging delinquency involved the son of a man whom Washington had helped often and sometimes at a sacrifice. On the "Middle Neck" between the Rappahannock and the York, the Custis farms which Mrs. Washington had retained in the general lease to "Jack" Custis, had been under the care of James Hill, whom Washington had employed in 1772.[62] When Washington wrote to inquire why Hill had made no report since the General returned home in December, 1783, the reply of the manager was, in effect, that he had turned over to Price Posey, son of Capt. John Posey, all that had been paid for farm products and all the cash, presumably £400, that had been entrusted to Hill by persons in debt to Washington. Thereupon, Posey had run off and, it was said, had gone to Georgia.[63] There seemed little or no prospect of recovering anything from him.

Had Washington kept a set of books in which all these delinquent items had been entered on capital account, even he, the financially confident optimist, might have been alarmed for himself, and he certainly would have been distressed by the plight of his kinsfolk and friends. As the accounts stood in 1786, badly recorded and confused, he prob-

[58] 28 *G. W.*, 497.          [59] *Ibid.*, 342.

[60] The Armistead family had not taken up the protested bill of exchange (*ibid.*, 410; 29 *ibid.*, 133); the Mercer heirs could not or would not settle John Mercer's debt, though Washington was liable for executions made on part of their land for which he had given an indemnifying bond (*Ledger B*, f. 221; 28 *G. W.*, 373, 388, 389; 29 *ibid.*, 5, 57); the hard-pressed Baylor descendants had to sell thirteen slaves to repay the Custis estate the balance of £3385, with interest, due on an original debt of £6771 (*Baylor Papers*); see also *Caroline Order Book*, 1785-87, Nov. 10, 1786, f. 377.

[61] The firm of Balfour & Barrand, which owed Washington £2000 for flour, had disappeared during the war (28 *G. W.*, 249, 432). Clement Biddle, Washington's agent in Philadelphia, had been depressed in spirit because of his financial difficulties and had been unable, temporarily, to remit to the General (232 *Papers of G. W.*, 31, LC).

[62] Vol. III, p. 286, 301. It will be remembered that Hill was the man who protested in 1773 that he never had "been right well since for I was catchd in a squall" (S. M. Hamilton, ed., *Letters to Washington and Accompanying Papers*, cited hereafter as *Hamilton*, v. 4, p. 239).

[63] 28 *G. W.*, 527; 29 *ibid.*, 76, 143 ff. Posey long had been under suspicion in some undescribed control he had over Custis properties, presumably by "Jack" Custis's prior appointment. Judge Dandridge had written Washington of Posey, Mch. 13, 1784: "his cunning is considerable, and his villainy more than I can describe or you can conceive" (229 *Papers of G. W.*, 77, LC). Richard Henry Lee wrote, Sept. 13, 1787, that Price Posey had been "found out" and had been sent "in chains to Richmond to be tried for his life" (2 *Ballagh, Lee Letters*, 437).

ably did not realize the full extent of his involvement. He did what he could to collect by persuasion and even by threats of litigation, but he continued unwilling to institute action if any excuse was offered. His lack of money was not to be concealed. A little later, when it looked as if necessity might require the sale of his brother Samuel's slaves in order that the dead man's debts might be paid, the General lamented his inability to supply needed funds to remove the possibility: "I cannot get [money] from those who owe me without suit, and I hate to sue them." He added: "I have offered lands for sale at very moderate prices, but have not been able to sell them." [64] In another letter of the same week he wrote, awkwardly but earnestly: ". . . my expenses, not from any extravagance, or an inclination on my part to live splendidly, but for the absolute support of my family and the visitors who are constantly here, are exceedingly high, higher indeed than I can support without selling part of my estate which I am disposed to do rather than run in debt, or continue to be so; but this I cannot do without taking much less than the lands I have offered for sale are worth." [65]

He had a surprising number of obligations, some of them pressing, and some of them embarrassing because, though small, they had not been settled long previously. When, for example, the General came to examine his accounts with his old friend and former neighbor, George William Fairfax, he found he was in Fairfax's debt by £207, which he contrived to pay promptly.[66] Washington still owed £800, and current interest at 7 per cent,[67] on the Oriskany tract near Fort Schuyler, that he had purchased with the assistance of George Clinton.[68] Settlement had not yet been made with Lund Washington for the salary the manager had failed to draw during the latter part of the war.[69] Even old John Alton was creditor of his master at the time of his death in the sum of £74;[70] workmen on the new chamber and on the other improvements had to be paid;[71] still another debt to an undisclosed person was described only as larger than the one due for the New York land.[72] The situation in its entirety was the worst Washington had known at any time after he had become proprietor of Mount Vernon,

---

[64] To Charles Washington, Feb. 14, 1787; 29 *G. W.*, 158.
[65] To his mother, Feb. 15, 1787; *ibid.*, 159.
[66] *Ledger B*, f. 230; 28 *G. W.*, 473.       [67] 29 *ibid.*, 6.
[68] See Vol. V., p. 450 and n.       [69] See *supra*, p. 7.
[70] *Ledger B*, f. 249. John Alton served and lived in the Washington family for forty years; see Vol. II, p. 55, 58; Vol. III, p. 13, 75, 81.
[71] 29 *G. W.*, 6.       [72] *Ibid.*

and it was not improving. His corn crop of 1786 was 1018 barrels; his year's supply of pork, weighed fresh, was 13,867, perhaps 2000 pounds less than he had "for family consumption" in good years.[73] Almost the sole gain of the year, with respect to his estate, was the judicial establishment of his title to his lands in Washington County, Pennsylvania.[74]

Along with the embarrassment of debt, Washington had on August 31 an attack of "ague and fever." He knew from unhappy prostration of earlier years what this might forecast and the next day he gave himself the staggering treatment of eight doses of red bark. This broke the fever, but it or some concurrent ailment produced so violent an eruption on the skin of the face that he could not shave. A fortnight passed before he was himself again, and then he had rheumatic pains that continued into the winter of 1786–87.[75] He was uncomfortable, rather than alarmed, and he insisted that he was reconciled to a general decline in his health, because he was "descending the hill" and, though "blessed," as he said, "with a good constitution," was "of a short-lived family."[76] In a frequently employed metaphor, he spoke of Martha and himself as past "the noon-tide of life" and gliding "gently down a stream which no human effort can ascend."[77] Why should he wish it otherwise, and how could it be more pleasant than it was? James Rumsey might perfect that strange double boat with which batteaux that had come down the Potomac might return by harnessing the current. Ships might sail up the river with favoring wind almost to the Great Falls and, when laden with the products of a widening new world, might transport them to the old. It was not so with life. After the high tide of endeavor—after the Trenton and the Yorktown of all-consuming effort—one moved with the ebb, always with the ebb, but so slowly that the landmarks faded softly into memories and the shouts from the shore came so gallantly over the water that grateful ears never were quite sure when the sound died in the wind. The ease of that outward adventure with the tide, Washington and Martha had earned by anxious winter-long vigils, by painful separation, by overcoming the demons of doubt, by holding unflinchingly fast to the ideal of American liberty. Their bark must never drift on the shoals. To raise the sail and tack and turn—that was the labor of youth. For the soldier who had won his final battles and had fixed his fame, there should be the slanting sun and then the silent sea.

In this spirit he began to make plans for the future of George Augustine Washington, but when he came to tell his nephew that he would leave the young man the land on Dogue Neck, he made a remark which indicated that he was far from expectation of early death: If he survived Mrs. Washington, there was no prospect that he would have issue and deprive his young kinsman of the property, "for," said he, "whilst I retain the reasoning faculties, I shall never marry a girl; and it is not probable that I should have children by a woman of an age suitable to my own, should I be disposed to enter into a second marriage." [78]

In connection with his own plan for the future of the family, Washington had new reminders of the ancestral truth that war did not terminate its toll when the bullets ceased to whine. During September, 1785, he had heard of the death of Gov. Jonathan Trumbull, patriot, prophet and politician, who had aided Washington valiantly during the war. In May, 1786, he learned that Tench Tilghman had expired on the 18th of April; June and July brought tidings that Alexander McDougall and Nathanael Greene had received their last leave. A heavy quadruple blow it was, to lose a faithful State executive, a cherished staff officer, a useful Major General, and the dauntless Greene, the lieutenant whom he had trusted above all others in counsel and in command. Had any of these men died in the course of hostilities, Washington would have announced it in a few words with a composure so stern that critics might have called it callous. It was different now. He wrote a careful eulogy of Trumbull,[79] he praised McDougall as a "brave soldier and disinterested patriot" [80] and he apparently made no less than three attempts, all of them futile, to express his feeling at the death of Tilghman, the bearer of the "victory dispatch" to Congress, a man who "left as fair a reputation as ever belonged to a human character." [81] Gloomy restraint in speaking of Greene [82] was followed by warmer praise,[83] and, at length, by this clumsy confession to Lafayette:

[78] Letter of Oct. 25, 1786; 29 *ibid.*, 29. Needless to say, this letter indicates clearly that Washington did not think his failure to beget children by Martha was due to sterility on his part.

[79] 28 *ibid.*, 284.  [80] *Ibid.*, 506.
[81] *Ibid.*, 506; cf. *ibid.*, 417, 450.  [82] *Ibid.*, 485.
[83] *Ibid.*, 494, 506.

# TOBIAS LEAR, A FORTUNATE CHOICE

Almost from the day of his return to private life, Washington felt desperately the need of secretarial assistance. His own papers and accounts were woefully disordered, his personal correspondence remained heavy and, unexpectedly, he was deluged with requests, queries and applications of every kind. Early in 1785 the General began to inquire among his friends for a reliable person to "live in the family" and serve as his private secretary. Specifically, he wanted "a gentleman who can compose a good letter," handle accounts, "examine, arrange and properly methodize my papers" and devote occasional time to the fundamental schooling of the two small Custis children. Young William Shaw came to Mount Vernon in July, 1785, and lightened the burden somewhat, but Washington was vexed at once by his employee's frequent recreational excursions to Alexandria. For a brief moment it appeared that the services of the grammarian, Noah Webster, might be procured, but in the fall of 1785 the General was composing detailed letters to George William Fairfax and George Chapman in England: perhaps a retired clergyman, single and "with a small living," would suit best.

Precisely at this time Benjamin Lincoln suggested that some graduate of one of the New England colleges might fill Washington's need. Then, in January, 1786, a letter arrived from Lincoln: "I have at last found a Mr. Lear, who supports the character of gentleman and scholar." Six months later Tobias Lear walked into Washington's home for the first time. Lear at twenty-four had honors from Harvard, a year's broadening travel in Europe and, most welcome, proficiency in French. The search had ended. Washington employed him at the annual wage of 200 dollars and reported to Lincoln that the new secretary seemed "a genteel, well-behaved young man." The General could not know that this son of a Portsmouth shipmaster would become, over the eight years to follow, his most intimate associate. Personable, industrious, discreet and highly intelligent, Lear carried out his duties at Mount Vernon in so exemplary a fashion that Washington in 1787 wrote of him to President Joseph Willard of Harvard in glowing terms. His service, however, came to full fruition after 1789 as private secretary to the Chief Magistrate. As Lear's responsibilities multiplied, his talents grew with them—but his loyalty and self-effacement remained the same. When Lear resigned in 1793 to go abroad on a business venture, Washington introduced him to Gouverneur Morris as "a person who possesses my entire friendship and confidence."

(From a print supplied by Stephen Decatur of a pastel by James or Ellen Sharples in the collection of Anna Decatur Wright. Authenticated by Katharine McCook Knox.)

# DAVID HUMPHREYS, "BELOV'D OF WASHINGTON"

"For God's sake," wrote Washington in urgent tone to David Humphreys late in 1786, "tell me what is the cause of all these commotions?" Then he reiterated: "Do write me fully, I beseech you." Greatly agitated by reports of insurrection in Massachusetts and hungry for accurate news, he well might look to Humphreys for an illuminating account. In the final days of the War the General had come to depend often and unreservedly upon the facile pen of this florid Lieutenant Colonel. As courtly in demeanor as he was corpulent of figure, this son of a Connecticut minister had his Master of Arts from Yale at 18. On Washington's staff his craftsmanship was generally employed in the composition of graceful, tailored replies to the flood of addresses received by the General in the years following Yorktown. In 1786 he visited briefly at Mount Vernon and revived an earlier proposal that the General undertake an autobiography or a volume of war memoirs. To this end Humphreys produced a draft, and Washington made additions from his recollections of the French and Indian War. In 1788 the Colonel returned on Washington's warm invitation, to stay at length as a guest "occupied with literary pursuits." He escorted the President-elect to New York in April, 1789, and Washington's esteem was evidenced four months later in the appointment of Humphreys as special commissioner to the Creek Indians. Not on poetic or diplomatic achievements, however, did Humphreys fasten his fame. He was "belov'd of Washington," and this was enough in his own time.

(After the Original by Gilbert Stuart and reproduced by courtesy of the Yale University Art Gallery.)

## "NELLY" CUSTIS—SO YOUNG, SO LOVELY

Among the guests at Mount Vernon in the fall of 1789 were the French Minister, the Comte de Moustier, and his sister, the Marquise de Bréhan. Whereas the lady's claim to distinction in society was generally, if ungenerously debated, her skill with brush and pencil was both generally and generously acknowledged. The charming profile miniature of Eleanor Parke Custis, reproduced here, was painted during this visit, when Madame de Bréhan executed similar portraits of the little girl's step-grandfather, George Washington. Better known as "Nelly," the child was in her tenth year, the youngest of three daughters born to "Jackie" and Eleanor Calvert Custis. After her father's death in 1781, and her mother's subsequent remarriage, "Nelly" and her small brother remained with the General and Mrs. Washington, whose outpouring of parental affection, once devoted to Martha's own "Patsy" and "Jackie," now centered on these grandchildren.

(After the miniature done in 1789 by the Marquise de Bréhan and reproduced by courtesy of the Yale University Art Gallery.)

"General Greene's death is an event which has given so much general concern and is so much regretted by his numerous friends that I can scarce persuade myself to touch upon it, even so far as to say that in him you lost a man who affectionately regarded and was a sincere admirer of you." [84] In all his letters about the death of these comrades, Washington could disregard the reservations he would have shown in wartime, lest he discourage soldiers who had lost their leaders, but he still felt embarrassment over the awkward inadequacy of what he wrote. He showed in another way than by words the depth of his feeling over the loss of Greene, who died with his financial affairs wretchedly entangled.[85] In explicit terms, Washington wrote Jeremiah Wadsworth that if Mrs. Greene and the executors thought "proper to entrust my namesake G: Washington Greene to my care, I will give him as good an education as this Country (I mean the United States) will afford and will bring him up to either of the genteel professions that his friends may choose, or his own inclination shall lead him to pursue at my own cost and expense." [86] This offer was made in October, 1786, when Washington's distress for money was acute.

He had special annoyances as well as grief and financial hardship during the year—for example, certain false allegations attributed to Capt. Charles Asgill, the man wrongly selected for reprisal in the Huddy case,[87] and a report that Washington had paid fifteen guineas a pair for imported, live pheasants that were in reality a gift from Louis XVI through Lafayette.[88] For this petty misrepresentation, and for all the hard decision between ejecting and crediting delinquent tenants, Washington found compensation in full labor for himself and for his country, humbler than that of army command but honorable and interesting. ". . . I divide my time," he wrote Jefferson, "between the superintendence of opening the navigations of our river and attention to my private concerns." [89] Wise use of his hours had been a rule

---

[84] 29 *ibid.*, 185.

[85] This is sketched in *DAB* and was unrelated to the affairs of Barnabas Deane & Co. which remained in 1786 a subject of discussion among some of the correspondents whose papers are mentioned in Vol. V, Appendix 2.

[86] 29 *G. W.*, 25.

[87] Asgill was quoted as saying falsely that a gallows had been erected outside his quarters and that he had been held *in terrorem*. David Humphreys answered this with a full statement of the facts. See *New-Haven Gaz., and Connecticut Magazine*, Nov. 16, 1786, p. 309–12; *Columbian Magazine*, January, 1787, p. 206–09 and February, 253–55; Humphreys to Washington, Sept. 24, Nov. 16, 1786, 236 *Papers of G. W.*, 86, 133; 28 *G. W.*, 450–52, 481; 29 *ibid.*, 2–4, 26, 102, 125.

[88] *Ibid.*, 94.          [89] 28 *G. W.*, 505.

of his early career: it now had become so fixed a habit that interruption of his well-ordered day was painful. Ambition had harnessed the great energies of his youth; this discipline had taken so lofty and so pleasant a place among the satisfactions of life that he would have been restless and unhappy had he loosened the reins. Duties as President of the Potomac Company during 1786 demanded attendance at six meetings of directors or committees,[90] where some complicated questions of canal locks at the falls of the river had to be considered.[91] Washington felt that a qualified engineer should be procured, preferably for all the contemplated developments of southern rivers.[92] Because of adverse weather[93] he had to get the consent of the Legislatures of Maryland and Virginia to an extension of the authorized period of three years during which the company was expected to improve navigation in specified details between Fort Cumberland and Great Falls;[94] but he continued altogether optimistic that the great design could be executed.[95] How could he fail to hope and to work for success in so inspiring and rewarding a labor as that of opening the markets of Europe to the "new empire" of the West? Were not vessels to and from London passing Mount Vernon daily[96] as if they were inviting the Ohio to flow into the Thames?

Clearing the Potomac seemed to be a matter of adequate money, engineering knowledge, and patient labor only. In a manner Washington probably felt himself inarticulate to express, the development of the "River of Swans" was symbolic of what was happening, silently and not slowly, in the young American republic. Men who grappled wearily day by day with depreciated currency and deceptive prices might not see the progress that was being made, but those farther off, with better perspective, found in it mystery and amazement. Benjamin Franklin, returning from his long service in France, had been astounded by his country's rise in prosperity and by the increase in values.[97] Washington himself recorded for foreign correspondents[98] some of the advances that Franklin listed. The General was more familiar, of course,

---

[90] 3 *Diaries*, 10–11, 26, 44, 83–86, 102, 122–23.
[91] 6 *Madison Papers*, 68, LC; cf. 2 *Hunt's Madison*, 258.
[92] 28 *G. W.*, 439; 29 *ibid.*, 1–2.     [93] 28 *ibid.*, 459.
[94] See the printed copy of the petition of Nov. 10, 1786, *Va. Exec. Papers*, VSL; 29 *G. W.*, 53, 61, 129.
[95] Cf. 28 *ibid.*, 401–02.     [96] *Ibid.*, 459; 7 *V* 181.
[97] A typical letter is that of Mch. 20, 1786, to Jefferson, in 9 *Smyth's Franklin*, 499. This aspect of the period is emphasized repeatedly in Jensen's *New Nation*.
[98] Notably in a letter to Chastellux, Aug. 18, 1786; 28 *G. W.*, 523.

than was the old philosopher with the extent to which several of the American States were dominated by men who were jealously suspicious of every change that would weaken the power of politicians or reduce the profit of their allies in business. These men seemed to regard their States as their own. Fenced fields, in their eyes, were better than wide pastures; commercial restrictions that gave them easy command of local markets were to be preferred to cooperation that would involve hard-fisted competitions. Although this narrowness of interest had been as bad after the war as during the course of hostilities, and in several States perhaps had become worse, a few leaders had continued to plead for closer economic relations. In particular, there had been a promising development in the suggestion for an annual meeting of representatives of Virginia and Maryland. When this had been proposed at the Mount Vernon Conference of March, 1785,[99] nothing more had been contemplated than that the two States review new questions of commercial relation from year to year, precisely as they had considered the joint use of the Chesapeake and the Potomac; but when the ratification of the united agreement was taken up in the Maryland Legislature, the lawmakers decided[100] to invite Delaware and Pennsylvania to the conference. Some Virginians went further and asked, in effect, Why not invite *all* the States to be represented[101] at such a meeting? The answer was not unanimous, but at the very end of the session of the General Assembly of 1785–86, a resolution to this effect was passed, Jan. 21, 1786: "That Edmund Randolph, James Madison, Walter Jones, St. George Tucker, and Meriwether Smith be appointed commissioners, who, or any three of them, shall meet such commissioners as may be appointed by the other States in the Union at a time and place to be agreed on, to take into consideration the trade of the United States; to examine the relative situations and trade of the said States; to consider how far a uniform system in their commercial regulations may be necessary to their common interest and their permanent harmony; and to report to the several States, such an act relative to this great object as, when unanimously ratified by them, will enable the United States in Congress effectually to provide for the same."[102]    It

99 See *supra*, p. 30.
100 6 *Madison Papers*, 26, LC; 2 *Hunt's Madison*, 198–99.
101 Text in 2 *Rowland, Mason*, 379–80.
102 *Jour. H.D. Va.*, 1781–86, session October 1785–January 1786, p. 153; *Jour. Sen. Va.*, 1785–90, session Oct. 25, 1785–January, 1786, p. 103. The text of the resolution is published in part in 2 *Rowland, Mason*, 93.

was apparent, of course, that this diplomatically drafted measure might mean much or little, but as James Madison was quick to point out, there was a chance the conference might recommend an increase of the powers of Congress. This, said Madison, "may possibly lead to better consequences than at first occur." [103]

This hopeful possibility, it had to be admitted, was not heightened by the manner in which the action of Virginia was communicated to the other States. Either because Gov. Patrick Henry did not know the duty was his, in the absence of explicit legislative instructions, or else because he was indifferent to the enterprise, he did not transmit the Virginia resolution to the other Governors until Feb. 23, 1786, and then, after summarizing the proposal, he said merely: "I have to request your Excellency's attention to the subject, and that you will be pleased to make such communications of it as may be necessary to forward the views of the legislature." [104]

Washington said nothing of Henry's delay if, indeed, he knew of it; but at the beginning of spring, 1786, he was not hopeful the obstacles to better relations among the States could be removed quickly. His "sentiments" with respect to the Federal Union, he wrote Henry Lee, had "been communicated without reserve," but, he went on, "my *opinion* is, that there is more wickedness than ignorance in the conduct of the States, or, in other words, in the conduct of those who have too much influence in the government of them; and until the curtain is withdrawn and the private views and selfish principles upon which these men act, are exposed to public notice, I have little hope of amendment without another convulsion." [105] He did not explain what he meant by "wickedness," except as he pronounced it "selfish," nor did he specify the nature of the "convulsion" that might seize America. His deepest dread apparently was of the slow disintegration of a union held together by waning sentiment and by a Congress so pauperized and so powerless that the States did not even take the trouble to see that their Delegates attended.

By May, 1786, he found encouragement in the response to Virginia's invitation. He explained to Lafayette: "All the Legislatures which I

---

[103] Letter of Jan. 22, 1786, to James Monroe; 6 *Madison Papers*, 35, LC; 2 *Hunt's Madison*, 223. Cf. Madison to Jefferson, *ibid.*, 227. 6 *Madison Papers*, 47, LC.

[104] 3 *W. W. Henry*, 348.

[105] Letter of Apr. 5, 1786, to Henry Lee; 28 *G. W.*, 402; repeated substantially in a letter of May 18, 1786, to John Jay, *ibid.*, 431.

have heard from have come into the proposition, and have made very judicious appointments: much good is expected from this measure, and it is regretted by many that more objects were not embraced by the meeting. A General Convention is talked of by many for the purpose of revising and correcting the defects of the federal government; but whilst this is the wish of some, it is the dread of others from an opinion that matters are not yet sufficiently ripe for such an event." [106] Washington himself was not sure a general convention would be approved, and he saw the danger of collapse more readily than he could fashion the prop: "That it is necessary to revise and amend the Articles of Confederation, I entertain *no* doubt; but what may be the consequences of such an attempt is doubtful. Yet something must be done, or the fabric must fall, for it certainly is tottering." [107]

Hope was mingled with doubt. He assured Luzerne in August: "The greater part of the Union seems to be convinced of the necessity of federal measures, and of investing Congress with the power of regulating the commerce of the whole"; [108] at the same time the antithesis of politics—the antithesis of public indifference with which he had been contending since his days as a young officer on the Virginia frontier—continued to trouble his political conscience. "We ought [not] to have calculated that our young governments would have acquired in so short a time all the consistency and solidity which it has been the work of ages to give to other nations"; [109] *but*—once again "but"—he told John Jay: "I do not conceive we can exist long as a nation without having lodged somewhere a power which will pervade the whole Union in as energetic a manner as the authority of the State governments extends over the several States." [110]

In this attitude of mind and in the face of letters predominantly pessimistic,[111] Washington looked forward with much eagerness to the meeting which had been set for Annapolis in September.[112] "Have you

---

[106] *Ibid.*, 422, somewhat repunctuated. John Jay was among those who did not think the people were ready for a general convention. See 4 *LTW.*, 130–31.

[107] Letter of May 18, 1786, to John Jay; 28 *G. W.*, 431.

[108] *Ibid.*, 500.          [109] *Ibid.*          [110] *Ibid.*, 502.

[111] 236 *Papers of G. W.*, 49, LC; 4 *LTW.*, 138; 8 *Burnett*, 417, 463; 6 *Madison Papers*, 68, LC; 2 *Hunt's Madison*, 262; George Bancroft, *History of the Formation of the Constitution of the United States of America*, cited hereafter as *Bancroft, His. Cons.*, v. 2, p. 383.

[112] The Virginia commissioners chose the date and named Annapolis as the place of meeting because they wished to avoid "the residence of Congress and large commercial cities as liable to suspicions of an extraneous influence" (James Madison in his unfinished "Preface to Debates in the Convention of 1787," published in Max Farrand, ed., *The Records of the Federal Convention of 1787*, cited hereafter as *Farrand*, v. 3, p. 545).

heard from Annapolis since Monday," he wrote a neighbor on the 9th of that month; "have the commercial commissioners met?" He continued his queries: "Have they proceeded to business? How long is it supposed their sessions will last? and is it likely they will do anything effectual?" [113] When he learned that five States only had been represented,[114] he was disappointed and was puzzled, in particular, to know why the commercial States of the East had sent no one. His anger rose, too, at the report that some who had been designated to attend the meeting had lingered so long that the conference had ended before they reached the Maryland capital.[115] He soon had assurance that failure had not been complete: The fourteen Delegates unanimously [116] had agreed to a report, prepared by Alexander Hamilton, which recommended that the States send Delegates to a convention in Philadelphia on the second Monday in May, 1787.[117] This proposed assembly was to "take into consideration the situation of the United States, to devise such further provisions as shall appear to them necessary to render the constitution of the federal government adequate to the exigencies of the Union; and to report such an act for that purpose to the United States in Congress assembled, as, when agreed to by them, and afterwards confirmed by the legislatures of every State will effectually provide for the same." [118]

Was this recommendation to be taken seriously by public men, or was it to have the fate of Virginia's call for the commercial convention of all the States at Annapolis? Before Washington could form any

[113] To Col. John Fitzgerald; 29 *G. W.*, 4.

[114] Sept. 11, 1786; the States were New York, New Jersey, Pennsylvania, Delaware and Virginia. Cf. 2 *Hunt's Madison*, 271. Although the conference met in Maryland, no official representative of that State was present. A proposal had been made in the Maryland House of Delegates on Mch. 8, 1786, that seven commissioners be sent (*Votes and Proceedings, Md. H.D., Session of November 1785*, f. 77, Annapolis); but three days later the suggestion was rejected on the ground that such a meeting as Virginia was contemplating, however good the intentions, "may be misunderstood or misrepresented in Europe, give umbrage to Congress, and disquiet the citizens of the United States," causing them "erroneously to suspect that the great council of this country wants either the will or wisdom to digest a proper uniform plan for the regulation of their commerce" (*ibid.*, f. 85). The Governor was requested to inform Virginia of Maryland's negative decision with the hint that "unforeseen consequences may result from such a meeting" (*Votes and Proceedings, Md. Senate, Session of November 1785*, f. 88, Annapolis).

[115] 29 *G. W.*, 123, 127, 138.      [116] Madison in 3 *Farrand*, 546.

[117] Edmund Randolph subsequently became confused with respect to the date and thought the call was for May 2. See his letter of Mch. 8, 1787, to Thomas Nelson, Jr., *Exec. Letter Book*, f. 57, VSL.

[118] Jonathan Elliot, *The Debates in the Several State Conventions on the Adoption of the Federal Constitution, as Recommended by the General Convention at Philadelphia in 1787*, cited hereafter as *Elliot's Debates*, v. 1, p. 118. Part of this was printed in *The Federalist*, No. 40, p. 250. Another copy is in 2 *Hunt's Madison*, 399 n–400 n.

judgment of this through his correspondence, he was alarmed by news that reached him from Massachusetts. Gazettes told of discontent that had begun to take form at the end of August. On the 11th of September, at Concord, a crowd of 200 or 300 men had cowed the justices into an announcement that they would not attempt to hold court.[119]

Washington did not understand what lay behind this angry challenge of the law. He affirmed often, with a certain boastful humility, that he saw only his neighbors and his guests and that he heard little of what was happening in the larger world. Aside from the newspaper reports, all he had at first, concerning events in New England, was conveyed in a letter of David Humphreys that read: ". . . you will have seen by the public papers that every thing is in a state of confusion in the Massachusetts. Our friend [David] Cobb,[120] who is both a General of militia and a Judge of the court in the county where he resides, is much celebrated for having said 'he would die as a General or sit as a Judge.' This was indeed a patriotic sentiment. His firmness in principles and example in conduct effected a suppression of the mob—but the court was adjourned in consequence of the Governor's order. I have just now seen an account of the tumults in New Hampshire: General Sullivan has behaved nobly and put a period to a very considerable insurrection without the effusion of blood.[121] Rhode Island continues in a state of phrenzy and division on account of their paper currency." [122] Washington knew of the madness of Rhode Island's paper money, but when it came to the Bay State—was it believable that courts were suspended in Massachusetts—Massachusetts of all States? ". . . For God's sake," he wrote back to Humphreys, "tell me what is the cause of all these commotions: do they proceed from licentiousness, British influence disseminated by the Tories, or real grievances which admit of redress? If the latter, why were they delayed till the popular mind had become so much agitated? If the former, why are not the powers of government tried at once?" [123] The General did not have to wait for

[119] The fullest early report that could have come under Washington's eye was the one in the *Penn. Gazette* (Philadelphia) of September 27, p. 2, but as Washington did not read that paper regularly, he may have followed the fragmentary report in *Penn. Packet* (Philadelphia), Sept. 23, 1786, p. 2.

[120] Former Lieutenant Colonel and aide to Washington in 1781–83 and Brevet Brigadier General as of Sept. 30, 1783.

[121] Accounts of New Hampshire disturbances appeared in the Philadelphia newspapers, *Penn. Packet*, Oct. 3, 1786, p. 2, and in the *Penn. Gazette* of October 4, p. 3, and the *Penn. Mercury* of October 6, p. 2.

[122] Letter of Sept. 24, 1786, written at Hartford, Conn.; 236 *Papers of G. W.*, 86.

[123] 29 *G. W.*, 27.

Humphreys' answer. Other correspondents, notably "Light Horse Harry" Lee, then in Congress, sent him such information from Massachusetts as came to New York and to other cities below the Hudson.[124] Some of these reports discounted the seriousness of the outbreak, but the prevalent tone was one of alarm. The situation was going from bad to worse. There was talk of "the abolition of debts, the division of property, and reunion with Great Britain." Affairs might become so critical, Harry Lee intimated, that Congress might call on Washington to go to the Eastern States, because it was taken for granted that the disorders then would subside.[125] Other Delegates were asking whether it was not the duty of Congress to raise troops with which to support the government of Massachusetts if the authorities of that State could not put down rioting that now had many aspects of dangerous rebellion.[126] Even those members of Congress who did not believe the malcontents could challenge the government were willing to admit that steps should be taken to secure the arms in the Federal arsenal at Springfield, Massachusetts,[127] from seizure by the followers of Daniel Shays, a former Captain in the Continental Army, who had emerged as the leader of the trouble-makers. The compromise agreed upon in October by a thinly attended, penniless body of Delegates in New York was to enlist troops for service against frontier Indians but to use them, if necessary, to cope with the insurrection in Massachusetts.[128] Washington's reflections on all this combined humiliation, common sense and deliberate choice between dangerous alternatives. "I am mortified beyond expression," he wrote Harry Lee, "when I view the clouds that

[124] 236 *Papers of G. W.*, 90, LC; *ibid.*, 98; 8 *Burnett*, 474, 481–83.

[125] Partly printed in *ibid.*, 486; the full text, including the quotation, is in 236 *Papers of G. W.*, 100, LC.

[126] This discussion was sharpened by Rufus King's address to the Massachusetts Legislature, Oct. 11, 1786, for which see 8 *Burnett*, 479. Cf. Henry Lee to James Madison, Oct. 19, 1786 (6 *Madison Papers*, 89, LC; 8 *Burnett*, 489), and William Grayson to James Monroe, Nov. 22, 1786, *ibid.*, 510.

[127] 236 *Papers of G. W.*, 90, LC; 8 *Burnett*, 474. For this important phase of the uprising, see J. P. Warren, "The Confederation and the Shays Rebellion," 11 *A.H.R.*, 44 ff. The *Knox Papers*, MHS, contain numerous letters to the Secretary from men who were observing closely the events in Massachusetts. See particularly William North of October 29, Samuel Parsons of November 6, Nathaniel Gorham of November 29 and December 13, Rufus King of December 13, James Bowdoin of December 14, and Henry Jackson of Dec. 31, 1786. Knox's important papers in the same collection, insofar as they relate to Shays's Rebellion are: to John Jay, October 3, to Maj. Joseph Williams, October 14, to Henry Jackson, December 3, to Jere. Wadsworth, December 13 and 30, to Nathaniel Gorham, December 24, and to Robert Morris, December, n.d., 1786. Knox's important letter of Oct. 28, 1786, to Washington, is cited in a later paragraph.

[128] Cf. *McLaughlin*, 165–66; cf. E. Carrington to Edmund Randolph, Dec. 8, 1786; 8 *Burnett*, 516. Warren (*op. cit.*) maintained that the danger on the frontier was real and was ample justification for the action of Congress.

have spread over the brightest morn that ever dawned upon any country." As for remedy, "you talk," he continued, ". . . of employing influence to appease the present tumults in Massachusetts. I know not where that influence is to be found and, if attainable, that it would be a proper remedy for our disorders." Then he wrote solemnly: "Influence is no government." If the insurgents had grievances, correct them or acknowledge them and say that cure had to wait for better days; but if the uprising represented no real complaint, "employ the force of government against [it] at once." He insisted: "If this [force] is inadequate, *all* will be convinced that the superstructure is bad, or wants support. To be more exposed in the eyes of the world, and more contemptible than we already are, is hardly possible . . . Precedents are dangerous things; let the reins of government then be braced and held with a steady hand, and every violaton of the constitution be reprehended: if defective let it be amended, but not suffered to be trampled upon whilst it has an existence." [129]

Thus was Shays's Rebellion linked, in the logic of Washington's reasoning, with the appeal for a stronger Federal government. Every development thereafter tightened the tie. From Henry Knox, Secretary of War, who had gone to Massachusetts to see the situation for himself, Washington received a long, careful letter on the uprising. The creed of the insurgents, said Knox, "is that the property of the United States has been protected from confiscation of Britain by the joint exertions of *all*, and therefore ought to be the *common property* of all. And he that attempts opposition to this creed is an enemy to equity and justice and ought to be swept from off the face of the earth." Further, said Knox of the insurrectionists: "They are determined to annihilate all debts public and private, and have agrarian laws, which are easily effected by the means of unfunded paper money which shall be a tender in all cases whatever . . . The numbers of these people amount in Massachusetts to about one fifth part of several populous Counties . . ." When reckoned with like-minded faultfinders in other New England States, they were said by Knox to constitute a body of 12,000 or 15,000 "desperate and unprincipled men," chiefly of "the young and active part of the community." [130] Washington confessed later that when he read this and similar reports of the uprising in

[129] Letter of Oct. 31, 1786; 29 *G. W.*, 34–35.
[130] Letter of Oct. 28, 1786, in *ibid.*, 51–52. The original is in 236 *Papers of G. W.*, 102–03, LC.

Massachusetts,[131] he felt as if he were in a dream. "Good God," he exclaimed, "who besides a Tory could have foreseen or a Briton predicted" such a situation? He asked Knox: "Were these people wiser than others, or did they judge of us from the corruption and depravity of their own hearts?" It was difficult to believe that the America which had won independence could be, in his simple language, "far gone in everything ignoble and bad"; [132] but it no more was his inclination in retirement than it had been during the war to accept an evil that could be corrected. The unavoidable must be endured; the circumstantial must be overcome.

Washington did not waste time in analyzing once again the conditions that rendered the Federal government helpless, or almost helpless, in dealing with Shays's Rebellion. Manifestly, the political machinery was too frail for the duty it was called upon to perform. It must be repaired or replaced. Virginia must begin that labor. Washington had observed with admiration the diligence, the patriotism and the high intelligence of James Madison, former representative in Congress and now, fortunately, a member of the House of Delegates of Virginia. Madison was the man to take the lead. On the 5th of November, with Knox's letter still burning in his mind, Washington wrote Madison to thank that Delegate for information regarding the legislative session. With applause for the refusal of the House to approve the emission of paper money,[133] he joined the hope that "the great and most important of all objects, the federal government" would be considered calmly and deliberately "at this critical moment." Fervently he pleaded: "Let prejudices, unreasonable jealousies and local interest yield to reason and liberality. Let us look to our national character, and to things beyond the present period . . . Wisdom and good examples are necessary at this time to rescue the political machine from the impending storm." Virginia had opportunity of setting the example and, he

---

131 Cf. David Humphreys to Washington, Nov. 9, 1786 (*ibid.*, 124), answering Washington's letter of October 22, cited *supra*: "In Massachusetts, particularly, I believe there are a few real grievances: and also some wicked agents, or emissaries, who have been busy in magnifying the positive evils, and fomenting causeless jealousies and disturbances—but it rather appears to me that there is a licentious spirit prevailing among many of the people; a leveling principle; a desire of change; and a wish to annihilate all debts, public and private." The similarity between this letter and that of Knox suggests the possibility that Humphreys may have seen the Secretary while Knox was returning to New York after his tour of inspection.

132 Letter to Henry Knox, Dec. 26, 1786; 29 *G. W.*, 122.

133 Washington had contributed indirectly to this by assisting in the election of the arch-enemy of paper money, George Mason, to the House of Delegates, even though Mason had said he would not serve (3 *Diaries*, 45; 2 *Rowland, Mason*, 96).

believed, had wisdom enough to lead. In deepest distress he gave warning: "Without some alteration in our political creed, the super-structure we have been seven years raising at the expense of so much blood and treasure, must fall. We are fast verging to anarchy and con-fusion." [134] Then he quoted, in proof, what Knox had written him.

Leadership? Virginia's? Madison's? The echo of Washington's words rolled back quickly from Richmond, where the General Assembly remained in session. Dark as was the outlook described by Knox, said Madison, he himself was "leaning to the side of hope." The Assembly had voted unanimously that it was expedient to comply with the recommendation of the Annapolis Convention in favor of a "general revision of the federal system." A good bill was pending and soon would be passed—a bill that gave the proposal a "very solemn dress and all the weight that could be derived from a single State." Next came the return challenge of leadership: Washington's name had been placed at the head of the list of Delegates to the Convention. "How far this liberty may correspond," said Madison, "with the ideas by which you ought to be governed will be best decided when it must ultimately be decided." [135]

That was not pleasant reading for a man whose love of retired detachment from controversies was second only to his love of country. Madison's respectful call to renewed public service was followed soon by plain-spoken, New England words from David Humphreys: "The troubles in Massachusetts still continue. Government is prostrated in the dust. And it is much to be feared that there is not energy enough in that State to reestablish the civil powers. The leaders of the mob, whose fortune and measures are desperate, are strengthening themselves daily; and it is expected that they will soon take possession of the continental magazine at Springfield, in which there are from ten to fifteen thousand stand of arms, in excellent order . . . Congress, I am told, are seriously alarmed and hardly know which way to turn, or what to expect. Indeed, my dear General, nothing but a good Providence can extricate us from our present difficulties and prevent some terrible convulsion." The heavy personal application followed: "In case of civil discord, I have already told you it was seriously my opinion that you could not remain neuter, and that you would be

[134] Letter of Nov. 5, 1786; 29 G. W., 51.
[135] Letter of Nov. 8, 1786; 6 Madison Papers, 94, LC; 2 Hunt's Madison, 283–84.

obliged, in self-defence to take part on one side or the other, or with-draw from the continent. Your friends are of the same opinion . . ." [136]

Washington had to admit the justice of at least a part of this: In such a crisis as he continued to think the Federal government faced,[137] he undeniably had his share of the duty he was invoking others to dis-charge; but he had an embarrassment of a sort on which his mind laid particular emphasis, even if some might term it an excuse and some might say he was deceiving himself in urging it seriously. It was this: As President of the Society of the Cincinnati, he had sent out a circular in which he had notified the State Societies that his private affairs, the presidency of the Potomac Company, and the affliction of rheumatism made it impossible for him to attend the triennial meeting of the Gen-eral Society.[138] As ill chance would have it, this meeting was to be held in Philadelphia during May, 1787—the town and the month set for the convention Virginia was calling. He had no other god before consistency and no code more compelling than courtesy. "Under these circumstances," he told Madison, "it will readily be perceived that I could not appear at the same time and place on any other occasion, without giving offence" to the Society.[139]

Washington's reasoning did not convince his friends if, indeed, it was quite conclusive in his own mind. Soon after the beginning of De-cember a long period of freezing weather in northern Virginia cov-ered roads and river with ice and cut Mount Vernon off [140] as completely as if it had been on the upper waters of the Monongahela, rather than a mere canter from the main North-and-South highway of America. When the post again was operating and mail could be brought from Alexandria, Washington learned that the Virginia General Assembly had passed the bill for calling a convention of the States; [141] that he had been elected unanimously to head a distinguished delegation of seven,[142] and that both Madison [143] and the new Governor, Edmund Randolph,[144] deferentially were urging him not to refuse immediately,

---

[136] Letter of Nov. 1, 1786; 236 Papers of G. W., 114, LC; 4 LTW., 148–49.

[137] See his observations in 29 G. W., 61, 68.

[138] Ibid., 31. He added that he did not wish to be reelected President because he would be compelled to decline. This letter was drafted by David Humphreys and was signed by Wash-ington substantially as written by the former aide (236 Papers of G. W., 109–10, LC).

[139] 29 G. W., 72; cf. ibid., 73, 76.     [140] Ibid., 115.

[141] 12 H 256.     [142] 2 W. W. Henry, 302.

[143] 7 Madison Papers, 3, LC; 2 Hunt's Madison, 295.

[144] 238 Papers of G. W., 19, 39, LC; 4 LTW., 152; contemporary copy, Dec. 6, 1786, in Executive Letter Book, 1786–88, f. 11, VSL.

because he could not be spared from attendance. His appointment, David Stuart wrote Washington, "appeared to be so much the wish of the House that Mr. Madison conceived it might probably frustrate the whole scheme if it was not done." [145]

The General read and pondered and could not bring himself to say "Yes" or to decline with a "No" so positive that someone else would of necessity be chosen in his stead. Carefully and painfully he reviewed the circumstances of his announcement to the Cincinnati that he would not attend its Philadelphia meeting; then, admitting the immense importance of the issue, he confided that he did not know what considerations might lead him to change his mind before the meeting in May. He concluded by leaving to Madison's judgment whether it "would be improper to let my appointment stand in the way of another." [146] In writing Governor Randolph, the General came a little closer to decision, but did not quite reach the finality of refusal: Because of circumstances from which there was little prospect of disengaging himself, he said, "it would be disingenuous not to express a wish that some other character, on whom greater reliance can be had, may be substituted in my place, the probability of my non-attendance being too great to continue my appointment." [147]

Wisely, Randolph and the Council decided not to act on Washington's declination—if declination it might be styled. Conditions might shift; another nomination could be made later, if necessary. "Perhaps, too," said the Governor, "(and indeed I fear the event), every other consideration may seem of little weight, when compared with the crisis which may then hang over the United States." [148] With superlative tact, Madison made the same appeal. [149] Washington referred the whole correspondence to David Humphreys with the query, "Should the matter be further pressed (which I hope it will not, as I have no inclination to go), what had I best do?"; [150] but in the same letter he argued earnestly for precisely such a stronger Union as Madison and the others hoped to assure at the Convention to which they knew the presence of Washington would give prestige. [151] His every impulse, all

[145] Letter of Dec. 19, 1786; 2 *Bancroft, His. Cons.*, 406. Also in 237 *Papers of G. W.*, 33, LC.

[146] 29 *G. W.*, 115.  [147] *Ibid.*, 120.

[148] Letter of Jan. 4, 1787, 237 *Papers of G. W.*, 46, LC; wrongly entered as of Jan. 4, 1786, in 4 *LTW.*, 124–25.

[149] 7 *Madison Papers*, 12 LC; 2 *Hunt's Madison*, 300–01.

[150] 29 *G. W.*, 127.  [151] *Ibid.*, 127–28.

the memories of frustration during the war, all his ambition to save America from humiliating collapse, made him an advocate of a constitution he said he would not assist in creating—lest he be regarded as inconsistent and discourteous in dealing with the Cincinnati. At the same time, his own fears for the future of the Union made him arouse the fears of others in the hope their sense of danger would assure a strong, representative convention in Philadelphia. The day after Christmas when the only flames should have been those of the Yule log, he warned Henry Knox: "There are combustibles in every State, which a spark might set fire to." [152] Just two days later in a letter to Thomas Johnson he apprehended the spring of 1787 might bring scenes that would "astonish the world." Then anxiously he concluded: "Nothing, I am certain, but the wisest councils and the most vigorous exertions can avert them." [153]

[152] *Ibid.*, 122.  [153] Letter of Dec. 28, 1786; *ibid.*, 130.

# PATRIOT FIRST—THEN OFFICER

Under the impulse primarily of General Knox, Continental officers at headquarters on the Hudson founded the Society of the Cincinnati in May, 1783. Taking its name from the Roman soldier who retired to private life after serving his country well, the Society declared certain purposes in an "Institution." Its intention was to perpetuate in peacetime the comradeship of eight years in arms, and to maintain a fund for the relief of distressed officers and their families. Washington as Commander-in-Chief was designated "President-General," and plans were drawn for organizing the Society in each of the States and in France.

Not a year was out before popular hostility to the Cincinnati climbed to threatening heights. One of the clauses in the Institution stipulated that membership pass down from father to son. This, Benjamin Franklin contended, would serve to create "an order of hereditary knights" in America. From their seats in Congress, Elbridge Gerry and Samuel Osgood expressed suspicion of financial designs on the part of the Society, and Jefferson in Paris could not wish it well. Then, in climax, Judge Ædanus Burke of Charleston gave vent to his ardent hatred of aristocracy with a vehement pamphlet which was translated in French by Mirabeau and later into German. In February, 1784, Knox wrote regretfully from Boston that Burke's publication had excited much antagonism and that New Englanders feared that foreign influence in the Society might distort American principles.

Washington had not anticipated this storm of opposition. To the founders, the eagle of the Cincinnati seemed scarcely more than a just, well deserved badge of faithful service in the Revolution—and was, perhaps, the only distinction a gallant officer could retain, now that the Army was disbanded. This thought, however, did not prejudice Washington. He had been a patriot before he became a soldier; he would be a patriot now before he was a veteran. If the people had criticism, the Cincinnati must so alter its Institution as to allay every apprehension; if antagonism persisted, the Society should dissolve itself in the best interest of the country. He pondered for weeks the several objections which had rung loudest. Action by the Society, he determined, must be "deliberate and wise." To this end, he drafted with care and precision a list of amendments to the Institution, with particular emphasis on the proposal to "strike out every word, sentence and clause which has a political tendency." Washington's first long journey after the war was to Philadelphia in May, 1784, to preside at a general meeting of the Cincinnati. His suggestions, with one exception, were adopted by the delegates. The soldier-patriot had again acknowledged civil supremacy.

(From the Papers of George Washington, Library of Congress.)

C

Strike out every word, sentence, and clause which has a political tendency

Discontinue the hereditary part in all its connexions, absolutely, without any substitution which can be construed into concealment, or a change of ground only; for this would, in my opinion, increase, rather than allay suspicions. —

Admit no more honorary Members into the Society. —

Reject subscriptions, or donations from every person who is not a citizen of the United States. —

Place the funds upon such a footing as to remove the jealousies which are entertained on that score. —   *

Authorize the foreign Officers to hold meetings in France, if it shall be permitted by their Government. — Empower them at these meetings to hear, & decide upon the pretensions ~~of foreigners whose claims are founded on~~ of those, of their own body, who, under the letter, or spirit of the Institution, claim the privilege of becoming members of the Cincinnati. — As also the pretensions of foreigners whose claims are founded on being Officers in the ~~french~~ American Army. — Americans in foreign Countries who belonged to the line of any State, are to make application to the Society of that State, who shall hear, & decide thereupon. —

Upon these principles let the Institution be formed in as clear, distinct & explicit terms as language can convey. — Let a Secret transmit the same to the Senior Foreign Member in France, or the Senior Land & Naval Officer in that Kingdom (if it shall be adjudged

and M$^{rs}$
GENERAL WASHINGTON presents
their Compliments to M$^r$ and
M$^{rs}$ Porter
and requests the favor of their
Company at dinner tomorrow
Monday 19$^{th}$ May
1788.

An answer is requested

## "A WELL-RESORTED TAVERN"

It was June 30, 1785, eighteen months after his homecoming, before Washington and his lady dined alone. The seven or eight regular "family" residents of Mount Vernon who sat at the General's table were joined by a continuing caravan of callers, overnight guests and visitors of doubtful duration. Old friends like "Mr. and Mrs. Porter," whose names appear on the invitation opposite, came usually on bidding; old comrades like Lafayette and Humphreys always were welcome. The vast majority of guests at Mount Vernon during the interlude of the General's retirement, however, were unknown to him. They arrived unexpected and unannounced except by the letters of introduction they bore: Europeans of title and Americans of every sort—the distinguished, the pretentious, the presumptuous, the curious; impressionable young travelers and jaded older ones. All found the master of Mount Vernon eminently hospitable. To Washington, this double rôle of national hero and national host was unavoidable. It was duty. Resignedly, he likened Mount Vernon to a "well-resorted tavern," at which "any strangers who are going from North to South or from South to North" were likely to pause a day or two.

(Courtesy of The Mount Vernon Ladies' Association.)


## WAS THIS DIVERSION—OR DISINTEREST?

Autumn of 1790 found Washington strangely preoccupied, his imagination captured by trifles. This turn of attention from serious matters of government manifested itself first in concern over redecoration of the Morris House, residence of the Chief Executive in Philadelphia. Washington assigned supervision of the repair to Tobias Lear, then proceeded to raise a hundred questions and resolve them himself in precise, ponderous letters to his secretary. Next, he wished to acquire a light, roadworthy carriage for travel and to transform his ten-year-old private coach into something "plain and elegant" for official use about town. David and Francis Clark, carriage makers of Philadelphia, provided the new vehicle, and were commissioned also to refurbish the "state" coach. Washington's interest was intense. He specified the color of the fresh paint, the interior fabric, the design of the harness—and submitted a pencil sketch of the "cypher," or personal crest, shown here, for the doors. Was the President seeking simple relaxation in these diversions, or did they carry a deeper meaning?

(After the Original in the Papers of George Washington, Library of Congress.)

# CHAPTER IV

## To Avert "Some Awful Crisis"

## (1787)

WASHINGTON HAD troubles enough in the early months of 1787 to have led a man of mind less resolute and ordered to put aside public affairs completely. John Augustine died at the beginning of the year, a loss the General sustained with heavy heart, because "Jack" of all his brothers had been next only to Lawrence in his affection.[1] The estate of Samuel Washington and the schooling of his sons Lawrence and George remained a concern of the busy "retired" soldier.[2] At home, Frances Bassett Washington had her first baby and lost it.[3]

These sorrows came when Washington still was suffering, sometimes acutely, from his "rheumatism"[4] and, in a different sense, from financial "hard times." His spirits certainly were not improved by a demand from his mother for fifteen guineas. He sent the coin in February with the unabashed statement that it was literally all he had in hand. Nor could he withhold a warm protest: he offered no excuse, he said, "for not paying you what may really be due . . . but it is really hard upon me when you have taken every thing you wanted from the plantation, by which money could be raised, when I have not received one farthing, directly nor indirectly from the place for more than twelve years if ever, and when, in that time, I have paid, as appears by Mr. Lund Washington's accounts against me (during my absence) two hundred and sixty odd pounds, and by my own account fifty odd pounds out of

---

[1] 29 *G. W.*, 141, 209. Death was attributed to "a fit of the gout in the head" (3 *Diaries*, 160).

[2] 29 *G. W.*, 158, 186, 268, 280–81. Many letters concerning these boys are in the *Papers of G. W.*, but scarcely call for specific listing.

[3] April 10–24; 3 *Diaries*, 192, 204. As noted (*supra*, p. 2, n. 10), Rev. Lee Massey's call to christen and then to bury this infant boy was Washington's only notation of a visit of his rector to Mount Vernon during the years immediately following the Revolution.

[4] On occasion, he could not turn over in bed without discomfort, and for a time he had to carry one arm in a sling (29 *G. W.*, 209). He did not state which arm it was. As of May 1, he made in his Diary an unusual reference to "my fatigue" (3 *Diaries*, 208), though his "rheumatism" by that time was waning (29 *G. W.*, 211. Cf. *ibid.*, 187, 195).

my own pocket to you, besides (if I am rightly informed) everything that has been raised by the crops on the plantation." [5]

Other demands were heavy. Currently, Washington had pressing bills for more than £500, of which £340, or something above that figure, was for taxes of 1786.[6] He found it exceedingly difficult to collect what was due him, even for flour, and from some of his tenants he could get nothing unless he took their horses.[7] Lund Washington had special need of his past-due salary: the best the General could do at the time was to tender him a bond he believed a borrower would pay on its maturity. "My estate for the last eleven years," he confessed, "has not been able to make both ends meet." He had the encumbrance of that deficit and, he told his kinsman, "I am not able to pay debts unless I could sell land, which I have publicly advertised without finding bidders." [8] Little or no effort was made to reduce expenses. Contracts for labor were negotiated with care, but if they involved service Washington desired, they were made almost without regard to plantation economy and, on occasion, in the face of strange stipulations. A new gardener had it written into his contract, for example, that he was to receive at Christmas four dollars, "with which he may be drunk four days and four nights" and so, in turn, for other holidays.[9]

Every day public questions obtruded and overshadowed farm and family and all else: Was the insurrection in Massachusetts spreading dangerously; were the States responding to Virginia's invitation; must Washington attend the Philadelphia Convention or could he hold in good conscience to his statement that as he had declined to attend the general meeting of the Cincinnati, he could not go to the same city for another purpose at the very same time? The three questions were related one to another: If Shays's Rebellion had proved the need of a stronger union, a convention of the States manifestly was the agent for recommending to each State changes in the system of government that would vest Congress with requisite powers; but if the Convention were small and unrepresentative, should Washington participate and give the prestige of his name to feeble, timid amendments? Conversely,

---

[5] Letter of Feb. 15, 1787; 29 *G. W.*, 159. Lund Washington's account book (*Mount Vernon MSS*) shows payments of £110 between Jan. 26, 1777 and Feb. 23, 1779 (f. 57, 66, 79, 82).

[6] 29 *G. W.*, 158.

[7] *Ibid.*, 156, 159, 166–67; B. Muse to Washington, Mch. 8, 1787, 238 *Papers of G. W.*, 13, LC. For the unprofitable spring run of fish, see 3 *Diaries*, 206–07.

[8] *Ibid.*, 212–13.          [9] *Ibid.*, 207.

in event a large assemblage of men struck out boldly for an effective Union, could he withhold his influence, which might be deemed essential to overcoming State prejudices and the jealousies of suspicious men of selfish ambition?

The mailbag at Mount Vernon was heavy for weeks with answers and arguments. Continued alarm over the discontent and violence in Massachusetts [10] was accompanied by a suggestion that it might be well for Washington to pay a "private visit" to that State,[11] but in mid-February it was hoped that a vigorous march by Benjamin Lincoln on Petersham, the stormy night of the 2nd, had broken the back of the rebellion.[12] Washington breathed less anxiously and at the appropriate time urged leniency for the insurgents,[13] though he shared Madison's fear [14] that discontent was spreading and that the affairs of the nation were approaching "some awful crisis." Gloomily the General exclaimed, "God only knows what the result will be!" [15] The threat of another flood of paper money engulfing America was, in the opinion of Washington, almost as serious as that of mobs closing Massachusetts courts.[16] He continued to assert that America was facing a final test as to whether she could survive "without the means of coercion in the sovereign"; [17] but insofar as this might require his own active participation as a Delegate to the proposed Convention, he held to his main argument for declining the appointment.[18]

On the 21st of February—the day before Washington was 55 years of age—Congress voted that it was "expedient" to hold a convention of

[10] *Ibid.*, 153.

[11] A. Campbell to James Madison, Jan. 4, 1787; 7 *Madison Papers*, 20, LC.

[12] 29 *G. W.*, 167–68. Knox's letters to Washington in January–March, 1787, were almost a connected history of the last phases of the insurrection. See letters of the following dates and folios (Knox to Washington) in 237 *Papers of G. W.*: December 17 (f. 27–28), January 14 (f. 52–54), January 21 (f. 63), January 25 (f. 69), January 29 (f. 81), January 30 (f. 82). In his letter of February 8 to Washington (f. 108), Knox included a dispatch from Gen. Benjamin Lincoln to Governor Bowdoin (237 *Papers of G. W.*, 76), and one from Lincoln to Knox (*ibid.*). Other letters (Knox to Washington) bear dates of February 12 (f. 111), February 27 (f. 124), March 5 (f. 132). See also, in 237 *Papers of G. W.*, B. Lincoln to Washington, Jan. 24, 1787 (f. 67); D. Humphreys to Washington, Feb. 11, 28, 1787 (f. 110, 126); Ezra Stiles to Washington, Feb. 7, 1787 (f. 107).

[13] 29 *G. W.*, 181–82, 184, 191.

[14] Madison to his father, Feb. 25, 1787; 7 *Madison Papers*, 42, LC.

[15] 29 *G. W.*, 169–70.

[16] *Ibid.*, 169. Cf. Edmund Randolph to James Madison, Apr. 11, 1787, 7 *Madison Papers*, 63, LC, and Edmund Randolph to Edward Carrington, Apr. 11, 1787; *Emmet Col.*, NYPL.

[17] 29 *G. W.*, 176; cf. *ibid.*, 189–90 and E. Randolph to Washington, Apr. 2, 1787; 2 *Bancroft, His. Cons.*, 416: ". . . everything travels so fast to confusion that I trust one grand effort will be made by the friends of the United States."

[18] 29 *G. W.*, 128, 151. For reports that he might or might not attend, see 2 *W. W. Henry*, 312; 8 *Burnett*, 527.

State Delegates in Philadelphia on the second Monday in May "for the sole and express purpose of revising the Articles of Confederation." [19] This action was justified, in Washington's opinion, even though it might not be strictly in accordance with the Articles themselves,[20] but he still doubted whether the Convention would be well attended by men of ability and courage. On the other hand, with the most sensitive regard for his own reputation, he began to ask himself whether his refusal to participate might not be considered a disclosure of lack of sympathy with republican ideals, if, indeed, his abstention might not be attributed to "other motives." [21] In frank acknowledgment that this question troubled him, he passed it on to Henry Knox and to David Humphreys for their counsel.[22] They were close friends and they were detached; the opinions of the younger, vigorous Virginia leaders he already knew: Madison and Edmund Randolph both continued patiently to urge that he go to the meeting of Delegates in Philadelphia or, at the least, that he should not say, unequivocally, he would not accept appointment.[23]

As late as March 15, Washington wrote as if it virtually were certain he would not attend,[24] but by that date, several developments were taking form: Congress's action in endorsing the Convention was approved widely and was condemned scarcely at all; most of the political leaders, certainly the younger of them, were agreed that a crisis was imminent or else that the Union, in its weakness and pauperism, soon would die of fiscal starvation and political neglect;[25] impressive appointments to the proposed Philadelphia Convention were being made unhesitatingly by several States.[26]

Washington read, wavered and reconsidered. On March 8, he had

[19] 32 JCC., 73–74; 1 Elliot's Debates, 119–20.

[20] 29 G. W., 67–68. The Articles could not be changed, it will be remembered, "unless such alteration be agreed to in a Congress of the United States, and be afterwards confirmed by the Legislatures of every State" (Article XIII; 19 JCC., 221).

[21] 29 G. W., 171. He did not specify what the "other motives" might be but Henry Knox's letter of April 9, infra, p. 85, suggested the General's nonparticipation might be regarded as indicating a belief that force should be employed to establish a new order.

[22] Ibid., 171, 172–73.

[23] Edmund Randolph to Madison, Mch. 7, 1787; 7 Madison Papers, 45, LC; Madison to Washington, Mch. 18, 1787, the original in ibid., 49, and printed in part in 2 Hunt's Madison, 325.

[24] 29 G. W., 180–81.

[25] See as typical, John Jay to Washington, January 7, 237 Papers of G. W., 46, LC; William Nelson to William Short, January 11, 2 Papers of William Short, 200–06, LC; David Humphreys to Washington, January 20; 237 Papers of G. W., 58–59, LC.

[26] Madison to Washington, Mch. 18, 1787, 7 Madison Papers, 49, LC, and in 2 Hunt's Madison, 321 (slightly abbreviated).

written David Humphreys he did not believe important changes could be effected "without great contention and much confusion." [27] A fortnight later he realized that the prospect was brighter in the North and in the East. Although he could not yet persuade himself that the Convention would be attended fully by unfettered Delegates,[28] he found a certain sense of shame making him more and more well disposed to the Convention. His own Virginia was holding back. While almost every mail brought reports of able men pledging themselves to go to Philadelphia, Patrick Henry [29] and Thomas Nelson, Jr., declined membership.[30] Governor Randolph proposed to name Richard Henry Lee in Nelson's place,[31] but Lee pled ill health [32] and said later that he did not think members of Congress should sit in the Convention.[33] Was the State that initiated the gathering to have all of her best known elder sons, Washington included, absent from that body? What would the other States think of that?

Pressure was becoming heavy.[34] Anxiously and painfully, Washington reviewed the arguments for and against attendance—arguments that seemed daily to become more complicated: On the one side was the formality and professed finality of retirement in December, 1783, the embarrassment of the Cincinnati meeting, the inconvenience of being from home, the chance that his "rheumatism" might cripple or confine him, and the probability that others, like himself, might decline attendance or appear in small numbers under hampering instructions. Even more personally, there was danger, he felt, that his reputation might suffer if a feeble convention ended with proposals that would not give the Union needed strength. Besides, the meeting might lead to a controversy of the sort he most disliked and always had avoided, if possible. The counter arguments set the beam squarely in balance: A desperate crisis appeared to lie ahead of the Union. What had happened in Massachusetts might be repeated in almost any other State. Government itself was challenged. A supreme effort seemed necessary to prevent the disintegration of the Federation into a congeries of rival States which might choke themselves with paper money. The Convention undeniably presented the best and perhaps the only means of

---

[27] 29 G. W., 173.                                 [28] Cf. ibid., 193, 198.
[29] 2 W. W. Henry, 311–14; 7 Madison Papers, 51, LC; an incomplete version in 2 Hunt's Madison, 324.
[30] Edmund Randolph to Madison, Mch. 22, 1787; 7 Madison Papers, 52, LC.
[31] Ibid.                                          [32] 2 Ballagh, Lee Letters, 415.
[33] Ibid., 434.                                    [34] Cf. 29 G. W., 229.

making this supreme effort. If Washington did not share in it, he might be accused of lack of sympathy with it. Abstention might be a far greater disservice to the nation than his presence would be an affront to the Cincinnati. The risk of odium from refusal might be greater than loss of popularity by taking sides in a dispute that might not, after all, be furious or defamatory. As for other personal considerations—poor health and financial embarrassment—should these stand in a patriot's way?

Washington balanced these arguments in their relation to his duty and to his reputation. Today he practically concluded he should stay at home and should not risk his fame; tomorrow, he would be almost convinced that he could not afford to absent himself from the Convention. If this evening the rheumatism discouraged him, in the morning he would feel he was overcoming his malady. At last on the 28th of March, still beset with misgiving, he wrote Governor Randolph an equivocal, overcautious and self-regarding letter: If the Governor had named nobody in his place and was not considering anyone, he would undertake to go to Philadelphia, provided his health made this practicable. He coupled with this qualified assent a new expression of his doubts concerning the outcome of the Convention, lest the failure of that body be construed as a reflection on his judgment,[35] and he took superlative pains not to commit himself beyond easy withdrawal.[36] In spite of ifs and provisos, the letter brought him reluctantly and begrudgingly closer to a favorable decision. Randolph took this view and let it be known that the General would attend if health permitted.[37] The Governor and James Madison became so nearly confident, in fact, of Washington's participation that they began to discuss whether he should be present at the opening of the Convention or should appear later.[38]

About the time his letter to Randolph arrived in Richmond, Washington received Knox's reply to his request [39] for advice on the course he should follow. The former Chief of Artillery previously had warned his old Commander against attendance on a convention that would be feeble in personnel, thin in representation or apt to involve the General

[35] *Ibid.*, 186–87.
[36] Cf. *ibid.*, 193–94.
[37] Two letters of Apr. 4, 1787, to Madison; 7 *Madison Papers*, 59–60, LC.
[38] *Ibid.*, 64, LC; printed in part in 2 *Hunt's Madison*, 341.
[39] Of Feb. 3, 1787; 29 *G. W.*, 151–52.

in dispute.[40] This time the answer of Knox was a somewhat inconclusive reminder that the effect of the venture on the reputation of the General would be determined by the magnitude of the Convention's accomplishment.[41] David Humphreys' counsel was discouraging: he did not favor Washington's attendance because he thought the Convention was certain to be small and apt to be a failure.[42] In circumstances less compelling, this counsel from trusted lieutenants familiar with sentiment in the Eastern States would have been influential and perhaps decisive with Washington. Coming when numerous other friends were urging him to go, the cautious letters of Knox and Humphreys probably had no other effect than to render him more unhappy. He had to make up his mind; this must not be a political Fort Washington campaign, when everything might be lost by hesitation.[43] On the 9th of April, most unwillingly and in an amazingly egocentric strain, he wrote Randolph that he was about to act contrary to his judgment. He apprehended, moreover, that his action would be regarded as inconsistent with his statement in December, 1783, that he never intended thereafter to "intermeddle in public matters." Once more, he reviewed the involvement of the Society of the Cincinnati and then he proceeded: "Add to these, I very much fear that all the States will not appear in Convention, and that some of them will come fettered so as to impede rather than accelerate the great object of their convening which, under the peculiar circumstances of my case, would place me in a more disagreeable situation than any other member would stand in. As I have yielded, however, to what appeared to be the earnest wishes of my friends, I will hope for the best . . ." [44]

He scarcely could have stated it more ungraciously or with more patent regard for himself, as distinguished from his country, but he said it and, after that, he did not turn back. A report of the extreme illness of his mother and of his sister sent him in great haste to Fredericksburg on April 27, and threatened to delay his departure for the North.[45] It might not be possible, he apprehended, for him to reach Philadelphia several days in advance of the Convention so that he might attend some, at least, of the meetings of the Cincinnati and ex-

[40] Letter of Jan. 14, 1787; 237 *Papers of G. W.*, 52, LC.
[41] Letter of Mch. 19, 1787; 238 *ibid.*, 27, LC.
[42] Letter of Mch. 24, 1787, *ibid.*, 32, LC. William Grayson was of this opinion, also, though Washington did not seek his advice at the time. See 8 *Burnett*, 581.
[43] See Vol. IV, p. 242 ff.        [44] 29 *G. W.*, 198.
[45] *Ibid.*, 209–10; Tobias Lear to Knox, Apr. 27, 1787; *Knox Papers*, MHS.

plain the "inconsistency" that had troubled him.[46] Fortunately, when he reached Fredericksburg, he found Mrs. Washington better and his sister's condition the result of strain from waiting on her mother, rather than of direct and dangerous illness. He returned home on the 30th [47] and soon had the satisfaction of finding that Henry Knox and David Humphreys had changed their opinion of the propriety of his participation in the effort to give America a stronger constitution. Knox wrote the very day that Washington sent his acceptance of his appointment as a delegate: "It is the general wish that you should attend. It is conceived to be highly important to the success of the propositions of the convention. The mass of the people feel the inconveniences of the present government and ardently wish for such alterations as would remedy them. The alterations must be effected by wisdom and agreement, or by force. A convention appears the only means to effect the alterations peaceably. If that should be unattended by a proper weight of wisdom and character, so as to carry into execution its propositions, we are to look to events, and force, for answer. Were you not then to attend the convention, slander and malice might suggest that force would be the most agreeable mode of reform to you. When civil commotion rages, no purity of character, nor services however exalted, can entirely shield from the shafts of calumny. On the other hand, the unbounded confidence the people have of your tried patriotism and wisdom would exceedingly facilitate the adoption of any important alterations that might be proposed by a convention of which you were a member (and as I before hinted) and president." [48] Humphreys was not so emphatic nor, indeed, convinced, but he reported that important men thought Washington should participate, and he admitted that he did not himself believe the General's attendance could "hazard such personal ill consequences as were to be apprehended before the proposed meeting had been legitimated by the sanction of Congress." If Washington went to the Convention, it was indispensable, in Humphreys' opinion, that he reach Philadelphia in time to attend the general meeting of the Cincinnati.[49] With this reassurance, and with the appreciative thanks of the men laboring for a successful convention,

---

[46] 29 *G. W.*, 187–88, 209. The Cincinnati were called to meet on the 2nd of May; the Convention was to assemble on the 14th.

[47] *Ibid.*, 210; 3 *Diaries*, 205, 206, 210. Washington did not count this time completely lost. On one or another of the Rappahannock plantations he visited, he learned of new, experimental methods of growing potatoes and clover. See *ibid.*, 210, 211.

[48] 238 *Papers of G. W.*, 46.           [49] Letter of Apr. 9, 1787; *ibid.*, 47.

Washington carefully gave full verbal instructions to his nephew, George Augustine, whom he intended to leave in charge of Mount Vernon.[50] Then, after a day's delay because of squalls and showers, he set out in his carriage, unaccompanied by Martha, early in the morning of the 9th of May.[51]

Often as he had traveled the road between the Potomac and the Schuylkill—to the First and Second Continental Congress, to Head of Elk in 1777, to Yorktown, to Annapolis for the return of his commission—he never had crossed its streams and skirted its mudholes with less credit to himself than now, unless it was early in 1756 when he was on his journey to Boston trying to establish his seniority over Capt. John Dagworthy.[52] In all the preliminaries of what may be regarded as a last effort to save the collapsing Union, he had been too zealously attentive to his prestige, his reputation and his popularity— too much the self-conscious national hero and too little the daring patriot. His formal retirement in 1783, like a man's previous statement that he will stay in his chamber at home, scarcely should have been binding now—the house was on fire. Consistency in his statements to the Cincinnati was a small thing compared with consistency in that which had been his greatest public quality, his readiness to put his country above himself. He had held off when he thought the Convention would be thinly attended by Delegates not of the first distinction and he had accepted only when satisfied that most of the States would be represented by able men, not unduly hampered by instructions.[53] He never could have won the war in the spirit he displayed in this effort to secure the peace.

Had all the disparaging circumstances of Washington's hesitation been known, they probably would not have shaken his popularity.

[50] 3 *Diaries*, 212. He probably determined before he left home to write George Augustine frequently from Philadelphia in answer to regular reports he told his nephew to forward, but no record of any such advance understanding has been found.

[51] 3 *Diaries*, 215. Martha, the General explained, "is become too domestic and too attentive to her two little grandchildren to leave home . . ." (29 *G. W.*, 211). Governor Randolph had offered to send some of the Delegates to the head of the Chesapeake on one of the Virginia inspection vessels (Randolph to George Wythe, John Blair and Thomas Nelson, Jr., Mch. 9, 1787; *Executive Letter Book*, f. 58, VSL).

[52] See Vol. II, p. 153 ff.

[53] "The latitude thus given, together with the generality of the commission from the States have doubtless operated to bring General Washington forward, contrary to his more early determination . . ." (Edward Carrington to Jefferson, June 9, 1787; 8 *Burnett*, 607). In a letter of Apr. 11, 1787, to Carrington (*Emmet Col.*, NYPL), Governor Randolph reported that Washington showed a reluctance to go to a convention where there was danger not all the States would be represented.

The people, as well as his friends, saw only that he had emerged from his cherished retirement to serve them in a time of difficulty and confusion. Henry Knox wrote Lafayette: "General Washington's attendance at the convention adds, in my opinion, new lustre to his character. Secure as he was in his fame, he has again committed it to the mercy of events. Nothing but the critical situation of his country would have induced him to so hazardous a conduct. But its happiness being in danger, he disregards all personal considerations." [54] From its different point of view, the *Pennsylvania Herald* announced Washington's purpose to attend the Convention. "This great patriot," said the Philadelphia paper, "will never think his duty performed, while anything remains to be done." [55]

He arrived on the 13th, after encountering weather more threatening than bad,[56] and was given a welcome that lacked nothing the affection of the people could bestow. Senior officers of his old Army met him at Chester and dined with him; at Gray's Ferry, the City Light Horse and many mounted citizens fell in as escort; the artillery fired a salute when he entered the town; the bells of Christ Church were rung; at the boarding establishment of Mrs. House [57] a crowd was awaiting him.[58] Although that lady operated what was regarded as "one of the most genteel" places of entertainment in the city,[59] the General was not permitted to remain there. Robert Morris and Mrs. Morris, whose invitation Washington gratefully had declined before he left Mount Vernon,[60] now urged him so warmly to lodge with them that he accepted and forthwith had his luggage removed to the financier's famous home.[61] Before he ended the day, Washington paid his first call—an official visit to Benjamin Franklin, now President of the Executive Council of Pennsylvania, whom Washington had not seen since 1776. The meeting of course was cordial, because each respected and admired the other, and it held out, also, the promise of close relations in the weeks ahead: Franklin had accepted appointment as one of Pennsylvania's Delegates to the Convention and, feeble though he admitted himself to be, he intended to take his seat. The old

[54] Letter of July 25, 1787; *Knox Papers*, MHS.
[55] Issue of May 12, 1787, p. 3.                    [56] 3 *Diaries*, 215–16.
[57] Said to have been at Fifth and Market Streets.
[58] 3 *Diaries*, 216; *Independent Gazetteer* (Philadelphia), May 14, p. 3; *Penn. Packet* (Philadelphia), May 14, p. 3; *Penn. Gazette* (Philadelphia), May 16, 1787, p. 3.
[59] *Independent Gazetteer*, loc. cit.
[60] 29 *G. W.*, 210–11.                    [61] 3 *Diaries*, 216.

diplomatist was philosophical and at the same time optimistic with respect to the meeting. ". . . if it does not do good," he wrote Jefferson, "it must do harm, as it will show we have not wisdom enough among us to govern ourselves . . ." [62]

With this visit to crown it, Washington's first day in Philadelphia could not be described with a lesser adjective than triumphant. He carefully recorded all the public occurrences of his entry, even to "on my arrival, the bells were chimed" [63] and he would have been justified in adding that, after three years and a half, there appeared to be no wane in the affection of the people for him, not a hint that he was "in the swallowing gulf of blind forgetfulness." Philadelphia had not welcomed him more eagerly when he arrived from Yorktown. The cordiality of the reception was all the more impressive because, in a sense, it was national. Five conventions, meeting simultaneously, had brought to the town representatives from nearly all the States.[64]

To the chagrin of the General, the most important of these conventions, the one to revise the Articles of Confederation, was the slowest in assembling. On the 14th, the date set for the opening, Pennsylvania and Virginia alone were represented. The next day, individual members from New Jersey, Delaware and North Carolina reported, but not in sufficient numbers to organize the delegations from those States. One Delegate only arrived on the 16th. While this was deplorable, James Madison cheerfully attributed members' tardiness to a long spell of bad weather that must have made every road a muddy mirror for the verdure of spring.[65] Washington apparently felt much the same disgust he had expressed over the tardiness of Delegates in going to Annapolis for the commercial convention,[66] but he believed that sooner or later a sufficient number of representatives would arrive to speak for a majority of the States and to organize the Convention. In this good hope he met daily with the other Virginians, who talked of the work to be done, and, no doubt, acquainted him with constitutional questions he had not considered in the quiet of Mount Vernon.[67] As

[62] Letter of Apr. 19, 1787, to Jefferson; 9 *Smyth's Franklin*, 574.
[63] 3 *Diaries*, 216.
[64] Besides the Federal Convention and the general meeting of the Cincinnati, the eleventh General Assembly of the Penn. Society for the Abolition of Slavery, the Presbyterian Synod and a convention of Baptists, not identified, met in Philadelphia at the same time during May (*Penn. Packet*, May 18, p. 2; *Penn. Mercury*, May 25, 1787, p. 3).
[65] 3 *Farrand*, 20.          [66] See *supra*, p. 68–69.
[67] Cf. George Mason in 2 *Bancroft, His. Cons.*, 421–22, May 20, 1787.

the able, vigorous men of the Virginia delegation proceeded with their discussions, they developed a "plan" of government, a paper based chiefly on proposals that James Madison and Edmund Randolph had brought with them.[68] Washington probably did not make any specific contribution of form or of substance to this plan, though his common sense and his experience doubtless were employed in determining what was necessary and what was practicable.

In addition to participating in these daily conferences, Washington visited friends, drew up a chair at their table, and perhaps not unwillingly changed his rôle of host for that of guest. His first dinner was *en famille* with the Morrises, his next was with the members of the Society of the Cincinnati,[69] a thin platoon of not more than a score of former officers, half of them distinguished and the other half little known.[70] These gentlemen understood readily why their President-General had come to Philadelphia when he had said he could not do so and they gave him as a matter of course their unhesitating and complete vote of confidence by reelecting him,[71] with the understanding that the active duties of the office were to be discharged by the Vice President, Thomas Mifflin.[72] This removed Washington's main ground of apprehension and doubtless was one consideration in reconciling him to delay that dragged on, day after day, to the wrathful disgust of his colleague George Mason, who was bored by "the etiquette and nonsense so fashionable" in Philadelphia.[73] Washington enjoyed, in his dignified manner, the social affairs that Mason detested, and in contrast to his youthful diffidence, he found no distress in drinking tea at the home of Benjamin Chew, "in a very large circle of ladies," who were guests at a wedding.[74] Perhaps the General's kindly impulses were tested on one occasion, at least, during this period of waiting. That was when Mrs. Morris "and some other ladies," in his helpless phrase, took him to a "charity affair," at which still another lady, one "in reduced

[68] 7 *Madison Papers*, 66, LC; partly printed in 2 *Hunt's Madison*, 344 ff; Edmund Randolph to Madison, Mch. 27, 1787, 7 *Madison Papers*, 56, LC, and frequently printed; Irving Brant's *James Madison*, cited hereafter as *Brant*, v. 3, p. 11–12; Moncure Conway, *Omitted Chapters of History Disclosed in the Life and Papers of Edmund Randolph, Governor of Virginia; First Attorney-General United States, Secretary of State*, cited hereafter as *Conway, Randolph*, p. 71 ff.
[69] 3 *Diaries*, 216, 217.
[70] The largest number of listed Delegates was twenty, as of May 16. See 1 *Proc. Cin.*, 26.
[71] *Ibid.*, 34. Henry Knox, Alexander Hamilton and Elias Boudinot constituted the committee that waited on him (*ibid.*).
[72] Mifflin succeeded Horatio Gates (*ibid.*).
[73] 2 *Rowland, Mason*, 103.          [74] 3 *Diaries*, 218.

circumstances," presented a reading. All that he could bring himself to say of it was, "Her performance was tolerable at the College Hall." [75]

Washington, the critic of elocutionary art, became Washington the planter, a more familiar part to play, in several visits to country places around Philadelphia; but when he wrote of these estates he never failed to mention in his diary the main business of the day—that Delaware "was represented" on Monday the 21st of May, that "the representation from North Carolina was completed" the next day, and that when the impatient Delegates assembled as usual on the 23rd and the 24th, "no more States" had spokesmen on the floor. [76]

At last, upon the arrival of another member from New Jersey, a qualified number of Delegates from seven States were counted on the 25th of May; and as seven were a majority of the States, men who had been waiting almost two weeks proceeded to organize the Convention. Most considerately and graciously, Robert Morris, a member from Pennsylvania, the hostess State, arose to perform a service Benjamin Franklin would have discharged if he had not been detained at home that day by weakness and bad weather. [77] In a few words, the financier said that on instructions from the Pennsylvania delegation and on its behalf, he proposed Washington as President of the Convention. John Rutledge of South Carolina seconded and expressed the hope that the choice would be unanimous. It was. Morris and Rutledge conducted the General to the chair, from which, briefly and modestly, he expressed his thanks for the honor done him, and asked the indulgence of members for the unintentional mistakes into which his ignorance of the requirements of the position might lead him. [78]

The other details of organization were completed quickly, a committee on rules was named, adjournment was voted to Monday the 28th. [79] Members lingered after that motion passed, to shake hands and to bow to the new presiding officer, or else they streamed out-of-doors into another bad day of the city's long period of unkind weather. It had been in a chamber not far distant, almost twelve years previously, that Washington had heard his name mentioned for another honor,

[75] *Ibid.*, 217; *Independent Gazetteer*, May 29, 1787, p. 2.

[76] 3 *Diaries*, 218.

[77] 1 *Farrand* (Madison), 4. In these references to *Farrand*, the parentheses will include the authority cited by that admirable editor. The page reference follows. A parenthetical "Journal" will contain reference to the formal record of the Convention, with Farrand's pagination.

[78] *Ibid.* (Madison), 3–4 and (Yates) 5–6. *Penn. Packet*, May 28, 1787, p. 3.

[79] 1 *Farrand* (Journal), 2.

and, in embarrassment, had hurried from the room. The Virginia planter and retired colonial field-officer had not wanted to be Commander-in-Chief in 1775, and the same planter from the Potomac, former head of the Army, did not desire this new post;[80] but there was a similarity of a sort between the two elections and a difference of some interest. Both were calls in a day of danger to America. Selection to lead the Army had put Washington in the tent where the decisions had to be made; designation as President of the Convention would take him off the floor for part of his time, away from the contention of rival advocates. He was committed to the work of the Convention by accepting membership in it; he was lifted above partisanship by the very nature of the duty he had to discharge. At the same time, having no speeches to prepare or committee meetings to attend, he could lend both ears to all spokesmen and thereby doubtless learn much that he had not acquired previously in camp or on his plantation. Presidency of the Convention was education and preparation.

The Convention itself was that and vastly more—if not in its seeding, then in its fruiting. Dull-eared Delegates, participants in the organization of many legislative bodies, might hear only the repetition of the old formulas of an initial meeting. Eyes dimmed by the reading of scrawled resolutions and ill-printed Journals might see little that was new in this assembly. Where memory ran back to vain appeals to stubborn States for the ratification of the feeble Articles of Confederation, or to the disregarded pleas of a penniless Congress for the right to levy an impost, Delegates might shake their heads and sigh as they walked from the convention hall that 26th of May. Their task might be hopeless—jealous States never would consent to create a government greater than their own. Every self-esteemed little Caesar had rather be first in an Atlantic village than second at a western Rome. If, by circumstance, experience were reversed—if shame or danger or calculation induced politicians to lay down powers a stronger Union might take up—what splendor the future would hold. Wisdom and righteousness would be America's! Washington did not have the eloquence of Delegate Rufus King to describe the nation's tomorrow, nor did he possess the skill of his young friend James Madison in arraying arguments as if they were a flawless line of battle; but he had glimpsed the edge of the great valley of America, which students might not see over the top

[80] 29 *G. W.*, 216, 225.

of their law books, and he had followed the routes by which the restless and the landless could enter and occupy that bountiful empire. He believed that if America had power to maintain the law, and revenue with which to pay her public debts, she could prosper, could assure a larger life for her sons and daughters and could recover the place she had in the good opinion of the world when she was struggling for independence. A government strong enough to enforce the will of a free people would not be a tyrant. It would be a protector. America's shores would be unassailable; but her ports would be open as an asylum, in Washington's own words, for "the oppressed and needy of the earth." [81] Where so much might be gained, or lost when almost in the people's grasp, who could begrudge the days of waiting, the weeks of debate, that agreement in the Convention would require?

Monday and part of Tuesday, May 28 and 29, were spent in adopting rules of procedure.[82] Later in the transactions of the 29th, speaking for the Virginia delegation, Edmund Randolph, in the stiff language of the Journal, "laid before the House, for their consideration, sundry propositions, in writing, concerning the American confederation and the establishment of a national government." [83] These "propositions," which Randolph explained in a long, formal speech, embodied the "Virginia Plan" that had been developed in the daily meetings Washington had attended. A government of three branches, legislative, executive and judicial, was to be created. The Legislature was to consist of two chambers, one elected by the people of the several States, the other chosen by the elected branch from a list of nominees submitted by the individual State Legislatures. This central bicameral law-making body was to have all the relevant powers vested in Congress by the Articles of Confederation and, in addition, the power to pass laws where the States were unable to act or were not in harmony. All State laws that contravened the terms of union could be "negatived" by the "National Legislature" which likewise could "call forth the force of the Union against any member of the Union failing to fulfill its duty under the articles thereof." A "National Executive" would have the powers suggested by the title, insofar as the Articles of Confedera-

---

[81] Letter of Mch. 30, 1785, to Lucretia Wilhemina van Winter, 28 *G. W.*, 119–20.
[82] 1 *Farrand*, 7–16.
[83] 1 *Farrand* (Journal), 16. The text of the "Virginia Plan" was believed by Farrand (*op. cit.*, v. 3, p. 594), to have been copied correctly by Madison in *ibid.*, 20 ff. No original is known to exist.

tion conferred authority of this type on Congress. "A general authority to execute the national laws" was added. The "National Judiciary" was to have particular regard to "questions which may involve the national peace and harmony." [84] Again and again that word "national" recurred, without specific definition.

These proposals and another plan of government prepared by Charles Pinckney [85] were referred that same Tuesday afternoon to the Committee of the Whole. When the committee began its sittings on the 30th with Nathaniel Gorham of Massachusetts as its chairman, Washington could take a seat temporarily with the other members. Nine States now were represented by thirty-seven members. [86] No less than seven of them had served along with Washington in the Continental Congress of 1774 or 1775 or both; [87] four had been on his personal staff during the Revolutionary War—Thomas Mifflin, Edmund Randolph, Alexander Hamilton and James McHenry. At least thirteen others, besides Washington himself, had been officers in the Continental Army; [88] an additional thirteen had been officers of the militia. [89] A total of twenty-one members were college graduates, [90] twenty-nine were or had been lawyers or judges; nearly all had held political office or

[84] 1 *Farrand* (Madison), 20–23, based on an abstract supplied by Randolph. Although the "Virginia Plan" is described in some detail in the text, because it was the basis of the long opening debate, the present work will not follow in detail the evolution of the constitution through the long deliberations of the Delegates. This has been done often and adequately in books by able men. Essential purposes would appear to be served if this narrative is limited to the main events as they concerned the outcome of the Convention and the actions and opinions of Washington.

[85] For the confusion of Pinckney's original plan with one apparently drawn up at a later time, see 3 *Farrand*, Appendix D, 595 ff.

[86] Rhode Island, New Hampshire and Maryland had no spokesmen on the floor. Doctor Franklin, who would have been the thirty-eighth member, apparently had not attended as of this date. The total number who participated in the Convention as members, according to *Farrand* (v. 3, p. 387–90), was fifty-five. In the textual summary, those who attended after May 25 are included along with those who were present when deliberations began.

[87] These were Benjamin Franklin, John Langdon, William Livingston, George Read, John Rutledge, Roger Sherman and James Wilson. Members who came to Congress in 1775, after Washington left Philadelphia to assume Army command, are not counted among the seven.

[88] Including commissioned members of Washington's staff, this brought the total of ex-officers to eighteen, or almost exactly one-third of the total attending membership.

[89] Besides these, John Dickinson had served, probably, for a few days as a private of militia; Gunning Bedford, Jr., who often is confused with his martial cousin of the same name, may also have been a militiaman. Washington's published writings and orders contain nothing to bear out the assertion that Bedford was aide to the General. The only extensive study of the little known Jacob Broom of Delaware (W. W. Campbell, *Life and Character of Jacob Broom*) mentions no military service.

[90] Included is James Wilson who, on application, received his honorary M.A. from the College of Philadelphia. Princeton (College of New Jersey) had graduated nine, Yale four, and Harvard and Pennsylvania (College of Philadelphia) three each. Samuel Johnson is credited to Yale, at which he won his Bachelor's degree, and not to Harvard, where he later became a Master of Arts.

had served on Revolutionary committees. The average age of members was 44, but four were under 30 or approaching that age.[91] While a considerable part of the membership was unknown personally to Washington when the Convention assembled, he soon had ample proof of what had been written him previously about the men elected in the different States: they represented high ability and at the outset impressed George Mason, who was somewhat suspicious, as men "of the purest intentions." [92] Madison wrote: ". . . [the Convention] in general may be said to be the best contribution of talents the States could make for the occasion." [93] It was pleasant to sit among these men during the day and, in the evening, to meet them socially.[94] Conversation had to be casual and guarded because the Convention voted on the 29th that "members only be permitted to inspect the journal" and that "nothing spoken in the house be printed, or otherwise published, or communicated without leave." Although this rule occasionally was violated,[95] most members were conscientious and close-mouthed. They would not talk of the one subject every guest at a tea and every frequenter of taverns wished to discuss. Washington himself exercised so much care that he made no notes even in his diary of what happened behind the doors of the convention hall.[96]

[91] Jonathan Dayton, 27; John Francis Mercer, 28; Richard Spaight and Charles Pinckney in their thirtieth year. Hamilton already had reached 30 in January, 1787. As the exact date of Gunning Bedford's birth in 1747 is not known, there is a possibility he had attained 40 by the time the Convention met. William Houstoun of Georgia was about 41; his birth date is given in DAB as c. 1746.

[92] Letter to George Mason, Jr., June 1, 1787; 2 Bancroft, His. Cons., 425.

[93] Letter of June 6, 1787, to William Short, 2 Papers of William Short, 354, LC.

[94] Washington's diary records most of these gatherings. The morning after the Convention opened, he returned all his calls (3 Diaries, 219), including one on Noah Webster (Ford, Notes on Life of Noah Webster, v. 1, p. 215); on Sunday, May 27, he went to high mass at "The Romish Church" (3 Diaries, 219; Penn. Herald, May 30, 1787, p. 3); Monday he dined at Robert Morris's and drank tea "in a large circle at [Tench] Francis's"; Tuesday he dined "at home" and went to a concert; the remaining days of the week were spent in the same whirl (3 Diaries, 220). On June 4, he reviewed the City Troop and the infantry militiamen, but the people were so anxious to see him that they did not leave room enough for maneuvers (Penn. Mercury, June 8, p. 3; Independent Gazetteer, June 8, 1787, p. 3). After that, for a few days, Washington's social activities diminished and his time alone at the Morris home increased. The General needed early morning and evening hours, because he went as far as he could in managing his plantations by letter from Philadelphia.

[95] 3 Farrand, 48–49, 54, 66, 80. Someone communicated extensively to Henry Knox, also. His letter of August 14 to Washington (239 Papers of G. W., 2, LC) could not have been written by a man uninformed, or misinformed, concerning the plan of government before the Convention. Rufus King's letters of May 27, June 3 and July 11 to Knox are in the Knox Papers but they contain no information that violated the rule.

[96] Cf. 3 Diaries, 220. In Madison's letters to his friends were several references to the rule of secrecy. He wrote to Jefferson of "the malefaction of being restrained from disclosing any part of their proceedings" and he promised to make up for this when the ban was lifted (Letter of July 18, 1787; 7 Madison Papers, 102, LC). Often Madison merely stated that

The General could have written much that was optimistic had he felt free to confide to his journal an outline of the first ten days' deliberations. Everything went well. Washington would take the chair each morning and, after the usual preliminaries would turn over the gavel to Judge Nathaniel Gorham, who acted as Chairman of the Committee of the Whole. For nearly the entire day's sitting, the members would debate the successive items of the Virginia Plan, which they approved in broad outline with disarming alacrity. Progress was rapid and in accordance with the proposals the Delegates of the Old Dominion had made initially.[97] After one or another of the involved principles was discussed on a given day for three hours or more, the committee would rise, Washington would resume the chair, and Judge Gorham would report progress, with a request for leave to sit again in committee. Adjournment usually followed at once. Among nearly all members, the disposition was to find the largest basis of agreement and to defer the issues on which there was wide disagreement. The spirit of accommodation seemed so pervasive that echoes of accord were audible in the newspapers, along with rumbling criticism of Rhode Island for ignoring the Convention.[98] Much of the hope that newspapers voiced for its success was founded on the presence and influence of Washington. "Ye men of America," shouted the *Massachusetts Centinel*, "banish from your bosoms those daemons, *suspicion* and *distrust* . . . Be assured the men you have delegated . . . are men in whom ye may confide . . . Consider, they have at their head a Washington," the mention of whose name tempted the editor to trail off into verse.[99]

Men of differing political background in dissimilar States could not hope to continue in accord. By the second week in June, members were divided on the question, Should the first branch of the National Legislature [100] be elected by the people or by the Legislatures of the several States? Other issues of wider import were shaping themselves: Should the equality of State representation that had prevailed in the Conti-

---

members were forbidden to say anything (cf. his letter of June 10 to Monroe, *ibid.*, 90). See also George Mason in 2 *Rowland, Mason*, 104. Col. Edward Carrington expressed his regret over the rule but admitted its propriety (Letter of June 13, 1787, *ibid.*, 93).

[97] 1 *Farrand* (Journal), 30–31, 46–47; *ibid.* (Madison), 64; *ibid.*, 35, 54.

[98] *Penn. Herald*, June 9, p. 3, June 20, 1787, p. 3. *Newport Herald* (R.I.), June 7, 1787, p. 2.

[99] Issue of June 13, 1787, p. 3. Cf. *Independent Chronicle* (Boston), June 14, 1787, p. 3.

[100] In all these discussions, the body that subsequently became the House of Representatives consistently was termed the "first branch," and the Senate the "second branch."

nental Congress be continued—one State, one vote, whether Rhode
Island or Virginia? If the first branch of the new lawmaking body
was to be elected by the people, should slaves be counted in determining
the basis of representation? To maintain the authority of the national
government, must its Congress of necessity be vested with power to
coerce the States or to "negative" their laws? Indeed, why should the
new government be national? Could it not remain federal, with the
largest freedom to the States, great and small?

After the Virginia Plan was reported, in substance, by the Committee of the Whole on the 13th of June,[101] these questions, one after
another, became the spearheads of attack on the plan. Debate on the
floor of the Convention was as searching and detailed as if the Committee of the Whole had not discussed the "propositions" at all. Delegates from the smaller States immediately found a rallying post in
resolutions introduced on the 15th of June by William Paterson, a New
Jersey Delegate. He proposed the amendment of the Articles of Confederation in such a manner as to increase substantially the powers of
Congress while preserving federal, as distinguished from national government, except in two particulars: With the consent of an unspecified
number of States, a delinquent member of the Union might be forced
to meet its obligations; second, the acts of Congress and all ratified
treaties were to be the "supreme law of the respective States" [102]—a new
doctrine, admirably phrased, that probably made an instant appeal to
some of the ablest intellects in the Convention. The Committee of the
Whole proceeded to debate this plan and to listen to an excursus by
Alexander Hamilton on proposals of his own that commanded little
following.[103] Powerful speeches by Edmund Randolph,[104] James Wilson [105] and James Madison [106] led to the rejection, June 19, of Paterson's
outline, seven States to three,[107] and put the Virginia Plan before the
Convention again.

This procedure returned Washington to duty as presiding officer
after he had sat as a silent member from the 30th of May onward,
except for the time spent during that period in opening and in closing
the sittings. He voted with the majority of the Virginia delegation in

---

101 1 *Farrand* (Journal), 224–32, with particular reference to p. 224, n. 4.
102 1 *Farrand* (Madison), 244–45. Differences between the Virginia and the New Jersey
Plans were given succinctly by James Wilson in a speech of June 16. *Ibid*. (Madison), 260.
103 1 *Farrand* (Madison and others), 282 ff.    104 *Ibid*. (Madison), 255.
105 *Ibid*. (Yates), 260.                        106 *Ibid*. (Madison), 314.
107 *Ibid*. (Journal), 313. Maryland was divided.

most of the divisions,[108] but on the embarrassing question of vesting the Federal government with power to negative all State laws, his colleagues most thoughtfully did not call on him to commit himself.[109] As for speeches, he felt that in his capacity as President he should not express opinions on matters pending in the Convention,[110] though his previous record as a lawmaker would indicate that he probably would have spoken seldom and briefly, if at all, had he been under no restraint. His only remarks to the house, during this period of the Convention, were a warning to members not to be careless with papers that concerned their work, an admonition he thought he should voice after Thomas Mifflin stumbled upon a copy of some of the secret "propositions" a Delegate carelessly had dropped.[111]

Washington had been pleased, at the beginning of the Convention, to find members more in accord than he had expected,[112] but when the basic differences developed during the second week in June, he wrote home for additional clothing because, he said almost glumly, "I see no end to my staying here." [113] Work was as hard, too, as the task was long. He had motions to put and points of order to settle during a fortnight of close and vigorous discussion that had to be followed attentively. Social activities, for some reason, were increasingly frequent also,[114] and added to the weariness he felt at the end of the day's sitting. Debate was becoming ill-tempered and tedious, particularly on the question of State representation in the proposed legislative branch of government. By the 28th the frowning factions were caparisoned for battle in a mood that made Doctor Franklin appeal unsuccessfully for prayers at the opening of each day's session.[115] On the 29th, fighting to the last, the spokesmen of the small States were outvoted, six to four, with Maryland divided, on a resolution that established an "equitable" instead of the "equal" basis of representation they sought in the first chamber.[116] In the analogy of their own Legislatures, this meant

---

108 1 *Farrand* (Madison), 97; 2 *ibid.*, 121.
109 *Ibid.* (Madison), 168. Madison specifically noted, "Genl. W. not consulted."
110 2 *ibid.* (Madison), 644.
111 3 *Hunt's Madison*, 56 n, with the quotation from 3 *A.H.R.*, 324–25, reprinted in 3 *Farrand*, 86–87.
112 29 *G. W.*, 228.
113 *Ibid.*, 233. A few days later he sent for his umbrella (*ibid.*, 235).
114 He described them briefly when he explained to Mrs. Richard Stockton why he had been delayed for a few days in acknowledging a "poetic performance" of hers. See *ibid.*, 236.
115 1 *Farrand* (Madison), 450–52. The account of this incident credited by William Steele in 1825 to Jonathan Dayton (3 *ibid.*, 467–73) was denied by Madison (*ibid.*, 531) and is apocryphal beyond all possible defence.        116 *Ibid.* (Journal), 460.

to members that the House of Representatives of a new Congress would be elected, by methods as yet undetermined, in proportion to population.

The men who spoke for the less populous areas continued to argue for equal representation in both chambers, but naturally they mustered their forces anew to win in the second chamber what they had failed to procure in the first. Washington stood with the other Virginia Delegates who favored representation on the basis of population for both houses of the National Legislature, but he did not lose his sense of reality. He was as convinced as ever that the stubborn selfishness of some of the State governments was responsible both for the weakness of the Union and for resistance to making it stronger. His counsel was simple: "To please all is impossible, and to attempt it would be vain. The only way, therefore, is . . . to form such a government as will bear the scrutinizing eye of criticism, and trust it to the good sense and patriotism of the people to carry it into effect." [117] In discussing this once with members of the Convention, "his countenance," said Gouverneur Morris, "had more than usual solemnity; his eye was fixed and seemed to look into futurity." His words were firm: "It is too probable that no plan we propose will be adopted. Perhaps another dreadful conflict is to be sustained. If, to please the people, we offer what we ourselves disapprove, how can we afterwards defend our work? Let us raise a standard to which the wise and the honest can repair. The event is in the hand of God." [118]

It looked the very next day, July 2, as if the time had come to raise the standard. Prolongation of the debate over representation in the Legislature of the new government had served only to array small States against large more stubbornly than ever. In the absence of several members, five State votes were mustered for a resolution to equalize representation in the second chamber. Defeat of the small States in the contest over the composition of the first chamber thus was offset, but at the price of a threatened impasse. When neither side would

---

[117] Letter of July 1, 1787, to David Stuart; 29 *G. W.*, 239.

[118] Morris, *An Oration, Upon the Death of General Washington*, 21, quoted at length in 3 *Farrand*, 381–82. As related by Morris in 1800, this incident may have occurred before the Convention began its work, but his language is not positive. To record it in connection with the similar though less rhetorical statement to Stuart manifestly is justified and chronologically may be correct. There is no good reason for questioning the substantial accuracy of the remarks quoted by Morris whenever made. Washington employed the same metaphor, in reverse, when he spoke, Sept. 22, 1788, of the circular of the New York Convention (see *infra*, p. 143) "as a standard to which the disaffected might resort" (30 *G. W.*, 96).

yield, Charles Cotesworth Pinckney proposed and nearly all the delegations agreed that a "grand committee" [119] of one member from each
State be appointed to fashion a compromise. Hugh Williamson of
North Carolina spoke for the cool-headed element when he said, "If
we do not concede on both sides, our business must soon be at an
end." [120] As the committee would require many hours for its deliberations, the Convention adjourned over the 3rd and 4th of July.

Washington took no part in the debate, but as Pinckney's motion accorded precisely with what he had written Doctor Stuart, he almost certainly voted for the South Carolinian's recommendation, even though
Madison [121] opposed. During the adjournment for the festivities of
the 4th, the General shared in patriotic services at the Reformed Cal-
vinist Church, and dined with the Pennsylvania Cincinnati at the State
House. That afternoon he "drank tea" with Mr. and Mrs. Samuel
Powel, whose intelligent and considerate company he enjoyed often in
Philadelphia; [122] but good food and even better company had not relieved his apprehension when, on the morning of the 5th, he returned
to the Convention hall. He found that Doctor Franklin with much
difficulty [123] had prevailed on the "grand committee" to recommend
this compromise: representation in the first chamber was to be on the
basis of one member for each 40,000 population of each State, with one
member for any State that counted fewer than 40,000 heads; the
chamber elected on this principle was to have exclusive authority to
originate bills levying taxes, appropriating money and fixing salaries;
the second chamber should not be empowered to amend these bills, but
with respect to no other legislation was it to be subordinate; finally—
this was the core of the compromise—in this second branch, each State
was to have "an equal vote." [124]

These proposals were regarded by the small States as a victory [125] and

119 The phrase was not Pinckney's but was used in the Convention and frequently in other
assemblies to distinguish large from small committees.
120 See the debate in 1 Farrand (Madison), 511 ff.
121 Ibid., 515.
122 Next only to Robert and Mrs. Morris, his host and hostess, the Powels were apparently
his closest friends in the city. For the ceremonies of the 4th, see Independent Gazetteer, July 6,
p. 3 (the most comprehensive account), copied in Penn. Journal (Philadelphia), July 7, p. 3.
See also, Penn. Journal, July 4, p. 3 and Penn. Packet, July 6, 1787, p. 3. In his journal entry,
3 Diaries, 226, Washington gave the name of the orator of the day as "a Mr. Mitchell, a
student of law." Newspapers referred to him as "James Campbell, Esq." Before attending the
exercises at the church, Washington visited the anatomical display of Dr. Abraham Chovet or
Chavet. See 3 Diaries, 226 n.
123 1 Farrand (Yates), 523; ibid. (Madison), 526 n.
124 1 Farrand (Journal), 524.        125 Ibid. (Madison), 526 n.

they forthwith were attacked by two of the most powerful debaters in the Convention, James Madison and Gouverneur Morris,[126] who employed experienced parliamentary maneuver along with skillful argument. Some phases of the compromise were turned over on the 6th of July to a special committee for review;[127] when this group reported, its findings were referred to another "grand committee."[128] Even the patient and innately optimistic Washington became gloomy. Affairs, he wrote Alexander Hamilton, were "in a worse train than ever; you will find but little ground on which the hope of a good establishment can be formed." Then he added, in a tone of depression he scarcely had employed since the gloomiest days of his most disastrous military campaigns: ". . . I almost despair of seeing a favorable issue to the proceedings of our Convention, and do therefore repent having had any agency in the business."[129]

Most of the occurrences of the next week were of a sort to deepen Washington's disgust with those he described as "narrowminded politicians or under the influence of local views."[130] He witnessed a seesaw of advantage between the spokesmen of the large States and the champions of the small, in the matter of representation in the Federal Legislature,[131] until, on July 16, there was a balance of five to five that apparently could not be shifted.[132] Some of the members were for adjournment and for immediate report to the country on the differences that had arisen; others still pleaded for a compromise; a few stated frankly their belief that equality of representation in the second chamber had to be conceded if the Convention was to avoid failure.[133] Discussion was renewed at an informal conference held before the house was called to order the next morning, July 17, but so much diversity of opinion was expressed that Madison thought the listening members from the smaller States would conclude they had no reason to fear their

---

[126] *Ibid.* (Madison), 527.                    [127] *Ibid.* (Journal), 538.
[128] *Ibid.* (Journal), 558.
[129] Letter of July 10, 1787; 29 *G. W.*, 245. Hamilton had left the Convention in the belief that it would do little and that he personally was powerless because he was opposed consistently in his own delegation by the other members in attendance, John Lansing and Judge Robert Yates. Although Hamilton declared himself willing to return to the Convention if service there would not be a waste of time (9 *A. Hamilton*, 418), he apparently realized that the influence of George Clinton and of the Governor's strong following was to be thrown against any recommendation to increase the Federal prerogative. See *Penn. Journal*, July 21, p. 3; *Daily Advertiser* (New York), July 21, p. 2; *Penn. Packet*, July 26, 1787, p. 2.
[130] 29 *G. W.*, 245–46.
[131] 1 *Farrand* (Journal), 538, 549, 557, 558, 563, 565; 2 *ibid.*, I, 13.
[132] *Ibid.* (Madison), 17.                    [133] *Ibid.* (Madison), 17–20.

opponents could agree on any plan of opposition to equality in the second chamber.[134]

From that very day, as if in acceptance of the inevitable, a spirit of reconciliation began to show itself even though there was irony in the report of a Philadelphia paper that men were saying the room in which the Convention held its meetings appropriately could be called "Unanimity Hall." [135] On July 17–21, more progress was made in framing a constitution than in any previous period of five days. Final decision on representation in the second branch was deferred; the motion to give the new Congress power to "negative" State laws was abandoned in favor of the clause first sketched in the "Jersey Plan"—that the acts of the Federal Legislature should be the "supreme law of the respective States." [136] Fundamental agreement was reached on the form and function of the judiciary, on the admission of new States, on the guarantee to the States of a republican form of government,[137] on a complicated scheme for the election of the Executive,[138] and, unanimously, on the grant to the Executive of power to negative all laws of the National Legislature.[139]

Washington must have been pleased with this and perhaps was refreshed for his daily ordeal in the chair by a brisk round of social activities.[140] After a Sabbath in the country, he enjoyed on the 23rd of July perhaps the most satisfying day he had spent, to that date, in the Convention. Members still had under consideration the powers and term of the National Executive and they wished to conclude this discussion and to reach a meeting of minds. Everything else that had been decided on the floor—a surprising range of accord—was referred to a committee of five "for the purpose of reporting a constitution conformably to the proceedings aforesaid." The unimaginative language could not conceal the shining fact: a constitution, complete in all its parts, was to be put on paper! Three more days, July 24–26, sufficed to effect agreement on the Executive; the accepted resolutions on that

---

[134] *Ibid.* (Madison), 20. While there is no record, one way or the other, of Washington's attendance at this conference, it is improbable that he was present.

[135] *Penn. Journal*, July 21, 1787, p. 3.

[136] 2 *Farrand* (Journal), 22. This supremacy was to apply, also, to "all treaties made and ratified under the authority of the United States" (*ibid.*).

[137] *Ibid.* (Journal), 37–39.　　[138] *Ibid.* (Journal), 50, 60.

[139] *Ibid.* (Journal), 71. When the Executive did this, the challenged legislation could not be made effective otherwise than with the concurrence of two-thirds of the members of both legislative chambers.

[140] All of them, including a visit to Spring Mill and to General Mifflin's estate, July 22, are listed in 3 *Diaries*, 227–28.

branch were given the new "Committee on Detail," as it was termed; and the Convention itself adjourned to the 6th of August, in order to allow the committee ample time for its difficult work.[141]

During this ten-day intermission, while the committee labored,[142] Washington played many parts—guest, traveler, veteran, planter, fisherman, patron of industry. Two days were given to rest and correspondence.[143] Then on the 30th of July, in Gouverneur Morris's phaeton, to which his own horses were hitched,[144] the General rode out to Mrs. Jane Moore's property, a part of which had been within the Valley Forge encampment. On Trout Creek, which Mrs. Moore's farm adjoined, Morris wished to try his hand at the shrewd act of casting[145] for the fish that gave their name to the creek. While his companion stumped along the bank of the stream on the 31st of July,[146] Washington rode over the whole of the cantonment of 1777–78, which he never had seen in summer's green. He looked at the mouldering fortifications and at the camps in the woods, near fields that still had not been brought back to duty under the disciplinary plow. Cheerful or gloomy as his reflections may have been, Washington did not set them down in his diary, but as he was riding back to Mrs. Moore's, he saw some farmers at work and he asked them about the growing of buckwheat, with which he had been experimenting at Mount Vernon. Their ob-

[141] 2 *Farrand* (Journal), 118. Washington mistakenly dated adjournment July 27. See 3 *Diaries*, 229.

[142] Its members were Nathaniel Gorham, Oliver Ellsworth, James Wilson, Edmund Randolph and John Rutledge. 4 *Farrand*, 72.

[143] 3 *Diaries*, 229.

[144] Washington's carriage was being painted and relined. See Washington to Samuel Powel, July 25, 1787; *Powel Papers*, Mount Vernon.

[145] 3 *Diaries*, 230. Jane Moore's tract of 275 acres in Upper Marion Township, Montgomery County, Pennsylvania, must not be confused with Moore Hall and its 340 acres, located in Charlestown, later Schuylkill Township, Chester County, three miles West of Valley Forge on Nutt Road. Mrs. Jane Moore's house was about two miles East of Valley Forge. (Information supplied by Mrs. Margaret D. Roshong, of the staff of the Valley Forge Park Commission, through Gen. Norman Randolph, Executive Secretary.)

[146] The presence of Gouverneur Morris with Washington on this excursion is an almost conclusive refutation of the story that Morris, on a dare, slapped Washington on the back during the Convention and, for his presumption, received "for several minutes . . . an angry frown" until he "retreated abashed and sought refuge in the crowd" (*Parton*, as below). Had Morris received this treatment prior to July 31, even he would not have had the temerity to go on a journey with Washington. If the alleged incident had occurred later in the Convention, it is improbable that Morris would have been on the cordial footing shown in the letters that passed between him and Washington that autumn and later. See 1 *Sparks's Morris*, 288 ff and 29 *G. W.*, 490. Morris, besides, was a welcome guest at Mount Vernon in November, 1787 (29 *G. W.*, 322; 3 *Diaries*, 269–70). It should be added that the back-slapping story, of which there are two versions, never appeared in print, so far as is known, until 1870, and then as a second-generation old man's tale (see 3 *Farrand*, 85 and 85–86 n, with quotations from W. T. Read's *Life and Correspondence of George Read* . . . , 441 n, and James Parton's *Life of Jefferson* . . . , 369).

servations he wrote out fully as soon as he could, in space more than four times as great as that which he gave to the scene of some of his blackest misery.[147] From the vicinity of Valley Forge, Washington returned to Philadelphia and, on the 3rd of August, went up to Trenton with a party to see whether the perch in the Delaware were interested in bait. This time the General himself used a rod with little luck one day and more success the next. He dined with Col. Samuel Ogden at the Trenton Iron Works,[148] and on the 4th at Gen. Philemon Dickinson's "Hermitage" which had been a Jäger picket post that thrilling "day after Christmas," 1776, when Sullivan's men had stumbled or slid past it in the surprise attack on Trenton.[149] Not a reminiscent word of this did Washington put in his diary. As always, tomorrow interested him vastly more than did yesterday.[150] He was back in Philadelphia, late in the evening of August 5, to be certain he did not miss the proceedings of the 6th, when the Committee on Detail was expected to report.[151]

Printed copies of the draft constitution were ready for members when John Rutledge rose to speak on behalf of the committee. Washington and all the other members listened and some followed the type across the page, line after line, as the Secretary read the entire text. With little argument, the Convention adjourned till the next day and, individually or as delegations, praised the committee or pointed to the sections they disapproved.[152] Washington himself spent the evening at Robert Morris's[153] and no doubt studied the committee's proposals. The next day, August 7, rejection of a motion to go into Committee of the Whole for consideration of the text[154] gave Washington the hard assignment of presiding during a floor debate that might be more tangled and retarded than ever, because of endless motions to amend.

Members now began with vigor and with some impatience a detailed scrutiny, day after day, of the suggested text, though some of them

---

[147] 3 Diaries, 230.

[148] Ibid., 231. The Penn. Packet of August 4, p. 3, and the Penn. Herald of the 8th, p. 3, must have been mistaken in stating that on the 3rd Washington also visited the Philadelphia steel furnace of Nancarrow and Matlack, for which see A. C. Bining, Pennsylvania Iron Manufacture in the Eighteenth Century. Washington undoubtedly went to this furnace but he could not have given time to such a visit in Philadelphia and have been in Trenton the same day for dinner at Ogden's Forge and Iron Works, the changed ownership of which is described in C. S. Boyer, Early Forges and Furnaces in New Jersey, 231.

[149] Vol. IV, p. 316 ff.

[150] Cf. 3 Diaries, 231.      [151] Ibid.

[152] 2 Farrand (Madison), 177, 189; cf. ibid. (McHenry), 190–92.

[153] 3 Diaries, 232.      [154] 2 Farrand (Madison), 196

realized that the completion of their task still would be a work of weeks.[155] Progress was steady, if not swift. Washington, rising early, walked daily from Morris's home to the State House alone and by this time was a familiar if still an awesome figure—in a blue coat and a cocked hat, with his hair in a queue, crossed and powdered. He was composed but, said an observer, he "seemed pressed down in thought."[156] In the chair, he presided with what was termed "his usual dignity,"[157] and, as he had the respect and consideration of all members, he was saved from the pitfalls of parliamentary law. Almost hourly, during the early days of August, he listened as voices from the floor reached the "aye" or "no" of decision that went far beyond the time and the vision of the participants. From the 7th through the 11th, the Convention plodded toward agreement. The pace was slower the next week because members were critically of two minds over the admission of foreign-born citizens to the National Legislature, and over the origin of appropriation bills.[158] During the days of this verbose debate, Washington conserved his strength, going out seldom in the evening, and he did not miss an hour from his duties.[159] He accorded emphatically, no doubt, in a resolution of August 18 that fixed the hours of the daily sittings from 10 to 4 o'clock and ruled out all motions to adjourn before the scheduled hour.[160]

That Saturday, August 18, an armful of proposals to give specific powers to Congress was turned over to the Committee on Detail, and the involved question of Federal assumption of State debts was referred to a special committee.[161] Then the Convention discussed the relation of the new government to the defence of America.[162] On adjournment that afternoon to Monday, the 20th, it was to the credit of Washington's endurance that he still had energy for an excursion on Sunday. With his friend Samuel Powel, he rode out to White Marsh, went over his old encampment there,[163] proceeded to Germantown and probably

---

155 James Madison to his father, July 28, Aug. 12, 1787 (7 *Madison Papers*, 105, 117, LC; 29 *G. W.*, 258). It was known generally that the Convention was debating a constitution, paragraph by paragraph (*Penn. Herald*, Aug. 8, 1787, p. 3). Correspondents reported the public impatient for news. Rumbles of possible disunion and of the organization of separate confederacies circulated. See, as typical, Rev. James Madison, Sr. to his cousin, August 1, and James McClurg to Madison, Aug. 5, 1787; 7 *Madison Papers*, 106, 112, LC.

156 Memoir of Maj. Samuel S. Forman by L. C. Draper in Forman's *Narrative of a Journey down the Ohio and Mississippi in 1789–90*, p. 15.

157 *Newport Herald*, Aug. 16, 1787, p. 3.

159 Cf. 3 *Diaries*, 232–33.

161 *Ibid.* (Journal), 321–22.

163 See Vol. IV, p. 526, 553.

158 2 *Farrand* (Journal), 265–67, 294–96.

160 2 *Farrand* (Journal), 322–23.

162 *Ibid.* (Journal), 323.

visited the Chew House, scarred with bullet marks and reeking still in memory with the burned powder of British muskets and American six-pounders.[164] The entire day was sombre—even if its shadows were of yesterday. Either the special circumstances of the journey or the analogy of the struggle for a better government prompted Washington to reflect "on the dangers which threatened the American Army" at White Marsh.[165] That camp site and Germantown exemplified the cruel vigils and the tortured hours of Washington during the dreadful months between the landing of Howe at Head of Elk, late in August, 1777, and the debouch of the lean American forces from Valley Forge when Howe evacuated Philadelphia in May, 1778. Those days of defeat and of hunger had been preceded by anxious, futile and wasteful campaigns and they had been followed by long waiting, by sinister cheating in the market places, and by every form of sloth and evasion in the seats of government. Independence had been won in woe; the dark forces that had prolonged the contest still lived. ". . . there are seeds of discontent in every part of the Union," Washington warned, "ready to produce other disorders if the wisdom of the present Convention should not be able to devise, and the good sense of the people be found ready to adopt a more vigorous and energetic government . . ."[166]

In that spirit he returned from Germantown to Philadelphia and, the next day, Monday, August 20, began another hard week as presiding officer of the Convention. Members apparently had lost none of their positiveness and they divided readily on the detail of the constitution, but few of them wasted the time of their colleagues in long orations. They would argue, object, defend, vote—and take up the next section of the draft constitution. On the 22nd, they paused for a time to debate the ethics and economy of the slave trade and, in so doing, disclosed more clearly the differences between North and South, between commercial and plantation States, between those that found slave owning uneconomical and those that thought it profitable. The cleavage was as deep as that between large States and small and was vehemently outspoken. At the moment, the Convention agreed to accept the proposal of Gouverneur Morris to refer the question of the slave trade and

---

[164] See *ibid.*, 508. The supposition that Washington went to the Chew House is based on the statement in his diary that he "visited Mr. Blair McClenegan" [McClenacham], owner of the property. See 3 *Diaries*, 233.

[165] *Ibid.*

[166] Letter of Aug. 17, 1787, to Lafayette; 29 *G. W.*, 260.

other disputed clauses to a committee. "These things," said Morris, "may form a bargain among the Northern and Southern States." [167]

Then, on Thursday the 23rd, in discussing the draft, the Convention reached the seventh article,[168] which made the legislative acts and existing and future treaties of the United States "the supreme law of the several States." After scrutinizing and simplifying the language, the Convention adopted this article unanimously, perhaps to the surprise and certainly to the relief of the old soldier in the chair, who during the war had pleaded often and vainly with unheeding States. Simultaneously with this decisive and inclusive action, the Convention, by a majority of one State, rejected the much discussed alternative, the amendment that would have empowered the National Legislature to negative any State law if two-thirds of the members of both branches so voted.[169]

An awkward obstacle was out of the way! The road was getting better. On the 25th, a busy day for Washington, the members accepted another major compromise, one that forbade Congress to prohibit the importation of slaves prior to 1808.[170] When Washington put this motion and not long afterward announced adjournment, the day being Saturday, he could have told himself that the week's labor had been as productive as any of the Convention's life. He had much reason for satisfaction and for rekindled hope when he rode out into the country eight or ten miles on Sunday.[171] Most of the remaining hours of his day of rest were given to the composition of a long letter of instruction for George Augustine Washington on the farm at home.[172]

Briskly on Monday, the 27th of August, the members began discussion of the committee's draft provisions regarding the judiciary. Despite the presentation of a theme on which every one of the twenty-nine lawyers in the Convention had opinions, the debate was mild and agreement was not difficult.[173] By the last day of the month, consideration of the draft had reached the stage where it seemed desirable to name a committee to review all postponed questions and to report them for final action.[174] An even better augury of the early completion of the text was the drafting of clauses on the ratification of the constitution

167 2 *Farrand* (Madison), 374.

168 Text in 2 *Farrand* (Journal), 381–82. See also *ibid*. (Madison) 389, and *ibid*. (Journal), 409. These provisions became the second section of the article finally numbered VI.

169 *Ibid*. (Madison), 390.    170 2 *Farrand* (Journal), 408–09.

171 3 *Diaries*, 234.    172 29 *G. W.*, 263–66.

173 2 *Farrand* (Journal), 423–25; 434.    174 *Ibid*. (Journal), 473.

by the States. The Articles of Confederation provided that amendment had to be by the unanimous consent of the States,[175] but it so manifestly was impossible to prevail on all of them, Rhode Island, in particular, to approve any strong central government that few members, if any, favored adherence to this requirement. Washington himself had encountered again and again the indifference and procrastination of the States in days when delay seemed a death sentence to America, and he was willing to make the constitution effective when a majority, a bare seven of the States, approved. The Convention voted, more conservatively, to require the assent of nine States.[176]

The last major article of the draft constitution awaiting decision was that which set forth the method by which the Executive was to be elected and was to be vested with power.[177] Discussion of this had become so involved that final action had been deferred. Now, in the week of September 3, the Convention resumed the debate and in four days reached agreement.[178] On Saturday the 8th of September, Washington and his companions had the satisfaction of referring their document to a committee of five "to revise the style of and arrange the articles agreed to by the House." The Delegates selected for this task were most admirably equipped for it—William Samuel Johnson, Alexander Hamilton, Gouverneur Morris, James Madison and Rufus King, men of clear heads and precise pens.[179] A happy description of their larger assignment appeared fortuitously, and at almost this very time, in the *Pennsylvania Packet*: "The year 1776 is celebrated," says a correspondent, "for a revolution in favor of Liberty. The year 1787, it is expected, will be celebrated with equal joy, for a revolution in favor of Government." [180]

Unaware of the scope of this new "revolution," the Spanish Minister, Don Diego de Gardoqui, arrived in Philadelphia from New York, about September 8, primarily to meet Washington,[181] who, of course, welcomed the representative of a government with which delicate nego-

---

175 See *supra*, p. 81, n. 20.
176 2 *Farrand* (McHenry), 482; *ibid*. (Journal), 472.
177 Originally Article X on the report of the Committee on Detail; *ibid*. (Madison), 185.
178 2 *Farrand* (Journal), 493–96, 505–08, 517–21, 532–34.
179 2 *Farrand* (Journal), 547. The text, as referred to the committee, was reconstructed with much care by Professor Farrand and was printed in *ibid*., 565 ff. Some doubt exists concerning the action that immediately followed the appointment of the Committee on Style. A motion to reopen the question of congressional representation may have been voted down, six States to five, though this maneuver may have been on the 10th. See *ibid*., 580 n.
180 Issue of Sept. 6, 1787, p. 3.            181 3 *Diaries*, 235.

# "I WILL HOPE FOR THE BEST"

From detached retirement Washington watched the ebb and flow of national affairs with ever-increasing apprehension through 1784 and 1785. Early in 1786 he expressed to John Jay a sentiment embryonic in the minds of America's best patriots: "That it is necessary to revise or amend the Articles of Confederation, I entertain no doubt." The General had no panacea to prescribe, but "something must be done or the fabric will fall, for it certainly is tottering." The "commercial" convention scheduled for September 1786, at Annapolis, was attended by delegates of five States only, and news of its failure was disheartening. Yet out of this frustration had come Alexander Hamilton's forceful call for a general convention in Philadelphia the following May "to take into consideration the situation of the United States" and to render the Articles of Confederation "adequate to the exigencies of the Union."

Washington realized at once that this summons had come none too soon. From the gazettes and through his correspondents he had learned of the rebellion of Massachusetts farmers under Daniel Shays. Was the new nation breaking asunder in anarchy? Lament yielded to imperative advice in November as Washington urged James Madison, brilliant young member of the House of Delegates, to sponsor Virginia's leadership in an action to save "the great and most important of all objects, the federal government."

Back from Richmond by the first post came Madison's affirmative response. Virginia was ready to lead and had, in fact, chosen its slate of representatives for the Philadelphia Convention—with Washington at the head. This last move the General apparently had not anticipated. He congratulated the House of Delegates on its initiative, then regretfully declined his own nomination. The excuses were manifold—rheumatism, the press of personal business, the finality of his retirement and, foremost, the fact that he already had refused the triennial meeting of the Society of the Cincinnati, planned also for May in Philadelphia. The positive arguments and deferential persuasions of Madison and Governor Edmund Randolph sufficed, after several months, to alter Washington's decision. With some reluctance still, he set out for Philadelphia on the 9th of May, 1787. Before the month was out, Charles Willson Peale had solicited the General to sit again for his portrait. From it was engraved the last mezzotint ever wrought by the artist. The painting was done in early July and perhaps reflects Washington's mood during those hours of national crisis. To Randolph he had written passively, "I will hope for the best."

(From the Original by Charles Willson Peale, in the
Pennsylvania Academy of the Fine Arts.)

No state shall, without the consent of Congress, lay imposts or duties on imports or exports, ~~without such consent, but to the use of the treasury of the United States~~ keep troops nor ships of war in time of peace, nor enter into any agreement or compact with another state, nor with any foreign power, nor engage in war, unless ~~it be~~ actually invaded ~~by enemies~~, or the danger ~~be so~~ imminent, ~~as not to~~ admit of delay ~~until Congress can be consulted.~~

### II.

**Sect. 1.** The executive power shall be vested in a president of the United States of America. He shall hold his office during the term of four years, and, together with the vice-president, chosen for the same term, be elected ~~_____~~ : as follows

Each state shall appoint, in such manner as the legislature thereof may direct, a number of electors, equal to the whole number of senators and representatives to which the state may be entitled in Congress: but no senator or representative ~~_____~~, ~~nor~~ any person holding an office of trust or profit under the United States, shall be appointed an Elector The electors shall meet in their respective states, and vote by ballot for two persons, of whom one at least shall not be an inhabitant of the same state with themselves. And they shall make a list of all the persons voted for, and of the number of votes for each, which list they shall sign and certify, and transmit sealed to the seat of the ~~_____~~ government, directed to the president of the senate. The president of the senate shall in the presence of the senate and house of representatives open all the certificates, and the votes shall then be counted. The person having the greatest number of votes shall be the president, if such number be a majority of the whole number of electors appointed; and if there be more than one who have such majority, and have an equal number of votes, then the house of representatives shall immediately chuse by ballot one of them for president; and if no person have a majority, then from the five highest on the list the said house shall in like manner choose the president. But in choosing the president, the votes shall be taken by states ~~_____~~, the representation from each state having one vote. A quorum for this purpose shall consist of a member or members from two-thirds of the states, and a majority of all the states shall be necessary to a choice. In every case, after the choice of the president ~~_____~~, the person having the greatest number of votes of the electors shall be the vice-president. But if there should remain two or more who have equal votes, the senate shall choose from them by ballot the vice-president.

The Congress may determine the time of chusing the electors, and the day on which they shall give their votes; ~~which days~~ shall be ~~one~~ the same ~~day~~ throughout the United States.

No person except a natural born citizen, or a citizen of the United States, at the time of the adoption of this constitution, shall be eligible to the office of president; neither shall any person be eligible to that office who shall not have attained to the age of thirty-five years, and been fourteen years a resident within the United States.

In case of the removal of the president from office, or of his death, resignation, or inability to discharge the powers and duties of the said office, the same shall devolve on the vice-president, and the Congress may by law provide for the case of removal, death, resignation or inability, both of the president and vice-president, declaring what officer shall then act as president, and such officer shall act accordingly, until the disability be removed, or ~~a~~ president ~~_____~~ shall be elected.

The president shall, at stated times, receive for his services a compensation, ~~_____~~ which shall neither be encreased nor diminished during the period for which he shall have been elected. and he shall not receive within that period any other emolument from the United States, or any of them.

Before he enter on the execution of his office, he shall take the following oath or affirmation: "I ~~_____~~, do solemnly swear (or affirm) that I will faithfully execute the office of president of the United States, and will to the best of my ~~judgment~~, ~~power,~~ preserve, protect and defend the constitution of the United States."

**Sect. 2.** The president shall be commander in chief of the army and navy of the United States, and of the militia of the several States, when called into the actual service of the United States, he may require the opinion, in writing, of the principal officer in each of the executive departments, upon any subject relating to the duties of their respective offices, ~~_____~~, and he shall have power to grant reprieves and pardons for offences against the United States, except in cases of impeachment.

He shall have power, by and with the advice and consent of the senate, to make treaties, provided two-thirds of the senators present concur; and he shall nominate, and by and with the advice and consent of the senate, shall appoint ambassadors, other public ministers and consuls, judges of the supreme court, and all other officers of the United States, whose appointments are not herein otherwise provided for, and which shall be established by law. But the Congress may by law vest the appointment of such inferior officers as they think proper in the president alone, in the courts of law, or in the heads of departments.

The president shall have power to fill up all vacancies that may happen during the recess of the senate, by granting commissions which shall expire at the end of their next session.

**Sect. 3.** He shall from time to time give to the Congress information of the state of the union, and recommend to their consideration such measures as he shall judge necessary and expedient: he may, on extraordinary occasions, convene both houses, or either of them, and in case of disagreement between them, with respect to the time of adjournment, he may adjourn them to such time as he shall think proper: he shall receive ambassadors and other public ministers: he shall take care that the laws be faithfully executed, and shall commission all the officers of the United States.

**Sect. 4.** The president, vice-president and all civil officers of the United States, shall be removed from office on impeachment for, and conviction of treason, bribery, or other high crimes and misdemeanors.

### III.

**Sect. 1.** The judicial power of the United States, ~~both in law and equity,~~ shall be vested in one supreme court, and in such inferior courts as the Congress may from time to time ordain and establish. The judges, both of the supreme and inferior courts, shall hold their offices during good behaviour, and shall, at stated times, receive for their services, a compensation, which shall not be diminished during their continuance in office.

**Sect. 2.** The judicial power shall extend to all cases, ~~both~~ in law and equity, arising under this constitution, the laws of the United States, and treaties made, or which shall be made, under

their

# A CONSTITUTION—ESTABLISHED IN CONVENTION

The bells of Christ Church, announcing Washington's arrival in Philadelphia on May 13, 1787, rang out their welcome into skies weighted with rain and ominous with uncertainty. Wet spring weather was a reason for failure of the Federal Convention to open on schedule the next day—only Virginia and Pennsylvania so far were "represented" —but Washington could easily have wondered, in the week and a half following, if apathetic tardiness was not defeating the "grand" Convention even before it had begun. The General took quarters in the home of Robert Morris, renewed his acquaintance with Franklin, visited much about town and at nearby country places, met daily with his fellow Virginians to study the proposals of Madison and Edmund Randolph—and waited. Finally, on May 25, seven of the thirteen States had delegates in the city. A motion by Morris, seconded by John Rutledge of South Carolina, and unanimously affirmed, established Washington as presiding officer of the Convention.

Whether or not he expected it, the General's elevation to the chair provided at once the ideal rôle for him. Parliamentary argument had never been among Washington's skills; his value would rest more in presence than in active participation. Washington's colleagues knew this—some of them surely anticipated crucial junctures at which his prestige might hold the Convention in session even while the bonds of patience, common endeavor and selfless patriotism were snapping one by one.

As it happened, the voice of Washington in the formation of the Constitution was small. He delivered but one speech, and this in brief support of another member's plea for minor revision on the day before the formal signing. Conversely, the influence of his presence at the Federal Convention can be described in no less a term than fateful. As hostility generated against the "Virginia Plan" in the latter days of June, as the crises of July 2 and July 17 surged to the threat of immediate adjournment, Washington was there. Each morning he walked alone to the State House. As the first draft was tediously debated by paragraphs for a month and a day in the oppressive heat of the Philadelphia summer, each day he was in the chair. On September 15, just before six in the evening, the roll was called and the delegations without exception gave assent to the revised draft. The Convention had accomplished a Constitution. Washington ordered the text to be engrossed, and his gavel fell for the last time. The interlineations on the chairman's copy of the final draft reveal his consuming interest to the last day.

(After the Original in the Papers of George Washington. Library of Congress.)

tiations over the free navigation of the Mississippi were being conducted. Philadelphians of station shared this sense of responsibility toward Gardoqui and they entertained him sumptuously. Washington attended these affairs, September 13–15, and a dinner given in his own honor by the City Light Horse,[182] but he did not permit anything to interrupt materially the final labors of the Convention. Monday, the 10th, was given to debate on amendment and ratification;[183] on the 11th, the Committee on Style[184] not being ready to report, the Convention merely assembled and adjourned.[185]

Waiting was rewarded: an admirable text was presented on the 12th by the chairman, Judge William Samuel Johnson,[186] and, once read, was sent to the printer so that every member might familiarize himself with the precise letter of the text and with titles and terms.[187] The "first branch of the Legislature" was, for example, to be styled the House of Representatives; the second was to be known as the Senate. "President" was the designation recommended for the Chief Executive; the court of last resort was to be called the Supreme Court of the United States. While the compositors set the type that recorded these changes, the Convention debated various issues concerning which there was no basic disagreement between North and South, or large States and small. On one such question, Washington differed from the majority and voted unsuccessfully against an amendment that reduced from three-fourths to two-thirds the majority required to pass a law over the President's veto.[188] Then, as always, he favored a strong Executive. He probably believed that a President would not withhold approval in other than the most extreme cases, and that when laws were so defective or so vicious that they had to be disapproved, three-fourths of the members were not a larger part of the whole than should be required to override the President.

---

[182] *Ibid.*, 235–36.                    [183] 2 *Farrand* (Journal), 555–57.

[184] Madison termed it the Committee on Style and Arrangement; the Journal mentioned it as the Committee on Revision; in American constitutional history it usually is known as the Committee on Style.        [185] *Ibid.* (Journal), 581.

[186] It was, needless to say, primarily the work of Gouverneur Morris (3 *ibid.*, 170, 420). "A better choice could not have been made," said Madison long afterwards, "as the performance f the task proved" (*ibid.*, 499). Morris himself never was satisfied with his language in part of the article (III) on the Judiciary (*ibid.*, 420).

[187] 2 *ibid.* (Journal), 582. It should be noted that for the last few days of the Convention the surviving records are so confused and fragmentary that Farrand wrote (*ibid.*, n) it was "impossible to reach any satisfactory conclusion with regard to the various questions and votes."

[188] 2 *Farrand* (Madison), 587. It will be remembered that the word "veto" does not appear in the Constitution. The Journal and Madison's Notes usually employ the term power or right "to negative."

Several close votes followed on numerous sections, some of them long contested, but in no instance did the majority fall below the minimum of six.[189] The balance at last had been stabilized and was not to be shaken.   On his own copy of the printed text, Washington inserted changes made through section 10 of Article I in the debate of September 14.[190] The next day, September 15, Washington noted various other verbal amendments and, as presiding officer, he put no less than twenty-five motions.[191] Before the last and most fateful of these was reached, Edmund Randolph took the floor and announced to the distress if not to the surprise of the General that he would not sign the constitution unless it included a provision, which he thereupon submitted, for another general convention to pass on amendments that might be proposed by the States to the text now ready for final action.[192] Washington's neighbor, George Mason, made a similar statement; [193] Elbridge Gerry, who had pursued an erratic course throughout the Convention, gave a number of reasons why he would not subscribe.[194] Nothing could be done to satisfy these men otherwise than by jeopardizing far more than was risked as a result of their opposition. All the States unflinchingly voted "No" on Randolph's motion for a second convention.[195]

It was now almost 6 o'clock, nearly two hours beyond the usual time of adjournment. The last proposal from the floor for change in the text had been made. Washington waited quietly and without visible emotion for the great moment. When it came, he arose: the motion is to agree to the constitution as amended; [196] the Secretary will call the roll of the States. From every delegation the answer of the majority was "Aye." [197] Engrossment of the text was ordered; the gavel fell.[198] The first stage of the battle for sound, strong American government had ended, more wisely and more easily than had seemed possible. From

---

[189] See, for example, Hugh Williamson's proposal on the 14th to increase by 50 per cent the membership of the House of Representatives (*ibid.* (Madison), 612).

[190] 2 *Farrand* (Journal), 610. A sheet of Washington's amended copy appears as an illustration in this volume.

[191] There may have been others not covered by the table in *ibid.* (Journal), 622.

[192] *Ibid.* (Madison), 631.                     [193] *Ibid.* (Madison), 632.

[194] *Ibid.* (Madison), 632–33.               [195] *Ibid.* (Madison), 633.

[196] It is much to be regretted that neither the name of the mover nor the exact form of the motion is known.

[197] 2 *Farrand* (Madison), 633. Madison's entry was: "On the question to agree to the Constitution, as amended, All the States ay."

[198] *Ibid.* Washington walked back to Robert Morris's and spent the evening there (3 *Diaries*, 236).

the Convention floor the issue must be carried to the thirteen States, in a wide, charging and decisive campaign.

Sunday, the 16th of September, was given by Washington to letter writing [199] and to a ride with Robert and Mrs. Morris to their country home for dinner.[200] Monday, the 17th, found Washington in the chair for the final ceremonies of signing the engrossed Constitution and, perhaps, for one proposal that was much on his mind. He found, if he did not already know, that a last-minute effort was to be made to persuade the three dissenters to join the majority in signing the Constitution. Doctor Franklin was present and, though too feeble to make a speech, he had written one which James Wilson read for him with the permission of the house. It was a wise and spirited appeal for the subordination of individual opinion to the nation's good, and it contained both an admission of Franklin's dislike of some articles and the cheerful declaration of his faith in the document as a whole. "It . . . astonished me, sir," he said, "to find this system approaching so near to perfection as it does; and I think it will astonish our enemies, who are waiting with confidence to hear that our councils are confounded like those of the builders of Babel; and that our States are on the point of separation, only to meet hereafter for the purpose of cutting one another's throats." The old philosopher ended with a motion which Gouverneur Morris had drafted in the hope it would satisfy Gerry, Mason and Randolph—that the enacting clause be: "Done in Convention, by the unanimous consent of the States present the 17th of September, &c, in witness whereof we have hereunto subscribed our names." [201]

Before this motion was put, Judge Gorham proposed that, even though the final text was engrossed, one line be scratched and the basis of representation in the House be reduced from 40,000 to 30,000. Rufus King and Daniel Carroll supported Gorham and urged the members to make the concession. This was what Washington had been waiting for. When he rose to put the motion, he explained that his position as president had kept him from expressing his views and that perhaps it still should impose silence, but he could not forbear voicing his wish that Judge Gorham's motion prevail. Objections to the constitution

---

[199] Six are represented by copies in Washington's Letter Book. Three of these had to do with his business affairs; three were notes introducing Charles Pinckney to friends in France.
[200] 3 *Diaries*, 236.                [201] 2 *Farrand* (Madison), 642–43.

should be as few as possible. One of them was involved here. Many members believed the House so small it gave "insufficient security for the rights and interests of the people." A basis as high as 40,000 always had seemed to him among the most objectionable parts of the constitution. Late as it was in the proceedings of the Convention, he thought amendment would give much satisfaction.[202] With that, he ended the only speech he had delivered during the session,[203] and he had immediate reward. The desired change was made unanimously and without further discussion [204]—not because all members agreed but because all of them wished to do what Washington desired.

This was the last and most gracious *nem. con.* of the meeting. The rest was appeal, explanation, expostulation, assent, then the adoption of Franklin's motion. Although the dissenters and two of the South Carolina members were in opposition,[205] the Constitution was accepted "by the unanimous consent of the States present." A resolution was adopted for the transmission of the finished document to Congress, with the expressed opinion that it should be submitted to popular conventions in the States. Other sections of the same resolve set forth the views of the Delegates on the manner in which the Constitution should be put into effect after nine States had ratified it.[206] The covering letter was a persuasive appeal for a Constitution that was "liable," the members affirmed, to as few exceptions as could reasonably have been expected. This letter was signed "Your Excellency's most obedient and humble Servants, George Washington, President. By unanimous Order of the Convention." [207]

The rule of secrecy was repealed, and the papers of the Convention were entrusted to Washington for disposition, in accordance with the order of the new Congress "if ever formed under the Constitution." [208]

---

202 *Ibid.* (Madison), 644. The quotation is from Madison and may not be of Washington's exact words.

203 Madison's note, as *supra*.

204 2 *Farrand* (Madison), as *supra*.          205 *Ibid.* (Madison), 647.

206 *Ibid.*, 666–67. See also, *infra*, p. 126.

207 2 *Farrand*, 667. The letter almost certainly was the work of Gouverneur Morris, in whose autograph is the copy now among the *Papers of G. W.*, LC. 2 *Farrand* (Journal), 583 n; cf. 3 *ibid.*, 499. For action of the Convention in directing that the address be prepared, and in declining to make a public appeal in advance of a decision by Congress on the Constitution, see 2 *ibid.* (Journal), 556–57, 582; *ibid.* (Madison), 564, 622–23. As neither the Journal nor Madison's Notes mentions the letter in the final proceedings, the precise place of the reading and signing of the document in the day's proceedings is not known.

208 *Ibid.* (Madison), 648.

Formal signing of the document followed. It was during this ceremony that Franklin said he was satisfied the sun painted on the back
of the President's chair was the rising, not the setting orb. Continued
refusal of Mason, Gerry and Randolph to attach their signatures did
not dampen the satisfaction with which members completed their difficult labor, adjourned *sine die*,[209] streamed to the City Tavern, had
dinner together and said farewell to one another. Washington walked,
after that, to Morris's house, where he received the Convention records
from the Secretary, and at last, in quietness, to quote his words, "retired
to meditate on the momentous work which had been executed . . ."[210]

The next day, September 18, after brief visits to the homes of friends,
he had an early dinner, and with Delegate John Blair as companion in
his chariot, he set out for home.[211] Near Head of Elk, on the 19th, he
found a ford swollen beyond all possible use, and, as he was in his
usual hurry of travel, he decided to cross on an old bridge. He and
Blair went over on foot, probably to lighten the load, and they suffered
no injury, but one of the horses broke through the weak flooring and
almost dragged the other animal and the carriage into the water. By
good fortune, abundant aid was at hand promptly, the horse was
rescued,[212] the journey proceeded. About sundown, on the 22nd, Washington reached Mount Vernon "after an absence of four months and
fourteen days," precisely reckoned and set down in his diary.[213]

They had been days during which his largest contribution was not
that of his counsel but that of his presence. His votes, where recorded,
were often on the losing side. Although he favored bringing the new
government into operation when seven States ratified, the Convention
decided to make nine the number. It must have been known that he
thought a three-fourths vote should be required to override a Presidential veto, but the majority insisted on two-thirds. Letters from
members seldom mentioned him among those at the forge where the
Constitution was hammered out, blow on blow. Madison, Gouverneur
Morris, James Wilson, Rufus King, Edmund Randolph—these were
the men, not Washington, who shaped the Constitution. Oliver Ells-

[209] *Ibid.* (Madison), 649.
[210] 3 *Diaries*, 237.                  [211] *Ibid.*
[212] 3 *Diaries*, 237–38. The accident alarmed Washington's admirers. Said the *Delaware
Gazette* (Wilmington), the "fortunate circumstances" of the General's crossing on foot "probably saved a life so dear to the country." Quoted in *Penn. Packet*, Oct. 3, p. 2 and *Penn.
Herald*, Oct. 4, 1787, p. 3. See also *Independent Gazetteer*, Oct. 11, 1787, p. 3.
[213] 3 *Diaries*, 238.

worth [214] may not have been far in error when he said, late in life, that Washington's influence in the Convention was not great.[215]

Outside the Convention, the reverse was true. In giving the body prestige and maintaining public confidence in it while deliberations dragged slowly, Washington had no peer and no second other than Franklin. It had been so from the early days of the Convention, when skeptics were asking whether the assembly would be representative or respectable even. Madison assured Jefferson that Washington's attendance was "proof of the light in which" the General viewed the Constitution; [216] Col. Edward Carrington's opinion was that the participation of Washington disclosed the "deep impression upon his mind of the necessity of some material change." [217] As public curiosity rose, and impatience with it, while the Delegates argued, copies of Washington's farewell circular to the States were offered the public; [218] Charles

---

[214] 3 *Farrand*, 396–97.

[215] In that remarkable collective estimate of Washington, the eulogies delivered immediately after his death and during the period of national mourning, Dec. 26, 1799, to Feb. 22, 1800, his part in the Federal Convention is mentioned in twenty-nine only of the 210 addresses and orations now preserved in LC of the 300 and more delivered and printed in pamphlet form. That of Gouverneur Morris (see *supra*, p. 98) was, of course, authoritative. Eight other speakers affirmed that Washington contributed materially and conspicuously to the work of the Convention. With the titles of their addresses eliminated but the place of delivery and the specific page reference in each pamphlet given, these eight were: Timothy Bigelow, Boston, p. 11; Peleg Burroughs, Tiverton, R. I., p. 6; John Carroll, Baltimore, p. 19; Enos Hitchcock, Providence, R. I., p. 28; James Wilson, Providence, R. I., p. 12; Thomas (later Robert Treat) Paine, Newburyport, Mass., p. 16; David Ramsay, Charleston, S. C., p. 15; and Gunning Bedford, Wilmington, Del. (a member of the Convention), in *The Washingtoniana . . . A Collection of Elegant Eulogies, Orations, Poems, &c . . .* (Lancaster, 1802), p. 145, cited herein as *Washingtoniana* (*Lancaster*). Thirteen memorial speakers merely noted that Washington was a member of the Convention or else they referred in generally vague and complimentary terms to the part he played: Abiel Abbot, Haverhill, Mass., p. 18; Oliver Everett, Dorchester, Mass., p. 14; Charles Pinckney Sumner, Milton, Mass., p. 15; Samuel Taggart, Colrain, Mass., p. 15; Cotton Tufts, Weymouth, Mass., p. 14; Daniel Appleton White, Methuen, Mass., p. 14; James Morris, Litchfield, Conn., p. 14; Roswell Shurtleff, Westmoreland, N. H., p. 6; Samuel Stanhope Smith, Trenton, N. J., p. 30; Henry Lee, Philadelphia, p. 7; Robert Davidson, Carlisle, Penn., in *Washingtoniana* (*Lancaster*), p. 283; William Clark Frazer, Lancaster, Penn., in *Washingtoniana* (*Lancaster*), p. 130; and Elisha Cullen Dick, Alexandria, Va., in *The Washingtoniana . . . An Account of the Various Funeral Honors . . .* (Baltimore, 1800), p. 202. One oration, delivered by John Brooks at Medford, Mass., placed emphasis (p. 13) on the General's dissatisfaction with the feeble government that existed under the Articles of Confederation. Washington's influence in the achievement of ratification was stressed in the orations of four men—Adam Boyd, Nashville, Tenn., p. 8; Daniel Dana, Newburyport, Mass., p. 14; Thomas Cushing Thacher, Lynn, Mass., p. 7; and David McKeehan, Greensburgh, Penn., in *Washingtoniana* (*Lancaster*), p. 273. The titles of these eulogies, as well as all others delivered after Washington's death in some 200 American towns, may be traced in Margaret B. Stillwell, "Checklist of Eulogies and Funeral Orations on the Death of George Washington," *NYPL Bulletin*, May, 1916, p. 403–50.

[216] Letter of June 6, 1787; 3 *Farrand*, 36.

[217] Letter of June 9, 1787, to Jefferson, *ibid.*, 38. Cf. Louis Otto, Chargé d'Affaires, to Comte de Montmorin, June 10, 1787, *ibid.*, 45.

[218] *Evening Chronicle* (Philadelphia), June 12, 1787, p. 1 and several times later.

Willson Peale painted a new portrait [219] which soon was reproduced for sale as a mezzotint.[220] Again and again, the General was presented as the man to be trusted. "A Washington," the New York *Daily Advertiser* asserted, "surely will never stoop to tarnish the lustre of his former actions, by having an agency in anything capable of reflecting dishonor on himself or his countrymen . . ." [221] Said a correspondent of the *Pennsylvania Packet*: "In 1775, we beheld [Washington] at the head of the armies of America, arresting the progress of British tyranny. In the year 1787, we behold him at the head of a chosen band of patriots and heroes, arresting the progress of American anarchy, and taking the lead in laying a deep foundation for preserving that liberty by a good government, which he had acquired for his country by his sword." [222] In Washington's own State, a Petersburg journal printed a correspondent's sketch of what he believed the powers of Congress should be: ". . . the grand federal convention it is hoped will act wisely, for on their determination alone, and our acquiescence, depends our future happiness and prosperity, and if there lives a man equal to so arduous a task, it is a Washington." [223] A writer in the *Independent Gazetteer* of Philadelphia suggested that the States which approved a new plan of government or the amendment of the old should confederate under Washington's leadership. "This," he said, "would probably stimulate the refractory states to comply also." [224]

Washington read some of this with satisfaction and some of it with dismay because it suggested the possibility that his retirement at Mount Vernon might again be interrupted. He did not flatter himself that he and his colleagues in Philadelphia had devised a perfect form of government, but he knew the Convention had given the country the best Constitution on which a majority could agree. In his papers he had, too, a letter written him by Henry Knox, when that loyal lieutenant was leaving the Quaker City. It probably was a letter for which Washington was grateful but not one he would have regarded, perhaps, at its real worth as a precise evaluation of his accomplishment in Philadelphia: "In every event respecting the reception of the propositions of the convention," said Knox, "you will enjoy the high satisfaction of

219 3 *Diaries*, 226, 227.
220 *Penn. Herald*, Sept. 20, 1787, p. 3.          221 Issue of July 26, 1787, p. 2.
222 Issue of August 23, p. 3; reprinted in *Penn. Mercury*, Aug. 24, 1787, p. 3.
223 This undoubtedly was from the *Virginia Gazette* (Petersburg), and was quoted in *Newport Mercury* (R. I.), Aug. 27, 1787, p. 2.
224 Issue of Aug. 17, 1787, p. 3.

having performed everything that could possibly be expected of you." [225]

Knox undoubtedly meant this encomium to include not only Washington's conduct in Philadelphia but also his reluctance to emerge from retirement and to risk criticism at a time when he had the fervid gratitude of nearly all Americans. In the eyes of the sympathetic Secretary of War, the hesitation of Washington, his half fretful, half fearful regard for his reputation was natural and in no sense unbecoming a patriot. Washington himself never wrote anything to indicate that he thought his yes-and-no attitude toward the Convention was in any way unworthy of him. Once the work had been taken in hand, his mind was fixed on his task, not on his fame; and for his achievement, surely, he deserved all that his former Chief of Artillery said of him. In retrospect, the document there on the desk in Washington's office represented dim portent and slow progress up to a certain point. The conference at Mount Vernon on the commercial harmony of Virginia and Maryland had shown that annual meetings would be desirable; out of that proposal had come the enlargement of the conference; the meeting at Annapolis in September, 1786, had been disappointing in itself and doubtful in its promise. After that, everything went more rapidly. Once the call for the Philadelphia Convention became audible, the States acted as if they had slept overlong and were waiting for reveille. Between the first resolution for the Maryland-Virginia conference on their joint waters, June 28, 1784, and the opening of the Philadelphia Convention, not quite three years had elapsed. The Constitution was completed and sent to Congress within approximately thirty months after the Virginians and the Marylanders signed their navigation report in the very room, probably, where Washington read over the text of the new plan of government. If a restless man, eager for change, chose to condemn this apparent delay in the achievement of national harmony, he would have been given sufficient answer when reminded that the Articles of Confederation had been reported to Congress July 12, 1776 and had not become effective till Mch. 1, 1781.

A new spirit, undefined but unmistakable, was stirring the people of America. It had shown itself not only in the ready action of the States in sending Delegates to the Convention but also in the temper and the standard of debates on the floor. Daily, for the greater part of the session, members had seemed to plod along and to halt often in stub-

[225] Letter of Sept. 14, 1787; 239 *Papers of G. W.*, 17, LC.

born, futile contention. Again and again even Washington had feared that differences were irreconcilable but always the spirit of accord had triumphed over pride of opinion. If a few small-minded men had sought to defend "principles" which, by their own argument, proved to be prejudices, these men were less numerous and less noisy than the like element in Congress had proved to be. The level of leaders' argument had been so high in the Convention that only the most obtuse of the men of small ability had taken the floor often. Nothing had been so inspiring, some would have said so mysterious, as the rearing of a constitutional structure, stone by stone, while the eyes of masons had been intent on the course they were laying today, not on the larger design. Almost contrary to their expectations, they finished it and when they stood off and looked at it, they were surprised by the strength and the symmetry of their handiwork. From modesty or from special devotion to some rejected proposal it became popular for members to say the Constitution was "not perfect." Politicians used this language, no doubt, to establish a basis of compromise with those who objected to provisions of the plan. Actually, critics would have found it difficult to justify material change, otherwise than for the advantage of one or another category of States; and critics would have found it equally hard to find favor for any additions, other than a bill of rights.

Twelve years had elapsed since Washington had assumed command of the American Army, perhaps the most valuable years of his full maturity, those between his forty-third and his fifty-fifth birthday. Nearly nine of those years, in the aggregate, had been given to the country. Was there now the promise, "first the blade, then the ear, after that the full corn in the ear"?

# CHAPTER V

## THE BASIC ARGUMENT FOR RATIFICATION
### (Sept. 22, 1787–June 28, 1788)

PERSONALLY, THE comments on the Constitution that most disturbed Washington were predictions that he would be chosen without opposition as first President of the United States;[1] but he told himself it was neither necessary nor modest to think of an unfilled office in a government not yet created, and he gave his thought to the reception of the document by the people rather than to its possible interruption of his retired way of living.[2] The text was printed widely;[3] Congress acted promptly and to the surprise of some in this non-partisan language: "Resolved, unanimously that the said report [of the Convention] with the resolutions and letter accompanying the same be transmitted to the several legislatures in order to be submitted to a convention of Delegates chosen in each State by the people thereof in conformity to the resolves of the convention made and provided in that case."[4] Washington himself had sent copies of the Constitution, immediately after adjournment, to Jefferson and to Lafayette in a detachment rival-

---

[1] *Daily Advertiser* (New York), September 26, p. 2; *Penn. Packet* (Philadelphia), September 27, p. 3; *Penn. Herald*, Sept. 27, 1787, p. 3. Benjamin Rush had quoted as early as August 30 a report that Washington would be placed at the head of the new government (1 *Butterfield*, 440; 4 *Farrand*, 75). Pierce Butler wrote, May 5, 1788, that he did not believe the powers of the President would have been made so extensive if members had not cast their eyes on Washington and had not shaped their ideas of the office according to the virtues of the man (3 *Farrand*, 302). Cf. Lafayette to Washington, Jan. 1, 1788; *LOLTW.*, 334; L. G. Otto, French Chargé to the Comte de Montmorin, June 10, 1787, 3 *Farrand*, 45; Gouverneur Morris to Washington, Oct. 30, 1787, 239 *Papers of G. W.*, 44, LC; unidentified correspondent of Jefferson, Oct. 11, 1787, 3 *Farrand*, 105.

[2] See *infra*, p. 147. Cf. Washington to Lafayette, Apr. 28, 1788; 29 *G. W.*, 479.

[3] Among the journals publishing it in full were the *Independent Gazetteer*, September 19, p. 1–3; the *Pennsylvania Packet*, September 19, entire issue; the *Pennsylvania Journal* (Philadelphia), September 19, p. 2–3; the *Pennsylvania Herald*, September 20, p. 2; *Connecticut Courant* (Hartford), Oct. 1, 1787, p. 2–3. An interesting study might be made of "editorial policy" with respect to the debate over the Constitution. Oswald's *Independent Gazetteer* appears to have been one of the few papers that threw open their columns for discussion, pro and con. Most of the journals, themselves advocating acceptance of the Constitution, gave the greater part of their open space to communications that favored ratification.

[4] This was on Sept. 28, 1787; 33 *JCC.*, 549. Cf. the confused entry of the 27th, *ibid.*, 540–44. See also 8 *Burnett*, 650–52.

ing that of Congress, without praise or criticism of the proposed system of government;[5] but he did not deceive himself into thinking that when the issue was presented to the States, he or any other American who had an interest in the future of the country could be neutral. He planned and hoped to do his part for ratification and he did not leave his position in doubt for a moment. When he sent a report of the Constitution to Patrick Henry, the most powerful man politically in Virginia, he said in plain words: "I wish the Constitution . . . had been made more perfect, but I sincerely believe it is the best that could be obtained at this time; and, as a constitutional door is opened for amendment hereafter, the adoption of it under the present circumstances of the Union is in my opinion desirable." He elaborated only to the extent of adding that the "political concerns of the country" were "in a manner, suspended by a thread" and that if nothing had been done by the Convention, "anarchy would soon have ensued, the seeds being richly sown in every soil."[6]

There he stood. His correspondence from the Middle States and from the East led him to believe a large element of the country stood with him in judgment both of the crisis and of the Constitution as the weapon for combating ruin. Henry Knox summarized all this: "Every point of view in which I have been able to place the subject induces me to believe that the moment in which the convention assembled, and the result thereof, are to be estimated among those fortunate circumstances in the affairs of men, which give a decided influence to the happiness of society for a long period of time." The Constitution, Knox said, was "received with great joy by all the commercial part of the community." Boston, New Jersey and Connecticut were enthusiastic.[7]

Of all the arguments that were being advanced in behalf of the Constitution, which was the most effective? Answers from the North and from New England were surprising and, to a man of Washington's temperament, disconcerting. In the taverns, the shops and the markets, and on the street corners, the chief reason given for support of the new Constitution was this: Washington and Benjamin Franklin had signed it and had approved it. ". . . the arguments, if they be arguments,

[5] 29 *G. W.*, 276, 277.
[6] Letter of Sept. 24, 1787, *ibid.*, 278.
[7] Letter of Oct. 3, 1787; 239 *Papers of G. W.*, 25, LC. For more restrained judgment of the public response, see Madison to Washington, Oct. 14, 1787, 8 *Madison Papers*, 23, LC, and Madison to William Short, Oct. 24, 1787, 3 *William Short Papers*, 481, LC.

most insisted upon, in favor of the proposed Constitution," wrote a correspondent of the *Pennsylvania Herald*, "are that if the plan is not a
good one, it is impossible that either General Washington or Doctor
Franklin would have recommended it . . ." The writer maintained
that the two leaders might have been of the minority and might not
have favored the text submitted to the country, but he did not attempt
to deny that their participation was the prime argument advanced for
the acceptance of the work of the Convention.[8] Praise of Washington
flooded newspapers sympathetic with the Constitution, in a manifest
effort to identify him with the document, so that it would gain strength
from his popularity.[9] "Is it possible," asked a writer, "that the deliverer
of our country would have recommended an unsafe form of government for that liberty, for which he had for eight long years contended
with such unexampled firmness, consistency and magnanimity?"[10]
The *Connecticut Courant*[11] at Hartford printed a Philadelphia dispatch
in which it was proposed "that the Federalists should be distinguished
hereafter by the name of Washingtonians, and the Anti-Federalists by
the name of Shayites, in every part of the United States." One Boston
correspondent had a still different opinion of the place Washington and
Franklin had won: "The military virtues of the former," he said, "and
the philosophic splendour of the latter will be obscured by the new
lustre they will acquire as the legislators of an immense continent."[12]

Any contrary view was no mere difference of opinion; it was regarded as something far more serious. A correspondent, signing himself "Centinel," argued in the *Independent Gazetteer* of October 5 that
the "wealthy and ambitious" who sought the control of the government "flatter themselves they have lulled all distrust and jealousy of
their new plan by gaining the concurrence of the two men in whom
America has the highest confidence." He then wrote: "I would be very
far from intimating that the two illustrious personages alluded to have
not the welfare of their country at heart; but that the unsuspecting

[8] *Penn. Herald*, Oct. 27, 1787, p. 2.
[9] Cf. *Penn. Mercury* (Philadelphia), Oct. 26, 1787, p. 3, with quotation from the *Worcester Magazine* on Washington as "the political saviour of America." In the *Daily Advertiser*, Oct. 20, 1787, p. 2, was a poem of eighteen stanzas in praise of the Constitution. One quatrain read:
> "Yes, Patriots, by experience taught,
> (Their country's guardian-guides)
> Concert a plan, with wisdom fraught,
> And WASHINGTON presides."

[10] *Independent Gazetteer*, Oct. 15, 1787, p. 2.
[11] Oct. 22, 1787, p. 3.
[12] *Salem Mercury* (Mass.), Oct. 9, 1787, p. 2, a reprint from the *American Herald* (Boston).

goodness and zeal of the one has been imposed on, in a subject of which he must be necessarily inexperienced, from his other arduous engagements; and that the weakness and indecision attendant on old age, has been practiced on in the other." [13] This utterance was snatched up instantly as an insult to Washington and Franklin, and, *ipso facto*, to the country. Both men, a Federalist thundered, were portrayed by "Centinel," that "insidious enemy to his country," as *"non compos mentis* when they concurred in framing the new Federal Constitution." [14] The next defender of the national heroes accused "Centinel" of representing Franklin "as a fool from age, and General Washington as a fool from nature," an "infamous libel," as all men knew.[15] Doubtless the next assertion, said one friend of the new system, would be that Daniel Shays was the best patriot in the United States and that John Franklin should be King of Pennsylvania.[16] The fury of this denunciation of "Centinel" rolled eastward; everywhere the argument was that Washington's approval of the Constitution justified acceptance. Gouverneur Morris sent the General this summary at the end of October: "I have observed that your name to the new Constitution has been of infinite service. Indeed, I am convinced that if you had not attended the convention, and the same paper had been handed out to the world, it would have met with a colder reception, with fewer and weaker advocates, and with more and more strenuous opponents." [17] David Humphreys had voiced the same view with different emphasis: "What will tend, perhaps, more than anything to the adoption of the new system will be an universal opinion of your being elected President of the United States and an expectation that you will accept it for a while." [18]

Strangely, the outlook for ratification seemed most doubtful in the two States where Washington's long presence and shining service might

---

[13] *Independent Gazetteer*, Oct. 5, 1787, p. 2–3. This article subsequently was charged against "a certain superannuated George Bryan of Pennsylvania" (*Mass. Gazette*, Nov. 30, p. 3, *Penn. Journal*, Dec. 19, 1787, p. 3), actually a man of some distinction, Vice President of the Supreme Executive Council of Pennsylvania in 1777–79. It was alleged (*Daily Advertiser*, Nov. 3, 1787, p. 2) that when this article was translated for a German publication in Philadelphia, the offending words were eliminated. Nothing has been found in the *George Bryan Papers* of this period (PHS) to confirm the allegation that he was "Centinel."

[14] *Independent Gazetteer*, Oct. 10, 1787, p. 2.

[15] *Ibid.*, Oct. 10, 1787, p. 3.

[16] *Ibid.*, Oct. 13, 1787, p. 2. John Franklin, now an almost forgotten figure, was a pioneer of the Wyoming Valley, who defied all challenge of his land-titles. At this time he was in a Philadelphia prison.

[17] 239 *Papers of G. W.*, 44, LC.      [18] Letter of Sept. 28, 1787; *ibid.*, 22.

have made his advocacy of the new government immediately influential and perhaps decisive. In New York, by general report, the adherents and the adversaries of the Constitution were, in Gouverneur Morris's words, "nearly balanced"; [19] in Virginia, Washington found most of the older and a few of the younger leaders in opposition at least to the extent that they demanded the earliest possible amendment of the Constitution, preferably by another general convention called for that purpose. Richard Henry Lee came to this view; [20] Arthur Lee suspected that in the Constitution various "errors," as he termed them, were made deliberately in order to facilitate control of the government by an oligarchy; [21] Benjamin Harrison thought the new government vested with excessive powers to levy taxes and to regulate trade, and he distrusted "the jurisdictions that are to be established in every State altogether independent of their laws." [22] George Mason had left Philadelphia "in an exceeding ill humor," according to Madison, [23] and had published detailed "Objections" to the Constitution, a copy of which he sent Washington. [24] With the exception, perhaps, of Luther Martin's denunciation, no protest by a member of the Convention aroused so many resentments and provoked so many counter-attacks as these "Objections" did. Mason was alleged to have been told by the Mayor and Aldermen of Alexandria, on his return from Philadelphia, that he must leave town within an hour, as they could not be answerable for his safety at the hands of the populace. [25] A critic demanded: "Where was Mr. George Mason from 1775 to 1783—What was the part he then took? Of his colleague, who did *sign* the *Constitution*, the *admiring world* well knows." [26] One reason only can be attributed for the vehe-

---

[19] *Ibid.*, 44. For Washington's later information concerning New York, see 29 *G. W.*, 350, 376, 377, 389.

[20] 8 *Burnett*, 648–50, 658; Madison to Washington, 8 *Madison Papers*, 16, LC; 239 *Papers of G. W.*, 23, LC; 2 *Ballagh, Lee Letters*, 438–40, 440–44, 456–58.

[21] See Charles Francis Adams, ed., *The Life and Works of John Adams*, cited hereafter as *John Adams*, v. 9, p. 554–55.

[22] Letter of Oct. 4, 1787, to Washington; 239 *Papers of G. W.*, 27, LC.

[23] 8 *Madison Papers*, 29, LC.

[24] 3 *Farrand*, 102, from 4 *Documentary History of the Constitution*, 315. The "Objections" were substantially those urged by Mason in the Convention on Sept. 15, 1787. See 2 *Farrand*, 629 and 2 *Rowland, Mason*, 178. Madison's analysis of them in a letter to Washington is in 239 *Papers of G. W.*, 35, LC.

[25] *Mass. Gazette*, Oct. 26, 1787, p. 3. Denial of this was published in the same paper Nov. 20, 1787, p. 3. The charge may have originated in the fact that twenty-nine of the most prominent Alexandria constituents of Mason called on him and David Stuart, the other Fairfax member of the House of Delegates, to declare that the County favored the immediate issuance of a call for a ratifying State convention. See *Va. Journal* (Alexandria), Oct. 11, 1787, p. 2.

[26] *New-Haven Gaz.*, Dec. 6, 1787, p. 5.

mence of these assaults: Mason was an influential figure and was the neighbor and friend of Washington; his dissent was, in the public mind, disloyalty to the national hero.

In Virginia, Mason would prove a troublesome adversary as well as a State legislator who sometimes displayed a vulnerable lack of patience;[27] but the man who would have the largest, perhaps the decisive influence was Patrick Henry. He had an extensive following in the Legislature and usually seemed able to control its actions. At first there was hope that he might favor the work of the Philadelphia Convention,[28] but some of those who knew him best gave warning that his antagonism must be taken for granted.[29] These observers were correct. The great orator's objections to the Constitution were set forth with restraint in a letter to Washington,[30] but his acts were vigorous. "Mr. Henry," said Archibald Stuart, "has upon all occasions, however foreign his subject, attempted to give the Constitution a side blow." [31]

Washington counted the foes of the Constitution and, as in war days, did not underestimate the strength of his opponents; but he found encouragement in the approval shown the document by residents of northern Virginia,[32] in the support pledged it by Edmund Pendleton,[33] wise Chancellor of Virginia, and in some indications that Edmund Randolph was not happy in the political camp where he had pitched his tent.[34] The greatest encouragement of all was in the fact that James Madison, Henry Lee, Alexander Hamilton and other young leaders of first-rate ability were vigorously active in behalf of stronger government for the United States. Washington took fullest advantage of this. It was unpleasant to be estranged from old friends, even on political grounds only—distasteful to differ from Benjamin Harrison, who had been his spokesman in Congress, and from Mason, who had been the most discerning of his counsellors in the early days of the Revolution. It would have been an uplifting experience to consult and to toil with

---

[27] He had written William Cabell, May 6, 1783, that he had been driven out of the Legislature "by their poor measures" (*Emmet Col.*, NYPL).

[28] Cf. 29 *G. W.*, 286; 239 *Papers of G. W.*, 35, LC.

[29] Edward Carrington to William Short, Oct. 25, 1787; 3 *William Short Papers*, 482–85, LC.

[30] Dated Oct. 19, 1787; 2 *W. W. Henry*, 320.

[31] Letter of Oct. 21, 1787, to James Madison; 8 *Madison Papers*, 26, LC.

[32] 29 *G. W.*, 291; cf. Edmund Randolph to Madison, Sept. 30, 1787; 8 *Madison Papers*, 17, LC.

[33] "His support will have great effect"—Madison to Washington, Oct. 18, 1787, 239 *Papers of G. W.*, 28, LC. For the details see David J. Mays, *Edmund Pendleton, 1721–1803*, v. 2, p. 218 ff.

[34] See Randolph to Madison, Oct. 23, 1787; 8 *Madison Papers*, 28, LC.

these men in opening a new domain of government, but if they were weary or content or timid and would go no further, then Washington must leave them and must undertake his adventure in the company of those who, like himself, were more concerned with securing the future than with enjoying the past. Most of these young pioneers were twenty, even twenty-five years younger than the retired Commander-in-Chief. What if they were? Interest, not age, created comradeship. Had it not been so that icy winter's night in 1776 when the shivering ranks of a shrunken Army had been drawn on the right bank of the Delaware? Youth and resolution and the patience of Washington [35] had carried the troops to victory at Trenton: The call again was to youth under the same captain. Without hesitation, Washington made common cause with these young men, chose them as his principal correspondents,[36] and, in particular, for the battle in Virginia, looked to James Madison. Prior to 1783, the General never had close contact with Madison, and, during the period between the close of hostilities and the assembly of the Convention of 1787, he had written ten letters only to the young legislator. The debates in Philadelphia had shown Washington that Madison possessed superlatively the type of mind that could meet with calm, cold skill both the logic and the maneuver of a parliamentary opponent. Washington did not excel in compliment and sometimes he admitted an awkwardness in seeking to express his appreciation of men, but now, as he contemplated the prospect of a convention in Virginia, to ratify or to reject the Constitution, he wrote Madison: ". . . I hope you will make it convenient to be present. Explanations will be wanting, and none can give them with more accuracy and propriety than yourself." [37] This was the judgment of the country. In the *Massachusetts Gazette* [38] a correspondent acclaimed Madison "Virginia's young Washington for patriotism."

The General prepared for the contest, with Madison in some sense his Chief of Staff, and he mustered his own arguments and resources. In his opinion the strongest practical appeal that could be made for the

---

[35] See Vol. IV, p. 311.

[36] Washington wrote a known total of 159 political letters to Americans from January, 1784, to April, 1789. Of this total, seventy-six, or almost half, were to seven men in their twenties or thirties, as follows: Alexander Hamilton, six; David Humphreys, twelve; Henry Knox, seven; Henry Lee, three; James Madison, eighteen; Edmund Randolph, fifteen; David Stuart, fifteen. In accepting these figures, the reader will not forget that individual judgment had to be applied in deciding whether a letter was or was not to be classified as political.

[37] Letter of Oct. 10, 1787; 29 *G. W.*, 286.

[38] Issue of Oct. 26, 1787, p. 3.

Constitution was one he had used from the day of adjournment—that it was the best on which the Convention could agree, that a second such gathering could achieve nothing, and that, in effect, America's choice was between the recommendations of the Philadelphia Convention and a continued drift toward ruin.[39] He wanted Mason answered and the Constitution explained and defended in the newspapers,[40] and he hoped the whole queston of the navigation of the Mississippi might be postponed. It could not be settled acceptably—and need not be—for some years, though meantime, he reasoned, agitation might create western antagonism that would extend, however unreasonably, to eastern proposals for a change in government.[41]

The first clash in Virginia proved to be what Washington in making his plans had assumed it would be [42]—nothing more than a skirmish. Without criticism or commendation, the General Assembly of Virginia referred the Constitution to a State convention that was to be elected in the counties and cities on the first day of the March court and was to be called to order on the 1st of June, 1788.[43] Perhaps the only sensation of the debate was the statement of George Mason that he would have considered himself a traitor to his country if he had subscribed to a Constitution he thought repugnant "to our highest interests." He was quoted as saying, "I would have lost this hand before it should have marked my name to the new government." [44] In spite of these angry words, the issue was not joined in the Legislature. The real contest would begin when friends and hostile critics of the Constitution offered themselves as candidates for the convention.

While the preliminary stage of the campaign in Virginia was ending with this resolution of the General Assembly, Edward Carrington wrote from Congress: "There perhaps never was a period of time at which reforms and revolutions in government were so general as now, and it is much for the honor of America, that while the more ancient nations in Europe are shaken to their very centre in the operation, hers

---

[39] See, as typical, his letter of Oct. 15, 1787, to Henry Knox; 29 *G. W.*, 288–89.
[40] *Ibid.*, 287, 290.          [41] *Ibid.*, 292.
[42] *Ibid.*, 286. Cf. John Dawson to Madison, Oct. 19, 1787; 8 *Madison Papers*, 24, LC.
[43] Proceedings of Oct. 25, 1787, *Jour. H.D. Va.*, October, 1787–January, 1788, Proceedings of October 25, p. 14–15; *Jour. Sen. Va.*, same session, 9, 10, 12; 2 *W. W. Henry*, 322 ff, with citation (p. 324 n) from *Penn. Packet,* Nov. 10, 1787, p. 2. See also John Pierce to Henry Knox, Oct. 21, 1787, *Knox Papers*, MHS.
[44] The original of this report probably appeared in the *Virginia Gazette* (Petersburg) of Nov. 1, 1787. It was copied in the *Virginia Journal* of Nov. 8, 1787, p. 2, and in the *New-Jersey Journal* (Elizabethtown), Nov. 21, 1787, p. 3, as well as in the issue of the *Pennsylvania Packet* cited by W. W. Henry.

is taking thorough effect, by peaceable convention, without interrupting for a moment the existing administration. The governors and the governed act in concert for producing the change, and the former look forward to no act with more desire than the surrender of the old, upon the maturity of the new government." [45]

Almost every political letter that came to Mount Vernon confirmed Carrington's observation, but those from some States showed that cleavage was wide and argument angry. The use of Washington's name as a slogan for ratification continued. One correspondent shouted: ". . . are the gentlemen who have withheld their assent from the Federal Constitution superior to Washington or Franklin, either in abilities or in patriotism—men whose names, borne on the wings of fame, are known throughout the world—and whose merit is universally acknowledged?" [46] These sentiments found expression again and again.[47] "Centinel" was attacked not only for his alleged abuse of Washington but also in a personal way for pleading the statute of limitations with respect to a debt.[48] Defenders of "Centinel" protested against the "old hackneyed argument of 'it is General Washington's opinion and advice'"; but even as they took their stand against the Constitution, they were excessively careful to make it plain they did not intend to depreciate the fame of Washington.[49] Arguments that the General had little part in the deliberations in Philadelphia [50] were met with the fanciful assurance that in the Convention, Washington held the floor "two hours at a time, in speaking upon some parts of the proposed system" and that "he advocated every part of the plan with all those rhetorical powers which he possesses in so eminent a degree." [51] An equally remarkable appeal for ratification was based on a widely circulated report that as Washington signed the contested document he "pronounced

---

[45] Letter of Oct. 25, 1787; 3 *William Short Papers*, 482–85, LC.

[46] New York dispatch in *Penn. Journal*, Nov. 24, 1787, p. 3.

[47] *New-Hampshire Spy* (Portsmouth), Nov. 30, 1787, p. 1, with quotation from *Albany Gazette*, n.d.; *Salem Mercury*, December 4, p. 1; *New-Jersey Journal*, Dec. 5, 1787, p. 3.

[48] *U. S. Chronicle* (Providence), Dec. 6, 1787, p. 2.

[49] See "Vir" in *ibid.*, Dec. 13, 1787, p. 2. Even in Rhode Island, which was under the domination of an element opposed to the new Constitution, this article was the only one of any significant Anti-Federalism, hostile to Washington, that appeared in available papers of that State during 1787. For a general disclaimer of any intention to lower Washington's prestige by defending "Centinel" or by criticizing the Constitution, see also "An Officer of the Continental Army" in a full-page letter to "The Citizens of Philadelphia," a document that is remarkably similar in style to the Newburgh addresses (*Independent Gazetteer*, Nov. 6, 1787, p. 2. Answers appeared in *ibid.*, November 9, p. 3 and Nov. 10, 1787, p. 3).

[50] *American Herald* (Boston), Nov. 19, 1787, p. 3.

[51] *Mass. Gazette*, Nov. 20, 1787, p. 3, reprinted in the *Daily Advertiser*, Nov. 30, 1787, p. 2.

these words, too remarkable to be forgotten or unknown—'Should the States reject this excellent Constitution, the probability is, an opportunity will never again offer to cancel another in peace—the next will be drawn in blood.' "[52] In different, accurate strain, voters were reminded that the General had been responsible for changing the basis of representation in the House from 40,000 to 30,000. ". . . This critical interference (which, we are well assured, was all the share he had in the business of the late convention)" said one newspaper, "tended to promote the interest and dignity of the people."[53]

Washington received more newspapers than he read,[54] but he doubtless saw something of the use to which his name was being put, reasonably or otherwise. No complaint came from him. He had signed and had endorsed the Constitution and he had no desire that his advocacy be kept secret. Now that contest mounted, his blood rose with it. Henry Lee correctly said, late in the autumn, that Washington continued "firm as a rock" in support of the new plan of government.[55] The General's arguments remained simple—that the will of the majority should prevail over a selfish minority, that the Constitution was the best the country could hope to get at the time, that a new general convention could accomplish nothing, and that the course of wisdom and of safety was to ratify the document drafted at Philadelphia and, if it were found defective in operation, to amend it later in the manner prescribed in Article V.[56] The presentation of more detailed reasons he wished to leave to those active in the debate, and, particularly, to the men writing the fine articles that were issued over the signature *Publius*, and were soon to be styled "The Federalist."[57] In Virginia,

[52] Apparently this originated in the *New-Jersey Journal* of Nov. 7, 1787, p. 2. See *Penn. Journal*, November 14, p. 3; *New-Hampshire Spy*, November 23, p. 3; *Mass. Gazette*, December 4, p. 2, and *Conn. Gazette* (New London), Dec. 7, 1787, p. 2.

[53] *Daily Advertiser*, Nov. 14, 1787, p. 2.

[54] Cf. 28 *G. W.*, 419, 430. His favorite seems to have been Dunlap and Claypoole's *Pennsylvania Packet*, then published daily except Sunday. Another that he read for a time was the *Pennsylvania Herald* (29 *G. W.*, 438, 439); still another was the *Virginia Gazette* of James Hayes, Jr. (*ibid.*, 113). Washington had been anxious not to be placed under any sort of obligation to Gen. Charles Lee's champion, Col. Eleazer Oswald, publisher of the *Independent Gazetteer*; see 28 *ibid.*, 349.

[55] Letter of Dec. 7, 1787, 8 *Madison Papers*, 52, LC.

[56] The fullest statement of his views was in a letter of Nov. 10, 1787, to Bushrod Washington, 29 *G. W.*, 309–13. See also, *ibid.*, 316, 323, 339–40.

[57] 9 *A. Hamilton*, 425; 29 *G. W.*, 308; 239 *Papers of G. W.*, 67, LC; 5 *Hunt's Madison*, 54–55, 59. Washington guessed, apparently, that one of the authors was Hamilton and he may have concluded from Madison's letters that his fellow-Virginian, leader in the fight for ratification, also was writing some of the articles.

which had few newspapers,[58] the debate was in the taverns, across the fence, at church, in the correspondence of public men, at the shops and on the lawn of every seat of justice when the farmers gathered on "court day." The echoes of this discussion that reached Washington during the last ten weeks of 1787 did not change his belief that Virginia would ratify the Constitution, but they indicated that enthusiasm for the new government was waning while antagonism was rising.[59] Jefferson's opposition was voiced in letters from November 13 onward, though these communications probably were not known in Virginia until January, 1788.[60] Reports circulated that Washington himself would be a candidate for the Virginia Convention,[61] but, so far as is known, not even those leaders who were becoming doubtful of the result in the State urged this on him. Outside the Old Dominion, the strength of the hostility to the Constitution in Washington's own State was variously explained. The newspaper that mistakenly announced his intention of going to the Virginia Convention remarked, almost casually, that the Anti-Federalists in the Commonwealth included two men only who were not in debt. The *Connecticut Courant* gave space to a controversialist styling himself "The Landholder," who maintained that "in Virginia the opposition wholly originated in two principles—the madness of Mason, and the enmity of the Lee faction to General Washington."[62]

The General did not permit the increasingly difficult situation in Virginia to blind him to the new encouragement coming from the States that held out the hope of ratification by the required nine. Madison predicted as early as October 28 that this number would come into the new Union. The dangerous doubt, in his mind, concerned the

[58] Apparently, eight were being published in 1787; a ninth, the *Virginia Centinel* of Winchester, was added in April, 1788. No less than four of these papers called themselves *Virginia Gazette*, with or without additional designation.

[59] The references are sufficiently numerous for this period to make possible a summary for each week, if this were not superfluous. During parts of the early months of 1788 there literally are day-by-day reports of one sort or another. The following are confirmatory of the statement in the text: 8 *Madison Papers*, 33, 34, LC; 29 *G. W.*, 308, 323, 327–28, 333–34; Washington to Samuel Powel, Nov. 30, 1787, *Powel Papers*, Mount Vernon; 8 *Madison Papers*, 53, LC; *Penn. Herald*, Dec. 19, 1787, p. 3. Washington's personal relations with George Mason remained friendly during this period (4 *LTW.*, 190–91; Mason to Washington, Nov. 27, 1787; 239 *Papers of G. W.*, 73, LC).

[60] See 6 *Jefferson*, 370, 372, 394.

[61] *Penn. Gazette* (Philadelphia), Nov. 21, 1787, p. 2.

[62] Issue of Dec. 24, 1787, p. 2.

future of the States that abstained.[63] Hamilton reported New York still uncertain;[64] Daniel Carroll was confident of Maryland's "Aye";[65] John Langdon of New Hampshire reported a favorable prospect in his part of the country.[66] Then, on the 6th of December, prediction became reality: the Delaware Convention ratified the Constitution unanimously; Pennsylvania followed with a convention vote of two-to-one, on the 12th.[67] Six days later, New Jersey with one voice approved the stronger Constitution. At the year's end, Connecticut seemed certain to be the fourth State; Massachusetts was expected to debate furiously and, in the end, to accept;[68] confidence was unshaken that New Hampshire was favorable;[69] New York remained in doubt; North Carolina was expected to follow Virginia's lead; South Carolina and Georgia were believed to favor adoption.[70] Washington, reading these reports,[71] scarcely could have asked for stronger testimony of the popularity of the Constitution than was offered by Pennsylvania and New Jersey which had known the miseries of war and had seen the need of union.

In Virginia the situation was obscured, especially for outsiders, by a threatening sentence in the act of the General Assembly that provided funds for the State convention: if the Delegates voted to hold communication with other States or conventions or should "incur any expense in collecting the sentiments of the Union respecting the proposed

[63] 239 *Papers of G. W.*, 42; also in 4 *LTW.*, 185. William Short posed this problem from the other angle—that the ratifying States might be widely separated. See his letter of Dec. 21, 1787, to Madison; 8 *Madison Papers*, 61, LC. Henry Knox wrote Lafayette, Dec. 14, 1787: ". . . on the whole it is highly probable that [the Constitution] will be adopted in the course of the year 1788 by nine States and more" (*Knox Papers*, MHS).

[64] 9 *A. Hamilton*, 425.

[65] Letter of October 28 to Madison; 8 *Madison Papers*, 31, LC; cf. 29 *G. W.*, 305.

[66] See *ibid.*, 327–28.

[67] S. Powel to Washington, Dec. 12, 1787; 239 *Papers of G. W.*, 87, LC; cf. *ibid.*, 93. When twelve guns were fired in honor of this ratification, Philadelphians wondered at the number—why twelve? The answer was, "twelve States were represented in the late Federal convention, and their system was adopted by this State, on the twelfth day of the twelfth month, in the twelfth year of the independency of America" (*Penn. Packet*, Dec. 17, 1787, p. 2).

[68] See *Mass. Centinel* (Boston), October 17, p. 2; November 14, p. 2; Nathaniel Gorham to Knox, October 30, December 16; Knox to James Swan, October 30; Henry Jackson to Knox, November 11 and Nov. 18, 1787 (*Knox Papers*, MHS).

[69] Madison to Washington, Dec. 7, 1787; 8 *Madison Papers*, 51, 63, LC, and same to same, Dec. 26, 1787; 239 *Papers of G. W.*, 98, LC; *New-Hampshire Spy*, Dec. 11, 1787, p. 3.

[70] Henry Knox to Washington, Dec. 11, 1787; 239 *Papers of G. W.*, 85, LC.

[71] In some, perhaps in most instances, he received his first information from the *Pennsylvania Packet* which published the news of the early ratification as follows: Delaware's of December 7 in issue of December 10, p. 2; Pennsylvania's of December 12 in issue of December 13, p. 2; New Jersey's of December 18 in issue of Dec. 21, 1787, p. 3.

Federal Constitution," this was to be paid.[72] Rufus King wrote: "to me, I confess [this action] appears to proceed in the present instance from no good motive . . ."[73] Newspapers from New Hampshire southward expressed some concern but they relied on the influence of Washington,[74] who, for his own part, experienced from day to day a rise or wane in his apprehension but held, on the whole, to the belief that Henry and Mason would not succeed in their effort to defeat the Constitution or to amend it before ratifying it. To assist in making certain that the Old Dominion would vote to accept the new Union in spite of these strong adversaries, Washington took advantage of freezing weather [75] and even of a bad cold [76] that kept him housebound or close to home throughout January,[77] and wrote many letters in support of the Constitution. In doing this he doubtless had the aid of David Humphreys, who had come back to Mount Vernon as a guest,[78] though he was following "literary pursuits" of his own.[79] Even with leisure and Humphreys' help, Washington on occasion wrote hurriedly of the document on which he believed the future well-being of America depended. In one instance, he lamented his haste. A letter he addressed on Dec. 14, 1787, to Charles Carter [80] was copied in part by that zealous

[72] 12 H 463; Jour. H.D. Va., session October, 1787–January, 1788, Proceedings of November 30, p. 77; Jour. Sen. Va., 1787, p. 45–46. The Connecticut Gazette interpreted this to mean that the Virginia Convention was authorized to approve, reject or amend the Constitution (Nov. 23, 1787, p. 3).

[73] Letter of Dec. 23, 1787, to Jere. Wadsworth; Wadsworth Papers, Wadsworth Athenaeum.

[74] Essex Journal (Newburyport, Mass.), Oct. 31, 1787, p. 3. In the Pennsylvania Herald, Dec. 26, 1787, p. 2–3, appeared a roster of the leaders on both sides, by Charles M. Thruston, in a letter to the Mayor of Winchester, Virginia, with the familiar conclusion, "the signature and approbation of our great Washington will give [the Constitution] a preponderency to weigh down all opposition." Cf. ibid., Dec. 29, 1787, p. 3, for a returned traveler's report that the "nabobs or great men (falsely so called) of Virginia" were the "only enemies" of the Constitution in the State "and that nineteen-twentieths of the yeomanry of Virginia are on the side of General Washington, the Man of the People, in favor of the new government." The "Nabobs," said Rufus King, ". . . begin to be alarmed" (Letter to Jere. Wadsworth, Dec. 23, 1787, as supra). The debate in Virginia newspapers of the autumn and early winter of 1787 may be worth a monograph or doctoral dissertation. Particularly useful are the files of the Virginia Journal for sentiment in the northern counties, and the Virginia Independent Chronicle (Richmond), which sponsored a free discussion. See also John Paine to Henry Knox, Nov. 19, 1787, and Edward Carrington to Knox, Jan. 12, 1788 (Knox Papers, MHS).

[75] 29 G. W., 389, 401, 403.          [76] Ibid., 367.

[77] On Feb. 5, 1788 he wrote: "I have not been ten miles from home since my return to it from Philadelphia" (ibid., 400).

[78] Newspapers reported him proceeding southward early in November, 1787 (Daily Advertiser, November 10, p. 2; Penn. Journal, November 21, 1787, p. 2). He reached Mount Vernon on the 18th (3 Diaries, 269) and remained there, with occasional visits to nearby homes and towns, until April, 1789.

[79] 29 G. W., 519; F. L. Humphreys, Life of David Humphreys, v. 1, p. 427 ff.

[80] 29 G. W., 339–40.

advocate of the Constitution and was distributed confidentially among friends, one of whom gave a transcript to a newspaper.[81] This soon was reprinted in Baltimore as Washington's creation.[82] The General complained to Carter, "Could I have supposed," said he, "that the contents of a private letter (marked with evident haste) would have composed a newspaper paragraph, I certainly should have taken some pains to dress the sentiments . . . in less exceptionable language, and would have assigned some reasons in support of my opinion and the charges against others." [83] Carter's explanation was forthcoming at once, in full, and was satisfactory to Washington,[84] who had no intention of writing controversially on the new plan of government.[85] The incident had significance, not because it showed once again Washington's unhappy consciousness of his awkward style, but because the General said at the time and repeated to James Madison [86] that he had no objection to the proper "communication of my sentiments on the proposed government, as they are unequivocal and decided." In the struggle for ratification, America's interest demanded that Washington abandon his position as the retired, non-partisan veteran who had told Lafayette in February, 1784, that he was "determined to be pleased with all . . ." [87]

The outlook in Virginia during January was unchanged, so far as Washington could observe or could ascertain from his correspondence,[88] except for a promising effort, which he shared, to bring Edmund Randolph back into the camp of the Federalists.[89] In this maneuver, the active leader was James Madison, who himself faced threat of a contest for a seat in the convention.[90] Before the end of the month, Washing-

---

[81] First publication almost certainly was in Timothy Green's *Virginia Herald* (Fredericksburg) of Dec. 27, 1787, but no copy of that issue has been found. Brigham listed none of that date.

[82] *Maryland Journal* (Baltimore), Jan. 1, 1788, p. 2. The letter may have appeared in the *Maryland Gazette* (Baltimore) of approximately the same date, but the pertinent issues are not available at LC. Oswald printed the letter in his *Independent Gazetteer* of Jan. 4, 1788 (p. 2), but he did not name Washington as the author. Printed versions vary perceptibly from the text in 29 *G. W.*, 340.

[83] *Ibid.*, 380.

[84] *Ibid.*, 387–88, 390, 396, 404. Cf. 5 *Hunt's Madison*, 106. 8 *Madison Papers*, 117, LC.

[85] 29 *G. W.*, 380.                                    [86] *Ibid.*, 373.

[87] 27 *ibid.*, 318 and *supra*, p. 2.

[88] 29 *G. W.*, 349–50, 376, 377, 389, 396; 8 *Madison Papers*, 66, LC; 2 *Bancroft, His. Cons.*, 456; James Madison to Tench Coxe, Jan. 30, 1788, 8 *Madison Papers*, 90, LC.

[89] *Ibid.*, 79, 84; 29 *G. W.*, 357; Edmund Randolph to Madison, Feb. 29, 1788; 8 *Madison Papers*, 123, LC.

[90] James Madison, Sr., to James Madison, Jr., Jan. 30, 1788; *ibid.*, 92, LC.

ton received news [91] that Connecticut had fulfilled expectations and, on the 9th, had ratified the Constitution by a vote of 127 to forty. This success strengthened his belief that there was the "highest probability" of ratification by more than nine States,[92] but the prolongation of the eventful campaign in Massachusetts soon gave concern. A favorable beginning of the Bay State Conventon had degenerated into a bulldog fight, the outcome of which threatened to be politically ferocious. Although a slight improvement in the strength of the Federalists was sensed in February,[93] almost the only prediction on which foe and defender agreed at the time was that the decision, one way or the other, of the most powerful New England State would have great influence on closely divided New York.[94] Washington rallied his patience and fortified his hope with more cheerful letters from Boston and New York. By the 8th of February, he had heard, though not officially, that Georgia had ratified—the fifth State.[95] One vote was as good as another, of course, in making the count of nine; Georgia's was as good as Pennsylvania's; but Massachusetts, New York and Virginia still were outside the ranks and, if they refused to ratify, they would leave the new Union so weak it probably would succumb. Massachusetts' action might be decisive. If the Bay State refused—but the Bay State did not. During the last week in February,[96] the watchman at Mount Vernon had good tidings: On the evening of the 6th the Massachusetts Convention had accepted the Constitution by a vote of 187 to 168.[97] Washing-

[91] The announcement appeared in the *Pennsylvania Packet*, Jan. 17, 1788, p. 2, but the date of the arrival of the paper at Mount Vernon is not known. See, for comment, etc., 4 LTW., 200–01; 240 *Papers of G. W.*, 232; Jere. Wadsworth to Knox, January 9, and Samuel Parsons to Knox, Jan. 19, 1788; *Knox Papers*, MHS.

[92] Washington to Samuel Powel, Jan. 18, 1788, *Mount Vernon MSS*; 29 *G. W.*, 376.

[93] This interesting contest is heavily documented with letters of Rufus King, Henry Knox and Benjamin Lincoln in the correspondence of Washington and of Madison. See 239 *Papers of G. W.*, 122, 125, LC; 240 *ibid.*, 6, 18, 27; 8 *Madison Papers*, 76, 80, 83, 91, 94, LC; 240 *Papers of G. W.*, 6, LC; 8 *Madison Papers*, 89, 93, LC; 29 *G. W.*, 396, 399–400. The most fascinating of the day-by-day reports are in the *Knox Papers*, MHS. See, in particular, N. Gorham to Knox, January 16; Knox to Sullivan, January 19; Henry Jackson to Knox, January 20; Knox to E. Benson, January 20; Henry Jackson to Knox, January 23; Rufus King to Knox, January 27; N. Gorham to Knox, January 30 and February 3; Constant Freeman to Knox, February 3; Rufus King to Knox, February 3; Henry Jackson to Knox, February 6; Knox to R. R. Livingston, Feb. 10, 1788.

[94] 8 *Madison Papers*, 78, LC; John Jay to Washington, Feb. 3, 1788, 240 *Papers of G. W.*, 19, LC; Henry Knox to Washington, Mch. 10, 1788, *ibid.*, 47; 29 *G. W.*, 349, 377, 389.

[95] *Ibid.*, 411; 8 *Madison Papers*, 102, LC. The news was printed in the *Pennsylvania Packet* of January 30, p. 3, and January 31, p. 3.

[96] The news was in the *Pennsylvania Packet* of Feb. 18, 1788, p. 3.

[97] 240 *Papers of G. W.*, 22, LC; Henry Knox to Washington, February 10 and Feb. 14, 1788, *ibid.*, 27, 31, LC, two most informative letters on conditions in Massachusetts.

ton felt the greatest satisfaction,[98] only to find, as usual, a sour cup offered him after a sweet. Maryland Anti-Federalists were urging that their State convention adjourn until Virginia acted;[99] conditions in North Carolina were said to be similar to those in Virginia;[100] the outlook in New Hampshire did not appear to be as favorable as had been assumed.[101]

In the eyes of most observers, even after the victory in Massachusetts, happenings elsewhere made the outcome in Virginia more important at the same time that it became more uncertain.[102] Prior ratification by nine States might rally a majority in the Old Dominion, but Henry and other opponents of an unamended Constitution were said to be using "very bold language" and to talk of Virginia's self-sufficiency. Some of them were charged with mysterious allusions to "external props."[103] Washington listened to all these reports and concluded that as Virginia's action might have the largest influence on her two nearest neighbors, the possibility of rejection by the Old Dominion must be brought to the absolute minimum by wise leadership on the floor of the convention. The man for this was James Madison, beyond all rivalry or comparison even. He could present the Constitution with a convincing clarity the most cunning adversary could not becloud. Without him, the advocates of ratification had no speaker who could stand up against Henry and Mason. The General consequently was much pleased when he learned that Madison had yielded to appeals and was willing to be a candidate for the Virginia Convention.[104] In the great fundamental of faith in the decision of his own people, the firmness of Washington went, if possible, beyond that of most of the younger men. With something of his old art in the analysis of intelligence reports, he interpreted his correspondence in terms of his own knowledge of Vir-

[98] 29 G. W., 426–27. Edward Carrington, writing Henry Knox on the 13th of March, made this observation: "The decision of Massachusetts is perhaps the most important event that ever took place in America, as upon her in all probability depends the fate of the Constitution. Had she rejected I am certain there would be the most remote chance for its adoption in Virginia" (Knox Papers, MHS).

[99] Daniel Carroll to Madison, Feb. 10, 1788; 8 Madison Papers, 104, LC.

[100] Ibid., 118; cf. Benjamin Hawkins of Warrenton, N. C. to Madison, Feb. 14, 1788; ibid., 109.

[101] Benjamin Lincoln to Washington, Feb. 20, 1788; 240 Papers of G. W., 33, LC.

[102] Edward Carrington to Madison, Feb. 10, 1788, 8 Madison Papers, 106, LC, an excellent letter.

[103] Madison to Jefferson, Feb. 19, 1788; ibid., 116, LC; cf. 29 G. W., 425.

[104] Ibid., 431. For the appeals to Madison and the urgent counsel that he conduct an active canvass, see James Gordon, Jr., to Madison, February 17, Joseph Jones to Madison, February 17, Joseph Spencer to Madison, Feb. 28, 1788; 8 Madison Papers, 113, 114, 122, LC. See, also, ibid., 117.

ginia, and he wrote Rufus King: ". . . no doubt, from the first, has been entertained in my mind of the acceptance of [the Constitution] here, notwithstanding the *indefatigable* pains which some very influential characters take to oppose it." [105]

During the second week in March, while the Virginia elections were in progress, Washington learned that the convention in New Hampshire had met on the 13th of February and, after debate, had adjourned on the 22nd until June 3. [106] This reverse—the only one sustained thus far by the advocates of the Constitution—caused some disappointment and surprise in Washington's mind, [107] until it was explained to him [108] that the convention had risen on the motion of friends of the new government. They knew that the majority against them included some men who favored ratification but had instructions from their constituents to oppose. Advocates reasoned that if time elapsed and other States meantime accepted, the hampering instructions might be withdrawn. [109]

With this, the battle swung back to Virginia where, by the end of March, the last of the elections to the convention had been held. Along with many weak Delegates, conservative and suspicious majorities in some counties had chosen able spokesmen who, in Washington's words, would throw a "greater weight of abilities" against the Constitution than opponents had mustered in any other State. [110] Mason was elected and was more violently hostile than ever to the document he had helped to draw. Patrick Henry also was to be a member and was believed to be implacable. [111] With an exceedingly hard contest ahead and the margin of advantage for the Constitution dangerously narrow, friends of a stronger central government began reluctantly to admit that prior ratification by nine States manifestly was desirable before the Virginia Convention met. Some, in fact, were fearful the Old Dominion might reject if her Delegates were not certain the new government could become operative without Virginia. [112] Even with this

[105] Letter of Feb. 29, 1788; 29 *G. W.*, 428.

[106] Madison to Washington, 9 *Madison Papers*, 2, LC; John Langdon to Washington, 240 *Papers of G. W.*, 41, LC; Benjamin Lincoln to Washington, Feb. 24, 1788; 9 *Sparks*, 335 n (the original in 240 *Papers of G. W.*, 40, LC).

[107] 29 *G. W.*, 441, 449–50.        [108] Cf. *ibid.*, 452 ff.

[109] See 240 *Papers of G. W.*, 42, LC; 9 *Madison Papers*, 3, LC; Benjamin Lincoln to Washington, Feb. 24, 1788, 240 *Papers of G. W.*, 40, LC; Henry Knox to Washington, Mch. 10, 1788, *ibid.*, 47.

[110] Edward Carrington to Madison, Apr. 8, 1788; 9 *Madison Papers*, 14, LC; 29 *G. W.*, 459.

[111] Madison to Jefferson, Apr. 22, 1788; 9 *Madison Papers*, 10, LC.

[112] George Nicholas to Madison, Apr. 5, 1788; *ibid.*

possibility undeniable, and doubt existing with respect to the views of the Kentucky members,[113] Washington's conclusion was that the foes of the Constitution had made a "grand push" at the polls and had failed, though narrowly, to win. He believed the opposition weaker than before the polling [114] and he maintained realistically that neither Virginia nor any other State could afford to remain outside the Union after nine made it a certainty.[115]

Preparations had to be made for the next phase of the campaign. Madison went to work to form a coalition with Edmund Randolph,[116] from whom Washington now expected feeble opposition, if any.[117] The General, for his part, undertook as a precautionary measure the somewhat delicate task of urging Maryland friends to prevent a move some of the adversaries of the Constitution had in mind—to adjourn their convention and to await the action of Virginia, which Maryland might wish to duplicate. Postponement would be equivalent to rejection. That was the argument Washington advanced,[118] and with some confidence, because indications were that if Maryland acted at all, she would ratify.[119] Luther Martin was not succeeding in his furious fight against the Constitution, nor was he convincing Marylanders when he insisted that great as Washington and Franklin were, these two had the wrong and he and his friends the right view of the Constitution.[120]

By the 28th of April, when Washington could count six ratifying States—Delaware, Pennsylvania, New Jersey, Georgia, Connecticut and Massachusetts—he reasonably could expect favorable action in South Carolina as well as in Maryland.[121] That would make eight. A ninth assuredly would approve.[122] The prospect stirred Washington's pride. He wrote: "Should [the Constitution] be adopted (and I think it will be) America will lift up her head again and in a few years become respectable among the nations. It is a flattering and consolatory reflec-

---

[113] 9 *Madison Papers*, 17, LC. Charles Lee, Apr. 11, 1788, wrote Washington (240 *Papers of G. W.*, 77, LC) the majority would be ten or twelve, exclusive of the Kentucky Delegates.

[114] 29 *G. W.*, 459, 490.                    [115] *Ibid.*, 500.

[116] Madison to Randolph, Apr. 10, 1788; 9 *Madison Papers*, 16, LC; Randolph to Madison, Apr. 17, 1788; *ibid.*, 19.

[117] 29 *G. W.*, 477.

[118] See James McHenry to Washington, Apr. 20, 1788, 240 *Papers of G. W.*, 86, LC; 29 *G. W.*, 463, 471, 472. Cf. 30 *G. W.*, 77–78, for Washington's expression of concern that he may have been regarded as intervening improperly, which Johnson denied in fine, friendly terms. See Edward S. Delaplaine, *Life of Thomas Johnson*, 459–60—an excellent book.

[119] Daniel Carroll to Madison; Apr. 28, 1788; 9 *Madison Papers*, 22, LC.

[120] 3 *Farrand*, 294.                    [121] 29 *G. W.*, 475.

[122] *Ibid.*

tion that our rising republics have the good wishes of all the philosophers, patriots and virtuous men in all nations, and that they look upon them as a kind of asylum for mankind. God grant that we may not disappoint their honest expectations by our folly or perverseness." [123] Maryland did not contribute to such a defeat. On the contrary, she fulfilled Washington's expectations by a decisive vote for the Constitution and thereby, in the General's opinion, aided the cause in Virginia, where Henry's followers had predicted their sister State would reject the new plan of government.[124] Although it continued to be taken for granted that South Carolina would follow Maryland and be the eighth ratifying State,[125] the uncertainty in Virginia alarmed Northern and Eastern friends of the Constitution [126] and stirred Anti-Federalists to make common cause.[127] Washington conceded nothing to panic. "The sentiment of this State will soon be known," he said calmly,[128] and he wrote Lafayette with something approaching awe: "A few short weeks will determine the political fate of America for the present generation and probably produce no small influence on the happiness of society through a long succession of ages to come. Should everything proceed with harmony and consent, according to our actual wishes and expectations, I must confess to you sincerely . . . it will be so much beyond anything we had a right to imagine or expect eighteen months ago that it will demonstrate as visibly the finger of Providence as any possible event in the course of human affairs can ever designate it. It is impracticable for you or anyone who has not been on the spot to realize the change in men's minds and the progress toward rectitude in thinking and acting which will then have been made." [129]

Five days after Washington wrote this, the Virginia Convention met in Richmond. The General waited eagerly for news of its organization and initial debate, and when it came, he had to restrain himself lest he

[123] Letter of April 25–May 1, to Chastellux, *ibid.*, 485–86.
[124] *Ibid.*, 488, 490. The vote in the Maryland Convention, Apr. 26, 1788, was sixty-three to eleven (E. S. Delaplaine, *Life of Thomas Johnson*, 447). Washington knew of this result within a day or two. For the fight in the convention and for the political situation in Maryland, see Daniel Carroll to Madison, May 28, and Alexander Contee Hanson to Madison, June 2, 1788; 9 *Madison Papers*, 47, 51–53, LC.
[125] 29 *G. W.*, 507.
[126] Tench Coxe to Madison, May 19, Rufus King to Madison, May 25, 1788, 9 *Madison Papers*, 41, 43, LC.
[127] See 2 *Ballagh, Lee Letters*, 466; and John Lamb to Nathaniel Peabody, May 18, 1788, a circular letter as "Chairman of the Federal Republicans Committee," *Personal Papers, Misc.*, LC.
[128] 29 *G. W.*, 501.
[129] Letter of May 28, 1788; *ibid.*, 507–08.

mistake a good beginning as assurance of a happy ending: [130] A large number of Delegates had been present on the opening day and had voted to consider the Constitution paragraph by paragraph. On the 4th of June, Patrick Henry had begun the attack with a demand for justification of the opening words, "We, the people." Why was it not "We, the States"? That question, said the leader of the opposition, he would have put to Washington had the General been present.[131]

This challenge forecast a hard fight over every line of the Constitution, but there were two encouraging items in the first report Washington received: Edmund Randolph had declared himself for ratification,[132] and—glorious if expected tidings—South Carolina had ratified.[133] Washington rejoiced: "The Ratification by eight States without a negative. By three of them unanimously. By six against one in another. By three to one in another. By two for one in two more; and by *all* the weight of *abilities* and *property* in the other is enough to produce a cessation of opposition." [134] South Carolina's action and prospective ratification in New Hampshire, he said, "will make *all*, except desperate men look before they leap into the dark consequences of rejection." At the least, "I think it is enough to produce some change in the conduct of any man who entertains a doubt of his infallibility." [135]

This joyful intelligence from South Carolina was followed by less favorable reports from Richmond. Madison had fallen sick soon after the convention opened, though he had recovered in a few days; Col. Eleazer Oswald had appeared in Richmond, perhaps as the emissary of Pennsylvanians and New Yorkers who opposed the Constitution; while Federalists appeared to have the advantage, a lag in enthusiasm was observable.[136] Debate still was polite and powerful, but outside the convention hall, men did not bow before they struck. Patrick Henry

---

[130] 29 *G. W.*, 510. The news reached Mount Vernon about the 7th of June.

[131] 9 *Madison Papers*, 54, LC; 2 *W. W. Henry*, 348; 29 *G. W.*, 514. The debates of the Convention were recorded stenographically by David Robertson, with perhaps more accuracy than has been allowed, and they were printed separately in two editions, as well as in *Elliot's Debates*. Henry's speeches are reproduced in 3 *W. W. Henry*. The reference to Washington and "We, the people" is p. 433. By no means all these details were supplied Washington in the first communication he received but they soon were known to him.

[132] *Conway, Randolph*, 107; 29 *G. W.*, 512.

[133] This action was taken May 23 by a vote of 149 to seventy-three. See C. C. Pinckney to Washington, May 24, 1788, 240 *Papers of G. W.*, 128, LC. Washington's first news of this probably came through Madison. See 29 *G. W.*, 510-11. The *Pennsylvania Packet* carried the information in its issue of June 3, p. 3.

[134] 29 *G. W.*, 511, verbatim.          [135] *Ibid.*, 510-11.

[136] Madison to Alexander Hamilton, June 9, 1788; 7 *Hamilton Papers*, 851, LC; Madison to Tench Coxe, June 11, 1788; 9 *Madison Papers*, 57, LC; 29 *G. W.*, 517-19.

was a chosen target. "That gentleman," Rev. John B. Smith wrote Madison, "has descended to lower artifice and management upon the occasion [of the election to the convention] than I thought him capable of." [137]

Washington himself continued to escape criticism, except for the half-compliment paid him by Colonel Grayson, who asserted on the floor, "I think that were it not for one great character in America, so many men would not be for this government." [138] In a few instances—Washington called the names—the General felt that politics were straining old ties. "With some," he said, "to have differed in sentiment is to have passed the Rubicon of their friendship . . .," [139] but much as he loved the good opinion of men, he would not withdraw a word of endorsement or concede an adjective of compromise. Too much of the future of America was at stake. While the debate in the Convention was at its heat, he wrote Lafayette: "When the people shall find themselves under an energetic government, when foreign nations shall be disposed to give us equal advantages in commerce from dread of retaliation, when the burdens of war shall be in a manner done away by the sale of western lands, when the seeds of happiness which are sown here shall begin to expand themselves, and when everyone (under his own vine and fig-tree) shall begin to taste the fruits of freedom, then all these blessings (for all these blessings will come) will be referred to the fostering influence of the new government whereas many causes will have conspired to produce them." [140]

Some of Washington's friends in the North, though not direct parties in the struggle of the Virginia Convention, were sharers with him in his hope and in his enthusiasm. The vote in the Old Dominion, said Tench Coxe once more, would have great effect on New York; [141] Anti-Federalists in that State, the observant Edward Carrington reported, manifestly were shocked at the prospect that Virginia would ratify; [142] the outlook in New Hampshire was favorable, said Rufus King [143] and

[137] Letter of June 12, 1788; 9 *Madison Papers*, 59, LC. Smith added that Henry misrepresented the Constitution and the designs of its authors. Further, "he has found means to make some of the best people here believe that a religious establishment was in contemplation under the new government."

[138] 2 *W. W. Henry*, 364, with citation from 3 *Elliot's Debates*, 616.

[139] 29 *G. W.*, 431.

[140] *Ibid.*, 525–26. In the original, "whereas" begins an incomplete sentence, but the proper connection would seem to be clear.

[141] Letter of June 11, 1788, to Madison; 9 *Madison Papers*, 58, LC.

[142] Letter of June 17 to Madison, *ibid.*, 62.

[143] Letter of June 12, 1788, to Alexander Hamilton, 7 *Hamilton Papers*, 853, LC.

Washington's young secretary, Tobias Lear;[144] there might be a race between Virginia and New Hampshire for the honor of bringing the new government into being with the ninth State vote.[145] In contrast, Gouverneur Morris chanced to be in Richmond during the struggle over ratification, and he wrote Alexander Hamilton, June 13, that "matters" were "not going as well in this State as the friends of America could wish." He told of the arts of Henry and of certain dark modes of operating on the minds of members, but he concluded: "Be of good Cheer. My Religion steps in where my understanding falters and I feel faith as I lose confidence. Things will yet go right but when and how I dare not predicate . . ."[146]

Madison was more confident than Morris. On the 20th, he wrote Hamilton that the article on the Judiciary was being discussed. "At present," he said, "it is calculated that we still retain a majority of three or four and if we can weather the storm against the part under consideration, I shall hold the danger to be pretty well over."[147] For two days he was troubled by rumors of maneuvers on the party of Henry. "Our calculations," Madison reported this time, "promise us success by three or four, or possibly five or six votes." He added cautiously: "But were there no possibility of mistaking the opinions of some, in reviewing those of so many, the smallness of the majority suggests the danger from ordinary casualties which may vary the result."[148] To Washington, on the 23rd,[149] he wrote that the discussion of the Constitution by paragraphs had been concluded that day. "Tomorrow," he said, "some proposition for closing the business will be made." The conversation of Anti-Federalists "seemed to betray despair," but he repeated, in substance, what he had told Hamilton, and he concluded: "It is possible . . . that some adverse circumstance may happen."[150]

This was not pleasant news for the master of Mount Vernon who was having trouble with his plowing and, on the 27th, had a guest whose overstay denied Washington even the solace of his usual ride around his plantations. Besides, the official who received the lists of taxable property in Fairfax County paid a call. That also was on the 27th.[151] Next morning early, amazing news was brought to the door.

---

[144] 241 *Papers of G. W.*, 4.                          [145] *Ibid.*
[146] Letter to Alexander Hamilton; 7 *Hamilton Papers*, 855, LC.
[147] *Ibid.*, 859, LC.                          [148] Letter to Hamilton; *ibid.*, f. 861.
[149] Wrongly dated the 25th by Madison; 241 *Papers of G. W.*, 27, LC; 3 *Elliot's Debates*, 586 ff; 5 *Hunt's Madison*, 226 n.
[150] 9 *Madison Papers*, 68, LC.                          [151] 3 *Diaries*, 378.

The previous evening's mail to Alexandria from Richmond had contained the glorious report that on the 25th the Virginia Convention had rejected by a vote of eighty-eight to eighty a motion to propose amendments to the Constitution prior to ratification. Then the Constitution had been accepted, eighty-nine to seventy-nine.[152] On receipt of this information, the town was illuminated, cannon were fired,[153] and plans immediately were made in Alexandria to celebrate on the 28th the birth of the new government. Virginia completed the requisite nine; the State that had moved for independence had made certain the full operation of the Philadelphia Constitution. At least that was the joyful boast in the Potomac port until two hours before daylight on the 29th. Then an express[154] arrived from the North with the intelligence that New Hampshire on the 21st had accepted the Constitution by a vote of fifty-seven to forty-six.[155] Ten States, not nine, had ratified; Virginia was the tenth, not the ninth.

The messenger who conveyed these happy tidings[156] presented, also, an invitation for the family to attend the celebration, which was to include a dinner in Alexandria that afternoon. Washington decided to go and, with Colonel Humphreys and George Augustine Washington, he set out; but even on this holiday errand, he shaped his ride so that he visited all the farms and observed what was being done on each of them.[157] A few miles outside Alexandria, Washington found a mounted group of townsmen awaiting him as an escort of honor. Nearer the town was the Light Infantry Company; a salute of ten guns announced his arrival. At Wise's Tavern, thirteen toasts were drunk after an elaborate dinner, each draft with the loud "Amen" of a cannon shot. Washington himself was not toasted but the convention was, and the ratifying States and the Potomac development, and other men and causes the General loved.[158]

During the festivities, someone recalled to Washington that the date

152 Madison to Washington, June 25, 1788; 9 *Madison Papers*, 71, LC. The final votes are recorded in 3 *Elliot's Debates*, 653–55.
153 *Penn. Packet*, July 11, 1788, p. 3.
154 Probably one sent by Philip Schuyler to James Madison, June 14, 1788, 9 *Madison Papers*, 70, LC; 9 *A. Hamilton*, 436.
155 241 *Papers of G. W.*, 24, LC.
156 The circumstances are not altogether certain; Washington's two references, *infra*, are vague.
157 3 *Diaries*, 378–79.
158 Details in the *Pennsylvania Packet*, July 11, 1788, p. 3, probably reprinted from the *Virginia Journal* of July 3, 1788, no copy of which is known to be in existence. A ball concluded the festivities on June 30. *Ibid.*

was that of the action on Sullivan's Island in 1776 and of Monmouth in 1778. The General might have blanched at the memory . . . Monmouth! Thirst and blasting heat . . . Charles Lee's strange retreat . . . the rally on the ridge . . . ten years ago . . . "I think," Washington wrote, in his earnest clumsy style, when he got home, "we may rationally indulge the pleasing hope that the Union will now be established upon a durable basis, and that Providence seems still disposed to favor the members of it, with unequalled opportunities for political happiness." [159]

That was one view, the reverent, impersonal view. Another was expressed by James Monroe to Thomas Jefferson: "Be assured [General Washington's] influence carried this government." [160]

[159] Letter of June 28, 1788, to C. C. Pinckney; 30 *G. W.*, 9–10.
[160] Letter of July 12, 1788, *The Writings of James Monroe*, S. M. Hamilton, ed., cited hereafter as *Hamilton's Monroe*, v. 1, p. 186.

# CHAPTER VI

## "My Reputation to Be Put in Risk"
### (July, 1788–April 16, 1789)

Ratification by New Hampshire and by Virginia relieved but did not remove the concern of Washington for the successful organization of Federal government under the compact adopted at Philadelphia. Three States—Rhode Island, New York and North Carolina—had not yet accepted the Constitution. From such information as came to him, the General thought Virginia's nearest Southern neighbor would accede,[1] and he did not attempt to predict what might occur in Rhode Island, whose dominant faction he denounced for "infamy" that "outgoes all precedent." He added in disgust: "There is no State or description of men but would blush to be involved . . . with the paper-money junto of that Anarchy."[2]

With respect to the powerful State of New York, Washington had hopes that rose or fell as the reports of Federalist correspondents now were cheerful and now were doubtful;[3] but in spite of his own reasoning, which told him that New York must remain with her sister States, he somehow feared that she might withdraw from the Union.[4]

Another uncertainty dogged him daily as he rode over his plantations and reflected on the future of America: In the States that had ratified the Constitution, would the Anti-Federalists continue to agitate for

---

[1] 30 *G. W.*, 12, 32. News from Carolina was meagre. "We are," Rufus King wrote Madison, "without any accounts or opinion concerning North Carolina . . ." Letter of July 20, 1788; 9 *Madison Papers*, 83, LC. See also Edmund Randolph to James Madison, July 27, 1788: "Not a syllable has transpired from the North Carolina Convention," 9 *Madison Papers,* 92, LC.

[2] Letter of July 20, 1788, to Jonathan Trumbull; 30 *G. W.*, 21. Cf. *ibid.*, 12, 32.

[3] Some of this correspondence has gripping interest and deserves publication or reprinting. See Jay in 241 *Papers of G. W.*, 37, LC; Knox to Rufus King, July 13, 1788, *Knox Papers*, MHS; Rufus King to James Madison, July 20, 1788, 9 *Madison Papers*, 83, LC; Madison to Washington, July 21, 1788, 8 *Burnett*, 763–64; 9 *Madison Papers*, 85, LC, and conveniently reprinted in 5 *Hunt's Madison*, 237–39; Alexander Hamilton to Madison, July, n.d., 1788, 9 *Madison Papers*, 96, LC; Jay to Washington, July 23, 1788, 241 *Papers of G. W.*, 50, LC; Knox to Washington, 241 *Papers of G. W.*, 95, LC; Tobias Lear to Washington, July 31, 1788, *ibid.*, 61.

[4] 30 *G. W.*, 34.

crippling amendments, and would they attempt to obstruct the organization of the government? Personally, Washington had not "much objection," as he wrote Thomas Jefferson, to any of the amendments, except to the one that would deny Congress the right of direct taxation [5]—the very amendment, in Tench Coxe's words, "most dear to [the] opposition" in Pennsylvania [6]—and for a time after Virginia accepted the Constitution, he felt relief because of the apparent acquiescence of Patrick Henry in the decision of the convention.[7] It was gratifying, also, to hear that many of those who had voted against ratification had now rejected a plan for a protest some of their leaders had intended to draft.[8] This satisfaction lasted a few days only. Then the report from Richmond was that Anti-Federalism might be languishing but was far from dead, despite the rumor that certain opponents of the Constitution now were recommending a "patient trial." [9]

Washington accepted this reversion in the spirit he usually displayed in dealing with hard actualities he could not soften. ". . . We ought not to be too sanguine," he wrote John Langdon, "or to expect that we shall be entirely exempted from the ills which fall to the lot of humanity." [10] When James McHenry reported a whisper of a secret plan "to suspend the proper organization of the government or to defeat it altogether," [11] Washington's counsel was realistic: In States where opposition was threatened, those "who are well-affected to the government [should] use their utmost exertions that the worthiest citizens may be appointed to the two houses of the first Congress." Adversaries should be reconciled by "candid and honest measures." Without overturning the new system of government, proper amendments to the Constitution should be approved.[12]

[5] *Ibid.*, 83.

[6] Letter of July 23, 1788, to James Madison, 9 *Madison Papers*, 87, LC.

[7] 30 *G. W.*, 12.

[8] Madison to Hamilton, June 30, 1788; 7 *Hamilton Papers*, 865, LC. A "spectator to the meeting" reported the lively details in the *Va. Independent Chronicle* (Richmond), July 9, 1788, p. 3. According to that witness, George Mason organized the meeting.

[9] James Madison to Washington, July 25, 1788, 9 *Madison Papers*, 71; Edmund Randolph to Madison, July 27, 1788; *ibid.*, 92, LC.

[10] Letter of July 20, 1788; 30 *G. W.*, 19.

[11] Letter of July 27, 1788; 241 *Papers of G. W.*, 55, LC. See also McHenry to Madison, July 26, 1788; 9 *Madison Papers*, 90, LC.

[12] Letter of July 31, 1788; 30 *G. W.*, 29. To a doubting Virginian his assurance was: "That all questions of this kind are . . . viewed through different mediums by different men is as certain as that they have existence; all that can be expected in such cases, therefore, is charity, mutual forbearance and acquiescence in the general voice, which, though it may be wrong, is presumably right" (Letter of Aug. 3, 1788 to Thomas Nelson, *ibid.*, 34).

Two days after he wrote this, Washington received news that was as pleasant as it was unexpected.[13] On the 26th of July, New York unconditionally ratified the Federal Constitution by a vote of thirty to twenty-seven [14]—a victory for the Union and for Alexander Hamilton; a defeat for the Governor, whom Hamilton had accused of ambition "to establish Clintonism on the basis of Anti-Federalism." [15] Ratification by New York was more than political, more even than a pledge that the Federalist States of New England would not lose their bridge across the Hudson to Jersey, to Pennsylvania, and to the South. New York symbolized struggle—Long Island, Kip's Bay, White Plains, Fort Washington, Stony Point and Verplanck's, West Point and Arnold, hunger and hope, the Newburgh address and threats of reprisal by ragged officers, an impregnable island city and a ravaged countryside. The very name New York was one of memories like those of nightmares, and yet all the associations had been those of triumph over perplexities and factional politics. Never had New York endured so dark a day that hope had been dead when night fell. Her action now confirmed Washington in his belief that the Constitution could be put into operation without dangerous friction or strife; [16] but he was displeased and perplexed when the New York Convention unanimously adopted and sent out, over the signature of George Clinton as President, a circular letter in which they called on the States to demand an early second convention to remove the defects of the Constitution.[17] Washington agreed, substantially,[18] with Madison that this circular had a "most pestilent tendency" [19] which Virginia Anti-Federalists might aggravate,[20] though he felt that acquiescence in the dispatch of the circular

[13] *Ibid.*, 32.
[14] Henry Knox to Washington, July 28, 1788, 241 *Papers of G. W.*, 59, LC; James Madison to his father, July 27, 1788, 9 *Madison Papers*, 91, LC; Clement Biddle to Washington, July 30, 1788, 241 *Papers of G. W.*, 60; Madison informed his father, incorrectly, that the vote was thirty to twenty-five. For a full discussion of the work of the Poughkeepsie Convention, see Clarence E. Miner, *The Ratification of the Federal Constitution by the State of New York* (1921), Chap. 5. See also, E. Wilder Spaulding, *His Excellency George Clinton, Critic of the Constitution*, 181, and Alexander C. Flick, ed., *History of the State of New York*, v. 5, p. 51–61.
[15] Letter of July, n.d., to Madison; 9 *Madison Papers*, 96, LC.
[16] See Washington to Hamilton, Aug. 28, 1788; 30 *G. W.*, 66.
[17] The text of the circular of July 28, 1788, is most conveniently accessible in 2 *Elliot's Debates*, 413–14.
[18] 30 *G. W.*, 52.
[19] Letter of August 15—sometimes cited as of the 11th—in 8 *Burnett*, 778–79, 4 *LTW.*, 232–34, 5 *Hunt's Madison*, 248–50; 9 *Madison Papers*, 104, LC.
[20] See James Gordon to James Madison, Aug. 31, 1788, *ibid.*, 112. Edmund Randolph was willing to have such a convention (see his letter of Aug. 13, 1788, to James Madison, *ibid.*, 102); Madison himself was increasingly if reluctantly of opinion that such a meeting might be necessary. See *ibid.*, 108, 110.

probably had been the price of New York's ratification and he accepted it as a hard bargain.[21] Nor did he waver when, to his disappointment, he learned that the North Carolina Convention had voted decisively against ratifying the Constitution, and then had adjourned with a declaration that it neither ratified nor rejected the new system of government.[22] Unaccountable as this course appeared to Washington,[23] it was not a subject on which he dwelt.[24] The refusal of Rhode Island and North Carolina to go forward with their sister States would not prevent the organization of the Union on foundations that would support "much purer civil liberty and greater public happiness than have hitherto been the portion of mankind." [25]

He and hundreds of other Americans could hope that private as well as public happiness might be enlarged also, at least insofar as happiness depended on gold. In August Washington confided to Doctor Craik: "I never felt the want of money so sensibly since I was a boy of 15 years old as I have done for the last twelve months and probably shall do for twelve months more to come." [26] To his humiliation he had to put off the Sheriff of Fairfax County three times when that official came to collect the money due on Mount Vernon [27] and he had received warning that his lands in Greenbrier County would be sold unless his taxes there were paid.[28] He could not remit the whole of what he owed Doctor Craik for medical attendance; [29] the rector of his church was to send in November for pew rent of £5 that should have been forwarded in August.[30] Washington had to devote many hours, in unconcealed

---

[21] 30 G. W., 66.

[22] 4 Elliot's Debates, 250–51. Earlier rumors had been that North Carolina had rejected the Constitution (John Langdon to Nicholas Gilman, Aug. 25, 1788, Personal Papers, Misc., LC; E. Randolph to Madison, Aug. 13, 1788; 9 Madison Papers, 102, LC) or had insisted on "prior amendment" (5 Hunt's Madison, 253, 256).

[23] 30 G. W., 52.

[24] He wrote no more about it until Oct. 26, 1788, when he remarked, "The constant report is that North Carolina will soon accede to the new Union" (ibid., 118).

[25] Ibid., 69. He added the hope that America would "prove an asylum for the persecuted of all nations."

[26] Ibid., 36; cf. 29 ibid., 335.                     [27] Ibid., 379; cf. ibid., 468.

[28] Ibid., 500–01; Ledger B, f. 267.            [29] 30 G. W., 36.

[30] David Griffith to Washington, Nov. 3, 1788; 242 Papers of G. W., 11, LC. Dr. Griffith, an eminent figure in the Episcopal Church, was elected first Bishop of Virginia but was impelled to decline consecration (2 Brydon, Mother Church, 464 ff). The special reasons for Washington's more acute financial distress at this time were: (1) the failure of his grain crop and the necessity of laying out at least £500 for corn to make good the shortage (see 29 G. W., 294, 303, 459–60); (2) his continued extravagant living and unavoidable entertainment (cf. as typical, his purchase of a watch at 25 guineas, 30 ibid., 142, and his own reflections in ibid., 148); (3) his inability to sell his western lands at figures he would accept, and his non-success in trying to collect rents due him (cf. 29 ibid., 283–84; Ledger B, f. 213, and the numerous references in 30 G. W., index entry Land); and (4) widespread shortage of money

harassment, to finding money for day-by-day expenditures,[31] but he maintained the confidence he always had about his own finances: his difficulties would be overcome in time, his peaceful life on the Potomac could be resumed in its quiet opulence and content. He told himself that he had performed his last public service in the Philadelphia Convention and had discharged it at the call of his country and in a willingness to accept all the criticism that might be stirred.[32] ". . . Although I shall not live," he had written Nathaniel Gorham, "to see but a small portion of the happy effects which I am confident this system will produce for my country, yet the precious idea of its prosperity will not only be a consolation amidst the increasing infirmities of nature and the growing love of retirement, but it will tend to soothe the mind in the inevitable hour of separation from terrestrial objects." [33]

This was his hope, this his expectation, but discussion of the Presidency which he had tried to disregard in the autumn of 1787 became brisker after the New Year. The *Pennsylvania Packet*, one of the two or three most important papers of the country, mentioned Washington frequently as President-to-be—and never once spoke of anyone else for the office.[34] In the New York celebration of Massachusetts' acceptance of the Constitution, one toast—doubtless of deep draught—was, significantly, "General Washington—may his wisdom and virtue preside in the councils of his country." [35] Many towns observed his fifty-sixth birthday with enthusiasm; in the mailbag brought down from Alexandria, Washington found letters from old and distinguished friends whose appeals for his acceptance of the Presidency he could not ignore. Gen. John Armstrong, comrade of three decades and more, wrote as if

---

that forced his debtors to ignore his appeals for payment or else to send trivial sums (cf. 29 *ibid.*, 301, 379). In commenting on the situation, Edmund Randolph wrote James Madison, Sept. 12, 1788: "The scarcity of money in Virginia can hardly be conceived by those who sojourn in a large city" (10 *Madison Papers*, 4, LC).

[31] He made a long effort to collect from the State of Virginia, in accordance with existing law, for a Negro slave executed for crime in 1781 (29 *G. W.*, 335, 429, 460). In the absence of other assets, he had to accept Negroes and livestock at a valuation of £1341 from the estate of Bartholomew Dandridge, and even then he could not bring himself to do otherwise with this property than to leave it where it was, for the use of Mrs. Dandridge. A balance of £2328 remained due from the estate of his brother-in-law (*Ledger B*, f. 280). For his later purchase of some inferior Dandridge land in Gloucester County, see John Dandridge to Washington, Dec. 6, 1788; 242 *Papers of G. W.*, 36, LC, and 30 *G. W.*, 166, 252, 272–73, 281–82). Washington's desperate need of money induced him to press anew for the payment of a bill of William Armistead, drawn in his favor and protested as long previously as 1763 (*ibid.*, 94, 231, 272, 282–83).

[32] Letter of Aug. 16, 1788, to Charles Pettit, *ibid.*, 42.

[33] Letter of July 21, 1788; *ibid.*, 24.          [34] This continued true to April, 1789.

[35] See specifically, the *Pennsylvania Packet* of Feb. 22, 1788, p. 2.

the hand of the Almighty had been placed on Washington's head;[36] a letter from Lafayette expressed some alarm over the magnitude of executive powers under the Constitution but voiced the belief that if Washington exercised the authority of the office and found it dangerously great, he would reduce it. For this and other reasons, Washington must consent to be President.[37] A like wish that he head the new government concluded a friendly letter of Jan. 18, 1788, from Rochambeau, who wrote of the unhappy end of de Grasse.[38] The answers of Washington to these three letters were shaped somewhat by the special nature of his relationship with each of the men, but the same wish was voiced with candor in all of them:[39] He did not say he would refuse to accept the Presidency; he affirmed only, in effect, that he did not desire the office, that he hoped it would not be offered him, and that if acceptance were unavoidable, it would represent the heaviest possible sacrifice. All this was written with composure, in much the spirit he had displayed many times during the war when he had refused to cross a bridge until he had come to it.[40]

The American people were not so philosophical. Without any prearrangement, their celebration of the 4th of July, 1788, became in large part a general call for the election of Washington as President. At Wilmington, Delaware, a toast was drunk to "Farmer Washington—may he like a second Cincinnatus, be called from the plow to rule a great people."[41] Citizens of Frederick, Maryland, lifted their glasses with the sentiment, "May the Saviour of America gratify the ardent wishes of his countrymen by accepting that post which the voice of mankind has assigned him."[42] At York, Pennsylvania, loyal participants in the festive ceremony listened to a "new Federal song" in five stanzas, each of which concluded:

[36] Letter of Feb. 20, 1788; 240 *Papers of G. W.*, 34, LC.

[37] Letter of Jan. 1, 1788; *LOLTW.*, 334–35.

[38] "I long, my dear General, to see your convention passed upon the plurality of the States and to see you President of a confederation strongly settled" (239 *Papers of G. W.*, 128, LC).

[39] His letter of Apr. 25, 1788, to Armstrong is in 29 *G. W.*, 464 ff. For the answers to Rochambeau and Lafayette, see *ibid.*, 474–75, 475–80.

[40] His only flash of resentment was over an application made as early as June, 1788, by Samuel Hanson, a financially distressed resident of Alexandria who applied for a position in the government he assumed Washington would head. With his usual consideration Washington spared the man's feelings as far as he could but he said plainly he thought an application "altogether untimely and improper" (29 *G. W.*, 509). Hanson's letter of June 4 is in 241 *Papers of G. W.*, 10, LC—a carefully written statement of his needs and an attempted justification of his action on the ground that he wished, if assured a public office, to have time in which to prepare himself for it.

[41] *Penn. Packet*, July 12, 1788, p. 2.　　　　　[42] *Ibid.*, July 19, 1788, p. 3.

"Great Washington shall rule the land
While Franklin's counsel aids his hand." [43]

New York City's observance of the 4th was postponed in the hope that the State convention would ratify the Federal Constitution in time for a joint festival. When the Delegates wrangled overlong, friends of the new order staged a great procession on the 23rd of July with floats, transparencies and patriotic banners and a mass of marching men. Several of the emblems honored Washington,[44] but that of the Tallow Chandlers outdid the others. It was "a flag with thirteen stripes —under them the figure of General Washington, with these words placed over him, 'the illustrious Washington, may he be the first President of the United States.' " [45]

Public men echoed the public demand. Appropriately, the first who spoke in words that stirred and alarmed Washington proved to be Alexander Hamilton. In reply to that friend's argument for the General's acquiescence in the call of the country, Washington went a little beyond the language he had used when he answered Armstrong: ". . . the event alluded to may never happen, and . . . in case it should occur, it would be a point of prudence to defer one's ultimate and irrevocable decision, so long as new data might be afforded for one to act with the greater wisdom and propriety." Then he admitted a scruple: persons familiar with his inclination would understand why he might consent if a "different line of conduct" proved "indispensable," but after all he had said about retirement from public life, "the world and posterity"—he never forgot posterity in his later years— "might probably accuse [him of] inconsistency and ambition." [46] He scarcely could have confessed more plainly both his regard for public esteem and his absolute dedication to duty at any price.

Hamilton, of course, regarded Washington's concern as ill-founded, though he agreed that prudence justified his old commander in deferring a decision. With his usual persuasive logic, Hamilton reviewed the circumstances and maintained that ". . . every public and personal consideration will demand from you an acquiescence in what will *cer-*

---

[43] *Ibid.,* Aug. 5, 1788, p. 2. This and several other references to the popular call for Washington as President appear in David M. Matteson, *Washington and the Constitution,* hereafter cited as *Matteson,* 201 ff.

[44] *Penn. Packet,* Aug. 6, 1788, p. 2.

[45] *Ibid.,* Aug. 7, 1788, p. 2.

[46] Letter of Aug. 28, 1788; 30 *G. W.,* 66–67.

*tainly* be the unanimous wish of your country." [47] Those were sombre, arresting words. In like conviction that duty ran with public demand, Henry Lee [48] and Benjamin Lincoln [49] made their plea.

The newspapers, too, renewed their appeals, not so much this time in order to win Washington's consent as to assure a unanimous vote for him [50] and to rally weak-kneed doubters and lukewarm patriots with the confident statement that he would accept.[51] Even before these articles began to appear, Washington had to admit to himself that he almost certainly would be the choice of the electors. ". . . I have always felt a kind of gloom upon my mind," he confessed, "as often as I have been taught to expect I might, and perhaps must ere long be called to make a decision" and he added in manifest distress of spirit: ". . . if I should receive the appointment and if I should be prevailed upon to accept it, the acceptance would be attended with more diffidence and reluctance than I ever experienced before in my life." [52] He did not set down in one-two-three order the arguments for and against assumption of the office, if it were tendered him, but in his answers to Hamilton to Lincoln and to Henry Lee he stated all the considerations that are known to have carried weight with him.[53]

[47] Letter of Sept., n.d., 1788; 7 *Hamilton Papers*, 905, LC, and in 9 *A. Hamilton*, 444. In thorough knowledge of the man he was addressing, he said: "In a matter so essential to the well-being of society as the prosperity of a newly-instituted government, a citizen of so much consequence as yourself to its success has no option but to lend his services if called for. Permit me to say it would be inglorious in such a situation not to hazard the glory, however great, which he might have previously acquired" (*ibid.*, 445).

[48] Letter of Sept. 13, 1788; 241 *Papers of G. W.*, 90, LC.

[49] *Ibid.*, 104; original in 241 *Papers of G. W.*, 104–05, LC. Jefferson wrote: "I presume there will not be a vote against him [i.e. Washington] in the United States." (Letter of Aug. 12, 1788 to William Carmichael; 7 *Jefferson*, 125.)

[50] The *Pennsylvania Packet* (Oct. 9, 1788, p. 3), calls for unanimity on the part of Pennsylvania electors in support of Washington. With this was coupled endorsement of John Adams for the Vice Presidency.

[51] *Penn. Packet*, Nov. 3, 1788, p. 3, a quotation from a letter written at Augusta, Georgia, October 6: "Let it ever be remembered that a Washington is to guide the helm." Cf. *Penn. Packet*, Nov. 6, 1788, p. 3: ". . . The universal voice of America is prepared to call to the chair of President of the United States the venerated President of the Federal Convention." Cf., a letter from Massachusetts in *ibid.*, Nov. 13, 1788, p. 2: "General Washington is universally talked of for President of the United States," and the "judicious and sensible" elements in Massachusetts favor John Adams as Vice President. A quotation in the *Pennsylvania Packet*, Nov. 25, 1788, p. 2, from a letter to the *Albany Register*, n.d., dealt with the "operation of the new government under the auspices of our illustrious Washington" as if he already had been elected.

[52] Letter of Oct. 3, 1788, to Alexander Hamilton; 30 *G. W.*, 111. Cf. a letter of similar import to Benjamin Lincoln, Oct. 26, 1788, *ibid.*, 119.

[53] The most detailed of these statements—perhaps the fullest exposure of his mind at this time—were in his letter of Sept. 22, 1788, to Henry Lee (*ibid.*, 97–98), and in an equally comprehensive and candid letter of Oct. 26, 1788, to Benjamin Lincoln (*ibid.*, 118–20).

The five prime arguments in his mind, at this time, against acceptance of the office were:

1. His age, his interest in agricultural pursuits and his love of retirement—in short, his personal circumstances and inclination.[54]

2. Fear that a return to public life after his deliberate retirement in 1783 might be regarded as inconsistent, if not, indeed, as evidence of rashness and ambition.[55]

3. Disinclination to assume new and unfamiliar duties, though he was resolved that this "terror of encountering new fatigues and troubles" should not be decisive with him.[56]

4. Doubt whether his election would be acceptable to the Anti-Federalists.[57]

5. The absence of any proof that the duties of the office could not be discharged as readily by someone else as by him.[58]

The arguments for acceptance were represented primarily by these four unanswered questions:

1. Much as he prized the good opinion of his fellow-Americans, would he not be violating principles to which he had adhered since young manhood if he sought to retain his popularity at "the expense of one social duty or moral virtue"? [59]

2. If clamor were raised against him and censure were imposed, could he not endure these plagues of public life, so long as he gave no just occasion for public disapproval? [60]

3. Was the good of the country involved? If it was, did he not have a duty to discharge, even though he might risk the reputation he had earned and cherished? [61]

4. Might it not be possible to answer the call, to hold the office briefly and, when the government was in operation, to resign and to return to Mount Vernon, there "to pass an unclouded evening after the stormy day of life"? [62]

In these terms, informally, he stated the case to his friends but he did not come finally to grips with it. He would continue in retirement

---

[54] *Ibid.*, 98.          [55] *Ibid.*, 97.          [56] *Ibid.*, 98.
[57] *Ibid.*, 97.          [58] *Ibid.*, 98, 111.     [59] *Ibid.*, 97.
[60] *Ibid.*, 98.
[61] *Ibid.*: ". . . certain I am, whensoever I shall be convinced the good of my country requires my reputation to be put in risk, regard for my own fame will not come in competition with an object of so much magnitude."
[62] *Ibid.*, 111.

unless convinced that this would have "very disagreeable consequences" to America and to himself. If those close to him wished it otherwise, they must demonstrate the absolute necessity that he, and not someone else, should assume the burden of the Presidency.[63] With this, he tried to slip from the rack. Persuasive letters of friends did not cease, but, as it chanced, he had a quiet period at Mount Vernon.[64] Only a few of a diminished number of guests—Madison, and Robert and Gouverneur Morris [65]—were men with whom Washington could discuss the future of the Union and, perhaps, his part in it. Most of the others who came from a distance were chance travelers or foreigners who could not, or did not, presume to give Washington an answer to the question uppermost in his mind—whether it was necessary for him to accept the Presidency.[66] He did not even have frequent meetings of the Potomac Company, at which some things besides the progress of dredging and the need of new capital might have been discussed.[67] Service to friends

[63] *Ibid.*, 98.

[64] Thirty-five thousand brick were fired in the kiln on the 25th of June (3 *Diaries*, 377); a well was dug for the new barn (*ibid.*, 392); in an exceedingly violent storm of July 23–24, much damage was done to trees and the fifteen-foot miniature ship *Federalist*, a gift from Baltimore merchants and shipowners, was sunk in the Potomac (*ibid.*, 365 n, 393; *Penn. Packet*, Aug. 6, 1788, p. 3; Edmund Randolph to Madison, July 27, 1788, with particular mention of the damage done to corn and tobacco from the Atlantic coast to Louisa County; 9 *Madison Papers*, 92, LC).

[65] 3 *Diaries*, 384, 387, 388.

[66] Francis Adrian van der Kemp, introduced by Lafayette (*LOLTW.*, 339) was displeased with Washington: "There seemed to me," he wrote, "to skulk somewhat of a repulsive coldness, not congenial with my mind, under a courteous demeanor; and I was infinitely better pleased by the unassuming, modest gentleness of the lady, than with the conscious superiority of her consort" (*Francis Adrian van der Kemp, 1752–1829: An Autobiography*, Helen L. Fairchild, ed., 116. The visit was on July 29, 1788). Elisha Ayers, an itinerant school-master, went uninvited to Mount Vernon late in the summer but apparently he had a short conversation only with the General (Elisha Ayers, *A Journal of Travel in Different Parts of the United States . . .*, 8–9). The new French Minister to the United States, Éléanor-François Élie, the Comte de Moustier, reached Mount Vernon on the 2nd of November with his sister-in-law, styled the Marchioness de Brehan, her son, and their escort, Victor Marie du Pont (3 *Diaries*, 441). Washington previously had written the Minister a letter on the possible development of trade between the United States and France (30 *G. W.*, 43), a letter that was most carefully prepared because it was understood that de Moustier was not pleased with America. Although the Minister and the Marchioness tried Washington's legs and perhaps his patience by a seven-mile walk around the plantation, he felt that de Moustier's mood would be better in future dealings with America (30 *G. W.*, 139). Gossip concerning the relations of the Minister and the lady will be found in 8 *Burnett*, 812–13, but this perhaps was unjust (see 6 *Jefferson*, 335).

[67] Apparently, Washington attended one meeting only of the Company during the summer and fall. That one was at Alexandria, August 4–5 (3 *Diaries*, 398–99). Two minor discussions of Company business were held at Mount Vernon (*ibid.*, 384, 432). Washington continued optimistic of the future of the river development (30 *G. W.*, 15, 80). For its financial needs (see *ibid.*, 57–58), and, as an investment, he commended to James Madison, unequivocally and almost enthusiastically, a share in the site at the Great Falls in which Lee was trying to interest Madison (H. Lee to Madison, Oct. 29, Nov. 19, Dec. 8, 1788, 10 *Madison Papers*, 35, 50, 63, LC; Madison to Washington, Nov. 5, 1788, *ibid.*, 42; Madison to H. Lee, Nov. 30, 1788, *ibid.*, 57; Washington to Madison, Nov. 17, 1788; 30 *G. W.*, 128–30).

and neighbors was neither particularly interesting nor unusually irksome,[68] and it did not take him far from home. He had many a day when, as he rode alone from one of his farms to another, he had time in which to fight the battle between conscience and desire—between Hamilton's "In a matter so essential . . . a citizen of so much consequence as yourself . . . has no option but to lend his services if called for" [69] and his own "I have no wish which aspires beyond the humble and happy lot of living and dying a private citizen on my own farm." [70] If the call were commanding and the welfare of the country required that he forgo his ease and risk his reputation he would do so, but was there someone else who could serve? [71] Did his friends say no one else could act? Did they urge necessity? Let them demonstrate it.

The Congress of the Confederation, moving slowly, by this time had carried out the recommendations made to it by the Philadelphia Convention.[72] Presidential electors were to be chosen in the different States on the first Wednesday in January. These electors were to meet and cast their votes on the corresponding date in February. The similar Wednesday in March had been set "for commencing proceedings under the said Constitution." [73] New York soon was named as the meeting place.[74]

Washington believed in the free, untrammeled choice of electors but he had taken seriously the warning of Madison that the Anti-Feder-

[68] It included so humble an assignment as that of procuring ass's milk for a sick lady (ibid., 117).
[69] 9 A. Hamilton, 445, and supra, p. 147–48 and n.
[70] 30 G. W., 42.     [71] Ibid., 98
[72] 2 Farrand, 665–66; (Sept. 17, 1787). The various stages in the formulation of this measure, prior to its adoption on the final day of the Convention, may be traced in Farrand's index, v. 4, under the heading "Introduction of new government."
[73] 34 JCC., 359. The original report of the committee, July 8, 1788, fixed all these days one month earlier (ibid., 304). An additional month had been allowed at the instance of the Delegates of the Southern States who had doubted whether the frontier counties could act within the prescribed term. Final action was delayed until Sept. 13, 1788 by the long and familiar wrangle over the seat of government (ibid., 367–68, 383–88, 392–404, 415–19, 455–57, 481–84, 487–88, 495–97, 515–19; Rufus King to James Madison, July 20, 1788; 9 Madison Papers, 83, LC; 8 Burnett, 763; 241 Papers of G. W., 57; Madison to his father, July 27, 1788, 9 Madison Papers, 91, LC). The details are given in Matteson, op. cit., 144 ff. Washington thought that the choice of a permanent seat of government would be contested vehemently but he did not consider the selection of a temporary meeting place a matter that deserved the time spent in debate and parliamentary maneuver. The decision rested, in his opinion, between Philadelphia and New York, with the stronger case for Philadelphia. See 30 G. W., 32, 52, 53, 83, 91, 95, 99, 100.
[74] 34 JCC., 521–23; Madison to Washington, Sept. 14, 1788, in 8 Burnett, 795. See, also, H. Lee in 241 Papers of G. W., 90, anticipated in S. Powel to Washington, Sept. 9, 1788, ibid., 87. Congress had moved to New York after adjournment at Trenton, Dec. 24, 1784. Delegates had reassembled at their new headquarters on the 11th of January, 1785, and by the 17th had arrived in sufficient number for Congress to organize (27 JCC., 704; 28 ibid., 1, 5)

alists' plan might be to "get a Congress appointed in the first instance that [would] commit suicide on their own authority." [75] The surest way of preventing this was the one already advocated by Washington and others—to confront the Anti-Federalists boldly, to resist premature amendment, and to elect friends of the Constitution in sufficient number to control both Houses of Congress.[76] In Virginia, it soon was apparent that the choice of Senators by the General Assembly was completely under the control of Patrick Henry. He gave his endorsement to Richard Henry Lee and William Grayson, and assured their election over Madison, whom Henry denounced as "unworthy of the confidence of the people in the station of Senator." [77] Henry's antagonism did not end here. He probably was the author of an appeal by the Virginia Legislature to Congress for an immediate second convention to consider amendments; [78] he was alleged, also, to have said he would oppose all measures to organize the new Federal government, unless legislation was attended by proposals to amend the Constitution.[79] Henry was charged, further, with arranging the congressional districts in such a fashion that Madison's county of Orange was put with others so strongly Anti-Federalist that Madison would have the utmost difficulty in procuring election [80] to the House of Representatives, which, in reality, he preferred to the Senate. Madison took his senatorial defeat in good spirits and said frankly he would prefer the House to the Senate but would not electioneer to get there.[81] Washington was indignant, though, as always, he took care to distinguish between what he knew and what he heard: "The whole proceedings of the Assembly, it is said, may be summed up in one word, to wit, that the edicts of Mr. H— are enregistered with less opposition by the majority of that

[75] Letter of June 27, 1788, to Washington; 9 *Madison Papers*, 75, LC.

[76] 30 *G. W.*, 29, 62, 96, 100–01, 118, 147, 171; 4 *LTW.*, 235; cf. Edward Carrington to Madison, Oct. 19, 1788, 2 *Bancroft, His. Cons.*, 480, also in 2 *W. W. Henry*, 415.

[77] Henry Lee to Madison, Nov. 19, 1788, 10 *Madison Papers*, 50, LC. For this interesting and well-documented contest, which is not, properly speaking, a part of the biography of Washington, see Edward Carrington to Madison, Oct. 19, 1788 (2 *Bancroft, His. Cons.*, 480); same to same, Oct. 22, 1788 (10 *Madison Papers*, 26, LC); same to same, Nov. 9, 1788 (2 *Bancroft, His. Cons.*, 483); Joseph Jones to Madison, Oct. 20, 1788 (10 *Madison Papers*, 22); Edmund Randolph to Madison, Sept. 12, 1788 (*ibid.*, 4); same to same, Oct. 23, 1788 (*ibid.*, 28).

[78] Text in 2 *W. W. Henry*, 423–25.

[79] C. Lee to Washington, Oct. 29, 1788; 242 *Papers of G. W.*, 8, LC.

[80] Francis Corbin to Madison, Nov. 12, 1788, 10 *Madison Papers*, 46, LC; Tobias Lear to John Langdon, Jan. 31, 1789, 2 *Bancroft, His. Cons.*, 489; Edward Carrington to Madison, Nov. 15, 1788; 10 *Madison Papers*, 47, LC.

[81] Letter of Nov. 23, 1788; *ibid.*, 55.

body than those of the Grand Monarch are in the Parliaments of France. He has only to say, let this be law and it is law." [82] Throughout, in Washington's opinion, the Assembly displayed a "most malignant . . . most unwarrantable disposition toward the new government." [83] Virginia was divided into parties as hostile as if they had been piling up grievances or planning revenge for a generation. The old contention between the aristocratic junta and Henry's upcountrymen never had been as violent as this. Washington did not lead the new battle but he was in the midst of it, heart and soul, on the side of the Federalists. This was true, most emphatically, of his views on the Presidency. He suspected that an effort would be made to have an advocate of destructive amendment of the Constitution placed at the head of the government. In October he wrote of these adversaries, ". . . the seeming moderation by which they appear to be actuated at present is neither more nor less than a finesse to lull and deceive. Their plan of opposition is systematized . . ." [84] To this opinion he held, even though his informed political friends continued to assume that he would be chosen President as a matter of course [85] and their effort was not directed to winning electors but to gaining his consent to serve. "We cannot, Sir, do without you," wrote ex-Governor Thomas Johnson of Maryland, "and I and thousands more can explain to anyone but yourself why . . ." [86]

Washington's position remained substantially the same. He told Benjamin Lincoln: ". . . nothing in this world can ever draw me from [retirement], unless it be a *conviction* that the partiality of my countrymen had made my services absolutely necessary, joined to a *fear* that my refusal might induce a belief that I preferred the conservation of my own reputation and private ease to the good of my country. After all, if I should conceive myself in a manner constrained to accept, I call Heaven to witness that this very act would be the greatest sacrifice of my personal feelings and wishes that ever I have been called upon to make. It would be to forgo repose and domestic enjoyment for trouble,

[82] Letter of Nov. 17, 1788 to Madison; 30 *G. W.*, 131.
[83] Letter of Dec. 2, 1788; *ibid.*, 146.
[84] Letter of Oct. 3, 1788, to Alexander Hamilton; *ibid.*, 112.
[85] Madison to Jefferson, Oct. 8, 1788; 10 *Madison Papers*, 14, LC.
[86] Letter of Oct. 10, 1788; 9 *Sparks*, 438 n. The full text is in *Delaplaine*, op. cit., 459–60. See also A. Hamilton's incisive appeal of Nov. 18, 1788; 9 *A. Hamilton*, 453; 7 *Hamilton Papers*, 920, LC.

perhaps for public obloquy: for I should consider myself as entering upon an unexplored field, enveloped on every side with clouds and darkness." [87]

In this same letter, Washington expressed in odd circumstances a decision that marked a definite change in his attitude toward the presidency. Benjamin Lincoln and others had been working industriously and with political skill to have John Adams chosen as Vice President, and they sounded out Washington on his attitude toward the Massachusetts leader.[88] The General's answer was that Massachusetts might reasonably be expected to supply the Vice President. Any "true Federalist" who sufficiently enjoyed the confidence of faithful Americans to be named to that office, could not be "disagreeable" to the General. ". . . I would most certainly treat him," said Washington of this hypothetical Vice President, "with perfect sincerity and the greatest candor in every respect. I would give him my full confidence and use my utmost endeavors to cooperate with him, in promoting and rendering permanent the national prosperity; this should be my great, my only aim, under the fixed and irrevocable resolution of leaving to other hands the helm of the State, as soon as my services could possibly with propriety be dispensed with." [89]

There he stood: If he had to accept, he would hold the office no longer than manifest national need required. He had mentioned that possibility previously but he never had adopted it as his main line of defence. At the end of November, he still permitted himself to hope that he would not be elected and that, if he were, he might contrive to decline.[90] All the while, he showed in his letters that his reason did not sustain his hope. When he went over the familiar argument once again in a letter to Jonathan Trumbull during the first week of December, he confessed in bewilderment: ". . . I would fain do what is in all

[87] Letter of Oct. 26, 1788; 30 *G. W.*, 119.

[88] Lincoln to Washington, Sept. 24, 1788, 241 *Papers of G. W.*, 104–05, LC; same to same, Oct. 25, 1788, 242 *ibid.*, 3. Hamilton and Madison thought it well to have the Vice President from New England if the President was from Virginia, the only possible objection to Adams being his alleged unfriendliness to Washington. On this point, see Hamilton to Theodore Sedgwick, Oct. 9, 1788, 7 *Hamilton Papers*, 909, and printed in 9 *A. Hamilton*, 447; Madison to Jefferson, Oct. 17, 1788, 10 *Madison Papers*, 18, and printed in 5 *Hunt's Madison*, 270; Sedgwick to Hamilton, Oct. 16 and Nov. 2, 1788, 7 *Hamilton Papers*, 910–11, 912, LC; Madison to Jefferson, Oct. 8, 1788, 10 *Madison Papers*, 14, LC. By early November, Hamilton had come to the conclusion that Adams should be the man; Hamilton to Sedgwick, Nov. 9, 1788, 9 *A. Hamilton*, 452.

[89] Letter of Oct. 26, 1788; 30 *G. W.*, 121.      [90] *Ibid.*, 143.

respects best. But how can I know what is best, or on what I shall determine?" Then, with an emotion he seldom permitted himself to show, he cried, "May Heaven assist me in forming a judgment; for at present I see nothing but clouds and darkness before me." [91]

The country did not share his doubt and confusion. While public-minded friends continued to urge him to accept the Presidency,[92] the electors were chosen [93] on the assumption that they would cast their votes for Washington who would not refuse the duty. Where contests were staged, they were for seats in Congress. All the Senators elected in the seven States and reported by the second week in December were advocates of the Constitution or, at the least, could not be counted as Anti-Federalist,[94] except for the two from Virginia.[95] "The appointment of Senators, taken collectively," Washington wrote Henry Knox, "is certainly very happy." [96] No less encouraging, on the whole, was the outlook for a sympathetic House of Representatives.[97] Washington's chief concern was for the Representatives from his own State, where he thought the Federalists negligent [98] and the enemies of the Constitution united and vigorous, particularly in their effort to defeat James Madison with James Monroe. Fortunately, when the contest was hottest, Madison let it be known that as the Constitution had been ratified and would be put into effect, he thought needed amendments could and should be made. This announcement destroyed the chief basis of opposition and contributed to a victory for Madison on February 2 by a

91 Letter of Dec. 4, 1788; *ibid.*, 149.
92 Under date of Dec. 6, 1788, Gouverneur Morris wrote: "I have ever thought and said that you *must* be President; no other man can fill that office. No other man can draw forth the abilities of our country into the various departments of civil life . . ." 242 *Papers of G. W.*, 37, LC.
93 Electors of some States were named by voters at the polls; elsewhere the Legislature designated them or combined appointment and election; in New Jersey, the Governor and Council picked them (*Matteson*, 199).
94 Madison to Jefferson, Dec. 8, 1788; 10 *Madison Papers*, 62, LC.
95 For the varying reports that the Virginia Senators might have moderated their views and would give the new government a chance of proving its worth before they insisted on amendments, see 30 *G. W.*, 126, 173. Cf. 2 *Ballagh, Lee Letters*, 477–80.
96 30 *G. W.*, 173.
97 Benjamin Lincoln to Washington, Jan. 4, 1789 (242 *Papers of G. W.*, 55, LC); Tench Coxe to Madison, Jan. 27, 1789 (10 *Madison Papers*, 86, LC); 30 *G. W.*, 195. Samuel Powel, on the other hand, wrote Washington Jan. 6, 1789 (242 *Papers of G. W.*, 56, LC) that the Anti-Federalists in Pennsylvania still were doing all they could to defeat the Constitution. For the dates of the State elections to the House, which were held from Nov. 24–25, 1788 in South Carolina, to Mch. 3, 1789 in New York, see *Matteson*, op. cit., 159 ff. The final election in one disputed Massachusetts district was on May 11, 1789 (*ibid.*, 166–67).
98 30 *G. W.*, 146–47, 174.

majority of 336 votes in the district.[99] Somewhat to Washington's surprise,[100] though in accordance with the forecast of various observers,[101] five more Federalists, perhaps six, triumphed in the ten districts of Virginia.[102] News of the choice of Representatives in other States came slowly [103] but it continued to point to the election of a Congress willing and perhaps zealous to support the Constitution.[104]

Washington already had abandoned his position as a detached observer and he had committed himself to the Federalist cause in the belief that it was the only means of guaranteeing America a strong government under an adequate Constitution. Now he went even further because he still hoped that if he had to accept the Presidency, he could resign it as soon as he got the wheels of the new government spinning. Anti-Federalists still did not oppose Washington for President but they appeared to be concerting for the election of a man of their own political creed for second place in the Executive. The individual most often mentioned as their candidate for Vice President was George Clinton, to whom Washington was bound by many ties of wartime memory and of personal obligation. Washington had every impulse to remember Clinton's service and consideration, but he knew that Clinton sponsored the "New York circular" that demanded immediate and dangerous amendment of the Constitution. Clinton, or any man of like views, might seek, as Madison previously put it, to have the new government commit suicide. The most practical method of dealing with such a possibility was to make common cause with John Adams in whose candidacy for Vice President Washington had been increasingly

99 Henry Lee to Madison, Nov. 19, 1788 (10 *Madison Papers*, 50, LC); George Nicholas to Madison, Jan. 2, 1789 (*ibid.*, 80); Madison to Washington, Jan. 14, 1789 (*ibid.*, 83); Madison to George Eve, Jan. 2, 1789 (*ibid.*, 79); Henry Lee to Madison, Jan. 14, 1789 (*ibid.*, 84); Edmund Randolph to Madison, Mch. 27, 1789 (11 *ibid.*, 28); 4 *LTW.*, 244–45; 10 *Madison Papers*, 83; 3 *Brant*, 242, with a citation from the Diary of Francis Taylor, v. 4, entry of Feb. 2, 1789; *VSL*. Edward Carrington wrote Henry Knox Feb. 16, 1789, that he did not believe Madison could have been elected earlier. Madison, he said, had to face "every species of misrepresentation respecting both himself and the constitution." The outcome in Madison's district and in other parts of Virginia was a successful if temporary rebellion, Carrington thought, against Patrick Henry and a rebuke to the compliant Legislature. Said Carrington: "the measures of our Assembly have done great good to the Federal cause—the people discover the intemperance with which they are marked and this discovery leads them to reflect on the deceptions before practiced on them." (*Knox Papers*, MHS). For the Virginia law governing the House elections of 1789, see 12 *H* 653 ff.

100 Cf. 30 *G. W.*, 146, 194, 195.

101 *Ibid.*, 146; Tobias Lear to John Langdon, Jan. 31, 1789, 2 *Bancroft, His. Cons.*, 489.

102 30 *G. W.*, 219. The doubt concerning one member was due to the fact that he came from the Kentucky District and was of unknown political affiliation, though he was believed to be a supporter of the Constitution. *Ibid.*

103 *Ibid.*, 190–91, 194, 195.                     104 *Ibid.*, 184–85, 195.

pleased, though without any pledge on the General's part of public support.[105] Adams was a safe man to whom the Presidential office could be entrusted; no Anti-Federalist was. Quietly, therefore, Washington let it be known in Virginia and in Maryland that votes for Adams would be agreeable to him and seemed to him "the only certain way to prevent the election of an Anti-Federalist." Benjamin Lincoln, one of Adams's principal advocates, was informed of this.[106]

It now was the end of January, 1789. The electors already had been named and, on February 4, were to meet in designated cities of the ratifying States to cast their ballots for President and Vice President. A month after that the new Congress was expected to meet and formally to announce the names of the two men the electors had chosen. ". . . my difficulties increase and magnify," Washington confided to Lafayette, "as I draw towards the period when, according to the common belief, it will be necessary for me to give a definitive answer, in one way or another," and he repeated once again the statement of his reluctance to reenter public life.[107] Soon Washington began to receive, piecemeal, the news that the electors in the Eastern, Northern and Middle States had done the expected thing[108] and, to a man, had cast their votes for him as President. The fullest statement of the result that reached him was the oddest. Washington had read in an advertisement that "superfine American broadcloth" was on sale in New York and he had asked Henry Knox to buy him enough for a suit and a sufficient yardage, also, to make a riding-habit for Martha.[109] Delay was encountered because the cloth had to be sent from the factory; but on the 16th of February Knox wrote: "The cloths have not yet arrived although expected by the first wind. The moment they come to hand

---

[105] *Ibid.*, 174. Madison wrote Jefferson, Dec. 8, 1788 (10 *Madison Papers,* 62, LC) that Adams was "pledged to support" Washington. See, also, Knox to Washington, Dec. 21, 1788, *Knox Papers,* MHS.

[106] 30 *G. W.*, 190. Henry Knox, another influential figure in Massachusetts, was assured some weeks later that Washington was pleased to hear "the votes have run in favor of Mr. Adams" (Letter of Mch. 2, 1789; *ibid.*, 219). The maneuvers to procure a suitable vote for Adams were an interesting example of the quick adaptation to Federal affairs of the methods the politicians had used in New England and in New York. There seems to have been the closest cooperation between Jere. Wadsworth of Connecticut and Alexander Hamilton, who apparently was directing operations jointly for Washington and for Adams. See Wadsworth to Hamilton, Feb., n.d., 1789: "Your favor of the 25th. January came in good time—our votes were given agreeably to your wishes: Washington, 7; Adams, 5; Governor Huntington, 2 . . ." (7 *Hamilton Papers,* 942, LC).

[107] 30 *G. W.*, 185.

[108] Noah Webster to James Greenleaf, Feb. 15, 1789, Ford, *Notes on Life of Noah Webster,* v. 1, p. 198; Henry Jackson to Henry Knox, Mch. 1, 1789, *Knox Papers,* MHS.

[109] 30 *G. W.*, 183-84.

I will forward those for you and Mrs. Washington." Then, with no ado or transitional sentence Knox proceeded in this "of-course" and casual statement: "It appears by the returns of elections hitherto obtained, which is as far as Maryland southward, that your Excellency has every vote for President and Mr. John Adams twenty-eight for Vice-President exclusive of New Jersey and Delaware, whose votes for Vice [President] are not known." [110]

When Virginia's vote was added to those reported by Knox, the result was beyond change by anything South Carolina and Georgia might do. Washington had been elected and, so far, unanimously! Even Patrick Henry, as a Virginia elector, had voted for him.[111] The agonizing question had to be answered: Must he accept, at least for the time required to bring the new government into peaceful operation? Was there no alternative, no escape?

Most of Washington's correspondents assumed that he could not resist so overwhelming an appeal. A British merchant who was returning home set forth one of the most alarming reasons for acceptance. Said he: ". . . I am satisfied you cannot resist the unanimous wish of United America, especially if you could be brought to think, as all other good men do, that the happiness and prosperity of the thirteen United States depend on your acceptance of the President's chair." Then the merchant wrote these solemn, deferential words: "Allow me to add that it is the general opinion of the friends to the new government that if you decline being at the head of it, it never can or will take effect." [112]

This, in all probability, was an exaggeration. The government doubtless could be brought into operation if Washington declined . . . but was there danger that all the misery of the Revolutionary War would have been endured for naught, and that the vigorous new Constitution would be stripped of the essential articles on taxation and effective control of commerce and trade? Would the Congress lapse again into impotence and public contempt, until the Union fell apart and thirteen feeble States separately faced conquest or bankruptcy? If there was even a chance that this might happen, then . . .

Washington had not yet said "Yes" and he did not intend to make

110 242 *Papers of G. W.*, 78, LC.
111 George Clinton received Henry's vote for Vice President (2 *W. W. Henry*, 441).
112 Alexander Donald, then in Richmond, Virginia, to Washington, Feb. 28, 1789; *Thom Collection*, Mount Vernon.

any public announcement until the electors' votes had been counted officially and he had been notified of the result. All his private references to the unhappy subject still hung on an "if," but he had, of course, to make preparations, financial and other, in event he was to be absent from Mount Vernon for a long period of time. He would need £500 or £600 to pay pressing debts and the expenses of a journey to New York. On the very day the wheels of the new government were supposed to turn for the first time, March 4, Washington applied for a loan from a wealthy citizen of Alexandria and offered security and 6 per cent interest.[113]

Three days later, Washington made what he told himself probably would be his final visit to his mother, the "last act of personal duty," as he termed it, "I may (from her age) ever have it in my power to pay [her]."[114] She still was at Fredericksburg, about 80 years of age[115] and in what appeared to be the fatal stage of long suffering from a slowly devouring cancer of the breast. Washington found her in the little house he had provided for her, not far from the rear of Kenmore, the home of her daughter Betty Lewis.[116] It was part of the independent nature of Mary Washington to live in her own establishment and to dress, eat, sleep and manage her servants in her own way, even though her daughter, like her son, was willing to do everything possible for her. Washington knew his mother's habits, but he did not know how fixed they were. Two years previously, on one of the occasions when her demands on him for money had been particularly embarrassing, he had urged that she "break up housekeeping" and live with one of her children. In the same letter he had said frankly that he did not believe residence at Mount Vernon would ever "answer [her] purposes in any shape whatsoever."[117] The house was "to be compared to a well resorted tavern, as scarcely any strangers who are going from North to South, or from South to North, do not spend a day or two at it."[118] If she lived there, he said, she would always have to be dressed for company, or appear in dishabille, or remain in her room—none of which

---

[113] Letters to Richard Conway, 30 *G. W.*, 220–21, 222–23. The 4th of March was a day of rejoicing among the Federalists, particularly in Boston. See Henry Jackson to Henry Knox, Mch. 7, 1789, *Knox Papers*, MHS.

[114] 30 *G. W.*, 222.

[115] The date of her birth is not known but probably was in the winter of 1708–09. See Vol. I, p. 43 n.

[116] Vol. III, p. 297.

[117] Letter of Feb. 15, 1787; 29 *G. W.*, 160–61.

[118] See *supra*, p. 34.

arrangements would be agreeable. "Nor, indeed," he said, "could you be retired in any room in my house; for what with the sitting up of company, the noise and bustle of servants, and many other things, you would not be able to enjoy that calmness and serenity of mind, which in my opinion you ought now to prefer to every other consideration in life."[119] She read this, no doubt, and perhaps had pondered it but she had remained where she was, and there, manifestly, she would die, probably while her son was discharging in New York the duties of his Presidential office. He and she would have no more disputes over rents due her; an end would be set to painful protests by her first-born that she was taking both rent and the farm products from the sale of which the rent was to be raised. On money matters, mother and son never had agreed; now the only subject of likely contention would be, possibly, her last will and testament. He owed her more, perhaps, than he had realized—his physical endurance, his resolution, his ambition to make his own way. Quiet words, then, at her bedside, a smile, a clasping of hands and peaceful preparation for the Great Silence that soon was to fall.[120]

Back at Mount Vernon, Washington probably began, about this time, to formulate in his mind the instructions he was to give his nephew, George Augustine Washington, for the management of his farms in his absence.[121] This was a troublesome labor and it had to be discharged when he painfully was answering the applications of those who assumed he would take office and would have vast patronage to dispense at pleasure.[122] Sadly he wrote Samuel Vaughan, to whose son he knew he could not offer a desired post: ". . . from the moment when the necessity [of accepting the Presidency] had become more apparent and, as it were, inevitable, I anticipated in a heart filled with distress, the ten thousand embarrassments, perplexities and troubles to which I must again be exposed in the evening of a life already nearly consumed in public cares. Among all these anxieties . . . I anticipated

---

119 29 G. W., 161.

120 A report of Mch. 12, 1789, from Fredericksburg, printed in the Pennsylvania Packet of the 24th, p. 3, stated that Washington arrived Saturday evening, March 7, and left Monday morning, March 9. This may have been the correct chronology, but a long, careful letter to Benjamin Harrison in 30 G. W., 223, is dated Mount Vernon, March 9, and scarcely seems the sort of communication a tired man could have written at the end of a day's hard journey.

121 These instructions were completed, in writing, by the end of March. See ibid., 256–60. He may likewise have started work on the recommendations he would present to Congress. For these, see infra, p. 188, 30 G. W., 176, 203, and 3 Brant, 242–43.

122 Cf. 30 G. W., 238.

none greater than those that were likely to be produced by applications for appointments . . . my apprehensions have already been but too well justified." [123] Once, in the spring of 1787, the General had talked of buying a slave bricklayer, but when the Negro was made unhappy by the prospect of living at a distance from his wife, Washington had changed purchase to hire with the statement, "I am unwilling to hurt the feelings of anyone." [124] Now, when there might be no more than one position for a hundred applicants,[125] the dreams of many an impoverished former soldier would be shattered and the ambitions of faithful lieutenants frustrated, because their old commander had to say "No." Deliberately and conscientiously he laid down seven rules for his guidance, though he never formulated or phrased them in specific order:

1. He would take office free of all advance commitments, to the end that he could "act with a sole reference to justice and the public good" when he considered the applications of different men.[126] This was dictated by regard for his own reputation as well as by the interest of the community.[127]

2. He would not permit himself to be affected in public affairs by his private inclinations but in his personal relations he felt he should be "indulged in the continuance of his former attachments." [128]

3. "Connections of blood or friendship" must not "have the least sway on decisions of a public nature." [129]

4. "Due regard" should be had "to the fitness of characters, the pretensions of different candidates and, so far as is proper, to political considerations." [130]

5. "I conceive . . . it will be found no pleasant thing, possibly very much the reverse, to displace one man, under these circumstances of actual occupancy, merely to make room for another, however considerable his abilities or unimpeached his integrity may appear in the public eye." [131]

---

[123] *Ibid.*, 238. Cf. *ibid.*, 240. The senior Vaughan had given Washington the handsome chimney piece for the "new room" (27 *ibid.*, 390, 425; 28 *ibid.*, 63). For the General's sense of obligation to Vaughan, see 29 *ibid.*, 6–7.
[124] Letter of Apr. 10, 1787, to John Lawson; 29 *ibid.*, 199.
[125] 30 *ibid.*, 239.      [126] *Ibid.*, 221.
[127] *Ibid.*, 228.      [128] *Ibid.*, 222.
[129] *Ibid.*, 224.
[130] *Ibid.*, 225. At the time he wrote this, Mch. 9, 1789, he did not define "political considerations."
[131] *Ibid.*, repunctuated.

6. Appointments should be distributed "(so far as that matter might be conveniently arranged) among inhabitants of the various States in the Union." [132]

7. "There are some . . . who have shed their blood and deserved all that a grateful country has to bestow. Nor are they, in my judgment, incapable of reflecting lustre on the most dignified stations." [133]

The hour was approaching when Washington would know officially that he had been sentenced by the electors to apply these rules. Congress had been expected to assemble in New York on the 4th of March, and, at a time of its choice, to have the certificates of the electors opened and counted by a temporary President of the Senate, chosen for that purpose. Actually, as Washington learned from newspapers and from a letter of Henry Knox's,[134] eight Senators only and no more than seventeen Representatives had made their appearance by the 5th.[135] Frequent letters thereafter, long delayed by mud and bad weather,[136] told of a disappointingly slow increase in the number of Representatives and Senators in attendance.[137] Washington went on with his preparations, as careful of detail as he was unhappy at heart.[138] More March days passed. On the farms,[139] the workers were sowing and har-

---

132 *Ibid.*, 236.               133 *Ibid.*, 240.

134 Dated Mch. 5, 1789; 242 *Papers of G. W.*, 91, LC. It is almost impossible to determine at this period precisely when Washington received at Mount Vernon some letters of known date, written in New York. As noted in the text, the roads were exceedingly bad, the post was slow and uncertain. Madison's letter of March 19 was not acknowledged by Washington until the 30th (30 *G. W.*, 254); on the other hand, Knox's of March 23 reached Mount Vernon on the 30th (*ibid.*, 268).

135 On the 4th, according to the Journals, the number had been: Senators, eight; Representatives, thirteen.

136 Knox to Washington, Mch. 19, 1789; 242 *Papers of G. W.*, 109, LC.

137 Knox to Washington, Mch. 23, 1789; *Knox Papers*, MHS.

138 He considered the employment of his nephew, Robert Lewis, to record his letters (30 *G. W.*, 228); he tried to clear his account with Thomas Newton, Jr., of Norfolk, Virginia, for fish and flour sold through that agent (*Ledger B*, f. 85) and he gratefully but firmly declined George Clinton's fine and friendly invitation of March 10 (242 *Papers of G. W.*, 97, LC) to use the Governor's house when he came to New York to discharge the duties of President. Carefully, as always, he laid down the proviso of his journey—". . . if it should be my lot (for Heaven knows it is not my wish) to appear again in a public station"—and then he explained that he would take lodgings "Because it would be wrong, in my real judgment, to impose such a burden on any private family as must unavoidably be occasioned by my company . . ." (30 *G. W.*, 251). To Madison he explained that he would go to a tavern if lodgings could not be found, and that he was "not desirous of being placed *early* in a situation for entertaining" (*ibid.*, 255), one of the few occasions on which he ever wrote anything which could be interpreted to mean that his financial conditions restricted his hospitality.

139 No Diary of Washington's period Feb. 3–Sept. 30, 1789, is in any known collection, though one was kept for at least a part of this time (see 4 *Diaries*, 6 n). Previous journals show this to have been the season for these particular labors.

rowing oats, barley and grass seed; the General sadly continued his efforts to put his affairs in order at Mount Vernon,[140] and by one act, in particular, he tacitly admitted that he despaired of finding any way of escaping the Presidency: Early in April he dispatched his secretary, Tobias Lear, and his body servant, Will, to New York. Still there was no report of a quorum for the organization of Congress,[141] a delay that might be considered, he said, a reprieve for him. Resolutely he wrote: ". . . in confidence I assure you, with the world it would obtain little credit, that my movements to the chair of government will be accompanied by feelings not unlike those of a culprit who is going to the place of his execution, so unwilling am I, in the evening of a life nearly consumed in public cares, to quit a peaceful abode for an ocean of difficulties, without that competency of political skill, abilities and inclination which is necessary to manage the helm." [142]

Probably on the 10th of April, when the General was busier than ever with his personal affairs,[143] an anxiously awaited regular post brought news that the House of Representatives had a quorum on the 1st and had organized.[144] Perhaps by the 13th, Washington learned that the count of the electors' ballots might have been made on the

[140] As noted, his detailed instructions to George Augustine Washington bear date of Mch. 31, 1789 (30 *G. W.*, 256 ff). Those to Thomas Greene, head carpenter, and to the chief overseer, John Fairfax, were drafted at approximately the same time (*ibid.*, 260). Much ink and effort were expended by Washington in trying to collect money due him, and in renewing matured and unpaid bonds of his debtors. Precisely as when he left home in 1775, he had to wrestle with the affairs of Mrs. William Savage, though the unfortunate woman was dead by this time. The Colville estate, also, was still almost as much of a vexation as it had been fourteen years previously (*ibid.*, 275). Washington had embarrassment, too, in his farm operations because of the non-receipt of grass seed ordered from New York and shipped via Baltimore (*ibid.*, 278–79). A most unusual duty was that of telling William Hartshorne, a well-known Quaker merchant of Alexandria, that he did not think he could intervene to prevent the illumination of Philadelphia on his arrival there. Hartshorne had written that Friends in the Pennsylvania city were fearful the celebration might draw together a mob that would seize the town (*ibid.*, 266).

[141] Knox to Washington, Mch. 30, 1789; *Knox Papers*, MHS, acknowledged Apr. 10, 1789 (30 *G. W.*, 280). The Secretary remarked that the delay in the assembly of Congress already had cost the new government the spring imposts, estimated at £300,000. Washington confessed himself humiliated and alarmed by the apparent indifference of members to the fulfilment of their obligation to be on time (*Ibid.* Cf. *Matteson*, 231).

[142] Letter of Apr. 1, 1789, to Henry Knox, 30 *G. W.*, 268.

[143] *Ibid.*, 281 ff.

[144] Knox to Washington, Apr. 2, 1789; 243 *Papers of G. W.*, 3, LC. This letter bears no endorsement of the date of receipt but it should have been in the mail of the 10th. The *Federal Gazette* (Philadelphia), which Washington did not see often, contained in its issue of April 4 (p. 3), an announcement that the "House of Commons" had a quorum on the 1st. The *Independent Gazetteer* (p. 2) and the *Pennsylvania Packet* (p. 2) reported on Monday, the 6th, that the House was ready to transact business. If this was known in Philadelphia on the 4th, it should have been transmitted to Mount Vernon by the 10th.

6th,[145] but he did not know officially whether this had been done or whether, as stated many times in advance, the poll for him had been unanimous. He wrote two letters that day and doubtless thought of the form of a certain document he regretfully had prepared in answer to the inevitable spokesman of the people. On the 14th of April, about noon, a clatter of hoofs and the sound of an unfamiliar voice told him that a guest had arrived. When he went to the door and recognized the visitor as the old patriot Charles Thomson, Secretary of Congress, he knew what to expect: Henry Knox had written in his letter of the 2nd: "Mr. Thomson will set off to announce to the President the unanimous choice of the people of the United States as soon as the votes shall be opened and counted." [146]

The axe had fallen. Thomson exchanged greetings and compliments [147] and then addressed Washington:

Sir,

The president of the Senate chosen for the special occasion having opened and counted the votes of the Election in the presence of the Senate and House of Representatives, I was honored with the commands of the Senate to wait upon your Excellency with the information of your being elected to the office of President of the United States of America. This commission was intrusted to me on account of my long being in the confidence of the late Congress and charged with the duties of one of the principal civil departments of government. I have now, sir, to inform you that the proofs you have given of your patriotism and of your readiness to sacrifice domestic separation and private enjoyments to preserve the liberty and promote the happiness of your country did not permit the two Houses to harbour a doubt of your undertaking this great, this important office to which you are called not only by the unanimous vote of the electors, but by the voice of America, I have it therefore in command to accompany you to New York where the Senate and House of Representatives are convened for the dispatch of public business. In executing this part of the commission where personal gratification coincides with duty I shall wait your time and be wholly governed by your convenience . . .[148]

---

[145] Madison to Washington, Apr. 6, 1789, 11 *Madison Papers*, 34, LC, date of receipt not known. First news of this in Philadelphia papers was published on the 8th by the *Federal Gazette*, p. 2.

[146] 243 *Papers of G. W.*, 3, LC.

[147] Thomson to John Langdon, Apr. 14, 1789; 21 *Early N. H. State Papers*, 865–66.

[148] *Ibid.*, with some change of capitalization. The original of this famous document is in 243 *Papers of G. W.*, 19, LC.

Then Thomson read the formal notification:

Sir, I have the honor to transmit to your Excellency the information of your unanimous election to the Office of President of the United States of America. Suffer me, Sir, to indulge the hope, that so auspicious a mark of public confidence will meet your approbation, and be considered as a sure pledge of the affection and support you are to expect from a free and an enlightened people.

I am, Sir, with Sentiments of Respect,
                          Your obedient humble servant,
                                              JOHN LANGDON [149]

The General was prepared. From his pocket or from a table he took a paper he had made ready for the occasion.[150]

Sir, I have been long accustomed to entertain so great a respect for the opinion of my fellow-citizens, that the knowledge of their unanimous suffrages having been given in my favor, scarcely leaves me the alternative for an option. Whatever may have been my private feelings and sentiments, I believe I cannot give a greater evidence of my sensibility for the honor they have done me, than by accepting the appointment.

I am so much affected by this fresh proof of my country's esteem and confidence, that silence can best explain my gratitude—while I realize the arduous nature of the task which is conferred on me, and feel my inability to perform it, I wish there may not be reason for regretting the choice. All I can promise is, only that which can be accomplished by an honest zeal.

Upon considering how long time some of the gentlemen of both Houses of Congress have been at New York, how anxiously desirous they must be to proceed to business, and how deeply the public mind appears to be impressed with the necessity of doing it immediately, I cannot find myself at liberty to delay my journey. I shall therefore be in readiness to set out the day after tomorrow, and shall be happy in the pleasure of your company; for you will permit me to say that it was a peculiar gratification to have received the communication from you.[151]

[149] Letter of Apr. 6, 1789; *ibid.*, 13.

[150] See *supra*, p. 164. Thomson wrote Langdon, Apr. 14, 1789, from Mount Vernon that the President made a short reply and "concluded informing me that he would be ready to set out the day after tomorrow . . ." This would seem to identify the paper as the one that follows. There remains a possibility that Washington made a brief statement and subsequently that day wrote Thomson in letter form what here is presented as a verbal statement read to the Secretary.

[151] Thomson to the President of the Senate, Apr. 24, 1789; *American State Papers*, cited hereafter as *ASP., Misc.*, v. 1, p. 5–6. A different version, from Washington's Letter Book, appears in 30 *G. W.*, 285–86. The principal variation is in the second sentence, from which, in the Letter Book, has been stricken the clause, "Whatever may have been my private feelings and sentiments."

That was the end of formalities. Washington prepared a brief conventional letter to President Langdon in which he said he had "concluded to obey the important and flattering call of my country . . ." Then he repeated substantially what he already had told Thomson,[152] and, with his usual thoroughness, he completed his arrangements for departure. On the morning of the 16th of April about 10 o'clock he entered his carriage with Thomson and Humphreys. Not a word that he spoke and not a glance that he gave his beloved fields was recorded by either of his companions. His own reflections were confided to his diary: "I bade adieu to Mount Vernon, to private life, and to domestic felicity, and with a mind oppressed with more anxious and painful sensations than I have words to express, set out for New York . . . With the best disposition to render service to my country in obedience to its call, but with less hope of answering its expectations." [153]

At Alexandria, citizens gave him a dinner. Thirteen toasts were drunk and a most affectionate, laudatory address was delivered by Mayor Dennis Ramsay.[154] In his peroration Ramsay said: "Farewell!— Go and make a grateful people happy, a people who will be doubly grateful when they contemplate this recent sacrifice for their interest. To that Being, who maketh and unmaketh at His will, we commend you; and, after the accomplishment of the arduous business to which you are called, may He restore to us again the best of men and the most beloved fellow-citizen." [155] Washington's reply was a cordial and candid statement of the struggle through which he had passed in deciding whether he would accept or decline the Presidency. ". . . words, my fellow-citizens fail me!" he said at the last: "Unutterable sensations must then be left to more expressive silence: while, from an aching heart, I bid you all, my affectionate friends and kind neighbors, farewell!" [156]

[152] 30 *G. W.*, 284–85.　　　　　[153] Lost Diary quoted in 10 *Sparks*, 461.

[154] The report of this first welcome on the journey northward was printed widely in numerous papers. See Frank Monaghan, *Notes on the Inaugural Journey and the Inaugural Ceremonies of George Washington as First President of the United States*, cited hereafter as *Monaghan*, 8–9. This is a mimeographed publication of material collected for the New York's World's Fair of 1939.

[155] *Monaghan*, 9.　　　　　[156] 30 *G. W.*, 287, punctuation unchanged.

# CHAPTER VII

## "WELL, HE DESERVES IT ALL"
## (April 17–23, 1789)

THE EVENTS that followed Washington's leave-taking at Alexandria offered the happiest possible contrast to his own gloomy foreboding. Everywhere the welcome was warm and the auguries favorable. Some of his hosts at the farewell dinner at Wise's Tavern crossed the Potomac with him and his carriage on the ferry boats sent from Georgetown [1] and they shared the reception given by the Maryland community. As soon as the General could depart without offending the people who sought to do him honor, he climbed back into his vehicle, and, in the company of Charles Thomson and Col. David Humphreys, started on the long, rumbling ride northward [2] over the familiar road of his life's greatest adventures. His escort on the first leg of the journey proved to be what such guards of honor usually were, a hindrance to swift passage, but, of course, there could be no denial of the privilege the friendly Marylanders asked, that of seeing their neighbor on his way. [3] When twilight overtook the travelers, after the gentlemen from George-town had said farewell, the most convenient resting place for the night was Spurrier's Tavern, approximately twelve and a half miles South of Baltimore. Spurrier's was a familiar resort, with which Washing-ton's most memorable associations had been those of the southward press of the Army in September, 1781; [4] but, for the usual reason, he now had little pleasure in the place or in the memories it revived. Always, when he was on the road, he put himself under strain to cover the maximum distance possible on a given day, because time in the saddle, spent otherwise than on business or needed exercise, seemed to

---

[1] *Times, and Patowmack Packet* (Georgetown), Apr. 23, 1789, p. 3.
[2] The most useful authorities on the events of Apr. 17–23, 1789, are *Monaghan*, and W. S. Baker, *Washington After the Revolution, 1784–1799*, hereafter cited as *Baker*.
[3] This body of mounted citizens was under William Deakins, Jr., Georgetown merchant and militia Colonel.
[4] Vol. V., p. 325; 23 *G. W.*, 108 n.

him to be wasted. Now he had a longer whip for his lead horses: Congress was waiting for him; some of its most conscientious members had been in vain attendance since the 4th of March; he must hurry on so that he would put no further shackle of delay on their procedure. He resolved that he would start every morning at sunrise, if possible, and would travel the entire day.[5] Ceremonies were of course to be expected—and within the bounds of modesty to be enjoyed—but they must be kept as brief as possible. If he could mount and get off in the early morning, he might save, at the least, the time spent in forming and moving an escort. Immediately ahead was a test of these arrangements at Baltimore. Otho Williams, former Brigadier, wrote to say that "a number of respectable inhabitants" wished to welcome the General. Most thoughtfully this officer who had commanded the First Maryland Infantry wrote Washington: "To avoid as much as possible every circumstance which might occasion delay or solicit too much of Your Excellency's attention, the gentlemen will move in files and on meeting you, will open to the right and left. And if Your Excellency will please to pass through, they will wheel into the rear and follow your suite to town. The gentlemen also propose to have the honor of conducting Your Excellency out of town." [6]

On to Baltimore, then,[7] to a welcoming salute on the afternoon of the 17th by its artillery, and to a supper at Fountain Inn.[8] After the meal, Washington was presented an address to which some cherished "fighting names" were attached. Besides that of Williams himself, who had been captured in the disaster at Fort Washington, the document carried the signature of Washington's friend and aide, James McHenry, and the autograph of Capt. Paul Bentalou, of the First Cavalry, Pulaski's Legion. Still another signer was Capt. Joshua Barney of the Navy, hero of the famous action between *Hyder-Ally* and *General Monk* in April, 1782. Nicholas Rogers also shared this written welcome, Rogers who had served with du Coudray and with de Kalb.[9] To read these names and to see the men themselves was to relive dark

[5] Charles Thomson to the President of the Senate, Apr. 24, 1789; *ASP.*, 1 *Misc.*, 5–6.

[6] Letter of Apr. 17, 1789; 243 *Papers of G. W.*, 21, LC.

[7] *Times, and Patowmack Packet*, Apr. 23, 1789, p. 3, stated that Maryland escort met Washington at Spurrier's Tavern, but no confirmation of this statement has been found.

[8] Often called Grant's Tavern. For a history of this famous hostelry, see Matthew Page Andrews, *The Fountain Inn Diary* (New York, 1948). Washington must have been compelled to wait somewhere on the road, else he would have arrived earlier in Baltimore.

[9] Rogers was born in Baltimore and was the owner of the Druid Hill estate. See *Baltimore, Its History and Its People*, v. 3, p. 833.

days with hope confirmed. ". . . we behold," the address said, "a new era springing out of our independence, and a field displayed where your talents for governing will not be obscured by the splendor of the greatest military exploits." The committee added this observation, which had large meaning: "We behold, too, an extraordinary thing in the annals of mankind; a free and enlightened people, choosing, by a free election, without one dissenting voice, the late Commander-in-Chief of their armies to watch over and guard their civil rights and privileges." [10] Washington's reply was in the same spirit: "It appears to me that little more than common sense and common honesty in the transactions of the community at large, would be necessary to make us a great and a happy nation. For if the general government, lately adopted, shall be arranged and administered in such a manner as to acquire the full confidence of the American people, I sincerely believe they will have greater advantages from their natural moral and political circumstances, for public felicity, than any other people ever possessed." [11] At the supper he said nothing of old soldiers and faithful civil servants to suggest it, but the address and the answer were fulfilment of the hope he had voiced and the pledge he had made in New York, almost fourteen years previously, on his way to Cambridge to take command: "When we assumed the soldier, we did not lay aside the citizen; and we shall most sincerely rejoice with you in that happy hour when the establishment of American liberty, upon the most firm and solid foundations, shall enable us to return to our private stations in the bosom of a free, peaceful and happy country." [12]

Washington retired at ten o'clock, was in his coach at 5:30 the next morning, April 18th, and, with the roaring "goodbye" of the volunteers' cannon, left Baltimore for Wilmington.[13] For seven miles of this long journey, until he alighted and insisted that they turn back, he had the company of some of Baltimore's best.[14] An unsensational two-day

[10] *Monaghan*, 13. Some accounts leave the impression that two addresses were delivered Washington in Baltimore but this seems to have been due to a confusion over the terms "citizens" and "burgesses" used in the address. Only one document, with the reply, appears in the first MS volume of Washington's "Addresses and Answers," 334 *Papers of G. W.*, 3–4. This Letter Book original does differ from Monaghan's version of the address in two or three words.

[11] 30 *G. W.*, 288.

[12] Vol. III, p. 470; 3 *G. W.*, 305.

[13] *Maryland Journal* (Baltimore), Apr. 21, 1787, p. 2.

[14] *Baker*, 123, with quotation from the *Pennsylvania Packet* of Apr. 28, 1789. Washington's halting place for the night of the 18th–19th is not known. If he "split the distance" between Baltimore and Wilmington, he stopped in the vicinity of Havre de Grace. Lodging was available at the town and probably at the ferry house on the opposite side of the river. See 3

journey through a thinly settled country brought him to the Delaware port Sunday evening, the 19th,[15] for a needed quiet night's rest in reminiscent contrast to the anxious hours of darkness he had endured in September, 1777, when he had been encamped on the left bank of the Brandywine, not far from the town.[16] To what depths the fortunes of America had fallen then, when nothing had sufficed to halt the steady, confident advance of Howe's Brigades on Philadelphia, the city that now was bestirring itself to welcome Howe's adversary!

On the morning of the 20th, the Burgesses and Common Council of Wilmington presented officially an address which Washington and Humphreys had seen informally long enough before the ceremonies to prepare a suitable answer. The theme was one already becoming a bit tedious—the call of the country for the General to head the new government and his acceptance of the summons in spite of a deep desire to continue in the retirement he had hoped to enjoy to the end of his days.[17] When these felicitations had been exchanged, the coach was started for Philadelphia, again with a mounted escort of gentlemen, honorable but hampering. At the Pennsylvania boundary line, a new guard appeared. Representatives of Delaware, with the warm thanks of Washington, entrusted him and his vehicle to Philadelphians, some of whom had come down the previous evening in expectation that the General would arrive then.[18] Most of the men at the head of the column were veterans of the Revolution, either as soldiers or civilian officials. Among them were two long-time members of the Board of War, Thomas Mifflin, now President of the Supreme Executive Council of Pennsylvania, and Richard Peters, who had become Speaker of

---

*Diaries*, 215, 238. He doubtless "baited," that is, fed and watered his horses on the 18th at Skerritt's Tavern, twelve miles north of Baltimore. See also Journal of William Loughton Smith, 51 *MHSP.*, 58–59, for description of Havre de Grace.

[15] It is traditional that citizens of Wilmington wished to illuminate their homes and stores on his arrival, but as the 19th was the Sabbath, they refrained. The only decoration was of a ship in the river (*Monaghan*, 15). There is a possibility that this incident occurred at Philadelphia and that it was related to the previous protest of the Quakers and not to the observance of the Sabbath. In any event, reference was made in the *Pennsylvania Journal* (Philadelphia), Apr. 22, 1789, p. 3, to the illumination of a ship precisely in the manner attributed to the observance at Wilmington.

[16] Vol. IV, p. 472–73.

[17] Text in *Monaghan*, 16–18; probably after the copies in 334 *Papers of G. W.*, 5–6. The Delaware Society for Promoting Domestic Manufactures also presented an address to which Washington replied (*ibid.*, 7–8). All these papers are dated April 19.

[18] The *Federal Gazette* of April 22, p. 2, the *Pennsylvania Packet* of the 24th, p. 3, and *Freeman's Journal* (all of Philadelphia) of Apr. 29, 1789. each printed an extract of a letter by "a gentleman in Philadelphia" to his nephew "in the country." This is the most comprehensive account of the day's events now extant.

the Pennsylvania Assembly. Washington greeted this delegation, along with the City Troops of Horse, and in their company, he made the best time he could to Chester. His arrival there was at the disconcerting hour of 7 A.M., but most of the veterans were in the streets or at the inn where the General had breakfast, spent a couple of hours,[19] and listened to a polite, brief address.[20] Apparently he was not given a copy of this in advance and consequently was compelled to reply extemporaneously in a few grateful words.

The men who had come out from Philadelphia must have brought with them a finely caparisoned white horse for the General,[21] and acceptable mounts for Humphreys and Secretary Thomson. These animals were provided in order that Washington might be seen by everyone when he entered Philadelphia and not remain half hidden from public view in his coach. He obediently went to the head of a column that steadily was growing longer, and from Chester he took the familiar road to the Lower Ferry Bridge across the Schuylkill. It was not long before Washington's party came face to face with more mounted Philadelphians, this band led by General Arthur St. Clair, who had come out from the city to join the welcoming procession. The horsemen fell in, and roadside spectators increased constantly in number until, at once, there was in sight the bridge at Gray's Ferry. Then he beheld what the bridge owners, the Brothers Gray,[22] had planned as a surprise for him and, doubtless, as an advertisement for the crossing.[23] With the help of Charles Willson Peale they had adorned amazingly the unstable structure. At each end of the bridge was an arch of laurel; the sides were lined with more of that shrub and with cedar. The ferry boat and the ferry barge were anchored in the stream. All the approaches were graced with large flags—one that proclaimed "The New Era," another that portrayed the rising sun of empire, a white standard

[19] Philadelphia papers, as cited *supra*, p. 170. See also *Monaghan*, 23–24, for a detailed list of some of those Henry G. Ashmead mentioned in "The Chester Washington Knew" as present at the brief reception.

[20] Text in *Monaghan*, 25.

[21] *Independent Gazetteer* (Philadelphia), April 21, p. 3.

[22] Gray's Garden, or Gray's Ferry, became a popular resort soon after the Revolution. The proprietors, G. and R. Gray, patterned it after the public gardens in London, with "shaded walks, beautiful flowers, artistic decorations" and "refreshments of every kind." The city poets often were inspired to write verses about it which were printed in the "Poets' Corner" of the *Columbian Magazine*. (J. Thomas Scharf and Thompson Westcott, *History of Philadelphia, 1609–1884*, v. 2, p. 492.)

[23] The history of these bridges over the Schuylkill is sketched in Scharf and Westcott, *op. cit.*, v. 3, p. 2141.

with the motto, "May Commerce Flourish," and a fourth under a tremendous Liberty cap, with the familiar warning, "Don't Tread on Me." Along the north side of the bridge were banners for each of the eleven States that had ratified the Constitution; on the south side, midway the crossing, the flag of the American Union rode high. Such a scene it was, an observer wrote in enthusiastic hyperbole, "that even the pencil of a Raphael could not delineate" it.[24]

Washington observed, admired, and rode to the western end of the bridge. Just as he came under the first arch, a child in garlanded dress let go a wreath that descended, unobserved by the General, to a point not far above his head. Philadelphia symbolically was crowning him with the hero's laurel.[25]

After he crossed the river and came to the stretch between the Susquehanna and the city, Washington found "every fence, field and avenue" lined with people of every age and station. More cannon barked,[26] the church bells rang, vessels in the river ran up all their flags and joined in the salute. He rode flawlessly, as always, and bowed again and again when spectators cheered or clapped their hands or shouted their welcome. It was incredibly different from his march through the city that day in August, 1777, when he had been pushing his ragged men southward, to meet General Howe, and had been able to give their tatters no other uniform than a sprig of green, the "emblem of hope." [27] Now, while 20,000 citizens seemed to contend for a sight of him, he kept astride the white horse, down Market and Second Streets to the City Tavern.[28] A great dinner had been prepared there at the expense of private citizens who invited "all the clergy and

24 Philadelphia papers, as *supra*, n. 18.

25 One report, cited in *Monaghan*, 26, was that Angelica Peale, daughter of Charles Willson Peale, "lowered on the hero's brow a wreath of laurel." The detailed, contemporary accounts in the newspapers did not mention Angelica by name. One narrative told of a "child, clad in white," who lowered the wreath. Another report included reference to "a lad, beautifully ornamented with sprigs of laurel" who "let drop above the Hero's head, unperceived by him, a civic crown of laurel." Nothing in these descriptions warrants the statement sometimes made that the wreath was dropped *on* Washington's head. He was spared that embarrassment.

26 Jacob Hiltzheimer, at that moment in the town of Bristol on his way home from Trenton, reported that even at such a distance he could hear "the great guns" in Philadelphia sounding their welcome. (*Extracts from the Diary of Jacob Hiltzheimer, 1765–1798*, p. 152, J. C. Parsons, ed.)

27 See Vol. IV, p. 462.

28 Charles Biddle noted in his MS Autobiography (*PHS*) that the "road and streets were . . . so dusty that there was no telling the color of [Washington's] clothes." As no other writer mentioned the dust, Biddle perhaps confused this incident with some other appearance of the President in Philadelphia.

respectable strangers in the city."[29] Approximately 250 men gathered at 3 o'clock while a band played and waiters made ready the wine with which fourteen toasts were to be washed down.[30] Some of these were Federalist toasts, too, stout and uncompromising—"the members of the late General Convention" and "May those who have opposed the new Constitution be converts, by the experience of its happy effects" and a final "Government without oppression, and liberty without licentiousness."[31]

Washington remained to the end of the dinner and, "as usual, captivated every heart,"[32] though he must have been weary long before the last clinking of the glasses. From the tavern he went directly to the home of Robert Morris and probably to the very chamber he had occupied in the summer of 1787 when he had wondered what sort of government the members of the Convention would offer the country. He had written often, in those uncertain days, to his youthful steward at Mount Vernon, concerning farm affairs. Now he had to inform President Langdon of his plans to press on to New York—in abandonment of that beloved plantation life.[33] He wrote: ". . . knowing how anxious both houses must be to proceed to business, I shall continue my journey with as much dispatch as possible. Tomorrow evening I purpose to be at Trenton, the night following at Brunswick and hope to have the pleasure of meeting you at Elizabeth Town Point on Thursday at 12 o'clock."[34] The distance to be covered in two days and a half was about seventy-five miles—not an overtaxing journey if the weather was favorable and the halts in the towns were short. To get an early start was

[29] *Federal Gazette*, Apr. 22, 1789, p. 2. Incidentally, that afternoon newspaper "held the presses" on the 20th in order to include in that day's issue a brief announcement, p. 2, that Washington had arrived.

[30] *Monaghan*, 27. Participation in this dinner evidently was esteemed. Ashbel Green noted proudly in his *Life*, p. 166, that he "was an invited guest and was formally introduced to the President."

[31] *Monaghan*, 27.

[32] *Federal Gazette*, Apr. 22, 1789, p. 2.

[33] Langdon had enclosed him on the 17th, resolutions of Congress, April 15 (*Journal of the House of Representatives of the United States* . . . , cited hereafter as *JHR.*, session March, 1789 [–March, 1793], v. 1, p. 15; *Journal of the First Session of the Senate of the United States* . . . , cited hereafter as *JS*, session March, 1789 [–March, 1793], v. 1, p. 12) for the appointment of a joint committee to wait on the General at his place of embarkation in New Jersey. The acting senior officer of the Senate had written to inquire when and whence Washington would be ready to proceed from New Jersey to New York. See J. D. Richardson, ed., *A Compilation of the Messages and Papers of the Presidents, 1789–1908*, cited hereafter as *Richardson*, v. 1, p. 45, 46.

[34] 30 *G. W.*, 289.

imperative but that might be difficult, especially in leaving friendly Philadelphia. The General had to attend a display of fireworks that evening; [35] the next morning, he was told, various addresses were to be presented.

Threatening weather on Tuesday the 21st did not deter five com-mittees from presenting addresses, to all of which Washington replied briefly.[36] While these gentlemen were complimenting the General, the City Troops of Horse were parading in order to escort him to Trenton,[37] but Washington considerately wrote President Mifflin that he could not consent for the volunteers to attend him on a day of forbidding skies. Between the lines of this letter was discernible the feeling of a prompt old soldier that inexperienced troops or untested horses might not be ready to start on the minute or able to keep his pace on the long road.[38]

As it was, the hands of the clock were nearing 10 when Washington had thanked all his hosts and could give a nod to his coachman. Off rolled the vehicle on what proved to be a damp, swift and uneventful ride up the right bank of the Delaware past villages that had witnessed many a painful march by the vanished Continental Army.[39] When he arrived at Colvin's Ferry, during the afternoon, he did not have to wait for the boat, and when he reached the left bank, he found a Troop of Horse, a Company of Infantry, and a large body of citizens ready to escort him into Trenton. After huzzahs and salutes, Washing-ton took a handsome mount, thoughtfully provided for him, and rode to his assigned place in the procession. If martial memories were stirred

[35] Newspaper accounts, as *supra*, n. 18

[36] These addresses were from: (1) The President and Supreme Executive Council of Penn-sylvania, 334 *Papers of G. W.*, 9; (2) The Mayor, Recorder, Aldermen and Common Council of Philadelphia, *ibid.*, 13; (3) the Judges of the Supreme Court of Pennsylvania, *ibid.*, 11; (4) the Pennsylvania Society of the Cincinnati, *ibid.*, 17; and (5) the Trustees and Faculty of the University of Pennsylvania, *ibid.*, 15. Addresses and answers were printed in the *Pennsyl-vania Packet*, Apr. 22, 1789, p. 2.

[37] *Federal Gazette*, Apr. 22, 1789, p. 2.

[38] The *Independent Gazetteer* of April 22, stated, p. 3, that Washington had "expressed a wish the day before [i.e. on the 20th] that no parade might take place on his departure." This may be statement of fact, but it is manifest that the Light Horse made preparation on the morn-ing of the 21st to attend the General. Jacob Hiltzheimer recorded in his Diary (*loc. cit.*) that Washington was escorted as far as Frankford by one Troop of Horse and that another "went on further" with him.

[39] The reported speed of the ride—approximately thirty-three miles in four hours—makes it certain, at the least, that no halt was made except, probably, to water the horses. It well may be doubted whether, even by pressing rapidly on, it would have been possible to reach present-day Morrisville at 2 P.M. As the time of leaving Philadelphia is fairly well established and the hour of arrival at Morrisville is traditional only, chances are that Washington reached the river, opposite Trenton, later in the afternoon than has been supposed.

by a sight of the ground where his Army had defied the advancing British on the 2nd of January, 1777, he said nothing. The moment he reached the top of Mill Hill, he could see the bridge over Assunpink Creek and the post he had taken from which to deploy the troops who had been falling back in the face of the British advance. Some had been fearful, that desperate afternoon twelve years previously, that he was leading his men into a trap, where the redcoats could envelop and destroy him. Now the bridge had been transformed—but how? What had been done to it? An arch of greenery had been placed on it, an arch no less than twelve feet long and twenty feet high, a veritable covertway, adorned as never one had been in all of Washington's campaigning. Closer to it, he could read the words painted on the southern face of the arch, "The Defender of the Mothers will also Defend the Daughters." [40]   Above this were the commemorative dates [41] of the actions that liberated Trenton. The crowning central adornment of the arch was a great artificial sunflower, "which, always pointing to the sun, was designed to express this sentiment or motto—'To you alone'—as emblematic of the affections and hopes of the people being directed to him, in the united suffrage of the millions of America." [42]

Washington observed gratefully and started across the bridge; but in a moment on either side of the roadway, as if in open ranks, he saw little girls in white, young ladies in spring costume and the most prominent matrons of Trenton, in living exemplification of the words written on the arch. These representatives of their city had a song for the General:

> "Welcome, mighty Chief! once more
> Welcome to this grateful shore!
> Now no mercenary foe
> Aims again the fatal blow—
> Aims at thee the fatal blow.

[40] The text is variously given but with essentially the same meaning.

[41] Two contemporary descriptions of the arch, and two only, are known to exist. One is in the account of Washington's reception printed by the *Pennsylvania Packet*, May 1, 1789, p. 2, and republished in *Columbian Magazine*, May, 1789, p. 288–90; the other is in a letter of Mrs. James Ewing to James Hunter, Jr., Apr. 23, 1789, printed in part in 30 *G. W.*, 291 n. Adjutant General William S. Stryker published in 1882 a brief pamphlet, "Washington's Reception by the People of New Jersey in 1789." This was based in part on traditions of varying probability collected by General Stryker. Some have credibility; others had been handed down, unwritten, in New Jersey households until the fabric of fact was lost under the embroidery of fancy. It has seemed best to follow the contemporary documents.

[42] Letter of April 21; *Penn. Packet*, May 1, 1789, p. 2.

"Virgins fair, and Matrons grave,
Those thy conquering arms did save,
Build for thee triumphant bowers
Strew, ye fair, his way with flowers—
Strew your Hero's way with flowers." [43]

As the last two lines were sung, girls who had baskets of flowers stepped forward and strewed the blossoms in the General's way. Washington scarcely made an effort to conceal the emotion he felt when he contrasted the beautiful scene before him with that of the January afternoon when the rearguard under Col. Edward Hand sullenly fell back across the little stream after their fight on Five Mile Run and Shabbakonk Creek.[44] He had sat on his horse that wintry day not fifty feet from the point where he now had drawn rein when he had perceived that the song would not be finished in his presence if he let his steed go on. After the girls emptied their baskets, he bowed deeply and audibly thanked the ladies for the great honor done him, and then he touched his mount and completed the crossing.[45]

A public dinner followed at Samuel Henry's City Tavern,[46] and after that, a reception. The evening was spent at his lodgings with a company of gentlemen,[47] but the General found time to write in the third person his acknowledgments to the ladies "for the exquisite sensation he experienced" in the "affecting moment" on the bridge. He continued: "The astonishing contrast between his former and actual situation at the same spot, the elegant taste with which it was adorned for the present occasion, and the innocent appearance of the white-robed choir who met him with the gratulatory song, have made such impressions on his remembrance as, he assures them, will never be effaced." [48] This was not phrased in rhetorical politeness. Washington so cher-

---

[43] Stryker, who printed this, *op. cit.*, 7, gave also the arrangement of part singing. His statement was based on tradition but may have been correct. The sole improbability is that the little children, according to Stryker, had no voice in the song. As will be observed from Washington's letter, presently to be quoted, it is at least permissible to infer that the little girls were the "choir."

[44] Vol. IV, p. 342–43.          [45] *Penn. Packet*, May 1, 1789, p. 2.

[46] C. W. Bowen, ed., *The History of the Centennial Celebration of the Inauguration of George Washington as First President of the United States*, cited hereafter as *Bowen*, 26.

[47] Mrs. Ewing to James Hunter, Jr., as *supra*, n. 41. In addition to Mrs. Ewing's remark that Washington "stayed all night at Vandigrifts," there is incidental testimony in the newspaper report that from the bridge over Assunpink the procession moved to the General's "lodgings," a term that assuredly would not have been used if, as tradition has it, he went on to Princeton that evening and stayed at President Witherspoon's. *Stryker*, op. cit., 18.

[48] 30 *G. W.*, 290–91; facsimile in *Bowen*, 27.

ished the song in his honor [49] that he later copied it in his Letter Book, along with a note on the circumstances and the text of his thanks to the ladies. These were the only papers he personally wrote in that volume of what he intended to be his permanent record.[50]

The next morning he was off at sunrise, with an escort that attended him for eight miles on the road to Princeton.[51] There, probably, he ate breakfast and received the formal address of the college to which he spoke in brief acknowledgment.[52] After the short ceremony he proceeded on the familiar road to New Brunswick. Some miles South of the Raritan, he was met by the Mayor and leading citizens, and as he approached the town, the sound of the church bells and the "b-o-o-m" of saluting cannon were audible. Along the main street, the volunteer Companies of Infantry and Artillery, with a detachment of Cavalry, formed a line past which Washington admiringly rode. A band of music played martial airs that heightened the enthusiasm of the townsfolk, nearly all of whom came out to welcome the General. Through the cheering, smiling throng, he went to the home of Thomas Egbert, who had been a Major of New Jersey militia in 1777.[53] Here, probably, he received a note from Jonathan Dayton and others who wished to know when he would leave New Brunswick the next morning, April 23, so that citizens of Elizabeth Town might set the hour for a cold collation they wished to tender him before he embarked for New York.[54] The General's answer doubtless was that he intended to push on another ten miles that evening and would get an early start the next day. Under cavalry escort, he left New Brunswick at 5 P.M. in the company of Jersey notables and with the affectionate acclaim of the crowd. The night of the 22nd–23rd was spent at Woodbridge.[55] In delicate compliment to him, the Light Horse from New Brunswick remained nearby to share in the ceremonies of the 23rd.[56]

[49] The author is supposed to have been Maj. Richard Howell, formerly of the Second New Jersey, and later, Governor of that State. Rev. James F. Armstrong selected the air to which the poem was set, and he instructed the choir that sang it. *Stryker*, op. cit., 7.

[50] 334 *Papers of G. W.*, 17–18; 30 *G. W.*, 291 n.

[51] Mrs. Ewing's letter of Apr. 23, 1789, as *supra*, n. 41.

[52] 334 *Papers of G. W.*, 19–20, LC.

[53] *Penn. Packet*, May 2, 1789, p. 2–3. Volume 334 of the *Papers of G. W.* contains no New Brunswick address. In the absence of all mention of a public dinner, the assumption is that Washington and his party ate at Major Egbert's.

[54] 243 *Papers of G. W.*, 28, LC. The other signers were Aaron Ogden and Jonathan W. Lawrence.

[55] Although positive proof is lacking, the probability is strong that he lodged in a tavern. For the day's events, see the *Pennsylvania Packet*, May 2, 1789, p. 2–3.

[56] *New-Jersey Journal* (Elizabeth Town), Apr. 29, 1789, p. 3.

The General's departure from Woodbridge on the last stretch of his journey may not have been as soon after sunrise as he had wished, but even with short waits by the roadside, while detachments fell in at Bridgetown and at Rahway,[57] the procession made good speed and reached Elizabeth Town before the clocks struck 9.[58] Through a throng that overflowed the streets, Washington passed a saluting line of militia and volunteers of all arms of the service, and went to the Red Lion Inn, the public house of Samuel Smith,[59] where he broke his fast in the company of the leading men of the community.[60] He met there the town officials and a committee of three from the governments of New York State and City,[61] but he punctiliously arranged that he would call on the three Senators and the five members of the House of Representatives who had come to Elizabeth Town to receive him on behalf of Congress.[62] These gentlemen were at the home of Elias Boudinot, himself one of the joint committee in his capacity of a New Jersey member of the House. Among the committeemen were, also, some who had participated conspicuously in the Philadelphia Convention of 1787 and two former officers of the Continental Army, a Colonel of Cavalry under Washington and a Surgeon in the Southern Department.[63] The entire group were men of such ability that if they were typical of Congress, the President could be sure of intelligent, patriotic cooperation. Every face was good augury.

After pleasant conversation at Boudinot's residence, Washington proceeded to Elizabeth Town Point—and the whole population, as it seemed, with him. At the dock, all the troops who had welcomed him on arrival that morning were drawn up. Other Companies had marched directly to the waterfront. The General reviewed them and after thanking their officers and his hosts, he walked to the craft that had been prepared for him with pride and pleasure at the expense of

[57] *Ibid.* and *Penn. Packet*, May 2, 1789, p. 2–3.
[58] *New-Jersey Journal*, as *supra.*
[59] F. B. Kelley, *Historic Elizabeth, 1664–1932*, p. 15, 21.
[60] Vagueness here is unavoidable. The *Pennsylvania Packet* reported (May 2, 1789, p. 2–3) that he had breakfast; the *New-Jersey Journal* (Apr. 29, 1789, p. 3) stated that he "partook of a repast provided by the gentlemen of the town." George Adams Boyd explains that Elias Boudinot had invited Washington to a "late breakfast" at noon but found that the committee had won the guest (George Adams Boyd, *Elias Boudinot, Patriot and Statesman, 1740–1821,* cited hereafter as *Boyd's Boudinot,* 161 n).
[61] The Chancellor and Adjutant General of the State, and the Recorder of the City, *Daily Advertiser,* Apr. 20, 1789, p. 2.
[62] Resolution of Apr. 15, 1789; 1 *JHR.,* 15; 1 *JS,* 12.
[63] Theodorick Bland and Thomas T. Tucker.

forty-six of the leading men of New York [64]—a new barge, with a keel of forty-seven feet, a mast and sail, an awning, festooned red curtains and thirteen oars on either side.[65] An experienced New York pilot was to handle each of these oars; the men and their coxswain, Thomas Randall, were in waiting, all of them dressed alike in white smock and black, fringed cap. Washington observed admiringly both craft and crew and got aboard with the joint committee of Congress and the three representatives of the civil government of New York.[66] It was then about noon; the wind was blowing strongly, auspiciously, some would have said, towards the city up the Bay.[67] As the little vessel got underway, the Artillery began its farewell salute and the troops on the waterfront remained rigidly in line as a martial background that faded gradually before the eyes of their old Commander-in-Chief.[68]

By the time the barge crossed Newark Bay and had reached the "Kills" opposite the southern end of Staten Island, the New Haven and Rhode Island packets and a collection of small craft, all with flags flying and in fanciful decoration, fell in behind Washington's boat, as if to form a naval parade.[69] Soon after the barge turned into the Upper Bay, a similar handsome vessel was nearby, ready to serve as special escort. Flags and familiar faces quickly identified it as the barge of Secretary Knox, who had with him the Secretary of Foreign Affairs, John Jay, and the members of the Board of Treasury.[70] As Washington approached the Battery on Staten Island, the oarsmen changed their strokes and the familiar work on shore was wreathed with the smoke of a salute that echoed over the water. These thirteen guns seemed to be taken as a summons by every owner of a small boat who could

[64] Their names are attached to their letter of Apr. 20, 1789, to Thomas Randall, 243 *Papers of G. W.*, 24, LC. They contributed between £200 and £300 for the craft; Stephen Decatur, Jr., *Private Affairs of George Washington from the Records and Accounts of Tobias Lear, Esquire, his Secretary*, cited hereafter as *Decatur*, 75.

[65] *Decatur*, loc. cit.; Thomas E. V. Smith, *The City of New York in the Year of Washington's Inauguration, 1789*, cited hereafter as *T. E. V. Smith*, p. 221. From the *Pennsylvania Packet*, Apr. 13, 1789, p. 3, it is manifest that the barge had been completed shortly before April 7. See also Letter of Dr. James Cogswell, an eyewitness, in 4 *Historical Magazine*, 244, and reprinted in part in *Bowen*, 30.

[66] *Daily Advertiser*, Apr. 24, 1789, p. 2.

[67] Elias Boudinot to his wife, Apr. 24, 1789, cited hereafter as *Boudinot letter*, and now most conveniently accessible in Boyd's *Boudinot*, 162 ff. See also the informative report in the *New-York Daily Gazette*, Apr. 25, 1789, p. 2. These two sources and the contemporaneous accounts in the *Daily Advertiser* and in the *Gazette of the United States* (New York), supply almost all the known details of Washington's arrival.

[28] *Boudinot letter*, op. cit., 162.

[69] *Ibid.*; letter of Dr. James Cogswell in 4 *Historical Magazine*, (1) p. 244, and reprinted in *Bowen*, 30–32.

[70] *Boudinot letter*, op. cit., 162, and *New-York Daily Gaz.*, Apr. 25, 1789, p. 2.

push it into the deep water.[71] Minute by minute the column grew wider and longer; everywhere was color, in enthusiastic compliance with the request previously made by the corporation of New York City, that all vessels display their flags as soon as the first salute was fired.[72]

Sturdily, the pilots pulled the barge through the Upper Bay. As they approached Bedloe's Island on their left, a finely handled sloop came up on the starboard bow, under full sail. When she was close in, Washington saw preparations aboard her and then in the wind he heard a familiar tune with new words—"God Save the King" with five stanzas of welcome and of praise directed to him.[73] Washington and his party lifted their hats; the gentlemen aboard the sloop returned the compliment,[74] while the sopranos and the contraltos doubtless beamed. This was not the end of song. From another craft, which pulled directly to the stern of the barge, the foremost of about a dozen male passengers leaned forward and handed the coxswain a number of copies of an ode, which the gentlemen on the rear boat began immediately to render in four parts.[75] A few minutes later, porpoises began to play around the prow of the barge [76] as if they, too, wished to do honor to the tall man in the cocked hat, the blue suit and the buff underdress.[77]

As the barge continued to spring forward in the favoring wind, the colors in the decorations of the ships near the southern end of New York Island became clearer. Vaguely, beyond them, could be seen the masses of people who lined the waterfront all the way from the fort to the end of Wall Street, where the barge was to land. Washington looked at the shipping and at the crowd and could not conceal his emotion. He had not expected any such reception as this!

The barge was now approaching the vessels anchored north of Governor's Island—*Galveston,* which was a Spanish sloop of war, Arnold H. Dohrman's ship *North Carolina,* the British packet, and others [78]

[71] *Daily Advertiser,* Apr. 24, 1789, p. 2.
[72] *Ibid.*
[73] *Boudinot letter,* op. cit., 162. The *Gazette of the United States* printed this ode, seven lines to the stanza, in its issue of April 25, p. 3. Authorship was attributed to "Mr. L**," that is, to Samuel Low.
[74] *Boudinot letter,* op. cit., 162.
[75] *Ibid.*
[76] *Ibid.,* 163.
[77] For the General's costume, see *T. E. V. Smith,* 222.
[78] Among these was the schooner *Columbia,* with the Revolutionary poet Philip Freneau on the bridge as master. Freneau's ship was "dressed and decorated in the most superb manner." *Daily Advertiser,* Apr. 24, 1789, p. 3. See also Lewis Leary, *That Rascal Freneau, a Study in Literary Failure,* cited hereafter as *Leary, Freneau,* 162. On board was "Dr. King from

that traded along the coast or ventured overseas. Most of these already were dressed; his Catholic Majesty's representative and Dohrman's pride merely showed their colors. Presently the British packet spoke out in a salute of thirteen guns, which an American battery forthwith answered. Then, on signal by her Captain, the Spanish vessel suddenly broke the flags of more than a score of countries, simultaneously manned her yards and let go her salute.[79] *North Carolina* equalled the display.[80] Never, it seemed, had so many friendly flags been flying.

Close now to the landing, Washington looked at thousands and thousands of New Yorkers.[81] The city almost had stopped work for the day;[82] everyone who could do so had crowded to the vicinity of the fort to see the barge come in. When cannon of the Battery fired another salute of thirteen guns, the spectators gave three huzzahs[83] and then nearly all of them started to Murray's Wharf, at the bottom of Wall Street, to see the General. So great was the din, after the landing salute had been fired, that probably few heard the church bells which loyally were to be rung for half an hour.[84] The flawlessly handled barge was made fast sometime between 2 and 3 o'clock;[85] the committees climbed out and started up the carpeted steps, the rails of which had been draped with crimson. Then, after a fitting pause, Washington went ashore and mounted to the landing, where Gov. George Clinton and a coterie of officials welcomed and congratulated him.[86] Washington thanked them with his dignified regard for each individual. Thereupon an officer stepped up, saluted, and ceremoniously announced that

South Africa, with a collection of natural curiosities, particularly a male and female ourang outang" (*Gazette of U. S.*, April 25). "As the escort for Washington proceeded up the bay, Captain Freneau, poet, seaman and scholar, brought his ship—with its cargo of monkeys—into line and sailed along with the gorgeous procession that was escorting the President-elect to the capital city" (G. H. Payne, *History of Journalism in the United States*, 152).

[79] *Galveston*, stationed precisely at the confluence of the North and East Rivers, fired fifteen cannonshot. The first of these was "so powerful in its detonation" that it surprised "the immense pageant by land and sea" and drew five cheers instead of three from the spectators. The Spanish minister reported that Washington later "confessed" to him a great satisfaction in the performance of *Galveston* (Gardoqui's dispatch of Apr. 24, 1789, to the Conde de Floridablanca; Arc. His. Nac., Madrid, *Estado*, Leg. 3894, Apart., No. 2, Letter 314, p. 705. A rather free translation of a part of this letter is in *Bowen*, 33).

[80] *Daily Advertiser*, Apr. 24, 1789, p. 2; *New-York Daily Gazette*, Apr. 25, 1789, p. 2; *Boudinot letter*, loc. cit., 163.

[81] "The whole city of all descriptions were out to meet him," wrote Samuel B. Webb, "and in all my life I never saw such unfeigned joy in every countenance." *Correspondence and Journals of Samuel Blachley Webb*, cited hereafter as *Webb*, v. 3, p. 128.

[82] *Daily Advertiser*, Apr. 24, 1789, p. 2.

[83] *T. E. V. Smith*, 221.          [84] *Daily Advertiser*, Apr. 20, 1789, p. 2.

[85] *New-York Daily Gazette*, Apr. 25, 1789, p. 2; 1 *JHR.*, 19.

[86] *Ibid.*, and *Daily Advertiser*, Apr. 24, 1789, p. 2.

he commanded the guard assigned the General and that he awaited orders. Washington's unstudied reply was almost as effective as his remarks at the Newburgh meeting or at the farewell in Fraunces' Tavern: [87] "As to the present arrangement, I shall proceed as is directed, but after this is over, I hope you will give yourself no further trouble, as the affection of my fellow-citizens"—and he turned to the throng as he spoke—"is all the guard I want." [88]

A formal parade had next place in the order of exercises but it was not easily started. The crowd was so dense around Murray's Wharf and the adjoining streets that it was not to be moved otherwise than by waiting and coaxing and pushing and commanding.[89] When at last a narrow way was opened, progress through Queen Street [90] was so slow and difficult that half an hour was required [91] to move from the dock to Franklin House at No. 3 Cherry Street, previously used by the President of Congress and now assigned to Washington.[92] A full-dress salute was rendered by the militia as the General passed their ranks; [93] and even when finally indoors, Washington had to receive and thank the officers who had conducted the procession.[94] Wine and punch were served,[95] but time did not suffice for a change of dress.[96] Shortly Governor Clinton's coach was at the door,[97] and the General and the

[87] Vol. V, p. 435, 467.

[88] *Boudinot letter*, op. cit., 164, with a transposition from the third to the first person, a change that does not seem to involve undue liability to error in dealing with a communication written only one day after the event.

[89] *Ibid.*, 163. The most detailed order of the procession is in *Daily Advertiser*, Apr. 24, 1789, p. 2.

[90] *Bowen*, 35. The procession followed Queen Street and passed the Governor's mansion at the foot of Cedar Street. See *T. E. V. Smith*, 29, for the changing names of different parts of present-day Pearl Street, which was Queen Street in 1789.

[91] *Boudinot letter*, op. cit., 163. The pace, according to Dr. James Cogswell, was "very slow" and attended with "great solemnity"; *Bowen*, 30, from 4 *Historical Magazine*, 244.

[92] 1 *JHR.*, 15; 1 *JS*, 12; *Decatur*, 117; *T. E. V. Smith*, 224–25. For a description of Franklin House, owned at the time by Samuel Osgood, see *Bowen*, 36 n.

[93] Gardoqui's dispatch of Apr. 24, 1789, *loc. cit.*

[94] *Boudinot letter*, op. cit., 163.

[95] Moustier to the Comte de Montmorin, Arc. Nat., Paris. Aff. Étrangères, *Corr. Polit., États-Unis*, v. 34, f. 158–71. The French envoy recorded, somewhat pompously, that he followed the procession from Murray's Wharf in his carriage; and that, upon approaching Franklin House, he was recognized by Washington, who lifted his hand in greeting. Thereupon Moustier rode near the President, and followed him up to the squalid (*chétive*) house provided for his residence. Inside, Washington shook Moustier's hand and offered him refreshment from a great quantity of wine and punch. "But," said Moustier, "I reminded him how at Mount Vernon I had objected to that usage." See, also, *Bowen*, 34.

[96] *Daily Advertiser*, Apr. 24, 1789, p. 2.

[97] Van Dorsten, in Algemeen Ryksarchief, Staten General. *Register der ingekomen Brieven, memorien en Bylagen uit American, 1782–89*, f. 60; translation dispatch of May 4, 1789, in *Bowen*, 50.

Governor proceeded without ceremony to the latter's mansion where an honor banquet was waiting.[98]

Rain began to fall before the long, late dinner was completed,[99] but this did not prevent an illumination which the weary General could not decline to inspect.[100] When, finally, Washington bade the last of his hosts goodnight and retired to his chamber in the house on Cherry Street, he could have told himself that in the whole of his life, he never had spent a more amazing day. Emotionally, he was almost exhausted. "The display of boats . . ." he wrote, "the decorations of the ships, the roar of cannon, and the loud acclamations of the people . . . filled my mind with sensations as painful (considering the reverse of this scene, which may be the case after all my labors to do good) as they are pleasing." [101] Later, if he read what the newspapers and their correspondents, the orators and the rhymesters had to say of his journey and of his acceptance of the Presidency, he well might have asked himself whether any man could hope to maintain the esteem or fulfil the expectations represented by such flights as these:

"The joy of our whole city [of Philadelphia] upon this august spectacle, cannot easily be described. Every countenance seemed to say, Long, long live George Washington, the Father of the people." [102]

"His Excellency came in on a very elegant white horse" and then a footnote: "And behold a white horse; and he that sat on him had a bow, and a crowd was given unto him, and he went forth conquering, and to conquer. Revelation, Chap. VI, verse 2." [103]

"All ranks and professions expressed their feelings, in loud acclamations, and with rapture hailed the arrival [in New York] of the Father of his Country." [104]

[98] Clinton's invitation of Apr. 23, 1789, written in a manner that scarcely permitted declination, is in 243 *Papers of G. W.*, 29. Although Governor Clinton was probably the most powerful adversary of government under the Constitution of 1787, he was personally and officially attentive to Washington, whom he significantly put on his right in the procession. *T. E. V. Smith*, 222.

[99] *Boudinot letter*, op. cit., 164.

[100] For the changes of official decision regarding this illumination, see *Daily Advertiser*, Apr. 20, p. 2, Apr. 22, p. 2, Apr. 23, 1789, p. 2. The Spanish minister reported that the rain was heavy and lasted all night, preventing the display of fireworks planned by himself and the French minister. Gardoqui's dispatch of Apr. 24, 1789, to the Conde Floridablanca, *loc. cit.*; translation in *Bowen*, 33.

[101] Entry in a section of his Diary now lost but in existence as late as 1857 and quoted in 4 *Irving*, 511 (ed. 1856–59).

[102] *Penn. Packet*, Apr. 21, 1789, p. 3.

[103] *Independent Gazetteer*, Apr. 21, 1789, p. 3.

[104] *New-Jersey Journal*, Apr. 29, 1789, p. 3.

"Absorbed and agitated by the sentiment which our adored leader and ruler inspired, the printer apprehends that he cannot with perfect precision describe the various scenes of splendor which this event exhibited . . ." [105]

"Many persons who were in the crowd . . . were heard to say that they should now die contented—nothing being wanted to complete their happiness, previous to this auspicious period, but the sight of the Saviour of his Country." [106]

"May the Rulers of America feel the spirit of their station—feel their hearts beat strong for virtuous fame—feel that they are exalted to be Gods among men, and study to imitate the God of Gods." [107]

"Merit must be great, when it can call forth the *voluntary* honors of a free and enlightened people; but the attentions shown on this occasion were not merely *honorary*, they were the tribute of gratitude, due to a man whose life has been one series of labors for the public good upon a scale of eminence that Heaven never before assigned to a mortal. These labors have been achieved so perfectly that future ages shall acknowledge the justice of the poet when they read,

'So near perfection, that he stood
Upon the boundary line,
Of finite, from infinite good,
Of human from divine' " [108]

Along with tributes such as these, pitched to a loftiness never before employed in praise of an American, there were echoes of what the crowd had been saying on the streets of Philadelphia, and at the arch over Assunpink Creek,[109] and on Murray's Wharf. The same editor who wrote of the "boundary line" heard the homely reflections of men who could not speak in iambics but knew Washington and saw and approved what was done for him: All ranks appeared to feel the force of an expression that was reiterated among the crowd—'Well, he deserves it all.' " [110]

[105] *Daily Advertiser*, Apr. 24, 1789, p. 2.     [106] *Gazette of U. S.*, Apr. 25, 1789, p. 3.
[107] Boston letter to the editor, *ibid.*, Apr. 29, 1789, p. 3.
[108] *Ibid.*, Apr. 25, 1789, p. 3.
[109] See, as typical, letter of Joseph Jones to James Madison, [May 10], 1789: ". . . The General's journey to New York shows the people still retain the same respect and veneration for his person and character they heretofore entertained and although he is little captivated by ceremonial distinctions, yet he could not fail of being sensibly gratified by such universal demonstrations of affection as were exhibited through his progress; among them none I conceive could be more pleasing than his reception at Trenton bridge. . . ." 11 *Madison Papers*, 59a, LC.
[110] *Gazette of U. S.*, Apr. 25, 1789, p. 3.

# CHAPTER VIII

### Inauguration Day Is Not Without Clouds

### (April 24–30, 1789)

". . . I GREATLY apprehend that my countrymen will expect too much from me. I fear, if the issue of public measures should not correspond with their sanguine expectations, they will turn the extravagant (and I may say undue) praises which they are heaping upon me at this moment, into equally extravagant (though I will fondly hope, unmerited) censures." That was the reflection of Washington [1] on the events of April 23, 1789, and of the fortnight that followed. It was a shining and at the same time an exceedingly difficult period for a man who never had served in a public executive position otherwise than as a soldier. From long habit and regard for orderliness, he completed easily the arrangements Tobias Lear had made in advance for comfortable living in the house assigned him, the former residence of the President of Congress.[2] It had been, Washington's Secretary wrote later, "in a state of the greatest confusion, pulling down, putting up, making better and better—and making worse; however, by spirited exertions, it was got into good order by the arrival of the President, and a little noise we have since been subjected to has made a good house of it"; [3] he carefully visited the members of Congress; [4] he received the congratulations of

---

[1] Letter of May 5, 1789, to Edward Rutledge; 30 *G. W.*, 309. Cf. Paine Wingate to Timothy Pickering, Apr. 27, 1789: "Fortunately, our President has the affections and confidence of his countrymen more than any man whatever and this will go a good way toward giving efficacy to measures and stopping complaints. . . . If popularity should not be lost, yet strong and troublesome oppositions may arise." (2 *Paine Wingate*, 298–99.) See, also, Arthur Lee to R. H. Lee, May 9, 1789; *University of Virginia MS.*

[2] 1 *JHR.*, 15; 1 *JS*, 12.

[3] Lear's letter of May 3, 1789, to George Augustine Washington; *Duke Univ. MSS.* The only considerable items of expenditure set down in Lear's accounts were £28 for sundries ordered by Mrs. Osgood at the instance of Mrs. Washington, and £41 for "making livery clothes, &c." See *Decatur*, 14–16.

[4] This is a safe assumption from the statement of Senator William Maclay of Pennsylvania that Washington called: "We asked him to take a seat. He excused himself on account of the number of his visits . . . He made us complaisant bows—one as he mounted and the other as he went away on horseback." *Journal of William Maclay* (edition of 1890), E. S. Maclay, ed., cited hereafter as *Maclay*, 4–5.

the city Chamber of Commerce,[5] and he assured a joint committee of Congress that any arrangements that body made for his induction into office would be acceptable,[6] whereupon Congress voted to inaugurate him on the 30th.[7] Meantime, both House and Senate discussed and promptly disagreed on the titles by which he and the Vice President should be addressed. A majority of the Senate favored "His Highness, the President of the United States of America, and Protector of their Liberties" but the Representatives would consent to nothing beyond the simple title "President of the United States," as set forth in the Constitution.[8] Washington himself wished this discussion to be dropped, because he believed that exalted titles would arouse public resentment which opponents of the new government would seek to aggravate.[9]

Another concern of Washington's first days in New York was the ceaseless flow of visitors in numbers for which even his long service as unlicensed and unrequited tavern keeper at Mount Vernon had not prepared him. "I was unable," the General testified later, "to attend to any business whatsoever; for gentlemen, consulting their own convenience rather than mine, were calling from the time I rose from breakfast, often before, until I sat down to dinner." [10] Some public affairs demanded attention, regardless of hours. Official visits had to be returned, at least while he remained a private citizen. Lear probably told literal truth when he said, "There has not been a moment unemployed." [11] At the outset, nothing could be done about this drain on Washington's time, without giving offence to persons whose good will was unmistakable, even if the main reason for their visits was curiosity or vanity; but a man as conscientious as the General in the discharge of business could not even contemplate a life given over to handshaking and civilities. He resolved after a few vexatious days that as

[5] *New-York Daily Gaz.*, Apr. 27, 1789, p. 2, 3; *Monaghan*, 41. This was on the 25th.
[6] 1 *JHR.*, 20.    [7] *Ibid.*, and 1 *JS*, 16-17.
[8] Final action is described *infra*, p. 203. See 1 *JS*, 16, 17, 22, 23, 24, 25; 1 *JHR.*, 20, 27, 32. The Senate debate may be followed in *Maclay*, 1-38; House debate, May 11, 1789, is reported in *The Debates and Proceedings in the Congress of the United States . . . compiled from Authentic Materials by Joseph Gales, Senior*, usually styled *The Annals of Congress* and cited hereafter as *Annals*, v. 1, p. 332 ff. Of interest, also, are Madison to Jefferson, May 9 and May 23, 1789, 11 *Madison Papers*, 58, 69, LC, and cited in *Hunt's Madison*, 355 n and 369 n; David Stuart to Washington, 243 *Papers of G. W.*, 100, LC, mentioned in 30 *G. W.*, 363 n.
[9] Letter of July 26, 1789, to David Stuart *ibid.*, 363. This reference appears to be a specific denial of the often-published statement that Washington wished to be called "His Mightiness, The President of the United States"; cf. *T. E. V. Smith*, 226. For typical arguments for and against titles, see the *Gazette of the United States* (New York), May 9, p. 3, May 16, p. 1 and 3, May 20, 1789, p. 3; *Daily Advertiser* (New York), May 22, 1789, p. 2.
[10] 31 *G. W.*, 53; cf. 30 *ibid.*, 361.
[11] Letter of May 3, 1789, to George Augustine Washington, as cited *supra*, n. 3.

soon as he took office, he would lay down this rule: persons who came to transact public business would be received at any suitable hour, but those who merely desired to "see the President" or to "pay their respects" must call at a specified hour on one or two designated days of the week. By no less drastic requirement could the President hope to find time for the work that was accumulating while the plans for the inauguration were being perfected.[12]

By the 29th of April, these arrangements were so nearly complete that Washington knew what to expect.[13] If he was awake at sunrise the next day, he heard the bark of thirteen guns from the war-time fortifications at the southern end of New York Island, just thirteen years from another April day when he had caught the sound of a friendly gun from the Battery. On the last day of that same month in 1776—a little more than two weeks after his arrival from Boston—he had been detaching troops for what he considered "rather too late" an effort to reenforce the feeble American columns in Canada.[14] He had styled New York at that time the "Grand Magazine of America" and he had given warning to a perplexed, patriotic Congress that undue risk was being run in "trusting this important post . . . to the handful of men remaining here." [15] All his faith, all his resolution, all his love of America had not sufficed to save that warning from fulfilment on the terreplein of Fort Washington and in the mud of the retreat across New Jersey. Now, from the redoubts [16] that had symbolized British power in thwarting revolution for seven years, there was rolling, un-

[12] 30 G. W., 360; Lear's letter to George Augustine Washington, May 3, 1789, as cited. This letter states that the rule concerning visitors had been put in effect after the inauguration, but an announcement in the *Gazette of the United States*, May 2, p. 3, would indicate that the limitation on social visits was in effect by the day after Washington took office. It is not likely that the practice would have been introduced so promptly had it not been decided on prior to the inauguration. Other regulations, to be described in the next chapter, manifestly were in contemplation. The paragraph in the *Gazette* read: "We are informed that the President has assigned every Tuesday and Friday, between the hours of 2 and 3 for receiving visits; and that visits of compliment on other days, and particularly on Sunday, will not be agreeable to him. It seems to be a prevailing opinion that so much of the President's time will be engaged by the various and important business imposed upon him by the Constitution that he will find himself constrained to omit returning visits, or accepting invitations to entertainments." For popular approval of Washington's desire to have no visitors on Sunday, see the *Gazette of the United States*, May 6, 1789, p. 3.
[13] The details published in the *Daily Advertiser*, Apr. 30, 1789, p. 2, were said to be taken from the "proceedings of Congress, Wednesday, April 29," but neither the *Journals* nor the *Annals* contain reference under that date to any other aspect of the ceremonies than attendance on a proposed service at St. Paul's Chapel after the oath had been administered and the President's address had been delivered.
[14] Vol. IV, p. 84; 4 G. W., 530.       [15] 4 G. W., 519.
[16] Whether the salute was from Fort George or from nearby Battery seems undeterminable because of the conflict of testimony.

challenged, this salute of a free people to him, the patient Commander-in-Chief who had lost the fields and had saved the country.

Not long after the guns paid homage, he had his hair powdered and dressed himself with proud care in a suit of brown broadcloth spun at Hartford, purchased after much negotiation and forwarded to Mount Vernon through Henry Knox. This apparel was to advertise American industry; it was, also, in a homely way to proclaim American liberty since the device on the buttons was that of a wing-spread eagle.[17] The stockings were Washington's best, of white silk; his shoe-buckles were silver; [18] he was later to fasten on a dress sword in a steel scabbard.

When Washington had completed this toilet and had eaten his breakfast, the bells of city churches began to ring, some of them merrily at first and then all of them solemnly in a summons to prayer at 9 or 9:30 o'clock.[19] The General and his assistants doubtless listened sympathetically, but they were busy with last-minute details that had to be set in order before the ceremonies began.[20] Washington's inaugural address was not a concern. It was in final form, ready for delivery. He had put aside completely the long statement of needed legislation he had written some weeks before at Mount Vernon, for presentation to Congress. In its place, probably with some help from James Madison, he had prepared a paper that could be read at unhurried pace in less than twenty minutes. It was largely personal, with one recommendation only and that one carefully phrased. No further change in the text was considered now.[21] The sheets were folded and in the coat pocket of the specially made brown suit.

Soon the General had the smallest final detail properly set in the pattern of the day's proceedings. Before his door, crowds gathered and gaped. Every moment, these spectators increased in number. Militia

---

[17] *Decatur*, 8–10; *Matteson*, 260, 277; *Bowen*, 51. Two buttons, believed to be from the coat of this suit, are in the museum of Valley Forge Park.

[18] *Ibid.* Moustier wrote the Comte de Montmorin that Washington carried his hat in his hand. Arc. Nat., Paris. Aff. Étrangères, *Corr. Polit., États-Unis*, v. 34, f. 73.

[19] *Daily Advertiser*, May 1, 1789, p. 2; Diary of Moravian Church in New York, quoted in 13 *Penn. Mag. of His. and Biog.*, 245 ff.

[20] Lear's Diary, Apr. 30, 1789, quoted in 10 *Sparks*, 463.

[21] The manuscript of part of the proposed first draft was given away by Jared Sparks. Fragments industriously reassembled by Fitzpatrick appear in 30 *G. W.*, 296–308, with his disgusted note, p. 296–97, but the broader underlying arguments scarcely can be reconstructed. Consultation with Madison regarding both texts is suggested vaguely in *ibid.*, 176, 204, 310. Madison's own proposals at this time for the amendment of the Constitution (10 *Madison Papers*, 79, LC; 11 *ibid.*, 40, 107; conveniently cited in 5 *Hunt's Madison*, 319 n–320 n, 336, 346 n, 414–19 and n) corresponded roughly to the language used in the inaugural but did not duplicate it.

appeared in the roadway; shouted commands were audible in the residence; a parade was being formed. Expectancy was in the air, pervading everything, but no call came for Washington till noon was past. Then he heard the sound of horses' hoofs, the tramp of troops and the grind of carriage wheels: The joint committee of Congress was arriving to escort him to Federal Hall. Along with the eight members, whose chairman was Senator Ralph Izard [22]—a name of many memories—a like number of "assistants" reported and made their bow, all except one of them veterans of the Revolutionary War.[23] On Izard's announcement that Congress was ready to receive him, Washington immediately left the house and, alone, entered a grand coach that had been prepared for him.[24] At half past 12, off rolled the General in slow stateliness, his vehicle drawn by four fine horses. Ahead were the troops and the Senate members of the joint committee of Congress; behind Washington rode his secretaries, the representatives of the committee, Chancellor Livingston, who was to administer the oath, and, with him, the heads of the Federal Departments [25] and a few eminent citizens.[26] Down Cherry Street into Queen and along Queen to Great Dock Street the procession moved, past smiling crowds. At Great Dock the column turned westward and moved to Broad. Then it swung northward until the front rank halted about 200 yards [27] South of Wall Street, at which crossing, on the north side, Federal Hall was located.[28]

[22] *Bowen*, 44.

[23] *Ibid.*, 42. The exception was John R. Livingston, a New York merchant and brother of the Chancellor of the State. "Lieutenant-Colonel Franks," unidentified in Bowen's descriptive roster, may have been Arnold's former aide, the Major David Franks who had been at West Point on the 25th of September, 1780, when his traitorous General had fled. See Vol. V, p. 197 ff.

[24] The Minister de Moustier's dispatch of June 5, 1789 to the Comte de Montmorin (*loc. cit.*, f. 75; a translation is in *Bowen*, 47–49), is authority for the statement concerning Izard and also for the inclusion of "several corps of infantry" in the procession from Federal Hall to Washington's quarters. Lear noted in his Diary, 10 *Sparks*, 463, that Washington rode unattended in the State coach and that he and Humphreys followed "in the President's own carriage."

[25] For these officials, see *infra*, p. 190–91.

[26] Washington's "assistants" and constables of New York City flanked the coach of state. The full order of the procession will be found in the *Daily Advertiser*, May 1, 1789, p. 2. It has been reprinted frequently, perhaps most conveniently in *T. E. V. Smith*, 229. The Resident Secretary of the Dutch Legation, van Dorsten, was the witness who set down the interesting fact that Washington alone had four horses to his coach. All the other carriages used two horses only (*Bowen*, 50). Moustier also gave the order of procession. He mentioned that Washington's coach was drawn by four horses, and that three lackeys were in attendance.

[27] Lear's Diary, as *supra*. In his letter of May 3, 1789, to George Augustine Washington, the Secretary stated that the Presidential party walked 300 yards, but this probably was from the point where Washington left his coach and not from the spot where the front rank stopped.

[28] *Daily Advertiser*, May 1, 1789, p. 2. Cherry Street now is lost in the abutments of Brooklyn Bridge. "Pearl Street, which was originally on the water-line, in 1789, bore that name

When the procession ended its march, the militiamen opened ranks. Washington and the others left the vehicles and walked up Broad Street toward the meeting place.[29] Fortunately, after a cloudy dawn, the sun shone by 9,[30] and the temperature was not so low that it nipped the enthusiasm of the crowd through which Washington passed with the simple dignity that had a singular emotional effect on almost every assemblage. Inside the remodeled and newly decorated building,[31] the General was told that the two Houses of Congress were sitting together in the Senate Chamber and were awaiting him.[32] With the committee he mounted the stairs on the right of the entrance and came in a minute to the Senate Chamber door, which was opened ceremoniously. The room was handsome, almost as wide as long and with a motif of sun and stars on the ceiling.[33] At the northern end were three windows, draped in crimson damask and under the middle one was a dais raised a yard above the floor. On this were three chairs, that in the centre under a canopy similar to the drapery of the windows. Curtains of the same color were arranged around three doors that led from the southern end of the room to a portico that overlooked Wall Street.[34] As Washington walked toward the platform, he saw the Senators, the foreign diplomatic agents and sundry officials on the western side of a narrow

only from the present State Street to Broad Street. From Broad Street to Wall Street it was called Great Dock Street, and thence to its end at Chatham Street it was known as Queen Street, a name which it received in 1695 and retained until toward the close of the [eighteenth] century" (*T. E. V. Smith*, 29). In other words, the parade followed the existing Pearl Street down town to Broad and then went North on Broad to Wall and Nassau.

[29] Lear's Diary, as cited; Gardoqui to the Conde Floridablanca, the Spanish Minister of State, May 1, 1789; *Arc. His. Nac.*, Madrid, *Estado*, Leg. 3894, Lett. 314, f. 705. Also in *Bowen*, 46.

[30] R. W. Griswold, *The Republican Court, or American Society in the Days of Washington*, hereafter cited as *Griswold*, 138. As will appear later, rain fell in the evening. The probability is that sunshine was intermittent.

[31] T. E. V. Smith, *op. cit.*, 40 ff, wrote an admirable account of the transformation of this structure in accordance with the ambitious design of Maj. Charles L'Enfant.

[32] Embarrassed committeemen may not have confessed it, but the two Houses of Congress had been in idle joint session for more than an hour because the senatorial members of the committee for the reception of the President had lingered unduly on the floor to share in a debate over trifles. See *Maclay*, 8. There is an error in next to the last line on this page of Maclay's *Journal*: "while" is "until" in the manuscript (see William Maclay, MS *Journal*, v. 1, p. 9, LC).

[33] *Bowen*, 15. The Senate Chamber measured forty feet by thirty, with a pitch of fifteen, or perhaps twenty, feet, the latter figure given in one contemporary description (*New-York Magazine*, March, 1790, p. 132–35). Fireplaces of fine domestic marble adorned the walls, but Washington would scarcely have noticed them, in the circumstances.

[34] The arrangement of windows and doors is known, but the location of the dais, as given in the text, is not stated specifically in any document uncovered in this study. While this consequence is an assumption in the text, the northern end of the room seems the place that best fits the description of the dais, even though, as frequently happened in assembly rooms, this put northern light in the eyes of members. A. K. Baragwanath, Librarian of the Museum of the City of New York, and Gardner Osborne, Director of the Federal Hall Memorial Museum, are of opinion that the dais faced South (Letter of Mr. Baragwanath, Feb. 19, 1953).

aisle; to the General's right, on the eastern side, were the members of the United States House of Representatives. All these lawmakers and their guests rose instantly from the semicircle of seats;[35] Washington bowed to both sides[36] while he walked to the Vice President who was standing directly in front of the platform.[37] John Adams formally welcomed Washington[38] and escorted him to the central seat, under the canopy.[39] With an exchange of bows, Adams took a chair on Washington's right, and Speaker Frederick Muhlenberg on the General's left.[40] After a brief pause of complete silence,[41] Adams stood again to address the President, but he hesitated in some embarrassment, as if he had forgotten part of what he was to say.[42] At length the words came: "Sir, the Senate and House of Representatives are ready to attend you to take the oath required by the Constitution. It will be administered by the Chancellor of the State of New York."[43] "I am ready to proceed," Washington answered simply.

Adams bowed formally and led the way to the arched central door of the three that led into a small half-enclosed portico overlooking Wall and Broad Streets.[44] As Washington emerged, he saw in front of him an arm-chair and a small table draped in red, and on this a crimson velvet cushion that held a large, leather-covered Bible.[45] Beyond the portico, across the street, he looked at crowded roof-tops and at windows filled with his fellow-Americans. A second later, from the front of the portico, he beheld a multitude in the streets. Everywhere were upturned faces till walls shut them off or distance dimmed them. The General bowed as his eyes ran over the amazing scene; wholehearted welcoming cheers rolled up to him and did not decrease in volume until he bowed again and again with his hand on his heart and

[35] Moustier's dispatch, *loc. cit.*; see also *Bowen*, 48.

[36] *Maclay*, 9.

[37] The shorter, east-and-west axis of the chamber was thirty feet; the pitch was fifteen (*Bowen*, 15) or twenty feet (contemporary description quoted in *T. E. V. Smith*, 46). The ceiling was arched, with no other adornment than a painted sun and thirteen stars).

[38] Gardoqui to Floridablanca, May 1, 1789, *loc. cit.*, f. 708; a translation in *Bowen*, 46.

[39] *T. E. V. Smith*, as *supra*.

[40] *Ibid.*, 227, with citation of the official arrangements, as *supra*, n. 6; 1 *JS*, 18.

[41] Lear's Diary, as cited.          [42] *Maclay*, 9.

[43] 1 *JS*, 18. "Sir" is not in the Journal, nor is it certain that Adams used two sentences. The Journal entry is a quotation but is in the form of indirect discourse. In Lear's letter of May 3, 1789, as cited *supra*, the language is: ". . . the Vice-President arose and informed the President that all things were prepared to administer the oath whenever he saw fit to proceed to the balcony to take it."

[44] Matteson, *op. cit.*, 228, noted that the floor of this "gallery" covered 480 square feet only. On either side of this portico was a window.

[45] *Memoir of the Life of Eliza Susan Morton Quincy*, cited hereafter as *Mrs. Quincy*, p. 51

then stepped back to the arm-chair where he took his seat.[46] By this time, the portico was jammed, but places had been left at the front for the Chancellor, for the Vice President and for Governor Clinton.[47] Immediately behind the table stood Henry Knox and Arthur St. Clair, the one still Secretary of War and the other Governor of the Northwest Territory. Both were Major Generals of the Continental Army though they did not appear in that capacity.[48] As soon as these and a few other guests were in their assigned places, Washington perceived that the historic moment was at hand. He arose and came forward again, close to the iron rail and in unobstructed view of the crowd. Opposite him stood Chancellor Robert R. Livingston, who had been a member of Congress when the Virginian had been named almost fourteen years previously as Commander-in-Chief. Samuel Otis, the "small, short" [49] Secretary of the Senate, lifted the Bible and the red cushion from the table and took his station between Washington and the Chancellor. Otis stood with his face to the throng; the Judge and the President were in profile when seen from the street. After the briefest of pauses, when Washington saw that the Judge was ready, he put his right hand on the Bible. "Do you solemnly swear," asked the Chancellor, "that you will faithfully execute the office of President of the United States and will, to the best of your ability, preserve, protect, and defend the Constitution of the United States?"

"I solemnly swear," Washington answered—and repeated the oath. Reverently he added, "So help me God." He bent forward as he spoke and, before Otis could lift the Bible to his lips, he kissed the book.

"It is done," Livingston announced, and, turning to the crowd, he made a broad gesture with his hand and shouted, "Long live George Washington, President of the United States!" The roar of the throng came back on the instant, joyful and sustained. Livingston's cry was taken up, and with it came clearly, "God bless our President." [50] Wash-

---

[46] *Ibid.*, 52.

[47] *Ibid.*

[48] The presence or absence of von Steuben has been asserted by different writers with a puzzling vehemence. An old engraving reproduced in 2 *Paine Wingate*, 304, shows Steuben directly behind John Adams but this is no more than traditional evidence. Matteson remarked there was "no proper authority" for Steuben's attendance among guests limited altogether to officials; *op. cit.*, 276.

[49] *Griswold*, 140. Samuel Otis was the brother of the patriot James Otis and the father of Harrison Gray Otis.

[50] Lear's letter of May 3, 1789, as *supra*.

ington bowed. The answering cheers were louder and more emotional than ever.[51] While the rejoicing continued, many eyes were lifted to the cupola of the Federal Hall, where the flag was being raised. It was a signal to the Battery which answered quickly with the bang-bang of thirteen guns. Soon this was amplified: *Galveston*, the Spanish sloop of war in the harbor, loosed her fire.[52] In the intervals of this pulsing, keener ears than those of Washington heard again the church bells of the city.[53] The President had not intended to address the crowd and, if he had planned to do so, he could not have made his voice audible above the congratulatory din. He bowed his acknowledgments, which evoked still more cheers, and before the ovation ended, he reentered the Senate Chamber, took his seat on the dais and waited for the members and guests to resume their places.[54] Then, after a pause, he got on his feet to read his inaugural address. All spectators rose with him [55] and, after he had bowed again, sat down intently. "Fellow Citizens of the Senate and House of Representatives," Washington began in a deep, low voice [56] and with manifest embarrassment,[57] "Among the vicissitudes incident to life, no event could have filled me with greater anxiety than that of which the notification was transmitted by your order . . ."

[51] Harrison Gray Otis, writing sixty years later, had a vivid recollection of the response of the spectators at this moment: "No one can describe the silent tearful ecstacy which pervaded the myriads who witnessed that scene, succeeded only by shouts which seemed to shake the canopy above them." S. E. Morison, *The Life and Letters of Harrison Gray Otis, Federalist, 1765–1848,* v. 1, p. 34. See, also, *Griswold,* 141.

[52] *Mrs. Quincy,* 52; *T. E. V. Smith,* 232; *Daily Advertiser,* May 1, 1789, p. 2; Gardoqui's dispatch of May 1, 1789, in Arc. His. Nac., Madrid. *Estado,* Leg. 3894, 314, f. 708. Cited in *Bowen,* 46. Although a considerable number of witnesses may be cited, there remains an element of doubt whether Washington repeated the oath clause by clause or waited until Livingston had read the whole of it. The text is believed to be correct but reservation on this point has to be made. The familiar "letter from New York," printed in the *Federal Gazette* (Philadelphia) of May 8 and republished in the *Gazette of the United States,* May 13, 1789, p. 3, still deserves quotation, in part, because it shows, as dramatically as any contemporary evidence, how the mere public appearance of Washington aroused emotions that were almost religious: "It would seem extraordinary that the administration of an oath . . . should, in so great a degree, excite the public curiosity. But the circumstances of [Washington's] election, the impression of his past services, the concourse of spectators, the devout fervency with which he repeated the oath, and the reverential manner in which he bowed down and kissed the sacred volume—all these conspired to render it one of the most august and interesting spectacles ever exhibited on this globe. It seemed, from the number of witnesses, to be a solemn appeal to Heaven and earth at once. Upon the subject of this great and good man, I may perhaps be an enthusiast; but I confess that I was under an awful and religious persuasion that the gracious Ruler of the universe was looking down at that moment with peculiar complacency . . ."

[53] *Mrs. Quincy,* 52.

[54] *Ibid*; Moustier to the Comte de Montmorin, May 1, 1789 (*loc. cit.,* f. 75). See translation in *Bowen,* 48.

[55] *Maclay,* 9.

[56] *Works of Fisher Ames, With a Selection from his Speeches and Correspondence,* Seth Ames, ed. (cited hereafter as *Fisher Ames*), v. 1, p. 34.

[57] *Maclay,* 9.

He repeated in well-fashioned phrases what he had said many times previously regarding the conflict of duty and inclinations and his consciousness of his "inferior endowments" and his lack of practice "in the duties of civil administration." He followed this with "fervent supplications to that Almighty Being who rules over the Universe." In paying homage "to the Great Author of every public and private good," the President said, he knew that he expressed the country's sentiment as well as his own. In reverent tones he spoke of the "invisible hand" and the "providential agency" that had guided the people of the United States in all their struggles and through the "tranquil deliberations and voluntary consent" that had wrought the "important revolution just accomplished in the system of their United Government."

After he had dwelt on these themes for about six minutes,[58] Washington turned to the duty imposed by the Constitution of making recommendations to Congress, but in this he deferred to Congress. He was sure, he said, that "no local pledges or attachments, no separate views nor party animosities" would "misdirect the comprehensive and equal eye which ought to watch over this great assemblage of communities and interests . . ." The one specific suggestion he made, as he went on, was that Congress should decide to what extent it should advocate constitutional amendments in order to meet objections and to relieve "inquietude." In this, said Washington, "I shall again give way to my entire confidence in your discernment and pursuit of the public good," but he added reflections that bespoke both his caution and his political judgment: "I assure myself that whilst you carefully avoid every alteration which might endanger the benefits of an united and effective government, or which ought to await the future lessons of experience, a reverence for the characteristic rights of freedom and a regard for the public harmony will sufficiently influence your deliberations on the question how far the former can be more impregnably fortified, or the latter be safely and advantageously promoted."

With this, he turned back the pages of his public service by renewing, in effect, the statement he had made when he had been named Commander-in-Chief in 1775: he would ask that his compensation "be limited to such actual expenditures as the public good may be thought to require." A minute sufficed for his conclusion: "Having thus imparted to you my sentiments, as they have been awakened by the occa-

[58] Assuming his delivery to have been slightly in excess of 100 words a minute.

sion which brings us together, I shall take my present leave; but not without resorting once more to the benign parent of the human race, in humble supplication that since he has been pleased to favor the American people, with opportunities for deliberating in perfect tranquility, and dispositions for deciding with unparalleled unanimity on a form of Government for the security of their Union and the advancement of their happiness; so his divine blessing may be equally conspicuous in the enlarged views, the temperate consultations and the wise measures on which the success of this Government must depend." [59]

When he folded his papers and bowed and sat down, his audience was as much moved as he had been. He had fumbled once or twice with the sheets and had not shown grace of movement in the single gesture he had made while speaking. Critical and experienced orators might have said that he did not know what to do with his hands while he was on his feet.[60] In spite of this and perhaps, in part, because of his manifest lack of familiarity with rhetorical tricks, he had stirred deeply the feelings of most of those who had listened. This was not because of the content of the speech any more than because of the delivery: the earnestness of the man, his sincerity, his simplicity and the memories that he personified, more than all, set hearts to beating faster and blurred responsive eyes. "I . . . sat entranced," said the greatest orator in Congress.[61] The French Minister, also a witness of the inauguration, reported to his government: ". . . never has sovereign reigned more completely in the hearts of his subjects than did Washington in those of his fellow-citizens . . . He has the soul, look and figure of a hero united in him." [62]

[59] 30 *G. W.*, 296, with the punctuation revised for clarity, but with the original capitalization preserved. New York papers printed the inaugural address in full. On May 5, the *Daily Gazette* (p. 2) republished it "at the request of a number of our subscribers."

[60] Cf. *Maclay*, 9.

[61] This was Fisher Ames. He wrote George Minot, May 3, 1789: ". . . it was a very touching scene and quite of the solemn kind. [Washington's] aspect grave, almost to sadness; his modesty, actually shaking; his voice deep, a little tremulous, and so low as to call for close attention; added to the series of objects presented to the mind, and overwhelming it, produced emotions of the most affecting kind upon the members. I, pilgarlic, sat entranced. It seemed to me an allegory in which virtue was personified, and addressing those whom she would make her votaries" (1 *Fisher Ames*, 34). The interjected word "pilgarlic" has been capitalized in some reprints, as if it were a proper name. Readers will recall it as a most interesting term, now almost completely obsolete, used to describe an individual as bald as a peeled garlic. By contemptuous application, the word became almost synonymous with the less formal phrase, "poor creature."

[62] Moustier to the Comte de Montmorin, June 5, 1789, *loc. cit.*, f. 75 and quoted in *Bowen*, 49.

From Federal Hall, after his inaugural had been delivered, the President walked with Congressmen and guests, through streets lined with militia, to St. Paul's Chapel, whither Congress had voted to go in order "to hear divine service, performed by the Chaplain of Congress." [63] The walk of about 700 yards was without other incident than new demonstrations of general good will and of rejoicing by the pious that the rulers of the people were showing themselves to be servants of God.[64] By this time, Washington had regained his grave, half-melancholy composure and, besides acknowledging the cheers of the crowd, he had an eye for individuals and if he saw a familiar face he made a personal bow.[65] At the end of the walk, which was as friendly as it was triumphant, he entered the crowded chapel where pews had been kept open for the President, the committee and the guests. In the dimly lighted edifice, Washington unconsciously and silently explained one of the reasons for the greater veneration shown him from the time he started North to assume office. To discerning eyes, at least, it was apparent that the nation's hero was growing old. The anxieties of war, the strain of the struggle for the Constitution, and the battle with his own spirit over a return to public life, had set the wrinkles and had deepened the lines. "Time has made havoc upon his face," wrote Fisher Ames, who sat near him,[66] and then the brilliant Massachusetts Representative confessed: "That, and many other circumstances not to be reasoned about, conspire to keep up the awe which I brought with me." [67] The President himself, as he bowed his head, shared in a strange commingling of the old and the new: the prayers read by the portly, dignified [68] Bishop, *in pontificalibus*, were those Washington had heard

[63] There were to be two Chaplains, of different denominations, one chosen by the House and the other by the Senate, with a transfer weekly of each clergyman to the other chamber. The Senate on the 25th of April had named Rt. Rev. Samuel Provoost, Episcopal Bishop of New York. Final action was not taken by the House until May 1, when a majority was found for Rev. William Linn (1 *JS*, 12, 14, 15, 16, 21; 1 *JHR.*, 12, 20, 26), a minister of the Collegiate Reformed Protestant Dutch Church (see *T. E. V. Smith*, 133, for Linn, and 139 for Provoost, who is sketched in *DAB*, also). Doctor Provoost was Rector of Trinity Church as well as Bishop, but as the reconstruction of Trinity after the fire of 1776 had not been completed, St. Paul's was designated for the service.

[64] *Daily Advertiser*, May 1, 1789, p. 2; *Maclay*, 9; *T. E. V. Smith*, 234.

[65] Cf. letter of "R— R—": "I must not forget to tell you that, on his way to church, through a numerous collection of spectators, I caught his eye and had the honor of a very gracious bow from him: this, from so great a man in so high a station, I thought myself highly honored by." 3 *Historical Magazine*, 184, cited in *Bowen*, 45.

[66] 1 *Fisher Ames*, 34.

[67] *Ibid.*

[68] *T. E. V. Smith*, 139.

since his boyhood days in the church at Fredericksburg; the *Te Deum* was as old [69] as the fame of St. Ambrose of Milan; [70] yet the minister read from a "Proposed" and not from an established Book of Common Prayer. Young as was government under the Constitution Washington had sworn that day to support, the American Protestant Episcopal Church was younger still in the sense that it had not yet adopted formally its prayers and its order of service.

The Bishop did not abbreviate the petitions he made to the Almighty, and the *Te Deum* was sung, not chanted; but as Doctor Provoost did not preach a sermon, Washington was soon out of doors again and in one of the carriages that awaited guests and committee.[71] When the horses stopped in front of his door, he had thanks to express to his escort and still more bows to exchange with officials who doubtless shared Henry Knox's opinion that "the business was conducted with the highest solemnity and propriety." [72]

Mercifully the President was left to dine privately and to reflect in his own chamber on events that would compel him at 57 years of age to face the perplexities inevitably attendant on the exercise by a central government of powers eleven States jealously had guarded as the symbols and the tools of their sovereignty. Had he been superstitious he would have found ill omen in the events of the evening. With Humphreys and Lear, he rode in his carriage that evening to Chancellor Livingston's and then to General Knox's residence to observe the illumination of the city and the display of fireworks [73] arranged by Maj. Sebastian Bauman at the Battery. The display was as fine as ingenious engineers could make it with lamps and thin cloth and fuses and flares at private homes and in the set pieces at public places. Between the old fort and the Bowling Green was a large transparency with a portrait of the President. Above him was an emblem of Fortitude; on his right

[69] For the inclusion of the *Te Deum* in the service, see Col. John May's letter of May 1, 1789, to his wife, as quoted in *Bowen*, 56, from May's *Journeys to the Ohio Country*, 123–34.
[70] In Washington's day, this renowned Latin hymn had not been credited, as now it generally is, to St. Nicetas, Bishop of Remesiana.
[71] *New York Daily Gaz.*, May 1, 1789, p. 2; *T. E. V. Smith*, 235.
[72] Letter of May 2, 1789, to John Hancock; *Knox Papers*, MHS.
[73] As cited in 10 *Sparks*, 464, Tobias Lear's Diary states that the three men went "in the carriages," carefully plural, but this may be a copyist's error. In his letter to George Augustine Washington, written May 3, Lear said nothing of two vehicles and left the impression that the three men proceeded informally together. The designer of the fireworks was the same Bauman to whom posterity owes the most useful of the maps of the fortifications at Yorktown, Virginia, in October, 1781.

hand was Justice, personifying the new Senate, and on the left was Wisdom, the House of Representatives.[74] It was remarkable but, like all transparencies, it faded in the night. The press of people was so great that Washington and his aides could not use their easy carriage in going home. They had to walk.[75]

Part of the way was dark.

[74] The fullest description of this transparency is in *Daily Advertiser*, May 1, p. 2. Both Gardoqui and Moustier gave interesting details of other features of the illumination. See their dispatches in *Bowen*, 47, 49.

[75] Lear's Diary, as *supra*, n. 20.

# CHAPTER IX

## WASHINGTON KEEPS HIS UNIFORM
### (May 1–July 4, 1789)

WASHINGTON'S FIRST task was not to ascertain his duties but to find time in which to discharge those awaiting him. He manifestly had to study all recent treasury reports and all foreign dispatches, and he had to confer with the heads of the departments that had existed when the Constitution became operative. In no other way than this could he so readily discover the poverty of the government and the state of negotiations with foreign powers and with the Indians. Good relations with Congress had to be established, and acceptable channels of communication had to be opened, perhaps by different approaches, with House and Senate. The executive branch of government had then to be organized, revenues had to be provided, courts set up, and appointments made—appointments that would tax his judgment and his patience and would antagonize a score for every person they would gratify.

These were duties of varying complexity but the least difficult of them would demand hours on hours of work every week and some would require long attention daily; how could this be given? If visitors were being ushered endlessly into the house all day, and the President went out every evening to return calls or to appear at civic entertainments, would not the public service suffer fatally and he, himself, disappoint popular expectation? The rule to receive "visits of compliment" on two designated days of the week and then for an hour only was made effective[1] forthwith. Invitations to dinner in the President's House, which usually was served at 3 o'clock, had not been issued between the date of Washington's arrival in New York and that of the assumption of office. It was decided to make no exception to this rule for the time being, though Lear, on reaching the city, had hired "Black Sam"[2] Fraunces

---

[1] Cf. *supra*, p. 187, n. 12.
[2] The name given Fraunces, who was a West Indian, by Philip Freneau. A sketch of Samuel Fraunces is in *DAB*.

as steward.[3] The former proprietor of the tavern where Washington had said farewell to his officers,[4] "tossed off such a number of fine dishes," according to Lear, "that we are distracted in our choice when we sit down to table, and obliged to hold a long consultation on the subject before we can determine what to attack." [5] Although it seemed bad to leave these viands untouched while members of Congress were eating poor meals at noisy taverns,[6] the General's tentative decision [7] to do no entertaining at dinner was approved and perhaps was prompted by old Federal lawmakers of taste and by conspicuous New Yorkers. They explained that some of the later presiding officers of Congress under the Articles of Confederation had been lavish in the invitations extended. ". . . the [President's] table," Washington subsequently explained, on the say-so of these informants, "was considered as a public one, and every person who could get introduced, conceived that he had a *right* to be invited to it. This, although the table was always crowded (and with mixed company, and the President considered in no better light than as a Maître d'hôtel) was in its nature impracticable and as many offences given as if no table had been kept." [8] To avoid this, the General was told that he would do well to extend no invitations and, further, to accept none.[9]

Washington wondered if this was altogether sound counsel. If he agreed to the whole of it, might he not be thought to ape a king, and would he not be a loser in that he would close "the avenues of useful information from the many," as he put it, "and make [himself] more dependent on that of the few"? [10] In electing to defer entertainment under his own roof, he felt it prudent to continue public appearances temporarily—and at what immediately proved to be an excessive price. On the 6th of May he attended the commencement of Columbia College and subjected himself to ten orations by graduating students at the same time that he heard the final exhortation by the clear-headed President William Samuel Johnson, an appeal doubtless better than the description in ancestrally familiar terms as "affectionate, pertinent and

---

[3] On May 4 Fraunces gave public notice to the merchants of the city that all purchases for the President's household would be strictly in cash, and cautioned against the advancement of credit to any who might represent themselves as the President's servants (*Gazette of U. S.* (New York), May 6, 1789, p. 3).

[4] Vol. V, p. 466 ff.

[5] Letter of May 3, 1789, to George Augustine Washington, as *supra*.

[6] 30 *G. W.*, 360–62; Lear, as *supra*.          [7] 30 *G. W.*, 360–62.

[8] Letter of July 26, 1789, to David Stuart; *ibid.*, 361.

[9] *Ibid.*          [10] *Ibid.*, 361–62.

elegant." [11] The next night, Washington went to a great ball at the Assembly Rooms.[12] The evening of the 11th was given to the theatre, with several members of Congress as guests of the President.[13] By the 14th, the strain of long days and late evenings may have been severe, but Washington had to go, as a matter of course, to a ball given in his honor by the French Minister, the Comte de Moustier.[14] Manifestly, for Washington to continue this measure of social activity was out of the question; but if he could not say "No" to the French diplomatic representative and would not decline to go to the Assembly, how could he refuse other invitations? As for the levees he was holding, they were well attended [15] and were disapproved by none except the most vehement foes of aristocratic trends [16]—but were two such gatherings a week necessary? Might not one suffice? These questions suggested others to Washington's mind and led him to review what had been done and what seemed next in order. Before he had ended his experimental round of attendance on social affairs, he asked John Adams, Alexander Hamilton, John Jay and James Madison for their advice: Might he safely reduce the levees? Could he with propriety set an early morning hour each day—say 8 o'clock—for calls by persons who had public business to discuss? Would it be in order for him to invite six, eight or ten men in public office, and no private citizens to dine with him on the days he held levees? Were all large entertainments better barred than held? Might not a few be arranged annually at the President's house, and if so, when? Was it permissible for him to make occasional informal visits or to attend tea parties at the homes of personal friends? Should he undertake journeys to other parts of the country to observe conditions and perhaps needs? This manifestly must be done at public expense, but by what form of appropriation?

Hamilton's answer was austere: One levee a week would be sufficient and should be open only to those who were introduced properly; Washington's appearance at these affairs ought not to extend beyond half an hour; during the reception, invitations to dinner should be extended

[11] *Gazette of U. S.*, May 9, 1789, p. 3.
[12] *Daily Advertiser*, May 8, 1789, p. 2; in *Griswold* is a long quotation, 155 n, from "Colonel Stone's"—probably Col. William Leete Stone's—description of the gowns worn by some of the ladies.
[13] *Maclay*, 30–31; *New-York Daily Gaz.*, May 11, p. 2; *Daily Advertiser*, May 9, p. 2; *Gazette of U. S.*, May 13, 1789, p. 3.
[14] *Ibid.*, May 16, 1789, p. 3. An account of this affair will be found in *Griswold*, 157–58.
[15] Cf. *Gazette of U. S.*, May 6, p. 3, May 9, p. 3, May 13, 1789, p. 3.
[16] Notably Sen. William Maclay. See his *Journal*, 30–31.

## "STREW YOUR HERO'S WAY WITH FLOWERS"

On the 16th of April, 1789, the President-elect left Mount Vernon for New York in a lone carriage, his family and entourage to follow when ready. For Washington and his two companions, Charles Thomson and Col. David Humphreys, the familiar journey northward must have been this time a revelation. America had hailed her heroes before, often with adulation rich enough to embarrass a humble man or to turn the head of a vain one. Now, however, Washington was evoking something altogether unique, something far beyond the usual measure of public acclaim. Here was something from a page in Roman history, something very like the triumphal return of a Caesar to his capital. The distinction was that Washington rode at the head of no legion—he was a private citizen, five years out of the Army, and his chariot was a plain traveling coach. Yet he was welcomed at every stage of the journey as though only yesterday he had emerged from battle with fresh achievement. Towns seemed in rivalry to do him unprecedented honor with escorts, salutes, parades, dinners, addresses, fireworks, fêtes of every description—and everywhere were the applauding voices and admiring eyes of thousands of his countrymen.

Some of this must have been tedious and much of it physically exhausting during the eight days of the trip. The parade into Philadelphia, for example, actually commenced at Chester about ten in the morning of April 20. After a banquet in the afternoon and a pyrotechnic display in the evening, Washington had to listen to five addresses before he could leave the city on the 21st. Later this same day, however, the President-elect received a tribute which struck a deep vein of emotion in him. Once on the Jersey side of the Delaware, he was given a handsome horse on which to lead the procession into Trenton over ground and past landmarks impressed in his memory by the desperate action of January 2, 1777. To his surprise, the simple bridge at Assunpink Creek was now elaborately adorned with a high arch of greenery and a motto to the effect that Washington had protected American mothers and would protect their daughters also. As he started across, he was surrounded by ladies and little girls dressed in white, who sang an ode and sprinkled flowers in his path. Washington bowed from his saddle and thanked them from his heart. For him, the "affecting moment" on Trenton bridge remained the high point of the inaugural journey.

(Engraving by T. Kelley. From Washington Irving's *Life of George Washington*, Vol. IV.)

# MADISON AND HAMILTON, A COALITION DIVIDING

Conditioned by experience to full appreciation of able lieutenants, Washington could contemplate the future of the Federal government with satisfaction and shining hope as the First Congress recessed on September 29, 1789. Never in the War had the General undertaken a large task with so splendid a galaxy of subordinates. For once Washington had at hand men upon whom he could depend without reluctance, seasoned timber this time instead of green. All about him now the President saw statesmen, public servants sharpened and polished in the art of government by the strenuous councils of the Confederation. Two among these he could look upon as the expert engineers of the new Federal system—in the executive branch, Alexander Hamilton as Secretary of the Treasury; in the legislative, James Madison as majority leader of the House.

Every evidence pointed to the fruitful collaboration of these leaders in the momentous work ahead. Both had the indefatigability of youth—the Secretary was 32, the Representative but six years his senior; both were admirably educated, practiced in debate, bold and brilliant political theorists; both were afire with patriotism, single-minded in their dedication to perpetuate America's independence at all costs. It augured well, further, that

(James Madison: After the Original by Gilbert Stuart. Reproduced by courtesy of The Bowdoin College Museum of Fine Arts.)

Hamilton and Madison had shared tribulation and triumph. Together in the Continental Congress, they had chafed at the feebleness of that body and had arrived substantially at the same criticisms. Out of their meeting at Annapolis in 1786 had come Hamilton's recommendation for a Federal Convention, and in Philadelphia the next year Madison's genius distinguished him as the principal architect of the Constitution. Parallel effort for ratification was the surpassing accomplishment of their political intimacy—authorship of the Federalist Papers, Madison's uphill struggle against the towering influence of Patrick Henry in Virginia, Hamilton's climactic victory over the organized and articulate supporters of Governor Clinton in New York.

It seemed a certainty, in autumn of 1789, that these men would continue to work together. On October 12, Hamilton asked Madison for suggestions "as to any modification of the public debt." When, however, the Secretary presented to Congress in January, 1790, the first of his comprehensive financial reports, Madison stood at the head of a conscientious, determined opposition. Within a few months the ground had split irreparably between Hamilton and Madison, the pillars of Federalism upon whom Washington had rested his fondest anticipations.

(Alexander Hamilton: After the Original by John Trumbull, in the Great Hall of the Chamber of Commerce of New York City; by permission of that Institution.)

informally to six or eight guests, with whom, when the meal had been concluded, the President would not linger overlong. No invitations were to be accepted, nor were any visits to be returned. From two to four entertainments might be held yearly.[17] John Adams's views were much more liberal: Two levees a week would be necessary to accommodate the crowds; access to them should be allowed with proper scrutiny of those persons who sought admission. The President should not have large social gatherings but he should remain free to receive unofficial guests in his house and be at liberty to visit informally, because his private life should be lived at his own discretion. Public entertainment was not necessary. Tours of the country were desirable, but the expense of them ought to be separate from the compensation of the President.[18]

On the basis of this and probably other advice, Washington chose, as he said, "that line of conduct which combined public advantage with private convenience and which in my judgment, was unexceptionable in itself"; [19] he would continue two levees a week,[20] but he would make no visits; [21] on occasion he would indulge his fondness for the theatre; [22] and as an interested planter he would drive out to see some of the farm implements developed by the Baron de Poellnitz, who was operating a small property near New York; [23] other decisions on social life could await the arrival of Martha from Virginia. She almost certainly would have associations and entertainments that must be fitted into his. In more extended activities, as in those of the frame he fashioned, the aim of Washington never was in actual doubt however much it might be misrepresented; he did not seek the glorification of his office but the simplification of his work. He precisely stated the fact when he said later of his regimen, ". . . had I not adopted it, I should have been unable to have attended to *any* sort of business unless I had applied the hours allotted to rest and refreshment . . ." [24] So clear was his line of

---

[17] 8 *A. Hamilton*, 83–84, probably of May 15 but misdated May 5, 1789. The original of this letter has not yet been located.

[18] *John Adams*, 491–93. The answers of John Jay and of James Madison, if made in writing, have not been found.

[19] 31 *G. W.*, 53.

[20] The hour of these was changed, May 26, from 2 to 3 P.M.; *Gazette of U. S.*, May 27, 1789, p. 3.

[21] Apparently he was not present at Gardoqui's "elegant entertainment" of May 22; *ibid.*, May 23, 1789, p. 3.

[22] Cf. *Baker*, 138–39 and *Gazette of U. S.*, June 6, 1789, p. 3.

[23] *Ibid.*, May 27, 1789, p. 3; 30 *G. W.*, 485–86; 31 *ibid.*, 23–24.

[24] Letter of July 26, 1789, to David Stuart; 30 *ibid.*, 361.

duty in the eyes of New Yorkers that the leading men of the city did not embarrass him by extending a single invitation to dinner. Except for his meal with Governor Clinton on the day of his arrival, he did not sit down at table outside the house assigned him by Congress.[25]

That body shared the feeling of New York about extensive entertainment and, in addition, it decided the question of titles in a manner to satisfy the staunchest supporter of republican simplicity. A majority of the Senate still adhered to the view of Vice President Adams that titles were proper, but on the 14th of May they announced themselves "desirous of preserving harmony with the House of Representatives" and therefore willing "for the present" to accept the practice of the other branch and to address the chief executive as " 'President of the United States,' without addition of title." [26]

"The President," then, with briefest title, had in the shortest possible time to organize his personal office and, through it, first of all, to thank those who had congratulated him or had facilitated his journey or had shared in the welcome accorded him.[27] He had admirable assistance in the experienced literary veteran, David Humphreys, and in Tobias Lear, whose wide abilities and fine disposition made him useful at almost every important task that had to be performed in the Presidential establishment. With amiable ease, Lear could effect a good bargain or have repairs executed quickly; he could write an excellent letter or manage a pleasant dinner. No young man since the days of Tench Tilghman and John Laurens had served so acceptably in Washington's household. Lear grew but so did his duties, which soon exceeded all

---

[25] *Ibid.*, 362.

[26] 1 *JS*, 25. Cf. *ibid.*, 16, 17, 22, 23, 24 and 1 *JHR.*, 20, 27, 32. Senator Maclay, the most vigorous adversary of titles, wrote in his *Journal* that he had no "clew" to Washington's feelings with respect to titles, though he wondered if the President had not dropped some hint to his confidants. The Pennsylvanian concluded: "But no matter. I have, by plowing with the heifer of the other House, completely defeated them" (*Maclay*, 35). For newspaper comment, see *Federal Gazette* (Philadelphia), April 2, p. 3, and Apr. 7, 1789, p. 2. See "Argos" in *Mass. Centinel* (Boston), reprinted in *Gazette of U. S.*, July 8, 1789, p. 1: "Let us (I mean true uncontaminated Whigs) lisp nothing but the pure names of men . . . plain John Anybody should be our address . . . *Mr.* signifies *Master* and leads to slavery; therefore away with it." Cf. Joseph Jones to James Madison, May 28, 1789, 11 *Madison Papers*, 72, LC: "I am pleased with the plain manly style of address, George Washington, President &c. The present name wants no titles to grace it, and should the office be filled by an unworthy person, the style will not dignify the man, or cast a beam of light around his head." Virginia Republicans felt some embarrassment because R. H. Lee vigorously supported John Adams's appeal for titles. See James Madison to Edmund Randolph, May 10, 1789; Randolph to Madison, May 19, 1789; 11 *Madison Papers*, 48, 59, 65, LC. Of interest, also, was Fisher Ames's amused comment, 1 *Fisher Ames*, 36–37. For the revival of the dispute over titles after Mrs. Washington's arrival in New York, see *infra*, p. 212.

[27] See 30 *G. W.*, 308 and n, 323 ff.

that even his diligence could accomplish on a given day. The President had to look for another senior secretary and two juniors. It took him some months to find and to make arrangement with Maj. William Jackson, who had served in Lincoln's South Carolina campaign and in 1787 had been Secretary of the Philadelphia Convention. Washington, like almost everyone else, found the Major personally so attractive and so skillful in dealing with all manner of men that he well might have lamented his failure to acquire the services of Jackson earlier.[28] One junior addition to the establishment was Thomas Nelson, son of the Virginia Governor of the same name who had commanded the Old Dominion militia in front of Yorktown. On the death of that fine-spirited leader, in January, 1789, fears that he had lost nearly all his fortune were confirmed: on the small farm to which he had moved from his fine house in Yorktown [29] he left a widow and eleven children—and debts of £35,000. When Washington received news of this, along with a request from David Stuart that a government clerkship or a place in the President's entourage be found for young Thomas,[30] he could promise no official position and he hesitated to put on his secretarial staff a man he did not know personally; but appreciation of the father's patriotic sacrifices outweighed his doubts. By his own hand he sent Thomas an invitation that was accepted gladly.[31] Still another young Virginian, Washington's nephew Robert Lewis, was to come to New York with Mrs. Washington. How many hours he could devote to the proposed copying [32] for the General, and how many to the Lady of the House, time and not advance planning alone would show.

Lear, Humphreys and Jackson were to be an able trio of helmsmen; Lewis and Nelson might prove useful. Meantime, there was need of political pilots—at least until Washington learned the parliamentary channel—to keep the executive bark away from shoals and shallows. The men to whom Washington looked for this assistance were James

[28] Although the date when Jackson joined Washington's family does not appear in the certificate the General gave him (320 Papers of G. W., 13-14, LC) after he had left the executive staff, Robert Lewis recorded in his Diary (Mount Vernon MSS) on Sept. 1, 1789: "Major Jackson came to live with us today." The first of Washington's letters signed by him bears date of Sept. 25, 1789 (30 G. W., 412). There is no positive reference to him before that date in Lear's financial accounts as set forth in Decatur.

[29] See Vol. V, p. 363, n. 18.

[30] 243 Papers of G. W., 88, LC; printed in 4 LTW., 267.

[31] 30 G. W., 365, 367; Thomas Nelson, Jr., to Washington, Aug. 13, 1789; 243 Papers of G. W., 115, LC. According to Lear's books, Decatur, 57, 148, Nelson did not join the family until Oct. 1, 1789, but he was paid from the time he accepted the place.

[32] See supra, p. 162, n. 138.

Madison and Alexander Hamilton—the Virginian for the drafting of papers too intricate for the secretaries, and the New Yorker for information on the higher political strategy, so to say, of New York and the East.[33] Both men could be valuable, exceedingly so, in Washington's next large task, the establishment of cordial relations with Congress.

This would not be difficult insofar as cordiality and cooperation called for deference and an understanding of the minds of Congressmen. Eight and a half years of negotiation with lawmakers while he was Commander-in-Chief had been added to his own training in the Virginia House of Burgesses and in the Congresses of 1774 and 1775. This long instruction gave him experience at least equal to that which any other American could employ in dealing, from the outside, with the new bicameral system of Federal legislation. The only unfamiliar phases of his official duty with respect to Congress were, first, a determination of the precise function of the Senate, and second, the establishment of a balanced relationship of the executive departments to Congress and to him. Immediately—and of necessity—he would use the four existing Departments—Foreign Affairs, War, Post Office and Board of Treasury—until others were created. In the absence of contrary precedents, he would have the heads of these divisions report directly to Congress on matters committed to them by resolution of the lawmakers.[34] In what he styled the "unsettled state of the executive departments" Washington did not feel, at the outset, that it was "expedient" to call officially for information from the departments;[35] but as soon as the pressure on him lightened in June, he began reading the dispatches and reports on file and he asked Jay, Knox and the members of the Board of Treasury to prepare a summary that would give him "a full, precise and general *idea*" of the work entrusted to them.[36] Within a few days, he began to assume a more positive direction of foreign affairs, the control of which was vested in him by the

[33] See 30 *G. W.*, 310 and n; Washington to A. Hamilton, May 5, 1789, 7 *Hamilton Papers*, f. 957, LC., quoted without specific reference in 30 *G. W.*, 311 n.

[34] The first instances of this were the submission to the Senate of certain treaties negotiated with the Indians before Washington took office. He turned over the papers to Knox for report (30 *G. W.*, 313) because he understood that relations with the natives had been under the Secretary of War. Later the treaties were sent the Senate "by the hands of General Knox . . . who will be ready to communicate to you information upon such points as may appear to require it" (*ibid.*, 332–33).

[35] *Ibid.*, 343.

[36] *Ibid.*, 343–44. For his care in making extracts from Jefferson's dispatches, see *ibid.*, 343 n. Washington's habit of taking notes was old and fixed, where important papers, public or personal, had to be considered. See a description of his practice in 10 *Sparks*, 473–83.

Constitution, no matter what might be the form of administration set up by Congress. Secretary Jay, he wrote the Senate, "has my orders to communicate to you whatever official papers on the subject [of a commercial convention with France] he may possess and you may require." [37] In this interpretation of his powers, the President from the outset wrote directly to foreign diplomatic agents who raised a question on which he alone could pass. [38]

In substance, then, Washington continued the service of the executive departments while he waited for Congress to decide how numerous these should be and how they were to operate. He gave no counsel on either of these subjects to the Senators and Representatives. In careful deference, he neither made recommendations to Congress at this time, nor discussed what the lawmakers debated. Most scrupulously he adhered to the stand he had taken at his inaugural—that amendment of the Constitution was proper but that in everything else he would rely on "the talents, the rectitude and the patriotism" of members. [39] The separation of the three branches of government was to be respected by him. He would administer but he would not interfere—that was the basis of his executive policy.

Congress was quick to assert the prerogatives he was careful to respect. Addresses to him in response to his inaugural were prepared, delivered and answered in accordance with colonial usage and with little disagreement over time and place for the exchange of friendly and respectful phrases. [40] The first bill passed by Congress was one that prescribed how oaths were to be administered, an act to which Washington attached his approving signature, June 1. [41] An imperative measure for levying imposts had been taken up in Committee of the Whole as early as April 8 [42] but members had much to say on this and

[37] Message of June 11, 1789; 30 *G. W.*, 346-47.

[38] See his careful letters of May 25 and June 2, 1789, to the Comte de Moustier, who undertook—improperly, as Washington thought—to open regular channels of oral communication with him. *Ibid.*, 333-35, 342. Both these are from Letter Book copies which give no indication of original authorship. If Washington did not have assistance in drafting them, he wrote with unwonted clarity and smoothness, though some passages appear to be in his style. If he followed his usual practice, he had Secretary Jay prepare drafts which he reviewed and perhaps changed in small particulars.

[39] *Ibid.*, 294.

[40] 1 *JHR.*, 26, 27, 28, 30, 31; 1 *JS*, 22, 26-27; *Gazette of U. S.*, May 9, 1789, p. 3; *Baker*, 134.

[41] 1 *JHR.*, 43; 1 *JS*, 30; *The Public Statutes at Large of the United States of America from the Organization of the Government in 1789 to March 3, 1845 . . . .*(ed. of 1845), v. 1, p. 23, cited hereafter as *Statutes at Large*.

[42] 1 *Annals*, 106-07.

on almost every other subject mentioned on the floor. Procedure was more or less unfamiliar; all the orators had to try their wings.[43] Debate over duties on imported goods soon developed many clashes of sectional interest and numerous complicated disputes over such issues as the proper ratio between the duty on rum and that on molasses.[44] In conditions then existing, it was encouraging, rather than disappointing, that the House agreed on the imposts, which were understood to be temporary, within little more than two weeks after the inauguration.[45] Senate acquiescence, with many disputable amendments, was reported to the House on the 12th of June.[46] Bills for the creation of executive Departments of Foreign Affairs, War and Treasury were authorized by the House on the 21st of May,[47] were presented early in June [48] and soon were involved in an interesting debate on the question, whether the right of the President to remove the heads of these departments was inherent in his office.[49] This was discussed with solemn and frequent reference to the text of the Constitution, almost as if the appeal were to the most venerable principles of the common law. Details might be amended but dispute over the precise meaning and the clear implication of the nation's organic law was reassuring proof of its acceptance.

Washington always had believed in a strong Executive, but he did not possess the type of mind that relished constitutional analysis, and even if he had been adept in this, he would have been put temporarily out of the debate by developments of mid-June. These occurrences had

[43] James Madison wrote Jefferson, June 30, 1789: ". . . the Federal business has proceeded with a mortifying tardiness, chargeable in part to the incorrect draught of committees and the prolixity of discussion incident to a public body . . . but principally resulting from the novelty and complexity of the subjects of legislation. We are in a wilderness without a single footstep to guide us. Our successors will have an easier task, and by degrees the way will become smooth, short and certain" (11 *Madison Papers*, 99, LC). Similar views were expressed by Madison to his father, July 5, 1789, *ibid.*, 103. Equally of interest, in judgment of the First Congress, are the fascinating letters written at this time by Fisher Ames, who was jealous and perhaps a bit suspicious of Madison. See 1 *Fisher Ames*, 35–36, 42, 47–49. Ames made a brilliant analysis of Congress in a letter of July 8, 1789, to George Richards Minot. See *ibid.*, 62–64.

[44] James Madison to Edmund Randolph, May 10, 1789, 11 *Madison Papers*, 59, LC. This bill was the predominant subject of debate in the House from April 8 through May 16 (1 *Annals*, 105–381). For the argument over rum and molasses, see *ibid.*, 131–44, and Hugh Williamson to Madison, May 19, 1789; 11 *Madison Papers*, 65, LC. Williamson wrote that wherever his vessel stopped on the way from North Carolina to New York, he heard complaints about the tax on molasses. He had not expected this sentiment in the South, he said, but he found that the poor—according to his informants—were dependent on molasses in their diet.

[45] 1 *JHR.*, 36–37.

[46] *Ibid.*, 48.

[47] *Ibid.*, 39.

[48] *Ibid.*, 44, 46.

[49] The greater part of the debate was June 16–27 and is summarized in 1 *Annals*, 473–613.

a happy prelude. After much careful preparation, Martha left home during the afternoon of May 16, with a tearful goodbye on the part of the servants. She rode in the family carriage with her two grandchildren and she had the General's nephew, Robert Lewis of Fredericksburg, as mounted [50] escort and major domo.[51] The team was of Mount Vernon horses but by previous arrangement, these animals were to be replaced with others that belonged to the operator of the stagecoach line, Col. Gabriel P. Van Horne.[52] The halt for the first day was at Alexandria in order that Mrs. Washington might visit her daughter-in-law and the two grandchildren who had remained with their mother when "Jack" Custis's widow had married Dr. David Stuart. On the 18th, the carriage without the horses was ferried over the Potomac, Van Horne's team was harnessed, and the journey was resumed. Nothing worse than the bolt of the animals and the badness of the road slowed the northward grind of the wheels until the party, attended by Van Horne, reached Hammond's Ferry, not far from Baltimore.[53] At the crossing, several eminent citizens of the town made their bow and conducted Martha to the home of Mrs. Charles Carroll, who had extended an invitation through a messenger. The gentlemen of Mrs. Washington's escort observed that the Carroll mansion appeared to have many guests; Robert Lewis and Colonel Van Horne consequently suggested that they proceed to the town and return later for the President's lady. Mrs. Carroll would not have it so: the gentlemen must refresh themselves, if only for a few minutes. "We found," Robert Lewis wrote later, "a large bowl of salubrious iced punch, with fruits &c which had been plucked from the trees in a green house, lying on the tables in great abundance; these, after riding 25 or 30 miles without eating or drinking, was no unwelcome luxury; however, Mrs. C could not complain that we had not done her punch honor, for in the course of 1 quarter of an hour (the time we tarried) this bowl, which held upwards

[50] 30 G. W., 318.

[51] Robert Lewis's Journal, 881 Papers of G. W., LC. This is a Toner Transcript, 18 pages in length, of a fragment of the journal kept by Lewis on his trip to New York. The original is at Mount Vernon. Cf. Martha Washington to Frances Bassett ("Fanny") Washington, June 8, 1789; Decatur, 20. Subsequent references to Decatur, 20 and 21, are to this chatty letter. For Washington's offer to Robert of a personal secretaryship, see supra, p. 162, n. 138, and 30 G. W., 228, 250.

[52] See Col. William Heth to Washington, May 3, 1789; Thom Coll., Mount Vernon. Van Horne's title was in militia service.

[53] The details of Martha's stay in Alexandria, the crossing, etc., will be found in Robert Lewis's Journal, 11–12, and in Decatur, 20.

of two gallons was entirely consumed to the no little satisfaction of us all." [54]

During the afternoon, Martha went with her escorts to the home of Major and Mrs. James McHenry, where she was to drink tea and renew happy associations. After nightfall, some fireworks were displayed for her and were, as always, a diversion; but a serenade in Martha's honor, lasting until 2 o'clock on the morning of the 20th, scarcely was good preparation for a journey that was supposed to be resumed at 5 A.M. [55] The fame of Martha's husband and a desire to pay her tribute —to say nothing of other stimulation—could have explained, though it scarcely could have justified, this musical marathon. Had the performers been put to the test, they doubtless would have maintained, gallantly, that Mrs. Washington deserved the full repertoire of the band on her own account. Furthermore, as citizens of a town that was advancing American industry with zeal, the Baltimoreans gave her of their best because, "like her illustrious husband, she was clothed in the manufacture of our country, in which her native goodness and patriotism appeared to the greatest advantage." [56]

Early or late, deafened or delighted, Martha left Baltimore that day, the 20th of May, and proceeded without accident through Wilmington to Chester, where she had breakfast on the 22nd. [57] About 10 miles from Philadelphia, she was met by General Mifflin, President of the Council, with other celebrities and the two Troops of City Horse. At Derby, her unfailing hostess, Mrs. Robert Morris, bade her welcome. When Gray's Ferry was reached, approximately 100 men and women, the leading personages of the city, were host and hostess at a cold collation. From the Schuylkill to the Morris mansion, Mrs. Washington's ride was a triumph. Although she came at the drowsy and inconvenient hour of 2 in the afternoon, the streets were crowded. The bells clanged cheerfully; Artillery gave her the same salute of thirteen guns that the President had received. [58] Not for a moment did any of this turn her head. She remained, as in Baltimore, simple, appreciative, human and—grandmotherly. After reaching her room, she sent almost

[54] *Robert Lewis's Journal*, 13–14, verbatim except for a few changes of punctuation.
[55] *Ibid.* Numerous details of entertainment at James McHenry's residence are omitted.
[56] Baltimore dispatch in *Gazette of U. S.*, May 30, 1789, p. 3.
[57] *Gazette of U. S.*, May 30, 1789, p. 3. It is to be presumed that she spent the night of the 20th–21st in the vicinity of Havre de Grace and the next night at Wilmington, but no confirmatory records have been found.
[58] *Penn. Packet*, May 26, 1789, p. 3.

immediately for the stay-maker, in order that she might discharge a commission entrusted to her by Frances Washington, back at Mount Vernon, and one of her first purchases was of shoes for Frances, for Nellie Stuart and for the Custis grandchildren she had left on the Potomac.[59] Needless to say, the people of the city did not know of these personal matters, but the more thoughtful of the elders remembered her previous visits in black days. The *Pennsylvania Packet* doubtless spoke for the citizens of Philadelphia when it said: "The present occasion recalled the remembrance of those interesting scenes, in which, by her presence, she contributed to relieve the cares of our beloved Chief, and to soothe the anxious moments of his military concern— gratitude marked the recollection, and every countenance bespoke the feelings of affectionate respect." [60]

A few days with fashions and friends prepared Philadelphia's guest for the last stage of her journey. On the morning of the 25th of May the Troops of Light Horse paraded in her honor with the intention of escorting her all the way to Trenton. Mifflin and other celebrities were in attendance. Martha permitted them to start, but as the skies were ill-favored and rainy, she insisted gently that all her guards turn back after a few miles, while she continued northward with Robert Lewis, the servants, and the entourage of Mrs. Robert Morris who, with her daughters, was going to New York in their family carriage.[61] No other ceremonials were observed on the road to Elizabeth Town Point, where the two vehicles and the horsemen arrived on the 27th. Washington, Robert Morris and David Humphreys had the President's new barge in waiting with thirteen "eminent pilots," [62] and soon they conveyed the ladies and the two Custis children to Peck's Slip, on New York Island. Previous notice of the expected arrival of Mrs. Washington that afternoon had been published; [63] a salute of thirteen guns was given her as she passed the Battery; Governor Clinton stood at the dock to meet her; a large crowd had assembled to observe and to smile.[64] Mrs. Washington drove at once to the President's House, which she found "a very good one and . . . handsomely furnished all new for the General." In spite of help from an excellent staff, she perceived quickly that she had heavy duties as mistress of a busy mansion

[59] *Decatur*, 20–21.                              [60] *Penn. Packet*, May 26, 1789, p. 3.
[61] *Ibid.; Decatur*, 21.                          [62] *Baker*, 137.
[63] *Daily Advertiser*, May 27, p. 2, and, less specifically, *Gazette of U. S.*, May 27, 1789, p. 2
[64] *Decatur*, 21; *Gazette of U. S.*, May 30, 1789, p. 3; *Baker*, 137–38.

and as hostess at diversified affairs. After almost a fortnight, she wrote her niece: "I have not had one half hour to myself since the day of my arrival. My first care was to get the children to a good school, which they are boath very much pleased at . . ." [65] She left it there: her correspondent could decide for herself, on the basis of a somewhat close knowledge of little Nellie and Master Washington, whether they were "pleased at" going back to school or pleased with the particular seat of juvenile knowledge which they were "at."

Besides her grandchildren's study, appearance and regard for the amenities of a conspicuous social position, Martha had to give her own dress and her own social obligations literally flawless and ceaseless attention. Her hair was set and dressed every day; she discovered, of course, that she had left at home various apparel for which she had somewhat laboriously to write; [66] scores of visits had to be acknowledged and were most satisfactorily disposed of, she soon found, if they were returned on the third day, without fail. It was a life as far removed as decent existence could be from the routine of Mount Vernon, where the greatest excitement of the day usually was the clatter of a strange horse's hoofs on the driveway. To be sure, there were at least two embarrassing situations. In one of them, the General had made arrangements to entertain guests at the afternoon meal on the 28th, the day after Martha's arrival; but perhaps because the servants were confused, the affair was neglected. Senator Paine Wingate, like the General, did not consider himself particularly "nice," [67] but even he wrote: "It was the least showy dinner that I ever saw at the President's . . . After the dessert a single glass of wine was offered to each of the guests, when the President rose, the guests following his example, and repaired to the drawing-room, each departing at his option, without ceremony." [68] Martha's activity and experience changed all that. Before the summer was over, a none-too-friendly Senator was to write of a meal at her table, "It was a great dinner, and the best of the kind I ever was at." [69]

The other recorded unpleasantness that attended the early days of Mrs. Washington's residence on Cherry Street had its origin in the zeal of John Fenno for the Federal cause. Fenno was a Massachusetts

[65] Letter of June 8, 1789, to Frances Bassett Washington, *Decatur*, 20–21.
[66] *Ibid.*, 28.                    [67] Cf. *supra*, p. 20.
[68] *Baker*, 138; also in 2 *Paine Wingate*, 277.
[69] *Maclay*, 137; reprinted in *Baker*, 144. This was August 27.

man of 38 who had served his apprenticeship on the widely read
*Massachusetts Centinel,* had come to New York and had begun in
April the *Gazette of the United States,* a semi-weekly newspaper that
he hoped to make the organ of Federalism and of the administration.
His tone in dealing with Washington always was reverently laudatory,
as if he believed the people would support the government more loyally
if they venerated its head.[70]  In Fenno's mind, as in John Adams's, respect for public men depended in a measure on public titles. When
Martha came to New York, this theory was applied in a list of "the
principal ladies of the city" who, "with the earliest attention and respect,
paid their devoirs to the amiable consort of our beloved President." [71]
Fenno began with "The Lady of His Excellency the Governor" and
proceeded with "Lady Stirling, Lady Mary Watts, Lady Kitty Duer,
La Marchioness de Brehan, the Ladies of the Most Hon. Mr. Langdon,
and the Most Hon. M. Dalton, the Mayoress"—and only at this point
did he drop to plain "Mrs." in naming the wives of New Yorkers and
of members of Congress who called on the "President's consort." It
was a bit silly, of course, to persons who knew that three of the most
impressive names near the top of the list were those of the widow
and daughters of Lord Stirling, the American General, whose title had
not been accepted by the House of Lords as valid. Continentals had
awarded what the peers had denied, and Washington himself, times
unending, had addressed him, "My Lord"; but for one of his daughters

---

[70] It is easy to see, in retrospect, how Fenno's adoration of Washington irritated men of
independent mind. No poem in any of Fenno's exchanges was too fulsome in phrase or too
limping in metre if it had Washington as its subject. In writing on his own account, Fenno
had an unmistakable awe in every reference to the President who, he almost said, could do no
wrong. Often the editor "broke into verse" when he had said in prose everything that plain
grammar would convey. Typical utterances were, May 16, p. 3, an eleven-stanza "ode" styled
"The Vision," said to have been written soon after Yorktown; June 10, p. 2, an "ode" sung
at a meeting of the Ancient and Honorable Artillery of Boston with this extraordinary quatrain:

> Fill the bowl, fill it high
> First born son of the sky,
> May he never, never die
> Heaven shout, Amen.

On the 4th of July, p. 3, Fenno indulged himself at length in prose and verse; in his previous
issue (July 1, p. 3) he had given space to an extravagant "ode" by Daniel George. Absurd as
much of this was, Fenno was by no means the sole culprit. It seems to have been overlooked
that other editors went as far as he did, though less persistently. A few examples are: *Maryland
Journal* (Baltimore), Apr. 24, 1789, p. 4, a ninety-one-line "ode" to Washington; *Daily Advertiser,* May 8, p. 2, copied in Fenno's issue of May 13, 1789, p. 2, a seven-stanza poem in honor
of the President; *Daily Advertiser,* June 26, 1789, p. 2, a fifty-eight-line effusion by "a young
lady of New York" on Washington's arrival there. The climax was:

> The man's divine—let angels write his name
> In the bright records of eternal fame.

[71] *Gazette of U. S.,* May 30, 1789, p. 3.

to be called Lady Kitty Duer, when she was the wife of Col. William Duer, and for the spouse of Robert Watts to be styled Lady Mary Watts . . . well, friends of the Federalist editor did not have to complete the sentence. His rivals did. The *Albany Register*, printed by Robert Barber, ridiculed the titles in an article which Francis Childs's *Daily Advertiser* republished for consumption in New York. Care was taken to speak of Washington as that "great and good man" and Martha was mentioned with a respect that was above all possible offence; but, said Barber, "of all the titles thus ostentatiously obtruded on the public, I can observe only one which is properly introduced, viz. that of La Marchioness de Brehan"—at which name, if the article were read aloud in a fashionable feminine circle, there might have been an exchange of glances and, perhaps, a delicate lifting of eyebrows. The fiery editor roared on: "We also find Levees, Drawing-Rooms, &c. are not such strange, incomprehensible distant things as we have imagined; and I suppose, that in a few years, we shall have all the paraphernalia yet wanting to give the superb finish to the grandeur of our AMERICAN COURT! the purity of republican principle seems to be daily losing ground; and was it not that VIRTUE itself fills the Presidential chair, I should almost be persuaded we are on the eve of another revolution. . . . *The Gazette of the United States* might then vie with the *London Gazette* for adulatory pomp and . . . every reader would become a master of etiquette." There followed an extravagant forecast, clumsily put together, of what the "court" would be like in 1800.[72] If Martha was puzzled by these political tactics, and was not especially qualified to participate in the debate over titles, real or burlesque, she was able to do something much finer: she quickly made scores of friends in her new position. "I took the earliest opportunity . . .," wrote Abigail Adams, "to go and pay my respects to Mrs. Washington." The wife of the Vice President warmed her page as she went on: "She received me with great ease and politeness. She is plain in her dress, but that plainness is the best of every article. She is in mourning. Her hair is white, her teeth beautiful, her person rather short than otherwise . . . Her manners are modest and unassuming, dignified and feminine, not the tincture of hauteur about her." [73] In her next letter, Abigail confirmed her judgment: "Mrs. Washington is one of those unassuming char-

[72] *Daily Advertiser*, June 15, 1789, p. 2.
[73] Letter of June 28, 1789, to her sister, Mary Cranch; *New Letters of Abigail Adams, 1788–1801*, Stewart Mitchell, ed., cited hereafter as *Abigail Adams*, 13.

acters which create love and esteem. A most becoming pleasantness sits upon her countenance and an unaffected deportment which renders her the object of veneration and respect. With all these feelings and sensations I found myself much more deeply impressed than I ever did before their Majesties of Britain." [74]

From the very beginning of her residence in New York, Martha emerged as a personality. During the war, stifling her timidity, she had traveled to the General's headquarters as soon as winter put an end to field operations and she had felt both the freezing blast that rolled over Massachusetts Bay and the savage wind that blew down the Hudson. She had come; she had ministered; she had gone southward when redcoats began to stir again and the roll of the drum had a threatening overtone. Visiting officers saw her and mentioned her casually. In passing through Philadelphia she sometimes had lingered and had made friends, but even there she had been shadowy, and to all except her intimates had seemed a name, rather than a person. Guests at Mount Vernon had pronounced her amiable and more sympathetic than her preoccupied husband. Visitors had remarked her caps and her clean, plain dress, but none of them had grown enthusiastic about her or had thought it worthwhile to sketch her even for a paragraph. Nobody had spoken of her teeth as beautiful—until now when she was old enough to have lost them, had she been less careful of them. The country's notables esteemed her, after the summer of 1789 when they could see her clearly, and not in the smoke of war.

Washington seldom had found himself more fortunate in her coming. He did not realize it, perhaps, but she humanized him in the eyes of his guests. What was more, she was at hand when, with little warning, he suddenly needed her in a particular manner. About the middle of June, when Congress was in tangled and contentious debate, the President developed a fever that did not yield to normal treatment. Soon there was a tenderness over the protuberance of his thigh on the left side.[75] Medical aid was summoned by the 17th;[76] Dr. Samuel Bard, a leading practitioner, and his consultants were unable to make a

[74] Letter of July 12, 1789; *ibid.*, 15.
[75] That it was his left side is not set forth in any of the numerous references to his "thigh," but the fact is established by his own remark (30 *G. W.*, 366) that he had to lie for six weeks entirely on his right side.
[76] *New-York Journal*, June 18, p. 3; *Baker*, 139.

diagnosis. Concern was general;[77] rumor spread that the President
had a malignant tumor or else was a victim of anthrax,[78] "wool sorters'
disease." His condition became so serious and he suffered such acute
pain that ropes were stretched across Cherry Street to save him, at least,
from the noise of passing vehicles.[79] The tumor grew fast and took
on a dangerous fiery hue; soreness spread to such an extent that he
could not sit down otherwise than in acute pain. About the 20th[80] the
fever disappeared and the tumor showed itself as an abscess. Doctor
Bard opened it but had to make a large incision, which manifestly
would heal slowly and, meanwhile, would keep the General aggra-
vatingly uncomfortable, night and day.[81] As an apostle of exercise,
comfortable or otherwise, Washington had the seats of his carriage adjusted in such a fashion that he could stretch out full length, under
Martha's soothing hands, while driven about the city;[82] and when he
wished particularly to see a guest, he could make himself presentable,
half sitting and half reclining.[83]

His progress was slow, very slow, but by the 3rd of July he could
write a letter, or at least revise a draft on official business of importance;[84] but, of course, he bestirred himself to extra effort for the observance of the 4th of July. The New York militia were to be paraded
and reviewed that day; the State Society of the Cincinnati planned a
meeting and an address to him. He must be prepared for its delivery.
So, on the thirteenth anniversary of the Declaration of Independence,
he dressed with care and probably kept on his feet as much as he could,
in order to escape the embarrassment of sitting down painfully and
awkwardly. The day had historic beginning. To Washington's house
was brought the text of "a bill for laying a duty on goods, wares and

[77] Clement Biddle, Philadelphia, to Tobias Lear, June 22, 1789; Clement Biddle Letter
Book, *PHS*, unpaged; *Penn. Packet* of June 22, cited in *Baker*, 139.

[78] See F. A. Willius and T. E. Keys, "The Medical History of George Washington," *Proc.
Staff Meetings, Mayo Clinic*, v. 17, p. 92 ff.

[79] *Baker*, 139; *Decatur*, 27. The rope was stolen and had to be replaced; *ibid.*, 32.

[80] Cf. *Gazette of U. S.*, June 20, 1789, p. 3. Fenno's paper of this date, doubtless to allay
public concern, reported Washington "much better" after only a "slight fever."

[81] James Madison to Edmund Randolph, June 24, 1789, 11 *Madison Papers*, 94, LC; Tobias
Lear in 30 *G. W.*, 348, 349, 350–51; Washington to McHenry, July 3, 1789, *ibid.*, 351. The
General's steady response to this treatment has led historians of medicine to conclude that he
did not have anthrax but a large carbuncle. See *supra*, n. 78. It may be permissible to suggest
that perhaps his thigh was irritated and later was infected by the rubbing of his scabbard. He
wore his sword often after he came to New York and had not carried it previously for many
months.

[82] *Gazette of U. S.*, July 4, 1789, p. 3; 30 *G. W.*, 351.

[83] *Abigail Adams*, 15.                    [84] E.g., 30 *G. W.*, 352–53.

merchandizes imported into the United States"—the "impost bill," contested in every line but adopted at last by Congress.[85] Washington signed it [86]—without a word to indicate that he reflected on the interesting connection between political independence declared on the 4th of July, 1776, and the fiscal independence assured by the simple bill made law thirteen years thereafter.

Next, the committee of the New York Cincinnati, fresh from their business meeting and with their "eagles" on their chests. Good soldiers and shining figures all of them were—Steuben, Alexander Hamilton, Samuel Blachley Webb, Sebastian Bauman, the artillerist and topographer, and William S. Smith, who had been aide to Sullivan, to Lafayette and then to Washington himself.[87] As president, Steuben delivered the address, which was considerately brief: "The Society of the Cincinnati of the State of New York have instructed this delegation to present to you, sir, their sentiments of the profoundest respect. In common with all good citizens of the United States of America, they join their ardent wishes for the preservation of your life, health and prosperity. In particular, they feel the highest satisfaction in contemplating the illustrious Chief of our armies, by the unanimous vote of an independent people, elected to the highest station that a dignified and enlightened country can bestow. Under your conduct, sir, this band of soldiers was led to glory and to conquest, and we feel confident that under your administration our country will speedily arrive at an enviable state of prosperity and happiness." [88]

For once, the General undertook to make an extemporaneous answer: "I beg you, gentlemen, to return my most affectionate regards to the Society of the Cincinnati of the State of New York, and assure them that I receive their congratulations on this auspicious day with a mind constantly anxious for the honor and welfare of our country; and can only say that the force of my abilities, aided by an integrity of heart, shall be studiously pointed to the support of its dignity, and the promotion of its prosperity and happiness." [89]

That was part of his plain, political philosophy: The dignity of this country must be maintained as surely as its prosperity was to be measured in larger harvests and its happiness mirrored in the faces of a

[85] 1 *Statutes at Large*, 24 ff.　　　　　　　[86] *Gazette of U. S.*, July 8, 1789, p. 2.
[87] The list is in *Gazette of U. S.*, July 8, 1789, p. 3.
[88] *Ibid.*, and perhaps more conveniently in *Griswold*, 177.
[89] After the copy in the Diary of Robert Lewis; cited in 30 *G. W.*, 353 n.

free people. He would labor for these things in the mansion on Cherry Street as faithfully as he had in the Ford House at Morristown when cause and Army had been starving.

By ths time, the rope across the roadway had been taken down. Vehicles were moving, music was audible, spectators were lining the street. The militia were coming with their band. He must go to the door to take their salute. Louder the band—perhaps with "General Washington's March"—and then the head of the column was in front of the house. The President straightened into the soldier. Militiamen and pedestrians and printers all saw him and did not fail to observe that he was "in a suit of regimentals." [90]

[90] *Gazette of U. S.*, July 8, 1789, p. 3.

# CHAPTER X

## "THE LINE OF MY OFFICIAL CONDUCT"
### (July 5–October 14, 1789)

AFTER THE 4th of July, 1789, Washington's recovery continued but, as he was beginning to find in matters less sensitively personal, progress was slow.[1] Had convalescence been more rapid, he could not have completed quickly the organization of the Executive, because Congress persisted in long debates on nearly all subjects presented.[2] The establishment of the Departments of Foreign Affairs, War and Treasury was by separate bills, not by a single measure. All three became the object of vigorous contention, because they gave the President the power to remove the heads of Departments. Was this in accordance with the Constitution, and if it was not inherent in the office, was it necessary for the control of the Departments? Should Congress have a voice in displacing an officer? Opinion differed honestly both on principle and on the issue of sound administrative practice. Although the argument went on for days and days, Congress continued so closely divided that the outcome remained in doubt.[3] The bill to set up "judicial courts for

---

[1] Although the *Gazette of the United States* announced July 11 (p. 3), that he was restored to his usual health, the incision on his thigh was draining slightly as late as September 8. See 30 *G. W.*, 396 and cf. *ibid.*, 359, 366, 369. By August 1 (1 *Paine Wingate*, 187–88) he was attending his levees again. Doctor Bard's bill was £84 (*Decatur*, 68). For Doctor Craik's advice from Virginia that the President take more exercise—advice he followed rigorously (e.g., 4 *Diaries*, 14)—see 244 *Papers of G. W.*, 5, LC. As late as autumn a visitor reported that the General did not look as well as he had expected (*Griswold*, 211). Washington's fine reply to Benjamin Franklin's congratulations on recovery appears in 30 *G. W.*, 409. Franklin's letter of Sept. 16, 1789 is in 12 *Bigelow's Franklin*, 137–38.

[2] See the complaint of this in C. Gore to Rufus King, Sept. 13, 1789; 1 *Rufus King*, 368.

[3] On the course of the bill for a Department of Foreign Affairs, the first to pass either House of Congress (June 23, 1789) see 1 *JHR.*, 52–53, 1 *JS*, 37, 41, 42, 43, 44, 45. The Senate debate over the power of removal is summarized in *Maclay*, 110 ff. It was on June 27 (1 *JHR.*, 54) that the bill to establish a War Department received the approval of the House. For Senate consideration, see 1 *JS*, 39, 44, 51, 52. Discussion of the measure to create a new Treasury Department came to a conclusion July 2. See 1 *JHR.*, 46, 47, 50, 52, 54, 56, 57; 1 *JS*, 39, 44, 49, 50, 53. Outside comment on this legislation was interesting. See *Daily Advertiser* (New York), May 26, 1789, p. 2, for argument on a division of responsibility in the Treasury. Prediction was made early in Philadelphia that the head of this Department would be Alexander Hamilton (*Gazette of U. S.*, June 17, 1789, p. 3). In a letter of June 10, 1789, Henry Lee expressed to James Madison the opinion that the country should be served by a three-man Board of Treasury, not by a single Secretary (11 *Madison Papers*, 79). On the general issue of removal by the President, see 1 *Fisher Ames*, 51–52; *Gazette of U. S.*, May 27, 1789, p. 3; James

the United States" passed the Senate July 17,[4] after debate that forecast long contention in the House.

Delay in the enactment of these fundamental laws was embarrassing to Washington. He could not set the foundations of the new executive structure, though the market-place was full of laborers awaiting hire.[5] Many men had come to New York in the hope of procuring public employment;[6] others let it be known they were willing to serve if called; and it was intimated that some modest individuals would not wish to be considered applicants.[7] Washington might well have been appalled to observe how much more numerous were the conspicuous men who sought offices than were the offices that would be available. Among applicants, direct or presented by friends, were Benjamin Lincoln, who was financially distressed;[8] James Wilson, who asked for the position of Chief Justice;[9] Arthur Lee, who explained that he had been called to the bar at Westminster Hall and wished to resume that profession as a Justice of the Supreme Court;[10] Thomas McKean, former President of Congress;[11] Maj. Gen. William Heath, and others no less well known.[12] Some of these grew impatient as weeks passed with no distribution of shining offices and exalted titles.[13] Washington filled promptly the positions established or continued under the temporary acts for levying and collecting imposts and tonnage taxes.[14] Beyond this,

---

Madison to Edmund Randolph, June 17, 1789 (11 *Madison Papers*, 84); James Madison to Edmund Pendleton, June 21, 1789 (*ibid.*, 91); James Madison to Tench Coxe, June 24, 1789 (*ibid.*, 95); Edward Carrington to James Madison, July 30, 1789 (*ibid.*, 119); Thomas Hartley to Jasper Yeates, Aug. 1, 23, 1789 (*Yeates Papers*, PHS); Edmund Randolph to James Madison, June 30, 1789 (11 *Madison Papers*, 100); same to same, Aug. 18, 1789 (12 *ibid.*, 9); Benjamin Huntington to his wife, June 20, 1789; W. D. McCrackan, ed., *The Huntington Letters, in the Possession of Julia Chester Wells*, 73.

[4] 1 *JS*, 36, 37, 38, 39, 40, 41, 42. For a calm discussion of the judiciary bill at the height of the debate, see Edmund Randolph to James Madison, June 30, 1789; 11 *Madison Papers*, 100, LC.

[5] These applications fill thirty-two manuscript volumes of 4807 pages, and they must number between 2500 and 3000. They are listed in Gaillard Hunt, *Calendar of Applications and Recommendations for Office During the Presidency of George Washington*. An annotated copy of this 1901 publication, with additions and corrections, is in the MS Division of LC.

[6] Henry Knox to Edward Carrington, June 16, 1789; *Knox Papers*, MHS.

[7] Letter from Boston in *Gazette of U. S.*, June 17, 1789, p. 3.

[8] Lincoln to Henry Knox, May 31; Knox to Lincoln, June 5, 1789; *Knox Papers*, MHS.

[9] 30 *G. W.*, 314. Wilson's letter of Apr. 21, 1789 (30 *Applications for Office Under Washington*, f. 4602, LC) is a clever document that will amuse anyone interested in Wilson.

[10] See Gaillard Hunt, *op. cit.*, 72.   [11] 30 *G. W.*, 315.   [12] *Ibid.*, 316.

[13] *Gazette of U. S.*, July 1, 1789, p. 3; 1 *Rufus King*, 368.

[14] 1 *Statutes at Large*, acts of July 4, 20, and 31, 1789, p. 24–27, 27–28, 29–49. Robert Lewis noted in his Diary, Aug. 4, 1789 (*Mount Vernon MSS*) that he and Lear had 120 letters to write to the first appointees, whose names were printed in the *Gazette of the United States*, Aug. 5, 1789, p. 3. Benjamin Lincoln was named Collector of the Port of Boston (Knox to Lincoln, Aug. 4, 1789) and, with assured income, seemed "a new man" (H. Jackson to Knox, Aug. 13, 1789) *Knox Papers*, MHS).

he reminded applicants, Congress had not yet gone into the creation of offices.[15] He let it be known, also, that subordinate posts would not be assigned in any of the Departments till the chiefs had been appointed,[16] and he reiterated what he had said again and again before leaving Virginia—that he had made no commitments and would seek the best man who offered, as far as his judgment guided him.[17] Three points that had not been anticipated in Washington's earlier decisions were stressed now: All applications would be regarded as confidential; those who sought positions should state specifically what work they desired; [18] if a man were discharging acceptably a State office that was transferred to the Federal government, he would not be displaced, and if a division of duties occurred, the incumbent would be regarded with favor for the better of the positions created.[19] In passing on official requirements and on men about whom he knew nothing, the President usually consulted the Senators from the applicant's State, though he made no sort of pledge to do this.[20] Even with these safeguards, applications proved a worse ordeal, if possible, than Washington had expected them to be. On occasion, too, some who should have known better made a particularly embarrassing request. Bushrod Washington, then a young lawyer of 27, calmly applied to his uncle for appointment as United States District Attorney for Virginia. The President's reply combined regard for the young man's feelings with a candid statement of his own duty: ". . . however deserving you may be of the [office] you have suggested, your standing at the bar would not justify my nomination of you . . . in preference of some of the oldest and most esteemed General Court lawyers [21] in your own State, who are desirous of this appointment." [22] Then he displayed the caution of a man long disciplined to respect both his public trust and his personal reputation: "My political conduct in nominations, even if I was uninfluenced by

[15] 30 *G. W.*, 323 ff.

[16] Cf. Steuben to William North, May 30, [1789]. Personal relics of the Baron von Steuben. "American Art Association Catalogue, 1929," p. 25, n. 151.

[17] Knox to Mrs. Mercy Warren, July 9, 1789; Knox to Edward Carrington, June 16, 1789, a comprehensive statement of Washington's policy of appointments (*Knox Papers*, MHS; see also 30 *G. W.*, 310, 314, 315, 316).

[18] Knox to Carrington, June 16, 1789, as *supra*.

[19] R. H. Lee to Charles Lee, June 7, 1789, 2 *Ballagh, Lee Letters*, 490; 30 *G. W.*, 353–54; 2 *Paine Wingate*, 339–41.

[20] For consultation of R. H. Lee, see 30 *G. W.*, 368–69.

[21] That is, lawyers practicing before the General Court, the jurisdiction of which was substantially what it had been in the youth of Washington. See Vol. I, p. 179–80.

[22] 30 *G. W.*, 366.

principle, must be exceedingly circumspect and proof against just criticism, for the eyes of Argus are upon me, and no slip will pass unnoticed that can be improved into a supposed partiality for friends or relatives." [23]

This same caution—so deep as almost to be instinctive—marked Washington's steps in exploring his relations with Congress. He regarded the executive branch as a "department" [24] distinct from the Federal legislature, but on parity with it and bound by oath and by the letter of the Constitution to show proper deference toward it. If he made any suggestion for action by Congress the occasion had to be one of importance. With measures of general legislation he would make himself acquainted, and he might form a personal opinion, but he would not voice this otherwise than in confidence to trusted friends. [25] The initiative, the choice, the form, the scope and the prompt enactment or deliberate postponement of legislation were for the determination of Congress, unhindered by the Executive.

The President's power over lawmaking, as he saw it, was confined to his veto. Washington held unswervingly to this view from the first, but he did not understand, at the outset, exactly how he should proceed with respect to subjects that called for joint action by the President and the Senate. Among the names he sent in for revenue posts was that of Benjamin Fishbourne as Naval Officer at Savannah, Georgia. Fishbourne had served in the main Continental Army from October, 1776, to June, 1783, and had won so fully the admiration of General Wayne that he had been assigned to carry to Washington the famous dispatch on the successful midnight action at Stony Point. [26] As far as Washington's knowledge went, Fishbourne had a clean record after the war. On moving to Georgia, he had acquired public good will and, in fact, was serving as Officer of the Port of Georgia when nominated. [27] To Washington's surprise, the nomination of Colonel Fishbourne was rejected by the Senate on a secret ballot, for no reason that was explained to the President. [28] Washington's chagrin shaped this question: Would it not be well, when doubts arose, for the Senate to communicate with

[23] Ibid.  [24] Ibid., 424.
[25] See, for example, his familiarity with the disputed question of discrimination in the tonnage tax on shipping, 30 G. W., 363, and the opinion he expressed to David Stuart on the Quakers' anti-slavery memorial, 31 ibid., 30.
[26] See Vol. V, p. 113.  [27] 30 G. W., 370-71.
[28] Ibid., 370; Journal of the Executive Proceedings of the Senate of the United States of America, ed. 1828, cited hereafter as EJS., v. 1, p. 16.

the President and to give him opportunity of explaining why he made a nomination? He decided to present this suggestion to the Senators and in doing so, not only to make another nomination but also to state why he had sent in Fishbourne's name originally. His message was tactful: "Whatever may have been the reasons which induced your dissent," he wrote, "I am persuaded they were such as you deemed sufficient." [29]

Before this disarming communication reached the Senate, a three-member committee of that body—Ralph Izard, Rufus King and Charles Carroll—informed him of their appointment to "confer with him on the mode of communication proper to be pursued between him and the Senate in the formation of treaties and making appointments to office." [30] The whole affair then took on a formality that most certainly is tedious in retrospect and scarcely could have been excusable, even at the time, had it not dealt with a new subject on which precedents would be based. As always, when he faced a new issue that did not require instant decision, Washington postponed a meeting with the three Senators until he could prepare himself for questions that might be raised.

As it chanced, too, he had been considering the procedure to be followed with respect to treaties, because he planned, if Congress approved, to undertake a settlement with the Southern Indians. A written message on the subject was sent both Houses the day after the Senate committee was named.[31] Further study clarified some of his conclusions on methods of dealing with the upper House, but his survey soon involved questions of ceremonial on which he was beginning to put undue emphasis. Two conferences with the Senate committee convinced Washington that inflexible procedure was not wise, nor was it, he discovered, so much a concern to the committee as was the substitution of voice votes for secret ballot in passing on nominees.[32] Washington favored direct, open voting and said so. As between written

---

[29] To the Senate, Aug. 6, 1789; 30 G. W., 370. The tradition that he went in person to the Senate, unannounced, asked for an explanation of the reasons for rejecting Fishbourne and received a vigorous answer from Senator James Gunn of Georgia, cannot be reconciled with existing documentary evidence. According to 1 Annals, 59–60, Henry Knox, not Washington, appeared with the letter. It is entirely possible that substantially the answer attributed to Gunn was made—it would have been entirely in character (see Charles C. Jones, Biographical Sketches of the Delegates from Georgia to the Continental Congress, 44 ff)—but he did not speak in the presence of Washington.

[30] 1 EJS., 16.

[31] 30 G. W., 371–73; for his consultation of Madison on the preliminaries, see ibid., 369–70.

[32] Ibid., 375.

messages and personal appearance before the Senate, he told Madison
he would advocate the one that would seem "most conducive to the
public good." [33] His preference was for the black and white of a permanent record on nominations; his judgment dictated personal appearance
occasionally before the Senate in order to explain the provisions of
treaties and to ask directly for "advice and consent." He thought it
might even be possible sometimes to dispatch to the Senate the text or
headings of a treaty and then to come before that body and to get forthwith its "yes" or "no" on the points he raised.[34] In the end, he proposed
that "the Senate should accommodate their rules to the uncertainty of
the particular mode and place that may be preferred, providing for the
reception of either oral [or] written propositions, and for giving their
consent and advice in either the presence or absence of the President,
leaving him free to use the mode and place that may be found eligible
and accordant with other business which may be before him at the
time." [35]

The Senate acquiesced in most of this with the proviso that all questions be put by the Vice President and that Senators "signify their assent
or dissent by answering, viva voce, aye or no." [36] No sooner was this
procedure tested than it was found in part unworkable. Relations between the powerful Creek Indians and the State of Georgia were at a
confused pass which called for the friendly intervention of the United
States to settle boundary differences and, if possible, to wean the savages
from their vague but long sustained alliance with the Spanish in
Louisiana. On the 7th of August, Washington suggested that Congress
approve an effort to reach an accord with the Creeks through "a temporary commission . . . to consist of three persons, whose authority
should expire with the occasion." [37] The two Houses agreed and appropriated twenty thousand dollars for the negotiations,[38] whereupon
Washington called on Benjamin Lincoln to head the commissioners,[39]
and, with Knox as active penman, prepared to draft instructions. On

[33] *Ibid.*
[35] *Ibid.*, 378–79.
[37] 30 *G. W.*, 372; 1 *JS*, 55; 1 *JHR.*, 73–74.
[38] 1 *JS*, 59, 60, 61, 62; 1 *JHR.*, 74, 75, 77; 1 *Statutes at Large*, 54; 30 *G. W.*, 391.
[34] *Ibid.*, 373–74, 375, 378.
[36] 1 *EJS.*, 19; Aug. 21, 1789.
[39] *Ibid.*, 379–80; 1 *EJS.*, 18. The other members were Cyrus Griffin and David Humphreys,
30 *G. W.*, 404. Senator William Few of Georgia on his own motion and with Washington's
approval accompanied the party which sailed August 31. See Knox to Few, Aug. 27, 1789
(*Knox Papers*, MHS); *Gazette of U. S.*, Sept. 2, 1789, p. 3. The commissioners' instructions
are in *ASP.*, 1 *Ind. Aff.*, 65–68. Few's autobiographical notes on the episode are in 7 *Mag. Am.
His.*, 352–54. For Humphreys' later reports and subsequent references, see *infra*, p. 245–46.

the scope of these, Washington thought he should have the "advice and consent" of the Senate and, by prearrangement,[40] he went to the Chamber on Saturday, the 22nd of August, attended by Knox, and presented his questions in a paper which he passed to the Vice President. In the midst of noise from the street and confusion on the floor, Adams read this document and another that Washington had prepared, and then, after a re-reading, put the question on giving consent to the first of seven propositions submitted in the President's summary. As the subject was a complicated one with which few Senators had any familiarity, it should have been manifest that approval would be perfunctory, but most of the Senators hesitated to say anything that would cast doubt on the wisdom of Washington's proposals. At length William Maclay, the most vigorous dissenter in the Senate, protested against immediate action and sought to have the questions sent to committee or, failing that, to have action deferred. Washington disapproved. "This," he said, "defeats every purpose of my coming here," and he maintained that Knox had all the information required for a sound decision then and there; but as he went on, he evidently saw that postponement would be welcome, and he accordingly consented to have the whole subject deferred until Monday, the 24th. That day, in a calmer session, he received the Senate's approval of all he asked, though the debate was laboriously dull.[41]

The experience, as a whole, was not one that made it possible for Washington to set with assurance his future course. He ended the incident far less disposed than he had been at the outset to consult in person with the Senate on diplomatic affairs. Written communications would be easier and less subject to misunderstanding. If one result of the experiment with the presentation of the Indian negotiations was to establish viva-voce action in the place of secret balloting by the Senate, that was a desirable gain, as the President saw it,[42] but it concerned Congress and not the Executive. Between the two, Washington drew a clear line. Said he: ". . . as the Constitution of the United States, and the laws made under it, must mark the line of my official conduct, I could not justify my taking a single step in any matter, which appeared to me to require their agency, without its being first obtained . . ."[43]

40 1 *EJS.*, 20.          41 *Maclay*, 128–32.          42 30 *G. W.*, 375.
43 Letter of Feb. 11, 1790, to Edmund Randolph, 31 *ibid.*, 9. There is no reason for thinking this statement would have been different in August, 1789.

Adherence to that rule was one of several factors that simplified Washington's labors during the summer of 1789. Congress gradually became more familiar with the larger issues under consideration, though it still indulged too generously its loquacious and contentious members. Washington signed on July 27 the bill for the establishment of a Department of Foreign Affairs [44] and on August 7, a similar measure for a Department of War. [45] Debate and subsequent conference over the form and function of a Treasury Department delayed final action until August 28; [46] agreement on the salary of the President and Vice President was in prospect, though the allowance for Adams was the subject of argument between the two houses. [47] Pay for the members of Congress became involved with this discussion, though indirectly. [48] The bill for the compensation of the two senior executive officers, as signed Sept. 24, 1789, [49] fixed Washington's allotment at 25,000 dollars and that of the Vice President at 5000. Washington continued to act on the principle that he was receiving his expenses only, but he let these mount almost precisely to the figure set by Congress as his salary. [50] Vigorous argument over proposed constitutional amendments was underway, with the Federalists determined to approve no change in the basic structure. [51] The bill for setting up Federal Courts was encountering less violent opposition than might have been anticipated. [52]

[44] 1 *Statutes at Large*, 28–29.

[45] *Ibid.*, 49–50.

[46] 1 *JHR.*, 70, 71, 72, 73, 76, 89, 90, 91, 94–95; 1 *JS*, 50, 65, 67. Washington's signature was attached Sept. 2, 1789; 1 *Statutes at Large*, 65–67.

[47] 1 *JHR.*, 26, 40, 43, 64, 71, 104, 105, 113, 116, 117, 119, 120; 1 *JS*, 52, 54, 55, 56, 72, 84. Cf. Joseph Jones to James Madison, July 2, 1789, 11 *Madison Papers*, 101, LC.

[48] Cf. *Boston Gaz.*, Aug. 24, p. 3, Sept. 7, 1789, p. 3.

[49] 1 *Statutes at Large*, 72.

[50] For analysis of his expenditures, see *Decatur*, 328–33. Sometime after July 15 Lear drew up a statement of Washington's expenses for the first eleven weeks of the Presidency. The total cost was computed at $3656; Lear then used this figure to project an estimate of one year's expenses at $17,282. At the same time, he noted that such items as house rent, furniture, and firewood in particular, had not been incorporated into the reckoning. This undated document is in 243 *Papers of G. W.*, 2, LC.

[51] 1 *JHR.*, 81, 82–83, 85–86, 87–88, 89; 1 *JS*, 64, 69, 70, 72, 73–76, 77, 87; 1 *Annals*, 730 ff. Contemporary comment was of large interest, especially to the Virginians in New York who knew how far short of Patrick Henry's demands the proposed amendments fell. See 2 *W. W. Henry*, 444; 1 *Fisher Ames*, 52–53, a hostile view of Madison and of the amendments; Tench Coxe to Madison, June 18, 1789 (11 *Madison Papers*, 87–88, LC); Madison to Coxe, June 24, 1789 (*ibid.*, 95); Edmund Randolph to Madison, Aug. 18, 1789 (12 *ibid.*, 9)—an important note on Henry's attitude toward the amendments. Thomas Hartley was close to the reality when he wrote: "The Antis do not want any [amendments] at this time—we are obliged, in fact, to force [the amendments] on them" (Letter of Aug. 16, 1789, to Jasper Yeates; *Yeates Papers*, PHS).

[52] It passed the Senate July 17 (1 *JS*, 42), but was postponed by the House in order that constitutional amendments might be aired. Debate on the judiciary bill was not begun by the lower branch of Congress until August 24 (1 *JHR.*, 90) and after that single day's discussion,

Arrangements for seeing visitors increasingly served their purpose in saving time, but this was at the price of some grumbles and misunderstanding. Washington himself contributed unintentionally to this. He was coming more and more to love display and he had ambition to make the Presidency "respectable"—the word was one he used often in the eyes of the world. He thought it befitted the dignity of the office to drive with six cream-colored horses attached to his carriage,[53] and when Mrs. Washington desired particularly to honor the wife of some public man, the President saw no reason why she should not use the same team.[54]

In the stable, from twelve to sixteen horses were kept;[55] Washington apparently did not think he was making himself unduly conspicuous when he rode a white steed with leopard skin housing and saddle cloth that had a gold binding.[56] Fourteen white servants and seven slaves from Virginia were employed in the house on Broadway;[57] dinners were large, frequent and elaborate;[58] the pomp of entry was heightened by the presence in the hall of powdered lackeys;[59] food was consumed in amazing quantities; orders for wine ran to twenty-six dozen claret and a like volume of champagne.[60] New England folk read of these things and did not rebuke their national hero, but some doubtless were of one mind with the writer who lamented that his "old General" was "being taken over" by the great. He insisted, half humorously: "These

was not renewed until the 29th (*ibid.*, 94; 1 *Annals*, 826 ff). The measure thereupon gave place to a varied discussion and, in particular, to a wrangle and maneuver over the location of the seat of government. Further consideration was given the judiciary bill on September 8 (1 *JHR.*, 105; 1 *Annals*, 921). Approval of the Senate bill with amendments was voted on the 17th of that month (1 *JHR.*, 113); differences then were settled quickly (*ibid.*, 115, 117, 118; 1 *JS*, 83, 84, 85); the act was signed by the President Sept. 24, 1789 (1 *Statutes at Large*, 73–93). Interesting comment on the excellences and deficiencies of the legislation will be found in 2 *Paine Wingate*, 318; Jeremiah Wadsworth to Pierpont Edwards, July 26, 1789 (*Emmet Col.*, NYPL); Edward Carrington to James Madison. Aug. 3, 1789 (12 *Madison Papers*, 2, LC); James Monroe to James Madison, Aug. 12, 1789 (*ibid.*, 6); Thomas Hartley to Jasper Yeates, Sept. 13, 1789 (*Yeates Papers*, PHS). It is interesting to see how mistaken some of the able critics of this act proved to be. Edward Carrington, for example, assured Henry Knox, Oct. 25, 1789, that the statute for the "Establishment of the Judicial Courts of the United States" was so defective it doubtless would be altered at the next session of Congress (*Knox Papers*, MHS).

[53] See *Abigail Adams*, 20–21. The most renowned of the President's coaches, the famous yellow one, apparently was not used until 1790 or 1791. Nathaniel Burt stated in his "Address . . . on the Washington Mansion in Philadelphia" that this vehicle, the history of which he gave in some detail, was presented to Mrs. Washington "by the government of Pennsylvania," but he cited no authority for this statement. See *infra*, p. 295.

[54] 1 *Paine Wingate*, 187–88.  [55] *Decatur*, 42.

[56] *Ibid.*, 25.  [57] *Ibid.*, 39.

[58] After Oct. 1, 1789, they are listed in Washington's *Diary*, usually with the names of the guests.

[59] *Abigail Adams*, 26.  [60] 30 *G. W.*, 381.

fine folks would spoil our General if they could. He never was a greater man than when he rode among us with his dusty boots." [61] A Boston paper thought it desirable to insist, "Our beloved President stands unmoved in the vortex of folly and dissipation, which the city of New York represents." [62]

No less a person than the Vice President's lady denied the charge against New York. "Not a single public amusement is there in the whole city," she said, "no, not even a public walk, and as to dinners, I believe there are six made in Boston to one here, unless it is for some particular person to whom a number of families wish to pay attention." [63] Abigail Adams, in this, was defending herself and the six wives of Senators then living in New York. Indirectly she was defending also the President and more especially her friend Martha, with whom she was on terms of intimacy. Martha had begun to hold levees Friday evening each week, with varying attendance that her husband carefully set down after he resumed his Diary.[64] He usually came into the room to greet his wife's guests and if by chance he found some other lady sitting on the right of Martha, where he thought Mrs. Adams should be placed, he tactfully led the misplaced guest to some other part of the room.[65] It was natural after receiving this delicate attention that Abigail should consider Washington's regard for ceremonial as proper, but she could not forget her upbringing in Massachusetts, nor could she ignore the suggestion that her John Adams was living ostentatiously. Washington's equipage with its large team, its four servants and two gentlemen outriders, was, said Abigail, "no more state than is perfectly consistent with his station, but then I do not love to see the newswriters fib so" in asserting "he is perfectly averse to all marks of distinction . . ." [66] As for the allegation against her husband, "The Vice President ten times to one goes to Senate in a one-horse chaise, and levees we have had none." [67]

Along with the provoking questions of who drove what and who entertained whom, those interested in such matters continued to ask

---

[61] *Essex Journal* (Newburyport), Mch. 10, 1790, p. 4, with article from *Independent Gazetteer* (Philadelphia).
[62] Quoted in *Gazette of U. S.*, Aug. 1, 1789, p. 3, from *Boston Gaz.* of July 27, 1789, p. 3.
[63] Letter of Aug. 9, 1789, to her sister; *Abigail Adams*, 19.
[64] E.g., 4 *Diaries*, 53, 55.
[65] See Abigail Adams to her sister, Jan. 5, 1790; *Abigail Adams*, 35.
[66] To her sister, Aug. 9, 1789, *ibid.*, 20.
[67] To her sister, Sept. 1, 1789, *ibid.*, 26.

how the President and his second-in-command should be entitled. With every argument they could devise, the *New-York Journal* and the *Boston Gazette* continued to denounce titles of any sort,[68] but the only interesting addition to the argument was another of the countless tributes to Washington: as proof of his assumed disregard for titles, his continued inflexible stand as the "man of the people," it was reported in Virginia that during the debate on the subject, Washington had informed Adams in writing of his purpose to resign if any title were attached to the office of President.[69] This was not true, of course, but it was evidence of the manner in which the people detached Washington from the growing contest over titles and ceremonial and social ostentation that were alleged to be part of a trend toward monarchy.

On the 1st of September, Washington had a dinner at which General von Steuben was one of the guests. "The Baron" was in a cheerful and facetious mood and made everyone merry. About the time the laughter was at its highest, Washington received a letter that had just arrived,[70] a letter that put an end to jest, to dinner and to all social activities of the next few days. Late in July, the General's sister, Betty Lewis, had written him that their mother's physical condition was grave. "God only knows how it will end; I dread the consequence. She is sensible of it and is perfectly resigned—wishes for nothing more than to keep [her breast] easy. She wishes to hear from you; she will not believe you are well till she has it from your hand . . ."[71] After that, it was no surprise to hear that Mrs. Washington had become speechless about the 10th of August, had lost consciousness on the 20th, and had died at 3 P.M. on the 25th.[72] Washington's reflection was the natural one: "Awful and affecting as the death of a parent is, there is consolation

[68] *New-York Journal*, June 18, p. 3, Sept. 10, 1789, p. 2; *Boston Gaz.*, May 18, p. 2, July 27, p. 3, August 3, p. 2, 3; Aug. 17, 1789, p. 3. See, in similar vein, *Independent Chronicle* (Boston), July 16, 1789, p. 3.

[69] Edmund Randolph to James Madison, Sept. 26, 1789; 12 *Madison Papers*, 35, LC. David Stuart wrote Washington July 14, 1789 (4 *LTW.*, 265–66, and 243 *Papers of G. W.*, 100, LC) that some Virginians were alarmed by titles and ceremonials; to this letter Washington sent the reply, 30 *G. W.*, 356 ff, quoted *supra*. See, also, Edmund Randolph to James Madison, July 23, 1789, 11 *Madison Papers*, 114, LC; *Gazette of U. S.*, July 15, p. 2, July 29, p. 3, and Aug. 1, 1789, p. 3.

[70] Diary of Robert Lewis, *Mount Vernon MSS*.

[71] Letter of July 24, 1789; 243 *Papers of G. W.*, 104, LC. Robert Lewis's Diary of August 22 contained a note that a letter from his mother indicated his grandmother was "exceedingly ill and unlikely to recover" (*op. cit.*).

[72] Burgess Ball to Washington, Aug. 25, 1789; 244 *Papers of G. W.*, 6, LC. Ball wrote: "The cause of her dissolution (I believe) was the cancer on her breast" but he followed with the statement made in the text concerning loss of speech and later of consciousness. His language, needless to say, makes it appear probable that she had a brain hemorrhage.

in knowing that Heaven has spared ours to an age beyond which few attain, and favored her with the full enjoyment of her mental faculties and as much bodily strength as usually falls to the lot of fourscore. Under these considerations and a hope that she is translated to a happier place, it is the duty of her relatives to yield due submission to the decrees of the Creator. When I was last at Fredericksburg, I took a final leave of my Mother, never expecting to see her more." With that he skipped a line and, in a new paragraph, began a generous discussion of her will, a copy of which had been sent him in the letter that brought the news of her demise.[73] He ordered black cockades, sword knots and arm-ribbons for the men of the household,[74] but he did not "go into deep mourning" for her.[75] The regular levees were suspended for a

[73] 30 *G. W.*, 399; Burgess Ball's letter as *supra*; *Gazette of U. S.*, Sept. 2, 1789, p. 3. Mrs. Washington's Will (14 *Ford*, 416–18) incorporated her specific bequests which were described in her own words, together with a formal introduction and a conclusion written, probably, by her attorney, James Mercer. She disposed equitably of three male and three female slaves, a phaeton, a riding chair, three horses and a quantity of household furnishings, but she mentioned no silverware except eight tablespoons. Some other undescribed spoons were among her bequests but nothing was said of the metal. Along with other property of no great value, the General received the only land to which she still had title, that on Accokeek Run, in Stafford County. Washington thought at first that his sister Betty was entitled to a share of the slaves, but he was reminded by his nephew, Bushrod, that his mother held these Negroes under his father's will and that they were to be distributed among the male heirs only (30 *G. W.*, 435, 450). It was better, the General thought, to sell and to divide the proceeds of property not specifically bequeathed, than to apportion the articles (*Ibid.*). His attitude toward the other heirs to the estate was one of generosity. He was patient, also, with respect to the sale of the house and land he had bought in Fredericksburg for his mother's use (*ibid.*, 456–57, 508; 31 *ibid.*, 19; Burgess Ball to Washington, Oct. 8, 1789, 244 *Papers of G. W.*, 41, LC; Charles Carter, Jr., to Washington, Feb. 6, 1790, 245 *Papers of G. W.*, 123, LC). An advertisement of the farm in Stafford, signed by Bushrod Washington, appeared in the *Virginia Herald* (Fredericksburg), September 10, p. 3, September 17, p. 4, and Sept. 24, 1789, p. 4. This described "that valuable tract of land" as "containing 400 acres, situated on the north side of Rappahannock River, about three or four miles below Fredericksburg, and adjoining the lands of Col. Burgess Ball and Mr. Joseph B. Downman." The advertisement continued: "This land is well timbered and the soil of an excellent quality, particularly the low grounds lying on the river . . . Jesse Hill, living on the land, will show the same . . ." A subsequent advertisement (*ibid.*, Oct. 15, p. 3, Oct. 22, 1789, p. 4), printed over the signature of Betty Lewis, announced the proposed sale on October 29, "at the plantation, about four miles below the town, late the property of Mrs. Washington deceased" of "all the stocks of horses, cattle, sheep and hogs, plantation utensils of every kind, carts, hay and fodder."

[74] *Decatur*, 60. These items cost in excess of £5.

[75] The *Gazette of U. S.*, Sept. 9, 1789, p. 3, observed that this decision was in conformity with the resolution adopted by the Continental Congress in 1774. Reference was so specific that one is disposed to think the editor, John Fenno, received his information from the President's entourage, but no positive evidence of this has been found. Fenno remarked that conformity to the practice established in 1774 had diminished and that "the force of former habits . . . gradually prompted so many to relapse into the preceding fashion" that the simpler mourning might have been forgotten "had not the example of our patriotic President interposed to revive it." The "resolution" mentioned by Fenno was in reality part of the "association" adopted by the Continental Congress, Oct. 20, 1774: ". . . on the death of any relation or friend, none of us, or any of our families, will go into any further mourning-dress, than a black crape or ribbon on the arm or hat, for gentlemen, and a black ribbon and necklace for ladies, and we will discontinue the giving of gloves and scarves at funerals" (1 *JCC.*, 78).

week,[76] but after that, social life flowed on as before. The old lady was buried where presumably she wished to be, but her grave was not marked and, in time, might have been confused with those of other persons laid to rest there.[77]

From her renowned son in his manhood, she never had elicited the warm love a man usually has for his mother. She had seemed to him grasping, unreasonable in her demands and untidy in her person. Doubtless, too, he had been irked by her poor management, and when he had been close enough for her to know what he was doing, he must have been irritated by her ceaseless concern for him.[78] She had unstinted care at the hands of her daughter, Betty Lewis,[79] but if she was beloved in the community where she lived, no echo of affection for her has survived in the writings of travelers or in the four extant letters of her townsfolk. In old age she may have been unlovely and unlovable, yet, when she bore her son George, she must have possessed qualities that reappeared in him, some of them softened, perhaps, and some of them disciplined. There is no valid reason for doubting the tradition that she had fine physique and figure and that she was a skillful horsewoman. At least a measure of her acquisitiveness was possessed by George, especially during his early manhood, and this similarity was perhaps the chief reason for misunderstanding between the two. Persistence in the mother was perseverance in the son. It was from her, also, that he probably received his love of trees, of rivers, of beautiful prospects and of fruitful nature.

The most attractive picture of her is that given by one of her grandsons, Lawrence Lewis, in explaining why she was buried on the ground where her ashes most appropriately have remained: "I remember it was a favorite spot. She frequently visited it with her only daughter and grandchildren. Nature had seldom formed one more beautiful, the

---

[76] *Gazette of U. S.*, Sept. 12, 1789, p. 3; *Baker*, 146. See also Gardoqui to Knox, Sept. 2, 1789, a diplomatic inquiry concerning proper action during the period of mourning (*Knox Papers*, MHS).

[77] Lawrence Lewis to George W. Bassett, May 5, 1831: "My knowledge of the spot where my Grandmother was deposited and an examination of her bones will enable me to identify her remains, as for many years before her death she had no teeth or at least not more than one before tooth; [other persons] deposited in that place were all much younger; therefore it is not likely a mistake will occur, although it may be attended with some trouble" (*Mount Vernon MSS*).

[78] Had the words been used in this particular sense during her lifetime, she could have been described as a "notorious worrier," where her son George was involved.

[79] Cf. *supra*, p. 85, for the discovery by Washington that the daughter was exhausted by waiting on the mother.

approach to it a perfect level although considerably elevated above surrounding grounds. The hill forms a perfect angle, from the point of which project two large, shelving rocks, separated about two feet. [These] evidently from their corresponding sides formed at some period one mass. Seated upon this rock, with those she most loved, she would point out the beauties of the place—the distant hills overlooking the town of Falmouth, crowned with everlasting verdure by its tall cedars, the distant view of the river Rappahannock, foaming over its rocky bed, whose distant murmurs seemed but to heighten the delight of viewing the rocky summits above. It was upon this spot, rendered forever dear to my recollection, she impressed upon our infant minds the wonderful works of the Great Creator of all things, his goodness, his mercy to all who love and obey him." [80] If, in this, memories of youth had enchantment, that was part of her fortune. When the generation that knew her was dead, without leaving its recollections of her, the glory of her son's name gave glamor to hers. The well-to-do matron of 1781 might complain of high taxes and might inspire thereby a proposal for pensioning her, but a lifetime later she became the "Spartan mother." Her fearsome concern for the safety of the nation's leader was forgotten; the scene of Washington's farewell in April, 1789, to the pathetic but indomitable old lady was painted over and over with affectionate, imaginative strokes until Mary Washington was portrayed as the sibyl of the American union. If still later, the clatter of horses' hoofs disturbed her sleep, she would have forgiven the lovely, laughing young riders, because they were students of Mary Washington College, the women's undergraduate branch of her State's university.

Her son needed in the late summer and autumn of 1789 all the endurance in which he resembled her. The House of Representatives entered vehemently, if prematurely, into a debate over the permanent seat of government which was proposed, at one time or another, for almost every town of any size between the Delaware at Trenton and the Potomac at Georgetown. As former president of the Potomac Company [81] and a planter of that river valley, Washington of course wished

[80] Letter of May 15, 1831, to George W. Bassett; *Mount Vernon MSS.*

[81] According to Pickell, *op. cit.*, 114, Washington declined reelection as president of the Potomac Company in 1788, but consented to remain a director that year. The post of president was not filled until August, 1789 (cf. *Gazette of U. S.*, Aug. 22, 1789, p. 2), when Thomas Johnson was named to head the company. Washington then ceased to be a director (*Pickell*, op. cit., 114; *Mrs. Bacon-Foster*, 83–84), but he kept his deep interest in the enterprise. For the progress of the work, see, in addition to the published works, Alexander White to James

# JOHN ADAMS, A MAN OF NO PARTY

"The history of our Revolution," wrote this round-faced man to a favorite correspondent in 1790, "will be one continued lie from one end to the other. The essence of the whole will be that Dr. Franklin's electrical rod smote the earth and out sprang General Washington; that Franklin electrified him with his rod—and thence forward these two conducted all the policy, negotiations, legislatures, and war."

So ungenerous a reflection exhibits perfectly the scythe-edged mind of John Adams cutting its careless swath through a bountiful field of illustrious contemporaries. As a young lawyer in Boston, Adams had displayed prodigious pride in his growing library and in his encyclopedic professional knowledge, and had taken inordinate delight in the exposure of intellectual flaws among his associates. His tongue and his pen were as acid as his mind was keen, and experience accentuated these characteristics until Adams in middle age could view, as Jefferson said, "all parties and all men" with a measure of contempt. This was his habit, and behind it was lost irretrievably the truly amiable nature of the man. Lighthearted and temporary as many of his judgments were, they cost him friends by the score. Through thirty years Adams had been accumulating enemies, and it was scarcely a surprise in 1789 when his election to the Vice Presidency was secured by thirty-four only of the sixty-nine votes cast. As it was, Adams's candidacy was genuinely promoted by Benjamin Lincoln and just a few others in Massachusetts; Hamilton and Madison were not enthusiastic, and Washington endorsed Adams primarily because George Clinton was aspiring to office and the New York Governor had disclosed himself vehemently hostile to the new Constitution. Adams at least was a safe choice and eminently qualified, a thorough student of government and a pioneer advocate of the three-branch system. Realizing that his rôle would be a mute one, Adams mocked himself with the observation, "My country has in its wisdom contrived for me the most insignificant office that ever the invention of man contrived or his imagination conceived."

Avoided by Hamilton as an unmanageable individualist, and sharply distrusted by Jefferson and Madison as a potential monarchist, Adams stood apart—in reality, a man of no party. Where it was needed, his support went consistently to the administration—but always as an independent and never as the arch Federalist, the Hamiltonian collaborator depicted by the Republicans in the vitriolic campaign of 1792. Some years earlier Jefferson had delineated Adams accurately: "He is as disinterested as the Being Who made him."

(After the Original by C. W. Peale, Independence Hall, Philadelphia.)

12589

# ABIGAIL ADAMS, "SEATED HIGH"

"I hope you will see our worthy President. He is much a favorite of mine, I do assure you." So wrote Abigail Adams to her sister in September, 1789. She was George Washington's advocate from first acquaintance, and ever afterward his champion. Following his recovery from grave illness in the spring of 1790, she made a discerning comment: "It appears to me that union of the States, and consequently the permanency of the Government depend upon his life. . . . His death would, I fear, have had most disastrous consequences." No less was she Martha's loyal lieutenant. Indeed, the Washingtons and the administration had no more ardent adherent.

It was to her husband's welfare and interests, however, that she consistently devoted her fullest efforts. Surely, whatever John Adams accomplished, he did the better because of his admired and admiring Abigail—his chief informant, wise counsellor, defender. If she assumed command in many matters of home and state, she commanded at the same time the respect of all. Her right "to be seated high" never was seriously disputed, but it was herself, not her position, that won esteem.

A sickly child, according to her own account, and for most of her adult life in "delicate health," her activities and accomplishments contradict this background of physical frailty. Affliction she wore with grace as readily as she wore the becoming garments of a lady of station and charm. Of high native intelligence, blessed with endurance and determination, she seemed fitted for the "bravest or most delicate duties." She could master with equal assurance the demanding details of a dairy farm or the elevated, exacting assignment as wife of the first American envoy to Great Britain. A certain masculinity of mind gave force and direction to her thinking, and an unusual perception of the people and politics around her. The dangers and difficulties in the struggle to establish a new government were as understandable to her as were those of earlier years in the struggle for independence. Whether, as in 1776, the roar in her ears was that of nearby Revolutionary cannon on Dorchester Heights or, as in the nineties, that of fervent Anti-Federalists on the streets of Philadelphia, she reacted with courage.

Abigail Adams was quick to praise and to extol the virtues of others, but she did not spare, in spoken or written words, those who incurred her disapproval. Brilliant in conversation, this remarkable woman was apt of phrase and, happily for posterity as for her contemporaries, she was facile and picturesque of pen. The flavor and vitality of her letters were monumental then; they are her best monument now.

(After the Original by Gilbert Stuart, now in the Adams House, Quincy, Mass., and reproduced by permission of the owner, Mrs. Robert Homans, Boston.)

that the decision of Congress would be for a site on the stream that separated his own State from Maryland; but there was not a complaint from any quarter that he attempted to influence the action of the lawmakers,[82] who, in the end, after much futile maneuver, deferred the issue to the next term.[83] Other legislation was pushed forward under the spur of impatience to adjourn the long session. The constitutional amendments were adopted finally on the 28th of September[84] in a form that met every strong demand for the guarantee of individual right and provided, in particular, that "the powers not delegated to the United States by the Constitution, nor prohibited by it to the States, are reserved to the States respectively, or to the people." No change in the division of specified powers or in the organization of the Federal government was submitted to the States. During the climactic period of this debate, the bill for the establishment of "judicial courts" was signed by Washington.[85] The Secretary of the Treasury was directed to report to the next session of Congress a plan for the support of public credit.[86] With these major enactments supplemented by numerous measures of less importance, Congress formally recessed on the 29th of September to meet again on the first Monday in January, 1790.[87]

Washington regarded the session as a success. He wrote Gouverneur Morris: ". . . national government is organized, and, as far as my in-

Madison, Aug. 25, 1789 (12 *Madison Papers*, 17, LC); Henry Lee to James Madison, Sept. 8, 1789 (*ibid.*, 24), and an excellent letter of George Gilpin's to Washington, Sept. 2, 1789 (244 *Papers of G. W.*, 12, LC).

[82] Thomas Hartley wrote somewhat awkwardly: "The President was put in a critical situation. It is true he has a strong bias for the Potomac, but the rules of candor and honor which have ever governed him in life would not have been deviated from upon this occasion and even a mistake would have been exposed" (Letter of Sept. 20, 1789, to Jasper Yeates; *Yeates Papers*, PHS).

[83] 1 *JHR.*, 98 ff, 117, with a decision, 28 to 21 and later 31 to 17, for a permanent seat on the Susquehanna and the retention, meantime, of New York as temporary capital; 1 *JS*, 86–87, 88, 89, 93. This last entry is to the Senate's vote, September 28, without a division, to postpone all action to the next session. For amusing and informative comment on the various maneuvers, see Thomas Hartley to Jasper Yeates, August 31, September 6, 13, 20, *Yeates Papers*, PHS. For a diversity of reasons, most of the Virginia members thought the prospect for a site on the Potomac would be improved if the question were deferred. Some of these men thought the "enumeration" of 1790 would show the centre of population farther South than advocates of a capital in the North predicted. See Alexander White to James Madison, Aug. 25, 1789 (12 *Madison Papers*, 17, LC); Henry Lee to Madison, Sept. 8, 1789 (*ibid.*, 24); David Stuart to Washington, Sept. 12, 1789 (244 *Papers of G. W.*, 19–21, LC). The scope of some attempted combinations to win a majority for a particular site is sketched in 1 *Fisher Ames*, 71; 4 *LTW.*, 291–94; 1 *Rufus King*, 381–83.

[84] The conference report was adopted by the House September 24 (1 *JHR.*, 121) and by the Senate the next day (1 *JS*, 86, 88).

[85] On Sept. 24, 1789. See 1 *JS*, 87; 1 *Statutes at Large*, 73–93.

[86] Resolution of Sept. 21, 1789; 1 *JHR.*, 117.

[87] 1 *JS*, 95; 1 *JHR.*, 130.

formation goes, to the satisfaction of all parties . . . opposition to it is either no more, or hides its head." [88] To a similarly cheerful view, most members of Congress already had come [89] with the somewhat humiliating observation that much antagonism to the new government still was observable in Washington's own State.[90]

Next, perhaps, to general acceptance of the new system, without crippling amendment, the most important achievement of the session was the creation of Federal Courts. In the executive branch of government, the great gain had been the acquiescence of Congress in the doctrine that the President should have the power to name and, if necessary, to remove the men who would be, so to say, his divisional commanders. The desired three Departments of State, Treasury, and War had been established.[91] Provision had been made, also, for an Attorney General [92] and for the continuance of the Post Office.[93] Subject to Senate confirmation, the President had, likewise, the responsibility of nominating the Justices of the Supreme Court and of the lower Federal tribunals.

Appointments consequently became the most pressing as well as the most vexatious task Washington faced during the last days of the session and for some weeks after adjournment. Applications had con-

[88] Letter of Oct. 13, 1789; 30 *G. W.*, 442.

[89] See Thomas Hartley to Jasper Yeates, July 29 (*Yeates Papers*, PHS); Alexander White to James Madison, August 17 (12 *Madison Papers*, 8, LC); David Stuart to Washington, September 12 (244 *Papers of G. W.*, 19–21, LC); John Brown to Harry Innes, Sept. 28, 1789 (19 *Innes Papers*, f. 18, LC). Abigail Adams was satisfied (*Abigail Adams*, 29) that her husband's use of his casting vote as presiding officer of the Senate had saved the Constitution from a death wound that would have been inflicted if Congress had tied the hands of the President by refusing him the power of removal.

[90] James Craik to Washington, Aug. 24, 1789, 244 *Papers of G. W.*, 5, LC; Henry Lee to James Madison, Nov. 25, 1789, 12 *Madison Papers*, 49, LC. Two interesting letters, Edmund Randolph to Washington (244 *Papers of G. W.*, 40, LC) and Madison to Washington, Dec. 5, 1789 (12 *Madison Papers*, 52, LC) show how the President's friends kept him informed of the political situation in Virginia. These are printed in 4 *LTW.*, 294–97, 297–99. As early as July 1, 1789, Henry Lee wrote Washington: "The political schism, which divides our countrymen, is, I fear, deep planted . . . and, however respect to a majority and affection to the President may quiet them now, yet, on the first inviting occasion, the spirit of opposition will show itself strongly . . . Instead of striving to court the good will of opposition . . . I would disarm them, by complying with the rational views of the advocates for amendments spontaneously . . . If it is not done under your auspices, it will never be effected; and, if never effected, we shall be a divided, distressed people" (*ibid.*, 263).

[91] As noted *supra*, the bill for "establishing an executive department to be denominated the Department of Foreign Affairs" was signed July 27 (1 *Statutes at Large*, 28–29) and the measure for a Department of War, August 7 (*ibid.*, 49–50). The bill for the Treasury Department was approved Sept. 2, 1789 (*ibid.*, 65–67). For the final legislative stages of this measure, see 1 *JHR.*, 57, 69, 70, 71, 72, 73, 76, 89, 90, 91, 95; 1 *JS*, 50, 65, 67, 69.

[92] This was a part of section 35 (1 *Statutes at Large*, 93) of the act of Sept. 24, 1789, for the establishment of judicial courts.

[93] *Ibid.*, 70; act of Sept. 22, 1789.

tinued to pour in, though the flood was not quite so great as in the spring.[94] After he had nominated about 110 men, chiefly in the revenue service,[95] the President prepared a summary that showed a geographical distribution of what he styled "offices of a general nature already filled" and in this he included the names of the men who held diplomatic posts. The States were not unequally recognized, except for Georgia and New Hampshire, but, in Washington's judgment, the balance would be more nearly correct if one member of the Supreme Court was assigned to each of six States: Massachusetts, New York, Pennsylvania, Maryland, Virginia, and South Carolina.[96] On another list he wrote the names of thirty-five men of varying distinction whom he selected, as he explained, "from a great variety of characters who have made a tender of their services for suitable offices . . ." Seven of these were citizens of New York State.[97] Besides filling available posts with some of these men, Washington wished to enlist for the public several men who had not applied for office and, in one instance at least, might be unwilling to serve.[98] The General waited until the bill for the establishment of the Treasury Department had been passed, then he made his principal appointments. As Secretary of War he designated the faithful man who held the corresponding office under the "old" Congress, his former Chief of Artillery, Henry Knox. Nobody else seems even to have been mentioned otherwise than on the hypothesis that Knox might decline. The Secretaryship of the Treasury went to Alexander Hamilton, who had been the individual most frequently mentioned as Washington's probable choice.[99] Almost as late as the time he nominated Hamilton, he wrote: ". . . I leave myself entirely free until the office is established and the moment shall arrive when the nomination is to be made; then, under my best information and a full view of all

[94] See Gaillard Hunt, op cit., as supra.     [95] 1 EJS., 9–11, 18.

[96] 8 Hamilton Papers, 1014, LC. This list is in the autograph of Tobias Lear with additions by Washington.

[97] Robert R. Livingston included, though not assigned on the list to New York. See 30 G. W., 413–14.

[98] Ibid.

[99] Cf. C. Gore to Rufus King, Sept. 13, 1789; 1 Rufus King, 368. Both the tradition (J. C. Hamilton, History of the Republic of the United States of America, as Traced in the Writings of Alexander Hamilton and of his Contemporaries, hereafter cited as J. C. Hamilton, v. 4, p. 30) that this appointment was on the recommendation of Robert Morris, and the further tradition (ibid., 29 n–30 n) that Washington selected Hamilton immediately after assuming office, are without documentary basis. It is entirely probable that Morris urged the appointment of Hamilton, and it is likely that the President talked with Hamilton in general terms, as he did with John Jay, about entering the public service, but it is altogether unlikely that Washington offered the position before it was created.

circumstances, I shall endeavor to the best of my judgment to combine justice to individuals with the public good, making the latter my primary object." [100] The next appointments were those of the Chief Justice and five Associate Justices of the Supreme Court, and those of the Judges, District Attorneys and Marshals of the eleven District Courts.[101] Here Washington had to select the best men he could find, at the same time that he made a geographical distribution and ran the risk of offending some of the powerful applicants he had to pass over. He compromised in the case of James Wilson by giving the Pennsylvanian one of the seats as Associate Justice, instead of the post of Chief Justice for which Wilson had applied; Arthur Lee he declined to name to the Court, though he kept on the list the name of the former Commissioner to France.[102] The other places as Associate Justice went to John Rutledge of South Carolina, William Cushing of Massachusetts, John Blair of Virginia and Robert H. Harrison of Maryland,[103] the beloved "old Colonel" of Washington's military staff in the years 1775-81. Washington wrote each of these men a letter in which he expressed his hope of their "ready acceptance" and he made particular appeals to Colonel Harrison and to Governor Rutledge,[104] who, he understood, were least disposed to take the positions tendered them. Choice of a Chief Justice had been considered carefully. As early as the first week in August Washington had talked in general terms with John Jay about office, and he later had discussed with Madison what Jay had told him.[105] No hint subsequently was dropped in the President's correspondence or in his reported conversation that he thought it desirable to shift Jay from the office of Secretary of Foreign Affairs to the post of Chief Justice. If Washington felt that Jay's policy with respect to the navigation of the Mississippi had created antagonisms, he said nothing about it, nor did he assign any other reason for making the shift. He sent in Jay's nomination as head of the Supreme Court, Sept. 24, 1789,[106] before he informed the appointee and Hamilton and Madi-

100 Letter of Sept. 8, 1789, to Edmund Randolph; 30 G. W., 398. For the nomination see 1 EJS., 25; proceedings of Sept. 11, 1789; Gazette of U. S., Sept. 12, 1789, p. 3. Complaints over the subordinate Treasury appointments are voiced in Memoirs of the Administrations of Washington and John Adams, Edited from the Papers of Oliver Wolcott, Secretary of the Treasury, George Gibbs, ed., hereafter cited as Gibbs, Wolcott Papers, v. 1, p. 20; the failure of Washington to reappoint officials of the former "Board of Treasury" with a single exception is noted in 2 Paine Wingate, 333.
101 1 EJS., 29; list submitted Sept. 24, 1789.
102 30 G. W., 393-94, 413.
103 Ibid., 424-25 and n.
104 Ibid., 417, 421-22.
105 Ibid., 375.
106 1 EJS., 29.

son that he had in mind to name a different man as Secretary of State. When Congress had confirmed Jay, the President wrote him: "In nominating you . . . I not only acted in conformity to my best judgment; but I trust I did a grateful thing to the good citizens of these United States; and I have a full confidence that the love which you bear to our country, and a desire to promote the general happiness, will not suffer you to hesitate a moment to bring into action the talents, knowledge and integrity which are so necessary to be exercised at the head of the department which must be considered as the key-stone of our political fabric." [107]

The man whom Washington selected to fill the office that corresponded to the one previously held by Jay was the United States Minister to France, Thomas Jefferson, then about to start home on leave.[108] The President had seen comparatively little of this fellow-Virginian and had not communicated extensively with him, except during the years when Jefferson was war-time Governor of Virginia,[109] but Washington had served with Jefferson for five years in the Virginia House of Burgesses [110] and, as he once wrote Lafayette, he had "early imbibed the highest opinion" of the master of Monticello.[111] The "readiness and zeal" with which Jefferson had furthered military operations in the Old Dominion had been acknowledged gratefully at the time,[112] and the Marquis de Chastellux had later been reminded of Jefferson's "talents and worth." [113] All the relations of Jefferson with the government of America's ally, France, had appeared to be cordially sympathetic; his dispatches on commercial affairs had been read and abstracted by Washington.[114] By the time he sent the nomination to the Senate, the President had learned of the incredible occurrences in

[107] Letter of Oct. 5, 1789, 30 G. W., 428–29. The nomination of Jay had been confirmed Sept. 26, 1789, at the head of the list of judicial appointments, not one of which was rejected by the Senate (1 EJS., 29–32). Jay's written acceptance, dated Oct. 6, 1789 (3 John Jay, 378–79), does not have a shadow of chagrin that he was named to the Court instead of to the portfolio of State.

[108] For the leave, see 7 Jefferson, 349, 432, 436, 453, 480; 1 EJS., 6–7. William Short was nominated and confirmed as Chargé in Jefferson's absence though the formal title was not used (ibid.).

[109] As listed by Matteson, 39 G. W., 829; the total number of letters from Washington to Jefferson, prior to October, 1789, was fifty-seven, of which thirty-eight bore dates of Jefferson's gubernatorial administration.

[110] Technically for the six years, 1769–1774, but Jefferson did not attend the session of 1772.

[111] Letter of May 10, 1786; 28 G. W., 424.

[112] Letter of June 8, 1781, to Jefferson; 22 ibid., 190.

[113] 27 ibid., 413.

[114] 244 Papers of G. W., 9, LC; Aug. 27–30, 1789. Washington made no entry on anything Jefferson had said of political affairs in France.

Paris that had culminated in the seizure by a Parisian mob on July 14 of a prison about which Washington probably knew nothing, a gloomy old place called the Bastille.[115] Although Jefferson's official report of these astonishing events may not have been at hand,[116] Washington knew that the information of the American representative would be of the largest value to the government in any situation that might develop in a country on whose support America in large, if lessening, measure still was dependent. Any disaster to France involved danger to the United States. Washington hoped for a happy issue, but he could not believe any great change in the government of France could be completed with such small loss of life as had been mentioned in reports that had reached America during the late summer.[117] Jefferson could give information and counsel on many subjects besides France. He seemed the ideal man for Secretary of State—an able, useful teammate for Hamilton in the Treasury and Knox in the War Department. The only hitch was the possibility that after so long an absence from his beloved mountain-top home in Virginia, Jefferson might not be willing to reside in a city. On the other hand, if he were going to continue in public service, he might wish to return to Paris. Washington consequently planned to write Jefferson and to express hope the Minister would accept, but until he heard of Jefferson's decision, he would not fill the French post.[118]

The last of the four executive positions of highest rank was that of Attorney General. This would not be a burdensome office during the early years of the government, and it might not even call for day-by-day attendance, but manifestly the man appointed to the office must be a highly competent lawyer, sympathetic with the Constitution. Such a man, in Washington's opinion, was Edmund Randolph, 36 years of age, former Governor of Virginia, and one of the shining figures in the Convention of 1787. Although Randolph had refused to sign the Constitution, he had promoted greatly the ratification of that document in his own State where his opposition, if added to that of Patrick Henry, might have been fatal. Nothing that Washington said about the appointment indicated that Randolph was being rewarded for his return

---

[115] The first report printed in New York apparently was in the *Daily Advertiser*, September 16, p. 2, from a Philadelphia paper of the 12th—a report brought by *Young Eagle*, thirty-five days out of St. Sebastian.

[116] His account was dated July 19, 1789. See 7 *Jefferson*, 409. The narrative was extended in a letter of July 22, 1789, to James Madison, *ibid.*, 424 ff; 11 *Madison Papers*, 113, LC.

[117] 30 *G. W.*, 443, 448.      [118] *Ibid.*, 446; letter of Oct. 13, 1789.

to the fold of Federalism. On the contrary, Washington's letter to Randolph was one that urged him to make the sacrifice for the public good,[119] though he was not sure that Randolph could afford to accept.[120] When this uneasiness was removed by Randolph's decision to serve, Washington had some embarrassment because the Attorney General was anxious to be excused from his new duties until March 1, and certainly until Jan. 15, 1790.[121] As Jefferson presumably was at sea, the President would not know whether his cabinet was complete until the nominee had landed.[122]

Although the greater part of the list of desirable candidates remained,[123] and a few declinations were to come,[124] at the same time that some hurt feelings had to be soothed,[125] the major appointments had been made by the time Congress adjourned, September 29. Washington's duties decreased because he left the administration of the departments to the men temporarily or permanently in charge. Entertainment became less elaborate when all the members of Congress, except a few New Yorkers, left the city. The French Minister and the Spanish agent were returning home, also.[126] This circumstance already had led Washington to inquire whether the representative of Spain should depart without receiving notice that failure to press vigorously for the free navigation of the Mississippi did not mean that the United States had yielded on that score or had decided to let the issue slumber indefinitely.[127] Another diplomatic question of more immediate bearing concerned the relations of Britain and the United States. Congress had shown a disposition to levy discriminating duties on British imports because no commercial treaty between the two countries existed.

[119] Sept. 28, 1789; *ibid.*, 418–19.

[120] *Ibid.*, 414. For the financial obstacles to Randolph's partial surrender of a profitable practice, in return for a low official salary, see *Conway, Randolph*, 129, 135; 244 *Papers of G. W.*, 40 ff, LC.

[121] *Ibid.*; Randolph to Washington, Nov. 22, 1789, *ibid.*, 113, and *Conway, Randolph*, 130–31.

[122] Cf. Washington to Jefferson, Nov. 30, 1789; 30 *G. W.*, 468.

[123] *Ibid.*, 413.

[124] Among them, R. H. Harrison's of a place as Associate Justice of the Supreme Court (*ibid.*, 466–67, 470; James Craik to Washington, Feb. 3, 1790, 245 *Papers of G. W.*, 122, LC), John Marshall's of District Attorney for Virginia (30 *G. W.*, 463) and Gov. Thomas Johnson's of the Federal judgeship in Maryland (*ibid.*, 415, 470, 484).

[125] *Ibid.*, 419–20, 472–73. For some instances of delicate consideration for the feelings of aspirants and nominees, see *ibid.*, 417–18, 468, 470–72, 484; *Steiner's McHenry*, 123–24.

[126] *Gazette of U. S.*, Oct. 14, 1789, p. 3; *Baker*, 148 n.

[127] Cf. the undated queries in 30 *G. W.*, 486–87. It is possible that Jay to the Spanish Chargé, July 27, 1789 (Nat. Arc. IV *Am. Letters*, f. 52–53) may represent the answer to these queries, but both the date and the mild, vague tone of the communication make this doubtful.

The future of America's important trade with the West Indies was in doubt; slaves carried away by the British had never been restored or paid for; the western posts had not been evacuated; Americans had resented the failure of Britain to send a Minister to the United States, though their country had been represented by John Adams for more than three years at the Court of St. James's.[128]  Before these bad conditions drifted to worse, Washington thought it desirable to sound out the London government and to ascertain whether relations could not be improved and a commercial treaty negotiated without discrimination, reprisal or trade war. John Jay and Alexander Hamilton were called separately into conference on this,[129] with the result that Washington took the advice of the Secretary of the Treasury and decided to ask Gouverneur Morris, who was then in England, to ascertain the views of the ministry, to the end that "harmony and mutual satisfaction between the two countries" might be achieved.[130]

[128] Washington to Gouverneur Morris, Oct. 13, 1789, 30 *G. W.*, 439–42.
[129] 4 *Diaries*, 16–17.          [130] 30 *G. W.*, 439–40, 440–42.

# CHAPTER XI

## "ALL FRAGRANT WITH THE ODOR OF INCENSE"
### (October 15, 1789–March 21, 1790)

THE APPOINTMENT of Gouverneur Morris to take the temperature of the British Ministry finished the tasks that held Washington in New York. While he had been consulting about foreign affairs, he had been asking his advisers for their opinion on a personal mission that had interested him for months[1]—a tour of the Northeastern States.[2] He told himself that this would help to restore him to full health,[3] would acquaint him with those parts of the region he had not seen, and would disclose, as he put it, the "temper and disposition of the inhabitants towards the new government."[4] His admirers realized, if he would not himself admit, that he would be the symbol of that government and of the struggle that had established American freedom. Strong as was support of the Constitution East of the Hudson, it would be stronger still after a visit by him.

If he anticipated a tour similar to his triumphal progress from Georgetown to New York Island in April, he was not disappointed. Much that occurred during the twenty-nine days from October 15 to November 13 was, in effect, a repetition of the festivity of the spring—addresses and odes and parades and dinners[5]—most of it delightful to

---

[1] See 30 G. W., 319–20.
[2] 4 Diaries, 14–16.
[3] Cf. 30 G. W., 436, 446, 502.
[4] 4 Diaries, 14.
[5] He was attended by Maj. William Jackson, Tobias Lear and six servants (4 Diaries, 20–21). For the greater part of the way he traveled in his carriage but for ceremonies he frequently mounted one of the horses. The itinerary follows, with references after each place named to contemporary newspaper accounts of Washington's reception, etc. October 15: New York to Rye, through East Chester, New Rochelle and Mamaroneck; October 16: Rye to Fairfield, via Horse Neck (now Greenwich), Stamford and Norwalk; October 17: Fairfield to New Haven (Conn. Journal, October 21, p. 2), with Stratford (Gazette of U. S. (New York), October 21, p. 3) and Milford en route; October 18, a Sunday, was spent in New Haven; October 19: New Haven, Wallingford, Durham, Middletown, Wethersfield, and on to Hartford; October 20: Hartford (Conn. Courant, October 26, p. 3); October 21: Hartford to Springfield, Mass., with a halt at Windsor; October 22: Springfield, then glimpses of Palmer and Brookfield, which Washington sometimes called Brookland, and lodging at Spencer; October 23: Spencer to Leicester to Worcester (Thomas's Massachusetts Spy, October 29, p. 3), then to Marlborough and on to Weston for the night (ibid.); October 24: Weston, Cambridge (ibid.), and on to Boston (ibid.); October 24–28 were spent at Boston (for preparations, see Gazette of U. S.,

experience but dull to read about now. Until he reached Stratford, Connecticut, on the 17th of October, there were no ceremonies, and when he left Portsmouth on the 4th of November, he headed directly for New York. En route, he usually left his tavern lodgings early in the morning so as to avoid all salutations, public dinners and drum-beating.[6] The eighteen intervening days were crowded with visits and ceremonies that Washington enjoyed zestfully. On his arrival at Cambridge, Saturday, October 24, the militia were slow in taking position—as if in strict regard for wartime precedent—but they formed close to the spot where the General had dismounted that historic 2nd of July, 1775, when he reached the college town and took command of the troops that were trying to besiege Boston.[7] From Cambridge, hosts and

October 21, p. 3; *Mass. Centinel* (Boston), October 17, p. 3; *Boston Gaz.*, October 19, p. 3; and *Independent Chronicle* (Boston), October 22, p. 3; for reception and major events, see *Mass. Centinel*, October 28, p. 3, October 31, p. 2, and November 14, p. 2; *Boston Gaz.*, October 26, p. 2, and November 2, p. 2; *Independent Chronicle*, October 29, p. 3; and *Herald of Freedom* (Boston), October 27, p. 2–3, and November 24, p. 3); October 29: from Boston to Charlestown and Cambridge, thence through Malden, Lynn and Marblehead to Salem; October 30: Salem (*Salem Mercury*, November 3, p. 2–3, and November 10, p. 3, and *Mass. Centinel*, October 31, p. 2) to Beverly, Ipswich and Newburyport (*Essex Journal*, November 4, p. 1, and November 11, p. 1); October 31: Newburyport to Portsmouth, N. H.; November 1–3 were spent at Portsmouth (*New-Hampshire Gaz.*, November 5, p. 2–3; *Essex Journal*, November 11, p. 3; *Independent Chronicle*, November 12, p. 3; *Mass. Centinel*, November 4, p. 2; and *New-York Daily Gaz.*, November 16, p. 3, and November 17, p. 3); November 4: Portsmouth to Exeter and Kingston and on to Haverhill, Mass.; November 5: Haverhill to Andover, Lexington and Watertown; November 6: from Watertown by way of Needham and Sherborn, which he called Sherburn, to Taft's Tavern, one mile beyond Uxbridge; November 7: from the vicinity of Uxbridge to Ashford, Conn.; November 8, a Sunday, was passed at Ashford; November 9: Ashford, past Mansfield and Coventry to East Hartford; November 10: East Hartford to New Haven; November 11: New Haven to Milford, and thence to Major Marvin's tavern, nine miles southwest of Fairfield; November 12: Marvin's to Stamford and on to the pleasant inn of Mrs. Tamar Haviland at Rye; November 13: Rye to New York and home before 3 P.M. This itinerary is set forth clearly in 4 *Diaries*, 20–51. Miscellaneous details appear in *Gazette of the United States*, November 4, p. 3, November 18, p. 3, and November 21, p. 3. Some unfamiliar details of the journey from Worcester to Boston will be found in Joseph Barrell to Samuel Webb, Nov. 1, 1789 (3 *Webb*, 142–44). Letters to Washington concerning his reception, etc., in Boston and at Portsmouth are printed in 4 *LTW.*, 289–90 and 290–91. The bulk of the correspondence, which is of little more than antiquarian interest, survives in 244 *Papers of G. W.*, covering many sheets between folios 61 and 106. See also Joseph Crocker to Henry Knox, Nov. 1, 1789 (*Knox Papers*, MHS); Ford, 1 *Notes on the Life of Noah Webster*, 246; *Decatur*, 80; 3 *Literary Diary of Ezra Stiles*, ed. 1901, p. 369. Samuel B. Webb repeated a rumor, Nov. 15, 1789, that Washington had intended to visit Albany "but hearing of the fall of snow there had been to the northward, he was anxious to get back and therefore pursued the most direct route" (3 *Webb*, 144).

[6] *Mass. Centinel*, Nov. 11, 1789, p. 2; *Thomas's Massachusetts Spy*, Nov. 12, 1789, p. 3. He manifestly was irked by the Connecticut law that forbade travel on the Sabbath. When forced to spend Sunday, November 8, at Ashford, he told himself that his horses needed the rest, but he found the tavern "not a good one" and the sermons of the parson of a nearby church "very lame discourses" (4 *Diaries*, 50).

[7] See Vol. III, p. 476. The committee welcoming Washington evidently thought that he had been received fourteen years previously by troops in open ranks (John Brooks to Washington, Oct. 21, 1789; 244 *Papers of G. W.*, 64, LC), but actually the soldiers of 1775 had been dismissed from parade before Washington arrived.

guests came to Boston. Washington's description of what followed in
the Massachusetts capital was not lacking in appreciation, nor was it
marked by the modesty attributed to him: ". . . preceded by the town
corps, very handsomely dressed, we passed through the citizens classed
in their different professions and under their own banners, till we came
to the State House from which, across the Street, an Arch was thrown;
in the front of which was this Inscription, 'To the Man who unites all
hearts' and on the other, 'To Columbia's favorite Son,' and on one side
thereof, next the State House, in a panel decorated with a trophy, composed of the Arms of the United States, of the Commonwealth of
Massachusetts and [of] our French Allies, crowned with a wreath of
Laurel, was this Inscription, 'Boston relieved, March 17th, 1776.' This
Arch was handsomely ornamented, and over the Centre of it a Canopy
was erected 20 feet high, with the American Eagle perched on the top.
After passing through the Arch and entering the State House at the
Southern End and ascending to the upper floor and returning to a
Balcony at the Northern End, three cheers was given by a vast con-
course of people who by this time had assembled at the Arch. Then
followed an ode composed in honor of the President and well sung by
a band of select singers; after this three Cheers," followed by a parade.[8]
Washington would not have set this down if he had not liked it.[9] He
was pleased, also, by what he saw of mills in New England [10] and by
the beauty and fine dress of the ladies he met at formal assemblies in
Boston, Salem and Portsmouth.[11] His stay in New Hampshire included
a landing in Maine, an unsuccessful fishing expedition and, of course,
much pleasantness in meeting old friends. Almost daily, in somewhat
extensive notes in his Diary, he described unusual or beautiful land-
scapes. As always, the excellence or badness of the roads and of the
agricultural land interested him. So did the condition of the taverns at

---

[8] 4 *Diaries*, 34–35, with the punctuation and elisions revised for clarity but with capitalization preserved.

[9] For similar observations on the honors paid him in other towns, see *ibid.*, 42, 43, 44.

[10] 4 *Diaries*, 37, 40, 41, 47. On visiting a sail manufactory, Joseph Barrell wrote Samuel
Webb, "His Majesty made himself merry . . . telling the overseer he believed he collected the
prettiest girls in Boston" (3 *Webb*, 144).

[11] 4 *Diaries*, 38, 40, 45. The last of these references, covering the Assembly at Portsmouth,
New Hampshire, contains this observation: ". . . there were [present] about seventy-five well
dressed and many of them very handsome ladies, among whom (as was also the case at the
Salem and Boston assemblies) were a greater proportion with much blacker hair than are
usually seen in the Southern States."

which he stopped consistently.[12] Not once on the tour did he spend a night at a private home, though several invitations were received and more doubtless would have been forthcoming had not his intentions been known to most of his friends.[13] When he was in Boston, bad weather prevented a visit to Lexington;[14] but on the way back to New York, he stopped on the 5th of November at the scene of the initial military engagement of the Revolutionary War.[15] As he viewed the positions the men of Massachusetts had occupied, he told his companions that various British critics had protested to Doctor Franklin, who was then in London, that it was ill usage for the Americans to hide behind stone walls and to fire at the King's soldiers; whereupon Doctor Franklin asked if there were not two sides to a wall. The "degree of good humor" with which Washington repeated this story[16] was typical of the spirit in which he finished what almost every observer considered a completely successful tour.[17] It was marred—if that is not too strong a word—by nothing more serious than Washington's careful insistence on the limitations and on the dignity of his office. When he learned on the 23rd of October that plans were being made for a review by him at Cambridge of the militia of Middlesex County, he sent the commanding officer a message he was careful to summarize in his Diary—". . . that as I conceived there was an impropriety in my *reviewing* the Militia, or seeing them perform maneuvers otherwise than as a private man, I could do no more than pass along the line, which,

[12] One incident at an inn was made the occasion for a plea by *Thomas's Massachusetts Spy* that an appropriate title be given Washington whom, for its own part (*supra*, p. 241, n. 6) it proposed to style "His Highness, the President General." Said the paper in its issue of Nov. 12, 1789, p. 3: "The President . . . on his return to New York, towards the close of one day last week, sent forward a messenger to an inn to bespeak a lodging, etc. The innkeeper was absent; and the landlady, supposing by 'the President' was meant the President of Rhode Island College . . . and being unwell, said she could not entertain the President, and that he must go on to the next tavern. When the landlady found it was the great Washington who had intended to be her guest, 'Bless me,' exclaimed she, 'the sight of him would have cured my illness and the best in my house and in the town should have been at his service.' Does not this show the necessity of a title to distinguish our first magistrate from the chairman of a common tavern club?" This tale was denied by the *Boston Gazette*, Nov. 23, 1789, p. 3: "There was no person of the innkeeper's family at home who was suitable to, or would undertake to entertain him."

[13] Hancock to Washington, 244 *Papers of G. W.*, 74, LC.; 30 *G. W.*, 451; George Cabot to Washington, Oct. 24, 1789, 244 *Papers of G. W.*, 75, LC.

[14] 4 *Diaries*, 36.    [15] *Ibid.*, 48.

[16] *Independent Chronicle*, Nov. 27, 1789, p. 3.

[17] 1 *Fisher Ames*, 74; *Mass. Centinel*, Nov. 4, 1789, p. 2; H. Jackson to Knox, Nov. 15, 1789 (*Knox Papers*, MHS). Fenno wrote (*Gazette of U. S.*, Oct. 28, 1789, p. 3) that Washington's approach, "like the glorious luminary of Heaven, appears to have totally dissipated the fog of Anti-Federalism."

if he thought proper, might be under arms to receive me at that time." [18]
The "impropriety," he did not think it necessary to explain, arose from
the fact that the militia were under the control of Governor Hancock
and consequently not subject to his direction or orders in any sense.

If he bowed in this to the authority of the Governor of the Bay State,
he expected, in turn, as much deference on the part of His Excellency
of Massachusetts. Washington had accepted an invitation to dine informally with Hancock on the afternoon of the day of his arrival in
Boston, but he took it for granted that the Governor would call on him
at the tavern beforehand. Instead, Hancock sent word that he was too
much indisposed to come in person to pay his respects. This meant
that if arrangements were carried out, the President would go to Hancock's for dinner and thereby would have made the first call. Washington most emphatically did not intend to have it so. He excused
himself from attending the dinner and ate at his lodgings with Vice
President Adams, whose entire attitude had been one of deference and
consideration.[19] The significance of this was not lost on Hancock. During the evening, the Lieutenant Governor, who was no less a person
than Samuel Adams, came to Washington's lodgings [20] with Gen. William Heath and Thomas Russell, members of the Council, "to express
the Governor's concern," in Washington's own words, "that he had not
been in a condition to call upon me as soon as I came to town." The
President's politeness did not restrict his candor. "I informed them in
explicit terms," he wrote in his Diary, "that I should not see the Governor unless it was at my own lodgings." [21] Hancock promptly capitu-
lated—or recovered. The next day, the Sabbath, he sent Washington a
note to inquire when he might call. He was prepared, he said, to
"hazard everything" as respects his health, "for the desirable purpose."
Washington had gone to morning service and he intended to hear Rev.
Peter Thacher that afternoon. The answer to Hancock consequently
was somewhat stiff in its requirement. Headed "Sunday 1 o'clock," [22]
it read: "The President of the United States presents his best respects to

---

[18] 4 *Diaries*, 32.

[19] Before leaving New York, Washington had learned that Adams was going to Massachusetts about the same date and he offered the Vice President a seat in his carriage, but
Adams, in the words of his admiring wife, "excused himself from motives of delicacy" (Letter
of Oct. 11, 1789, to her sister, *Abigail Adams*, 29).

[20] These were at "a widow Ingersoll's (which is a very decent and good house)." 4 *Diaries*,
35, duly identified in *ibid.*, n.

[21] 4 *Diaries*, 36.

[22] Incidentally misdated. Sunday was the 25th; the note assumed it was the 26th.

the Governor, and has the honor to inform him that he shall be at home 'till 2 o'clock. The President of the United States need not express the pleasure it will give him to see the Governor; but, at the same time, he most earnestly begs that the Governor will not hazard his health on the occasion" [23]—an unmistakable reference to the brave language of Hancock's note. When Hancock came, he insisted that sickness alone had prevented his making a call the previous day and that, as it had been suggested he expected to receive the first visit, which he knew was improper, he had come without regard to his condition. Washington wrote this down for the record and dropped the subject there.[24]

This may have been an amusing and not an irritating memory by the time Washington returned to New York on the 13th of November, "all fragrant," as John Trumbull remarked, "with the odor of incense." [25] The President had the expense of £280 charged up promptly [26] and he went to work on an accumulation of government mail so heavy that for a time he had to defer all personal correspondence.[27] His other tasks were more troublesome than numerous. Five days before Washington reached New York, the three commissioners sent to negotiate with the Creek Indians [28] returned to the city [29] from Georgia and reported failure. They had met the half-breed, powerful Chief of the natives, Alexander McGillivray, and after auspicious preliminaries on the 24th of September had offered him a treaty which was at least a reasonable basis of negotiation. Instead of remaining to discuss this, McGillivray and his men disappeared, with the excuse that they had to retire several miles in order to find better pasturage for their horses. Exchanges of letters after that had been in vain. McGil-

---

[23] 30 G. W., 453–54 and n.

[24] 4 Diaries, 36. Boston newspapers, in general, accepted the view that Hancock's illness was real, not feigned (Mass. Centinel, October 28, p. 3; Independent Chronicle, October 29, p. 2, 3; Boston Gaz., October 26, p. 2 and Nov. 2, 1789, p. 2), though subsequently a press dispute arose over the question whether the staunch Federalist, James Bowdoin, rather than the republican Hancock had not been Washington's most frequent companion in Boston (Mass. Centinel, Nov. 14, 1789, p. 2; Herald of Freedom, Nov. 24, 1789, p. 3). Public men were divided in opinion. Some were disposed to think Hancock pretended to be sick in order to have the honor of the first visit; others thought him genuinely ill (see 1 Fisher Ames, 73; 1 Rufus King, 369; H. Jackson to Henry Knox, Nov. 20, 1789, Knox Papers, MHS). On Jan. 20, 1788, Rufus King had written General Gates that Hancock had been ill since the meeting of the State convention called to pass on the Federal Constitution. As soon as a majority was shown on one side or the other, King observed, Hancock's health would improve (Emmet Col., NYPL).

[25] 1 Gibbs, Wolcott Papers, 26.

[26] Decatur, 76.

[27] 31 G. W., 17.

[28] See supra, p. 223.

[29] Nov. 10, 1789; Gazette of U. S., Nov. 14, 1789, p. 3.

livray, in the commissioners' opinion, was solely responsible for the failure of their effort, but as he insisted his people would commit no further acts of violence, the commissioners felt it proper to urge that Americans should keep the peace. Some suitable individual should be sent into the Creek country to negotiate; if he failed, the "arms of the Union should be called forth for the protection of the people of Georgia." [30] Washington doubtless received the substance of this when he entertained the commissioners at dinner on the 16th of November [31] and he must have been puzzled and disappointed. As the danger of a war with the powerful Creeks of the Southwest was only one and might not be the worst threat on the frontier, Washington began a study of relations with the unfriendly tribes beyond the American settlements. [32] On the basis of this and of new developments, he was to endorse, months later, a scheme to bring McGillivray to New York. If the Chief could be prevailed upon to come, it was hoped Washington and his lieutenants then could convince him that the Creeks had more to gain from an American than from a Spanish alliance. [33]

Until December, this was the most complicated of Washington's puzzles. Some of his other experiences were pleasant or, at least, rewarding. At the instance of Congress [34] he had proclaimed a day of Thanksgiving for the 26th of November [35] and he undertook to share reverently in the services. Objections by one or two Anti-Federalist newspapers did not deter him. [36] While attendance in New York churches was thin, because of adverse weather, [37] the observance appealed to many [38] and accorded with Washington's utterances on religious themes from the time he assumed the Presidency. [39] The day of

[30] The commissioners' report of Nov. 17, 1789, *ASP.*, 1 *Ind. Aff.*, 68 ff, includes all the essential documents.        [31] 4 *Diaries*, 52–53.

[32] *Ibid.*, 53–54, 57, 58, 60–61, 69, 74, 81, 88–90; 30 *G. W.*, 476 n, 479–80; 31 *ibid.*, 20, 21–22; Henry Knox to Arthur St. Clair, Mch. 3, 1790 (19 *Innes Papers*, LC).

[33] 4 *Diaries*, 95; Knox to Washington, Feb. 15, 1790, *Knox Papers*, MHS, and printed in 4 *LTW.*, 315–20.

[34] 1 *JHR.*, 123, 126; 1 *JS*, 90, 92.        [35] Text in 30 *G. W.*, 427–28.

[36] The complaint of the Boston *Herald of Freedom*, quoted in the *New-York Journal* of Oct. 29, 1789, p. 3, was that "The President can have nothing to do with the people, but through the governments of the federal states" and that he consequently should have "addressed himself to the supreme executives of the several states and recommended it to them to appoint a thanksgiving upon one particular day . . ."

[37] 4 *Diaries*, 55.        [38] *Gazette of U. S.*, Oct. 3, 1789, p. 3.

[39] 30 *G. W.*, 416 and n. Many of these broad expressions of belief in Providence will be found in the MS volumes of Addresses and Answers in the *Papers of G. W.*, LC. One incident of the late autumn that would have pleased the religious element in America, had it been known generally, developed from damage done the harness of the President's carriage. In a note to John Jay, Dec. 13, 1789, Washington mentioned this and asked for a seat in Jay's carriage if the Chief Justice were going to church that day (3 *John Jay,* 381).

remembrance was followed by a period of work over Mount Vernon affairs, pleasant in the memories they aroused if not in the current details;[40] Washington had, in addition, to be counsellor on numerous financial transactions for which he had a varying measure of responsibility as his wife's agent or as a trustee.[41] Before all these matters were settled, the President was deep in a study, with Knox and Steuben,[42] of plans for organizing the militia[43] and no less busy with preparations for an official reception of his own on New Year's Day from noon to 3 P.M., and for a social affair after dinner, tendered jointly by Mrs. Washington and himself.[44]

As the time for the reassembly of Congress approached, he extended his activities as host, but he still held rigidly to his rule to accept no invitations, not even to funerals.[45] Probably at his instance, Martha also had placed restrictions on her daily life. Visits had to be made with discretion; she must not go to "public places." Her coming and going was so regulated, in fact, that she professed herself "more like a state prisoner than anything else." In manifest good humor she added: "As I cannot do as I like, I am obstinate and stay at home a great deal."[46] More in detail she wrote Mercy Warren: "Though the General's feelings and my own were perfectly in unison with respect for our predilection for private life, yet I cannot blame him for acting according to his ideas of duty in obeying the voice of his country. The consciousness of having attempted to do all the good in his power, and the pleasure of finding his fellow citizens so well satisfied with the disinterestedness of his conduct, will doubtless be some compensation for the great sacri-

---

[40] Some tobacco now was being raised on the plantation (245 *Papers of G. W.*, 88, LC) and, of course, was of interest to the owner. The price of wheat (246 *ibid.*, 37) was a financial concern. Correspondence continued over the purchase of mares to be bred to the jackasses (30 *G. W.*, 356–57, 422, 459–60, 506–07; 31 *ibid.*, 18–19 and n); Thomas Hartley to Washington, Dec. 7, 1789 (*Thom Col.*, Mount Vernon); certificates of purchase, February 12 (245 *Papers of G. W.*, 131, LC) and Mch. 9, 1790 (246 *ibid.*, 34).

[41] Involved were: (1) "Jack" Custis's "Alexander lands" (30 *G. W.*, 408); David Stuart to Washington, Dec. 3, 1789 (244 *Papers of G. W.*, 131–32, LC), and Mch. 11, 1790 (246 *ibid.*, 28–29); (2) the suit of William Dawson against Col. George Mercer (30 *G. W.*, 456–57; Edmund Randolph to Washington, 1790, n.d., *Emmet Col.*, NYPL; Wm. Dawson to Washington, October 5, Nov. 4, 1789, *Thom. Col.*, Mount Vernon); (3) the transfer to Washington of Gloucester county land in partial settlement of Bartholomew Dandridge's debt (31 *G. W.*, 16–18); (4) a title dispute over a tract in Maryland (*ibid.*, 7); and (5) final withdrawal, after twenty-two years, from the effort to compel Dr. William Savage to reimburse the estate of his wife, Margaret (30 *ibid.*, 488–89); Bryan Fairfax to Washington, Feb. 7, 1790, 245 *Papers of G. W.*, 126, LC.

[42] For Steuben's new financial distresses and the political aspects of Congress's compliance with his appeals for further relief, see *infra*, p. 281.

[43] 4 *Diaries*, 59, 60, and *infra*, p. 251.　　[44] 4 *Diaries*, 65.
[45] *Ibid.*, 52.　　[46] *Decatur*, 46.

fice which I know he has made. With respect to myself, I sometimes think the arrangement is not quite as it ought to have been; that I, who had much rather be at home, should occupy a place with which a great many younger and gayer women would be prodigiously pleased . . . I know too much of the vanity of human affairs to expect felicity from the splendid scenes of public life. I am still determined to be cheerful and to be happy in whatever situation I may be; for I have also learned from experience that the greater part of our happiness or misery depends upon our dispositions, and not upon our circumstances." [47] She made friends at the same time that she yearned for the quiet life of Mount Vernon and she accepted with gentle grace all the accidents and mistakes of entertaining. Once at dinner a dessert was put on the table in most attractive form. The General served Mrs. Robert Morris who was sitting on his right, as she always did when present; [48] Mrs. Morris, on tasting it, discovered that the cream in the dessert was rancid and she so whispered to the President, who immediately changed her plate. Martha continued to eat as if she did not find the dessert unpalatable. [49]

Whether or not the New Year's reception was served with sweet cream or with rancid, the occasion was preliminary to a session of Congress that began four days late, January 7, [50] with a good taste, so to say, in almost every mouth. North Carolina had ratified the Constitution on the 21st of November; [51] the proposed amendments to that document had met with favor in most of the States. [52] At the beginning of his term, Washington had felt that he was walking "on untrodden

[47] Letter of Dec. 26, 1789, *ibid.*, 66.          [48] *Ibid.*, 134.

[49] Apparently, when Mrs. Morris told this tale to Senator William Maclay, she wished to indicate that Mrs. Washington was greedy of sweets or else was not of sensitive taste. The interpretation here put on the incident would seem much more in line with Mrs. Washington's reputation as a tactful hostess and as a superlatively good housewife. The quotation is from *Decatur*, 132, who found it in *Maclay*, 73–74. It would seem that Mrs. Morris was not given to kindliness; she was often uncharitable in her comments.

[50] 1 *JHR.*, 133–34. Twenty-six members only were present on the specified day, January 4, *ibid.*, 133; and John Brown to Harry Innes, Jan. 5, 1790, 19 *Innes Papers*, LC.

[51] 1 *JHR.*, 299. Washington had received through Alexander Hamilton on Jan. 3, 1790, full authentication of previous newspaper reports of the State's action.

[52] Maryland ratified Dec. 19, 1789, *ibid.*, 146; records of like, later action by other States appear in *ibid.*, 303 ff. The unconditional entry of North Carolina into the Union convinced Patrick Henry it would be futile to attempt to procure major amendments (2 *W. W. Henry*, 449, 451). For the contest in Virginia, see Edmund Randolph to Washington, November 22, 26 (244 *Papers of G. W.*, 113, 115, LC); Edward Carrington to Madison, Dec. 20, 1789, 12 *Madison Papers*, 56, LC); as he saw it, "the government of the United States" seemed "to want very little more than the sanction of time to give it all that stability which can be expected from any human fabric." Letter of Jan. 15, 1790, to Sir Edward Newenham (30 *G. W.*, 504).

ground" and that his conduct in almost any respect might set a precedent. He had been cautious at the same time that he had been anxious every move should advance the public interest. Now, he said with manifest relief, "I may indulge a hope that my labors have not been altogether without success . . ." [53] In that cheerful approach to self-confidence, Washington staged with superlative care the delivery of his message on the 8th of January. He had so much satisfaction in the spectacle that he entered the details in his Diary: ". . . at 11 o'clock, I set out for the City Hall in my coach, preceded by Colonel Humphreys and Major Jackson in uniform (on my two white horses) and followed by Messrs. Lear and Nelson, in my chariot, and Mr. Lewis on horseback, following them. In their rear was the Chief Justice of the United States and Secretary of the Treasury and [of the] War Departments in their respective carriages, and in the order they are named." He followed this with a recital of the rising and bowing and seating and ceremonial that attended the delivery of what he termed his "speech." [54]

This annual message had been expected to be an important presentation of policy,[55] but Washington's continuing caution deterred him from vigorous advocacy which, indeed, was contrary to his nature. The paper he read in the Senate chamber consisted merely of a congratulatory paragraph on "the present favorable prospects of our public affairs" and a series of unexciting proposals for common defence,[56] protection of the frontiers, naturalization laws, uniform weights and measures, the grant of patents, the extension of the post, and the "promotion of science and literature." This last suggestion he marred by straddling language: "Whether," said he, "this desirable object will be best promoted by affording aids to seminaries of learning already established, by the institution of a national university, or by any other expedients, will be well worthy of a place in the deliberations of the Legislature." [57]

When Congress had been in session a week, Secretary Hamilton submitted the plan he had prepared, on order of Congress,[58] for the sup-

[53] Letter of Jan. 9, 1790, to Catherine Macaulay Graham, *ibid.*, 496.
[54] 4 *Diaries*, 67–68.
[55] John Brown to Harry Innes, Jan. 5, 1790; 19 *Innes Papers*, LC.
[56] "To be prepared for war is one of the most effectual means of preserving peace" (30 G. W., 491).
[57] *Ibid.*, 494. For the addresses in reply to this message, see 4 *Diaries*, 69, 70; 1 *JHR.*, 139, 140–41; 1 *JS*, 104–05.
[58] See *supra*, p. 232.

port of public credit.[59] Hamilton had carried on this study with little
or no reference to Washington, who, for his part, had been entirely
satisfied to leave to the Secretary an enterprise that involved questions
of funding with which the President was unfamiliar. On the 2nd of
January,[60] he examined the report, which, when formally submitted to
the House of Representatives on January 14,[61] was recognized immediately and by all as a bold and strong document.[62] Its basic argument
and recommendation were, in summary, to this effect: For their honor,
their manifest advantage and their assurance of future credit in emer-
gencies,[63] the United States must pay defaulted interest on their continental debt and must fund the principal. To achieve this, the United
States must treat all creditors fairly and must avoid, in the funding,
any sort of discrimination between original purchasers and present
holders of these obligations.[64] Next, the United States must assume the
war-time debts and unpaid interest of the States because these were
incurred in support of the common cause and, unfunded, were a costly
drain on the resources of America.[65] Assumption would not confuse,
as some men insisted, the settlement of accounts between the States
and the central government. The terms of such a settlement were
equitable and available.[66] A reduction in the average, long-term interest rate of the domestic debt was justified and should be effected by
giving creditors a wide choice of honorable alternatives that included
annuities and, in most proposals, western lands at twenty cents an
acre.[67] Refunding should begin with the foreign and domestic continental debt; determination of the State debts in a form to make assumption practicable would take time.[68] Interest on the foreign debt
at the covenanted rate, and on the domestic continental debt at 4 per
cent would call for 2,239,000 dollars annually.[69] The foreign "instal-

---

[59] 2 *A. Hamilton*, 227–91; 1 *JHR.*, 136, 141–42.
[60] 4 *Diaries*, 65.                                    [61] 1 *JHR.*, 141.
[62] Perhaps the most available text is in 2 *A. Hamilton*, 227 ff, but this does not include
the appendices, several of which are essential to an understanding of the complicated part of
the report that deals with the credits and debits of the States. These appendices are in *ASP.*,
1 *Finance*, 26–37. A copy of the official fifty-one page printed report is preserved in 8 *Hamilton Papers*, 1021–37, LC.
[63] 2 *A. Hamilton*, 228–34.
[64] *Ibid.*, 236 ff. This is one of Hamilton's most careful arguments, but one that failed to
convince his friend James Madison, who regarded "discrimination" in payment as a prime
requisite of sound funding and fair settlement.
[65] *Ibid.*, 244 ff.
[66] *Ibid.*, 248 ff. Actually this was the most complicated part of Hamilton's plan and the
part presented with least clarity.
[67] *Ibid.*, 258 ff.                    [68] *Ibid.*, 268–70.                    [69] *Ibid.*, 271.

ments" should be met by new loans abroad; interest on the domestic debt could be provided by higher impost duties on wines, spirits, tea and coffee, together with the existing tonnage-tax on foreign shipping, and an increased excise on spirits distilled in the United States.[70] Twelve million dollars should be borrowed to refund foreign obligations [71] and—a shrewd stroke—to begin the purchase of American notes and certificates of debt as soon as the general plan was adopted. This was to be done to discourage speculation.[72] Finally, from the assumed profits of the Post Office, a sinking fund was to be created.[73]

This was a dazzling plan, and from the viewpoint of the Federalists, the most impressive possible device to demonstrate to the American people the vitality and good faith of their new government. Washington approved but he foresaw a bitter and perhaps dangerous controversy over assumption of State debts.[74] For this reason and in deference to the lawmakers who had the right to accept, to reject or to amend Hamilton's proposal, he wrote nothing about it and did nothing to commend it to Congress. Nor did he take sides in the arguments over "discrimination" and "assumption" that began to develop heat even before February 8, when debate on the report was opened in the House.[75] Members did not stint other legislation while exploring the tangled and fascinating problems of Federal finance and funding. Neither House looked with favor on the measure to organize the militia,[76] but bills to enact most of Washington's recommendations were given all the consideration they required.[77] The President left

[70] *Ibid.*, 276 ff.          [71] *Ibid.*, 284.          [72] *Ibid.*, 284 ff.
[73] *Ibid.*, 282.          [74] 31 *G. W.*, 84.

[75] 1 *JHR.*, 154. For the discussion of it from January 12 to the middle of March, see, among numerous references, N. Gorham to Henry Knox, Jan. 12, 1790 (*Knox Papers*, MHS; 1 *Fisher Ames*, 75 ff; 2 *Paine Wingate*, 347–48, 350); Thomas Hartley to Jasper Yeates, January 31, February 7, 14, 22, 28, Mch. 7, 14, 1790 (*Yeates Papers*); Oliver Wolcott to Nathan Strong, February, n.d. (1 *Gibbs, Wolcott Papers*, 39–40); Edward Carrington to James Madison, February 5, Mch. 2, 1790 (12 *Madison Papers*, 75, 86, LC); William Heth to Hamilton, February 21 (8 *Hamilton Papers*, 1050–51, LC); James Madison, Jr., to his father, Feb. 20, 1790 (12 *Madison Papers*, 83, LC); Adam Stephen to James Madison, March 3 (*ibid.*, 88); Henry Lee to Madison, March 4, 13 (*ibid.*, 89, 98; 1 *Jefferson*, 273); Alexander White to Horatio Gates (*Emmet Col.*, NYPL); Jonathan Trumbull to Gates, Mch. 17, 1790 (*Ibid.*).

[76] This plan for a "general arrangement" of the militia was laid before Congress Jan. 21, 1790 (30 *G. W.*, 512; 1 *JHR.*, 144, 199; 1 *JS*, 107; *ASP.*, 1 *Mil. Aff.*, 6–13). For the opposition, see 2 *Paine Wingate*, 353. After some preliminary shuffling, a bill was reported July 1, 1790 (1 *JHR.*, 254), and was referred to the Committee of the Whole, but was not considered further at that session. The militia bill must not be confused with the one for the regular military establishment of the United States, cited in the next note.

[77] Census act of Mch. 1, 1790. 1 *Statutes at Large*, 101–03; naturalization, Mch. 26, 1790, *ibid.*, 103–04; patents, Apr. 10, 1790, *ibid.*, 109–12; regulating the Army, Apr. 30, 1790, *ibid.*, 119–21; copyright, May 31, 1790, *ibid.*, 124–26.

Congress to choose its own course, to make its own decisions and, when it so desired, to call on the Secretaries: his was the duty to recommend and to administer; Congress must not be subject to any interference by him in debate and in enactment. He held strictly to his maxim, "the Constitution of the United States and the laws made under it must mark the line of my official conduct." [78] This was a protective as well as a considerate rule of conduct in dealing publicly with questions apt to divide Congress along any line of cleavage, such, for example, as Quaker memorials against the slave trade that precipitated a violent debate in the House of Representatives. [79] On the ground that he might have to act officially, Washington declined comment on an anti-slavery letter, [80] though personally he thought it regrettable that the question of the slave trade had been raised. [81]

Within his own "department," where authority had been vested by the Constitution or voted him by Congress, Washington did not hesitate to act. The Osgood residence on Cherry Street was not as commodious as Washington desired, nor was it as handsome as he thought the President's house should be. He continued to insist earnestly that he did not cherish "the glare which hovers around the external trappings of elevated office" except for the "lustre which may be reflected from its connection with a power of promoting human felicity"; [82] but he was in nothing more zealous at this time than in seeing that the Presidential office and all its trappings and appendages were "respectable." When Washington learned that the Macomb House on Broadway, which had been used by the departing French Minister, the Comte de Moustier, now might be vacated by the French Chargé d'Affaires, Louis Otto, he undertook negotiations for a lease and pressed these hurriedly, almost nervously. [83] Most generously, Otto agreed to surrender the property as soon as he could find another abode if he thereby could oblige the President. [84] Washington forthwith covenanted to pay 1000 dollars a year in rent [85] and, although the Osgood House had been refurnished the previous year at heavy expense, he bargained for some of the fittings of the Macomb residence at £665. [86] Nor did he consider

[78] See *supra*, p. 224, and 31 *G. W.*, 9.
[79] 1 *JHR.*, 157, 176, 177, 178, 179, 180–81; 1 *Annals*, 1224 ff, 2 *ibid.*, 1451 ff.
[80] 4 *Diaries*, 103–04.                    [81] 31 *G. W.*, 30.
[82] Letter of Jan. 9, 1790 to Mrs. Graham; 30 *ibid.*, 496.
[83] 4 *Diaries*, 83, 84.                    [84] *Ibid.*, 84.
[85] *Decatur*, 147. This was to be paid from his "compensation" of 25,000 dollars a year and was not, in any sense, an additional public charge.
[86] *Ibid.*, 123.

himself guilty of extravagance in improving a mansion he might have to abandon in a short time if Congress moved the seat of government southward as many predicted. By frequent personal visits, and through the diligence of Tobias Lear, he rearranged the contents of the rooms, ordered additional stabling and instituted a hurried search for a needed green carpet.[87] New serving plateaux [88] subsequently were purchased; lighting arrangements were improved; [89] efforts were made to procure a better cook; [90] the Council of New York promptly provided street lamps in front of the house; [91] as a final convenience, the ultimate in domesticity, two cows were purchased.[92] On February 22–23, before some of the improvements were completed, Washington moved into the large mansion [93] and on the 26th had his first levee there.[94] If the entries in his Diary were an accurate register of the employment of his time and were a precise gauge of his interest, they would compel the conclusion that in February, 1790, he gave more thought to his quarters than to Congress.

The lawmakers themselves were talkative, sometimes belligerent and usually deliberate, but they were accustomed by midwinter, 1789–90, to their procedure and they were familiar with most of their duties. On the 9th of February Washington sent to the Senate eight nominations to fill posts that original appointees had declined. Organization of the judiciary was completed [95] when these nominations were confirmed.[96]

[87] 31 *G. W.*, 8–9, 18.

[88] Strangely, this word "plateaux," familiar in the eighteenth century, seems to have no etymological kinship to "platter," for which it is almost a synonym. "Plateau" might be described, not inaccurately, as a decorated "platter."

[89] 31 *G. W.*, 15.

[90] Clement Biddle to Tobias Lear, February 10, Mch. 24, 1790; *Clement Biddle Letter Book*, PHS.

[91] 1 *Minutes of Common Council of New York, 1784–1831*, p. 525, proceedings of Feb. 19, 1790.

[92] May 10, 1790; *Decatur*, 131.     [93] 4 *Diaries*, 92.

[94] The house number was 39–41 Broadway, not far South of Trinity Church. Decatur (*op. cit.*, 148), wrote of the residence: "It was one of a block of three houses erected in 1787 and was four stories and an attic high, with a width of fifty-six feet. From the rear of the main room glass doors opened onto a balcony giving an uninterrupted view of the Hudson river. On entering, one found a large hall with a continuous flight of stairs to the top of the house. On each side of the hall were spacious, high-ceilinged rooms, used for the levees and dinners and always referred to by Washington as 'public rooms.' The house was so large that it was afterward converted into a hotel and for many years was known as Bunker's Mansion House." On occasion, as many as twenty-seven persons were seated together at Washington's dinner table (*Decatur*, 126).

[95] James Iredell was named Associate Justice of the Supreme Court in place of Robert H. Harrison, who adhered to his declination and died April 2, 1790. See 1 *EJS.*, 38; 31 *G. W.*, 10–11, 46 and n. As John Marshall had been unwilling to serve as District Attorney for Virginia, William Nelson, Jr., was named (1 *EJS.*, 38).

[96] *Ibid.*, 40, proceedings of Feb. 10, 1790. Some of the appointments to the revenue service were postponed.

No general act was presented for Washington's signature until the 8th of February and, after that, none till March 1.[97] In New York, therefore, the only condition to give new concern to Washington was the vehemence of the debate over Hamilton's plan and over the Quaker memorials against the slave trade. At home, the situation was different. From Virginia, David Stuart reported to the President: "A spirit of jealousy which may become dangerous to the Union towards the Eastern States seems to be growing fast among us. It is represented that the Northern phalanx is so firmly united as to bear down all opposition, while Virginia is unsupported even by those whose interests are similar with hers. It is the language of all I have seen on their return from New York. Col. [Henry] Lee tells me that many who were warm supporters of the government are changing their sentiments from a conviction of the impracticability of Union with States whose interests are so dissimilar from those of Virginia." [98]

This was a serious development, one most appropriately to be discussed, when opportunity offered,[99] with a gentleman who, after much hesitation and embarrassing delay,[100] had accepted office [101] and on March 21,[102] had reported in New York for duty—Thomas Jefferson, Secretary of State.[103]

[97] One was a measure extending Federal legislation to North Carolina (1 *Statutes at Large*, 99–101); the other was the first census act (*ibid.*, 101–03).

[98] Letter of Mch. 15, 1790; 246 *Papers of G. W.*, 32, LC. In contrast, on the 23rd of March, Fisher Ames wrote his friend George Minot: "The southern gentry have been guided by their hot tempers and stubborn prejudices and pride in regard to southern importance and negro slavery . . . and they have shown an uncommon want of prudence as well as moderation; they have teased and bullied the House out of their good temper, and driven them to vote in earnest on a subject which at first they did not care much about." 1 *Fisher Ames*, 75–76.

[99] Stuart's letter, dated March 11, was answered on March 23. See 31 *G. W.*, 24, 28.

[100] 30 *ibid.*, 468, 509–11; 31 *ibid.*, 1, 12; 8 *Jefferson*, 1, 12; Jefferson to James Madison, Feb. 14, 1790, 12 *Madison Papers*, 78, LC; Alexander White to Horatio Gates, Mch. 13, 1790, *Emmet Col.*, NYPL.

[101] Letter of Feb. 14, 1790; 8 *Jefferson*, 4.

[102] *Ibid.*, 7.

[103] Washington received Jefferson for the first time about 1 P.M. on the 21st, 4 *Diaries*, 106, and on the 23rd discussed with him a number of administrative questions relating to foreign affairs. The only one of first importance dealt with possible Spanish negotiations over the navigation of the Mississippi. The French Revolution is *not* mentioned in Washington's minutes of this conversation (*ibid.*, 107–08).

# CHAPTER XII

## LAWMAKERS IN A CONTENTIOUS MOOD
### (March 23–Sept. 11, 1790)

WASHINGTON FOUND Jefferson a wise and ready counsellor both on foreign affairs and on the diversified questions of public policy concerning which the President asked the opinion of the heads of departments, much as he had sought the opinions of his senior lieutenants during the war.[1] The Secretary had useful information, also, on the possibility of procuring the release of American seamen captured and enslaved by Barbary pirates.[2] Jefferson already had filed a report on the desirable location of consulates,[3] and, when questioned, he disclosed a strong opinion concerning the rank at which American diplomatic representatives should be accredited to European courts. It would be better, he thought, to send Chargés of prestige rather than Ministers of comparative lower standing in that category. The only exception, in his judgment, should be at Versailles.[4] Washington did not agree entirely with this. He was not without hopes that British official temper might cool and that an American Minister would be well received at the Court of St. James's,[5] but he had a particular reason at that time for getting all the advice he could: The House had under consideration a bill for "providing the means of intercourse between the United States and foreign nations." [6] This involved an important constitutional principle and the application of it in the vote of funds: Was it the prerogative of the President or the right of Congress to say at what rank diplomatic agents should be accredited, and if they were to have position that called for a considerable establishment, how was it to be financed within the compensation Congress apparently was disposed to allow?

---

[1] An interesting series of Jefferson's answers will be found in 3 *Jefferson*, 15 ff.
[2] 4 *Diaries*, 106. For the immediate antecedents and Jefferson's connection with them, see *ibid.*, 56; 30 *G. W.*, 357–58, 458–59, 474–76; Jay to Washington, Nov. 16, 1789, Nat. Arc., 14 *Am. Lets.*, 120, f. 108, and also in Nat. Arc. RG. 59. State Dept.: *Gen. Records.*
[3] 4 *Diaries*, 107 and n.  [4] *Ibid.*, 107.  [5] *Ibid.*, 128.
[6] 1 *JHR.*, 144, 146, 147, 182. This was House Bill 35, for which H.B. 52 was substituted.

Jefferson thought, as did Jay and Madison, that the Senate could do no
more than accept or reject the President's nominee and could not prescribe the rank.[7] The amount of the appropriation was, of course, for
Congress to determine, and so was the pay of State Department officials
of different grade; the President was free to decide whether he would
send an Ambassador, a Minister or a Chargé to a given post, provided
the total expenditures authorized by him did not exceed the appropriation. To have this view accepted in all its parts, and, in particular, to
get money enough for the men needed at foreign capitals, Washington
had "to intimate"—the verb was of his own picking—that he planned
to send to Britain, as well as to France, an agent with the rank of
Minister. Even after this cautious and reluctant intervention, the
requisite funds were not made available until months after Jefferson's
arrival.[8]

The incident was not the happiest with which Washington might
have welcomed his Secretary of State but it had no serious consequences,
though it occurred when the lawmakers were in a contentious mood.
The reason for heat and division was the bill "to protect the public
credit," the first measure to carry out the recommendations in Hamilton's report. After the defeat of Madison's amendment for discrimination between original creditors and later purchasers of continental
notes,[9] the debate in the House swung to the most disputable of all the
involved questions: Should the United States assume the debts contracted by the States on account of the war? This had been discussed
hotly before the arrival of Jefferson and it was destined to long, long
weeks of angry argument until the new Secretary had to admit regretfully that assumption had "created greater animosities than I ever yet
saw take place on any occasion."[10] The House was almost evenly
divided[11]—a condition that Washington thought particularly regrettable where the issue was one of high importance.[12] Privately, he be-

---

[7] 4 *Diaries*, 122. Jefferson's detailed opinion is in 3 *Jefferson*, 15 ff.

[8] The bill was signed July 1, 1790; 1 *Statutes at Large*, 128–29. For the legislative contest,
see 1 *JHR.*, 186, 202, 205, 224, 227, 237, 249, 251, 252, 253, 254; 1 *JS*, 136, 138, 144, 145,
169, 170, 173. See, also, 4 *Diaries*, 128, 130.

[9] The vote was in Committee of the Whole, Feb. 22, 1790; 2 *Annals*, 1298. Madison
mustered thirteen votes only; the opposition numbered thirty-six.

[10] Letter of June 27, 1790, to Doctor Gilmer; 8 *Jefferson*, 52.

[11] Letter of Samuel Johnston to Iredell, Apr. 6, 1790; G. J. McRee, *Life and Correspondence
of James Iredell*, v. 2, p. 286.

[12] 31 *G. W.*, 28–30.

lieved it wise that "assumption" should prevail,[13] but he wished to be in a larger majority—or a much smaller minority. The more numerous the men of one mind, the less the danger of an upheaval. Nothing, except the choice of a permanent seat of government, was so apt to cause a convulsion.[14] Cleavage was not sectional. Massachusetts' supporters of assumption were exceeded in the vehemence of their arguments by like-minded Representatives of South Carolina. "After wheedling us into the Union," cried Ædanus Burke of the State whose people had seen British martial rule in Charleston, "and wheedling us out of the impost, we must consider ourselves wretchedly duped if we are now abandoned to our fate," [15] with a debt the people could not support [16]—to which the reply of the Marylander, Michael Jenifer Stone, was terse: ". . . to attain imaginary equity, you are guilty of positive injustice." [17] Over and over the appeal was: These debts of the States were contracted for a common cause; the States were merely the agents of Congress; [18] debt was the price of liberty. Madison met this with a reminder that assumption did injustice to the States which had done their duty by their creditors and now were called on to contribute to those States that had not done like duty.[19] Almost without exception, the magnitude of the debt of a given State was the gauge of its Representatives' zeal for assumption. Men jealous of the rights of their States warned that assumption would increase the popularity of the Federal government and would weaken the States.[20] Daily, endlessly, the debate went on. If an orator exhausted his auditors, his arguments, or improbably, himself, a fellow-member would spring forward to whip up the same weary words. The patience of the House was outraged more than once by the petulance of wranglers. What the vote would be on assumption was as doubtful as was the time when the roll would be called.

Washington listened as the arguments were brought from Federal Hall and were repeated in the newly occupied house on Broadway, but he probably exemplified the complaint of the traveler that he was the one man who never felt called upon to make any reply to questions he

---

[13] *Ibid.*, 52.
[14] *Ibid.*, 84.
[15] 2 *Annals*, 1362.
[16] *Ibid.*, 1332.
[17] *Ibid.*, 1365.
[18] *Ibid.*, 1348.
[19] *Ibid.*, 1378.
[20] *Ibid.*, 1356. Needless to say, the whispered allegation, later on, was that this had been the chief reason Hamilton proposed assumption.

did not wish to answer. In his silence was strength and security. When debaters were looking everywhere for new witnesses and were turning every page for fresh evidence, nobody could quote a word Washington had spoken or written on assumption.

Had the President felt it necessary to explain his reserve during the last week of April, he could have said that he had the matter of diplomatic allowances to occupy his mind and, still more, that he faced now a new and perplexing problem. The State of Georgia was alleged to have sold to private land companies large tracts that lay beyond the line of territory reserved by treaty to the Choctaw and Chickasaw and to part of the Cherokee tribes.[21] This was done after Georgia had ratified the Constitution of the United States and thereby had relinquished all right to deal with the Indians. If the savages were to be restrained from violence and depredation, their rights under existing treaties must be respected, to the extent, at least, that if lands were occupied, payment should be made and new treaties negotiated. How was this to be done by the Federal government? Had not the Constitution been violated by Georgia's action, and if it had been, what proceedings should be initiated?[22] Washington sought the answer with characteristic caution. Knox's report was accompanied by a written opinion of Attorney General Edmund Randolph and also by the draft of a proclamation the Secretary of War thought the President should issue.[23] At first opportunity, April 30, Washington asked Hamilton to look over these papers and when the Secretary of the Treasury expressed doubts concerning the steps recommended by Knox, the President referred the entire question to the Secretary of State.[24] Jefferson concluded that Georgia prior to 1789 had possessed the exclusive right to acquire the native title but that when the State ratified the Federal Constitution and that document became effective, Georgia surrendered the means by which she could negotiate with the Indians on her own account. All, therefore, that Georgia could convey to the land companies in question was the right, even the exclusive right, to acquire; "but she could not convey what she had not herself, that is, the means of acquiring."[25]

[21] The Georgia act of Dec. 21, 1789, is in *ASP.*, 1 *Ind. Aff.*, 114. For the tribes involved, see *ibid.*, 112.

[22] The background of the controversy is sketched in Knox's report of Jan. 22, 1791; *ibid.*, 112–13.

[23] 4 *Diaries*, 123, 125. Neither Knox's report nor Randolph's opinion is in the *Papers of G. W.*, LC.

[24] *Ibid.*, 125.                                         [25] 3 *Jefferson*, 20.

Instead of coercion,[26] there should be "respect and friendship," an opportunity for Georgia to withdraw from her position and, meantime, to preserve the status quo. It might be well, in addition, to send a representative to the Indians in order "to explain to them the views of government, and to watch with their aid the territory in question." [27]

Nothing was said of it at the time, but the methods by which the opinions of department heads were assembled for Washington's decision on the main issue illustrated one phase of his conception of his office. Apparently he considered it entirely in order for Knox to seek the legal opinion of Randolph and then to draft a proclamation. Nor did Washington feel he had done anything amiss in conveying Knox's and Randolph's ideas to the Secretary of the Treasury, and then in having Jefferson pass on Hamilton's caveat. The President wanted the expression of each man's judgment,[28] and where the four were harmonious, there was no reason for special tact in dealing with sensibilities. Courtesy was a constant, but beyond that, cooperation did not depend on ceremony. Washington pondered the counsel given him and awaited development.

Not long after his conference with Jefferson, the President found himself with a bad cold and, as the day was the Sabbath, he decided to stay at home and to employ himself quietly in letter writing.[29] The next day he was worse. Mrs. Washington took charge of the sick-room, and, as Tobias Lear was absent on his honeymoon,[30] Major Jackson assumed direction of the office and made all arrangements for medical attendance. Besides Dr. Samuel Bard, he called in Dr. John Charlton and Dr. Charles McKnight,[31] but their combined treatment did not halt the progress of the malady which was diagnosed as a serious form of pneumonia.[32] Alarm seized the household. Washington "seemed

[26] The word was Jefferson's.          [27] 3 *Jefferson*, 21.

[28] See *infra*, p. 335.

[29] This was May 9, 1790. 4 *Diaries*, 129.

[30] He and Mary Long had been married at Portsmouth, N. H., on the 18th of April (*Decatur*, 128). For his absence until approximately June 1, see 31 *G. W.*, 43.

[31] For McKnight, who died the next year, see James J. Walsh, *History of Medicine in New York*, v. 1, p. 198, and Martha J. Lamb, *History of the City of New York*, v. 2, p. 284. She also mentioned Doctor Charlton, *ibid.*, 305. He was an English surgeon who had come to New York with the British Army. Doubtless these physicians were summoned at the request of Doctor Bard. For their presence at the bedside, see Mrs. John Jay to her husband, May 15, 1790, 3 *John Jay*, 399.

[32] Most of the reports of the illness have a puzzled note, as if the malady were not typical lobar pneumonia. Washington himself described it as "a severe attack of the peripneumony kind" (31 *G. W.*, 46). Madison's observation was not positive but undoubtedly echoed the opinion of attending physicians: "His complaint is a peripneumonia, united probably with the influenza" (Letter of May 19, 1790, to Edmund Randolph, 13 *Madison Papers*, 29, LC).

less concerned himself as to the result," Martha said afterwards, "than perhaps almost any other person in the United States." [33] By the 12th, the General's condition was becoming so critical that the physicians asked for the counsel of Dr. John Jones of Philadelphia. Major Jackson had an express dispatched immediately and he exerted every effort to have the famous surgeon make the journey with secrecy. "To relieve you from any extraordinary personal anxiety," he wrote Clement Biddle, "I am happy to inform you that the symptoms which attend the President's indisposition are not threatening," but the urgency of the call for Doctor Jones gave this reassurance the color of anxious doubt.[34] Within a few days, it was known in most of the cities of the East that Washington was dangerously ill and that his death was not improbable.[35] Doctor Jones arrived promptly but could suggest nothing effective.

On the 15th of May, six days after the appearance of the first symptoms of his "cold," the General seemed to be close to the end.[36] A caller at the house found "every eye full of tears" and the President's "life despaired of." [37] Doctor McKnight, who then was in immediate attendance, said frankly that he had every reason to expect the death of his patient.[38] Shortly after midday, Washington seemed to be at the last of his hurried and shallow respiration. Then, about 4 o'clock, he broke into a copious sweat, and his circulation improved. Within two hours, the change was definite: he had passed the crisis. Before the night was over, the character of his expectoration was different. On the

[33] Letter of June 12, 1790, to Mercy Warren; 2 *Warren-Adams Letters*, 319. The original of this letter is owned by Dr. Joseph E. Fields of Joliet, Ill.

[34] A typographical error in 31 *G. W.*, 41, n. 73, makes it appear that this letter was written May 2, instead of May 12. In *ibid.*, 57, n. 4, Jones is entered as Gardner Jones, but Matteson indexed him correctly as Dr. John Jones.

[35] Mercy Warren to Washington, May 18, 1790 (246 *Papers of G. W.*, 86, LC); Thomas Hartley to Jasper Yeates, May 17, 1790 (*Yeates Papers*, PHS); S. Ogden to Henry Knox, May 22, 1790: "There has been a universal gloom throughout this country on account of the President's illness" (*Knox Papers*, MHS). Cf. Henry Lee to Washington, June 12, 1790: "We have been all again made most miserable by the account received of the desperate state of your health" (246 *Papers of G. W.*, 111 LC). Few persons agonized more than did Abigail Adams, who knew something of the magnitude of the unfinished tasks the government faced. She did not believe anyone besides Washington could discharge them successfully and she wrote her sister: "I feared a thousand things which I pray I never may be called to experience. Most assuredly I do not wish for the highest post. I never before realized what I might be called to, and the apprehension of it only for a few days greatly distressed me . . ." (Letter of May 30, 1790; *Abigail Adams*, 49).

[36] Madison to Monroe, June 1, 1790; 13 *Madison Papers*, 34, LC, and cited in 6 *Hunt's Madison*, 15 n; Jefferson to Edward Rutledge, July 4, 1790; 8 *Jefferson*, 61.

[37] *Maclay*, 265.

[38] *Ibid.*; cf. John Brown to Judge Harry Innes, June 8, 1790 (19 *Innes Papers*, LC).

16th he was so much improved that members of the household began to hope he was out of danger.[39] By the 20th, this was the general opinion.[40] After that, though he could not shake off his cough immediately, Washington was himself again,[41] and Martha, in consequence, was restored, as she said, to her "ordinary state of tranquility and usually good flow of spirits." [42] Washington's reflections were calmly simple: He had suffered two illnesses of increasing severity within a year, he said; the next doubtless would be the last.[43] Meantime, physicians' orders to take more exercise and to do less work were hard for even so well disciplined a man as he to obey. "I cannot . . . avoid persuading myself," he confessed, "that it is essential to accomplish whatever I have undertaken (though reluctantly) to the best of my abilities." His comfort was the prospect of going to Mount Vernon for a vacation if Congress took a recess.[44]

Members had not advanced their legislation satisfactorily during the month Washington had been ill and convalescing. Seven acts had been passed, none of them of first importance,[45] but neither the bill to provide for the public credit nor the measure to establish the seat of government had received final legislative approval. On the contrary, the two had become entangled in a manner that excited the politician and made the citizen shake a puzzled head. When the close division of the House of Representatives [46] had been tested by a roll call on the 12th of April, assumption of State debts had been rejected in Committee of the Whole by a majority of two.[47] At first, after that defeat, the resent-

[39] For the sole detailed account of the successful passage of the crisis, posterity is indebted to Thomas Jefferson. See his letter of May 16, 1790, to his daughter, Martha Randolph, *The Jefferson Papers*, 1 MHS Cols., 7th Series, p. 36.

[40] Madison to Edmund Randolph, May 19 (13 *Madison Papers*, 29, LC); Thomas Hartley to Jasper Yeates, May 18, 23 (*Yeates Papers*, PHS); Richard Henry Lee to Thomas Lee Shippen, May 18, 23, 1790 (2 *Ballagh, Lee Letters*, 515–16, 517). Once it was a certainty that Washington would live, the *Gazette of the United States* waxed jubilant and demanded, in poetic style, that America offer solemn thanks. "From all let grateful incense rise," intoned "a Lady" in the issue of June 5, 1790, p. 3. The *Boston Gazette* had a contributor who sent the paper a thirty-line poem "On the Illustrious President Washington's Late Recovery to Health." This was published in the issue of Aug. 9, 1790, p. 4, but while flattering, it was not an exclusive tribute. Amazingly, in the issue of Aug. 14, 1790, p. 4, were thirty more lines "On the Illustrious Governor Hancock's Late Recovery to Health."

[41] 31 *G. W.*, 44, 55; 8 *Jefferson*, 33; Clement Biddle to Lear, June 16, 1790, *Clement Biddle Letter Book*, PHS.

[42] Letter of June 12, 1790, to Mercy Warren; 2 *Warren-Adams Letters*, 319.

[43] 31 *G. W.*, 55; cf. *ibid.*, 66.          [44] *Ibid.*, 46.          [45] 1 *Statutes at Large*, 122–26.

[46] Perhaps the best report of the narrow margin of votes, on one side or the other, is in Thomas Hartley's letters of March 29 and April 11, 1790; *Yeates Papers*, PHS.

[47] 2 *Annals*, 1525. The vote was 31 to 29. Elias Boudinot's doleful comment was: "The harmony of our House is broken up." (Boudinot to William Bradford, Apr. 15, 1790; *Boyd's Boudinot*, 185.)

ment of New Englanders and South Carolinians ran so high that they were suspected of planning to reject all funding at that session of Congress.[48] They were too wise and too much interested to be guilty of any such blunder. In the face of increasingly violent attacks by a few republican newspapers on Hamilton and his plan,[49] they rallied their forces [50] while the Virginians continued in united, unyielding opposition to every proposal that the debts of the States be assumed.[51] To the surprise of some members of Congress, tempers cooled quickly.[52] Hamilton, Jefferson, Robert Morris and others took advantage of this and, while the President was convalescing, they made common cause. The Secretary of the Treasury had resolute ambition to see his funding plan succeed, and he did not consider that his duty as head of a department under Washington should keep him from seeking congressional support for his proposals, but he did not deceive himself into thinking he had a majority in the House. He lacked a vote or two and he must find them.[53] Jefferson had made friends in every circle after he had taken up his duties as Secretary of State [54] and, like Hamilton,

[48] Thomas Hartley to Jasper Yeates, Apr. 13, 1790 (*Yeates Papers*, PHS). Massachusetts observers thought the adverse vote attributable in some measure to the bitter feeling aroused by the debate on the Quakers' memorial for the suppression of the slave trade (cf. N. Gorham to Knox, Apr. 17, 1790, *Knox Papers*, MHS). Henry Jackson wrote Knox, April 25, that the vote had thrown Boston into the greatest confusion and would weaken the Federal government in the estimation of the people (*ibid.*).

[49] The principal critics, in a campaign that probably will repay closer study, were the *New-York Journal* (March 25, April 15, 29, May 24, June 4, 11, July 2, 1790) and the *Independent Chronicle* (Boston) (Apr. 15, 22, 1790) with some support, for a time, from the *Boston Gazette* (cf. its quotation of amusing mixed metaphors, July 12, p. 1, from a Philadelphia newspaper of June 26). It may be assumed that the hostility of so venerable and widely regarded a newspaper as the *Pennsylvania Gazette* (Philadelphia) proved a particular irritant to Hamilton and his followers. In the issue of Mch. 17, 1790, p. 3, the editor levelled a poetic broadside at "Young Belcour":

> "Each day a fresh report he broaches,
> That Spies and Jews may ride in coaches,
> Soldiers and farmers, don't despair
> Untax'd as yet are Earth and Air."

This campaign continued through the summer of 1790, even after final action had been taken by Congress. See, in particular, *New-York Journal*, Sept. 3, 1790, p. 3: "The funding bill was founded on the dejected idea of our national poverty and imbecility."

[50] Their arguments at this time had been anticipated partially by Stephen Higginson in a wise letter of Apr. 7, 1790, to Henry Knox (*Knox Papers*, MHS). See, also, Henry Jackson to Knox, July 4, 1790 (*ibid.*).

[51] Perhaps the fullest statement of the "Virginia Case" is in Edward Carrington to James Madison, March 27 (12 *Madison Papers*, 110, LC). Of scarcely less interest are: John Dawson to Madison, Apr. 13, 1790 (13 *ibid.*, 9); Adam Stephen to Madison, April 25 (13 *ibid.*, 13); Edmund Randolph to Madison, May 20 (13 *ibid.*, 31); Beverley Randolph to Madison, May 26, 1790 (13 *ibid.*, 32).

[52] Thomas Hartley to Jasper Yeates, May 11, 1790; *Yeates Papers*, PHS.

[53] Boudinot was sure that Hamilton's proposal for assumption could never be passed in the current session "without a coalition" (*Boyd's Boudinot*, 185).

[54] Cf. Abigail Adams to Mary Cranch, Apr. 3, 1790: "Mr. Jefferson is here, and adds much to the social circle" (*Abigail Adams*, 44).

he saw no reason why he should not use his influence with members of Congress in what he considered good causes—such, for example, as locating the permanent home of the Federal government on the Potomac—though as yet he was not familiar with all the shoals and currents in the confusing waters of congressional politics. Robert Morris was desperately anxious to have the seat of government moved temporarily to Philadelphia, doubtless in the hope the choice might be *in perpetuo*. Out of these three interests, which were shared by the supporters of the three men, there came an agreement whereby the advocates of the assumption of State debts were to effect the conversion of a few doubters or unbelievers, in return for which, as a thank offering, Philadelphia was to be the seat of government until 1800. After that year, the capital was to be near Georgetown, on the Potomac.[55] As a result of this agreement, the bill "for establishing the temporary and permanent seat of the Government of the United States" was passed and was presented to him on the 12th of July.[56] Those who favored New York as the capital and those who opposed assumption of State debts were furious. "We may as well have a set of gamblers for rulers," remarked the disgusted printer of the *Boston Gazette*.[57] Elbridge Gerry already had protested: "I was in some expectation that the new government would have for a time risen superior to local views and prejudices, but confess to you that I am greatly disappointed . . . The two Houses are much divided . . . Intrigues, cabals and combinations are the consequences, and what will be the issue, time must determine."[58] John Brown in like strain lamented that assumption and the dispute over the seat of government had destroyed the disinterestedness that had marked the previous session

[55] In describing this familiar "bargain," Channing relied heavily on Maclay, who admittedly was not "in the secret," and questioned whether Jefferson's part in the transaction was as naive as the Virginian represented it to be in a labored explanation written in 1793 (see P. L. Ford, ed., *Writings of Thomas Jefferson*, v. 6, p. 172–74), and in the "Anas" (1 *Jefferson*, 274–76) of his twilight years. In a long and bitter commentary in 1792 on his mounting friction with Hamilton, Jefferson insisted that the only instance in which he attempted to influence legislation was the one "I was duped into by the Secretary of the Treasury, and made a tool for forwarding his schemes, not then sufficiently understood by me" (Jefferson to Washington, Sept. 9, 1792; 8 *Jefferson*, 396). For Channing's conclusion that the whole story perhaps would never be known in its entirety, see 4 *His. U. S.*, 77. One is inclined now to summon witnesses Channing did not call, and from their testimony, one is disposed to think the essential facts can be established. See Fisher Ames to Thomas Dwight, June 11, 1790 (1 *Fisher Ames*, 79–80); R. H. Lee to T. L. Shippen, July 1, 1790 (2 *Ballagh, Lee Letters*, 531); and Thomas Hartley to Jasper Yeates, May 11, June 2, 9, 11, 20, 1790 (*Yeates Papers*, PHS).

[56] 1 *JS*, 177.

[57] July 5, 1790, p. 3. Cf. *Conn. Courant* (Hartford) quoted in *New-York Journal*, July 2, 1790, p. 3; see, also, *New-York Journal*, July 13, p. 3, and July 16, 1790, p. 3.

[58] Letter of June 25, 1790; 49 *New England Historical and Genealogical Register*, 436.

of Congress.[59] In pleasant contrast later was the cheerful observation of General Maunsell to Knox: "Strange news indeed . . . Congress quite tired with looking at our pretty girls' faces and . . . our seabass banks, have resolved to go to Philadelphia." [60]

Being the sensitive, conscientious man he was, the President could not be indifferent to this, but the only article that raised a question in his mind was an argument in the New York *Daily Advertiser* [61] that the proposed adjournment of Congress to Philadelphia was unconstitutional and that he should veto the bill. When Jefferson reassured him on this,[62] he signed the bill on the 16th of July.[63] For his action Washington received now what was almost the first, and perhaps the very first, direct newspaper censure that had been leveled at him since he had taken office. It was mild, guarded censure. A writer, signing himself "Z," took his text from the plan of the Mayor and Council of New York "to raise a portrait, more lasting than brass to perpetuate the virtues of the President." The correspondent was bitter: "It is asked, which are the virtues that render him so respectable? Why are they not singled out? Is it for that inflexible justice, that distinguished gratitude to the city of New York, in giving his sanction to the unconstitutional residence bill?" That Washington had real virtues, "Z" was careful to admit. He even promised to portray these subsequently, but here his intimation was explicit if not damnatory: Washington lacked gratitude.[64] Doubtless in the conversation of disappointed members of Con-

---

[59] Letter of July 10, 1790, to Judge Harry Innes; 19 *Innes Papers*, LC.

[60] General John Maunsell received grants of land in New York and Vermont for his military services in Cuba and Canada, and came to New York City early in the 1770's in order to establish his claims. There he married Elizabeth Stillwell, widow of Peter Wraxall. On the outbreak of the Revolution he returned to England, but as he refused to serve in any army fighting his American friends, he was given a command in Ireland, where Mrs. Maunsell joined him in 1777. At the close of the War he came back to New York. His knowledge of affairs on both sides of the Atlantic made him a desirable adviser to both governments and on several occasions he acted as arbiter. He died in New York City in 1795. His correspondence with Knox (*Knox Papers*, MHS) and with other government officials bears witness to his intelligence in handling public affairs and to his personal charm. For an account of General Maunsell, see Charles Maunsell, *The Maunsell Family*, v. 2, part 2, p. 557 ff., and the *Mag. Am. His.* (ed. 1892), p. 519 ff. Letter of Sept. 1, 1790, *Knox Papers*, MHS.

[61] Issue of July 13, 1790, p. 2. This critique, written by "Junius Americanus," took the form of an open letter "To the President of the United States."

[62] 31 *G. W.*, 69–70; 3 *Jefferson*, 59 ff.

[63] 1 *Statutes at Large*, 130, and wrongly entered in the Table of Contents as of July 6.

[64] *New-York Journal*, July 23, 1790. Another controversialist, writing in the same paper, made the remarkable statement: "The residence bill was a political trap, set for the integrity of the executive . . . The hopes of the people may vanish, and the influence of opinion may be lost if the virtue of this illustrious character is exposed to the wiles and intrigues of faction . . . The enemies of the gospel . . . endeavored to injure it by tempting our Saviour into sin; the enemies of the new government mean to wound it, by leading our political Saviour into

gress, the President was criticized more sharply—and always *sotto voce*.
There is no record of any rebuke from the floor, nor does any known
letter by Senator or Representative allege that Washington was party
to the bargain. The nearest approach to such an assertion was in the
diary of the vehement republican, William Maclay. "It is, in fact," said
the junior Senator from Pennsylvania, "the interest of the President of
the United States that pushes the Potomac." In plainer terms: "He,
by means of Jefferson, Madison, Carroll and others urged the business . . ." [65] Later the Senator wrote: "The President of the United
States has (in my opinion) had a great influence in this business. The
game was played by him and his adherents of Virginia and Maryland
. . . and the President has become, in the hands of Hamilton, the dish-
clout of every dirty speculation, as his name goes to wipe away blame
and silence all murmuring." [66] Voluble as Maclay habitually was, and
rash though he often appeared to be, he did not say any of this openly.
He could have said justly that Washington personally hoped the valley
of the beloved Potomac would be chosen as the site of the new capital.
Beyond that, Maclay could not have cited any evidence, so far as it
now is known, that Washington sought to influence the decision of
Congress. If any member's resolve to vote for the Potomac seat was
affected by the President, it was because the individual wished to do
what Washington desired, and not because the General asked him to
do it. No criticism was directed against Washington because of the
part Hamilton and Jefferson played in this transaction. The two men
were praised or blamed for the political maneuvering but their right
to act independently of the President apparently was taken for granted.
Nor was the principal held responsible for these acts of his agents—another evidence of the almost monarchical detachment of the President
at this time.

The bill to move the temporary capital to Philadelphia and the
permanent capital to the Potomac was followed in little more than a
fortnight by the funding measure.[67] In the Senate, the closest vote on

---

error, and to destroy his popularity" (*New-York Journal*, July 27, 1790, p. 2). On the other
hand, of course, Fenno's *Gazette of the United States* was lavish in its praise and positive in its
prophecy. "Assumption," insisted one writer in the issue of July 28, p. 3, "rivets the chain of
union . . . By this, the monster with thirteen heads receives his death wound . . . The machinations of State demagogues to divert the people from a steady pursuit of their best interests
will prove in vain."

[65] *Maclay*, 312.                              [66] *Ibid.*, 328–29.
[67] Presented to Washington Aug. 2, 1790; 1 *JS*, 194.

the plan "making provision for the debt of the United States" had been
that by which the bill was passed [68]—fourteen to twelve; [69] the House
once had reached a decision by a majority of three [70] but usually it had
a majority of five or six for the main items.[71] In final form, the bill
embodied Hamilton's foundation of a new foreign loan, the payment
of accrued interest, and the assumption of State debts; but the super-
structure was simpler than in his design and on straight lines. If the
Secretary still might claim to be the architect, he owed more thanks
than he gave to the draughtsmen of Congress. Washington believed in
the bill [72] and, two days after it was delivered to him,[73] he signed it
with a sense of relief that the dangerous issues involved in it and in
the other part of the "bargain" had been settled.[74] Under this act, 600,-
000 dollars of annual revenue were set aside for the current expenses of
government. All other receipts, the faith of the United States, and the
proceeds of all sales of public lands were pledged to pay the principal
and interest of debts renewed or assumed.[75] The foreign debt was to
be funded again from an overseas, and presumably Dutch, loan of
12,000,000 dollars, which was to have a term not exceeding fifteen years.
From this loan, moreover, all accrued interest and past-due instalments
of the foreign debt were to be paid.[76] Every promise made European
creditors was to be redeemed. The domestic debt accumulated by the
Continental Congress and by the Congress under the Articles of Confederation was to be satisfied in this manner: The holder of any specified certificate of debt of the United States could present it at one of
the offices created for the purpose [77] and could get a new obligation of
the Federal government in a like sum.[78] If any person had the old
currency of Congress,[79] he could turn this in and get a debt-certificate
of one dollar for every 100 dollars of currency tendered.

---

[68] July 21, *ibid.*, 187.
[69] The same vote had been recorded on the sections dealing with assumption, July 20;
*ibid.*, 186.
[70] On certain Senate amendments, July 24; 1 *JHR.*, 277.
[71] *Ibid.*, 223, 281, 283.                    [72] See *supra*, pp. 251, 256–57.
[73] 1 *Statutes at Large*, 138–44, approved Aug. 4, 1790, in 22 sections.
[74] Letter of Aug. 10, 1790, to Luzerne; 31 *G. W.*, 84.
[75] 1 *Statutes at Large*, as *supra*, Sec. 1.
[76] Sec. 2.                                     [77] Sec. 6.
[78] Throughout this and contemporary statutes on public finance, the term "specie value" is
used in the sense of the modern words, "face value."
[79] The so-called "bills of credit issued by the authority of the United States in Congress
assembled." Sec. 3

The new obligations issued for the old evidences of debt were to be in two categories. Those for principal were to bear 6 per cent; those for accumulated interest were to yield 3 per cent. Further, the capital amounts represented by the 6 per cent certificates were to be divided into thirds. Interest on two-thirds was to be paid quarterly from Jan. 1, 1791 [80] at 6 per cent; interest at the corresponding rate on the remaining one-third was not to begin until after 1800. These certificates for principal could not be redeemed by government in an amount greater than 2 per cent of the amount outstanding in a given year. Even this long-term redemption was not compulsory.[81] Liquidation of certificates issued for past-due interest was to be at the discretion of Congress.[82] In event any holder of government certificates did not wish to accept these terms, he could deposit his paper (other than currency) and could get new certificates that conformed to the existing provisions for interest and redemption, whatever these might be.[83]

Such were the arrangements for funding the foreign and the continental debts. The plan for dealing with the debts of the States was based on the crude, unavoidable give-and-take of public finance during the Revolutionary War, when the States had supplied some of the necessities of "the continent" and Congress had paid for some of the supplies and equipment that should have been charged against the States. These accounts were supposed to be in process of settlement; the assumption of State debts was to be a part of the final accounting in the following manner: Holders of the securities of a State could turn them in to the office of the Federal commissioner who superintended the loans. In return, certificates of the United States would be issued. Two-thirds of the principal would bear 6 per cent interest. The remaining one-third would yield 3 per cent from Jan. 1, 1792; but there was a further provision: Of the amount that paid 6 per cent, two-thirds would bear interest from Jan. 1, 1792, and the other third from Jan. 1, 1801.[84] Provisions for retirement of the assumed State debts were similar to those for the continental debt.[85] Limits, moreover, were set on the amounts of State debts that could be presented for Federal funding. The total was reckoned roughly at twenty-one and a half million, apportioned

[80] Secs. 4, 8.      [81] Sec. 4.
[82] Sec. 5.      [83] Secs. 9–10.
[84] Sec. 15. In somewhat confusing terms a statute otherwise remarkably clear spoke of these classifications as "two-thirds of the aforesaid two-thirds" and as one-third thereof.
[85] Sec. 14.

according to the estimated war debts of the different States.[86] Georgia could tender 300,000 dollars only; Massachusetts and South Carolina, 4,000,000 dollars each.[87] If more than these amounts for any State were brought to the commissioners' offices, the issue of new certificates would be pro rata for that State; and if less than the specified amounts were forthcoming, the State would have an interest-bearing credit until final settlement of accounts with "the continent." [88] In such a conclusive balancing of accounts, each State was to have the amount of assumed debt charged against it as a Federal payment on account.[89] In furtherance of its pledge to guarantee revenue for this funding, Congress proceeded to raise existing imposts,[90] though it declined to carry out Hamilton's recommendation for a tax on spirits distilled in America.[91]

The weeks during which Congress had fought over debt settlement and the seat of government witnessed several developments that encouraged or puzzled the President in his convalescence. On the 29th of May, Rhode Island ratified the Constitution of the United States,[92] and forthwith received both blessing and exhortation from Washington: "Since the bond of Union is now complete," he said, "and we once more consider ourselves as one family, it is much to be hoped that reproaches will cease and prejudices be done away; for we should all remember that we are members of that community upon whose general success depends our particular and individual welfare; and, therefore, if we mean to support the Liberty and Independence which it has

---

[86] The act carefully defined these debts, Sec. 13, in order to make certain that the Federal government assumed no debts other than those of the war.

[87] Sec. 13.                                 [88] Secs. 14, 17.

[89] Sec. 19. In explanation of this long summary of the funding act of Aug. 4, 1790, it may be said that some of the narratives of this famous financial operation confuse Hamilton's proposals and the completed act, or describe the one as if it were the other.

[90] Act of Aug. 10, 1790; 1 *Statutes at Large*, 180–82.

[91] For the subsequent levy of an excise on spirits distilled in the United States, after June 30, 1791, see the act of Mch. 3, 1791, mentioned *infra*, pp. 293–94, 1 *Statutes at Large*, 219.

[92] A convenient text of the ratification will be found in 1 *JHR.*, 300–03. Washington's message to Congress, Jan. 28, 1790, covering the call for a State convention is in *ibid.*, 148, and in 1 *Richardson*, 72. For the President's continued warnings to the State and his reproach of the long-dominant element, see 30 *G. W.*, 442, 485, 504. The threat of commercial non-intercourse with Rhode Island was conveyed in a Senate bill passed May 18 (1 *JS*, 142) and denounced by Sen. John Steele of North Carolina as "tyrannical and arbitrary in the highest degree" (*Papers of John Steele*, H. M. Wagstaff, ed., cited hereafter as *Steele Papers*, v. 1, p. 61). This measure was received in the House May 19 (1 *JHR.*, 219) and the next day (*ibid.*), was set for hearing in Committee of the Whole on the 31st, by which date it doubtless was hoped the convention would have ratified. The 31st chanced to be an exceedingly busy legislative day. Before the Senate bill was reached after that, Rhode Island had resumed her place in the Union. Several letters on the ratification are in the *Knox Papers*, MHS.

cost us so much blood and treasure to establish, we must drive far away the dæmon of party spirit and local reproach." [93] In a broader governmental sense, Washington felt that Rhode Island's action made possible "a fair experiment of a Constitution . . . framed solely with a view to promote the happiness of a people." [94] In contrast, the safety, rather than the quiet happiness of the people, seemed to be involved the next month, after Major George Beckwith appeared in New York. This British officer, aide to Lord Dorchester, Governor of Canada, sought out Alexander Hamilton on the 8th of July and in a long conversation of traditional diplomatic indirection, hinted that Britain not only might settle differences with America but also might be willing to enter into an alliance. In event of war between England and Spain,[95] Beckwith remarked, the United States would find it to their interest to uphold Britain. There was much besides, in the Major's conversation, but these were the points of strongest emphasis. To suggestions that Lord Dorchester, formerly Sir Guy Carleton, gave no evidence of authority to discuss these matters, Beckwith's reply was that the very importance of the subject should be a guarantee that Dorchester knew the wishes of the British cabinet.[96]

Hamilton reported this to Jefferson, and went with the Secretary of State to inform the President of what had occurred. To Washington, the incident seemed entirely in accord with what he had seen of British dealings for twenty-five years. Usually he was cautious in his conclusions and did not clinch them until he had deliberated and had heard all that the best men around him had to say. This time his judgment was clear and was quickly shaped: The British had determined not to give an answer to Gouverneur Morris in London until they ascertained by Beckwith's indirect approach whether the United States were willing to make common cause with them against Spain. If America did this, then the British would negotiate a commercial treaty and, as Washington expressed it, would "promise perhaps to fulfil what they already stand engaged to perform" under the treaty of 1783. "However," Washington went on, "I requested Mr. Jefferson and Colonel Hamilton, as I intend to do the Vice-President, Chief Justice and Sec-

[93] Letter of June 4, 1790, to Gov. Arthur Fenner, 31 *G. W.*, 47–48.
[94] Letter of July 1, 1790, to the Comte de Segur; *ibid.*, 67.
[95] On the probability of war, see Jonathan Williams to Knox, May 5; P. Brett to Knox, July 4, 17, 1790. All three of these letters are from London and are in the *Knox Papers*, MHS.
[96] Hamilton's minute of this interview is in 4 *A. Hamilton*, 296–99. Washington copied it in his *Diary*. See 4 *Diaries*, 137–39.

retary at War, to revolve this matter in all its relations in their minds" and to advise him later.[97] The result of this and of another diplomatic fencing bout between Hamilton and Beckwith [98] was a decision by Washington to let it be impressed that the United States had no understanding with Spain and had not settled with that country the question of the navigation of the Mississippi. Beyond this, in the absence of any official British proposals, civility and reticence manifestly were the course of prudence on the part of a country that desired to remain neutral and at peace with all foreign powers.[99] Hamilton added: ". . . in case of rupture between Great Britain and Spain, the United States ought to be in the best situation to turn it to account, in reference to the disputes between them and Great Britain on the one hand, and Spain on the other." [100]

Thus the matter stood until mid-August, when there was intimation that if England and Spain opened hostilities, Lord Dorchester might wish to descend the Mississippi through the territory of the United States, and attack Louisiana or its outposts. If Britain made a request for her troops to have unhindered passage, what should Washington do? He thought such application would be made by Dorchester and he believed that no decisive answer should be given, but, once again, he sought the advice of Hamilton, Jefferson and Knox, and of the Vice President and of the Chief Justice as well.[101] The President found these counsellors divided. Jefferson was willing to face Britain in arms again if the alternative were England's conquest of Louisiana and the Floridas. He would remain neutral as long as possible, enter the war late, if at all, and try to evade a direct answer to any British request for passage.[102] John Adams advised his chief to maintain neutrality if it could be done and to avoid every appearance of wrong to either party. If Britain violated American neutrality, he would remonstrate.[103] John Jay was of opinion that an application for peaceful passage should be granted, and that, in theory, passage without prior application should be resisted, though actually if the march were from western posts through unoccupied territory to the Mississippi, which the British had the treaty-right to use, he did not think an effort should be made by

[97] *Ibid.*, 139, entry of July 8, 1790.

[98] Interview of July 22, 1790, reported to the President and printed in 4 *A. Hamilton,* 299–302.

[99] 4 *Diaries,* 142, 143.

[100] 4 *A. Hamilton,* 302.

[101] 31 *G. W.,* 102–03.

[102] 3 *Jefferson,* 79–81.

[103] 8 *John Adams,* 497–500.

force of arms to stop their troops. Serious danger to the United States would be created by British seizure of Louisiana and Florida, but this was not immediately an issue.[104] Secretary Knox advised refusal of the application, if made, but would not attempt to resist a march, though this would be *casus belli*. Washington's answer should exhibit caution and should include a statement of the government's wish to remain neutral in a little-understood dispute between two friendly nations.[105] Hamilton's reply was preceded by a long and careful review of the applicable international law, but as a matter of policy, he advocated nothing more positive than a protest unless the British forced some American post.[106]

The diversity of this counsel underscored the warning the President's own judgment gave him: he would have an unhappy decision to make —one that would outrage the West or divide the East—if the British "beat the general" at Detroit and started southward. He could not tell, as yet, whether the two powers who together hemmed in his country would go to war—with the prospect that British victory would set King George's ramparts North, West and South while the Royal fleet ruled the Atlantic.

In the exchanges between Hamilton and Beckwith there had been polite intimation and horrified denial that Britain had been exciting the northwestern tribes to violence and that American frontier officers had been threatening British posts verbally.[107] The fuel for a conflagration was scattered widely North of the Ohio. Although the Six Nations no longer were a firebrand, the Miami and the Wabash tribes were attacking boats on the Ohio and the Wabash and were crossing into Kentucky on raids of massacre and arson.[108] A particularly vicious band had established itself early in the spring of 1790 on the northern bank of the Ohio, a few miles above the mouth of the Scioto.[109] Previous efforts to make peace with these murderous incendiaries had been futile. Washington, St. Clair and Knox were of one mind in the belief that nothing short of a vigorous, punitive campaign would dispose of a danger that otherwise might be so serious it soon would stop all move-

[104] Letter of Aug. 28, 1790; 247 *Papers of G. W.*, 51, LC.
[105] Letter of Aug. 29, 1790, *ibid.*, 55–56.
[106] 8 *Hamilton Papers*, 1138 ff, LC, and printed in 4 *A. Hamilton*, 313–42.
[107] 9 *Hamilton Papers*, 1091 ff, LC; also printed in 4 *A. Hamilton*, 298–99, 301.
[108] Reports of depredations are assembled in *ASP.*, 1 *Ind. Aff.*, 84 ff. Several are described in the *Knox Papers*, MHS, and in 19 *Innes Papers*, LC.
[109] James Wilkinson to Gen. Josiah Harmar, Apr. 7, 1790, *ASP.*, 1 *Ind. Aff.*, 91–92.

ment on the Ohio River. Very quickly and with scarcely a word in writing, Washington had instructed St. Clair, as Governor of the Northwest Territory, to prepare the expedition and to call out militia to reenforce a small contingent of regulars, who were to have some artillery with them. St. Clair had sent out his requisition for militia on the 15th of July.[110] These troops, presumably about 1500 in number, were assembling now at Fort Washington, which had been established the previous year on the Ohio.[111] With good fortune and good leadership, they might strike a blow in the autumn that would clear the river and make the settlements secure. The commanding officer, Brevet Brig. Gen. Josiah Harmar, had served with Pennsylvania troops during the Revolution, but was not well known to the President.

South of the Ohio, most of the Cherokees, Choctaws and Chickasaws were thought to be well-disposed, though a handful of Cherokee and Shawanese bandits were proving troublesome.[112] As for the Creeks, after Benjamin Lincoln's commission had failed to induce them to make a new treaty, Henry Knox had gone to work and, through a shrewd and patient agent, Col. Marinus Willett, he at last had accomplished what had seemed impossible: he had prevailed on Alexander McGillivray to come to New York with twenty-nine Creek head men.[113] Washington never had any affection for Indians, but he had followed with some interest the journey of the natives toward the temporary capital.[114] On their arrival, July 20,[115] the Tammany Society undertook their entertainment, and Henry Knox supervised the negotiation of a solemn pact by which the Creeks yielded to Georgia the disputed lands on the Oconee but refused to give up their hunting-grounds southwest of the junction of that river and the Ocmulgee.[116] Washington shared in some of the entertainment of the Indians [117]—

---

110 *Ibid.*, 94–95.

111 The site was at Cincinnati, Ohio. For the mobilization there see *ASP.*, 1 *Mil. Aff.*, 20.

112 31 *G. W.*, 87.

113 The number is given in *Daily Advertiser*, July 22, 1790, p. 3. For the dispatch to Georgia, meanwhile, of the few troops available for service in the field, see Knox to Anthony Wayne, April 10 and Wayne to Knox, May 12, 1790; *Knox Papers*, MHS.

114 4 *Diaries*, 132–33, 135; 31 *G. W.*, 68. For the meeting of William Knox with McGillivray and the chief's mentor, Col. Marinus Willett, see William Knox to his brother Henry, July 14, 1790, *Knox Papers*, MHS.

115 *Baker*, 188.

116 31 *G. W.*, 77. It will be remembered that the confluence is on the northern line of the present Jeff Davis County, about fifty-two miles NNW of Waycross, Georgia.

117 The savages, McGillivray in particular, aroused much curiosity. Fisher Ames wrote of the half-breed, "He is decent and not very black" (1 *Fisher Ames*, 87). Abigail Adams apparently had not heard or else would not repeat the well-founded stories that McGillivray was a

a reception at his residence, a formal military review and a visit to the ship *America*,[118] which had completed a voyage to Canton, China [119]—and gave his approval to the various measures Knox desired at the hands of Congress.[120] When the treaty was completed, he attended the ceremonies in the Hall of Congress, signed the document in person and shook the hand of each of the Indians.[121] Apparently he did not think the United States had paid too heavy a price for the treaty which he proclaimed immediately [122] and followed with warning to all and sundry against violation of the earlier covenants with Cherokees, Choctaws and Chickasaws.[123] In manifest satisfaction over the achievement of Knox [124] and Willett, he wrote Lafayette that except for the crimes of a few bandits, the treaty "will leave us in peace from one end of our borders to the other." Even the destruction of the outlaws was to be avoided, if possible, because, he said, "the basis of our proceedings with the Indian nations has been, and shall be *justice*, during the period in which I may have anything to do in the administration of this government." [125] The only dissent immediately audible was that of a few Anti-Federalists. In giving up Georgia to the Creeks, said one writer in the *New-York Journal*,[126] the United States made allies of "10,000 Prussians of the forest." He concluded: "This treaty is founded on extended views . . . I seem to view the posterity of the present signers . . . forming the van of the Army of the United States, when it lays siege to Mexico."

The adjournment of Congress on the 12th of August, the day before the final ceremonies of the Creek treaty, left Washington free to attend

---

drunkard. Said she: "He is grave and solid, intelligent and much of a gentleman, but in very bad health" (Letter of Aug. 8, 1790, to her sister; *Abigail Adams*, 57). The details of their entertainment, which are not particularly interesting, are given in *Daily Advertiser*, July 22, p. 3, August 3, p. 2, August 14, p. 2, August 16, p. 2; *New-York Journal*, July 23, p. 3, July 30, p. 3, August 3, p. 2, August 17, p. 2; *Gazette of U. S.*, July 24, p. 3, July 28, p. 3, July 31, p. 3, Aug. 14, 1790, p. 3.

[118] The respective dates July 20, 27 and 29; *Baker*, 188–89.

[119] *New-York Journal*, July 30, 1790, p. 3.

[120] 31 *G. W.*, 74–77.

[121] *Baker*, 190. This was on the 13th of August. The treaty bore date of the 7th. It will be found in *ASP.*, 1 *Ind. Aff.*, 81–82.

[122] 1 *Richardson*, 80.

[123] Proclamation of Aug. 26, 1790; *ibid.*, 80–81; cf. 31 *G. W.*, 88–92.

[124] Among the interesting documents of this period in the *Knox Papers*, MHS, are questions "To the Tallisee King," August 6, the speech of the American commissioners prior to the signing of the treaty, August 7, and the minutes of the Spanish treaty with the Creeks in 1784 at Pensacola.

[125] Letter of Aug. 11, 1790; 31 *G. W.*, 87.

[126] Issue of Sept. 7, 1790, p. 3. Cf. *ibid.*, Aug. 20, 1790, p. 2.

to several matters, half personal, half official, and then to go back to Mount Vernon for the quiet he had craved. Before his illness he had made a five-day tour of Long Island, in part of which he had found little to praise either of soil or of forest.[127] Perhaps his most interesting experience was a visit to a paper mill, the first, probably, that he ever had seen in operation. At the request of the vatman, Washington dipped in the laid mould, brought it out again, and then couched the sheet. The General asked many questions about the process and remarked, as he surveyed the site, that it would be a good location for a fort.[128] An excursion of a different sort, and more enjoyable, was a fishing expedition with Jefferson and others on the 7th of June, the first time after his attack of pneumonia that the President ventured far from his doctors' care. He was "out" three days and had a good catch of sea bass and black fish.[129] On his return he took exercise, driving and walking, in patient obedience to his physicians' orders,[130] but he had no diversion until the 10th of July when he went on a picnic to Fort Washington, scene of the heaviest loss of prisoners sustained by the United States Army, Charleston alone excepted, during the Revolutionary War.[131] Washington made the meagrest reference to the military associations of the lofty position that was a skeleton, a tomb, a bleak reminder of the misery he had endured in November, 1776. All he had to record, when he had carefully listed the seventeen persons in the excursion, was this: ". . . we visited the old position of Fort Washington and afterwards dined on a dinner provided by Mr. Mariner at the house lately Col. Roger Morris', but confiscated and in the occupation of a common farmer." [132]

Later, when Congress had adjourned, he decided to execute a plan he must have fashioned from the time he had received news that Rhode Island had ratified the Constitution. He had not entered that State during his tour of New England in the autumn of 1789. Now that Rhode Island had reknit the old ties, he would go there, meet the leaders, see the people and make it plain that he no longer kept in his

---

[127] 4 *Diaries*, 116–21. The entries give his day-by-day movements. Nowhere is there any mention of the Battle of Long Island, though he crossed part of the field of action.

[128] This was "on what is now Silver Lake, a peaceful body of water that flows into the head of Hempstead Harbor, at Roslyn . . ." Dard Hunter, *Papermaking Through Eighteen Centuries*, 254–55, a reference supplied by the always generous John Bakeless. The same story is repeated in Hunter's *Papermaking; the History and Technique of an Ancient Craft*, 184–85.

[129] *Decatur*, 133; 8 *Jefferson*, 33; *Gazette of U. S.*, June 12, 1790, p. 3.

[130] 4 *Diaries*, 129–30.

[131] See Vol. IV, p. 252 and n.

[132] Entry of July 10, 1790; 4 *Diaries*, 142.

heart the resentments the petty spokesmen of the little State had aroused. The journey was begun on the 15th of August with Jefferson, George Clinton and other notables, and was in almost every detail the easiest Washington had made in many years. Travel to Newport and return to New York, via Providence, was by the comfortable packet through Long Island Sound; the reception at Newport on the 17th–18th and at Providence on the 18th–19th was altogether friendly and after the familiar pattern of parades, addresses and dinners. Washington drank his fill of the beauties of both places, and at Providence took a four-hour stroll "which," said one attendant stiffly, almost resentfully, "completely fatigued the company which formed his escort." [133] The President saw every attraction, wonder and point of interest the two cities offered and he appeared in so many places that citizens who did not have a look at him had themselves, and not the visitor, to blame. He even moderated his rule against personal visits to the extent that he stopped briefly at five private homes and sipped a glass of wine or drank festive punch.[134] The necessity of reviewing State troops he met by standing at the door of a tavern while the soldiers and accompanying citizens passed and saluted.[135] The most noteworthy occurrences of the brief visits were Washington's answers to three of the addresses delivered him. Instead of perfunctory, polite avowals, he made thoughtful statements, half philosophical and admirably phrased.[136] He told the representatives of the Jewish Congregation of Newport: "It is now no more that toleration is spoken of, as if it was by the indulgence of one class of people, that another enjoyed the exercise of their inherent natural rights. For happily the government of the United States, which gives to bigotry no sanction, to persecution no assistance, requires only that they who live under its protection should demean themselves as good citizens, in giving it on all occasions their effectual

---

[133] Journal of William Loughton Smith, the South Carolina member of the House of Representatives, one of his traveling companions, in 51 *MHSP*, 38. This is the fullest, most observant account of the friendly foray into Rhode Island. Newspaper accounts summarized or reprinted in *Baker*, 190–93, were those of *Daily Advertiser*, August 26, p. 2, *United States Chronicle* (Providence), August 19, p. 3, and *Providence Gazette*, August 21, p. 3. The first of these three is an adequate summary of the tour, and may be supplemented by *Gazette of the United States*, August 28, p. 3. Further details will be found in *Newport Mercury*, Aug. 23, 1793, p. 1.

[134] Smith, as *supra*, p. 36, 38.        [135] *Ibid.*, 37.

[136] As the President manifestly did not have time to write these answers during the few busy days he was in Rhode Island, the papers must have been prepared by one of his secretaries, and presumably by Humphreys, but Washington signed them, read them aloud at the ceremonies and thereby stamped them his own.

support . . ." [137] In answer to the Legislature of the thirteenth State he spoke of the change in government effected "by the influence of reason alone." He concluded: "It remains for the people themselves to preserve and promote the great advantages of their political and natural situation; nor ought a doubt to be entertained that men who so well understand the value of social happiness will ever cease to appreciate the blessings of a free, equal and efficient government." [138] Members of King David's Lodge of Masons received one of the few public acknowledgments he ever made of his faith in the Order: "being persuaded," he said, "that a just application of the principles on which the Masonic fraternity is founded, must be promotive of private virtue and public prosperity, I shall always be happy to advance the interests of the society, and be considered by them a deserving brother." [139] All these remarks, needless to say, strengthened the influence of Washington in Rhode Island, where, indeed, he apparently never had lost popularity during the time the State government was in the hands of the men who held paper money to be the means of paying every man's debts—the more the paper, the cleaner the sheet.

Washington left Providence in the late afternoon of August 19,[140] reached New York before sunset on the 21st,[141] and forthwith took up his part of another task: the transfer of the seat of government to Philadelphia. Shipment of records and funds was the work of the clerks of Congress or of the departmental secretaries; the President took it upon himself to supervise the moving of those contents of his residence that were not too bulky or too much a part of the house to be taken down. Economically, of course, the change from Cherry Street to Broadway now appeared wasteful, because the former abode of the French Minister had been used for six months only; but as an exercise in transportation and adornment, the labor was one that Washington performed zestfully. Rehabilitation, literal or metaphorical, made a peculiar appeal to him. Details were left to Tobias Lear, who had the rare and needful combination of diligence and patience.[142]

Lear's service was more difficult and more nearly indispensable be-

---

[137] 31 *G. W.*, 93 n.     [138] *Ibid.*, 94 n.     [139] *Ibid.*, 93 n.
[140] *Providence Gaz.*, Aug. 21, 1790, p. 3.
[141] *New-York Daily Gaz.*, Aug. 23, 1790, cited in *Smith's Journal*, as *supra*, 39 n.
[142] Correspondence on this subject after Washington left New York appears in 31 *G. W.*, 110 ff. Lear's numerous and lengthy answers are chiefly in 247 and 248 *Papers of G. W.*, LC. Various preliminaries in Philadelphia may be traced in *Clement Biddle Letter Book*, PHS. The interest of all these exchanges is more antiquarian than historical.

cause of Washington's third task, the reorganization at this time of his office staff. David Humphreys was going to Spain and thence to Portugal on diplomatic assignment; [143] Robert Lewis was returning to Virginia to act as steward while George Augustine Washington went "to the mountains" in hopes of physical recovery; [144] Thomas Nelson went, also, to Virginia on a vacation.[145] The President consequently was left with two secretaries only, Lear and Maj. William Jackson.

By the 30th of August, all these matters had been arranged; all necessary papers for the negotiation of the Treasury loans had been placed in the hands of Hamilton; [146] Knox had been instructed to complete all current transactions for Harmar's expedition, the Indian treaties and the defence of the frontier; [147] the amenities of departure were observed, and accounts were settled.[148] On the 28th of August, the Governor of New York, the Mayor of the city and the Aldermen were his guests at a dinner when, as Fenno's *Gazette* dutifully reported, "Mrs. Washington appeared greatly affected" [149] as, of course, she was expected to be. Her distress was more than civil. She had written cheerfully to Mercy Warren: ". . . I contrive to be as happy here as I could be at any place except Mount Vernon. In truth, I should be very ungrateful if I did not acknowledge that everything has been done which politeness, hospitality or friendship could suggest to make my situation as satisfactory and agreeable as possible." [150] Washington himself would have said the same thing and, particularly, on the 30th of August when, in spite of his request for an unceremonious leave-taking,[151] the Governor, the Chief Justice of the United States, the heads of Federal departments

[143] Decatur, *op. cit.*, 146, stated that Humphreys left Washington's employ on the 10th of August. For the Colonel's mission, see 31 *G. W.*, 219–22; 8 *Jefferson*, 70–76, 82–84. Humphreys' fine farewell letter to Washington, Sept. 1, 1790, is in 247 *Papers of G. W.*, 63, LC.

[144] Account in *Decatur*, 148.

[145] He was paid August 23 to Oct. 1, 1790, *Decatur*, 147. From Yorktown, Nov. 24, 1790, Nelson sent his polite and grateful resignation from Washington's staff. He did not explain the circumstances that prevented his return, 248 *Papers of G. W.*, 39, LC.

[146] 31 *G. W.*, 106–07. Cf. 3 *Jefferson*, 74 and 4 *A. Hamilton*, 302.

[147] 31 *G. W.*, 91–92.

[148] *Ibid.*, 107–08, concerning the return to the donors of the barge given Washington on arrival in New York; *ibid.*, 109, for a gift of twenty guineas for the relief of distressed debtors in prison. See, also, *Decatur*, 151–52. In *ibid.*, 156–57 is a good review of Washington's expenditures in New York.

[149] Issue of Sept. 1, 1790, p. 3.

[150] Letter of June 12, 1790, 2 *Warren-Adams Letters*, 319. She added that her grandchildren had enjoyed good educational opportunities in New York and she went on: "In their happiness, my own is, in a great measure, involved. But for the ties of affection which attract me so strongly to my near connection and worthy friends, I should feel myself indeed much weaned from all enjoyments of this transitory life."

[151] *New-York Journal*, Aug. 31, 1790, p. 3.

and the Executive officers, State and municipal, came to his house and
escorted him with the utmost good will to the wharf. The crowd at
that time was not large, because the exact hour of his departure from
Elizabeth Town Point had not been announced.[152] Although New
York had the humiliation just then of realizing that the city was losing
the "seat of government" and the prestige accompanying that honor,
the last minutes were impressive: "All was quietness, save the report of
the cannon that were fired on his embarkation . . . the heart was full
—the tear dropped from the eye; it was not to be restrained; it was
seen; and the President appeared sensibly moved by this last mark of
esteem . . ."[153]

For the long road southward, Tobias Lear had requested, in advance,
that there be "no more parade on [the President's] journey than what
may be absolutely necessary to gratify the people," because this was "to
him a most fatiguing thing."[154] The request had been repeated with
the further explanation that Washington desired his time in Philadelphia, as far as possible, to be his own.[155] The large party—a total of
sixteen persons [156]—traveled slowly at first because some of the horses
were young and the teams had been lacking hard exercise.[157] All went
quietly until, in the early afternoon of the 2nd of September, Washington reached the vicinity of Philadelphia. There, as usual, he was met
by a Troop of Light Horse, by militia companies and by numerous
citizens,[158] all of whom "testified their affection," the *Pennsylvania
Packet* reported, "for the Benefactor of Mankind."[159] The bells were
rung, a *feu de joie* was tendered—everything was as if the President
were visiting the city for the first time.[160] Dinners and other ceremonies were offered [161] but at least some of them would have been de-

---

152 *Ibid.*; *Gazette of U. S.*, Sept. 1, 1790, p. 3.

153 *Daily Advertiser*, Aug. 31, 1790, p. 3; Decatur, *op. cit.*, 150, pointed out that Washington never returned to New York.

154 Letter of Aug. 8, 1790; 31 *G. W.*, 77–78.

155 *Ibid.*, 99–100.

156 Included were "two maids, four white servants and four black d'o." Lear in *ibid.*, 100.

157 *Ibid.* Lear gave this schedule which probably was followed: Monday, August 30, to
Elizabeth; August 31, to New Brunswick; September 1, to Trenton; September 2, to Philadelphia.

158 This was not unexpected. Clement Biddle had written Lear, August 30, that the City
Troop of Horse would meet the President ten miles from the city (*Clement Biddle Letter Book*,
PHS).

159 Issue of September 4, p. 3, after the *Federal Gazette* (Philadelphia) of Sept. 2, 1790, p. 3.

160 *Federal Gazette*, as *supra*.

161 Cf. *Jacob Hiltzheimer's Diary*, 163; *Baker*, 195–96. A dinner on the 3rd with the
Pennsylvania Convention was reported in the *Federal Gazette*, September 4, p. 3; a garden
party on the 4th was described in *Pennsylvania Packet*, Sept. 8, 1790, p. 3.

clined with the excuse of a hurried journey, had not Martha fallen sick.[162] As it was, the President looked, bowed, enjoyed the various affairs and found time to satisfy himself concerning the matter for which he had wished to reserve his time, the details of arrangements for a residence at the new seat of government. The municipal corporation of Philadelphia had anticipated his search and had rented for him no less a mansion than the home of Robert Morris, probably the handsomest dwelling in the city. The financier and his wife most generously had acceded to the wishes of the City Fathers and were preparing to leave the premises in ample time. Washington did not find the place all that he felt he needed. He wrote Lear: "It is, I believe, the best *single House* in the City; yet, without additions it is inadequate to the *commodious* accommodation of my family"; [163] and with that, he went on to describe the changes he thought necessary and the servants he thought he would require.[164] He laid out work enough—hiring maids, moving property and directing repairs—to keep even the industrious Lear busy for many days. Then, on the 6th, Washington left the city for Mount Vernon without ceremony. As nothing further in the way of ceremonial occurred except a small dinner in Baltimore,[165] and no accident worse than a harmless overturn of the chariot and the wagon delayed the remainder of the journey, Washington and his entourage reached Mount Vernon on the 11th of September.[166]

During the seventeen months he had been away, he had been fortunate. No crisis had developed in America or in dealings with foreign countries. Equally had he been fortunate in the fact that, though his counsellors and heads of departments had not always agreed, they had not quarreled. While luck had been on Washington's side, he had deserved it. His achievements in the mass had been far more solid and numerous than a day-by-day recountal of them would indicate. It was "here a little and there a little." He had shared in putting the government in successful operation—that was to say, in making the theories of the Philadelphia Convention a reality. By his patience and pains he had organized the departments and had made the appointments with little resultant grumbling, even on the part of most of those who had been passed over. Through the ratification acts of North Carolina and

[162] 31 *G. W.*, 110.          [163] *Ibid.*          [164] *Ibid.*, 111–12
[165] *Baker*, 196, after *Maryland Journal* (Baltimore), Sept. 10, 1790, p. 3.
[166] 31 *G. W.*, 117.

of Rhode Island, he had seen the Union completed, and by intelligent and courageous choice on the part of Congress, he had found the country saved from amendments that might have weakened the Constitution. He had received the support of the legislative branch on everything he had advocated and on most of what had been put forward by his department heads; and when Congress had deferred or rejected measures advocated by his lieutenants, he had not been blamed for them.

Insofar as his success had been built on Congress, he owed it to his caution, his deference and his unfailing care in not overstepping the line drawn in the Constitution between his "department," as he termed the executive branch, and the sphere of the Federal legislature. It seemed scarcely believable, but the disputable legislation on the seat of government, on the refunding, and on the assumption of the State debts had been enacted without a single public challenge of his disinterestedness. Washington had said not long before he left New York: "In a government which depends so much in its first stages on public opinion, much circumspection is still necessary for those who are engaged in its administration." He had not exaggerated when he added: "Fortunately the current of public sentiment runs with us, and all things hitherto seem to succeed according to our wishes. In the meantime, population increases, land is cleared, commerce extended, manufactories . . .[167] and Heaven smiles upon us with favorable seasons and abundant crops."[168]

It was true, but the sky was not unclouded. Although the day was fair, the wind was blowing from a quarter where storms were brewed. From April onward, complaint had been made that Congress was too loquacious in its debates, too lacking in political wisdom,[169] and too slow in its decisions.[170] Extravagance had been alleged in various par-

[167] A word missing.
[168] Letter of Aug. 10, 1790, to Rochambeau; 31 G. W., 83–84. Rochambeau's letter of Apr. 11, 1790, is in 246 Papers of G. W., 60, LC.
[169] Cf. letter of Oliver Wolcott to his father, May 22, 1790: "What is most wanted here is stability and political knowledge. There are men of great abilities and extensive science; but they are in some instances prone to indulge their minds in fanciful theories of republican liberty. Some few mistake cunning for wisdom." 1 Gibbs, Wolcott Papers, 47.
[170] See Nathaniel Gorham to Henry Knox, Apr. 17, 1790, with the warning that unless Congress made greater dispatch in business, "they would sink in the estimation of the people" (Knox Papers, MHS); Independent Chronicle, May 27, p. 2; New-York Journal, June 11, p. 3; Henry Jackson to Henry Knox, July 4, Knox Papers, MHS; Boston Gaz., July 5, p. 2; "Junius" in Independent Chronicle, Aug. 19, 1790, p. 2.

ticulars, not excluding a Library of Congress [171] and, most offensively, in a grant to General von Steuben of a life annuity of 2500 dollars in final settlement of his services in the Revolution.[172] Grumbling had been confined, almost entirely, to a few newspapers avowedly or notoriously Anti-Federalist,[173] but questioning was audible in the assemblies of men who were not politicians, and doubts were rising when planters and frontiersmen read of the ceremonial at Washington's residence.[174] Sectionalism was creating suspicion in the minds even of some intelligent men.[175] Patiently and quietly, in occasional private letters, Washington reasoned against this feeling,[176] and deplored the habit some Representatives and Senators had developed of explaining their legislative failures by attributing to their adversaries the basest of motives.[177]

While the evil of these trends was manifest to Washington, he did not perceive as yet that his conception of his office might have in it elements that would encourage the ambition of subordinates and give room for the play of jealousies. He continued to believe that caution and slow extension of government were necessary if the permanent support of good citizens was to be assured. Nothing that he did at any time, in any way, must infringe on the prerogatives of Congress. He must remain detached; his heads of departments, in matters entrusted

[171] For criticism of the Library, see *Boston Gazette*, May 10, p. 2; *Independent Chronicle*, May 13, p. 3. More general allegations of extravagance appear in *New-York Journal*, May 18, p. 2, July 2, p. 3; *Independent Chronicle*, June 3, p. 1; *Boston Gazette*, July 12, 1790, p. 3.

[172] 1 *JHR.*, 207, 208, 209, 210, 211, 212, 213, 225, 226, 233, 234; 1 *JS*, 139, 144, 145, 146, 147, 148, 150, 151; 2 *Annals*, 1621–22; 2 *Laws of U. S.*, ed., 1815, p. 107. Von Steuben asked for 60,000 dollars but all capital payment was stricken from the bill by a close vote. For criticism of the appropriation, see Wingate to Samuel Hodgdon, June 2, 1790, 2 *Paine Wingate*, 363; *Boston Gaz.*, June 14, p. 2; *Independent Chronicle*, June 17, p. 2, July 1, p. 3, July 22, 1790, p. 2.

[173] With characteristic heavy contempt for "a press that teems with lies and slander," Fenno's *Gazette of the United States* (Sept. 4, 1790, p. 3) insisted that this brand of public paper "be execrated as a pestilent engine of mischief." This manifestly was a denunciation of Thomas Greenleaf's *New-York Journal*. It may be concluded that up to the time the government was removed to Philadelphia, Greenleaf had offended by vicious abuse as often as had Fenno by extreme adulation.

[174] According to David Stuart, there had circulated at the Governor's table in Richmond during the spring of 1790 "some extraordinary representations" of the "etiquette" which prevailed at the President's levees. The story-tellers had specified to Patrick Henry "that there was more pomp used there than at St. James's . . . and that [Washington's] bows were more distant and stiff." Stuart to Washington, June 2, 1790; given in 2 *W. W. Henry*, 451–52.

[175] For an alarming comment by a southern man on the power of "the Northern hives," see Henry Lee to James Madison, Apr. 3, 1790; 13 *Madison Papers*, 2, LC. On the other hand, Senator Paine Wingate of New Hampshire suggested broadly that the President's "nominations for [new] officers in the military establishment," made in early June, revealed a southern predilection. 2 *Paine Wingate*, 364.

[176] See, for example, his letter of June 15, 1790, to David Stuart, 31 *G. W.*, 49–55.

[177] *Ibid.*, 52.

to them, must be free to use their discretion. This was generous—was it dangerous?

The question might arise, ugly and ominous, but it ought not to be raised as a tired man came home to the Potomac in the second week of September, when every field displayed its ripening crops and the nights were cool enough for untroubled sleep. ". . . I had rather be at Mount Vernon," he said, "with a friend or two about me, than to be attended at the seat of government by the officers of State and the representatives of every power in Europe." [178]

[178] Letter of June 15, 1790, to David Stuart; *ibid.*, 54.

# CHAPTER XIII

## A Time of Reckoning
### (September 11, 1790–April 7, 1791)

RETURN TO Mount Vernon in September, 1790, raised the spirits of Washington and contributed to full restoration of his health.[1] He did not have any particularly involved problem on the plantation[2] other than his usual need of ready cash,[3] a need still so great that when he found an entry which reminded him of the failure of Col. Joshua Fry's heirs to pay their part of the cost of procuring the "bounty lands" in 1769–72,[4] he asked counsel to attempt collection, though he would not enter suit for the twenty-year-old bill.[5] This general review of accounts old and new brought to light, among other papers, a letter of James Henry's, in which, on June 2, 1785, Washington had been praised by his King and Queen County neighbor. To this pleasant communication, Washington by mischance and delay had failed to make an answer, and now, after five years, he apologized for his apparent discourtesy.[6] Correspondence necessitated by these private affairs did not take any large part of his time at Mount Vernon. He was able to make a leisured, twelve-day examination of what was being done in the improvement of the Potomac by the company he had organized and headed, and in the course of this inspection he was called upon once only to receive and to answer an address.[7]

[1] 31 *G. W.*, 142.
[2] Negotiations over the Dandridge lands in Gloucester were begun anew (*ibid.*, 127); the General Assembly of Virginia was petitioned to close the ferry on Posey's farm (*ibid.*, 134 n; 9 *T* 39–40; G. A. Washington to George Washington, Dec. 28, 1790, 248 *Papers of G. W.*, 84, LC); the suit against Robert Scott over the Gooseneck tract probably was pursued (247 *Papers of G. W.*, 19, LC); care was taken to protect Washington's interest in the land on Timber Ridge, Hampshire County, in event the claim of the Mullen family lapsed (31 *G. W.*, 78–79, 154–55); sale of part of the Custis land in King and Queen County to James Henry was completed (*ibid.*, 157–58); effort was made to assure the proper recordation of a deed from George Muse (*ibid.*, 158); above all, the settlement of the Colville estates, long delayed by confusion over the names of the legatees, seemed to be brought closer to a final settlement (*ibid.*, 137–38, 145–46, 149–50; *Ledger C*, f. 14).
[3] Cf. 31 *G. W.*, 114.          [4] See Vol. III, p. 237 ff.
[5] 31 *G. W.*, 158–59.          [6] *Ibid.*, 158.
[7] *Ibid.*, 134 n, 135. The inspection was Oct. 12–24, 1790. In 247 *Papers of G. W.*,

Little public business was submitted by department heads for his re-view. Jefferson troubled him not at all[8] and Hamilton transmitted routine papers with consideration. The Secretary of the Treasury did pass on a rumor that Spain had admitted the right of the United States to the free use of the Mississippi,[9] and he recounted, also, another con-versation with Major Beckwith, who intimated that Gouverneur Morris was consorting with the leader of the parliamentary opposition in Britain, and with the French Ambassador, none other than Chevalier la Luzerne.[10] Neither of these letters from Hamilton excited Wash-ington. From other sources, he had heard nothing of Spain's alleged action[11] and he did not believe the tale Beckwith had told.[12]

The President's one official concern was over the absence of any report from General Harmar, who by this time was supposed to have marched against the Miami Indians.[13] Doubt of success rose in Wash-ington's mind when he learned that General St. Clair had notified the British at Detroit of Harmar's expedition and had assured them the United States forces were not marching against that post.[14] The British, in Washington's opinion, might pass on this information to the Indians whom Harmar was to punish.[15] When Washington heard a little later that General Harmar was believed to be a heavy drinker, the President virtually abandoned hope of any substantial achievement by the American column.[16] Knox could say nothing to reassure his Chief. "Not a word," the Secretary of War wrote on the 10th of No-vember, "has been received relative to the preparations for, or the commencement or success of the Wabash expedition . . ."[17] The un-pleasant possibility that he might have to report a military failure gave

---

119, LC, is this address of Elizabethtown, now Hagerstown, Maryland. Another copy, with Washington's reply, is in 335 *ibid.*, 21–23. The address bears date of October 20. Details of the reception of Washington at Elizabethtown will be found in the *Gazette of the United States*, Nov. 3, p. 2.

[8] That is to say, the *Papers of G. W.* and the published writings of Jefferson contain no letter from the Secretary of State during this period, nor is there in 31 *G. W.* acknowledgment of any communication from Jefferson for the days in question.

[9] Letter of Sept. 21, 1790; 9 *A. Hamilton*, 469–70.

[10] Letter of Sept. 30, 1790; 9 *Hamilton Papers*, 1158, LC, and printed in 4 *A. Hamilton*, 343.

[11] 31 *G. W.*, 128–29. In the last week of October there may have circulated in Alexandria a false report that England and Spain were at war (see *Gazette of U. S.*, Nov. 3, 1790, p. 3), but Washington certainly did not hear it.

[12] *Ibid.*, 131–32 and n.          [13] *Ibid.*, 143.

[14] This letter of Sept. 19, 1790, is in *ASP.*, 1 *Ind. Aff.*, 96.

[15] 31 *G. W.*, 144.          [16] *Ibid.*, 156.

[17] Knox added that contractors reported they had made all necessary deliveries. 248 *Papers of G. W.*, 26, LC.

a somewhat grim touch to the instructions Washington sent Knox—to prepare papers that would explain to Congress why the enterprise was undertaken.[18] Hamilton and Jay were requested also—and without particular thought of the Indian operation—to make suggestions for the annual message, and the two men were urged to discuss general policies, if they would, as well as matters directly in their charge.[19]

Leisure and interest prompted Washington to spend hours and hours in planning how the Morris House in Philadelphia was to be enlarged, decorated and furnished as the official residence of the Chief Executive. No less than nine [20] of the forty-one letters written during his weeks of rest at Mount Vernon were addressed to Tobias Lear and were devoted to everything that concerned the move to the Quaker City and the adornment of the dwelling. Use of bran to prevent the breakage of ornaments,[21] the volume of wine consumed at the steward's table,[22] an exchange of ironing mangles with Mrs. Morris,[23] and even the color of curtains on the stairway [24] were the subject of earnest and detailed explanation. A less admiring correspondent than Lear might have wondered, as he read, if Washington's regard for trifles indicated any decline of mental power to cope with large questions. It was a strange, if not an ominous state of affairs, because the only important point in all the long letters was insistence by the President that the house be leased by him in regular form, at an agreed figure, and be not accepted with the rent paid by any public body in Pennsylvania.[25] Along with regard for a hundred details of the most trivial sort, Tobias Lear and Clement Biddle, as Philadelphia agent, were enjoined to survey Philadelphia schools and to recommend those suited to Mrs. Washington's grandchildren, to George and Lawrence, the General's nephews, and possibly to his niece Harriet, also.[26] In none of this long correspondence

18 31 *G. W.*, 143, 156–57.

19 *Ibid.*, 132, 155. For the answers of Jay and Hamilton, see *infra,* p. 287. It is possible that Washington wrote Jefferson, also, but as the Secretary of State was then at Monticello (see 8 *Jefferson,* 104), the absence from the President's Letter Book of such a communication would suggest that Washington respected Jefferson's vacation and waited until he could see in Philadelphia his official adviser on foreign affairs.

20 31 *G. W.*, 116, 120, 125, 128, 132, 135, 139, 146, 152.
21 *Ibid.*, 116.             22 *Ibid.*, 117.             23 *Ibid.*, 127.
24 *Ibid.*, 148.            25 *Ibid.*, 137, 153.

26 *Ibid.*, 129, 133, 140, 146–47. In view of the labor Biddle and Lear performed—Biddle chiefly before Washington's secretary came to Philadelphia from New York—they assuredly deserve to have their dutiful letters listed. These are as follows: Lear to Washington, September 12 (247 *Papers of G. W.*, 72–73, LC); September 17 (*ibid.*, 89), September 26 (*ibid.*, 102–03), September 30 (*ibid.*, 105), October 3 (*ibid.*, 109–10), October 6 (*ibid.*, 111), October 10 (*ibid.*, 114), October 14 (*ibid.*, 115), October 17 (*ibid.*, 117), October 24 (*ibid.*, 121–22),

was there a touch of boredom or a lack of zest on the part of the gentleman at Mount Vernon and in scarcely a line of it was there a reference
to Mrs. Washington, her wishes or her plans: The house in Philadelphia manifestly was to be the President's, not hers. In his attitude
there was no discourtesy and no disregard, because he was conspicuously and consistently mindful of his wife's comfort; but this particular
task had been assumed by him. As always was the case when he undertook anything, it must be discharged to the last detail and to the best
of his ability.

Whether the entire residence would be ready for use on his arrival in
Philadelphia remained doubtful,[27] but the 22nd of November had been
set for departure in a coach usually employed in public service,[28] and
neither uncertainty over quarters in the temporary capital nor the
frightful condition of the roads, after hard, incessant rains,[29] could
delay departure. With an incompetent, drunken driver, who made bad
conditions almost intolerable,[30] Washington pressed on and, at last,
about 11 in the morning of November 27,[31] he and his party reached
the Quaker City and went at once to the Morris House. Lear had made
it habitable even though the remodeling was not complete.

The condition of public affairs was good and bad—good in the general prosperity and content of the people, bad in the absence of news
from Harmar and in the continued hammering of the Anti-Federalist
newspapers, the *New-York Journal* in particular.[32] These complaints

---

October 28 (248 *ibid.*, 3), October 31 (ibid., 8–9), November 4 (*ibid.*, 14), November 7 (*ibid.*,
20–21), November 14 (*ibid.*, 28–29), Nov. 21, 1790 (*ibid.*, 34–35); Clement Biddle to
Lear, September 14 (247 *Papers of G. W.*, 77, LC), Sept. 23, 1790 (*Clement Biddle Letter
Book*, unpaged, PHS); Clement Biddle to Lear, September 14 (*ibid.*), September 22 (247
*Papers of G. W.*, 99, LC), September 27 (*Clement Biddle Letter Book*, PHS), October 6 (*ibid.*),
Oct. 17, 1790 (*ibid*).
   27 See Lear to Washington, Nov. 7, 1790; 248 *Papers of G. W.*, 20–21, LC.
   28 Negotiations for the exclusive use of this vehicle began October 29. See 31 *G. W.*, 138,
139–40, 152.
   29 *Ibid.*, 157.                        30 *Ibid.*, 159–60.
   31 *Jacob Hiltzheimer's Diary*, 165; *Penn. Packet*, Nov. 29, 1790, p. 3. Apparently Washington's coming was not generally known on this trip, for he escaped the usual festivities, both
in Baltimore (*Maryland Journal*, November 26, p. 3) and in Philadelphia (*Gazette of U. S.*,
December 1, p. 3).
   32 Its criticisms of alleged waste, aristocratic trends, disregard of republican obligations, etc.,
appeared as follows: September 17, p. 3; September 28, p. 3; October 1, p. 3; October 15, p. 3;
October 26, p. 3; October 28, p. 3; November 1, p. 3; November 4, p. 2; Nov. 15, 1790, p. 3.
The Boston *Independent Chronicle* fulminated September 23, p. 3, September 30, p. 3, and
was to voice hard words December 16, p. 2, December 23, p. 1, and Dec. 30, 1790, p. 1. After
the congressional election in Massachusetts on Oct. 4, 1790, in which the *Boston Gazette* and
its adherents worked without success to unseat Fisher Ames, this paper subsided and did not
renew its attacks until Aug. 15, 1791.

failed to raise a clamor or to defeat any considerable number of the members of Congress who stood for reelection that autumn.[33] The majority of thoughtful voters seemed to agree with Benjamin Lincoln's statement that the United States never had a brighter promise, and that nothing but extreme folly could cloud the prospect.[34] Washingon most heartily shared that conviction and proceeded with no waste of time to prepare for the coming session of Congress. John Jay's requested suggestions for the speech awaited the President on his return and ended in as cheerful a strain as Lincoln's assurance, but most of the Chief Justice's observations dealt with matters of law or with improvements that did not seem pressing.[35] The headings proposed by Hamilton were practical in form and in content and were incorporated, with few exceptions, directly into the text of the speech,[36] which was ready for delivery when both houses of Congress could count a quorum.[37] On the 8th, Washington drove to the Hall of Congress[38] and in the Senate chamber[39] made his brief address, which he devoted principally to finance and Indian affairs. On the one subject, he had favorable credit standing to report and the recommendation that the Federal debt be reduced "as far and as fast as the growing resources of the country will permit . . ."[40] As for Indian depredations, it probably was fortu-

[33] Five of the twenty-six Senators and twenty-seven of the sixty-five members of the House retired in 1791. While some of these men were defeated by more popular aspirants for public favor, many declined to seek reelection for reasons that probably differed in almost every instance. As far as is known, no detailed study of issues, either personal or political, in the election of the Second Congress has been published. For the active role of the Federalist editor, Fenno, see the *Gazette of the United States*, September 15, p. 3, and Sept. 18, 1790, p. 3. Retiring Senators included Philip Schuyler and William Maclay; the most interesting newcomer in the Senate was Aaron Burr of New York. Gen. Artemas Ward, 64 years of age, appeared as a Representative from Massachusetts.

[34] Letter of Dec. 4, 1790, to Alexander Hamilton, 9 *Hamilton Papers*, f. 1176, LC. "A new, happy series of years commences," extolled Franklin's grandson, B. F. Bache, in his *General Advertiser* (Nov. 27, 1790, p. 3). "The hands of the manufacturer are beneficially employed. Our ports abound in our own vessels. Agriculture is encouraged. A Washington presides over us with as much dignity and wisdom as a man is capable of exerting . . ."

[35] 3 *John Jay*, 405–08. His reflections on the "content and good humor" of New England are in *ibid.*, 408.

[36] 9 *Hamilton Papers*, 1175, LC; 8 *A. Hamilton*, 94–95. The only omission of importance was of a paragraph in which Hamilton spoke of the "utility and benefits of a national government" and attributed localized dissatisfaction with particular measures to "misapprehensions" (*ibid.*, 95). For the Secretary's rough draft, with corrections and interlineations, see 9 *Hamilton Papers*, f. 1175.

[37] The Senate had a quorum on the date set for the opening, Dec. 6, 1790; the House was able to organize the next day, 1 *JS*, 216; 1 *JHR.*, 329.

[38] This "plain brick building" at the southeast corner of Sixth and Chestnut is described in James Schouler, *History of the United States under the Constitution* (ed. 1908), v. 1, p. 352–53. The structure had been designed as a court house.

[39] For the legislative exchanges on the meeting place, see 1 *JHR.*, 330, 1 *JS*, 216.

[40] 1 *Richardson*, 81, 83; 31 *G. W.*, 164–65, 168.

nate that the flavor of an auspicious opening was not soured by knowledge of the failure of Harmar's expedition. At the moment, Washington could say only "the event of the measure is yet unknown to me," though he added immediately that the Secretary of War would report the information on which the offensive had been based and the expense it had involved.[41] The justification, in short, would precede, not follow, the details, which were certain to be disappointing. On the general subject of war, the President gave a paragraph to the situation in Europe and to the probable curtailment of available shipping for American exports. Deferentially he told the Senators and Representatives: "I recommend to your serious reflections how far and in what mode it may be expedient to guard against [shortage of vessels] by such encouragements to our own navigation as will render our commerce and agriculture less dependent on foreign bottoms . . ."[42] A more cheerful paragraph dealt with the admission of Kentucky to the Union; the remainder of the address was devoted, briefly, to mint and militia, to weights and measures, and the post office and the post roads.[43]

It was not a sensational occasion.[44] Addresses by the two houses and answers by the President were perfunctory.[45] Knox's report on Indian affairs, submitted on the 9th,[46] disclosed abundant reason for Harmar's expedition,[47] but gave no account of what had befallen Harmar and his men. When the official report at length was received and was forwarded at once by Washington, it was found to be a complacent review of operations represented as successful,[48] though actually they were a bloody failure in the defeat of two detachments and the loss of 180

[41] 1 *Richardson*, 82; 31 *G. W.*, 166.

[42] 1 *Richardson*, 82–83; 31 *G. W.*, 167.

[43] 1 *Richardson*, 81–82, 83; 31 *G. W.*, 165, 168.

[44] John Fenno, whose *Gazette of the United States* had followed the government to Philadelphia, failed to report in detail on the President's address until a rival paper, *Freeman's Journal*, printed a congratulatory paragraph and a twenty-line poem (issue of December 15, p. 3). Then Fenno, in his issue of December 18 (p. 3), unabashedly reproduced the entire paragraph, part of which read: "Washington appears in our great national council—his voice is heard—that voice, which gave vigor to war, gives animation to peace. He looks—and dissension is hushed. He speaks—and harmony returns on the wings of a cherub. Let Philadelphians and others who heard, felt, and revered his accents, acknowledge that, although virtue has been sometimes rewarded even in this world, never did she receive purer homage, than at the state-house of Philadelphia on the eighth day of December in the year 1790." To this Fenno added his own bouquet: Washington's "invigorating" speech revealed clearly that national affairs "engrossed a great share of his contemplations during the recess."

[45] 1 *JS*, 220–21; 1 *JHR.*, 334, 336; 31 *G. W.*, 172 n.

[46] 1 *JHR.*, 333.

[47] See *ASP.*, 1 *Ind. Aff.*, 83 ff, and particularly, Knox to St. Clair, Sept. 12, 1790 (*ibid.*, 100).

[48] *Ibid.*, 104.

men.[49] Washington's candor in keeping Congress informed and the apparent adequacy of Knox's preparations saved the President from criticism. Doubtless, too, the edge of disappointment was dulled by the slowness with which the failure was reported, after Harmar's defeat was a matter of accepted rumor and then of general knowledge.

Alexander Hamilton contributed most of all to the prompt suspension of congressional talk about Knox and Harmar. The Secretary of the Treasury took the centre of the stage a week after the session opened, and on the 13th and 14th he submitted two reports that forthwith made every member of Congress his advocate or critic, to the exclusion of almost every other subject of legislative debate. Both papers were in obedience to a resolution passed by the House of Representatives at the previous session, for a report on any further action the Secretary considered necessary for establishing the public credit.[50] Hamilton divided his answer into two parts, submitted on successive days, one a series of suggestions for new and higher excises, the other a plan for the establishment of a central bank.[51] The proposal for heavier taxes on imported spirits[52] was coupled with one for excises, ranging from nine to thirty cents per gallon, on liquors distilled in the United States.[53] The total of imported and domestic spirits was estimated at 10,500,000 gallons per annum;[54] the estimated net revenue would be 877,500 dollars.[55] As Hamilton designed the bank, which he frankly styled "national,"[56] it was to have a capital stock not exceeding 10,000,000 dollars,[57] of which the President was to subscribe 2,000,000 dollars on account of the United States. Funds for this purpose were to be obtained by a loan of like amount from the institution, repayable in ten equal yearly instalments. The bank was to establish branches throughout the country at its discretion and was to have an exclusive Federal charter; its notes and bills, if payable on demand in gold and silver

[49] *Ibid.* Some details of the actions of October 19 and 21 may be reconstructed in part from testimony at the court of inquiry on Harmar, Sept. 15–23, 1791, in *ASP.*, 1 *Mil. Aff.*, 20 ff, but the record is by no means complete. Harmar was vindicated by the court in everything he did, and was said to merit "high approbation." He resigned Jan. 1, 1792.

[50] 1 *JHR.*, Aug. 9, 1790, p. 295.

[51] Excises, Dec. 13, 1790, 2 *A. Hamilton*, 337 ff; bank, Dec. 14, 1790, 3 *ibid.*, 388 ff. An interesting view of Hamilton's mind at work is afforded by comparison of the finished reports, as printed, with the Secretary's original drafts in 9 *Hamilton Papers*, f. 1191–1227.

[52] 2 *A. Hamilton*, 338.      [53] *Ibid.*, 338–39.

[54] This was 2.6 gallons per capita, on the basis of the census of 1790. Present-day importation and production is 3.5 gallons. Both figures disregard exports of American spirits.

[55] 2 *A. Hamilton*, 351.      [56] 3 *ibid.*, 431.

[57] Divided into 20,000 shares, par 500 dollars.

coin, were to be receivable in all settlements with the United States.[58] Details were well considered, the Bank of England serving as a model, but no provision of the treasurer—no "thou shalt" or "thou shalt not" —had interest comparable to that of the exciting question: Did Congress have the power, under the Constitution, to charter any bank? This was a challenge to the study, the judgment, and the sympathy of members.

While legislators debated this fascinating issue in the taverns and in the boarding houses, before they so much as raised it on the floor, Washington labored over a small but a singularly perplexing series of tangles and wrangles. The reassurance of friendly Indians, alarmed by Harmar's expedition, was particularly difficult at a time when plans for new operations against the Miami scarcely were concealed.[59] Preliminaries had to be arranged for laying off the "Federal District" on the Potomac as the permanent seat of government.[60] Washington had to decide, also, what further instructions should be given Gouverneur Morris, whose unofficial inquiries in England had brought to light no inclination on Britain's part either to execute the provisions of the treaty of peace or to open friendly commercial relations on a basis of equality.[61] The President's conclusion, buttressed by Jefferson's analysis, was against further effort, for the time being, to press for any accord.[62] Later, in reporting the circumstances to Congress, he announced that he had instructed Morris to cease communication with the King's ministers [63]— a step that prompted an agitation by the lawmakers for the encouragement of self-dependent American shipping [64] in substantial accord with the President's suggestion at the beginning of the session.[65] A considerable volume of other legislation, including measures for the admission of Kentucky and Vermont to the Union,[66] occupied Congress more than it involved the President. The sole recommendation of Washing-

[58] 3 *A. Hamilton*, 435–37.

[59] See 31 *G. W.*, 179–84, 194–95, 197, 243, 259, 267, 273–74; 1 *JHR.*, 364; 1 *JS*, 236. See Knox to James Wilkinson, Mch. 10, 1791 (*Wilkinson Papers*, Chicago HS); Knox to Washington, and Lear to Washington, Mch. 27, 1791 (249 *Papers of G. W.*, 121, 122, LC). An act for raising another Regiment was signed Mch. 3, 1791; 1 *Statutes at Large*, 222–24; cf. 1 *JS*, 267, 274.

[60] 3 *Jefferson*, 82; 31 *G. W.*, 189, 191, 200, 201, 202, 204; 1 *JHR.*, 360–61; 1 *JS*, 235.

[61] The best summary of the situation is in Jefferson's review, December 15, for Washington's benefit, of the correspondence between the President and Morris (3 *Jefferson*, 90 ff).

[62] 31 *G. W.*, 172; 8 *Jefferson*, 115–16.

[63] Reports of Feb. 9, 14, 1791; 1 *Richardson*, 96; 31 *G. W.*, 213, 214–15.

[64] 1 *JS*, 269; 1 *JHR.*, 377–78, 379; *ASP.*, 1 *For. Rel.*, 128.

[65] 1 *Richardson*, 82–83; 31 *G. W.*, 166–67.

[66] 1 *Statutes at Large*, 189, 191.

ton's that met with virtual denial was for the uniform organization of the militia. This was debated at length in the House [67] and was killed by postponement.[68]

Although little of this legislation aroused heat, no essential part of the bill for the excise on spirits, and scarcely a clause of the measure for the establishment of the national bank failed to stir the coals of controversy. As Washington looked on, with equal regard for both regions, he felt that South and East were arrayed unpleasantly against each other—the southern delegations in opposition to bank and to excise and the New Englanders for the two measures—but even on these divisive subjects, it seemed to him that the debates were conducted with "temper and candor." [69] The bank bill originated in the Senate; [70] the excises, of course, were for the House to initiate.[71] Both branches went vigorously, almost furiously, to their assignments. The Senate passed the bank bill on the 20th of January, 1791,[72] and the House the excise legislation precisely a week later.[73] Then the two chambers exchanged bills in continuance of the struggle between South and East. The Representatives made short work of the measure to establish the bank and on the 8th of February accepted it, by a vote of almost two to one,[74] a victory for Hamilton that narrowed the final contest to the Senators' wrestling match over the excise bill.[75] Washington, meantime, had to decide for himself the constitutional question that had divided both chambers: Should he sign or disapprove the bill to charter the Bank of the United States? He sought the answer by his usual deliberate procedure. The Attorney General was asked for his opinion, which was adverse.[76] Next, Jefferson's observations were sought; they were forthcoming almost immediately with a convinced precision that indicated

[67] 1 *JHR.*, 337, 338, 339, 340, 341, 342, 345; 2 *Annals*, 1804 ff.

[68] 1 *JHR.*, 349, proceedings of Jan. 5, 1791.

[69] Letter of Mch. 16, 1791, to David Humphreys; 31 *G. W.*, 242.

[70] Debate commenced Jan. 11, 1791; 1 *JS*, 232.

[71] The first detailed review of these on the floor was Dec. 24, 1790; 1 *JHR.*, 343. Several bills to collect duties and to make provision for the debt were considered at this session and are confusing to the student. The excise bill was, by its title, specifically one for "repealing, after the last day of June next, the duties heretofore laid upon distilled spirits," etc. It was H. B., 110, and appears in 1 *Statutes at Large*, 199–214, and in 2 *Laws of U. S.*, ed. 1815, p. 203.

[72] 1 *JS*, 234.          [73] 1 *JHR.*, 365; the vote was 35–21.

[74] Feb. 8, 1791, vote 39–20; 1 *JHR.*, 371–72. Passage by an easy margin had been anticipated (1 *Fisher Ames*, 94).

[75] Cf. 1 *JS*, 262, 263.

[76] 31 *G. W.*, 216. Randolph's long written opinion, which is not among his strongest papers, appears in G. W. *Letter Book*, No. 23, "Communications with the Treasury, September 1790–October, 1792" (328 *Papers of G. W.*, 94–108, LC.)

he had made up his mind completely during the progress of the debate, perhaps even earlier. The bill, he said, manifestly was unconstitutional, because Congress was not vested with specific authority to create such a corporation, and under one of the amendments then in process of adoption,[77] "the powers not delegated to the United States by the Constitution, nor prohibited by it to the States are reserved to the States respectively, or to the people." This and other less relevant arguments were set forth succinctly and without admission of a single doubt concerning the absolute correctness of Jefferson's interpretation;[78] but at the end was this candid counsel: ". . . unless the President's mind on a view of everything which is urged for and against this bill, is tolerably clear that it is unauthorized by the Constitution; if the pro and the con hang so even as to balance his judgment, a just respect for the wisdom of the Legislature would naturally decide the balance in favor of their opinion. It is chiefly for cases where they are clearly misled by error, ambition, or interest, that the Constitution has placed a check in the negative of the President." [79]

Washington sent this opinion and that of the Attorney General to Hamilton and gave the Secretary "an opportunity of examining and answering the objections," but with the understanding that Jefferson's and Randolph's papers were to be returned and no copies made.[80] A few days later, Washington asked James Madison to draft a proper form for returning the bill to Congress in event the decision was to refuse approval. Madison responded with a brief document conveniently phrased for returning the bill either on the ground of unconstitutionality or on that of a lack of merit in the measure. The argument advanced by Madison against the constitutionality of the bank bill was condensed into a single long but clear sentence: "I object to the bill," Madison would have the President say, "because it is an essential principle of the government that powers not delegated by the Constitution cannot be rightfully exercised; because the power proposed by the bill to be exercised is not delegated; and because I cannot satisfy myself that it results from any expressed power by fair and safe rules of implication." [81] Hamilton's answer was written under heavy pressure and

---

[77] Jefferson spoke of this tenth amendment (3 *Jefferson*, 146) as if it already were adopted, but actually it was not in force until Dec. 15, 1791.

[78] *Ibid.*, 145–53. The germ of the Virginia and Kentucky Resolutions and of nearly the whole doctrine of States' rights is wrapped in a few sentences of this remarkable paper.

[79] *Ibid.*, 153.                              [80] 31 *G. W.*, 216.

[81] Feb. 21, 1791; printed in part in 6 *Hunt's Madison*, 42 n–43 n.

to the length of 15,000 words [82] in a complete review and attempted refutation of substantially everything Jefferson and Randolph had said. As the New Yorker wrote on and on, he shaped his sentences as if he were endeavoring to demolish an adversary rather than to answer a colleague. Hamilton's basic argument in positive support of the bill was covered by an early paragraph: ". . . it appears to the Secretary of the Treasury that this general principle is inherent in the very definition of government, and essential to every step of the progress to be made by that of the United States, namely: That every power vested in a government is in its nature sovereign, and includes, by force of the term, a right to employ all the means requisite and fairly applicable to the attainment of the ends of such power, and which are not precluded by restrictions and exceptions specified in the Constitution, or not immoral, or not contrary to the essential ends of political society." [83]

Thus were Washington's closest counsellors divided, to his distress and embarrassment, over the width and the reach of the foundations on which the structure of government was to rise. Could the high, thick walls of a secure fortress be set on such narrow footings as Jefferson and Randolph traced? Was the future of America to be similar to the most wretched aspect of her past, a hopeless struggle between a frail central government and powerful, self-willed States, jealous of their prerogatives and insistent on their sovereignty? Washington never wrote a line to indicate that he asked himself these particular questions, nor did he ever state what consideration was strongest with him, but from the beginning of the effort to give America a new Constitution, his controlling principle had been the simplest: the United States must have a strong central government if they were to keep their freedom. Because his reasoning and conviction were altogether on the side Hamilton championed, he signed the bill on the 25th of February.[84] The excise measure came to his desk on the 1st of March,[85] and, as it in-

---

[82] The Secretary's rough draft, with multiple alterations, is in 11 *Hamilton Papers*, 1402 ff. Printed in 3 *A. Hamilton*, 445–93.

[83] *Ibid.*, 446. This was applied more specifically in six principles laid down (*ibid.*, 471–72).

[84] 1 *JHR.*, 391; text in 1 *JS*, 282–85; 1 *Statutes at Large*, 191–96; 2 *Laws of U. S.*, ed. 1815, p. 194. The *Gazette of the United States* had been vigorously advocating Hamilton's bank plan (see issues of February 9, p. 2, February 12, p. 3, February 19, p. 2, and Feb. 23, 1791, p. 1), and now took occasion to laud "that judgment and prudence" which caused the President to devote so much thoughtful consideration to the question of constitutionality (*Gazette of U. S.*, Feb. 26, 1790, p. 3).

[85] 1 *JS*, 295. It had passed the Senate, with amendments, on the 12th of February (*ibid.*, 362) and subsequently went through the various stages of disagreement, conference and compromise over the rate of excise. See 1 *JHR.*, 379, 381, 384, 386, 388, 391. The last reference here is to acceptance on February 25 by the House of the conference report.

volved no constitutional issue, it received his signature the next day.[86]

The only other large question of sharp controversy on the floor of Congress was a French protest against the tax on tonnage of ships entering the United States. Troubled as the government of Paris was, in its desperate struggle at home against division, hate and greed of power, its ministry had prepared a "representation" that the treaty between France and the United States exempted American shipping in France from a tonnage tax, except in coastal trade. America had reserved the right to impose on French tonnage a levy equivalent to that which France had charged on coasting vessels. America had not laid this compulsory tax on tonnage, it was argued forcefully, and could exact no other of French commerce. The rates of the general tonnage act and the status of the "most favored nation" did not apply.[87] Washington asked Jefferson to report on this and, when the document was ready, he transmitted it to Congress.[88] The Secretary, friend though he was of France, found her contention invalid for reasons he set forth at length. He admitted that policy might dictate concession but he outlined explicitly the basis of what might be said in rejecting the protest.[89] Over this report by Jefferson the Senate wrangled at intervals and decided, February 26, to maintain "in the most friendly manner" the interpretation the Secretary put on the treaty.[90]

When Congress at length adjourned on the 3rd of March, 1791, amid much confusion in the Senate,[91] Washington felt that besides passing the great contested measures, the two houses "had finished," in his words, "much other business of less importance, conducting on all occasions with great harmony and cordiality." Some observers thought the sectional differences more serious than the accord on routine legislation,[92] but the majority probably agreed with Washington and shared Abigail Adams's belief: "Our public affairs never looked more prosperous."[93] Even the Boston *Independent Chronicle*, long in carping opposition, had praise for the session's labor of Congress, and praise, also, for the President.[94]

[86] 1 *JS*, 309.

[87] L. G. Otto's note to Jefferson, Dec. 13, 1790; 1 *Richardson*, 93. In *ASP.*, 1 *For. Rel.*, 109 ff, is the entire correspondence, of which part only appears in *Richardson*.

[88] *Ibid*.                                [89] *Ibid*.

[90] 1 *EJS.*, 72, 77; *Maclay*, 381 ff, 401 ff.        [91] Amusingly described in *Maclay*, 411–13.

[92] Cf. 2 *Paine Wingate*, 385.

[93] Letter of Mch. 12, 1791, to her sister; *Abigail Adams*, 71.

[94] Issue of Mch. 10, 1791, p. 3.

Philadelphia most certainly was pleased with him, personally and officially, and had been able to demonstrate often during the winter its old affection for him and its pride in being the seat of his administration.[95] He and Mrs. Washington held their levees as usual, and with no change of the arrangements that had been made in New York, except that when the President's lady had an unusual number of interesting guests, she entertained until 10 o'clock and, on occasion, even later.[96] The shining affairs were Mrs. Washington's Christmas Eve entertainment,[97] the New Year's Day reception,[98] and the ceremonious observance of the President's birthday on the 22nd of February.[99] Formalities were as strictly followed as ever and as offensive to an extreme republican, but most of them were accepted because they were established. Washington carefully walked the line he had set for himself, and respected all the amenities, even the least, but he was beginning to tire of the pomp of public appearance [100] and he was not insensitive to criticism of monarchical practices. A Philadelphia tradesman who planned to emulate British custom and to affix the Washington arms over his shop with the boast that he was "Silversmith to the President," promptly received notice that this would be "very disagreeable." [101]

One display that Washington could not bring himself to abandon was the distinguishing mark of the wealthy colonial planter in Virginia—great equipage. A coach and four—better still, six—appealed to him irresistibly; perhaps it represented the attainment of early ambition. When the Morris House [102] gradually was brought close to what Washington desired, he shifted interest from the renovation of the dwelling to the redecoration of his personal carriage. The badly worn "official" vehicle used in New York and subsequently brought to Phila-

[95] An excellent description of the city at this time will be found in 1 Schouler, op. cit., 250–51. Perhaps the most interesting account by a foreign visitor, approximately of this date, is Brissot de Warville, New Travels in the United States, 312 ff.

[96] Decatur, 194–95.          [97] Ibid., 177.

[98] Baker, 204, with citation of Maclay, 363.

[99] This was one of the earliest of great parties on that date. See the Gazette of the United States, Feb. 23, 1791, p. 3, for details and eighty-two lines of extravagant poetry by "Ella." The Maryland Journal (Baltimore), hailing Washington as "the founder of our empire" in its issue of February 11, p. 2, declared that "no citizen or crowned head of any age or nation ever attracted so vast a portion of public confidence, and at the same time so truly deserved it." For the practice of celebrating the 11th—which Boston followed in 1791 (Henry Jackson to Knox, Feb. 13, 1791; Knox Papers, MHS)—see the letter of Tobias Lear to Clement Biddle, Feb. 14, 1790; 31 G. W., 11, and Lear to Jefferson, Feb. 11, 1792, ibid., 479 n. By 1792, Washington had adopted February 22, NS, as his birthday.

[100] See infra, p. 375.          [101] 31 G. W., 177 n.

[102] For the precise location of the residence with relation to nearby properties, see Nathaniel Burt, "Address . . . on the Washington Mansion in Philadelphia," p. 12.

delphia had been sold there on September 30, and the £45 it brought on the market had been credited to the United States on Washington's books.[103] His own coach, ten years old now but still sturdy and very impressive because of its size,[104] was left in the Chestnut Street shop of David and Francis Clark for a complete restoration while the President sojourned at Mount Vernon in the autumn of 1790. This "old" carriage, freshly painted, reupholstered, with its trim re-plated and its harness replaced, became veritably a resplendent "coach of state";[105] but it was too heavy, as well as too handsome, for hard use on the roads. Travel through mudholes and over stumps, along slanting and slippery byways, called for a lighter vehicle. Fortunately, the Clarks were able to supply Washington's need at once, and this "new" carriage was soon to prove itself so stout and trustworthy that the President did not hesitate to recommend the coachmakers.[106] He might have added that they gave him diversion along with fine workmanship.

Another and far more interesting diversion had been in his mind.

[103] 31 *G. W.*, 126. Lear's accounts in *Decatur*, 153. On the 4th of December, 1789, Lear told William Duer the President would "keep the carriage provided for his use previous to his arrival in New York . . . as it will be considered upon the same footing with other articles furnished at that time and for that purpose" (30 *G. W.*, 476 n). This doubtless was the vehicle sold in Philadelphia.

[104] 18 *G. W.*, 128–29, 177–78, 233–34. Washington's continued regard for his "old coach," as he referred to it at the time of its rehabilitation, is a testimony to the skill of the builder, George Bringhurst of Philadelphia, to whom the General had paid £210 in 1780.

[105] The estimate for this work, together with the letter of the Clarks, dated Sept. 13, 1790, are in 247 *Papers of G. W.*, 74, 75, LC, and with these documents is a fine pencil sketch of the "cypher" or monogram to be used on the doors (*ibid.*, 76). For Washington's detailed directions and suggestions, see 31 *G. W.*, 111, 115–16, 154. The General observed, in the last of these references, "I had rather have heard that my repaired coach was plain and elegant than 'rich and elegant.'" The crest is shown as an illustration in the present volume.

[106] In a letter to William Washington on April 26, 1793 (32 *G. W.*, 433), the President remarked that David Clark "made the carriage which I had with me at Charleston on my southern tour." The *Gazette of the United States* reported (Mch. 23, 1791, p. 3) that Washington was starting South "in a new chariot and six . . . built by Mr. Clark . . . a superior specimen of mechanical perfection." In the absence of specific correspondence between Washington and the Clarks regarding this "new" coach, credence may be given to the assumption of Lossing in the first edition of his *Mount Vernon*, p. 235, that David Clark had just arrived from England with two identical brand-new vehicles—one sold to Washington and the other to Mrs. Samuel Powel, wife of the Mayor of Philadelphia. In his 1866 edition Lossing omits the reference to the English origin of the coach, and also deletes the remark that Mrs. Powel was owner of a companion carriage. The Powel coach survived the years, was exhibited at the Philadelphia Centennial Exposition of 1876, as "Washington's White Chariot," and came to Mount Vernon in 1901. Washington's coach, on the other hand, was sold by his executors in 1802 and probably was taken apart for souvenirs about 1814. The General's "old" coach was offered for sale at Philadelphia in 1797, and ordered broken up for the iron it contained in 1798 when no customer for it could be found (see 36 *G. W.*, 294, 373). The best coverage of the controversy of the Powel coach is in Mary Stevens Beall, *The Story of the Washington Coachee and the Powel Coach* (1908), with a supporting opinion by J. F. Jameson, p. 68–74. It should be noted, however, that this careful work tends to confuse the description of Washington's renovated 1780 carriage with that of his new 1790 vehicle.

Before he left New York, he had seen an advertisement in a Philadelphia paper of farms for sale near the city and had developed an idea
of trading land in western Pennsylvania for one or two of these tracts
in order that he might ride out to them for exercise and by renewing
his contact with good earth, lose some of his homesickness for Mount
Vernon. An exchange without cash was what he hoped might be
effected. He wrote Clement Biddle: ". . . to pay money is out of the
question with me. I have *none* and would not, if it was to be had, run
in debt to borrow, nor would it do for me to dispose of *real* property
to obtain it, when that species of property is brought to low ebb and
dull market." [107] He found nobody interested in such a transaction and
probably gained by his disappointment, because, had he acquired a
farm, he would have become ambitious to make it the best in the
countryside and, in attempting this, would have found dollars disappearing by the thousand before he even rivaled some of the fine agriculturists around Philadelphia.[108]

Instead of an exciting if costly trial of Virginia agricultural methods
in well-tilled southeastern Pennsylvania, he had another series of personal and family chores to discharge, some of them so tedious and
vexatious that they would have overtaxed even his patience, perhaps,[109]
if they had not included two gratifying events. One was the birth in
the President's own house of a baby boy to Tobias and Mary Lear, who
were residing there both comfortably and usefully on the hearty invitation of the General and of Mrs. Washington.[110] This young gentleman was christened Benjamin Lincoln Lear, with Washington as
godfather.[111] The other occurrence was an offer by John Joseph de

---

[107] Letter of July 20, 1790; *ibid.*, 71. The italics are George Washington's.

[108] Cf. his remark in his letter of June 18 [–21], 1792, to Arthur Young: "[Pennsylvania]
husbandry (though not perfect) is much better, and her crops proportionately greater" (32
*G. W.*, 68).

[109] The following perhaps are of interest: arrangement for the schooling of two nephews
in Philadelphia (31 *G. W.*, 177); reservation of a farm for a needy cousin (*ibid.*, 178) and
of a possible lease for his sister (*ibid.*, 212); consideration of an offer for the services of Royal
Gift as a stud, with some confidential and perhaps boastful observations on the prowess of
that esteemed jackass (*ibid.*, 217–18); various efforts to lease his unused Pennsylvania and
western lands (*ibid.*, 221–22, 252); a stiff and somewhat unpleasant exchange with the widow
of Theoderick Bland, who wished him to recover a runaway slave (249 *Papers of G. W.*, 51, LC;
31 *G. W.*, 246–47), and an effort, successful at last, to terminate personal correspondence with
the persistent Rev. William Gordon (31 *G. W.*, 224–25).

[110] *Decatur*, 128–29. Mrs. Lear, a splendid girl, familiarly was called "Polly."

[111] The boy was born Mch. 11, 1791, and was baptized within a few days. It was characteristic of Lear to name the infant after the soldier who had given him his start, "my true
friend and one of the best of men." The young father went on: "Many express their surprise
that a son of mine, born too in this family, should receive any other name than that of

Barth to purchase at a fair figure all of Washington's lands on the Ohio and the Kanawha, an offer promptly and gladly accepted. When warned that de Barth might not be able to make settlement, Washington replied: "I cannot be in a less productive situation by the engagement than I was . . ." [112]

Washington long had been making plans for a tour of the southern States [113] and as quickly as he could he disposed of the public business that had to be transacted if the wheels of government were to revolve smoothly during an absence of three months, part of which would be in remote areas of the country. With business-like order and experienced confidence, he disposed of these matters [114]—not forgetting to instruct Tobias Lear to see that Mrs. Washington had all the money she required; [115] and then, on the 21st of March, with Major Jackson, much equipment and a cumbersome entourage of five persons, he set out for the Potomac on what he regarded as the first stage of the southern journey. [116]

Never had Washington faced a more inauspicious start. Roads were so heavy with rain and so cut up by wheels that instead of proceeding via the Susquehanna and Baltimore, he went down the Eastern Shore of Maryland and undertook to cross the Chesapeake by boat from Rock Hall to Annapolis, which he intended to visit anyway. [117] Everything went wrong. A wagon animal went lame; Washington's saddle horse refused to eat; craft were so small that four had to be hired; [118] half a day was lost in loading at Rock Hall on the 24th; a gale sprang up during the sail to the mouth of the Severn River; the little vessel on which Washington had taken passage ran aground twice, and the second time, in darkness, it could not be budged. The President had to spend the night aboard, wrapped in his greatcoat, boots on, cramped in a berth too short by a head. [119] After that, the hospitality of Gov. John Eagef Howard, the attention of other Marylanders and the delayed

---

George Washington. But although I love and respect the great man who bears that name, yet I would not for the world do a thing that would savor of adulation toward him—and if I would not adulate him I am sure I would adulate no human being." Undated letter quoted in *Decatur*, 205.

[112] 31 *G. W.*, 266; cf. *ibid.*, 255–56. The transaction failed.

[113] 30 *ibid.*, 502; 31 *ibid.*, 192, 195–96, 229–32.

[114] *Ibid.*, 233–39, 240.

[115] *Ibid.*, 251. He added: ". . . and from time to time ask her if she does want, as she is not fond of applying."

[116] 4 *Diaries*, 149. The new chariot was drawn by four horses, the baggage wagon by two; the total number of draught animals and mounts was eleven.

[117] 31 *G. W.*, 245.    [118] 4 *Diaries*, 150.    [119] *Ibid.*, 151.

crossing of a servant and two horses [120] held Washington at Annapolis until the morning of the 27th. Even then, the formalities of escort and leave-taking kept him on the Georgetown road until breakfast time on the 28th,[121] a full week after departure from Philadelphia.

The duties Washington now had to perform on the Potomac were exceedingly interesting at the outset, especially to an old surveyor who, in youth, had helped to run the lines of the rival town of Alexandria, across the river. Under the law he had signed on the 16th of July, 1790, "for establishing the temporary and permanent seat of the government of the United States," [122] he was required to appoint three commissioners and to direct their survey of the district where the Federal City was to rise. The President was to decide, further, how much land was to be acquired on the Maryland side of the river for public use. This land was then to be purchased or accepted as a gift, and on it, "according to such plans as the President shall approve," the commissioners were to provide "suitable buildings." Before the end of the short session of Congress, Washington had named two citizens of Maryland—Thomas Johnson, an able former Governor, and Daniel Carroll of Rock Creek, retiring Senator,[123] and for thirty years a sterling leader in his State. The third commissioner was Washington's alert and trusted friend David Stuart, whose wife was "Jack" Custis's widow. Maj. Andrew Ellicott, an experienced boundary surveyor, had been sent to the Potomac in February to take a general view of the area and then to suggest "lines of experiment" for determining the exact "seat of government." [124] Ellicott had been followed by Maj. Pierre Charles L'Enfant, who was instructed to make detailed surveys, particularly with an eye to the location of public buildings.[125] These appointments of commissioners and of surveyors had been made at a time of intense excitement on the part of landowners. Almost every man who held

[120] They had been left accidentally at Rock Hall (*ibid.*, 150).

[121] *Ibid.*, 151–52.

[122] 1 *Statutes at Large*, 130; 2 *Laws of U. S.*, ed. 1815, p. 113. At Washington's instance and for public convenience (31 *G. W.*, 201–05, 206–07), this had been amended by an act of Mch. 3, 1791 (1 *Statutes at Large*, 214–15; 2 *Laws of U. S.*, ed. 1815, p. 223) which had extended to Hunting Creek, the eastern boundary of that part of the district to be located in Virginia. The law had not been changed in any other particular.

[123] He had drawn a two-year term.     [124] 31 *G. W.*, 203.

[125] L'Enfant was to concern himself more immediately with the area lying Northwest of the so-called "Eastern Branch," now styled the Anacostia River. It was taken for granted that this ground would be included in the district, no matter where the final lines were drawn (31 *G. W.*, 226–27; 4 *Diaries*, 153–54). See Fiske Kimball's sketch of L'Enfant in *DAB*, with citation of numerous interesting documents in *Records of the Columbia His. Soc.* (v. 2, 11, 13 and 17) and in Elizabeth S. Kite, *L'Enfant and Washington, 1791–1792.*

title to an acre in the vicinity was dreaming of fortunes to be made
when farms of undistinguished fertility became, overnight, priceless
lots in the very centre of a city. Where were the boundaries to be
drawn? Whose land would the Federal government buy, and at what
price? How could a speculator ascertain in advance the proposed location of capitol and offices—and buy for maximum profit the nearest
procurable tract? Was Georgetown or Carrollsburg to be closer to the
hub of the new town? [126] A settlement named Hamburg had been
laid out close to Georgetown: how valuable would its lots be, and how
could its streets fit into those of the future Federal City? [127] The most
interested freeholder and, it was feared, the most troublesome, bore the
name David Burnes.[128] Envious men said he thought the sun of good
fortune was shining so benevolently on him that he had only to bide
his time and reap his golden harvest.

In such a situation as this, George Washington, a veteran in land-
buying, could be a wise, perhaps even a shrewd guide, for the cautious
President of the United States. He deliberately had undertaken to
maintain tight-lipped secrecy concerning the final lots and bounds of
the district, and had reserved as much latitude of purchase as possible.
If one group of property owners demanded an exorbitant price, he
could make a show, at least, of looking elsewhere. He already had authorized purchase of certain tracts,[129] and had directed a suspension
and then a renewal of negotiations with Burnes [130] as if that gentleman's holdings were desirable but not indispensable. Before coming to
Georgetown, Washington, in a word, had created as much of an air of
buyer's independence as he could. After he reached the town and examined personally the various tracts under frowning skies,[131] he called
the landholders together and explained in clear, practical terms of
profit, that Georgetown and Carrollsburg might defeat their own ends
by rivalry or by excessive prices for property desired by the Federal government. If they made common cause and accepted moderate terms,
both towns would gain. The case was not one of competition but of

---

[126] Fitzpatrick noted, 31 *G. W.*, 256 n, that "Carrollsburg was bounded by the Eastern
Branch, or Anacostia River, and James Creek; it extended as far North as N Street, S.W."
[127] Cf. *ibid.*, 244.
[128] Burnes, a Scotsman, owned some 225 acres along the Potomac and apparently realized
that his land had high strategic value. He appears to have been an unambitious farmer and a
heavy drinker, who lived in an old cottage and kept but twelve slaves. See Allen C. Clark's
article in 22 *Records of the Columbia His. Soc.*, 128–43.
[129] 31 *G. W.*, 208.          [130] *Ibid.*, 225, 227.          [131] 4 *Diaries*, 153.

cooperation. Together, the towns did not cover more ground than would be required for the city. The wisdom of this counsel, with the weight of Washington's popularity behind it, was for the moment irresistible. Next day, March 30, Washington was informed that all the principal owners, including David Burnes,[132] would accept the terms he proposed.[133] A total of between 3000 and 5000 acres was to be ceded to the United States, with these provisos: the whole was to be included in the Federal City and was to be laid off in lots; alternate lots everywhere were to remain the property of the former proprietors, who were to donate the ground for streets and alleys; for the land taken by the Federal government, twenty-five dollars an acre was to be paid.[134] Much pleased with this, Washington gave instructions for making the survey and for taking other action necessary to execute the agreement [135] and then he crossed to Alexandria, had his dinner there and that same evening reached home.[136]

Instead of roaring cannon, he had barking dogs to welcome him, and in the place of state functionaries, the family servants; but the absence of formality did not imply any lack of historical importance. A period had been set; a time of reckoning had come. The First Congress had passed out of existence; its members had scattered and in their districts were explaining what had been done and why. Washington himself was pleased not only with the achievements of the Congress but also with his success in learning his new duties. Before he left Philadelphia, he had written Lafayette that the American public had accepted Federal laws, which had been moderate and wise. "The administration of them," said he, "aided by the affectionate partiality of my countrymen, is attended with no unnecessary inconvenience . . ." [137] He owed this

---

[132] One individual of some importance described as the "purchaser of Slater's property," did not attend (31 *G. W.*, 257). [133] 4 *Diaries*, 153–55.

[134] Various minor concessions of interim use, etc., were made. The whole arrangement was described by Washington in a letter of Mch. 31, 1791, to Jefferson, 31 *G. W.*, 256–58. As there delineated, the area to be "ceded to the public" consisted of "all the land from Rock Creek along the river to the Eastern Branch and so upwards to or above the ferry, including a breadth of about a mile and a half . . ." The ferry, according to Fitzpatrick's note, was "at the foot of Kentucky Avenue, SE." Fitzpatrick also pointed out, 4 *Diaries*, 155 n, that the full text of the agreement between Washington and the landowners appears in William Tindall's *Origin and Government of the District of Columbia*, 85–86.

[135] 4 *Diaries*, 155. Major L'Enfant was authorized to lay off the entire tract as a city.
[136] *Ibid.*, 155.

[137] He added: "and every circumstance is auspicious to the felicity of your fellow-citizens in this section of the globe" (Letter of Mch. 19, 1791; 31 *G. W.*, 248). A few days earlier he had written David Humphreys: "Our public credit is restored, our resources are increasing, and the general appearance of things at least equals the most sanguine expectation that was formed of the effects of the present government" (*ibid.*, 243).

lack of difficulty to the same five conditions that had aided him in 1789
—his own cautious, sound judgment, the absence of crisis, the consideration of legislators, the undiminished esteem in which Americans
held him, and, lastly, the success of his dealings with Congress and
with the men he had chosen as heads of the departments. Knox had
been in harness so long that he pulled his part of the load without kick
or balk, though he was beginning to gaze with dangerous eagerness on
the green pastures of land speculation. Attorney General Randolph
had not been called upon, as yet, to discharge difficult legal duties to an
extent that confirmed or shook Washington's favorable judgment of
his abilities. Alexander Hamilton and Thomas Jefferson, eager, ambitious individualists, were Washington's closest advisers by this time
and were the two executive lieutenants most esteemed by Congress.
Madison was less frequently consulted during the winter of 1790–91,
not because of any cooling of affection but because Madison was engrossed in his labors as a legislator. Although John Jay still was called
upon for counsel, it had to be remembered now that he might have
to pass as Chief Justice on questions presented in their first form to the
President. Jay must not be embarrassed or placed where he might be
compelled to disqualify himself in hearing a case. Inside Congress,
with the wane in his employment of Madison, the President had nobody
who spoke for him as Benjamin Harrison frequently had done in the
Continental Congress. Washington's unofficial communications with
Congress—and some of his regular reports—were through the heads of
departments. Always the approach was as deferential as when the
Commander-in-Chief had been in the field during the war, the appointee of Congress and dependent on it for recruits and supplies. In
his new position he lost none of his consideration for the pride and
prerogative of lawmakers. Early in December, 1790, for example, he
had received from the President and Members of the French National
Assembly a letter and a packet addressed to the President and Members
of the American Congress. Washington had refrained from opening
this and had transmitted it to the Vice President who then had returned it with the statement that the Senate was of opinion the President should break the seal and communicate to Congress such part of
the contents as he thought proper. Washington thereupon had sent the
papers to Jefferson, with directions to open and examine them.[138] An

---

[138] 31 G. W., 169 n. Jefferson's reply to the National Assembly is in 8 *Jefferson*, 137.

executive who took pains of this sort to respect the authority of the legislative branch was not apt to have a clash. His dealings with the Governors, the State Legislatures and officials in general conformed to the same criterion,[139] but he insisted, firmly if politely, that this golden rule of administration be followed by others as well as by himself, and he resented any encroachment by the States on the domain of the Federal government. Negotiations by New York with some of the Indian tribes seemed to him a particularly dangerous violation of the Constitution of 1787, a violation inspired by men who coveted the savages' land. Angrily Washington wrote: ". . . the interferences of States and the speculations of individuals will be the bane of all our public measures." [140]

It was different within the executive precinct of the Federal government. There the heads of departments might exercise the initiative and the freedom of thought that some of them must have in amplest measure if they were to do their best for their country. Hamilton went so far as to tell his senior, "it is always best for the chief magistrate to be as little implicated as possible in the specific approbation of a particular measure proceeding from a particular officer . . ." [141] Washington agreed. Department heads were at liberty to express their own views in papers they laid before Congress at his direction [142] as well as in reports prepared on order of Congress and transmitted directly to that body by these officials, without any covering letter by the President.[143] Nor was there the least complaint on the part of Washington when any document he sent to Congress was referred by that body to one of his subordinates for study and independent report.[144] In foreign

---

Another letter from that body had been sent directly to Washington, who handled it in the usual manner and dispatched an answer drafted by Hamilton (31 *G. W.*, 205–06, correctly dated Jan. 27, 1791; also printed in 4 *A. Hamilton*, 349, but dated 1792, a manifest error).

[139] See, for example, his tactful warning to Arthur St. Clair, Governor of the Northwest Territory, never to issue executive orders that usurped a legislative function (31 *G. W.*, 190–91).

[140] Letter of Apr. 4, 1791, to Alexander Hamilton; *ibid.*, 274.

[141] Letter of Dec. 22, 1790; 9 *Hamilton Papers*, f. 1230, LC.

[142] See, for instance, Knox's statement on Harmar's expedition, 1 *Richardson*, 82, and Hamilton's report on the terms of the foreign loan, 1 *JS*, 286–87. It is safe to say that these and similar reports might have been less factual and more opinionated without giving offence to Washington.

[143] Hamilton's reports on public credit were not enclosed by the President but were sent direct. So was Edmund Randolph's report of Dec. 27, 1790, on the judicial system (*ASP.*, 1 *Misc.*, 21 ff), and so were Jefferson's papers on weights and measures, July 4, 1790 (3 *Jefferson*, 26 ff), and on American fisheries, Feb. 1, 1791 (*ibid.*, 120 ff).

[144] A case in point developed over the Mediterranean trade, mentioned in his speech at the opening of Congress, in December, 1790. The entire subject was turned over to the Secretary

affairs, Washington had no unvarying policy of administration. He might conduct direct correspondence for a time with American representatives abroad and later might request the Secretary to act; or he might take over from Jefferson; or, still again, both he and his lieutenant might write a Minister or Chargé within the same week.[145] On occasion, too, the President would content himself with making suggestions to the Secretary of State.[146]

In the assignment of particular tasks, and in the consideration of public business of wide import, Washington employed the heads of departments substantially as he had used the members of his military family during the war. There was no secretarial seniority analogous to that which had prevailed in dealing with officers of the line. Each man was consulted if and when the President desired that individual's judgment on a given issue, whether or not it was in the department for which that person was directly responsible.[147] This had been accepted without murmur or misunderstanding and sometimes had been regarded as a convenience. Knox, for instance, once had written Lear that he did not wish to submit a certain paper to the President until he had consulted Hamilton and Jefferson.[148] On another occasion, Jefferson forwarded to Hamilton a French report on an alloy for coin and concluded with the expression of hope that the Secretary of the Treasury would "consider the liberty taken as an advance towards unreserved communications for reciprocal benefit." [149]

Differences over the banking bill had soured most of this amity between Jefferson and Hamilton. The opinions the two men had given Washington on the constitutionality of that measure had been those of men with a different philosophy of government, and not merely with contrary views of the implied powers of Congress. Friends of Hamilton had thought the ambitions of Jefferson's friends had been disclosed in

---

of State by the lawmakers for further examination, etc. 1 *JHR.*, 338; 3 *Jefferson*, 90 ff; *ASP.*, 1 *For. Rel.*, 104 ff.

[145] The correspondence with Gouverneur Morris at one time or another represented all three of these methods. See 31 *G. W.*, 169–70, 172–74; 3 *Jefferson*, 90 ff; 8 *ibid.*, 115–16.

[146] Cf. the matter of claims in the case of Joseph St. Marie, who was despoiled in 1787 by Spanish troops East of the Mississippi. 31 *G. W.*, 232 and n, 247.

[147] Jefferson, for example, was consulted on the Northwest Territory (3 *Jefferson*, 85 ff); he and Randolph, but not Hamilton and Knox, were asked for their opinion on the extent to which Washington should or should not go in encouraging the woollen industry in Virginia (31 *G. W.*, 193); Hamilton was chosen to draft numerous papers for which he, rather than Jefferson or Lear, seemed to be best suited.

[148] Letter of Jan. 15, 1791; *Knox Papers*, MHS.

[149] Letter of Dec. 29, 1790; 8 *Jefferson*, 121.

debate over the bill on the order of succession to the Presidency in event of death or vacancy on other account.[150] Jefferson, in his turn, was beginning to talk "of a sect who believe [the British Constitution] to contain whatever is perfect in human institutions" and that "the members of this sect have, many of them, names and offices which stand high in the estimation of our countrymen."[151] Domination of most of the newspapers by men alleged to belong to this pro-British "sect" had led republicans to wish for a strong, outspoken journal that would present their views of contested issues. Jefferson had this distinctly in mind when he offered the minor post of translator for the State Department to Philip Freneau, a writer of some skill, who shared his political opinions.[152] Another gain, Jefferson thought, probably would be the more intelligent and extensive presentation of foreign news. Regardless of newspaper support, or the lack of it, rivalry between Jefferson and Hamilton was becoming so apparent that Washington could not have been unaware of it, but he chose to ignore it, and he took pains to avoid any treatment of one or the other that might seem preferential or partial. After he had rested a few days at home, had transacted necessary public business, and had made all his preparations to start his southern tour on the 7th of April, 1791, he sent his itinerary to the three Secretaries. If important matters arose while he was on his journey, he said, the three should confer and, if they decided he should return forthwith, he would. In event they could act legally and properly in his absence, then, he wrote, "I will approve and ratify the measures . . ."[153] The great seal, so to say, was to be in commission. Neither of the rivals was to act as President. America's interest de-

---

[150] 1 *Fisher Ames*, 93.

[151] Letter of Feb. 4, 1791, to George Mason; 8 *Jefferson*, 124.

[152] Freneau was assistant editor of the *Daily Advertiser* in New York when Jefferson first had contact with him. The poet-journalist boasted he dealt "neither in court sycophantism nor in sublime dedications" (*Daily Advertiser*, Dec. 16, 1790, p. 3) and had poked satiric fun at Fenno's "official" *Gazette of the United States* (*ibid.*, Feb. 18, 1791, p. 2). Jefferson's offer of the translator's position, which then paid only 250 dollars a year, was made in a letter to Freneau on Feb. 28, 1791 (8 *Jefferson*, 133). "It gives so little to do," wrote the Secretary of State, "as not to interfere with any other calling the person may choose, which would not absent him from the seat of government." Jefferson's subsequent admissions concerning Freneau (1 *Jefferson*, 353; 8 *ibid.*, 133, 402, 403–05, 440; 19 *ibid.*, 79) confirm all the charges made against him of urging Freneau on, except the allegation that he wrote articles for Freneau's paper. On this, see John B. McMaster, *A History of the People of the United States, from the Revolution to the Civil War*, v. 2, p. 52–53. Jefferson's apparent conviction in early 1791 was that Freneau must come to Philadelphia and establish an active political paper to combat the influence of Fenno's *Gazette of the United States*.

[153] He added that if, contrary to his expectation, John Adams was in Philadelphia, the Vice President, also, should be party to the conferences. 31 *G. W.*, 272–73.

manded that if it could possibly be done, the office remain above politics, provided always that the Union be preserved in strength. It seemed a wise policy and it might be practical, also, but involved in it were a concept of the Presidency and a peculiarity of the mind of Washington that might give certain unreality to his share in the expanding government of a growing America. He had eyes to see, even if he put on glasses to read, and he had ears to hear, in spite of rumors that he was becoming deaf. Observant aides brought tales from the taverns and from the halls of Congress; he read the newspapers and he learned much from visitors and from correspondents. It was unthinkable that a man who had been his own best intelligence officer during the war should fail to know what was happening or should fail to sift critically and realistically the news that came to him. He knew, but was he willing to act? A thrilling drama was being played on a new stage; was he playing the leading rôle created for him, or was he becoming merely a spectator in a decorated box? He rode in state: would he become so accustomed to the carriage seat that he would cease to walk the common way? Would cold, just judgment bring dangerous detachment? Could he be above politics and still be able to cope with politicians?

# CHAPTER XIV

## NEW HOMAGE ON A SOUTHERN TOUR
### (April 7–June 12, 1791)

FOR HIS long journey through a region of notoriously bad, sandy roads, Washington had prepared carefully a list of distances and contingencies. He allowed himself eight days for what he termed "casualties"—the accidents of travel and the foundering of horses—and he fixed precisely the number of days he was to spend in each of the principal towns he planned to visit. The whole arrangement he termed his "line of march" [1] which he was to follow in his new, light chariot,[2] with no other companions than Major Jackson and the servants. The luggage was to go in a wagon which, like the chariot, was to have two horses hitched to it. Had he been superstitious he would have doubted at the very outset the wisdom of his venture, because in crossing the Occoquan, on the 7th of April, one of the animals harnessed to the chariot fell into the stream, fully harnessed, and so excited the others that all of them went overboard. Quick work prevented loss.[3] At Fredericksburg, where he spent two nights and a day,[4] he had a second disquieting experience: John Lewis, the only surviving son of Fielding Lewis by his first marriage, told of a recent interview with Patrick

[1] 31 *G. W.*, 294.
[2] Described as "a superior specimen of mechanical perfection"; *Gazette of U. S.*, Mch. 23, 1791, p. 3.
[3] 4 *Diaries*, 156. This account of the uneventful journey to Georgia and back again is summary, for the reason that Archibald Henderson, in *Washington's Southern Tour, 1791*, cited hereafter as *Henderson*, has devoted 340 pages to a detailed account. Readers who wish to identify all the stopping places of the General, and the exact language of the various addresses delivered him, in the usual familiar form, will find them in Henderson's fully documented narrative. Although Henderson does not cite specifically or consistently the pertinent newspapers, a comparison of his narrative with the *City Gazette* (Charleston), the *Georgia Gazette* (Savannah) and the *Augusta Chronicle* indicates that much of his detail was drawn from the reports in these journals. Needless to say, the *Gazette of the United States* reprinted the southern reports in its issues of late May and early June.
[4] He arrived in time for dinner at Kenmore, his sister's residence, on Friday, April 8, and left Sunday, April 10, about 6 A.M. 4 *Diaries*, 156–57. This Diary, a document more elaborate than most of his journals, is the primary source of the southern tour. In towns that had newspapers, surviving files usually elaborate Washington's entries. See, for example, the publication cited in 13 *V* 428.

Henry, who made no secret of his financial interest in the so-called Yazoo Company. When Lewis had inquired how the company expected to deal with the Indians, Henry had said that an appeal would be made to Congress for protection. If this was denied, the Yazoo proprietors would organize their own force under Brig. Gen. Charles Scott.[5] That was an ugly threat if it was not mere gasconade: how could peace with the Indians be preserved if every land company were to establish its own private army? "Schemes of that sort," Washington reflected a little later, "must involve the country in trouble—perhaps in blood." [6]

A third unpleasantness awaited Washington in Richmond, where he received ceremonious welcome on the afternoon of the 11th of April,[7] and, along with salute and salutation, mail from Philadelphia. Included was a letter in which Tobias Lear remarked that Attorney General Randolph was in danger of losing slaves brought from Virginia because of a Pennsylvania law which provided that adult bondsmen would be free six months after their owner, moving into the State, became a citizen.[8] Washington thought the difference between his situation and that of Randolph gave reasonable assurance that the law did not apply to him. In order to appear in Pennsylvania courts, Randolph had become temporarily a citizen of Pennsylvania; Washington had not. At the same time, the President felt that someone might "entice" his servants and that the Negroes might become "insolent" if they thought themselves entitled to their freedom. His old regard for his property asserted itself in the letter he wrote Lear: "As all [the slaves of the Presidential establishment] except Hercules and Paris are dower negroes, it behooves me to prevent the emancipation of them, otherwise I shall not only lose the use of them but may have them to pay for. If upon taking good advice, it is found expedient to send them back to Virginia, I wish to have it accomplished under pretext that may deceive both them and the public; and none, I think, would so effectually do this as Mrs. Washington coming to Virginia next month

---

[5] 4 Diaries, 157.

[6] Ibid., 192. In the original the word "schemes" does not begin a sentence.

[7] Ibid., 157–58. Washington dined at Bowling Green on the 10th and lodged at a tavern fourteen miles South of that pleasant village. For his reception and entertainment in Richmond, see W. A. Christian, Richmond, Her Past and Present, 44–45, wrongly dated.

[8] Decatur, 223. This act of Mch. 29, 1788, is in 13 Statutes at Large of Pennsylvania, ed. of 1908, p. 52–56. For the earlier defective law of Feb. 29, 1780, "for the gradual abolition of slavery," see W. F. Dunaway, A History of Pennsylvania, 221–22.

(towards the middle or latter end of it, as she seemed to have a wish to do) if she can accomplish it by any convenient and agreeable means, with the assistance of the stage horses etc. This would naturally bring her maid and Austin, and Hercules under the idea of coming home to cook whilst we remained there, might be sent on in the stage. Whether there is occasion for this or not, according to the result of your inquiries or issue the thing as it may, I request that these sentiments and this advice may be known to none but yourself and Mrs. Washington." [9] Slavery, in his eyes, was a wasteful nuisance, but so long as it existed in a country where the sentiment of honest men was divided over it, he would safeguard his rights with the least public offence. Even so, the words "pretext" and "deceive them" did not flow naturally from his pen.

He had time in Richmond for other letters, also, because the ceremonies followed a familiar pattern—a parade, a dinner, an illumination, an address and answer, and a formal leave-taking—and did not over-crowd the two days and a half that he gave to the capital of his native State.[10] With Gov. Beverley Randolph and the directors, he examined the canal the James River Navigation Company was constructing around the falls, and he had opportunity of talking with Col. Edward Carrington, former Deputy Quartermaster General, and his own appointee as Marshal of the District of Virginia. The Colonel thought the people well disposed to the Federal government and ready to approve action properly explained to them.[11] Washington heard this with much satisfaction. One of the reasons for making the tour was his wish to ascertain at first hand what the people thought of the government. He rejoiced to learn that the tree seemed to be taking root.

From Richmond, the President drove to Petersburg on the morning of the 14th and there received all the honors the town could bestow. "So great was the desire of the people to see him," Colonel Carrington wrote, "that by the time of his arrival there were not less than several thousands after him." [12] The dust kicked up by these men and their horses made the day a hard one. Apparently the 15th would be no

---

[9] 37 G. W., 573–74. Some of the punctuation has been revised but the reference to the servants has been retained as it is in the original, because the comma after "Austin" affects the meaning.

[10] He arrived during the afternoon of April 11 and left after an early breakfast on the 14th; 4 Diaries, 158–60.

[11] Ibid., 159.

[12] Letter of Apr. 20, 1791; 14 Madison Papers, 6, LC.

better because militiamen and citizens were preparing to canter in his company part of the way to the North Carolina boundary. Washington could not bring himself to decline this friendly attendance, nor could he contemplate otherwise than with rebellious nostrils the prospect of eating dust for twenty miles. His recourse was set down unblushingly in his Diary: "I caused [the citizens'] enquiries respecting the time of my setting out, to be answered that, I should endeavor to do it before eight o'clock; but I did it a little after five, by which means I avoided the inconveniences above mentioned." [13]

He had been warned that the next stages of his journey would be "dreary" [14] and he was not unprepared for the dull, flat pinelands through which he had to pass, mile on mile. [15] The weather changed while the country remained the same. In place of dust, he faced heavy downpours that filled the road. [16] Although he soon came into a region new to him, farther South than he had been even on his inspection tour of the frontier forts in October, 1756, [17] he found little to interest him except the river valleys and the possible improvement of navigation. [18] The villages were too thinly peopled and too poorly furnished for impressive entertainment. Reception at Halifax, [19] Senator Samuel Johnston admitted regretfully, "was not such as we could have wished, though in every other part of the country [Washington] was treated with proper attention." [20] The President took no offence [21] and after he reached Tarboro, he wrote—perhaps as much in homage as in amusement—"We were received at this place by as good a salute as could be given by one piece of artillery." Southward from Tarboro, with an escort of honor, Washington proceeded to Newbern, where he had what he described as "exceedingly good lodgings." The welcome fitted the

[13] 4 *Diaries*, 161, verbatim. Cf. "The Commonwealth," March, 1948, p. 17–18.

[14] 31 *G. W.*, 282.

[15] 4 *Diaries*, 162. He lodged on the night of April 15 "at the house of one Oliver," an estimated twenty-seven miles South of Petersburg (*ibid.*, 161). This must have been close to the Nottoway River.

[16] *Ibid.*, 162. The unpleasant journey of April 16 covered approximately forty-eight miles and ended at Halifax, North Carolina.

[17] See Vol. II, p. 216–19.

[18] 4 *Diaries*, 162–63.

[19] He arrived there April 16, at 6 P.M., remained there on Sunday the 17th, attended a dinner in his honor and left early the next morning (*ibid.*, 163).

[20] Letter to James Iredell, May 23, 1791; G. J. McRee, *Life and Correspondence of James Iredell*, v. 2, p. 332. Johnston usually was styled Governor but he was at this time United States Senator.

[21] Cf. 4 *Diaries*, 164.

quarters,[22] but the next stretch of the journey, the long one to Wilmington, was almost bad enough to efface the pleasant memories of the hospitable town at the confluence of Neuse and Trent Rivers. All of the six inns at which Washington halted on the 22nd and 23rd of April were listed sadly in his journal as "indifferent houses"; most of the road passed, in the President's own words, "through the most barren country I ever beheld." [23]

Wilmington itself was hospitable and was interesting because of its effort to maintain connection with the sea in spite of a mudbank in Cape Fear River below the city. As always, Washington looked upstream, too, and speculated on the possibility of extending transportation as far inland as Fayetteville, which was described to him as already a "thriving place" with large markets for tobacco and flax seed.[24] All this was pleasant to contemplate. After spreading a table for the reception committee on the 24th, Washington attended a public dinner and ball the next day.[25] He was particularly gratified to observe how many ladies danced in his honor and he wrote down the number with care—sixty-two. As it chanced, other numbers represented an unpleasant disclosure during Washington's forty hours in Wilmington: When he made his usual inquiry concerning the population of the town, he was told that the census listed about 1000, but that the Marshal's deputies had been most shamefully careless in their count. Wilmington was far larger than the enumeration indicated [26]—an avowal not unique to the city on the Cape Fear River or destined to be limited to the first census.

From Wilmington southward, the road traversed still more stretches of "sand and pine barrens"—in Washington's own words—though he was told of better farms and a population less sparse, back from the traveled route. For part of the way to Georgetown, there were no inns,

---

[22] The journey of the 19th was from Tarboro to "one Allan's," about thirty-nine miles. Henderson, *op. cit.,* 78, identifies the proprietor as Shadrack Allen, whose establishment was "just South of Turkey Swamp" and was styled Crown Point Inn. On the morning of the 20th, Washington sought breakfast at the home of Col. John Allen, about twenty miles South of Newbern, because he had been informed that Allen kept an inn. ". . . we were very kindly and well entertained," the President wrote, "without knowing it was at his expense until it was too late to rectify the mistake." It was from Colonel Allen's (whose seat is identified in *Henderson,* 82 n) that Washington proceeded to Newbern, which he reached that afternoon, April 20 (4 *Diaries,* 164). He left, with a large escort, on the 22nd (*ibid.,* 166).

[23] *Ibid.*                    [24] *Ibid.,* 167–68.

[25] *Henderson,* 118–24, gives many details, some of record and some traditional, of Washington's stay at Wilmington.

[26] 4 *Diaries,* 167.

but while this compelled Washington to violate his self-imposed rule against the acceptance of private hospitality, the absence of public houses added to the comfort of his travel. He was received most graciously, and once, he suspected, at an establishment which was a tavern, though the proprietor insisted it was a private home. "We therefore were entertained," Washington wrote, "(and very kindly) without being able to make compensation." [27]

On the 29th of April, approximately three weeks after leaving Mount Vernon, Washington had his first contact with the rich society of South Carolina. This was at Clifton House, the seat of William Alston, on a wooded hill above the Waccamaw River.[28] Alston had the reputation, admirers told Washington, of being "one of the neatest rice planters in the State of South Carolina and a proprietor of the most valuable ground for the culture of this article." [29] Washington consequently looked at the plantation with eyes that never were more keenly appreciative of trees and thriving crops; and he told himself there scarcely could be a more incredible contrast than that of Alston's green, well-watered rice fields and the thin, unpeopled district through which he had passed.[30]

At Clifton House were Gen. William Moultrie, Col. William Washington and John Rutledge, who had come out to escort their State's guest to Georgetown and thence to Charleston. All three were interesting men. Besides his kinship with the President, William Washington had the fine reputation he had acquired in the main Continental Army and the still greater fame he had won in the Southern Department. Moultrie was an officer of whom Washington had seen little or nothing,[31] but he had a shining reputation, valiantly won. Edward Rutledge was the brother of the Chief Justice of the State, John Rutledge. These gentlemen brought the written greetings of Gov. Charles Pinckney and invitations from him.[32] Doubtless, too, the committee

[27] *Ibid.*, 168. This was at "Mr. Vareen's," about sixteen miles below the North Carolina-South Carolina boundary. The date was April 27th. On the 28th, Washington had dinner at "Mr. Pauley's" and lodged at the residence of "a Doctor Flagg." Fitzpatrick noted, *ibid.*, 169 n, that the names of these hosts "do not appear in the 1790 census." Even Henderson did not identify the gentlemen.

[28] *Ibid.*, 169; *Henderson*, 126.          [29] 4 *Diaries*, 169.

[30] *Ibid.*

[31] Both the President and Col. William Washington were descendants of Col. John Washington, the "emigrant ancestor"; the former through Lawrence, the elder son of Colonel John; and the latter through the younger son, John. For Washington's "opinion" of General Moultrie, cf. 31 *G. W.*, 509-10.

[32] *Henderson*, 129.

told the President about other plans for entertaining him in the city that was, above all others, the one he wished most to see on his tour. Meantime, in Georgetown, on the 30th,[33] he attended a public dinner and during the afternoon he bowed at a tea party to "upwards of fifty ladies," a figure less precise than that of the female contingent at his reception in Wilmington. He interested himself in Georgetown and its waterways but he felt that the town was overshadowed by Charleston and was hampered by a bar that left only twelve feet of water except at the spring tides. "The inhabitants of this place," he wrote, "(either unwilling or unable) could give no account of the number of souls in it, but I should not compute them at more than 5 or 600." [34] He did not add the reflection that the smaller the town the greater the reluctance to come down to flat figures.

The 1st of May was given to travel from Georgetown to Gabriel Manigault's plantation, Marshlands, where Washington spent the night [35] and the next morning began an extraordinary week. A ceremonial crossing from Haddrel's Point to Charleston harbor was almost as spectacular as the passage up New York Bay for the inauguration of 1789. A twelve-oared barge was rowed by American sea captains; two boats conveyed musicians; almost all light craft in the vicinity of Charleston attended the President; on approaching Prioleau's Wharf, Washington received a hearty salute from the artillery of the town. After a formal landing and welcome, he was driven to the Exchange to see the procession pass—he was careful not to term it a review—and, when the last contingent had saluted him, he went to the residence of Judge Thomas Heyward, which had been leased and adorned for his occupancy.[36] Washington looked over the rooms and later wrote in his Diary: "The lodgings provided for me in this place were very good, being the furnished house of a gentleman at present in the country; but occupied by a person placed there on purpose to accommodate me, and who was paid in the same manner as any other letter of lodgings would have been paid." [37] He wished his record to show that he had

---

[33] He left Alston's fine plantation that morning. 4 *Diaries*, 169.

[34] *Ibid.*, 170. Since 1790, Georgetown's population has been multiplied tenfold.

[35] *Ibid.* Henderson noted, *op. cit.*, 141, that Manigault married the daughter of Ralph Izard, whom Washington knew as a member of the Continental Congress in 1782–83 and as one of the original Senators from South Carolina.

[36] *Henderson*, 148–49, 156–61; 4 *Diaries*, 172. Heyward was a signer of the Declaration of Independence and a distinguished figure in the life of his State.

[37] *Ibid.*; cf. *ibid.*, 195.

held to his resolution to put no private family to the expense of entertaining him except in those instances where no inn, however "indifferent," was available to travelers. This was particularly important in Charleston, because he had changed his original plan and, instead of allotting five days to the city,[38] had decided to spend a week there—a longer time than he ever had devoted to an official visit.[39]

Not even his "triumphant progress" from Mount Vernon to New York in 1789 equalled the entertainment that began the hour he arrived in the Carolina city. He held three receptions, attended two breakfasts, ate seven sumptuous formal dinners, listened and replied to four addresses, was the central figure at two assemblies and a concert, rode through the city, visited the scenes of military operations, went twice to church, observed and praised a display of fireworks and drank sixty toasts.[40] The visit proved that his social endurance at 59 years of age could not be sapped and overthrown. What was more, his interest in beautiful women was sharpened. Never had he devoted quite so much space in his unimaginative Diary to ladies' looks and attention to him. On the 3rd of May—the day after his arrival—he wrote proudly: "Was visited about 2 o'clock by a great number of the most respectable ladies of Charleston—the first honor of the kind I had ever experienced and it was as flattering as it was singular." [41] The next evening he had this delight to set down: "Dined with the members of the Cincinnati"— which seemed to him to call for no comment—"and in the evening went to a very elegant dancing assembly at the Exchange, at which were 256 elegantly dressed and handsome ladies"—256, as if he had counted and admired every one of them. From one superlative he climbed to another. On the afternoon of the 5th he "dined with a very large company at the Governor's and in the evening went to a concert at the Exchange at which there were at least 400 ladies the number and appearance of which exceeded any thing of the kind I had ever seen." [42] Such modesty as remained in him, with respect to ceremonials, well might have been washed away by a compliment this matriarchy paid him. At the assembly on the evening of May 4, "the ladies," according to the *City Gazette,* "were all superbly dressed and most of them wore

[38] 31 *G. W.*, 230.

[39] It will be remembered that his stay in Boston, October, 1789, was for five days (4 *Diaries*, 33-39 and *supra*, p. 240, n. 5.

[40] 4 *Diaries*, 172-74. Henderson devoted fifty-six printed pages (*op. cit.*, 144-200) to the events of these seven days and omitted no recorded detail of interest.

[41] 4 *Diaries*, 172.                          [42] *Ibid.*, 173.

ribbons with different inscriptions expressive of their esteem and respect for the President such as: 'long live the President,' etc." [43] Two evenings later, at the ball given by Governor Pinckney in Washington's honor, the homage of his feminine admirers was in their hairdress. Nearly all the coiffures included a bandeau or fillet on which was painted a sketch of Washington's head or some patriotic, sentimental reference to him.[44]

A different attraction of the charming Carolina city was the line of its defence in the campaign of 1780. At the time when Benjamin Lincoln was facing Clinton and Arbuthnot, it had seemed to Washington that the leader of the American forces had concentrated too large a part of his little army at Charleston and could hope for a success only if he could hold the bar, but at Morristown he had felt himself too remote to pass final judgment on a lieutenant whose courage and discretion he trusted.[45] With deepest interest, the old Commander-in-Chief went over the ground in the company of General Moultrie and of other veterans who knew every foot of it [46] and he concluded that the defence had been altogether honorable, but in his Diary he added vaguely that "the measure was undertaken upon wrong principles and impolitic" [47] —a reiteration, probably, of what he had thought in 1780. Another visit of military interest was to Fort Moultrie on Sullivan's Island, and Fort Johnson on James's Island. Although little remained of these earthworks, Washington had the privilege of hearing the repulse of the British fleet on the 28th of June, 1776, described by William Moultrie, who not only was responsible for it but was able to recount it with all the skill of a practiced raconteur. At parting, Washington expressed both thanks and satisfaction but in his Diary the comment was brief: Fort Johnson was "quite fallen," of Fort Moultrie, "scarcely a trace" remained.[48] Not a word did he write of a battle he had attributed at the time to the leadership of Charles Lee and had proclaimed an achievement the main Army should emulate.[49] How impossible seemed the transformation from 1776 to 1791! Events had been so complicated during the American Revolution, and the elements of success so confused that only the best informed of Washington's hosts in Charleston could have put them together; but, somehow, the people knew that the

[43] Quoted in *Henderson*, 178.
[44] *Ibid.*, 184, 196, with citation of Charles Fraser's *Reminiscences of Charleston*, 18.
[45] 18 *G. W.*, 151–52; see *supra*, Vol. V., p. 155.
[46] For the names, see *Henderson*, 172.
[47] 4 *Diaries*, 173.                     [48] *Ibid.*
[49] See Vol. IV, p. 141 and 5 *G. W.*, 314–15.

city's guest had done more than any man to make independence a reality. Now that he was leaving the city on the morning of May 9,[50] many of his old officers and "most of the principal gentlemen of the city," in Washington's own grateful words, rode to the crossing of the Ashley and there had breakfast with him before they said farewell.[51]

En route to Savannah, May 9–11, the President violated his rule against the acceptance of lodging at private homes; but he explained this carefully in his Diary: He spent one night at Col. William Washington's plantation, Sandy Hill, from "motives of friendship and relationship," as he expressed it, and he stayed at O'Brien Smith's on the 10th and at Thomas Heyward's on the 11th, because there were "no public houses on the road."[52] The next day, before breakfast, a ride of twenty-two miles carried him to the Savannah River, at Purysburg, where some of the notables of the fine city downstream were awaiting him[53] with boats for the vehicles and the luggage, and an eight-oared barge, rowed by native sea captains, for Washington and the committee. On the way, the President went ashore at Mulberry Grove for a brief visit to the widow of Nathanael Greene, the ablest of his war-time lieutenants. Adversity had overtaken this brilliant woman who had enlivened many a black night in Revolutionary winter quarters. Besides creating a tangle of private debts by mismanaged speculation, General Greene had become surety for John Banks and Company, who had contracted provisions for the troops of the Southern Department when all other sources of supply had failed. The emptiness of the Continental Treasury after the war and an unwarranted suspicion that Greene enjoyed a financial interest in the contract had combined to delay a settlement. He had been compelled to sell the landed property the State of South Carolina had presented him,[54] and now, almost five years after Greene's death, there was doubt whether his widow could hope to retain Mulberry Grove, the gift of the State of Georgia. In the brief time Washington had for this first call on her in her southern home, he could not discuss her business affairs, nor would he have talked of them, probably, had his stay been longer, because it was likely he might be called upon, as President, to sign or to disapprove legislation for her relief. Washington's entry in his journal may echo a deliberate

---

[50] 4 *Diaries*, 174.  [51] *Ibid.*, 174–75.  [52] *Ibid.*, 175.
[53] A footnote in *ibid.*, 175–76, identifies them.
[54] 3 *Greene's Greene*, 521.

but awkward effort to disregard the melancholy emotions the visit might have stirred: "In my way down the river," he wrote, "I called upon Mrs. Greene, the widow of the deceased General Greene (at a place called Mulberry Grove) and asked her how she did." [55]

He himself did none too well in the remainder of his passage along the river. With wind and tide against the bedizened sea captains at the oars, it was 6 P.M. on the 12th of May when he reached Savannah, but the townsfolk still were awaiting him. They had excellent quarters for him; they gave him a public dinner, late as was the hour, and they illuminated their houses in his honor. The next two and half days were crowded with ceremonial—another dinner, an assembly, "at which there was about 100 well-dressed and handsome ladies," and a third dinner "in an elegant bower erected for the occasion on the bank of the river below the town." After that was presented what the city's guest unenthusiastically termed a "tolerable good display of fireworks." [56] In addition, as the General carefully and proudly wrote, he received on the 14th and during the early afternoon of the 15th, "a number of visits from the most respectable ladies of the place." [57] The feature that should have been of largest interest was a visit to the scene of the attempt the Comte d'Estaing and General Lincoln made in September-October, 1779, to wrest Savannah from the British garrison. Although numerous informed residents of the town and a Brigadier who had participated in the attack were among the guides, Washington met disappointment and cautiously refrained from comments. He wrote: "To form an opinion of the attack at this distance of time, and the change which has taken place in the appearance of the ground by the cutting away of the woods, etc., is hardly to be done with justice to the subject, especially as there is remaining scarcely any of the defences." [58]

From Savannah, after attending church and bowing to the ladies who called on him, Washington returned by road to Mulberry Grove, dined with Mrs. Greene, and went on to a tavern where he lodged. Thence he rode to Augusta, which he reached on the 18th of May. Two days and a half were spent in the enjoyment of the town's hospitality, in dispensing which the President was pleased to find nu-

[55] 4 *Diaries*, 176. Washington here spelled the name "Green."
[56] *Ibid.*, 177. Henderson, *op. cit.*, 208–32, supplied a multitude of cherished small details of the events of these days.
[57] *Ibid.*, 177–78.
[58] *Ibid.*, 177. The Brigadier who accompanied the party was Lachlan McIntosh.

merous ladies. He described them as "well dressed" but—doubtless by oversight—he failed to say they were handsome also.[59] The town itself impressed him as well situated and destined to grow as a tobacco market.[60] Next on the way, after Washington left Augusta in the early morning of May 21, was a halt of a day and a half at Columbia and, unexpectedly, of a second day there because of the bad condition of a horse. Except for a welcoming escort and a public dinner at the unfinished State House, the visit to Columbia was without incident.[61] The miles stretched out northward. An overnight halt and a public dinner at Camden on the 25th were followed by a careful and interested examination of the ground of the action between Greene and Lord Rawdon on the 25th of April, 1781. Here Washington found it less difficult to pass judgment than at Savannah. It seemed to him that Greene had chosen a good position but had not established the American forces satisfactorily when the capture of a vidette gave Rawdon opportunity for a successful surprise attack. Farther on, Washington viewed the scene of the rout of Gates by Cornwallis, Aug. 16, 1780, and later wrote down his conclusion, with care and with generosity toward the American comrade he had distrusted for years: "As this was a night meeting of both armies on their march and altogether unexpected, each formed on the ground they met without any advantage in it on either side, it being level and open. Had General Gates been half a mile farther advanced, an impenetrable swamp would have prevented the attack which was made on him by the British army, and afforded him time to have formed his own plans; but having no information of Lord Cornwallis's designs and perhaps not being apprized of this advantage it was not seized by him." [62]

After Camden,[63] Washington found nothing of importance on the road to Charlotte, except a visit by a few disturbed Chiefs of the Catawba Indians who seemed to think some scheme was afoot to deprive them of their land.[64] Charlotte itself was disappointing [65] but the approaches to it were through better farm lands than Washington had

---

[59] 4 *Diaries*, 179.                            [60] *Ibid.*, 180.

[61] *Ibid.*, 182–83. Washington reached Columbia during the afternoon of May 22 and left at 4 A.M. on the 25th.

[62] *Ibid.*, 184.

[63] Washington left on the forenoon of May 26; *ibid.*, 183.

[64] *Ibid.*, 184–85. On crossing the line between the Carolinas, he was met by a detachment of volunteer horse. Henderson (*op. cit.*, 278–87) quotes a tedious account of this episode from the autobiography of one of the participants, Charles Caldwell, later a physician of distinction.

[65] 4 *Diaries*, 185. It was then, in Washington's words, "a trifling place."

seen in days and days,[66] and the district between Charlotte and Salisbury seemed to him "very fine," the soil "of a reddish cast and well timbered, but with very little underwood." [67] Salisbury offered him a public dinner, after which Washington drank tea "with about twenty ladies, who had been assembled for the occasion." Perhaps it was because he was troubled by the foundering of another of his horses that he failed in his usual compliment to the mesdames as well dressed or handsome or both.[68]

The last day of May brought a journey reckoned at thirty-five miles from Salisbury to Salem, a little Moravian town that gave Washington a somewhat unusual welcome, thus charmingly described in the diary of the community: "At the end of this month the congregation of Salem had the pleasure of welcoming the President of the United States, on his return journey from the Southern States. We had already heard that he would return to Virginia by way of our town. This afternoon we heard that this morning he left Salisbury, thirty-five miles from here, so the brethren Marshall, Koehler and Benzien rode out a bit to meet him, and as he approached the town several melodies were played, partly by trumpets and French horns, partly by trombones. He was accompanied only by his Secretary, Major Jackson, and the necessary servants. On alighting from the carriage he greeted the bystanders in friendly fashion, and was particularly pleasant to the children gathered there. Then he conversed on various subjects with the brethren who conducted him to the room prepared for him. At first he said that he must go on the next morning, but when he learned that the Governor of our State would like to meet him here the following day he said he would rest here one day. He told our musicians that he would enjoy some music with his evening meal, and was served with it." [69] The next day he visited the workshops of the Moravians and then had six of their leaders dine with him. Later, when Gov. Alexander Martin

[66] *Ibid*. He reached Charlotte before 3 P.M. on the 28th and left at 7 A.M. on the 29th. He lodged that night at Maj. Martin Phifer's residence, an estimated twenty-two miles from Charlotte on the road to Salisbury.
[67] *Ibid.*, 186.
[68] *Ibid*. Henderson, *op. cit.*, 207–308, assembled many details of this visit to the town where some of his ancestors lived. These incidents are not important but they constitute a most informative example of the manner in which a small town of homogeneous, long-resident population cherishes traditions and keeps them alive. Nowhere is American memory longer than in such a place.
[69] *Ibid.*, 310, with translation by Miss Adelaide L. Fries of the German of the original diary, published in *Records of the Moravians*, v. 4, p. 2319–24.

had arrived, Washington went to a concert of church music presented by men and women who during the day pursued humbler arts. Politics were mingled with music. As opportunity was presented that day and the next, Washington talked with Governor Martin about the attitude of the people of North Carolina to the new government in Philadelphia. Martin confirmed for his own State all that Colonel Carrington had said of public sentiment in Virginia: opposition and discontent were subsiding fast. The Governor said, moreover, that as soon as he received the Federal laws on the subject, he would issue his proclamation for State officials to take the prescribed oath. To Washington's relief, Martin seemed to be hostile to the land companies that were trying to procure vast tracts beyond the boundaries set by treaty with the Indian tribes.[70]

In the company of the suave, conciliatory Governor, Washington rode on the 2nd of June from Salem to Guilford, where apparently no arrangements of any sort had been made for entertaining him, though it was known he would arrive that day. Washington made no complaint. He simply remarked in his Diary: ". . . there was a considerable gathering of people who had received notice of my intention to be there today and came to satisfy their curiosity." [71] Near Guilford, before and after dinner, Washington examined the ground of the engagement, on the 15th of March, 1781, between Greene and Cornwallis, and he concluded that the first line was "advantageously drawn up" and that "had the troops done their duty properly, the British must have been sorely galled in their advance, if not defeated." [72]

The day after surveying the scene of a tactical defeat that became a strategical victory, Washington bade farewell to Governor Martin and started on the final stage of his journey, a stage broken by no ceremonial of any sort. From Guilford he rode to Dan River, and on to Col. Isaac Coles's plantation on Staunton River,[73] whence in a single day he proceeded to Prince Edward Court House. By the afternoon of the 10th, he was at Kenmore, his sister's home in Fredericksburg, and

[70] 4 *Diaries*, 192.　　　　　　　　[71] *Ibid.*, 191.

[72] *Ibid.* Henderson, *op. cit.*, 321–22, quotes a passage in Jefferson's "Anas" (June 7, 1793; 1 *Jefferson*, 355–56) where Washington is quoted as saying that he and Greene always had differed in their use of militia: Greene had put them in front; he had employed them "as a reserve to improve any advantage." He went on to say that if the troops behind the fence in Greene's front had stood their ground, they would have torn the enemy to pieces. As it was, the militia abandoned this position after a single volley.

[73] He went to Colonel Coles's on pressing invitation Sunday, June 5, and left at daybreak on the 7th. 4 *Diaries*, 196–97.

on the 12th of June, he ate dinner at his own table [74] in definite satisfaction over the accuracy of his timing and the sturdiness of his team: ". . . I performed a journey of 1887 miles without meeting with any interruption by sickness, bad weather, or any untoward accident. Indeed, so highly were we favored that we arrived at each place, where I proposed to make any halt, on the very day I fixed upon before we set out. The same horses performed the whole tour, and, although much reduced in flesh, kept up their full spirits to the last day." [75] He had himself gained, rather than lost weight [76] and he wrote almost with enthusiasm of the journey: ". . . it has enabled me to see with my own eyes the situation of the country through which we traveled, and to learn more accurately the disposition of the people than I could have done by any information. The country appears to be in a very improving state, and industry and frugality are becoming much more fashionable than they have hitherto been there. Tranquility reigns among the people, with that disposition towards the general government which is likely to preserve it. They begin to feel the good effects of equal laws and equal protection. The farmer finds a ready market for his produce, and the merchant calculates with more certainty on his payments." [77]

This seemed to him the great reassurance, the shining lesson of the tour.[78] He made no record of other things he had learned, some of them useful, some surprising and some in a measure disappointing. His wars, he believed, all were behind him, but had he planned to study that bloody art further, he now could say that he had seen all the more renowned battlefields of his country, except King's Mountain, Bennington and the scenes of maneuver North of Lake Champlain. Greene's campaigns no longer would be chess-board movements, or finger tracing on a map. The Commander-in-Chief had observed where his lieutenant marched and fought, retreated and returned in the operations that made possible the entrapment of Cornwallis at Yorktown.

Other lessons had been learned. The President of the United States might answer Southern addresses with confidently voiced hope that the

---

[74] *Ibid.*, 197–99. Cf. his letter of June 11, misdated June 12, 1791; 31 *G. W.*, 291–92.
[75] Letter of July 20, 1791, to David Humphreys; *ibid.*, 318.
[76] *Ibid.*, 321.                     [77] *Ibid.*, 318. Cf. *ibid.*, 325.
[78] Late in 1791 Washington wrote Gov. Alexander Martin regarding the recent tour: "My object in that journey was not to be received with parade and an ostentatious display of opulence. It was for a nobler purpose . . . to learn on the spot the condition and disposition of our citizens" (*ibid.*, 415).

countryside would blossom and the towns become thriving cities, but the proprietor of Mount Vernon had seen what previously he had not known fully—that the coastal plain was deep in sand, that much of it had thin soil, and that even inland there were long stretches of poor land. He must have realized, more than ever, that the richer meadows were beyond the mountains. It would be more in the interest of the nation to open the West than to people thickly the regions that grew nothing but gaunt pine.

The journey had shown that the President was as popular in the Southern States as he was in Federalist New England.[79] On the tour he had received at least twenty-three addresses, in answering which both he and Major Jackson well might have spent their stock of friendly phrases. Particularly noticeable had been the number of addresses from Lodges of Free Masons. Of the total, no less than three had come from the fellow craft. This probably had no significance otherwise than as it disclosed the strength of the Masons in the South and their pride in Washington as a brother. His answers, in turn, had been in good Masonic terms, with no casualness in his references to his membership in the Order.

Washington himself perhaps was unaware of it, but finally he was becoming increasingly fond of the homage paid him at assemblies and wherever he made his bow to ladies. Mounted escorts that deepened mud or raised dust were a nuisance, but ladies, handsome, well-dressed ladies who paid him the new honor of calling on him . . . well, the Presidency was not altogether without its compensations.

[79] The *Gazette of the United States* had prophesied, while the tour was in progress, that the President's appearance in the South would eradicate any "uneasiness" that might exist there. "Seeing him . . . will have a very conciliatory effect, and do more than a thousand arguments from even an Ames or a Gerry" (see issue of May 7, p. 3).

# CHAPTER XV

## "Faction Glows Within Like a Coal-Pit"

### (June 12, 1791–May 8, 1792)

Washington had transacted little public business while on his south-ern tour,[1] and, as he had missed a great part of the mail dispatched to him, he found a heavy accumulation of papers at Mount Vernon.[2] He encountered, besides, a multitude of plantation duties, sadly increased by the progressive illness of his nephew and steward, George Augustine Washington.[3] Some problems of domestic management at the Presi-dent's house in Philadelphia were posed, also, in Tobias Lear's faithful reports from that city.[4]

Care of these matters was made somewhat depressing by a drought that had ruined the hay crop and now threatened the oats;[5] but Wash-ington faced his labors with his usual, well-ordered self-discipline, and made the most of the eight days he felt he had saved on his southern tour by escaping accident and bad weather. As he had allowed for a six-day rest on his return, he had in reality a fortnight at home[6] before

---

[1] He had received news of an unexpected hitch in the acquisition of land for the Federal City (31 *G. W.*, 286–88), had approved various funding measures of Hamilton's (*ibid.*, 285–86), had undertaken further negotiations for the return of fugitives in Florida (*ibid.*, 288–90, cf. *ibid.*, 370–71; 4 *Diaries*, 180–81), had sought vainly to prevail on C. C. Pinckney or Edward Rutledge to accept a seat on the bench of the Supreme Court (31 *G. W.*, 290–91; 10 *Sparks*, 165 n), and, in amusing contrast, had yielded to a plea that he send one of his jackasses to South Carolina the next season (31 *G. W.*, 312–13, 341–42, 457–58).

[2] *Ibid.*, 292 ff, 299–300.

[3] For Major Washington's decline, see his letter of Aug. 1, 1791, to the General, 251 *Papers of G. W.*, 57, LC; Washington to Lafayette, 31 *G. W.*, 363; James Craik to George Washington, Aug. 31, 1791, 251 *Papers of G. W.*, 92; Washington to Lear, 31 *G. W.*, 377–78, 382. The personal correspondence of the President at this period offers a most interesting picture of the scene at Mount Vernon and of the endless details (cf. *ibid.*, 307–09) involved in keeping the estate in order. A long, vexatious search for about 200 blankets, required for the slaves (*ibid.*, 301, 377, 380, 383–84), was typical of the troubles encountered on an ill-supplied market. Improvements of some magnitude were in prospect at the mill (*ibid.*, 347–48, 355, 465–66, 472–74, 483–84); arrangements still had to be completed for the transfer of the Clifton prop-erty (*ibid.*, 331–32, 364).

[4] May 1, May 8, May 15, 1791, 250 *Papers of G. W.*, 58, 73, 88, LC; and June 12, June 19, June 23, 1791, 251 *ibid.*, 10, 14, 19. See also Mrs. Washington to Mrs. Samuel Powel, May 1, 1791; *Powel Papers*, Mount Vernon.

[5] 31 *G. W.*, 298.

[6] See his letter of June 13, 1791, to Hamilton; 31 *G. W.*, 294.

he started on the 27th for Philadelphia by an unfamiliar route. First he went to Georgetown and there speedily settled a misunderstanding and had the pleasure of announcing where the public buildings would be located.[7] Then he proceeded, via Frederick, Maryland, to York and Lancaster, Pennsylvania, two towns he never had visited. He found the countryside interesting to a Virginia farmer, and at York he had on Sunday, July 3, an experience that he described with what was, for him, a positive touch of humor: ". . . there being no Episcopal Minister present in the place, I went to hear morning Service performed in the Dutch reformed church—which, being in that language not a word of which I understood I was in no danger of becoming a proselyte to its religion by the eloquence of the Preacher." [8]

The weeks following Washington's return to Philadelphia on the 6th of July [9] brought a minor illness [10] and a move by Pennsylvania politicians to construct a new house for the President [11]—an involvement he avoided with some difficulty. These were mere annoyances, though,

[7] The misunderstanding arose over the extent of the conveyances of private property for the new Federal City. See 4 Diaries, 199–201; 31 G. W., 323. In the New-York Journal of Aug. 10, 1791, p. 3, appeared a reprint of a poem from Georgetown with a proposal that the new city be named Washingtonople. By this time, the President was beginning to divest himself of responsibility for the proposed seat of government and was passing on the details to Jefferson. See 8 Jefferson, 234–35; 31 G. W., 349, 351–52.

[8] 4 Diaries, 203, verbatim. The Diary appears to have been suspended on July 4, 1791, with an unfinished entry at Lancaster. No similar record is known to exist prior to Sept. 30, 1794. Receptions and addresses on the journey from Georgetown to Philadelphia were of the familiar order. Details will be found in Baker, 224–27.

[9] Ibid., 227.

[10] The reason was another carbuncle, less serious than that of 1789. See 31 G. W., 334; Jefferson to Madison, July 24, July 27, 1791; 14 Madison Papers, 32, 35, LC. Frances Washington wrote her father, Burwell Bassett, Sept. 21, 1791: "The President looks better than I expected to see him, but still there be traces in his countenance of his two last severe illnesses which I fear will never wear off. My Aunt, I think, looks as well as when she left home [for Philadelphia]." "Mount Vernon Ladies' Asso. Report, 1952," p. 67.

[11] So far as Washington himself was concerned, the matter began when he read in a newspaper that the Pennsylvania legislature was debating on appropriation for a suitable dwelling to be erected and placed at the disposal of the President. The statement was made that Washington felt dissatisfaction with the house he was occupying and that this was the reason for the proposal. The General was sorry this argument was advanced in a form personal to him because, after the workmen had left it, he made no complaints about the house he had leased. Were another and finer residence available, he explained, he would not undergo the expense of moving into it so late in his term of office. These remarks were quoted and disputed and when Washington made a visit home in the autumn, they were the subject of a rather stern inquisition of Tobias Lear by Samuel Powel and other advocates of a mansion. In the end, it was plain that the aim of these men was to build a handsome house that could be used ultimately by the Governor of the State. If such a building stood majestically in the Quaker City it would constitute an argument in dollars and cents against the transfer of the capital of Pennsylvania to an inland town. This and other arguments did not shake Washington's stand. Although an impressive residence was constructed, he never used it. See Lear to Washington, Sept. 21, 1791; 251 Papers of G. W., 121, LC; Sept. 25, 30, Oct. 2, Oct. 11, 1791, 252 ibid., 12, 17, 25, 38; 31 G. W., 372, 376–77, 380–81; cf. ibid., 374. This correspondence shows that the rent of the Morris House was £500, with the lease year calculated from Oct. 1, 1790.

compared with the ominous increase of tension among European countries that had fought one another again and again for centuries. The three powers that appeared to be on the verge of renewed conflict happened to be those whose holdings in the northern hemisphere were adjacent to the United States and constituted either a market or a threat or both. England still was in possession of northwestern posts and was suspected of inspiring the Indian raids, if, indeed, she was not supplying the savages with arms and officers. Spain's hold on the Mississippi and her occupation of New Orleans and Florida gave her a position as formidable as that of the British in Canada. There was ample reason to believe the Governor of New Orleans was dealing with greedy and reckless men on the frontier who were willing, for a consideration, to throw in their fortune with his. France was in convulsion at home and was facing a frightful slave insurrection in Santo Domingo, the richest of her West Indian possessions.

War among these powers might be ruinous to American foreign trade. Even the possibility of a coalition between Britain and Spain, with France as their common adversary, would expose all three of the land frontiers of the United States to danger at the same time that it might involve a call by France for America to fulfil the military alliance of 1778. These were contingencies Washington faced without any self-deception and with little or no prejudice. Although he never wrote down all the details of American policy in any single paper, he applied certain clear principles.

First: Efforts must be made everywhere on the frontier to effect peace with the Indians by formal treaties that acknowledged the natives' territorial rights and assured American recognition of them. Indians who chose war instead of peace were to be punished with a vigor and severity that would destroy them and would deter less aggressive tribes from emulating them.

Second: So young and weak a republic as America must keep out of foreign wars if this could be done with honor and self-respect. "The change of systems [in Europe]" Washington wrote Gouverneur Morris, ". . . will undoubtedly affect us in a degree proportioned to our political or commercial connections with the several nations of it." The President hastened to add: "But I trust we shall never so far lose sight of our own interest and happiness as to become, unnecessarily, a party in their political disputes. Our local situation enables us to keep that state with them which otherwise, could not, perhaps, be preserved by human wisdom." [12] Distance was a stronger bulwark than judgment could be in dealing with a situation the outcome of which no man could foresee.

Third: For these reasons, achievement of peace depended on drawing a distinction between conflicts with foreign interests in America and American interference in Europe. As Washington told George Clinton: ". . . the public welfare and safety evidently enjoin a conduct of circumspection, moderation and forbearance. And it is relied upon that the known good sense of the community ensures its approbation of such a conduct." [13]

Fourth: This balanced policy had to be pursued separately and patiently with each of the three powers. Methods might be different; the basis of bargaining might be shifted; the goal was the same—peace, progress and the deserved larger respect of European countries.

In applying these broad rules to Britain, Washington could not disregard the feelings of his fellow countrymen who were resisting what he believed to be the general desire for peace. Something had to be conceded to the old American resentment. Said Washington: "There are . . . bounds to the spirit of forbearance which ought not to be exceeded. Events may occur which may demand a departure from it. But if extremities are at any time to ensue, it is of the utmost consequence that they should be the result of a deliberate plan, not of an accidental collision; and that they should appear both at home and abroad to have flowed either from a necessity which left no alternative, or from a combination of advantageous circumstances which left no doubt of the expediency of hazarding them. Under the impression of this opinion and supposing that the event which is apprehended should be realized, it is my desire that no hostile measure be in the first instance attempted." [14]

An understanding with Spain manifestly was difficult: Obscurity surrounded the designs of Gov. Estéban Rodriguez Miró. Dr. James O'Fallon, who was perhaps the most active of the frontier adventurers identified at this time, had been operating for the South Carolina

---

[12] Letter of July 28, 1791; 31 G. W., 327.

[13] Letter of Sept. 14, 1791; ibid., 369.

[14] Letter of Sept. 14, 1791, ibid., 369-70, to George Clinton, apropos of rumors that the British planned to establish a new, advanced post in the Northwest. To ascertain whether this was true, Washington planned to send out a secret agent and Governor Clinton was so informed.

Yazoo Company and had been loud in his professions of loyalty to the United States; but there had been suspicion that he planned to seize a region that had been acknowledged by the American government to be an Indian possession. Concern had been felt that this man might precipitate a frontier war and even might involve the country in hostilities with Spain, but, apparently, Washington's advisers had not thought that O'Fallon was in collusion with Governor Miró.[15] A proclamation against O'Fallon's activities and an order for his arrest had seemed enough in the spring of 1791.[16] Thereafter, on the assumption that this schemer had been curbed, Washington gave first place in Spanish negotiations to removal of the suspicion the ministers of the Catholic King seemed to have that the young Western Republic was eyeing covetously the Spanish West Indies. The American Minister at Madrid was instructed to assure the government that the United States had no designs on these holdings in the Antilles, though America had reason to protest against the restrictions imposed on her trade with the Islands.[17]

What should be the policy of the United States towards their ally, France? Washington continued to follow the progress of the Revolution in that country with sharpest interest, of course, but he confessed his anxiety regarding the "indiscriminate violence" that was to be dreaded from the "tumultuous populace of large cities."[18] Jefferson might write of the flight to Varennes that "it would be unfortunate were it in the power of any one man to defeat the issue of so beautiful a revolution";[19] Washington took the more cautious view. Subsequently, it seemed to Jefferson that the President never had appeared so dejected as when informed of the flight, capture and return of Louis XVI to Paris.[20] Washington rallied quickly, as usually he did, and wrote of events in the land of his beloved Lafayette: ". . . however gloomy the face of things may at this time appear in France, yet we will not despair of seeing tranquility again restored; and we cannot help looking forward with a lively wish to the period when order shall be established by a government respectfully energetic and founded on the broad basis

[15] The fullest account of this strange affair is in J. C. Parish, "The Intrigues of Dr. James O'Fallon," reprinted from *Miss. Val. His. Rev.*, September, 1930, p. 230–63.

[16] 1 *Richardson*, 101–02; 31 *G. W.*, 250. This proclamation bore date of March 19. For a report on O'Fallon's earlier activities in the West, see Lieut. John Armstrong, Jan. 20, 1791; *ASP.*, 1 *Ind, Aff.*, 114 ff. See, also, 8 *Jefferson*, 191; *ASP.*, 1 *Ind. Aff.*, 172–73.

[17] 31 *G. W.*, 331 n.     [18] *Ibid.*, 324.

[19] Letter of Aug. 24, 1791, to Sir John Sinclair; 8 *Jefferson*, 231.

[20] 1 *ibid.*, 301.

of liberality and the rights of man,[21] which will make millions happy and place your nation in the rank which she ought to hold." [22] Patience was needed if this was to be achieved, and patience was the virtue America had to display in dealing with the abrupt changes of policy under the revolutionary government. Specifically, the National Assembly had voted a preferential rate on tobacco and oil when imported in French bottoms,[23] and thereby the lawmakers had discriminated against America if, indeed, they had not violated the commercial agreement with the United States. Washington took the friendly, tolerant view of this. He wrote Lafayette: ". . . If [the members of the National Assembly] have done anything which seems to bear hard upon us, at a time when the Assembly must have been occupied in very important matters, and which perhaps would not allow time for a due consideration of the subject, they will, in the moment of calm deliberation, alter it and do what is right." Meantime, he did not think America would make hasty reprisal.[24] The new French Minister to the United States, Jean Baptiste Ternant, was received cordially and with the personal consideration [25] due a man who brought commendatory letters of introduction from several of Washington's friends in France.[26] The utmost was to be done in complying with the request of France for money and arms to be used in combating the slave insurrection in Santo Domingo.[27] No advantage was to be taken of France by repaying the American debt in depreciated assignats.[28] Politeness, friendliness even, was shown in the rejection of a dubious refunding plan submitted by European speculators who had the blessing of the French Foreign Office.[29]

[21] This reference to the "rights of man" was an echo of Washington's interest in Thomas Paine's pamphlet of that title, which he had been anxious to get (31 *G. W.*, 302). The President quoted the title more than once (see *ibid.*, 327), but when he made belated acknowledgment of fifty copies sent him by the author, he thanked Paine and made no comment on the political philosophy advanced in paragraphs which many other Americans accepted almost as a creed (Letter to Paine, May 6, 1792; 32 *ibid.*, 38).

[22] Letter of Sept. 10, 1791 to the Marquis de la Luzerne; 31 *ibid.*, 361. Washington showed the same circumspection in writing to Lafayette, *ibid.*, 362–63; cf. *ibid.*, 356–57.

[23] 8 *Jefferson*, 182–83.  [24] Letter of July 28, 1791; 31 *G. W.*, 325.

[25] Cf. *ibid.*, 380.

[26] *LOLTW.*, 352–53, cf. 356; d'Estaing to Washington, May 30, 1791; 250 *Papers of G. W.*, 112, LC; 31 *G. W.*, 359–60, 362, 363.

[27] The French commissioner from the island, M. Roustan—first name unknown—arrived in New York, via New London, on the 20th of September, 1791. See F. J. Turner, ed., *Correspondence of the French Ministers to the United States, 1791–97, A. H. A.* Annual Report, 1903, v. 2, p. 45. For the loans, etc., see 4 *LTW.*, 382–83, 384–85; 31 *G. W.*, 374–75.

[28] 8 *Jefferson*, 247.

[29] This was the firm of Schweizer and Jeanneret. See James Swan (Paris) to Henry Knox, May 27, 1791, *Knox Papers*, MHS; 31 *G. W.*, 366 ff, a letter probably drafted by Hamilton.

Such was the simple, prudent foreign policy Washington adopted on his return to Philadelphia after the southern tour. It was a policy that had to be applied step by step, as opportunity offered, with respect to Britain and Spain, but it was imperative and immediate where Santo Domingo was concerned. Moreover, charges of British incitation of Indian warfare were about to be put to the test. When Arthur St. Clair, Governor of the Northwest Territory, had been in New York during the late summer of 1790,[30] he had discussed the next phase of frontier defence with Washington. The Commander-in-Chief knew that St. Clair had no experience in this type of warfare and he consequently repeated for the Governor the warning he so often had given officers entrusted with troops in the wilderness: Beware of surprise. St. Clair listened and, at the proper time, presented a plan for establishing a military post at the so-called "Miami Village," approximately 135 miles North-by-West from Fort Washington,[31] as a means of over-awing nearby Indian tribes and of showing the British that the United States had no intention of abandoning that rich area to the King. The proposal had been thought a good one, so good, in fact, that after being laid aside as beyond the military resources of the United States,[32] it had been taken up and entrusted to St. Clair, who was recommissioned at his wartime rank of Major General.[33] His instructions were to proceed to the Miami Village with a force of regulars and militia and a contingent of artillery, to a total of 2000 men. He was "to establish a strong and permanent military post at that place" and, after constructing and garrisoning it adequately, he was to "seek the enemy" and "endeavor by all possible means to strike them with great severity."[34] These orders were assumed by the autumn of 1791 to be in process of execution. Various communications with other tribes and some active negotiations meantime were conducted by Secretary Knox or his appointees.[35]

[30] He was there August 23 and had left prior to September 14. See 2 *St. Clair Papers*, 155, 162, 183.

[31] This principal Miami or Maumee village was KeKionaga, within the corporate limits of present-day Fort Wayne, Ind. It will be remembered that the particular Fort Washington mentioned here was within the bounds of the modern Cincinnati, Ohio.

[32] Knox to St. Clair, Sept. 14, 1790; 2 *St. Clair Papers*, 181–82.

[33] As of Mch. 7, 1791; 1 *EJS.*, 82. This made St. Clair the ranking officer of the active army. There was no other Major General of the regular establishment, though Richard Butler often is mentioned as "Major General of the United States levies."

[34] Knox's instructions to St. Clair, Mch. 21, 1791; *ASP.*, 1 *Ind. Aff.*, 172.

[35] As extended into the winter of 1791–92 this correspondence was voluminous. Much of it will be found in Knox's own papers, in *ibid.*, 225 ff, and in 2 *St. Clair Papers*, 230 ff. See,

Important as these relations with near and far neighbors might prove, determination of the main lines of policy did not require many days. Nor did Washington have to sit long at his desk in preparing notes for his message to Congress which, according to his calendar of events, was to assemble on October 31.[36] Requests were made of his counsellors for suggestions on subjects that should be included;[37] details were put aside for leisured review at Mount Vernon, whither the President turned his carriage again on the 15th of September.[38] This time, the reason was necessity: Major Washington, in a pathetic condition— spitting blood and tragically feeble—had gone to Berkeley Springs in the hope of regaining strength. The owner of Mount Vernon had to make arrangements for operating the estate during his nephew's absence.[39] Without accident or delay on account of any ceremonial, the General reached his home on September 20th[40] and commenced a survey of his affairs. His most important task after a deathly dry summer described to him as "the greatest drought in this country ever known,"[41] was the further instruction of his head farmer, Anthony Whiting, in the management of the property;[42] but, as always, scores of lesser matters awaited his decision.[43] In addition, Washington had

---

also, 4 *LTW.*, 366 ff, 379–80; 250 *Papers of G. W.*, 114–15, LC; 251 *ibid.*, 5, 12, 113; 31 *G. W.*, 386–87.

[36] *Ibid.*, 390.

[37] Cf. *ibid.*, 354 and 10 *Sparks*, 499–502. Letters similar to the one addressed to Jay doubtless were written the heads of departments, or else their assistance was sought verbally.

[38] *Baker*, 229. Included is an account the Viscount de Chateaubriand gave of a dinner with the President on the 14th.

[39] James Craik to George Washington, Aug. 31, 1791; 251 *Papers of G. W.*, 92; 31 *G. W.*, 336, 363.

[40] *Baker*, 230, with quotation from *Dunlap's American Daily Advertiser* (Philadelphia), Sept. 30, 1791.

[41] Battaile Muse to Washington, Aug. 22, 1791; 251 *Papers of G. W.*, 75. The wheat crop, wrote Muse, was exceedingly sparse, and no worse season for corn and tobacco could be remembered.

[42] Whiting had contracted May 20, 1790, to come to Mount Vernon as "an overlooker of one or more" of Washington's farms. He was, in effect, to take the place of James Bloxham (see *supra*, p. 53), who wished to return to England. Washington considered Bloxham "perfectly acquainted with every part of a farmer's business," but, as the General later wrote, Bloxham found it "a little troublesome to instruct the Negroes and to compel them to the practice of his modes" and he gradually slid into their careless practices (34 *G. W.*, 103–04).

[43] Not the least of Washington's concerns at this time was the affirmation of John Dandridge in a letter of Sept. 6, 1791 (251 *Papers of G. W.*, 99), that his father, the Judge, had died insolvent. Washington wrote on October 2 a thoughtful reassurance that Mrs. Dandridge need not feel pressed to sell or surrender her slaves immediately for the discharge of the old debt. He still was troubled with affairs pertaining to the Colville estate, though efforts toward its final settlement were being pressed (31 *G. W.*, 342). In addition, Robert Lewis, the General's nephew, had succeeded Battaile Muse as collector of rents (31 *ibid.*, 390 ff); various commissions had to be discharged for friends and kinspeople (*ibid.*, 407; 32 *ibid.*, 23–24, 39–40); a complicated plow had to be declined because such implements could not be entrusted to ignorant

considerable correspondence with officials in Philadelphia, though not on questions of large moment, and he continued to direct the preparation of material for his address to Congress. Most particularly, he wrote Tobias Lear to examine his previous speeches to the legislative bodies, in order to ascertain how many of his recommendations had been adopted, how many had not been considered, and how many had not been completed. Then he could decide whether to bring any of them to the attention of a new House of Representatives.[44]

Everything seemed to be in smooth progression, suited to an able, experienced administrator, when, from a letter received on the 13th of October, Washington discovered that he had made a mistake concerning the date of the meeting of Congress: it was to assemble on the 24th, not on the 31st.[45] He had a week less than he thought in which to complete his work at Mount Vernon, to get back to Philadelphia, and to draft the annual message. No time was lost after that. Word was sent to the Quaker City the very next day for speed in collecting the information he would require.[46] By the 21st he reached the temporary capital,[47] having paused at Georgetown just long enough to give instructions regarding the sale of lots.[48] Luckily, too, he met Jefferson and Madison on the site of the Federal City and received suggestions from them for the paper he was to read to the legislators.[49] These were passed on to Hamilton, who already had assigned to Knox the writing of some paragraphs of the President's address.[50]

Washington was ready, if by a margin of a few hours only, when Congress met on the 24th of October for a session that some observers expected to be important. "From this time," Oliver Wolcott wrote his

---

hands (31 *ibid.*, 410); high prices cut an order for clover seed from 1000 pounds to 400 (*ibid.*, 425, 427–28); vigilance had to be commanded in order to protect the estate against poachers (*ibid.*, 455, 485, 486); an inquiry concerning the family genealogy had to be passed on to a cousin interested in such matters—as Washington was not (32 *ibid.*, 10–11, 26–33); roof and portico floor soon were to require attention (George Augustine Washington to the General, Apr. 15, 1792; 254 *Papers of G. W.*, 59, LC) and so endlessly through the winter.

[44] 31 *G. W.*, 384; Lear to Washington, Oct. 16, 1791; 252 *Papers of G. W.*, 44, LC. Certainly by the fall of 1791 Lear had advanced, if unofficially, from the status of trusted private secretary to that of responsible administrative assistant. See his letter to Washington, Oct. 2, 1791 (*ibid.*, 25–26), in which Lear describes a recent interview with the French Minister who had called during the President's absence from Philadelphia. Lear's vast usefulness in personal matters, however, was suffering no diminution: On October 6 he reported that "the painting, whitewashing and cleaning" of the President's house "seems to have made a vast alteration in it" (*ibid.*, 33).

[45] 31 *G. W.*, 387, 390.　　[46] *Ibid.*, 388–89, 390.　　[47] *Baker.*, 230.
[48] 31 *G. W.*, 395.　　[49] *Ibid.*
[50] Hamilton to Knox, Oct. 17, 1791; *Knox Papers*, MHS.

father, "a Statesman will be able to judge what is the natural bias and inclination of the powers of government." Wolcott continued: "The struggle between States and the United States will now be perceived . . . The principles of dissension exist, but the principles are the merest trifles. Mr. H. [51] and Mr. J. seem much disposed to quarrel on the questions whether liberty can be maintained in a country which allows citizens to be distinguished by the additions, *Mr., Esquire* and *Deacon*; and whether Tom Paine or Edmund Burke are the greatest fools." [52]

A part only of this forecast was borne out. Washington's address on the 25th [53] had a cheerful opening [54] and prime emphasis on operations against the western Indians, but it contained no important suggestion on new legislation other than that the law imposing an excise on spirits be revised where valid objection was disclosed. Most of the later paragraphs dealt with recommendations previously made and not yet enacted—provision for uniform militia, improvement of the post office and post roads, execution of the plans for a mint, establishment of standard weights and measures, and a new system for the sale of vacant land ceded the government. [55] Congress's response was one of unenthusiastic approval [56] that slowly shaped itself into a few bills that were considered in leisured debate. Gradually, after that, there developed a new vigor of dispute and a closer approach to rival philosophies, advocated by those who believed in strengthening the pinions and by those who would clip the wings of government, but the earlier antagonisms of large States and small, eastern interests and southern, prevailed on occasion over the abstract question of the scope of Federal power.

While Washington permitted himself to be a partisan in no instance where he did not feel that national interest required him to take sides, he had, of course, to remain in Philadelphia throughout a session that proved inordinately long and, as always, he had to be vigilant in seeing that no careless step carried him over the line he drew between his constitutional rights and those of the legislative branch of government. [57]

[51] The published text reads "A."

[52] Letter of Oct. 14, 1791; 1 *Gibbs, Wolcott Papers*, 68–69.

[53] Text, 31 *G. W.*, 396–404; 1 *JS*, 324–27; 1 *JHR.*, 435 ff.

[54] Paine Wingate was particularly pleased that no additional revenue was asked. 2 *Paine Wingate*, 390.

[55] 31 *G. W.*, 402–04.

[56] See the addresses of the two Houses, Washington's answers, and the Senate's appointment of a committee to consider the scope of legislation; 1 *JS*, 331, 332, 335; 1 *JHR.*, 440, 442.

[57] Some interesting examples will be found in 31 *G. W.*, 411, 417 n, 477. For early emergence of the perennial question of the right of Congress to call for executive papers, see 1

This cautious policy was time-consuming, and so was the President's continuing official responsibility for the District of Columbia, though he used the services of Secretary Jefferson as far as practicable,[58] and insisted, furthermore, that all subordinate officials and employees be under the District Commissioners and report through them.[59] When the commissioners' principal surveyor, Maj. Pierre Charles L'Enfant, quarreled with the three men to whom he was responsible, and tore down a house without having it declared an encroachment, Washington tried several devices to retain for the enterprise the services of the brilliant designer,[60] but came with regret to the conclusion that L'Enfant could not work in harness. Dismissal of the engineer was a distressing task deferred as long as any hope of adjustment remained but then ordered firmly and in the conviction that no alternative existed,[61] even though it was expected that L'Enfant would play into the hands of those who were seeking to retain Philadelphia as the capital.[62]

Another continuing labor was presented the General personally by the ominous decline in the health of George Augustine Washington. "The Major," as his uncle usually called him, had gained but little, and that little temporarily, by a stay at Berkeley Springs, Virginia.[63] Willing though he was, he could not visit the Mount Vernon farms daily and keep all the records the absent owner required. Fortunately, Anthony Whiting, who had come to Mount Vernon as manager in the spring of 1790,[64] seemed to possess both intelligence and industry and he took over an increasing share of the work on the estate. Before many months, the busy gentleman in the Morris House on Market

---

*Jefferson*, 303–05; 32 *G. W.*, 15. An amusing exchange regarding Washington's refusal to pass judgment on a dispute of two officials appears in Peter Jaquett to Washington, and Lear to Jaquett. See Nat. Arc., RG 59. State Dept.: *Misc. Lets.*, 1791, f. 84–85. For Washington's belief that his private position could not be divorced from his public, see 31 *G. W.*, 454.

[58] 8 *Jefferson*, 251–52, 256, 257, 307–10, 322–24; 31 *G. W.*, 451–52, 458, 479, 480, 495, 497–99; Jefferson to Washington, Mch. 28, 1792; Nat. Arc. RG 59. State Dept.: *Misc. Lets.*, f. 205.

[59] 31 *G. W.*, 419–23; 32 *ibid.*, 3, 18–19.

[60] 31 *ibid.*, 429 ff, 432–33, 442–44, 451–52. The General did his utmost to analyze the peculiarities of L'Enfant, whose conduct puzzled him (*ibid.*, 445–46, 462–63).

[61] David Stuart to Washington, Feb. 26, 1792, 253 *Papers of G. W.*, 109, LC; 31 *G. W.*, 476, 482–83, 486, 487, 488–89; 19 *Jefferson*, 87–88.

[62] 31 *G. W.*, 495, 503–08. L'Enfant's dismissal was written by Jefferson, Feb. 27, 1792; 19 *Jefferson*, 87–88. Washington's review of the circumstances, in a letter of Feb. 28, 1792, to the engineer, is in 31 *G. W.*, 488–89. The plan for the city was submitted to Congress Dec. 13, 1791. See 1 *JS*, 355; 1 *JHR.*, 472; 31 *G. W.*, 444.

[63] *Ibid.*, 336, 354, 363, 377–78; 32 *ibid.*, 55. He returned home before Sept. 15, 1791, 31 *ibid.*, 377.

[64] *Ibid.*, 36, 37 n.

Street was addressing to Whiting a part, at least, of such instructions as previously were sent George Augustine.[65] The General's practice in writing these letters was economical of time because when he sat down at his desk he first would read over the last report from his manager and on a scrap of paper he would make memoranda of all the items he had to answer. As he wrote his reply he would check off one note after another till he had covered the whole, but even this method occupied his swift-running pen for many hours. It was difficult, when public business pressed, to find the time for these detailed directions about private business. Often it was interrupted, but, somehow, the long communications were dispatched with regularity and frequency, no matter how crowded the weeks might be.[66]

During the autumn, because of Congress, L'Enfant and Mount Vernon, Washington had a heavy load but he carried it without getting— to use his own words—"on a stretch." Some of the papers laid on the President's desk were interesting and some were encouraging. October brought a development in relations with England: a British Minister arrived in Philadelphia to take up his residence there, George Hammond, former Chargé in Vienna, Copenhagen and Madrid [67]—the first diplomatic agent to be accredited formally to America. As soon as practicable, Washington selected Thomas Pinckney, of South Carolina, for the corresponding post at the Court of St. James's,[68] but the President did not persuade himself that an exchange of Ministers forecast an early settlement. The extent of Hammond's powers was not known and was not assumed to be broad.[69]

For the consideration of whatever Hammond might propose, and for the scrutiny of any questions that might require common counsel,

[65] Some qualification may be necessary here, because most of Washington's correspondence on farm affairs is missing for the period from October, 1791, to July, 1792. A surviving letter of Jan. 16, 1792 to Whiting (*ibid.*, 460–61) reads as if Washington were writing him regularly, but the extant long series of informative directions does not begin until the following summer.
[66] Washington described this method of communication in his letter of May 19, 1793, to Whiting, 32 *ibid.*, 466, 467.
[67] He is sketched in *DNB*. For prediction that a Minister would be sent, see Lear to Washington, June 19, 1791 (251 *Papers of G. W.*, 15, LC; 31 *G. W.*, 311). See, also, the unsigned and undated note (14 *Hamilton Papers*, 1903) designating Gen. John Maunsell as Britain's unofficial observer until the arrival of a diplomatic agent. Hammond's calls on Jefferson are noted, Oct. 26, 1791, in 8 *Jefferson*, 249. His presentation of his credentials to Washington, Nov. 11, 1791, is described in *Baker*, 231.
[68] 8 *Jefferson*, 252; 31 *G. W.*, 413, 460. Pinckney to Washington, Nov. 29, 1791, Nat. Arc. State Dept.: *Dipl. Desp.*, Gt. Br., v. 3.
[69] Cf. Jefferson's memorandum of Nov. 26, 1791, Nat. Arc. RG 59. State Dept.: *Misc. Lets.*, f. 85; 19 *Jefferson*, 83; Maunsell to Knox, Feb. 9, 1792; *Knox Papers*, MHS.

Washington now had his advisers better organized. He still conferred with Hamilton individually about Jefferson's business or vice versa, and he did not hesitate to seek the judgment of either on the work of the Attorney General or of the Secretary of War.[70] Madison was consulted more frequently than anyone else on the drafting of public papers;[71] but by the autumn of 1791 the President began to bring Jefferson, Hamilton, Knox and Randolph together for the joint consideration of policy.[72] He did not style these men his cabinet, or speak of their presence in his office as a "cabinet meeting." Formality was not stressed; the reality was, he saved time and gained information by having his "heads of departments," as he termed them, present their opinions and air their differences vis-a-vis.

No question—not even the reapportionment of representation or the order of succession to the Presidency or any other subject of debate in Congress—so frequently was discussed at these conferences as was that of the country's relations with the Indians. Almost every informed public servant in the United States believed a settlement with Britain would put an end to most of the murderous raids along the Ohio and its tributaries. Peace with the Creeks would be easy when Spain no longer supplied them with powder and arms. Meantime, Washington continued to work, chiefly through Secretary Knox, for amity with well-disposed tribes and for victory over the hostile coalition against which Arthur St. Clair had been dispatched with regulars and militia.[73] In longer policy there was no change. Jefferson held to his view that the United States must give the Indians a "thorough drubbing" and afterwards must "take up the plan of liberal and repeated presents to them," a scheme he believed "much the cheapest in the end" and one that "would save all the blood which is now spilled."[74] Washington had neither love of the savages nor faith in them, but he maintained, as long he had, that when the aggressors in the Ohio Valley had been destroyed, the United States should make a firm, inclusive peace and should continue the effort to prevent encroachment on lands acknowledged to be the Indians' domain.

[70] For typical instances, see 31 *G. W.*, 428, 448, 461, 484; 1 *Jefferson*, 297; 8 *ibid.*, 319–20.
[71] 31 *G. W.*, 395–96, 479, 481; 32 *ibid.*, 35.
[72] 31 *ibid.*, 428, 453. The earliest meeting for which a call appears in *G. W.* was that of Nov. 25, 1791.
[73] For the submission, Oct. 26, 1791, of a new treaty with the Cherokees, see *ASP.*, 1 *Ind. Aff.*, 123, and for confirmation, see 1 *EJS.*, 88–89. Reports of successful small operations by Gen. Charles Scott and Gen. James Wilkinson are in *ASP.*, 1 *Ind. Aff.*, 129 ff; 1 *JHR.*, 441.
[74] 8 *Jefferson*, 179.

On the 8th of December, 1791, unofficial but plausible reports were received in Philadelphia of a costly defeat sustained by St. Clair, November 4, within fifteen miles of the Miami town where he was to establish a post. It was said, with a shudder, that his casualties reached no less than 600 and that Gen. Richard Butler and other senior officers were among the slain.[75] Washington undoubtedly heard this dark news. The next day, December 9, Philadelphia newspapers had another report that had come from Kentucky, by way of Richmond, Virginia.[76] That evening, Washington received dispatches from St. Clair that included one,[77] the opening words of which were enough to make Washington set his jaw: "Yesterday afternoon, the remains of the army under my command got back to this place, and I now have the painful task to give you an account of as warm and as unfortunate an action as almost any that has been fought, in which every corps was engaged and worsted, except the First Regiment. That had been detached . . ."[78] Washington did not have time to do more than give a hasty reading to the document, because he was entertaining guests; and as Mrs. Washington was holding her usual Friday reception that evening, he had to conceal his feelings until he had bowed to the last departing caller. Then he broke out in wrath and disappointment: St. Clair had been warned against surprise, yet he had permitted the Indians to gain overpowering advantage almost before the alarm could be sounded! It was infamous, but . . . Washington soon mastered himself and remarked that he had not scrutinized all that the defeated General had to say. A full statement must be awaited; justice must be done the unfortunate commander.[79]

[75] Timothy Pickering to his wife, Dec. 8, 1791, 3 *Pickering*, 22. The first news apparently was conveyed in a letter from Shippensburg, Penn., Dec. 5, 1791. See *Dunlap's American Daily Advertiser*, Dec. 9, 1791, p. 2.

[76] *Ibid.*; more details were printed on the 10th; *ibid.*, Dec. 10, 1791, p. 2.

[77] This was dated November 9, from Fort Washington.

[78] *ASP.*, 1 *Ind. Aff.*, 137; also in 2 *St. Clair Papers*, 262–67.

[79] This is believed to be all of the demonstrable fact that underlies the traditional story of the arrival at night of St. Clair's travel-worn messenger who refused to place his dispatches in any other hands than those of Washington. This story first was published, so far as is known, in 1827 by George Washington Parke Custis (see *G. W. P. Custis*, p. 406 n), and in a slightly different version by Richard Rush (*Washington in Domestic Life*, 65–69) in 1857, on the basis of what Rush remembered Tobias Lear to have related to him about 1816. These accounts are highly dramatic and detailed, even to the alleged direct quotation of Washington's words. Manifest errors are numerous: if the dispatches reached Washington on the day of his wife's reception, that would have been Friday, and as they were forwarded to Congress on the 12th, that particular Friday must have been December 9. By that date, the essentials were known to Washington from the newspapers. There could have been no sudden shock or surprise. Further, the dispatches were addressed to Knox, not to Washington, and must have come to the President

When all the facts had been sifted, Washington found that this, in substance, was what had happened: On the afternoon of November 3, St. Clair had encamped his army on commanding ground, behind a creek,[80] and in two lines on a front of 350 yards. His artillery was in the centre of his force which had been reduced by detachment and desertion to 1400 men. The militia had been placed in advance of the stream, from which position numerous Indians were flushed during the afternoon. Half an hour before sunrise on the 4th, as the troops protected by the creek were leaving the parade, firing opened from the ground occupied by the militia. In a few minutes, these untrained, frightened soldiers splashed back across the stream and created general disorder and confusion before the ranks could be formed. The field pieces were manned; the regulars stood firm; hostile fire enveloped the flanks; soon the Americans were almost surrounded. Moreover, they were helpless. The Indians, as of old, fired from the ground or from behind trees and seldom presented a target. Around the guns, which were served persistently, the dead piled up until almost every man who knew how to load and fire a cannon was lifeless or bleeding. Counter attacks were ordered and were bravely made but were of no avail: the moment the troops drew back to their lines, the savages sprang up, followed swiftly, dropped to the ground and renewed the deadly fire. Gradually the American force was beaten into a disordered mass, melted moment by moment. After about three hours of this, St. Clair realized that all his men, literally all, would be shot down and scalped unless he could organize a retreat. Himself ill and unable to get on a horse or to dismount without assistance, he could do little to rally his beaten troops and to form them for an orderly, stubborn withdrawal. When at length a final charge cleared the road temporarily, the militia took off to the rear, and the other troops followed, while one battalion tried

from the Secretary, not from St. Clair's messenger. Still again, Washington is quoted as saying that he warned St. Clair "here, on this very spot," when, in reality, Washington had not seen St. Clair after early September, 1790, when the conference, if held, was in New York. Finally, it has been supposed (1 St. Clair Papers, 190) that the messenger was Lieut. Ebenezer Denny, though it is apparent from Denny's own Journal (p. 379) that he did not reach Philadelphia until a week after Washington had transmitted St. Clair's dispatches to Congress. While these known circumstances invalidate much of the traditional story, it is probable that the official reports reached Washington on the 9th, through Knox, and that they disappointed and angered the President. St. Clair's later dispatch of November 17, brought by Lieutenant Denny, apparently has been lost.

[80] He thought this to have been the St. Mary's; but it was an upper stretch of the Wabash. The location is the present-day Fort Recovery, Mercer County, Ohio, almost on the Indiana line and about eighty-five miles North-by-West from Cincinnati.

to hold off the yelling, blood-mad Indians. "It was," St. Clair confessed, "in fact, a flight." Although the redmen ceased pursuit after following for something more than four miles, and the detached First Regiment came up, the defeated survivors staggered on to Fort Jefferson, about twenty-nine miles from the scene of the action. They rested there only about five hours and then started for Fort Washington. An all-night march brought the hungry men on the 5th to a supply of flour. After that, panic died away, and the unwounded survivors, who numbered not more than 580 men, were restored to the form, if not to the protective reality, of discipline.[81]

Washington, on reading St. Clair's report, could not have overlooked a postscript in which the ill-faring commander remarked that "some very material intelligence" had been communicated by Captain Slough to General Butler during the night before the action but was not forwarded to St. Clair or known to him for days.[82] It developed that during the night of November 3-4, Slough had made a reconnaissance which showed many Indians at hand. Butler received the report of this but had put aside a proposal of Slough's to convey this ominous information to St. Clair. The captain needed rest, Butler said; he would himself inform the commander—which he failed to do.[83] A man less self-mastered than Washington might have winced at that, because he had appointed Butler to command in the face of protests.[84]

Good soldier or poor, vigilant or forgetful, Butler was dead and, with him, thirty-eight other officers. Twenty-one who held commissions were wounded. Total casualties exceeded 900. All the cannon with

[81] St. Clair's candid and manly report, *ASP.*, 1 *Ind. Aff.*, 137-38, is supplemented by a variety of other contemporary sources, notably Col. William Darke to Washington, Nov. 9, 1791 (*Knox Papers*, MHS), the *Diary of Col. Winthrop Sargent*, and the *Military Journal of Ebenezer Denny*, which is separately printed and is in 2 *St. Clair Papers*, 251-62. The two Congressional reports on the causes of the failure of the expedition are not particularly informative on any matters other than those of supply. See *ASP.*, 1 *Mil. Aff.*, 36-39, 41-44. Chaplain John Hurt's observations are in a personal letter of Jan. 4, 1792, to Washington, Nat. Arc. RG 59. State Dept.: *Misc. Lets.*, 7-10. The Chaplain thought that the horses for the cavalry detachment had been misused shamefully, that some of the officers had been disgracefully at odds, and that muskets had been defective. Most of the documents tell the same tale concerning the battle itself; the conflict of testimony on this score is negligible. An interesting recent secondary account of the campaign is J. A. Johnston's "The War Did Not End at Yorktown," 60 *V*, 444-57.
[82] *ASP.*, 1 *Ind. Aff.*, 138. The name of Capt. Jacob Slough is here printed as Hough, but is correctly given in the text of St. Clair's report in 2 *St. Clair Papers*, 262-67.
[83] This became a question of angry dispute by Butler's family. Cf. 2 *St. Clair Papers*, 267, but Denny's statement, *ibid.*, 258-59, and St. Clair's own remarks, *ibid.*, 278, leave no room for doubt that the facts were as stated. Whether St. Clair could have organized a successful defence, if notified, is another matter. He knew already that the enemy was close at hand.
[84] 31 *G. W.*, 334-35.

the main force had been lost. Equipment of every sort had been left on the field. The "most disgraceful part of the business," said St. Clair, "is that the greatest part of the men threw away their arms and accoutrements, even after the pursuit . . . had ceased." He added: "I found the road strewed with them for many miles . . ." [85] Nothing so ghastly, so humiliating, to the white man, had been experienced in Indian warfare since that dreadful 9th of July, 1755,[86] when Braddock's bewildered redcoats had been the target of unseen marksmen on the Monongahela.

Washington, after the first wrathful outburst, took this defeat in the spirit he had shown when disasters had come to his arms in days far darker. Congress had adjourned on Friday, December 9, probably before the arrival of St. Clair's reports. When members reassembled Monday, the 12th, the President sent them a message that might have been dated in the sombre 'seventies, over the signature, "George Washington, General." It was brief: "Gentlemen of the Senate and of the House of Representatives: It is with great concern that I communicate to you the information received from Major General St. Clair, of the misfortune which has befallen the troops under his command. Although the national loss is considerable, according to the scale of the event, yet it may be repaired without great difficulty, excepting as to the brave men who have fallen on the occasion, and who are a subject of public as well as private regret. A further communication will shortly be made of all such matters as shall be necessary to enable the Legislature to judge of the future measures which it may be proper to pursue." [87] The copies of St. Clair's reports, covered by this message, were sent precisely as received, and when published, they were complete. Not even the ugliest line on the flight of the beaten troops was eliminated.[88] Washington had learned long previously the protective value of candor in dealing with the American people and he knew that one reason for their trust in him was their belief he would tell them the whole truth. Without further lament, he directed Knox to assemble all papers that showed what had and had not been done to win the support of friendly Indians, to placate the hostile, and to punish the aggressors. Most particularly did Washington see to it that the succession of long reports sent Congress should stress the magnitude and the

85 *ASP.*, 1 *Ind. Aff.*, 138.     86 See Vol. II, p. 64 ff.
87 1 *JHR.*, 471; 1 *JS*, 355; 31 *G. W.*, 442.     88 *Ibid.*, 444.

cost of what should be undertaken if the frontiers were to be secure.[89] Inquiry by Congress was not avoided,[90] nor was public criticism silenced by this forthright action. Washington himself was not blamed; Knox escaped with less abuse than he might have expected; there was sympathy, rather than obloquy, for St. Clair. Chiefly, the fault was laid at the doors of army contractors. The most vigorous discussion had to do impersonally with methods of Indian warfare and, somewhat surprisingly, with the ethics of occupying Indian territory. No sharp political issue developed from this debate.[91] Until that time, it has to be ad-

[89] For Jefferson's part in preparing the first papers, see his memorandum, dated Dec. 16, 1791, Nat. Arc. RG 59. State Dept.: *Misc. Lets.*, f. 87–88. His view that the defeat imposed the "necessity of stronger preparations than were before thought requisite" is set forth in 8 *Jefferson*, 284. As the first plan submitted by Knox did not find favor (31 *G. W.*, 450–51), it was revised and sent to Congress, Jan. 11, 1792 (*ibid.*, 456, 1 *JS*, 370; 2 *Paine Wingate*, 400). The text, which is in *ASP.*, 1 *Ind. Aff.*, 139 ff, presents a somewhat detailed account of all negotiations with the Northwestern Indians in 1791. Supplemented by 2 *St. Clair Papers*, 164 ff, it is adequate except, of course, for information which never can be recovered, concerning the Indians' plans and councils. Comment on the mistakes of the campaign and on the policy to be pursued in settling accounts with the savages will be found in John Armstrong to Washington, Dec. 23, 1791, 10 *Sparks*, 223 n; John Hurt to Washington, Jan. 4, 1792, Nat. Arc. RG 59. State Dept.: *Misc. Lets.*, 7–10—with particular reference to the employment of cavalry; Fisher Ames to Thomas Dwight, Jan. 13, 1792, 1 *Fisher Ames*, 109; John Brown to Harry Innes, Jan. 20, 1792, 19 *Innes Papers*, LC; Oliver Wolcott to his father, Feb. 14, 1792; Oliver Wolcott, Sr., to his son, Feb. 19, 1792, 1 *Gibbs, Wolcott Papers*, 73, 74; Otho Williams to Alexander Hamilton, Mch. 5, 1792, 15 *Hamilton Papers*, 2069–73; Timothy Pickering to Washington, Mch. 21, 1792, *ibid.*, 2075–76. Henry Knox's papers on this unhappy period are not illuminating. The Secretary had nothing better than this to say in his letter of Jan. 6, 1792, to Winthrop Sargent: "I pass over the event which gives you and all of us so much pain. It is in vain to regret the past. We must endeavor to remedy the evil in future . . . Some papers and plans will be laid immediately before Congress for their consideration and decision, which I hope will be such as shall be entirely adequate to the occasion" (*Knox Papers*, MHS). A further report by Knox on the 26th of January, 1792 (3 *Annals*, 1046 ff), at the instance of Washington (31 *G. W.*, 459), summarized the measures taken to establish peace with the Indians. By request, both Hamilton and Jefferson, on Jan. 25, 1792, submitted to the President what they regarded as suitable introductions to this paper (Nat. Arc. RG 59. State Dept.: *Misc. Lets.*, f. 39, 40).

[90] See *infra*, p. 341, n. 94.

[91] Knox to Winthrop Sargent, Apr. 11[?], 1792: "Captain Freeman will tell of the uproar the failure of the late expedition has excited" (*Knox Papers*, MHS); Henry Merchant to Benjamin Bourne, Dec. 24, 1791: "It looks as though . . . we must be involved in a long, bloody and very expensive Indian war" (*Peck Papers*, RIHS); Hubbard Taylor to James Madison, Jan. 3, 1792: "Our existence [in Kentucky] almost depends [on a vigorous war] in a two-fold point of view, first, as to defence, secondly, as to the circulating money amongst us, which is much less than would have been had the main army come down the last fall . . ." (14 *Madison Papers*, 107, LC). Correspondents of Bache's *General Advertiser* (Philadelphia) promptly raised the question of American right to invade Indian lands, especially when this involved heavy expense (December 14, p. 3; Dec. 29, 1791, p. 3). This newspaper reprinted, also, the "Braddock" letters in its issues of Jan. 4 and 10, 1792, p. 2 and 3. A sharper critic was "Braddock" in the *Independent Chronicle* (Boston), Dec. 29, 1791, p. 2. Freneau did not himself attack editorially the management of the campaign but he gave space to the reprint of comment from other papers, whether this comment was friendly or hostile. To cite a few examples, see *National Gazette* (Philadelphia), January 9, p. 2, 3; January 12, p. 2, 3; January 23, p. 3, 4; January 26, p. 3; February 2, p. 1 and Feb. 6, 1792, p. 3. *Dunlap's American Daily Adver-*

mitted, comment bore out abundantly the statement of Timothy Pickering, "There is much murmering [sic] on account of the manner in which the western war has been planned and conducted." [92] In the minds of those who were not party to the press war, feeling was moderated gradually by the successful outcome of negotiations with the Senecas and the Cherokees [93] and by the resignation of St. Clair as Major General.[94] A sharpened zeal was manifested, also, for peace with the Indians.[95] Such dealings would be enforceable by an adequate army,[96] the command of which stirred the ambition of soldiers and the partisanship of politicians.[97] Candidates and their friends hoped and hinted, assailed rivals and swore, after the manner of revolutionary days, that their "honor" would not permit them to serve under men

---

*tiser* (Philadelphia) likewise printed a number of critical letters, along with one or two in which the administration was defended. See issues of January 3, p. 2; January 4, p. 2; January 6, p. 2—a vigorous attack on Knox—January 10, p. 2; January 17, p. 2, and Jan. 27, 1792, p. 2. Fenno's defence included his own editorial articles and reprints from other papers. See *Gazette of the United States* (Philadelphia), January 4, p. 3; January 11, p. 1 and 3; February 1, p. 3; February 4, p. 3; February 8, p. 3 and Feb. 11, 1792, p. 3. The last of these was one of the most effective of Fenno's articles and apparently had influence in bringing the long newspaper discussion to an end.

[92] Letter of Jan. 7, 1792, to his wife; 3 *Pickering*, 23.

[93] 10 *Sparks*, 210 ff; Knox to Washington, Jan. 17, 1792, 253 *Papers of G. W.*, 52–53, LC; *ASP.*, 1 *Ind. Aff.*, 203 ff; 31 *G. W.*, 462, 481–82.

[94] He sought a court of inquiry, which Washington could not authorize because of the lack of officers who had the rank legally required for passing on the conduct of a Major General. See 32 *ibid.*, 13–14. St. Clair thereupon tendered his resignation; but when the House or Representatives proceeded to order an investigation of the disaster, after voting down a resolution to have Washington do so (1 *JHR.*, 551–52), St. Clair sought to retain his military status until the inquiry ended. Washington had to point out that one Major General only was allowed under the law and that an officer of that grade was required in the field. As St. Clair himself had mentioned this obstacle to his continuance in the army, he accepted the conclusion of the Commander-in-Chief without further argument. See 2 *St. Clair Papers*, 282–86; 31 *G. W.*, 494 and n; 32 *ibid.*, 12–13, 15–16. St. Clair's attitude in this exchange of letters was above criticism. After the committee of Congress pronounced him free of blame for the disaster (*ASP.*, 1 *Mil. Aff.*, 36 ff), Knox protested that the report was by indirection a censure of him and he asked a hearing. A second inquiry, undertaken the next year, with William B. Giles as chairman, confirmed the earlier findings (*ibid.*, 41 ff).

[95] 31 *G. W.*, 491; Knox to James Wilkinson, Feb. 11, Mch. 10, 1792, *Wilkinson Papers*, Chicago HS; Aaron Burr's observations, Mch. 13, 1792, Nat. Arc. RG 59. State Dept.: *Misc. Lets.*, f. 29.

[96] Three new Regiments, one of them including 320 dismounted light dragoons, were to be recruited for three-year enlistment; but the President was empowered to reduce the total number and was required to discharge all the new troops if peace with the Indians was concluded. See 1 *JHR.*, 499–501; 1 *JS*, 384 ff, 2 *Laws of U. S.*, ed. 1815, p. 256, signed Mch. 5, 1792; 2 *Paine Wingate*, 405, 406, 408; 3 *Annals*, 337 ff; 31 *G. W.*, 491 ff.

[97] An act of Mch. 28, 1792 (2 *Laws of U. S.*, ed. 1815, p. 263) authorized the President to appoint not more than four Brigadiers (cf. 32 *G. W.*, 8–9, 1 *JS*, 413, 415). Until this was a matter of law, Washington had felt that the less said about appointments, the simpler his task (31 *G. W.*, 463), but he went carefully over the list of men who seemed the best of those available (*ibid.*, 509 ff).

## RANDOLPH AND JEFFERSON, VIRGINIANS IN DISSENT

On December 14, 1790, the Secretary of the Treasury presented to Congress the most striking feature of a spectacular financial program which already had pleased many, alienated many and had awakened partisanship in every corner of the Union. Hamilton now asked for the establishment of a central, or "national" bank. Debate commenced in the Senate on January 11, 1791, and ended, affirmatively, nine days later; the House followed with approval, thirty-nine votes to twenty, on February 8. Passage had been easy, but a question of constitutionality was in the air—did Congress possess the power to charter a bank? Washington determined to settle this point before committing the bill to law by Presidential signature. The opinion of each of his principal advisers must be sought and studied. Most certainly the Secretary of War would join in advocacy, but what of Secretary of State Thomas Jefferson and Attorney General Edmund Randolph? In response to the President's specific solicitation, Randolph delivered a long, legal opinion in the negative. Jefferson's denial was more assertive—the bank bill stood clearly in excess of the Constitution and should go back to Congress unsigned.

By every qualification and for a myriad of reasons, the President had cause to rest large confidence in each of these men. Jefferson he had appreciated as patriot, statesman and diplomatist for almost twenty years; Randolph he had known as a boy, the scion of a famous Williamsburg family and a brilliant law student, then briefly as a military aide in 1775 and, more significantly, as an architect of the Constitution. Jefferson had authored the Declaration of Independence; Randolph had sponsored Madison's formula at the Federal Convention and, as Governor of Virginia in 1788, had exercised his influence for ratification despite reservations which prompted him to reject the Constitution in final form. After much negotiation, the President was gratified early in 1790 to procure for the Department of State the services of Jefferson, now 46 and admirably seasoned for this assignment by five years as envoy to France. Randolph, ten years younger but vastly experienced in public life and as competent a lawyer as Washington knew, accepted the Attorney Generalship at manifest personal sacrifice. The President valued the friendship and the association of these fellow-Virginians; he considered thoughtfully their objections, then gave Hamilton opportunity to answer. The logic and, even more, the urgency of the reply were devastating. Washington was convinced; he signed the bank bill on February 25, 1791.

(Thomas Jefferson: After the Original by C. W. Peale, Independence Hall, Philadelphia.)

(Edmund Randolph: From F. J. Fisher's copy, in the State Capitol at Richmond, of the original Gilbert Stuart.)

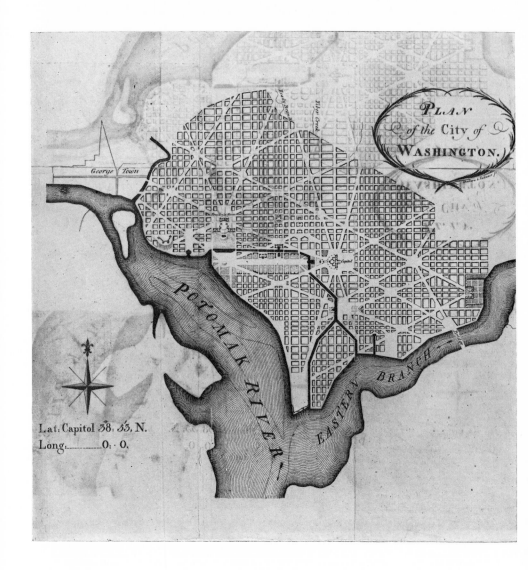

PLAN of the City of WASHINGTON.

George Town

POTOMAK RIVER

EASTERN BRANCH

Lat: Capitol 38: 53, N.
Long: 0 · 0.

# "A PLAN BOTH PROPER AND PROMISING"

In the summer of 1790, as Washington was convalescing from his second grave illness within a year, circumstances shaped themselves which soon were to yield the first great legislative "bargain" in American history. The Secretary of the Treasury was dogmatically determined to win Congressional acceptance of his funding proposal; the Secretary of State hoped to establish a permanent home for the Federal government at some point midway between New Hampshire and Georgia, perhaps on the banks of the accessible Potomac. Add to this the desire of a leading Senator to shift the seat of government, temporarily at least, from New York to Philadelphia, and every ingredient was at hand for production of political pudding. The funding measure became law in August, 1790—not, however, before Congress had passed a "residence bill" which provided for immediate transfer of governmental offices to Philadelphia and, further, selection of a "Federal" site near Georgetown, Maryland.

Had the complicity of Hamilton and Jefferson been generally known, the swell of criticism which came in the wake of these maneuvers might well have risen to imperil the good names of both Secretaries. It happened that Madison and even Washington were caught in small currents of journalistic abuse. The President had nothing to do with fashioning the "bargain," but a great deal to do with its fulfillment.

It was the Executive's task, under the act of July 16, 1790, to designate a specific location for erection of a "Federal City," to determine the acreage required and arrange for acquisition, then to direct the planning of streets and buildings—in a word, to supervise the entire project. By March, 1791, Washington had appointed three commissioners to oversee the detail of the work, and was himself studying Maj. Andrew Ellicott's preliminary survey of the Potomac region. Toward the end of that month, the President was at Georgetown for the first cautious negotiation with expectant landowners and, worse still, eager speculators. This delicate business satisfactorily concluded, authorization to lay out three to five thousand acres was given Maj. Pierre Charles L'Enfant, chief architect and engineer. Shortly, however, the talented Frenchman was displaying so arbitrary and unconciliatory a temperament that Washington regretfully had to order his dismissal. Before this day, happily, L'Enfant had submitted his masterful "Plan" of the future city, a simplified approximation of which, shown here, was etched for publication in the March, 1792, issue of the *Columbian Magazine*.

(From the Papers of George Washington, Library of Congress.)

who previously had been their subordinates.[98] The officers finally nominated were Anthony Wayne as Major General and Daniel Morgan, Marinus Willett, John Brooks and James Wilkinson as Brigadiers. When Morgan and Willett declined, Washington named in their stead Rufus Putnam and Otho Williams. All these were confirmed.[99] To strengthen still further the national defence, Congress passed the previously contested bill for uniform militia,[100] a useful measure that authorized the President to call out the militia to execute the laws, suppress insurrections and repel invasions.[101] All in all, then, St. Clair's defeat did not impair Washington's reputation and, indirectly, it gave the Federal government the means of making its will more effective in a day of danger.

At least one development of the winter likewise promised, in a favorite phrase of Washington's, to make the United States "more respectable." When one of the commissioners of the Catholic King had intimated to Jefferson that Spain was willing to discuss the free navigation of the Mississippi,[102] Washington nominated William Carmichael, Chargé at Madrid, and William Short, who held a similar post at Paris, to undertake negotiations which, he soon concluded, it would be possible to extend to commercial relations with Spain and perhaps even with those of her colonial possessions.[103] This proposal became snarled with a recommendation to send Gouverneur Morris to France with the rank of Minister, and William Short to The Hague with like status,

[98] James Wilkinson to Knox, Mch. 13, 1792, *Knox Papers*, MHS; Henry Lee to James Madison, Apr. 4, 1792, 15 *Madison Papers*, 30, LC; Anthony Wayne to Henry Knox, Apr. 1, 1792, *Knox Papers*, MHS; Jefferson to Washington, Apr. 4, 1792; Nat. Arc. RG 59. State Dept.: *Misc. Lets.*, f. 78; John Brown to Harry Innes, Apr. 13, 1792, 19 *Innes Papers*, LC; 32 *G. W.*, 13, 14–15, 24.

[99] 1 *EJS.*, 117, 121, 122, 123, 124. There was hesitation and a few days' delay in the case of Wilkinson, *ibid.*, 119, 120. For Wayne's declination, later reconsidered, see his letter of Apr. 1, 1792, to Knox. See also Knox to Otho H. Williams, May 3, and Williams to Knox, May 6, 1792. All three of these are in the *Knox Papers*, MHS.

[100] 1 *JHR.*, 457, 516, 523, 524, 525, 528, 573, 575, 585, 587, 591, 592, 606; 1 *JS*, 406, 407, 412, 413, 415, 417, 418, 434, 435, 443; 2 *Laws of U. S.*, ed. 1815, p. 293 ff, approved May 8, 1792.

[101] *Ibid.*, p. 284; approved May 2, 1792.

[102] Jefferson to Washington, Dec. 22, 1791; Nat. Arc. RG 59. State Dept.: *Misc. Lets.*, f. 96; see, also, *ASP.*, 1 *For. Rel.*, 130–31; Letter of Jan. 11, 1792.

[103] 31 *G. W.*, 456–57, 501–02; 32 *ibid.*, 12, 14; 4 *A. Hamilton*, 358, 359 ff; Jefferson to Washington, Mch. 7, Mch. 22, 1792, Nat. Arc. RG 59. State Dept.: *Misc. Lets.*, f. 13–17, 49–50; 8 *Jefferson*, 313–16, 326 ff; Gardoqui's proposals in 1 *EJS.*, 109–10. Various aspects of dealings with the Spanish colonies, including the vexatious question of fugitives in Florida, are presented in 4 *LTW.*, 385; in Charles Pinckney to unnamed correspondent, Jan. 8, 1792; Nat. Arc. RG. 59. State Dept.: *Misc. Lets.*, f. 12–13; and in Anthony Wayne to Washington, Mch. 13, 1792, *ibid.*, f. 30.

which some Senators thought pretentious and expensive. In the end all the nominations were confirmed.[104]

The contest over the rank of diplomatic agents and the differences of opinion concerning the policy to be employed in dealing with Spain were mild exchanges compared with the struggle in Congress over the reapportionment of representation to conform to the population shown by the census of 1790. Wisely the Constitution had imposed three requirements only: In the lower house of Congress, each State should have at least one Representative; the total number should "not exceed one for every 30,000"; in applying this basis, slave population was to have three-fifths only of the representation allotted a like number of white persons.[105] Now that reasonably accurate figures on the inhabitants of the States in 1790 were available,[106] changes from the provisional representation adopted in 1787 manifestly were required. The first Congress had sixty-five members of the House; Vermont added two more, and Kentucky, when admitted, would bring the total to sixty-nine. Those figures would be increased greatly by any apportionment Congress was apt to endorse, because the census gave a population of 3,893,000.[107] If the country's 697,000 slaves [108] were reckoned at three-fifths of their actual number, for purposes of representation, the

---

[104] 1 *EJS.*, 92, 93, 94–98, 99. Lear to Jefferson, Jan. 24, 1792; Nat. Arc. RG. 59. State Dept.: *Misc. Lets.*, f. 37. Morris was confirmed Jan. 12, 1792, Short on the 16th and the commissioners to Spain on the 24th. Thomas Pinckney, see *supra*, p. 334, was confirmed as Minister to Great Britain the same day the Senate voted in favor of Morris. The new Minister to France considered himself in debt to Alexander Hamilton for his appointment. See Morris to Hamilton, Mch. 21, 1792; 15 *Hamilton Papers*, 2074. In the general matter of appointments, Washington seemed to Edmund Randolph too rigid. The Attorney General wrote: ". . . the opinion of many respectable men has been strenuous in favor of relaxing that delicacy which is supposed to have restrained you in the distribution of offices with respect to those who are around you. I shall not dissemble my genuine sentiment that the propriety of departing from it seems to depend on the obvious fitness of the character nominated" (letter of July 13, 1791; 251 *Papers of G. W.*, 43, LC). For some of the numerous examples of the "delicacy" and care displayed by Washington, see 31 *G. W.*, 296, 313, 332, 359, 496–97. In an interesting note to Benjamin Lincoln, concerning two men under consideration as United States Marshal for Massachusetts, Washington said he did not wish to issue a commission on an uncertainty "because the refusal of commissions makes a bad impression on the public mind" (31 *G. W.*, 336). The only observed instance during the winter of 1791–92 when Washington permitted personal considerations to weigh with him was in the selection of Richard Harrison as Auditor of the Treasury Department. Harrison was the new son-in-law of Washington's long-time friend Dr. James Craik of Alexandria. See *ibid.*, 418–19.

[105] Art. 1, sec. 3.

[106] Washington, it will be remembered, had heard of shameful delinquencies of census-taking in South Carolina. See *supra*, p. 311.

[107] Exclusive of 35,000 in the Southwest Territory, which included the present State of Tennessee and some additional area. No enumeration was made of the Northwest Territory. See *A Century of Population Growth*, 47.

[108] *Ibid.*, 135.

net population entitled to have spokesmen in Congress would be approximately 3,614,000. With one representative for every 30,000 of these, the maximum membership permitted in the House would be 121. Many States would gain; none would lose representation. No sooner was this rough computation made than challenging questions were raised: By what authority was the rule of one Representative for every 30,000 laid down in terms of the total population of the United States? Should it not be applied State by State—every State divided by 30,000 and given the near number of Representatives, six, for instance, if it had 175,000 people, and five if it had, say, 160,000? The question provoked another: Was such an arrangement to be made without any regard to the remainder? Members of Congress went back to their school exercises in long division to determine on what basis their States would have the largest possible number of Representatives in the lower House and the lowest "remainder" of "unrepresented" population.[109] In nearly all their calculations, the mathematicians of every State found that gains for their own constituency involved concessions to other States they did not wish to strengthen.[110] First and last, House or Senate or both voted on representation at every rise of 1000 from 30,000 to 35,000,[111] but they could reach no agreement.[112] In February, 1792, some adroit members suggested a specific apportionment that was to stand until a new census was taken in 1797 for the benefit of the rapidly growing States.[113] This arrangement was acceptable to the House[114] and to the Senate, but the upper branch rejected the provision for another census in 1797.[115] In its final form, this legislation proposed a

---

[109] The fullest statement of the facts is in Jefferson's "Opinion on the Bill Apportioning Representation," dated Apr. 4, 1792, and prepared at the instance of the President (3 *Jefferson*, 201 ff). For the maneuvering over the bill, see Thomas Hartley to Jasper Yeates, Dec. 19, 1791: "At first I was for the ratio of one for 30,000 but really considering how this would operate compared with 33,000, I changed my sentiments" (*Yeates Papers*, PHS).

[110] Jefferson's table of the ratios from 30,000 to 33,000 for each State is in 3 *Jefferson*, 203.

[111] Benjamin Bourne to Governor Fenner, Nov. 20, 1791, *Peck Papers*, RIHS. Madison to Edmund Pendleton, Jan. 21, 1792; 14 *Madison Papers*, 114, LC.

[112] The entries in 1 *JHR*. and in 1 *JS* are hopelessly confusing unless it is understood that the first apportionment bill (No. 147) was presented in the House, November 18 and was passed Nov. 24, 1791 (1 *JHR*., 456, 459, 462, 470). The Senate received H.B. 147 on November 24 and passed it with amendments Dec. 8, 1791 (1 *JS*, 342, 345, 347, 349, 350, 357), but the measure was laid aside Dec. 20, 1791, when the majority in neither chamber would recede from its disagreement (1 *JHR*., 472, 475, 476, 478; 1 *JS*, 356, 358).

[113] Cf. Madison to Edmund Pendleton, Jan. 21, 1792; 14 *Madison Papers*, 114, LC.

[114] This was H.B. 163, presented February 6, debated at great length and passed Feb. 21, 1792 (1 *JHR*., 503, 507, 509, 510, 511, 516).

[115] 1 *JS*, 394, 396, 404, 405, 406, 408, 409. Passage on the 12th of March was by a vote of 14 to 13.

House of 120 members [116] and seemed to some opponents nothing more than a trick to enlarge the delegations from New England by bribing those from a sufficient number of other States to assure a majority for the measure. Richard Henry Lee gave this explanation: ". . . six Eastern States have one [member] apiece more than they ought, Jersey and Delaware the same, and North and South Carolina each one more than these States would have had, if the plain constitutional mode had been pursued of dividing the number of people in each *State Respectively* [117] by the agreed ratio of 30,000. But by a certain arithmetico-political sophistry an arrangement of six to two against the South has been made of the eight members gained by this sophism. They first divide the whole or aggregate number of people in the United States by 30,000, which produces 120 members instead of 122 which would have come from dividing the people in each State by 30,000, leaving large fractions with some States. After having obtained the 120 members, they apply different ratios in different States so as to give one member for that ratio which in each should approach nearest to one for 30,000 and leaving smaller fractions." [118]

When the bill was presented to Washington on March 26, 1792,[119] he had to ask himself, Shall this measure be signed or sent back to Congress? In the Federal Convention of 1787, he had been apprehensive that the basis of representation might be set too high, and he personally had prevailed on members to lower it to 30,000, in one of the last votes taken by that body, but of this he now said nothing. For about a week he kept his own counsel, and then, April 3rd,[120] when his time was running out, he called on Randolph for an opinion and directed the Attorney General to get the views of the heads of departments for his consideration the next day. Jefferson had seen or had himself prepared the tables that showed how the various ratios operated and he had no difficulty in putting his argument together in detail; [121] Hamilton was less ready but he was able to prepare a well-ordered if brief review.[122]

---

116 See Madison to Edmund Pendleton, Mch. 25, 1792; 15 *Madison Papers*, 22, LC.

117 The capitalization and italics are Lee's.

118 Letter of Mch. 25, 1792, to Henry Lee; 2 *Ballagh, Lee Letters*, 547. See also Madison to Edmund Pendleton, Mch. 25, 1792; 15 *Madison Papers*, 22, LC. Jefferson stated in his "Opinion" of Apr. 4, 1792, that the ratio was 30,026 in the States not allowed any representation in excess of their ratio, and 27,770 in the eight favored States. 3 *Jefferson*, 204.

119 1 *JHR.*, 551.   120 For the date, see 8 *A. Hamilton*, 96.

121 3 *Jefferson*, 201–11, with a bad typographical error in the last line of the opening paragraph. The figure for Massachusetts should be eight, not two.

122 8 *A. Hamilton*, 96–100.

Randolph, of course, had followed the bill through all its legislative stages and had formulated his views. Knox was disposed, as usual, to side with Hamilton. When the four opinions were summarized for Washington, he found his counsellors equally divided: Jefferson and Randolph held the bill unconstitutional, primarily because it did not apply the same fixed ratio to each of the States separately; Hamilton and Knox did not affirm the measure constitutional beyond all dispute, but they argued that as the interpretation put on it by the majority in Congress was tenable, the President would do well to accept the judgment of the legislative branch.[123]

This conflict of opinion disturbed and perhaps confused Washington, who had until the 6th of April to make up his mind. If he did not return the bill by the close of proceedings that Friday, it would become a law without his signature.[124] On the morning of the 5th [125] the President called on Jefferson before breakfast and, after a few preliminaries, described his dilemma: The principle applied in determining representation certainly was not the one the Delegates to the Philadelphia Convention had in mind, but it might be defensible. Besides, the final vote for and against the measure had been geographical: if he disapproved the bill, it might be thought that he was taking sides with a Southern party. Jefferson admitted this was an embarrassment but, he said, he did not think it justified action that would be fundamentally wrong. If the measure were approved, there would be a scramble over the "fractional members" in every future apportionment. Washington saw this, of course, at the same time that he sensed the full dangers of sectionalism. He even confessed, in answer to Jefferson, a fear that "there would be a separation of the Union, that the public mind seemed dissatisfied." Whereupon he left the Secretary's quarters, went home, and sent a messenger for the Attorney General. On arrival, Randolph was instructed by the President to find Madison and to go with the Congressman to the Secretary of State. The three were to confer and if they united in advising that he should disapprove the bill, they were to draw up a statement for him to send to Congress. Randolph obeyed instructions promptly and returned ere long with the draft of a brief message in which two reasons were set down for not favoring the

---

[123] Undated summary in the autograph of Tobias Lear; 254 *Papers of G. W.*, 84, LC.
[124] Art. 1, Sec. 7, par. 2; cf. 1 *Jefferson*, 307.
[125] Jefferson, as *infra*, mistakenly gave the date as the 6th.

bill.[126] In these arguments, said Randolph, the three men agreed. Washington listened and did not appear completely convinced. As Randolph prepared to leave, the President walked with him to the door.

"And you say you approve of this yourself?"

"Yes, sir," Randolph answered, "I do upon my honor."

This reaffirmed judgment of his legal adviser, buttressed by the opinion of Jefferson and Madison, was decisive. In a few minutes, the proposed message was copied and dispatched to the House, the first "negative" of any legislation passed by Congress.[127] The paper was received with protests, some of them angry, by certain of Washington's Northern supporters in Congress,[128] while most Southern members, Jefferson's followers in particular, expressed satisfaction.[129] Resulting action of Congress vindicated Washington's veto. A motion to pass the bill in spite of him failed in the lower chamber;[130] a revised bill that provided a House of 103 members on a basis of 33,000 was passed after discussion on two days only.[131] The Senate concurred the day this bill was laid before it;[132] Washington consequently had the satisfaction on the 14th of signing a measure[133] which increased House membership by thirty-six.[134] The representation of all the States, Delaware and

[126] These were: "First: The Constitution has prescribed that Representatives shall be apportioned among the several States, according to their respective Numbers: and there is no one proportion or division which, applied to the respective numbers of the States, will yield the number and allotment of Representatives proposed by the bill. Second. The Constitution has also provided that the number of Representatives shall not exceed one for every thirty thousand: which restriction is, by the context, and by fair and obvious construction, to be applied to the separate and respective numbers of the States: and the bill has alloted to eight of the States more than one for thirty thousand." (Message of Apr. 5, 1792, verbatim including the misspelling of a word; 32 G. W., 16–17. Under this same date, presumably before Washington sent for him, Randolph wrote the President of a chance meeting on the street with Justice James Wilson who, in answer to an observation on the challenged constitutionality of the apportionment bill, had remarked that the measure never would come before him as a judge. "Therefore," Wilson went on, "I will say that Congress appear to have forgotten the source from which representation flows." 254 Papers of G. W., 44, LC.)

[127] 1 Jefferson, 307–08. This is from the "Anas" but it is dated Apr. 9, 1792, and therefore seems in every way a bit of contemporary evidence, not a reminiscence of Jefferson's old age.    [128] Ibid.

[129] 2 Ballagh, Lee Letters, 550; National Gaz., May 10, 1792, p. 3.

[130] 1 JHR., 563. The vote was: for passage over the veto, twenty-eight; against, thirty-three. This is given wrongly in 3 Annals, 541, as twenty-three to thirty-three but the roll-call there is correct. Notification of the Senate that the House had not given the required two-thirds vote is in 1 JS, 422.

[131] This was H.B. 179. See 1 JHR., 569, 570–71, 573, 577, 579; 3 Annals, 542–48. The one extensive speech, arguing for maximum representation, was delivered just before the final vote, April 9, by William B. Giles.

[132] Apr. 10, 1792; 1 JS, 423. Cf. ibid., 424, 425, 426.

[133] 2 Laws of U. S., ed. 1815, p. 272–73.

[134] With the Vermont members already seated, the appearance of the two Kentucky Representatives in November, 1792, raised the total roster of the House to sixty-nine before the reapportionment became effective.

Georgia excepted,[135] was to be raised by numbers that ranged from one [136] to nine.[137] Twenty-nine of the thirty-six were to come from five States—Massachusetts (six), New York (four), Pennsylvania (five), Virginia (nine), and North Carolina (five). Twenty-one, net, were to speak for States North of the Potomac. Washington himself scarcely could have asked for a more equitable arrangement.

In this long contest, it had seemed natural, unhappily, that South should be arrayed against East, and that Jefferson's opinion had been the reverse of Hamilton's. This was becoming the daily order of politics. In November, 1791, Fisher Ames wrote that "tranquility has smoothed the surface" but that "faction glows within like a coalpit"; [138] before the end of January, 1792, he was saying, "I do not believe that the hatred of the Jacobites towards the House of Hanover was ever more deadly than that which is borne by many of the partisans of State power towards the government of the United States." [139] The feeling on the other side was voiced in its mildest, most polite form by Madison when he asked who were the "real friends" of the Union, and answered "Not those, in a word, who would force on the people the melancholy duty of choosing between the loss of Union, and the loss of what the Union was meant to secure." [140]

Both sides suffered from certain disadvantages. Jefferson had been embarrassed by an unintended endorsement of a proposed American edition of Thomas Paine's "Rights of Man" published in Fenno's *Gazette of the United States*.[141] He made no concealment of his admiration of the pamphlet,[142] but he was concerned lest he should be regarded as going out of his way to criticize publicly a series of articles known to have been written by Vice President Adams.[143] In addition, Jefferson was acquiring as much ill will politically as he was displaying towards Hamilton. Progress in government, said Oliver Wolcott,

---

[135] Delaware was left with one member; Georgia had hers reduced from three to two.

[136] New Hampshire, Rhode Island, New Jersey and South Carolina.

[137] Virginia was raised from ten to nineteen.

[138] Letter of Nov. 30, 1791; 1 *Fisher Ames*, 105.

[139] Letter of Jan. 23, 1792, *ibid.*, 110.

[140] *National Gaz.*, Apr. 2, 1792, p. 2, reprinted in 6 *Hunt's Madison*, 104.

[141] See 8 *Jefferson*, 193–95, 212 ff, 242–44; 19 *ibid.*, 77; Lear to Washington, May 8, 1791, 250 *Papers of G. W.*, 73–74, LC, partially printed in 10 *Sparks*, 160–61 n.

[142] For Washington's own reference to the "rights of man," in unmistakable echo of the political philosopher of the Revolution, see *supra*, p. 328.

[143] These were "Discourses on Davila," published in Fenno's *Gazette of the United States*; 8 *Jefferson*, 193–95, 212 ff, 242–44; 19 *ibid.*, 77; Lear to Washington, May 8, 1791, 250 *Papers of G. W.*, 73, LC, partially printed in 10 *Sparks*, 160–61 n.

would be more rapid if the administration were more united. "Mr. J[efferson]," he wrote, "appears to have shown rather too much of a disposition to cultivate vulgar prejudices; accordingly he will become popular in ale houses, and will do much mischief to his country by exciting apprehensions that the government will operate unfavorably." [144] Jefferson lost prestige, also, in the decision of the Senate on the final form of the bill to fix the succession in event both the President and the Vice President were dead, disqualified or incapacitated. Jefferson's friends "seemed to think it important," in Fisher Ames's words, "to hold [Jefferson] up as King of the Romans," [145] and they succeeded in having the House vote him the honor, but when the Senate stubbornly refused its assent, the republicans decided not to force an issue. The President pro tem of the Senate and the Speaker of the House were named.[146] To a less degree, Jefferson might have been hampered in his opposition to Hamilton's fiscal policy by the fact that in at least one instance he had spoken of the "unparalleled prosperity" of the country in the spring of 1791.[147]

Hamilton's disadvantages in the contest were as numerous and as serious. Although Aaron Burr, the new Senator from New York, had not yet begun to exert large influence, he hated Hamilton heartily.[148] The strongest Federalist in the House, Fisher Ames, was in wretched health; a temporary Senator from Virginia, John Taylor, was bowling over Hamilton's spol·esmen in debate.[149] Jefferson may have had some reason for saying, more broadly, that "on the whole . . . Treasury influence was tottering." [150] In the larger strategy of government—funding, assumption, excise and the protection of American manufactures by high duties—Hamilton still had the better of the struggle for power; but in the tactics of contest, he carelessly remained on the defensive while Jefferson enjoyed on four fronts all the rewards of a vigorous offensive. The fiscal policy of government, especially in giving a preferred position to the Bank of the United States, was alleged by the republicans to be responsible for the speculative mania that seized and

---

[144] Letter of Feb. 14, 1792; 1 *Gibbs, Wolcott Papers,* 73.

[145] 1 *Fisher Ames,* 114.

[146] Joseph Jones to Madison, Mch. 2, 1792; 15 *Madison Papers,* 16, LC; 6 *Hunt's Madison,* 95-96 n; 1 *JHR.,* 484-86, 509, 515; 1 *JS,* 341-42, 346; 2 *Laws of U. S.,* ed. 1815, p. 253.

[147] Letter of May 12, 1791, to Charles Dumas, 8 *Jefferson,* 197.

[148] See Isaac Ledyard to Hamilton, Feb. 17, 1792; 15 *Hamilton Papers,* 2058, LC.

[149] 6 *Hunt's Madison,* 123-25.

[150] 1 *Jefferson,* 293, a propos of the debate on whether Congress should make its calls for information directly to the heads of departments or through the President.

shook or ruined hundreds of men in the spring and summer of 1791.[151]
A second charge against Hamilton, and a most effective one in appealing to voters, was his alleged lack of sympathy with republican ideals
and his belief that monarchy was the one stable form of government.
Some intemperate observations by the Secretary of the Treasury, soon
after Jefferson's return from France, convinced the Virginian that
Hamilton was at heart an enemy of the institutions established by the
war for independence.[152] This suspicion of Hamilton burned more and
more hotly in Jefferson's heart and fired his opposition.

Jefferson's adherents directed their third attack against the excise
which they regarded as Hamilton's creation. Washington had been
sensitive to the political dangers the use of this source of revenue involved, and both on his southern tour and by subsequent inquiry he
had undertaken to gauge resentments. Although most reports to him
were encouraging, his reference to the subject in his address at the opening of Congress had disclosed his concern. This had been followed by
a statement on what had been done administratively under the excise
act.[153] Much later in the session, Congress sought to allay dissatisfaction
with the law by lowering slightly the excise on domestic spirits and by
simplifying its terms.[154] This neither satisfied nor silenced those who
believed they could wean support from Hamilton by continued denunciation of the tax on whiskey. The entire front page of the *National*

---

[151] An excellent brief description will be found in 2 *McMaster*, 38–41. A brief but effective
review is in Henry Knox to William Knox, May 15, 1792; *Knox Papers*, MHS. Clamor continued for months; every effort was made to array all the losers against the administration;
see Madison to Jefferson, July 10, 1791, 14 *Madison Papers*, 23, printed with variations in
6 *Hunt's Madison*, 55 n; *Independent Chronicle*, July 7, 1791, p. 2, part of a series of articles
by "Republican," in answer to "Publicola" of the *Columbian Centinel* (Boston); S. Breck to
Henry Knox, Aug. 7, 1791, *Knox Papers*, MHS; *Boston Gazette*, Aug. 15, 1791, p. 3; *New-
York Journal*, Aug. 17, 1791, p. 2 and 3—an article and poems from a paper that was now
less frequently vehement against the Federalists; Henry Lee to James Madison, Jan. 8, 1792
(14 *Madison Papers*, 109, LC); same to same, Jan. 17, 1792: "Sir, that funding system will
undo us" (*ibid.*, 112). The controversy reached the point where two rival editors argued in
verse, of a sort, whether public debts were blessings or curses. See *National Gazette*, May 3,
1792, p. 3; see, also, Return J. Meigs to Madison, Feb. 1, 1792 (15 *Madison Papers*, 2, LC)
and James Blanchard, Norfolk, Va., to Hamilton, Feb. 29, 1792 (15 *Hamilton Papers*, 2065, LC).

[152] 1 *Jefferson*, 284, with this quotation from Hamilton: ". . . the present government is
not that which will answer the ends of society, by giving stability and protection to its rights
and . . . it will probably be found expedient to go into the British form," though he wanted
a fair test made of government under the Constitution. This is substantially what Hamilton
himself affirmed in 9 *A. Hamilton*, 534. Cf. 1 *Jefferson*, 325. In *National Gaz.*, Feb. 27, 1792,
p. 3, was the remark: "Foreigners have observed, on *this* country, that the inhabitants . . . are
only republican in name."

[153] 31 *G. W.*, 409, a document of no large importance historically.

[154] 1 *JHR.*, 592, 594; 1 *JS*, 436, 438; 2 *Laws of U. S.*, ed. 1815, p. 289, compared with
excises in the act of Mch. 3, 1791, *ibid.*, 208.

*Gazette* was given over repeatedly to articles, signed "Sidney," that undertook to demolish every argument advanced in a report Hamilton had made on the principles and operation of the excise.[155] Enforcement was denounced, also. "The free citizens of America," said another writer in the same paper, "will not quietly suffer the *well-born few* to trample them under foot." These would-be masters of America "have brought forward a law to empower the President to make use of the militia of one State to put the excise law and other laws in force in another."[156] This sort of appeal was designed to create dissatisfaction and to contribute to the overthrow of the Federalists, but the case against the excise was not convincing even to some of Jefferson's unwavering supporters. "The excise," wrote James Monroe, "is generally disliked; but whether any tax more acceptable could be substituted to raise the same sum I have not been able to collect."[157]

Still another line of attack on Hamilton was the argument that many of his proposals defied the Constitution. The republicans, to be sure, did not have a patent on this weapon. Federalists, too, could wield it, but not usually with the broad sweep of the critic's blade. Fisher Ames probably described the duel with accuracy when he told Thomas Dwight: "The practice of crying out 'this is unconstitutional' is a vice that has grown inveterate by indulgence, and those cry out most frequently who were opposed to its adoption."[158]

Whether the contest was over fiscal policy or monarchism, over excise or constitutionality, the Federalists had their journalistic gladiator in John Fenno, who continued to edit the *Gazette of the United States*, and the republicans their champion in Freneau, whose *National Gazette* was becoming more outspoken. Although Fenno could hit hard on occasion—as in the controversy over St. Clair's defeat—he did not possess the resourcefulness and skill of Freneau in finding quickly and exploiting boldly a new line of attack on the opposition. Freneau, in addition, commanded before the end of the winter the services of two vigorous and ably equipped contributors. "A Farmer" began a series

[155] These articles, which are as dull as they are lengthy, began in the issue of April 23 and appeared at intervals through May 24, 1792.
[156] *National Gaz.*, May 7, 1792, p. 2.
[157] Letter of June 17, 1792, to Jefferson; 1 *Hamilton's Monroe*, 232.
[158] He added: "If they were more disposed to execute it according to their objections, the friends of union and order would have less cause to complain of delay, as well as of the hazard in which every good measure is kept hanging, as it were, with a rope round its neck, during its passage" (Letter of Mch. 8, 1792; 1 *Fisher Ames*, 115).

of critical articles on February 23;[159] and "Brutus" delivered between March 15 and April 9 a powerful, if partisan, assault on the entire funding program of Hamilton.[160] Fenno did not attempt to answer these polemics point by point. Instead, he voiced editorial generalizations that usually displayed less of logic than of warning and even of whimper. He seemed to think the administration could retain its hold upon Congress and the country by asserting its excellence rather than by demolishing the arguments of its critics.[161] Manifestly, Fenno was slowly losing the battle. His supporters must have realized that he needed reenforcements. "Brutus" must be answered.

Before the end of the session of Congress, Washington had achieved the state of mind in which he paid little heed to newspaper debate that was not offensively personal to him,[162] but he observed anxiously the widening of the rift between his two principal officers of administration. He listened when they talked of their differences of political opinion,[163] but, as yet, he made no answer to them and contented himself with setting an example of equal regard for all honest elements in politics. There was, he still believed, no personal ill will between Jefferson and Hamilton; their clashes were those of principle.[164] He would do what he could to confine divergent opinion and, needless to say, he would employ his most resolute endeavor to prevent a disintegration of the Union because of the antagonisms between North and South.[165]

On that longer road, he did not feel he would travel far. The birthday celebrated widely and ceremoniously on the 22nd of February[166]

[159] Other articles appeared February 27, p. 2; March 1, p. 4; March 15, p. 2; March 26, p. 4; Apr. 5, 1792, p. 1.

[160] The opening article, Mch. 15, 1792, p. 2, listed six alleged evils of the funding system. Leary (op. cit., 199) pronounced Brutus's articles "the earliest telling blow against Hamilton's influence."

[161] Of scores of examples, the following are typical: February 11, p. 3; February 15, p. 3; February 22, p. 3; February 25, p. 3; March 14, p. 3; March 17, p. 3; March 21, p. 3; April 4, p. 3; April 11, p. 3; April 14, p. 3; April 18, p. 3; April 21, p. 3; June 27, 1792, p. 3.

[162] Cf. his thanks to Mrs. Samuel Powel Apr. 23, 1792 for sending him a copy of certain "Strictures" that had appeared in print; they had not given him, he said, "a moment's painful sensation." 32 G. W., 22–23.

[163] Cf. 1 Jefferson, 289–92.

[164] In reading the "Anas" for this period, the spring of 1792, it is difficult to escape the conclusion that, in reality, personal jealousy on both sides was more of a divisive factor than was political philosophy.

[165] Cf. Abigail Adams to her sister, Apr. 20, 1792: "I firmly believe if I live ten years longer, I shall see a division of the Southern and Northern States, unless more candor and less intrigue, of which I have no hopes, should prevail." Abigail Adams, 83.

[166] Baker, 233–34; Gazette of the United States, Feb. 22, 1792, p. 1 and 3, with two long poems in Washington's honor. One diversion of Washington's birthday was a venture by him into literary criticism. His friend and admirer, Mrs. Samuel Powel, sent him a copy of some verses written in her honor on her natal day. Washington returned the paper with the mild

was his sixtieth. He felt that he was getting old and that his memory, which he always had depreciated, was unreliable. A fear possessed him that he might be showing to others a mental decline of which he was not conscious. On occasion he found himself less active and business in consequence more irksome. The prospect of retiring in March, 1793, was increasingly sweet. He would do his duty but he looked forward with eagerness and yearning to the time when, once again, his trust would be his plantation, not the nation.[167]

In this state of hope for himself and of anxiety for the peace of his colleagues and his country, he passed without visible impatience through the final weeks of a session that produced better legislation than had been expected of it.[168] Washington had made or had renewed seven major recommendations.[169] Those relating to the excise, to re-apportionment of representation, to the creation of a uniform militia, to the improvement of the postal service, and to the establishment of a mint, had been enacted into law. Nothing positive had been done with respect to the introduction of a system of standard weights and measures, or the disposal of vacant land.[170] On its own initiative, Congress had arranged for the succession to the Presidency, had revised the system of invalid pensions and had indemnified Nathanael Greene's estate for a bond he had given to supply his troops with provisions.[171] An extension to Mch. 1, 1793, had been granted for the tender of notes to be assumed by the Federal government;[172] an effort to have the United States Treasury pay for a further assumption of State debts was beaten in the face of hope, pressure and much maneuver.[173] By the terms of a most important measure, the President was authorized to call out the militia to execute the laws of the Union, suppress insurrections and repel invasions.[174] This was the record with respect to measures the

---

comment that the "thoughts are well conceived, the sentiments are just," etc. Reading these remarkably bad verses must have been an ordeal, even for a man who had not an ear particularly sensitive to poetry. All the related manuscripts are in the *Powel Papers*, Mount Vernon.

[167] See his remarks of Feb. 29, 1792, to Jefferson; 1 *Jefferson*, 287–88.

[168] 1 *Fisher Ames*, 118. Cf. Oliver Wolcott to his father, Jan. 30, 1792, 1 *Gibbs, Wolcott Papers*, 72; Jonathan Dayton to Dr. Elmer, Jan. 20, 1792; *Emmet Coll.*, NYPL.

[169] 31 *G. W.*, 399–403.

[170] A convenient list of the laws passed at the first session of the Second Congress appears in 1 *JS*, 445–46; the acts themselves are in 1 *Statutes at Large*, or, perhaps more accessibly, in 2 *Laws of U. S.*, ed. 1815.

[171] 2 *Laws of U. S.*, ed. 1815, p. 278–79.    [172] *Ibid.*, 306.

[173] Benjamin Bourne to Welcome Arnold, Mch. 1, 1792, *Peck Papers*, RIHS.; 2 *Paine Wingate*, 407; 1 *JHR.*, 556–60.

[174] 1 *Statutes at Large*, ed. 1845, p. 264; 2 *Laws of U. S.*, ed. 1815, p. 284.

President advocated or favored. On the other side, not a bill was passed that seemed to him imprudent, so far as he spoke of the session's accomplishment, nor had Congress voted adversely on any measure he was known to favor.[175] Some action that he had recommended to the legislative branch had been postponed but none had been denied outright. His veto had shaped the terms of the reapportionment. St. Clair's defeat had been charged to the commanding General, to Butler, to Knox, to the contractors—but not to Washington. Around him, conflict was rising but he still was apart from it. No influence approached his; he had no rival; his retirement would be the signal for the muster of opposing politicians whose hate of their adversaries might threaten the tranquility of the nation; yet Washington talked of retirement and of the drafting of a farewell address.

[175] He had no part in the effort made in the House to execute the resolution of Aug. 7, 1783 for the erection of an equestrian statue of him. This now was deferred on the ground of expense and, probably, because of lack of enthusiasm for the elaborate design proposed by the one sculptor who appears to have been active in seeking the commission, Giuseppe Ceracchi. See 1 *JHR.*, 468, 602; 1 *JS*, 349; 32 *G. W.*, 3.

# CHAPTER XVI

## OF THE PEOPLE'S OWN CREATION
### (May 10, 1792–March 4, 1793)

WASHINGTON HAD confided to Madison and to all the heads of departments separately his growing inclination to retire at the end of his term. Hamilton and Knox had done their utmost, with their urgent appeals, to dissuade him. Randolph had felt that Washington should accept reelection. Madison had said that the President's retirement would be a surprise and a shock to the people.[1] Jefferson had spoken against such a step but had not spoken as if he thought the President was to be shaken from his decision.[2] The judgment of the Secretary of State seemed to be warranted. As Congress approached its vacation, Washington found his duties more burdensome and the rising resentments of party more unreasonable. Newspaper criticism, he reflected, undoubtedly was aimed at him though ostensibly it was directed at some of his subordinates. Was he not responsible for the administration the editors assailed? If there were truth in the charges they made, and nothing had been done to correct them, would he not be judged careless or else be deemed too stupid to understand what was happening? He would be a fool indeed to forget this and to swallow the little sugar plums thrown out for him![3] "The fatigues and disagreeableness of his situation were in fact scarcely tolerable to him."[4] Some one else

---

[1] James Madison, "Substance of a Conversation held with the President," May 5, 1792; 15 Madison Papers, 42, LC. 6 Hunt's Madison, 107 n.

[2] "I knew that . . . before forming your decision you had weighed all the reasons for and against the measure, had made up your mind on full view of them, and that there could be little hope of changing the result. Pursuing my reflections, too, I knew we were some day to try to walk alone, and if the essay should be made while you should be alive and looking on, we should derive confidence from that circumstance, and resource, if it failed." Letter of May 23, 1792, to Washington; 8 Jefferson, 341–42.

[3] This is from Jefferson's note of July 10, 1792, in his "Anas," 1 Jefferson, 310. There is no reason to believe that Washington's quoted remarks at that time did not represent his state of mind in May. The two other contemporary accounts are in Madison's memorandum of May 5, 1792, loc. cit., 6 Hunt's Madison, 106 n, and Jefferson's references in his letter of May 23, 1792, to Washington, 8 Jefferson, 341 ff.

[4] 15 Madison Papers, 42, LC; reference in 6 Hunt's Madison, 108 n.

could do as well as he, with failing powers and impaired hearing,[5] could hope to do in the Presidency. If he had thought his withdrawal from public service actually would be inimical to the country's welfare, he would have "conquered his longing for retirement."[6] As it was, he believed "his return to private life was consistent with every public consideration,"[7] as surely as it accorded with his own inclination,[8] which was stronger day by day. He wished to settle as quickly as he could the question of how he should announce his intention in a manner to make it plain that he was not presuming he would be elected if willing to serve. Would it be permissible to make his statement at the next session of Congress, or would that be too late for public convenience, and would it prompt the legislators to present an address he might be embarrassed to answer?[9]

On this he decided to ask the counsel of James Madison, who also could be of highest help in preparing the text of a farewell address. In a long conversation with the Congressman on the 5th of May, Washington found Madison convinced that he should not retire. Madison's strongest argument, perhaps, was that the rise of party spirit was a reason for continuing as President, rather than a reason for declining reelection. A weak minority might wish to overthrow the government or, on the other side, to make an approach to a mixed monarchy; but the public was so averse to extremes that opposition of this sort could not survive long. It was reasonable to hope that ere another term of four years would run out, a temperate and wise administration would "give such a tone and firmness to the Government as would secure it against danger from either of these descriptions of enemies . . ."[10] Madison had much more to say that was logical but not convincing or persuasive. The two men separated with the understanding that Madison was to reflect on the question of when and how Washington's proposed retirement was to be announced, though the younger man repeated the hope that no decision would be necessary.[11]

Soon after this interview and the adjournment of Congress, Washington left Philadelphia, May 10, with Lear in attendance,[12] for a hur-

---

[5] 1 *Jefferson*, 309.                     [6] *Ibid.*
[7] Madison in 15 *Madison Papers*, 42, LC; 6 *Hunt's Madison*, 108 n.
[8] *Ibid.*                                  [9] *Ibid.*
[10] This quotation is from Madison's memorandum of the conversation and may not be his exact words. See *ibid.*, 109 n.
[11] *Ibid.*, 106 n.
[12] *Gazette of U. S.* (Philadelphia), May 12, 1792, p. 3.

ried journey to Mount Vernon,[13] where he found the crops flourishing in fine order. "The country generally," he wrote an Irish correspondent, "exhibited the face of plenty." [14] George Augustine Washington, however, had declined sadly since the last visit of his uncle. He was spitting much blood and, in the judgment of his doctors, could not expect any restoration of health unless he ceased all work and gave himself completely to rest.[15] The one available man to relieve "The Major" was the farm manager, Anthony Whiting, who already had taken over many of George Augustine's duties. Whiting's work had been commendable thus far, without the disclosure of any bad habit that would eat up his hours. Washington perforce decided to give him a trial, though this would call for much correspondence and a closer supervision from Philadelphia than had been required after the younger George had become proficient in handling plantation affairs.

Perhaps this circumstance increased Washington's desire to return home on conclusion of his term. The more he reflected on the question of a second administration, the more firmly did he find himself disposed to decline if it were offered him. Nothing, he resolved, should keep him in office after March 4, 1793, unless party spirit got out of hand, or some dangerous dispute over his successor developed. This was not a probable contingency, because he did not see how a threatening contest could develop before the actual election, which would be held after he had eliminated himself as a candidate. His dream might be fulfilled at last: he might spend his closing years in ease and tranquility.[16] In anticipatory quiet he let his mind dwell on a valedictory, a statement he might make to fellow citizens about their government and themselves. Could they be brought to see that they all were children of the same country, great and rich, which promised to be as prosperous and as happy as any in human annals? Americans must be reminded that diversity might mark their local affairs but that in every essential of their existence as a nation, their interests were the same. Diversity of climate and of soil, the varying production of different regions—all these created interdependence and held out the hope that America, in time, would be self-dependent. In this land of hope, government was of the people's own creation and theirs to amend by lawful process. If they acquired experience and displayed wisdom, good will

[13] He arrived May 14; *ibid.*, May 23, 1792, p. 2.
[14] 32 *G. W.*, 74.          [15] *Ibid.*, 55.
[16] Letter of May 20, 1792, to Madison; *ibid.*, 45-46.

and tolerance, they could bring their government as close to perfection as man might hope to reach. The only struggle among Americans should be an effort to stand foremost in labor toward the accomplishment of this end by supporting and cementing the Union. This was to be his message: Madison must be asked to put it in clear, plain words.[17] On the way back to Philadelphia, he met the Congressman on the road and delivered a letter in which he sketched his valedictory and described his dilemma: he still could not decide in what manner he could decline reelection without posing the assumption that a second term would be his if he desired it. This was compunction of a sort in which his mind was singularly apt to become entangled. In his eyes, arrogance was worse than ignorance, and bad manners second only to bad morals.

Back in Philadelphia on the 28th of May,[18] Washington found foreign relations and Indian affairs at a stage that called for much consultation with Jefferson and with Knox. After wasted weeks of finessing, Minister Hammond at last was ready to discuss with the Secretary of State the execution of the peace treaty. Washington shared in preparations for this meeting, though he was not optimistic. "I wish more favorable explanations than I expect," he wrote Jefferson, "from your interview with the British Minister." [19] The negative outcome of the first meeting [20] consequently did not disappoint Washington greatly, but he followed subsequent cautious exchanges with care.[21] Doubtless, too, he kept himself informed on Jefferson's instructions to Thomas Pinckney, the American Minister to Britain, who was about to leave for his station. Later in the summer, after Pinckney had established himself in London, he encountered much difficulty in dealing with the representatives of King George's government. Those who were not indifferent were absent in the country [22]—a state of affairs that did not surprise either Washington or Jefferson. The President did not look for an early settlement with Britain, but, with his exhaustless perseverance, he intended to continue his efforts, especially as the activity of a

[17] Letter of May 20, 1792, to Madison; *ibid.*, 47–48.
[18] *Gazette of U. S.*, June 2, 1792, p. 3.        [19] 32 *G. W.*, 51.
[20] It is described in Jefferson's letter of June 4, 1792, to James Madison; 15 *Madison Papers*, 51.
[21] 32 *G. W.*, 84.
[22] For Pinckney's instructions, see 8 *Jefferson*, 368 ff. Pinckney's dispatches to Jefferson are in Nat. Arc. State Dept.: *Dipl. Desp.*, Gt. Br., v. 3. The absence of British Ministers was reported in Pinckney's dispatch of Aug. 29, 1792 (*Ibid.*). He had embarked at New York June 18, 1792, and reached London August 3. See S. F. Bemis, "The London Mission of Thomas Pinckney, 1792–96," 28 *A.H.R.*, 228 ff, a reference followed from 2 *Malone*, 400.

Spanish agent in the Creek country was creating a suspicion that Madrid and London might be working together against America.[23] Patience, then, in dealing with them, patience and vigilance! Diplomacy demanded those virtues now as surely as war had called for them in the seventeen-seventies.

Whether England and Spain were or were not responsible, Indian affairs had reached a distressful state. On Washington's return, he found Henry Knox disturbed over the criticism and the alarm that St. Clair's defeat had evoked.[24] Kentucky was demanding protection against the savages; Washington unhesitatingly pledged it [25] and, in his old fighting spirit, awaited developments. For a time, to the surprise of many, the frontier was tranquil, though he continued military preparations as if an Indian war had to be faced.[26]

Washington's prime concern after he came back to Philadelphia remained the one he had brought with him from Mount Vernon, the question of retirement at the end of his term. Jefferson had written him, while he was on the road northward,[27] a most earnest plea that he consent to reelection. The letter indicted the speculators and the alleged monarchists and urged that Washington add "one or two more to the many years [he had] already sacrificed to the good of mankind." Within that time, said Jefferson, "an honest majority" might be established in Congress on the new basis of representation, and Washington might go back to private life with less danger to the country. "Your being at the helm," said the Secretary of State, "will be more than an answer to every argument which can be used to alarm and lead the people in any quarter into violence or secession." Then Jefferson added in a fine turn of phrase: "North and South will hang together if they have you to hang on." [28] That was an argument not easily dismissed, even though it rested somewhat on partisan denunciation of men with whom Washington wanted Jefferson and all other right-minded Americans to live in peace. The subject was so thorny that the President laid it aside, day after day, and did not take it up with Jefferson until almost

---

[23] 8 *Jefferson*, 388; 32 *G. W.*, 117 ff., 128–29. Cf. Jefferson to Washington, Sept. 9, 1792: "That Spain and Great Britain may understand one another on our frontiers is very possible; for however opposite their interests or disposition may be in the affairs of Europe, yet while these do not call them into opposite action, they may concur as against us." 8 *Jefferson*, 394–95.
[24] Knox to his wife, June 17; Knox to Edward Carrington, July 24, 1792; *Knox Papers*, MHS.
[25] Knox to Gov. Isaac Shelby, July 12, 1792; *Wilkinson Papers*, Chicago HS.
[26] 32 *G. W.*, 102, 103–04.          [27] 1 *Jefferson*, 309.          [28] 8 *ibid.*, 347.

the time he was to leave again for Mount Vernon. Then he went painfully over the familiar story of his reluctance to accept office and of his frustrated hope that he could retire in 1790 or in 1791. He explained his disabilities and his fear that if he continued as President, his earlier profession of a longing to leave public life would be regarded by the people as affectation. The country would say that he was like all the others: when he got office he could not bring himself to quit it.[29] With this he turned to what Jefferson had said about those who wished to overthrow the Federal government, or to change its nature. There might be a desire in some quarters to transform the republic into a monarchy but he did not believe there was any design to accomplish this. Newspaper articles recently published, Washington went on, particularly those in Freneau's paper, seemed to be intended to excite opposition to government. Pennsylvania was said to be astir already because of the excise. Agitation in the gazettes tended to produce a separation of the Union—the worst of calamities. From the resulting anarchy a return to monarchy might be expected.

Washington went on to insist that the hostile papers were attacking him indirectly, because he had signed the laws for which they were condemning the administration. He did not like every part of every law; he had approved none that he did not think eligible. Besides, he was not sure concerning the discontent on which the newspapers dwelt. He did not believe it extended far beyond the cities; personally on his recent journey he had talked with many Virginians and Marylanders, and he had found the people happy. On this, he said, he wanted more information: if dissatisfaction was widespread, the reported desire that he remain President might not be general.[30] Jefferson's reply went back to the arguments he had advanced in his letter of May 23 and particularly to the charge that assumption had increased the Federal debt unnecessarily and had furnished the means "of corrupting both branches of the legislature." Members who held the balance of power in Congress were "legislating for their own interests in opposition to those of the people." [31] Presumably, Jefferson asserted again that Washington alone could cope with this and subdue it; but his plea much resembled an invitation for the General to keep his camp fire burning in a powder magazine, while the kegs were being opened. Jefferson went about his business; Washington had a text to ponder, not only in

[29] 1 ibid., 309–10.    [30] Ibid., 310–11.    [31] Ibid., 311–12.

the Secretary's philippic but also in a carefully prepared draft by Madison on what a retiring President should say and when he should say it.[32] Daily he had, too, the papers that carried the salvos of rival editorial frigates. In most of this exchange between the Federalist *Gazette of the United States* and the republican *National Gazette*, there was more noise than damage,[33] but the editor who was translator in the Department of State dealt angrily with unnamed Congressmen alleged to be involved in speculation,[34] and prayed that "plain American republicans" might not be "overwhelmed by those monarchial writers on Davila, &c., who are armed with long wigs, long pens and caitiff printers, ready to disseminate their poisoned doctrines throughout this blessed continent."[35] Freneau seemed to be smacking his lips verbally when he wrote: "It is intimated in a Boston paper that the general government is under no small obligation to this man [Captain Shays] for its adoption, advancement and popularity."[36] Place was given, also, to the republication of an article by "Brutus" against the excise: "Since the glorious and honorable peace of 1783, artifice and deception" have wrought "one revolution in favor of the few. Another revolution must and will be brought about in favor of the people."[37] The boldness of these attacks was amazing to the Federalists. Francis Childs of New York was known to be one of the owners of the Philadelphia paper Freneau edited. In his own city, Childs was publisher of the *Daily Advertiser*,[38] and was, in Hamilton's eyes, "a very cunning fellow." The Secretary explained: "In Philadelphia, in the person of his proxy, Freneau, he is a good Anti-federalist and a Clintonian; in New York, he is a good Federalist and Jayite. Beckley[39] and Jefferson pay him for the first, and the Federal citizens of New York for the last."[40] If there was no way of preventing this, Freneau must be answered in the Quaker City by someone who spoke vigorously and effectively. Fenno's reenforcements had to be put into action. Washington probably knew nothing

---

[32] Letter of June 21, 1792; 15 *Madison Papers*, 53, and printed in 6 *Hunt's Madison*, 111 n.

[33] For example, a verbal tack and close over some derogatory observations of Fenno on those who, "having lately escaped from bondage, know not how to enjoy liberty." *Gazette of U. S.*, June 9, p. 3; June 13, p. 3; *National Gaz.* (Philadelphia), June 11, p. 3; June 14, 1792, p. 3.

[34] *Gazette of U. S.*, June 23, p. 3; *National Gaz.*, June 25, 1792, p. 3.

[35] *Ibid.*, June 21, 1792, p. 2.                    [36] *Ibid.*, July 4, 1792, p. 3.

[37] *Ibid.*, July 4, 1792, p. 2.

[38] Apparently the financial relationship of John Swaine to these two papers has never been established precisely. He was Childs's partner in the printing business but Leary (*op. cit.*, 191) seemingly concluded that Childs alone was liable for loss on the Philadelphia paper.

[39] This was John Beckley of Virginia, Clerk of the United States House of Representatives.

[40] Letter of July 25, 1792, to Rufus King; 10 *A. Hamilton*, 4-5.

of the plan to do this but he may have read in the issue of the *Gazette of the United States* for July 7 an article signed "Crito," in which the charge was made that Freneau's paper was the tool of a junto of politicians whose goal was "to oust from the government almost every man now in the administration." [41]

This was the opening gun in the second phase of the battle of the press. If it echoed, Washington did not hear it long: on the 11th of July he left Philadelphia again for Mount Vernon.[42]

It proved to be an inauspicious journey. One of his horses fell sick and had to be left behind; [43] as Washington approached his home he saw evidence of a drought so severe that the corn appeared to be ruined. As if in contrasting welcome, there was a fine rain on the night of his arrival and on the day following. Moreover, when he stopped, en route, at Georgetown, he had the gratification of seeing much better designs for the public buildings than previously had been offered.[44] "It was a pleasure indeed," he said, "to find, in an infant country, such a display of architectural abilities." [45] Pleasure there was, also, in being free of the endless appointments and unrelaxed inquisition of the temporary capital, but there was no escaping the correspondence of the Presidential office. It was brought in the mailbag from Alexandria as inexorably, if not as frequently, as it had been laid on his desk in Philadelphia. "The President," Henry Knox wrote his wife, "is buried in solitude in Mount Vernon"; [46] after a time Washington himself thought himself isolated. "The truth is," he said, "I go out nowhere; and those who call upon me observe a silence which leaves me in ignorance in all [political] matters." [47] He might have added that his nearest and most valuable informant on affairs in his own State no longer came to Mount Vernon. Regretfully, when he had occasion to mention George Mason, he had to speak of him as "my neighbor and quondam friend." [48] All this meant that Washington had much hard work to do with no clerical help,[49] in a household made unhappy by the extreme illness of Major

---

[41] *Gazette of U. S.*, p. 2.                    [42] 32 *G. W.*, 86–87.

[43] B. Dandridge to Colonel Van Horne, July 14, 1792; 255 *Papers of G. W.*, 42, LC; 32 *G. W.*, 86–87.

[44] *Ibid.*, 100–01. For his previous disappointment see *ibid.*, 85–86, 93–95.

[45] *Ibid.*, 101.

[46] Letter of July 24, 1792; *Knox Papers*, MHS.

[47] 32 *G. W.*, 142.                    [48] *Ibid.*, 95.

[49] Lear was in New England; Major Jackson had resigned in December, 1791, to try his hand at the law (31 *ibid.*, 449–50); Washington's two young assistants, Bartholomew Dandridge, who was his wife's nephew, and Howell Lewis, his own nephew, were allowed to go

Washington,[50] during a most unhealthy season [51] and at a time when the General's need of money was great.[52]

If, improbably, he had thought that private affairs could have first attention and public business be left to aestivate the summer through, developments on the frontier soon would have aroused him. It was reported that officers sent to the Western Indians to negotiate peace had been murdered,[53] and that Spanish agents, as previously, had been inciting the Creeks to hostility.[54] Reports that seemed to have some basis of truth told of the arrival in New Orleans of five Regiments of Spanish troops, each Regiment consisting of about 600 men, who were to be followed by a like number from Havana.[55] Simultaneously, negotiations were under way with friendly tribes, whose failure to be satisfied with American offers might lead them to look to the British or to the Spanish. War then might be inevitable.[56] At a distance from government offices, Washington did not feel sure of his information, and he consequently gave the largest discretion to the Secretary of War. The fundamental view of the President remained the same [57]—that every effort should be made to preserve or restore peace and that, meantime, recruiting, preparation, disciplining the troops and bringing up supplies must be pressed.[58] In all of this, Henry Knox was of one mind with

on visits to their friends (32 *ibid.*, 100). Dandridge had joined Washington early in 1791 (*Decatur*, 187); Howell Lewis had been added to the staff in the spring of 1792, primarily because Washington had heard that the young man "was spending his time rather idly" (32 *G. W.*, 43–44; cf. *ibid.*, 17–18). The appointment was temporary.

[50] *Ibid.*, 115; cf. *ibid.*, 140, 156, 173.          [51] *Ibid.*, 141, 156.

[52] He made a most vigorous effort to collect on the long-overdue loan to John Mercer, with the tangled trusteeship this involved. See *ibid.*, 79, 80, 89–92, 110 n, 111–12, 164–66, 175; and he sought actively to bring into his coffer the money due him from the sale of land held jointly by him and his dead brother-in-law, Fielding Lewis (*ibid.*, 88, 158). He could do little about rents of his small farms in Northern Virginia. Tenants were reported too poor to pay or to make the required improvements. See Robert Lewis to Washington, Feb. 7, 1792; *Thom Col.*, Mount Vernon.

[53] One was Maj. Alexander Trueman of the First Infantry, who had two companions, Instructions, *ASP.*, 1 *Ind. Aff.*, 229; finding of the bodies, *ibid.*, 243; reported to Washington, 32 *G. W.*, 107–08. The other slain emissary was Brigadier John Hardin of the Kentucky Militia. After he had been listed for weeks as dead, he was reported alive and back in the settlements. See *ibid.*, 172.

[54] *Ibid.*, 117.          [55] *Ibid.*, 129.

[56] *Ibid.*, 113, 129–30. Washington's careful summary of reports from Georgia and West Florida is in *ibid.*, 117–24. Many of the underlying documents will be found in a so-called "General View," a mass of poorly arranged correspondence, etc., in *ASP.*, 1 *Ind. Aff.*, 225 ff, particularly p. 295 ff.

[57] Nowhere had the desire for a just and general peace been set forth more clearly than in Knox's instructions from Washington to Wilkinson, Feb. 11, Mch. 10, 1792 (*Wilkinson Papers*, Chicago HS).

[58] 32 *G. W.*, 108, 113, 114, 127. See also Knox to Washington, Aug. 5, Aug. 7, 1792; 255 *Papers of G. W.*, LC, 83, 92. Two excellent statements of general policy in dealing with the Indians are those of Marinus Willett, 10 *Sparks*, 263–64 n; and Timothy Pickering, Mch. 21, 1792, 15 *Hamilton Papers*, 2075–76.

his Chief.[59] Representation should be made to the Spanish Commis-sioners in Philadelphia that the Spanish government was not suspected of unfriendly action in the Creek country but that the evidence against certain Spanish officers was too strong to admit of a doubt and too important to ignore.[60] Washington repeated that if the Spanish were intriguing as the American agent believed, this would make the President suspicious "that there is a very clear understanding in all this business between the courts of London and Madrid and that it is calculated to check, as far as they can, the rapid increase, extension and consequence of this country." [61]

This state of affairs—this threat of Indian war and of jealous powers encircling the young republic—seemed to Washington all the more sinister because of the partisan division that was deepening every hour. He knew a few details only of the dispute and he probably had accepted without personal study the more complicated aspects of funding and assumption as presented by Hamilton. Selfish and dangerous reasons for this policy had been alleged in Jefferson's letter of May 23.[62] It was a situation somewhat similar to those Washington had faced dozens of times during the war when military failure had been alleged in terms that made a court of inquiry proper both for the country's sake and for an accused officer's reputation. Hamilton must be given opportunity of explaining what he had done; but if further friction between him and Jefferson was to be avoided, it would be well not to mention to Hamilton the source of the criticisms. Carefully and in full detail, Washington copied or paraphrased under twenty-one headings all the objections made by the Secretary of State. Nothing was withheld and nothing softened. The President sent this long paper in his autograph to Hamilton with the simple, superfluous statement that he sought only "to obtain light and to pursue truth." Explanations as well as complaints, he said, were desired on measures in which "the public interest, harmony and peace is so deeply concerned, and my public conduct so much involved." Would Hamilton write out his "ideas upon the discontents here enumerated"? [63]

When Washington wrote this at Mount Vernon, the advantage that

---

[59] Cf. his letter of July 17, 1792, to James Wilkinson: "I hope to God that such a spirit will arise among the officers . . . that every officer who is a drunkard shall be expelled from the Army . . ." (*Wilkinson Papers*, Chicago HS).

[60] Almost Washington's own words; 32 *G. W.*, 120.

[61] Letter of Aug. 23, 1792, to Jefferson; *ibid.*, 130.

[62] See *supra*, p. 360.   [63] 32 *G. W.*, 95-100.

Freneau had won in Philadelphia over the *Gazette of the United States* was being lost. Fenno's sponsors had come to his support. If Washington's copy came regularly by the post, he received, about the end of July, the issue of July 25, in which a writer who signed himself "T. L." stated flatly that "the editor of the *National Gazette* receives a salary from government," and he posed the query "Whether this salary is paid [Freneau] for translations or for publications, the design of which is to vilify those to whom the voice of the people has committed the administration of our public affairs—to oppose the measures of government, and, by false insinuations to disturb the public peace?" Then "T. L." concluded: "In common life it is thought ungrateful for a man to bite the hand that puts bread into his mouth; but if a man is hired to do it, the case is altered." [64] The replies to this in Freneau's paper [65] may not have come under the eye of the gentleman at Mount Vernon, who had the deepest contempt for the republican editor. Freneau pronounced the charge "beneath reply," but he struck back with attempted ridicule and with the accusation that while he received a "small stipend for services rendered as French translator," a certain "vile sycophant" was receiving far more lucrative emoluments by "undermining another who was in possession of the employ"—by which he meant to indict Fenno as printer of the Senate Journal and Treasury documents.[66] Probably the next phase of the dispute reported at Mount Vernon was a letter by "Detector" in Fenno's paper of the 28th of July.[67] The attack was furious: "It is high time that the mask were torn from the faces of these professed friends, but real enemies of the United States. The effrontery of these men is now so brazen that it glares upon every eye." Furthermore, "these hypocritical republicans" had made the *National Gazette* "only the tool of faction, and the prostituted vehicle of party spleen and opposition to the great principles of order, virtue and religion." Freneau's contributors, said this unsparing critic, were distinguished primarily by "that dark designing envy which sickens at superior abilities and fame in others." To this "Brutus" replied somewhat ineffectually [68] on the very day "T. L." mocked in Fenno's pages the

---

[64] *Gazette of U. S.*, July 25, p. 3. See Appendix VI–2.          [65] July 28, 1792, p. 3.

[66] See Fenno's answer on this point in a letter to Freneau, printed in *National Gaz.*, Aug. 1, 1792, p. 3. Cf. also *National Gaz.*, Aug. 15, 1792, p. 3 and *Gazette of U. S.*, Aug. 18, p. 2. In the second of these references "Candor" explained that Fenno was one only of the printers engaged by the Treasury. Childs and Swaine, the backers of Freneau, had the printing for the House of Representatives, the State Department and New York State.

[67] Page 3.          [68] *National Gaz.*, Aug. 1, 1792, p. 2.

boastful statement of Freneau that he was the "editor of a free news-paper." Free it was, "T. L." allowed—"free to defame but never free to praise." Three days later, the guns were opened on Jefferson himself by name. Over the pseudonym "An American" this was said of the Secretary of State: "Can he reconcile it to his own personal dignity and the principles of probity to hold an office under [the existing government] and employ the means of official influence in opposition?" Jefferson, it was maintained, had attempted "an experiment somewhat new in the history of political maneuvers in this country: a newspaper instituted by a public officer, and the editor of it regularly pensioned with the public money in the disposal of that officer." [69] The defence was vigorous; Fenno was accused of receiving $2000 or $2500 as printer to the Senate and to the Treasury Department: Was not ten times more influence exerted through this than through the $250 paid Freneau as translator? [70] Much more that probably was not read by Washington appeared in Freneau's paper, but the initiative now was shifted. Besides the attacks on Jefferson, the Federalist organ soon began to publish a series of articles signed "Civis" and "Fact" which disposed of the argument that the funding of the public debt and the assumption of State obligations had been wasteful.[71] Unknown to the President, efforts were being made by both sides, behind the scenes, to determine the precise responsibility of republican leaders for the establishment of the *National Gazette*.[72]

While the tide of controversy was running strongly in Fenno's favor, Hamilton replied on the 18th of August to Washington's twenty-one inquiries.[73] The Secretary of the Treasury said in a letter that accompanied his 14,000-word answer: "You will observe that here and there

---

[69] *Gazette of U. S.*, Aug. 4, 1792, p. 2–3.    [70] *National Gaz.*, Aug. 15, 1792, p. 3.

[71] These articles appear most conveniently in 3 *A. Hamilton*, 28 ff. Probably unaware of the identity of the contributor, Freneau printed the "Civis" pieces in *National Gazette*, September 5, p. 3, and September 12, p. 2, with a rebuttal by "Mercator" on September 8, p. 3. "Fact" appears in *Gazette of the United States*, September 15, p. 1.

[72] These machinations can be traced in *Leary, Freneau*. Some of the more important articles in the press war, after Jefferson's name was brought into the dispute, were as follows: *Gazette of the United States*, August 8, p. 3; August 11, p. 2; August 15, p. 3; August 18, p. 2, 3; August 22, p. 3; Aug. 25, 1792, p. 3; *National Gazette*, August 8, p. 3; August 11, p. 4; August 15, p. 3; August 29, p. 4; Sept. 1, 1792, p. 3. Examination of these and other references may convince some investigator that the controversy merits a more detailed treatment than it received in S. E. Forman, *The Political Activities of Philip Freneau* (The Johns Hopkins University Studies in His. and Pol. Sc., Series 20, Nos. 9–10, 1902), or in *Leary, Freneau*. The responsibility of Jefferson, James Madison and Henry Lee for Freneau's appearance and support in Philadelphia may be traced in 9 *A. Hamilton*, 519; 8 *Jefferson*, 402–05; 19 *ibid.*, 79; 6 *Hunt's Madison*, 55 n, 69 n, 117 n; Jonathan Dayton to Hamilton, Aug. 26, 1792, 17 *Hamilton Papers*, 2315; Henry Lee to Madison, Feb. 6, 1792, 15 *Madison Papers*, 4.

[73] Text in 2 *A. Hamilton*, 428 ff.

some severity appears. I have not fortitude enough always to hear with calmness calumnies which necessarily include me, as a principal agent in the measures censured, of the falsehood of which I have the most unqualified consciousness. I trust I shall always be able to bear, as I ought, imputations of errors of judgment; but I acknowledge that I cannot be entirely patient under charges which impeach the integrity of my public motives or conduct. I feel that I merit them *in no degree*; and expressions of indignation sometimes escape me, in spite of every effort to suppress them. I rely on your goodness for the proper allowances." [74] The document was all denial or refutation, with the single exception that speculative dealings in government securities "had some bad effects among those engaged in it," though this doubtless was unavoidable.[75] Much of the paper echoed the keen reasoning of the earlier reports on public credit; the allegations of stock-jobbing were met with the statement that Hamilton did not know a single member of Congress who could "properly be called a stock-jobber or a paper-dealer"; [76] his reply to the favorite charge of republicans that the way was being prepared for a change to a monarchy, on the the model of Great Britain, was a flat denial, with the added remark "that the project, from its absurdity, refutes itself." Hamilton repeated on this point substantially what Washington himself already had said.[77] The Secretary wrote: "The truth unquestionably is, that the only path to a subversion of the republican system of the country is by flattering the prejudices of the people, and exciting their jealousies and apprehensions, to throw affairs into confusion, and bring on civil commotion. Tired at length of anarchy or want of government, they may take shelter in the arms of monarchy for repose and security. Those, then, who resist a confirmation of public order are the true artificers of monarchy." [78] Toward the end of his answer, Hamilton came to the objection, "The owners of the debt are in the Southern, and the holders of it in the Northern division." Said Hamilton: "If this were literally true, it would be no argument for or against anything. It would be still politically and morally right for the debtors to pay their creditors," [79] and from that

---

[74] *Ibid.*, 426–27. In reality, the language of his answer to the "Objections" was mild compared with that of a letter he had written May 26, 1792, to his long-time friend Col. Edward Carrington, 9 *A. Hamilton*, 513 ff, a most important paper for an understanding of the grounds of Hamilton's opposition to Jefferson and, regretfully, to Madison.

[75] 2 *A. Hamilton*, 453–54. The original draft of the lengthy document is in 17 *Hamilton Papers*, 2278–2309.

[76] *A. Hamilton*, 456.

[77] See *supra*, p. 360. *Infra*, 374.

[78] 2 *A. Hamilton*, 460.

[79] *Ibid.*, 466.

he proceeded to a discussion of economic differences between North and South and the effect of the war in determining debtors and creditors—the sort of argument most certain to impress so stoutly bottomed a nationalist as the President was.[80]

Perhaps before this letter reached Mount Vernon and certainly before it was read carefully,[81] Washington took occasion, in writing Jefferson concerning the danger of an Indian war, to appeal for political moderation and compromise: "How unfortunate," he exclaimed, "and how much is it to be regretted . . . that whilst we are encompassed on all sides with avowed enemies and insidious friends, that internal dissensions should be harrowing and tearing our vitals." Without more charity toward opposing opinion, he went on, "I believe it will be difficult, if not impracticable, to manage the reins of government or to keep the parts of it together . . ." If union were thrown away before its utility were justly tried, then, he said, "in my opinion, the fairest prospect of happiness and prosperity that ever was presented to man will be lost, perhaps forever." He made his appeal simply and, as he explained, without applying the case to any individual: "My earnest wish and my fondest hope . . . is that instead of wounding suspicions and irritable charges, there may be liberal allowances, mutual forbearances and temporizing yieldings on *all sides*. Under the exercise of these, matters will go on smoothly and, if possible, more prosperously."[82] A letter of similar import and, in part, of almost identical language was sent Hamilton.[83]

Both men answered on the 9th of September. Hamilton wrote regretfully of Washington's unhappiness and said plainly that if the President did not succeed in producing harmony, "the period is not remote when the public good will require substitutes for the differing members of your administration." He felt himself "the deeply injured party," said Hamilton, from the time Jefferson took office. "I have been the frequent subject of the most unkind whispers and insinuations" by the Secretary of State. "I have long seen a formed party in the Legislature under his auspices, bent upon my subversion. I cannot doubt from the evidence I possess that the *National Gazette* was instituted by him for political purposes and that one leading object of it has been to render me and all the measures connected with my department as

80 *Ibid.*, 468–71.
82 Letter of Aug. 23, 1792; *ibid.*, 130–31.
81 Cf. 32 *G. W.*, 132.
83 Aug. 26, 1792; *ibid.*, 132–34.

odious as possible." In spite of this, Hamilton continued, he had never struck back publicly, until of late. On the contrary, he had prevented an attack on Jefferson in return for what the Secretary had said about John Adams in the letter on Paine's pamphlet. Recently, Hamilton said, "I cannot conceal from you that I have had some instrumentality . . . in the retaliations which have fallen upon certain public characters and that I find myself placed in a situation not to be able to recede for the present." It had become his duty, he said, "to draw aside the veil from the principal actors," and he added, with unconcealed satisfaction, "[I] think events will prove that I have judged rightly." Then he made this pledge, ". . . if you shall hereafter form a plan to reunite the members of your administration upon some steady principle of cooperation, I will faithfully concur in executing it during my continuance in office. And I will not directly or indirectly say or do a thing that shall endanger a feud."[84] In this, Hamilton did not specify the nature of the "retaliations" he had begun, but he probably need not have done so. Familiar as the President had become by this time with the style of the Secretary of the Treasury, a hint doubtless sufficed to convince Washington that Hamilton was the author of some, at least, of the attacks made on Jefferson in Fenno's columns.

Jefferson's answer to Washington's appeal for compromise and conciliation was a long letter[85] that set forth Jefferson's chief basis of opposition to Hamilton in a broad, inclusive statement the verity of which he apparently did not think he needed to prove: "[Hamilton's] system flowed from principles adverse to liberty, and was calculated to undermine and demolish the Republic, by creating an influence of his department over the members of the Legislature."[86] Jefferson proceeded to denounce mildly Hamilton's concept of the right of Congress to legislate for the general welfare, and then the Secretary of State dwelt on the restraint he had shown in not opposing Hamilton's plan, though he disapproved of it. "Has abstinence from the department, committed to me, been equally observed by him?" asked Jefferson and, in answer to his own question, wrote of the manner in which Hamilton had undertaken on his own account to deal with the ministers of foreign countries. When Hamilton's views with respect to foreign policy pre-

---

[84] After the original in 256 *Papers of G. W.*, 61, LC. The printed text in 5 *J. C. Hamilton*, 71–73, contains several small inaccuracies.
[85] 8 *Jefferson*, 394–408.  [86] *Ibid.*, 397.

vailed, Jefferson wrote, "their execution fell, of course, to me; and I can safely appeal to you, who have seen all my letters and proceedings, whether I have not carried them into execution as sincerely as if they had been my own, though I ever considered them as inconsistent with the honor and interest of our country . . . So that if the question be by whose fault is it that Colonel Hamilton and myself have not drawn together, the answer will depend on that to two other questions, whose principles of administration best justify, by their purity, conscientious adherence? and which of us has, notwithstanding, stepped farthest into the control of the department of the other?" [87]

Jefferson might have elaborated the second of these questions to the disparagement of Hamilton, because the facts undoubtedly were that the Secretary of the Treasury had usurped many of the functions of the Secretary of State; but Jefferson's singular sensitiveness to criticism showed itself in his quick abandonment of this argument for a lengthy defence of his part in the press war. He blamed Hamilton for the "late charges against me in Fenno's *Gazette*; for neither the style, matter, nor venom of the pieces alluded to, can leave a doubt of their author." [88] Jefferson admitted that he had procured subscriptions for Freneau's paper but he denied that he had written or had procured anyone else to write for that publication or to suggest anything for the editor's consideration; [89] and he asked, "is not the dignity, and even decency of government committed, when one of its principal ministers enlists himself as an anonymous writer or paragraphist . . .?" [90] The Secretary concluded with the statement that he intended to retire at the end of Washington's term and that, until then, he would defer what he would feel free to do and to write thereafter *in propria persona*. He reiterated this in the final sentences, but he maintained: "I will not suffer my retirement to be clouded by the slanders of a man whose history, from the moment at which history can stoop to notice him, is a tissue of machinations against the liberty of the country which has not only received and given him bread, but heaped honors on his head." [91]

These letters from his two principal officers were of doubtful comfort to Washington. They contained weak promises to seek an armistice, but they showed deep personal animosity between the two men, and they disclosed the purpose of Hamilton to continue his attacks

[87] *Ibid.*, 399.        [88] *Ibid.*        [89] *Ibid.*, 403–04.
[90] *Ibid.*, 406.        [91] *Ibid.*, 407.

through the newspaper, to which Jefferson probably would reply after March 4, 1793.[92] The prospect of party strife was increasing. That scarcely could be denied. Washington had, therefore, to wait for better opportunity of making truce and, meantime, he had to consider to what extent the disputes in his official family would affect his retirement at the end of his term.

All his correspondence on the subject showed that his friends were convinced he should accept reelection, which they regarded as certainly his at the nod of his head. Tobias Lear wrote Washington that Robert Morris said he hoped the President "would not give up the government and the country to that fate which he clearly foresaw awaited them if you should determine to retire from the chair. He thought the reasons for your continuing were, if possible, more strong than those which first induced your acceptance of the office." [93] Substantially the same argument was advanced by Edmund Randolph,[94] and by Alexander Hamilton, who rejoiced because "there was," he thought, "some relaxation" in Washington's previously unyielding stand against reelection.[95]

Another involvement of the entire subject of Washington's continuance in office was presented by the rising opposition to the excise on whiskey, particularly in Pennsylvania. This raised two questions: Did it constitute an evidence of the unpopularity of the administration, in line with what Washington previously had said he would regard as a good reason for retiring; or was this discontent so serious that Wash-

[92] Cf. Jefferson to Edmund Randolph, Sept. 17, 1792: "Though I see the pen of the Secretary of the Treasury plainly in the attack on me, yet, since he has not chosen to put his name to it, I am not free to notice it as his. I have preserved through life a resolution, set in a very early part of it, never to write in a public paper without subscribing my name, and to engage openly an adversary who does not let himself be seen, is staking all against nothing. The indecency, too, of newspaper squabbling between two public ministers, besides my own sense of it, has drawn something like an injunction from another quarter" (8 *Jefferson*, 411). This underscores Malone's observation (2 *op. cit.*, 358): "ever since his governorship of Virginia [Jefferson's] dread of controversy had been little short of an obsession . . ." Jefferson evidently did not feel that his pledge to Washington barred him from making plans immediately to launch an effort for the amendment of the Constitution after his retirement. See his letter of Sept. 9, 1792, to Archibald Stuart; 8 *Jefferson*, 409.

[93] Lear to Washington, July 21, 1792, from Portsmouth, New Hampshire; 255 *Papers of G. W.*, 57, LC. Lear added observations he had made on his way to New England: "I found an eagerness of inquiry . . . mixed with an apprehension of what might be the consequence of your retiring. . . . The general idea seemed to be, to say nothing of the fatal effects expected from division of parties, that most of the important things hitherto done under this government, being as it were matters of experiment, had not yet been long enough in operation to give satisfactory proof whether they are beneficial or not, and that they could not under any other administration have the fair experiment which they would have under that which first introduced them." See, also, Lear to Washington, Aug. 5, 1792; *ibid.*, 85.

[94] 255 *Papers of G. W.*, 84, and printed in 10 *Sparks*, 512.

[95] 10 *A. Hamilton*, 7.

# AMES, ZEALOT ON THE FLOOR

"A pretty little warbling canary bird"—this was John Adams's recollection in old age of the foremost orator of the first years under the Constitution. Deeply read in ancient history and in the classics, endowed with sprightly imagination and beautifully modulated voice, Fisher Ames of Massachusetts enjoyed some distinction as a public writer in the Federal cause when elected over Samuel Adams to the House of Representatives in 1789. He was spare of frame and just turned thirty as he took his seat, but shortly Ames discovered an electric power of address which earned him acknowledgment as the outstanding spokesman of Federalism in Congress. Never among Hamilton's intimate friends, he became the vigorous champion of Federalist philosophy. "Law," Ames told the House in 1792 in typically graphic metaphor, "is in some countries the yoke of government which bends or breaks the necks of the people—but, thank Heaven, in this country it is a man's shield, his coat of mail, his castle of safety." His admirers compared him in speaking skill to Burke and in reasoning prowess to the elder Pitt—"My God! How great he is!" James Iredell was to exclaim. Broadened by study but not broken to discipline, the orator gave terse explanation of his own talent: "I am habitually a zealot in politics . . . I burn and freeze. . . ."

(After the Original by Gilbert Stuart and by permission of the owner, Henry Cabot Lodge, Jr. Reproduced through courtesy of the Frick Art Reference Library.)


## WILLIAM MACLAY, CANTANKEROUS CRITIC

"What a set of vipers I have to deal with!" His colleagues in the Senate might have identified the cheerless ring of William Maclay of Pennsylvania, but in 1789 they would hardly have recognized this likeness of a youngish man. Already in his fifties, balding and rheumatic, the lawyer from Harrisburg that year was elevated from obscurity to the First Congress. Failing reelection, he surrendered his seat in March, 1791. If Maclay conversed with anything like the venom which characterized the daily entries in his *Journal*, he must have been conspicuously unpopular among his contemporaries. Hamilton's sharpest critic and a consistent defamer of Adams, he was slightly more generous to Washington: "The creatures that surround him would place a crown on his head, that they may have the handling of its jewels." With his exit Congress was rid of its most cantankerous member and, as well, an arch-foe of Federalism.

(After a miniature portrait by an unknown artist.
Courtesy of the Frick Art Reference Library.)

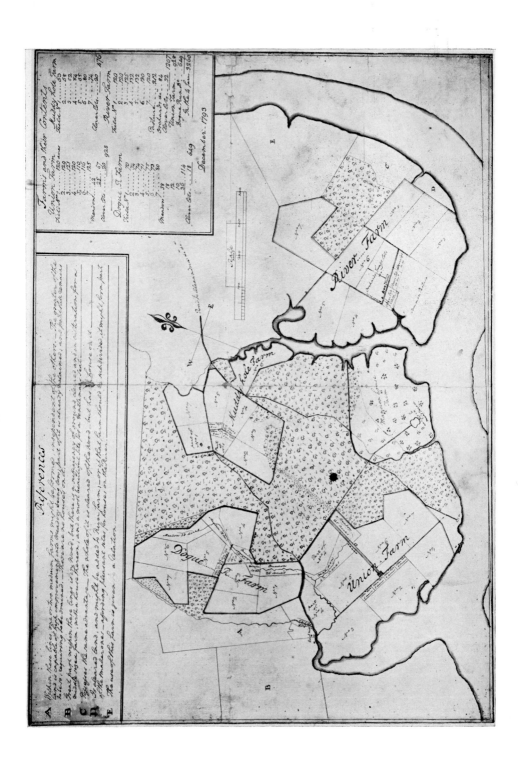

Whether patriot and statesman or patriot and soldier, Washington never ceased to be the planter. By far the greater part of the 8073 acres of the Mount Vernon estate was acquired before the Revolution, but from the Presidential office he planned enlargement and improvement of his property as constantly and as avidly as he had from the commander's tent in the field. What others derived from books and games, Washington took from the land. "I think with you," he wrote Alexander Spotswood in 1788, "that the life of a husbandman of all others is the most delectable . . . To see plants rise from the earth and flourish by the superior skill and bounty of the laborer, fills a contemplative mind with ideas which are more easy to be conceived than expressed." That same year he confided to Arthur Young, "The more I am acquainted with agricultural affairs the better I am pleased with them . . . I can nowhere find so great satisfaction as in those innocent and useful pursuits."

If the years immediately following the War were Washington's happiest, his "plantations" constituted a major source of that pleasure. The General could lose himself in the intricacies of a campaign in "cropping," experiment endlessly with foreign seed which came by multiple gift to his door, and every day of the growing season ride twenty miles around the circle of his cultivated land on a tour of inspection. He had enjoyment in

this life, certainly, but it was the delight of hope contrasted, inevitably, with frustration. There was no consistent success. Always, it seemed, the soldier of the Potomac was facing a formidable array of circumstance. The soil of Mount Vernon, indifferent by nature and worn down by successive crops of tobacco in the old style "ruinous mode of farming," could yield satisfaction to its master no more readily than harvest to his barns. Drought in 1785, lack of reliable clover seed, continual paucity of animal manure, less than good luck in the employment of managers, high mortality among his slaves —these typical obstructions led Washington to the evolvement, finally, of a six-year rotation plan for which high expectations were entertained. The results, of course, were meagre because the soil itself was meagre.

Away from Mount Vernon much of each year after 1789, the President returned there a thousand times in fancy. When Washington could spare a minute from his duties, his imagination might fasten upon some problem in a particular field. When he could spare an hour, he might draft a letter to the resident manager, write a memorandum to himself, construct minute entries in his ledger, or ponder some plat of his acres or master map to re-divide his five farms, such as the elaborate one, pictured here, which he finished late in 1793. Agriculture remained the only hobby of his life.

(From the Original, by courtesy of the Henry E. Huntington Library, San Marino, California. Copyright, 1931.)

ington might have to stay in the Presidency to suppress possible disorder?[96] Washington did not have the immediate answer but he said in plain, uncompromising terms that he had the duty of enforcing the law[97] and he proceeded to draft and to have Jefferson seal a proclamation in which all persons were admonished and exhorted to "refrain and desist from all unlawful combinations and proceedings" that might obstruct the operation of the excise laws. Courts and officials were charged and required to exert their respective powers in seeing that the object of the proclamation was executed.[98] Washington did not delude himself. "I have no doubt," he wrote Hamilton, "but that the proclamation will undergo many strictures; and as the effect proposed may not be answered by it, it will be necessary to look forward in time to ulterior arrangements . . ." The use of Federal troops was to be avoided, if possible, because, as he put it, "there would be a cry at once, 'The cat is let out; we now see for what purpose an Army was raised.'" Even so, if force was necessary as a last resort, the Army must be used to restore order and to uphold the will of the country, expressed through an act of Congress.[99]

Other collisions seemed possible, though they scarcely could be regarded as impending. With funds provided during the last days of the session of Congress, Washington authorized a new effort for the ransom of the American seamen held captive by the pirates of the Barbary States;[100] the uncertain situation in France gave Washington daily concern,[101] and, at the same time, it fired ardent republicans in Phila-

---

[96] On general conditions with respect to the excise and the course of action to be pursued by the Federal government, see 32 G. W., 137, 320–21, 469; 1 Gibbs, Wolcott Papers, 68, 72; 10 Sparks, 526 ff; 10 A. Hamilton, 18–19; 3 John Jay, 444–45; Jay to Hamilton, Sept. 8, 1792, 17 Hamilton Papers, 2331.

[97] 32 G. W., 143–44.

[98] Jefferson was then at Monticello, whither the proclamation was sent by express. See ibid., 149–51, 153–55, 169, 171; 8 Jefferson, 412. The proclamation, dated Sept. 15, 1792, will be found in 1 Richardson, 124–25 and in 32 G. W., 150–51.

[99] Letter of Sept. 16, 1792; ibid., 153.

[100] Ibid., 55–56, 125; Washington to Jefferson, Aug. 20, 1792; Nat. Arc. RG 59. State Dept.: Misc. Lets., f. 56 (not in G. W.); 8 Jefferson, 353, with the details of the capture of these men from the schooner Maria and the ship Dauphin in 1785. Cf. ibid., 366, 374. The story of the long correspondence and negotiation for the release of these captives may be traced in ASP., 1 For. Rel., 100–08, 117–20, 129–33.

[101] Knox to Washington, Sept. 16, 1792, Knox Papers, MHS; 32 G. W., 87–88. William Short, then at The Hague, was forwarding to his government a series of dispatches on the French Revolution. These were less skillfully written but scarcely less informative than the famous letters Gouverneur Morris was sending from Paris. Short's dispatches have the advantage of a certain detachment from the scene, even if they lack the color of Morris's. These interesting documents are filed in the National Archives with the Dispatches of United States Ministers to the Netherlands.

delphia to organize a Jacobin Club; the *National Gazette* was in a rapture; Fenno's teeth chattered as he wrote that the word "club" was "almost synonymous to faction."[102] Neither Federalist nor republican editors seemed to regard the fact—if indeed they discerned it—that relations with Britain were slowly approaching a settlement. Hamilton soon was to receive a confidential report that Lord Hawkesbury[103] had said, "as long as Washington is at the head of the executive and the Federal party prevail, there will be no war with this country, as peace is the interest and wish of both governments."[104] Further, after some maneuvering to prevail upon both Ternant and Hammond to visit Mount Vernon,[105] the British Minister arrived late in September.[106] Considerately, he did not tarry long, though doubtless the President extended his warmest hospitality to the young diplomat.[107]

After Hammond's departure, Washington completed his arrangements at Mount Vernon, as far as this was possible, and made preparations for his own leave-taking. Already he had called on several of his subordinates to give him their suggestions for his annual "speech" to Congress,[108] and, during spare moments toward the end of Hammond's visit, he had had opportunity of talking with Jefferson, who stopped on the Potomac en route to Philadelphia from Monticello. Before breakfast on the morning of the 1st of October, the two had a long, frank discussion of the desire both had to retire from public service. Washington explained his state of mind and confessed that he still was in doubt about a second term, though all his inclination was to return to Mount Vernon; only there was he happy.[109] He said the evidence he had from Tobias Lear, whom he had instructed to make inquiry, was that it seemed to be the wish of the people in the North for him

---

[102] *Gazette of U. S.*, June 23, 1792, p. 3. See *National Gaz.*, June 18, p. 2: "The patriotic French song of *Ça Ira* . . . may be considered as the funeral dirge of tyrants"; *ibid.*, June 21, p. 3: "Few people have a proper sense of the importance of the success of the French revolution to the welfare and happiness of America . . . Should the French Revolution eventually succeed, a moderate degree of vigilance on the part of the people of this country will preserve a pure republican system . . ."; *ibid.*, July 7, 1792, p. 2: The friends of the French Revolution are "the real friends to the revolution in America."

[103] This was Charles Jenkinson, later (1796) first Earl of Liverpool, usually known in British history of the seventeen-nineties as Lord Liverpool.

[104] Conversation of Aug. 19, 1792, with "Mr. Baring," almost certainly Francis Baring, who received a baronetcy in May, 1793; 17 *Hamilton Papers*, 2310.

[105] See Knox to Washington, Sept. 16, 1792; *Knox Papers*, MHS.

[106] 32 *G. W.*, 163.

[107] Hammond's dispatch to Foreign Secretary Grenville, dated Oct. 3, 1792, fails to elaborate on the details of the visit but does mention a tour of the proposed site of the Federal City; *British Photostats*, Foreign Office 4, v. 16, No. 39, LC.

[108] 32 *G. W.*, 132–36, 140, 172–74.      [109] 1 *Jefferson*, 315.

to remain in office. "Those who expressed a doubt of his continuance, did it in the language of apprehension, and not of desire." [110]

Jefferson took this to be a hint that Washington wished to draw from him a statement of the view of Southerners, if their opinion differed from that of the region above the Delaware; but he did not have to employ the diplomatic art in answering. He affirmed that the President was "the only man in the United States who possessed the confidence of the whole; that government was founded in opinion and confidence, and that the longer [Washington] remained, the stronger would become the habits of the people in submitting to the Government, and in thinking it a thing to be maintained; that there was no other person who would be thought anything more than the head of a party." [111]

This brought the conversation to the doubt that troubled Washington as much as any other—whether he could and should attempt to go on when deep division existed between Jefferson and Hamilton. The President had never been aware, he told Jefferson, of the magnitude of the rift. "He knew, indeed, that there was a marked difference in our political sentiments, but he had never suspected it had gone so far in producing a personal difference, and he wished he could be the mediator to put an end to it." [112] Washington proceeded to explain in complete candor that he thought it important to have Jefferson among the officers of administration "in order to keep things in their proper channel, and prevent them from going too far." [113] As for the idea of changing the government into a monarchy, Washington said, "he did not believe there were ten men in the United States whose opinions were worth attention, who entertained such a thought." [114] Here, of course, Jefferson dissented, and, in citing what he considered proof that the monarchist element was considerable, he reverted to the allegations he previously had made against Hamilton as one of this large number. A call to breakfast ended the discussion. [115]

The next move of Washington was back to Philadelphia, via Georgetown, where, on the 8th of October, he attended a sale of lots in the new Federal City. [116] The satisfactions of this evidence of public faith

---

[110] This is Jefferson's paraphrase of Washington's quotation of Lear and not the precise words of the General's secretary; *ibid.*, 316.

[111] *Ibid.*, 317.　　　　[112] *Ibid.*　　　　[113] *Ibid.*　　　　[114] *Ibid.*

[115] 1 *Jefferson*, 317–19. The quotations are from Jefferson's minutes of the conversation as set down later that day at Bladensburg and subsequently incorporated in the "Anas."

[116] 32 *G. W.*, 170. Original deeds and titles, with every lot and its purchaser accounted for, are compiled in Erastus Thatcher, *Founding of Washington City*.

in the future of the "permanent seat of government" were marred by the second report Washington had received of strange electioneering tales told by John Francis Mercer, a Maryland candidate for reelection to Congress. The first yarn, promptly and indignantly denied by Washington, had been to the effect that the President had endorsed Mercer as "the best representative that now goes or ever did go" to Congress from the State. Washington, of course, never had spoken for or against any candidate and he set down that fact stiffly in a letter to Mercer.[117] The second report, which Washington did not have time to hear in full at Georgetown, was that Mercer had charged Hamilton with attempting to bribe the Marylander to "vote for a further assumption of the State debts." Washington put this away in his mind, incomplete though the story was, so that, later on, he might investigate the charge.[118]

From Georgetown, with Martha and the other members of the family, Washington went to Baltimore and there on the 10th he received entertainment at the hands of gentlemen of the city, entertainment that included the inescapable toasts with artillery salute as the wine was drunk.[119] This sort of hospitality was becoming an embarrassment to Washington. He had told James McHenry: ". . . it oftentimes, if not always, proves inconvenient to some of the party bestowing, if it is not to the party receiving, the compliment of a public dinner, being a tax which I am as unwilling to impose, as many are to pay, if false delicacy would allow them to express their real sentiments." [120] The dinner had been arranged in spite of this protest, which had been voiced in advance. With thanks to his host, the President made the best speed he could to Philadelphia and arrived there on the 13th of October.[121]

As soon as he reopened his office, Washington found that the routine of his daily life had to be changed somewhat. Public duties, of course, still came first and would demand many hours, because Congress was to meet on the 5th of November and affairs in the Federal District had to be supervised. Without stinting here or in his general administration, Washington had to devote much thought to Mount Vernon and had to write many long, long letters to the manager, Anthony Whiting.

[117] *Ibid.*, 147 n, 165–66.
[119] Scharf, *The Chronicles of Baltimore*, 264.
[120] 32 *G. W.*, 110.
[118] *Ibid.*, 193–94.
[121] *Ibid.*, 177; *Baker*, 243.

In bulk, these communications represented more than half of Washington's total correspondence during the winter of 1792–93,[122] but they went southward every week in Washington's swift, clear autograph. The apparent marvel of conservation of time in finding privacy for drafting these letters was no marvel at all: Washington devoted to them a considerable part of each Sunday. His general direction of the Federal District was simplified by his insistence that a superintendent be chosen as soon as possible and that he personally deal with this new official and with all others through the District Commissioners only.[123] Administrative practice in Philadelphia was modified, also, to the extent that Washington conferred more frequently with the heads of departments as a whole and, further, that he increasingly turned over documents to these men for examination and report. He did not change his practice of seeking the advice of individuals when he needed it, even though the question at issue concerned the department of another.[124]

Where foreign affairs were involved, Washington might have wished for more papers of a positive nature to circulate among department chiefs. Relations with Spain scarcely were better, in spite of denials by the King's agents of any incitation of the Creeks against the Americans. The attitude of Spain in the probable event of war between Britain and France was the subject of much earnest consideration in Philadelphia, but, for weeks, the only result was anxiety.[125] It was manifest, also, that a new crisis was developing in France, and perhaps in that

[122] Between Oct. 14, 1792 and Mch. 3, 1793, he wrote Whiting twenty-one letters, most of them long. The first of these, penned the day after he reached Philadelphia, ran to approximately 2800 words. See 32 *G. W.*, 177–85. These papers show a most extraordinary knowledge of all activity and of every location on the Mount Vernon estate, and they constitute specific evidence that, at least so far as his personal affairs were involved, Washington erred when he protested that his memory was failing.

[123] The troubled affairs of the District—Judge Thomas Johnson's resignation, a renewed dispute with Burnes, misunderstanding with Andrew Ellicott and all the preliminaries of finding a superintendent—may be followed in Johnson to Washington, Jan. 16, 1793, Nat. Arc. RG 59. State Dept.: *Misc. Lets.*, f. 31; David Stuart to Washington, Dec. 10, 1792, 257 *Papers of G. W.*, 87, LC; David Burnes to Washington, Feb. 12, 1793, Nat. Arc. as cited, f. 66; Uriah Howell to Washington, Jan. 10, 1793, *ibid.*, f. 18; Lear to Jefferson, Jan. 11, 1793, *ibid.*, f. 20; Jefferson to Washington (third person), Feb. 14, 1793, *ibid.*, f. 69; David Stuart to Washington, Feb. 18, 1793, 258 *Papers of G. W.*, 81–82, LC; 32 *G. W.*, 308–09, 344 n. For the completion of the plat of the District and its transmission to Congress, Feb. 18, 1793, see Jefferson to Washington, Feb. 18, 1793, Nat. Arc. State Dept.: *Dom. Lets.*, v. 5, p. 57–58; 32 *G. W.*, 351; 1 *JS*, 489; 1 *JHR.*, 705.

[124] Supervision of the new mint, which Washington may have visited on Dec. 28, 1792 (*Decatur*, 323), was a case in point, 32 *G. W.*, 187. Cf. *ibid.*, 342, and Lear to Jefferson (third person), Jan. 16, 1793; Washington to Jefferson, Feb. 13, 1793; Lear to Jefferson, Feb. 26, 1793. Nat. Arc. RG 59. State Dept.: *Misc. Lets.*, 29, 67, 95.

[125] 1 *Jefferson*, 319–20; 8 *ibid.*, 416–18, 422, 423, 425; the correspondence with the Spanish agents is in *ASP.*, 1 *For. Rel.*, 138–39.

country's relations with the United States. The talk of the French Minister was of the abolition of privateering, a suggestion that prompted
Jefferson to propose general negotiations that would include revision
of the commercial treaty. Here again, nothing tangible seemed likely
to come out of the discussions until the course of the French Revolution was less obscured by doubt.[126] The one exception was the nature
and measure of assistance that could be given the French in suppressing
the slave insurrection in Santo Domingo.[127] With Britain, as with
France, it did not appear that negotiation would progress far, certainly
in America, until the issue of war or peace was determined. When
effort was made, during the winter, to pin down the British Minister,
his elusive answer was that he lacked instructions.[128]

Washington might have said, then, that he had too little business
with foreign powers, and too much with his manager at Mount Vernon
and his commissioners in the Federal District. Relations with Congress,
on the other hand, had now been established firmly and, in most particulars, involved little more than a continuing deference,[129] the delivery
of messages, and a steady compliance with the lawmakers' requests,
when reasonable. The session opened in the usual manner on the 5th
of November [130] with the familiar figure of Richard Henry Lee missing
because of his resignation.[131] Washington's annual message, which was
delivered on the 6th, had been prepared with the assistance of the heads
of departments and after some careful inquiry by Lear,[132] but it was a
matter-of-fact document in which Indian affairs had first place. Washington listed the various threats on the frontier, explained what had
been done, together with what was projected, and made the plea he so

[126] 8 *Jefferson*, 421; 32 *G. W.*, 188–90. Gouverneur Morris's notable letter of Oct. 22, 1792
to Washington, will be found conveniently in 4 *LTW.*, 409–14. Short's dispatches of Nov. 9,
16, 1792, as cited *supra*, n. 101, are informative for the reason there given.

[127] Concerning this, Hamilton and Jefferson disagreed (1 *Jefferson*, 323–24; 4 *LTW.*, 415.
See also 8 *Jefferson*, 419–20, 441–42). Washington's later decision to pay certain bills drawn
by the colonial administration was covered by Lear to Jefferson, Jan. 14, 1793; Nat. Arc. RG 59.
State Dept.: *Misc. Lets.*, f. 26.

[128] 9 *Jefferson*, 7; 32 *G. W.*, 284. Pinckney's dispatch of Dec. 13, 1792 (Nat. Arc. State
Dept.: *Dipl. Desp.* 3 G. B.) was interesting but not encouraging; that of Dec. 31, 1792, concerned chiefly routine matters (*ibid.*); in that of Jan. 7, 1793 (*ibid.*) he had to confess with
embarrassment that he "most unaccountably" had lost his cipher, which undoubtedly had been
stolen.

[129] As, for example, in his report on the use made of militia, 32 *G. W.*, 253.

[130] For the usual preliminaries, see 1 *JS*, 451–52.

[131] Oct. 8, 1792, on account of feeble health; 2 *Ballagh, Lee Letters*, 550–51. John Taylor
came back to the Senate Dec. 12, 1792, as successor to Lee. 1 *JS*, 463.

[132] Randolph's suggestions of Oct. 28, 1792, are in 257 *Papers of G. W.*, 20, LC, but were
not important; Knox's of Oct. 14, 1792 (*ibid.*, 4) were in the same category. Most of Hamilton's and Jefferson's proposals doubtless were oral. For Lear, see *supra*, pp. 373–74.

often had voiced for restraining those persons guilty of outrages on the Indians.[133] The one consoling note in this part of the address was the expression of opinion that if the scale of operations was not increased, the cost probably could be met from existing revenues.[134] Next came brief reference to what appeared to be diminishing resistance to the excise on whiskey,[135] an unpleasant subject, followed by recommendation that Congress revise the judiciary system [136] and enact laws to discourage aggression against the territory of other countries.[137] The nearest approach to a political issue was the unqualified observation that "the state of the national finances" made possible an arrangement to begin paying off the Federal debt and the loan issued for the Bank of the United States,[138] a course of action vigorously advocated by the republicans.

One bit of good luck attended the delivery of the address: The very next day, word was received that on the 27th of September, Gen. Rufus Putnam had signed with the Wabash and Illinois Indians a treaty that removed one threat to the settlers on the Ohio and some of its tributaries.[139] By chance, Knox had submitted to Congress that same 7th of November a "General View" of negotiations with the Indians. Those members who had the patience to wade through the deep documents would have to admit, in simple honesty, that the Federal government had done all that could be expected of it in trying to maintain peace, to punish murderers, and to protect peaceful settlers from raids.[140] Reports sent Congress the next week on conditions in Florida and the country of the Creeks were equally to the credit of the Federal government.[141]

Important as was the message in what it said of Indian affairs that led to these developments, the address was most notable, to some observers, for one omission: not a word did it include concerning Washington's wishes or intentions with respect to a second term. He was

---

[133] 32 G. W., 205–08. The text is also in 1 Richardson, 125–29, in 1 JS, 452–55, and in 1 JHR., 611–13.

[134] 32 G. W., 207–08.        [135] Ibid., 208.        [136] Ibid., 209.

[137] Ibid., 209–10.        [138] Ibid., 211–12.

[139] 8 Jefferson, 439; 2 Paine Wingate, 411; ASP., 1 Ind. Aff., 319 ff. The treaty itself was transmitted to Congress Feb. 13, 1793, ibid., 338.

[140] ASP., 1 Ind. Aff., 225 ff. Putnam's instructions are ibid., p. 234. Indian affairs in the South, including Florida, are presented along with those of the Northwest. The papers date from December, 1791.

[141] Ibid., 320, 325 ff; 1 Fisher Ames, 125; 2 Paine Wingate, 413. Cf. Thomas Hartley to Anthony Wayne, Jan. 27[?], 1793: "As the Indian war is very odious in several of the States, I am sure it will be your study to obtain peace" (Wayne Papers, PHS).

silent where it might have been supposed he would speak out if he had held to his purpose to retire. Truth was, he had not brought himself to announce his wish to quit public life. He recognized the force of the arguments that both Jefferson and Hamilton advanced when they urged him to accept reelection; nor could he deny either the gravity of the times or the advantage he alone could enjoy as the positive choice of two rival leaders who agreed on almost nothing else political. Was there danger of opposition in spite of what the Federalist chieftain and the republican spokesman assured him? Would he at 61 have to forgo, after all, the quiet ease of Mount Vernon and, in return, suffer the humiliation of a smaller vote than he had received in 1788-89? Day by day he put off the answer and would promise no more than that he would not make an announcement *then*. As late as November 17, an able woman, who knew him well, thought it necessary to exhort him to the favorable choice she felt he had not made at that time.[142] The sole assurance that electors would not be throwing away their votes for him was the fact that he had not said "No."[143] He had told Madison as long previously as May that he intended to make his announcement at a time most convenient to the public for choosing his successor; that he had thought of the opening of Congress as a suitable occasion but that he had laid this aside because, for one thing, the session would be late in starting.[144] Now the States were preparing to name electors, Congress had begun its session, and he still was silent.

No rival for the office had appeared, none was so much as mentioned. Unless Washington declined almost immediately, he would be reelected. That was certain. Equally was it certain, from the beginning of the session, that the contest for Vice President would be hard fought, that the rivalry of Jefferson and Hamilton would involve many men and numerous issues, and that the clash of parties would be louder and more violent. Washington took absolutely no part in the battle for the Vice Presidency, which became an ugly fight against John Adams by

---

[142] Elizabeth Powel to Washington, Nov. 17, 1792; *Powel Papers*, Mount Vernon.

[143] The key to his state of mind is in a remark to Henry Lee, early the next year: ". . . it was after a long and painful conflict in my own breast, that I was withheld (by considerations which are not necessary to mention) from requesting, *in time*, that no vote might be thrown away upon me; it being my fixed determination to return to the walks of private life, at the end of my term." Letter of Jan. 20, 1793; 32 *G. W.*, 310. His reference to the size of the vote, mentioned *infra*, p. 384, is in the same letter. Jefferson noted, Dec. 13, 1792, that he thought Washington made a remark to him, about the slow delivery of certain china, in order to indicate that he would retire within two years (1 *Jefferson*, 326-27). No supporting evidence of this has been found, though there is no inherent improbability to the story.

[144] See *supra*, p. 375.

George Clinton and the republicans.[145] Had Washington been in private life, he no doubt would have endorsed Adams as he had in 1788,[146] because the casting vote of the Vice President always had been on the side of adequate government and Adams's personal relations lacked nothing of civility or consideration. As it was, the President of all the people did not feel that he could be the advocate of even so admirable a public servant as he considered his second in command to be.[147]

Contention shifted in Congress from personalities to principles and back again, time after time. A Federal proposal to have the heads of departments appear on the floor by legislative permission, and to explain their acts, was defeated early in the session by a majority so large that Jefferson thought it an augury of republican gain already observable in the elections to the third Congress.[148] "I think," he said, "we may consider the tide of this government as now at the fullest, and that it will, from the next session of Congress, retire and subside into the true principles of the constitution." [149] He looked forward to the success of his developing party and insisted, all the while, that he wished to quit public life and to go back to his "little mountain." [150] Hamilton was of much the same mind with respect to private life,[151] but both he and his rival had too much fighting spirit [152] to decamp while the battle continued,[153]

[145] For endorsement of Washington and denunciation of Adams in the same breath, see reprints from *New-York Journal* in *National Gazette*, September 12, p. 4, and October 10, p. 2. *Dunlap's American Daily Advertiser* joined the attack on Adams in its November issues. Fenno's defence was spirited: "The calumniators of Mr. Adams pretend to be perfectly satisfied with the administration of the President . . . and while they discover great solicitude to depreciate the former in the public estimation, they scarcely risk a whisper against the latter" (*Gazette of U. S.*, November 21, p. 2). See also "Antonius" in *ibid.*, November 28, p. 1, and "Philanthropos," December 1, p. 1.      [146] See *supra*, p. 154.

[147] It seems probable that the campaign for the Vice Presidency in 1792 was a rehearsal that deserves more study than it has received. In addition to the newspapers, which contain much material, the following references may be found useful: 10 *A. Hamilton*, 25; 2 *Rowland, Carroll*, 181, 190; 2 *Paine Wingate*, 411–12; 1 *Gibbs, Wolcott Papers*, 83, 84; 1 *Fisher Ames*, 123, 125; 6 *Hunt's Madison*, 121 n; 8 *Jefferson*, 446; Joseph Jones to James Madison, Dec. 24, 1792, a vigorous argument against Adams, based solely on "what I have heard," 15 *Madison Papers*, 108. The Adams Papers on the election of 1792 have not been examined in the course of this study.

[148] 8 *Jefferson*, 439–40. The vote, Nov. 16, 1792, was 35–11. See 1 *JHR.*, 614, 619.

[149] Letter of Dec. 3, 1792, to Thomas Pinckney; 8 *Jefferson*, 443. Federalists were complaining that men who had been consistently hostile to the government were trying to seize power (Charles Carroll to Hamilton, Oct. 22, 1792; 2 *Rowland, Carroll*, 181) and that few of those who were most clamorous against the funding system had an understanding of it (David Stuart to Washington, Sept. 11, 1792; 256 *Papers of G. W.*, 65, LC).

[150] 8 *Jefferson*, 438–39.

[151] See John Jay to Hamilton, Dec. 29, 1792; 18 *Hamilton Papers*, 2444.

[152] See John Bard to Hamilton, Mch. 4, 1793; 18 *ibid.*, 2523, with quotation of Pope's epitaph on James Craggs the younger.

[153] 1 *Jefferson*, 330–32; 9 *ibid.*, 155 ff.

and neither could confine his energies to the department assigned him by Washington.[154] The President kept himself apart from their controversy, as far as he could, and showed no favoritism. Not long after his return to Philadelphia, for example, he had written to David Stuart in an effort to establish the facts concerning Col. John Francis Mercer's alleged statement that Hamilton had tried to bribe the Marylander.[155] At one time, too, early in the winter of 1792–93, he was much closer to Jefferson's point of view, with respect to France, than to Hamilton's.[156] He continued, also, his efforts to reconcile the two men [157] but without any success whatsoever.

When questions between the followers of Jefferson and of Hamilton were brought to a test in Congress, victory was more often with the Federalists than with the republicans. Consideration of the critical report of the committee that had investigated St. Clair's defeat [158] was referred to another committee which made several corrections of no great importance to the first report; but this document was not completed until late in the session and never was brought up for discussion, though its sponsor was the vehement republican Representative, William B. Giles, who would have spared no official and no contractor.[159] This was tactical gain for the Federalists in the sense that it was an escape from vindictive thrust and it was attended by numerous steps to place relations with the Indians where Washington had been urging them to be, on a basis of justice and fair dealing.[160] "In vain we may expect peace with the Indians on our frontiers, so long as a lawless set of unprincipled wretches can violate the rights of hospitality, or infringe the most solemn treaties, without receiving the punishment they so justly merit." [161]

[154] For Jefferson, see his letter of Jan. 3, 1793, to William Short, 9 *Jefferson*, 9 ff. Cf. 1 *Gibbs, Wolcott Papers*, 86; for Hamilton, see Gouverneur Morris, from London, Mch. 21, 1792, to Hamilton, an assurance that he will give Hamilton information that will be private and will not be disclosed to anyone else (15 *Hamilton Papers*, 2074). Hamilton's intimacy with George Hammond, British Minister, was a matter of common knowledge.

[155] See *supra*, p. 375. None of Stuart's answers to Washington, now in the *Papers of G. W.*, contains any acknowledgment of this letter or any references to the charge.

[156] 1 *Jefferson*, 327–28.

[157] 32 *G. W.*, 185–86; 1 *Jefferson*, 331–32.

[158] It had been presented May 8, 1792; 1 *JHR.*, 605.

[159] 1 *JHR.*, 614, 619, 620, 704 ff. Giles's report was presented Feb. 15, 1793. The first or "Fitzsimons" report of May 8, 1792, is in 3 *Annals*, 1106 ff; the second or "Giles" report is in *ibid.*, 1309 ff.

[160] See 32 *G. W.*, 260–61, 312–13, 327 n. Washington did his utmost to get three conspicuous men to serve as commissioners to negotiate with the savages. Cf. 2 *Rowland, Carroll*, 199; 1 *EJS.*, 135; 1 *Fisher Ames*, 122.

[161] 32 *G. W.*, 338.

A definite victory for the Federalists, Hamilton in particular, came late in the session after the impetuous Giles had moved and the House had directed, that Washington and Hamilton respectively supply information about loans and balances with the Bank of the United States. Although many of these facts had been requested and submitted two months previously,[162] Giles's resolutions were so worded that they might be considered an entirely proper call for statistics and records; they might likewise be regarded as heavy with innuendo that something was wrong.[163] Hamilton met the demand so promptly and with such detailed and inclusive papers that even Giles was almost silenced.[164] The largest minority he rallied for a vote of censure on Hamilton was fifteen against a majority of thirty-three;[165] one of Giles's accusations was supported by seven members only,[166] three of them Virginians. It must have pained Washington to learn that Madison had voted in every instance against Hamilton.[167]

The other contest of importance between the parties was over a proposal to extend the assumption of State debts. In those instances where adjustment of accounts showed a balance due a State by the Federal government for the expenses of war, the holders of State obligations could exchange them for Federal interest-bearing certificates similar, in most particulars, to those already issued in the assumption of State debts.[168] After the usual debate, maneuver and minor amendment, the bill passed the House by the casting vote of the Speaker, with substantially the whole republican contingent in opposition;[169] but in the Senate the measure was defeated, seventeen to eleven, on its second

---

[162] 1 *JHR.*, 631, 655; 3 *Annals*, 1162.

[163] Resolutions of Jan. 23, 1793, 1 *JHR.*, 677–78. See Jefferson's memorandum on the Hamilton report of Jan. 3, 1793, 15 *Madison Papers*, 114.

[164] Hamilton's reports, prepared with much hard effort (1 *Gibbs, Wolcott Papers*, 85), are most accessible, perhaps, in *ASP.*, 1 *Finance*, as follows: February 4, p. 192 ff; February 5, p. 200; February 13, p. 202; Feb. 14, 1793, p. 218. The final debates are in 3 *Annals*, 899 ff. Giles's only deliverance of any length at this time was on March 1 and was largely defensive (*ibid.*, 923 ff).

[165] 1 *JHR.*, 728.                          [166] *Ibid.*, 730.

[167] Chauncey Goodrich probably expressed the feeling of most Federalists when he wrote of Giles's rebuke: "He has now for his recompense to feel at least the confusion of detected rascality, whatever he may of remorse. One excellence of the chastisement is that it quickly follows the offence" (1 *Gibbs, Wolcott Papers*, 87). Thomas Hartley was content with the observation that Hamilton had given a "masterly answer to his adversaries" (Letter of Feb. 8, 1793, to Anthony Wayne; *Wayne Papers*, PHS). Jefferson's pale, approving comment on Giles's move is in 1 *Jefferson*, 345–46.

[168] Resolutions of Dec. 12, 1792; 1 *JHR.*, 637.

[169] *Ibid.*, 637, 669, 672, 676, 683–84. The debate is covered poorly in 3 *Annals*, 830 ff and, particularly, 844–51.

reading.[170] "There is no hope of doing anything for the State debts this session," wrote Fisher Ames in disgust, "nor will the faction from the South ever agree to provide for the balances." [171]

When defeats and victories for Hamilton and Jefferson had been set down, it might have been said, not unreasonably, that the Federalists had won the campaign but that the republicans might win the war. Washington observed the struggle with regret, and strove both to reduce personal animosities and to prevent damage to the new government. He winced as editorial darts were aimed increasingly in his direction, especially when the old charge of monarchical pomp was revived,[172] but he was philosophical even in this, and he was convinced that the "great body of the people now feel the advantages of the general government." Angry and exaggerated charges, he had written Gouverneur Morris soon after his return from Mount Vernon, "must be placed in opposition to the infinite benefits resulting from a free press; and I am sure you need not be told that in this country a personal difference in political sentiments is often made to take the garb of general dissensions." [173] He held to that, sometimes uncomfortably but always resolutely and, long before the party battles ended in Congress, he had evidence that the faith of Americans in him was undiminished. As the weeks had passed, he had made no statement concerning the election to the Presidency. In his own mind, he still had been restrained by what he termed "strong solicitations" in Philadelphia from saying that he would not accept reelection.[174] Silence had been taken as consent: On the 13th of February, 1793, when the vote was counted,

---

[170] Feb. 4, 1793; 1 JS, 479.

[171] 1 Fisher Ames, 127–28. To this list of important measures in which there was division between the parties, it may be proper to add the resolution of Dec. 28, 1792, for a reduction of the military establishment, but this was defeated promptly on Jan. 8, 1793, without any formal array of opposing factions, though most of the republicans favored the muster-out of part of the forces. See 1 JHR., 657, 661, 662, 664; 3 Annals, 762 ff, 773 ff.

[172] 1 Jefferson, 332–33. From mid-December on, Freneau dedicated space in almost every issue to mockery intended, doubtless, to fall at Washington's door rather than upon the head of Adams. See "Mirabeau" in National Gazette (December 12, p. 2), and "Fair Play" in the same number. "Cornelia" in the issue of December 26, p. 1, congratulates Freneau's contributors but adds that they "have not struck the evil at its root . . . witness the Drawing Room!" An intense criticism of "those apparent trifles, birthday odes" began on December 19 (p. 1), and was carried with zeal into 1793. Freneau himself on January 30 (p. 3), made a frontal assault: "It appears . . . that a new order of citizens has been created . . . consisting only of the officers of the federal government. The privileges of this order . . . consist in sharing exclusively in the profits of the 25,000 dollars a year allowed for the President's table, and in the honor of gazing upon him once a week at his levees." See, further, National Gazette, February 27 (p. 1), March 2 (p. 3), and "Mirabeau's" open letter to the President, March 13 (p. 1).

[173] Letter of Oct. 20, 1792; 32 G. W., 189–90.

[174] See his remarks of Feb. 7, 1793, to Jefferson; 1 Jefferson, 333.

John Adams was found the choice of seventy-seven electors and George Clinton of fifty,[175] but Washington had first place unanimously.[176] Not a voice had been raised for any other man at the head of the government. Celebration of his birthday, soon after the count of the electoral vote, was as hearty and affectionate as ever.[177]

He was 61 and he complained mildly of waning memory and of poor hearing, but few others saw any evidence of decline, and his daily life showed none, unless it was an increasing disposition to spend too much time on trifling matters of farm management. Was he not mounted and ready for four years more on the road of service to his country? The multitude of his followers and the handful of envious foes would have proclaimed the certainty with joy or reluctantly would have admitted the probability, but there were omens the road would be stony and cloud-covered, and there were voices prophesying strife.

[175] Virginia's entire vote of twenty-one had been given Clinton; 1 *JHR.*, 702.

[176] For the preliminaries and the formal count, see 1 *JS*, 479, 480, 484, 485, 487; 1 *JHR.*, 689, 699, 701–02. Much attention was given during the latter days of February, 1793, to the question, When and in what circumstances can an incumbent President take the oath of office for another term? See 32 *G. W.*, 336–37 n, 361 and n; 1 *Jefferson*, 344; Memorandum of Mch. 1, 1793, signed by Knox and Randolph, with appended note by Hamilton, 258 *Papers of G. W.*, 108, LC.

[177] *Baker*, 250–51. The same author quoted, p. 237, the statement by Edward Thornton, Minister George Hammond's secretary, that a dinner at Washington's table "is of all others the most dull and unentertaining." Thornton complained, as strange young male guests at the President's house often did, that "the President's reserve, the effect partly, I think, of pride, partly of constitutional diffidence, throws a restraint on the whole party." However that might be, Washington continued to entertain and had a staff adequate to most calls on it. Decatur, *op. cit.*, 277, calculated that Washington in June, 1792, had fifteen white servants and five slaves in the Presidential establishment.

# APPENDIX VI–I
## Growth of The Mount Vernon Tract

# APPENDIX VI–II
## American Newspapers and Editorial Opinion
### 1789–93

# APPENDIX VI-1

## Growth of the Mount Vernon Tract

(Washington's 1793 map of Mount Vernon is an illustration in this volume)

Through the will of Lawrence Washington, probated at the Fairfax County Court House on September 26, 1752,[1] his half-brother George came into possession of the Mount Vernon estate of some 2650 acres on the western shore of the Potomac between Little Hunting Creek and Dogue Run. This was almost exactly one-half of the original proprietary of 5000 acres in "the freshes" of the Potomac granted by Lord Culpeper to Col. Nicholas Spencer and Lt. Col. John Washington, March 9, 1674/75.[2] The large tract, which lay across the River from the Indian town of Piscataway, Maryland, was divided amicably and equally between the heirs of the grantees in 1690,[3] and the death of John Washington's son, Lawrence, in 1698 conveyed to his infant daughter, Mildred, the 2500 acres facing Little Hunting Creek.[4] It was years, however, before this land came under cultivation, for the Washingtons had settled seventy miles down the Potomac in Westmoreland County and had built their homestead, Wakefield, on Bridges Creek. Wakefield was in the occupancy of Lawrence's younger son, Augustine, when an opportunity came in 1726 to purchase from Mildred, now Mrs. Roger Gregory, the larger, unimproved tract up the River. The price was £180 sterling. Here was a bargain—2500 acres at slightly more than a shilling per acre—and Augustine concluded the transaction with his sister and her husband on May 17, 1726.[5] Nine years later Augustine moved his family up the River from Wakefield to a new seat on the lands, then called Epsewasson, on Little Hunting Creek.[6] The total acreage increased to 2700 in 1738 when Augustine's son Lawrence arranged for the purchase of 200 river-front acres from William Spencer, heir to the other half of the original Culpeper grant.[7] Lawrence conveyed this title to his father, but kept in his own name a section of fifty-six acres

[1] Lawrence died July 26, 1752. His will, dated June 16, 1752, appears in W. C. Ford, *Wills of George Washington and his Immediate Ancestors*, 73-79.
[2] *Va. Land Office Records*, Northern Neck, v. 5, p. 207. The grant was not recorded until 1677; see 6 *ibid.*, 615. See Vol. I, p. 22 and n.
[3] For the division, see original document in *Mount Vernon Collection* with a plat of the tract. See also Vol. I, p. 37.
[4] For this will, dated Mch. 11, 1697/98, see Ford, *op. cit.*, 33-38.
[5] Original deed is in *Mount Vernon Collection*. See Vol. I, p. 37.
[6] *Ibid.*, 52-53.
[7] Original deed, dated Mch. 1, 1738, is in *Mount Vernon Collection*.

on Dogue Run which he bought from Spencer in 1739.[8] Augustine's death in 1743 transferred to Lawrence, as eldest son, the 2500 acres on Little Hunting Creek, but the infant son Charles was bequeathed the 200 acres on the river acquired in 1739.[9] When Lawrence Washington adopted the name "Mount Vernon" for his lands in 1743, the acreage appears to have been 2556. In 1751, Lawrence added ninety-four acres on the south side of Dogue Run through purchase from Henry Frenn at five shillings per acre.[10] The Mount Vernon estate, therefore, totalled 2650 acres at the time title passed to George Washington in 1752.[11]

It was only natural for the new master of Mount Vernon to cherish the hope that some day the boundaries of his estate would be rounded out to conform to the lines of the original 5000-acre Spencer-Washington grant of 1674. This may have been a prime aspiration, but Washington knew that such an achievement would take years if it were possible at all. Meanwhile, no opportunity should be overlooked which would serve to enlarge Mount Vernon in other directions. Late in 1757 Washington purchased from Sampson Darrell a parcel of land on Dogue Run and another on Little Hunting Creek, paying £260 in current money and giving a note for £90 more.[12] A second negotiation two years later, rendered difficult by the tangled affairs and vacillation of the seller, and prolonged over several months, netted Washington the highly desirable 1806 acres held by William Clifton directly across Little Hunting Creek from Mount Vernon. "Clifton's Neck," the largest single acquisition in Washington's forty-seven years as a planter on the Potomac, cost £1210, Virginia currency, at auction in March, 1760.[13]

---

[8] Original deed was in possession of a New York dealer in 1948. This information was graciously furnished by Charles C. Wall, Resident Superintendent, Mount Vernon.

[9] Augustine's will, dated Apr. 11, 1743, was probated on May 6. It appears in Ford, *op. cit.*, 41–51.

[10] Original deed, dated Feb. 4, 1751, is in *Mount Vernon Collection*.

[11] Washington's own quit-rent records in *Ledgers A* and *B* (see statement for 1761 in 2 *G. W.*, 390; statement for 1765 reproduced opposite p. 436 in 2 *G. W.*) consistently credit only 2126 acres to that part of his property designated "Mount Vernon." If the total inheritance as calculated at 2650 acres is correct, it would appear that Washington had an imperfect knowledge of his boundaries and was estimating conservatively. A memorandum in Washington's hand, dated Oct. 1–2, 1759, emphasizes this possibility: "I endeavoured to find the true bounds of my Mount Vernon tract of land, but not knowing where it divided from the Spencers part on the river . . ." (*Mount Vernon Collection*). If the quit-rent figure of 2126 acres is correct, it is manifest that the Spencer "half" of the original 5000 acres was somewhat more than one-half and that Augustine's purchase from his sister Mildred in 1726 netted closer to 2000 than to 2500 acres.

[12] 1 *Diaries*, 127; *Ledger A*, f. 49, 89. See also Vol. III, p. 39. The section on Little Hunting Creek was the larger, a 300-acre parcel. For a history of Darrell's land, see his bond to Washington dated Dec. 20, 1757, in the *Mount Vernon Collection*.

[13] The frustrating negotiation with Clifton may be traced in 1 *Diaries*, 126, 128, 132, 135, 137, 140, 163–64 n. For the price, see *Ledger A*, f. 57, 101. The transaction is described fully in Vol. III, p. 39–41. For a sketch of the history of Clifton's Neck from the original patent of Capt. Giles Brent in 1653, see 1 *Diaries*, 125–26, n.3. This "Neck Plantation" (*ibid.*, 245) Washington designated "River Farm" on his 1793 map of the Mount Vernon lands which is reproduced in this volume.

That year Washington also purchased the 238 acres of George Brent on Little Hunting Creek for £250.[14]

During the next four years the master of Mount Vernon made a series of small purchases in the Dogue Run "quarter" which, in the aggregate, amounted to 658 acres of the old Spencer property. In 1761, though beset by unanticipated financial difficulties, Washington promised to deliver £150 for the 135-acre farm of William Ashford.[15] Settlement was made in 1762,[16] and in the same year the adjoining 135 acres of George Ashford came into the boundaries of the Mount Vernon estate.[17] From Simon Pearson, late in 1762, another parcel of 178 acres was added.[18] The "quarter" was filling out nicely, but 210 acres on the south side of Dogue Run remained in the possession of the heir of Henry Frenn who had released ninety-four acres to Lawrence Washington in 1751 at five shillings per acre. In the hope of acquiring the entire residue for £50 or £60, Washington commissioned his neighbor, Capt. John Posey, to negotiate with the orphaned Diana Frenn.[19] Posey at length reached an agreement with the lady and her husband, William Whiting, and on June 19, 1764, Washington contracted to pay £75 for the 210 acres.[20]

Posey's own property was the next addition, but it did not come until 1769. Washington's brother Charles, who as an infant had inherited the 200 river-front acres annexed to Epsewasson by Lawrence Washington's purchase from William Spencer in 1739, subsequently sold this land to Posey and the Captain incorporated it into his "Ferry Farm." Posey, however, had been constantly in Washington's debt for varying amounts since 1755, and in 1762 had borrowed £700 to satisfy the clamor of numerous creditors.[21] In 1767 Washington had to refuse Posey's request for an additional £300.[22] In desperation the Captain then claimed that his 200 acres of river frontage had been improved to the value of at least £700 and asked Washington to stand as surety for a £300 loan currently being negotiated with George

---

[14] See Washington's letter to Robert Cary and Company, Aug. 10, 1760 (2 G. W., 349–50), in which the seller is named incorrectly as "Robert Brent." Washington altered this to "George Brent" in his next mention of the transaction (2 G. W., 352). For the exact acreage, see Washington's quit-rent and tax memorandum for 1761 in 2 G. W., 390. Brent's land was the remainder of a 584-acre grant to his ancestor by Governor Jeffreys in 1677; see the original patent in *Mount Vernon Collection.*

[15] Vol. III, p. 64.

[16] 1 *Diaries*, 185 n; Vol. III, p. 76 n.

[17] That there were two distinct Ashford purchases, each for 135 acres, is indicated by Washington's quit-rent accounts for 1762; 2 G. W., 390.

[18] 1 *Diaries*, 154 and n; *Ledger A*, f. 132.

[19] 1 *Diaries*, 136.

[20] *Ibid.*, 139 and n. Washington's quit-rent records for 1765, reproduced opposite p. 436 in 2 G. W., show the acreage of the Mount Vernon tract at 5318. This figure included all acquisitions through 1764.

[21] Vol. III, p. 100.

[22] *Ibid.*, 184.

Mason.[23] To this Washington reluctantly gave his consent, but within two years more Posey's decline was complete. In July, 1769, Washington offered to buy from his bankrupt neighbor the 200 river-front acres,[24] but Posey clung to the hope that somehow he could redeem his fortunes and save his land as well. While Washington did not demand payment of the sums owed him and long overdue, other creditors had abandoned their patience and were entering suit against the distraught Captain. The reckoning came on Oct. 23, 1769, in a court sale at Posey's plantation. Washington bid in the 200 acres he had sought,[25] and two years later negotiated directly with Posey for the purchase of the six acres and buildings of the Captain's homestead, Rover's Delight.[26] Also in 1769 Washington bought from George Mason 100 acres on Dogue Run which adjoined the land acquired from Sampson Darrell twelve years before.[27]

Washington's tract was expanding—but considerable portions of the old Spencer property still lay in the Dogue Run "quarter" under various owners, resident or absentee. These lands proved irresistible to the master of Mount Vernon. One parcel of 118 acres was in the possession of Mrs. Valinda Wade, and Washington paid £175 current money for it in December, 1770.[28] Charles West's 484 acres, called the "Chappel Land," was acquired after a vexatious wait in October, 1772,[29] and Washington immediately sold seventy-two acres, which he did not want, to George William Fairfax.[30] Much negotiation through Lund Washington was necessary to accomplish the annexation, in 1779, of Thomas Marshall's tract of 500 acres directly North of the land formerly owned by Posey.[31] Mrs. Wade's sister, Mrs. Sarah Barry, held title to 118 acres, and the purchase of this parcel for £350 in

[23] Ibid., 191.

[24] Ibid., 231.

[25] Ibid., 233.

[26] The date of the transaction was June 8, 1772. Washington paid £50. Ledger B, f. 50. Posey's "Ferry Farm" formed part of the river frontage of the "Union Farm" as shown in Washington's 1793 map of Mount Vernon; see illustration in this volume.

[27] Ledger A, f. 61. Washington and Mason had surveyed this land on Apr. 19, 1769 (I Diaries, 321), prior to the transfer of title.

[28] For the transaction of Dec. 17–18, 1770 and the earlier history of the Wade property, see the deed of William and Sarah Barry, dated June 16, 1783, in Mount Vernon Collection. It is incorrectly noted in 1 Diaries, 233 n., that Washington purchased the Wade lands in 1773. Washington made a survey (2 ibid., 79) of these 118 acres on Sept. 18–19, 1772.

[29] Original deed, dated Oct. 27–28, 1772, is in Mount Vernon Collection. See also Ledger B, f. 59. In mid-1769 Washington was urging Charles West to sell his "cold wet ground"; see letter to West, June 6, 1769, in 2 G. W., 505–07. For the history of the "Chappel Land," later known as "Woodlawn," see the statement of Col. George Mason dated Apr. 29, 1805, in Mount Vernon Collection.

[30] Ledger B, f. 66. See Vol. III, 294.

[31] Ledger B, f. 156. For the source of 350 acres of this tract, see the deed of William and Sarah Barry, dated June 16, 1783, in Mount Vernon Collection. For Washington's instructions to Lund, see letters of Dec. 18, 1778 (13 G. W., 423 ff) and Sept. 14, 1779 (16 ibid., 290). See also the correspondence of Lund Washington for 1778, Mount Vernon Collection.

June, 1783,[32] filled out Washington's borders in the Dogue Run area. His acquisitions on and around Dogue Run since 1757 totalled more than 2000 acres.

Facing Little Hunting Creek and adjacent to the Clifton tract, John West's farm of 203 acres proved attractive enough to cause Washington to pay £436 for its title in September, 1772.[33] After the purchase of the last of the Dogue Run properties in 1783, Washington focused his attention on the 650-odd acres that lay between Little Hunting and Epsewasson Creeks. The greater part of this ground, some 500 acres, was held in absentia by Mrs. Penelope French, an aged widow; the remaining 142 acres had passed from Harrison Manley upon his death to an executor, William Triplet. Mrs. French's land was in the care of her son-in-law, Benjamin Dulaney, and late in 1781 Washington disclosed his interest in the French-Manley property by remarking to Dulaney that "it is my wish . . . to have in expectation . . . all the lands in this neck." [34] Washington feared at the time that Dulaney might bid successfully for Manley's acres at auction, but Dulaney assured him that the area in question was "entirely at the disposal of Mr. William Triplet, the executor." [35] In February, 1785, Dulaney visited Mount Vernon and concluded with Washington an agreement for the exchange of Mrs. French's property for equivalent acreage outside Alexandria.[36] The bargain, which Washington described as "long in agitation," [37] was further complicated by Mrs. French's "life interest" in the 500 acres, and it was not until late in 1786 that a positive date of occupancy could be foreseen.[38] Meanwhile, Washington proceeded to negotiate for the 142 acres held in executorship by William Triplet. On September 25, 1786, he wrote that his intention regarding the French-Manley property had never been mercenary. Rather, he hoped "to blend them and my other plantations together, and to form entire new ones out of the whole." [39] Referring to Manley's land, Washington asked: "Is there a single acre which can be converted into meadow? Is not the land much worn, greatly exhausted and gullied in many places?" [40] Before the year was out, the title to the property was in Washington's hands.[41]

[32] Original deed of June 16, 1783, is in *Mount Vernon Collection*. For an earlier boundary dispute with William Barry, see Vol. III, 287.

[33] Photostat of the deed, dated Sept. 22, 1772, is in 13 *Papers of G. W.* Cf. *Ledger B*, f. 31. Washington surveyed this land at West's request in July (2 *Diaries*, 76).

[34] Washington to Dulaney, Nov. 17, 1781, in 23 *G. W.*, 350.

[35] Dulaney to Washington, Feb. 28, 1782, in 24 *ibid.*, 70 n.

[36] 2 *Diaries*, 339–40. Deeds were exchanged at Alexandria on Feb. 21, 1785; *ibid.*, 344.

[37] *Ibid.*, 339.

[38] See memorandum, dated Oct. 24, 1786 and signed by John Robertson, in *Mount Vernon Collection*. Robertson, who was leasing the land from Mrs. French agreed to vacate before Jan. 1, 1787.

[39] Letter to William Triplet, Sept. 25, 1786, in 29 *G. W.*, 17.

[40] *Ibid.*, 20.

[41] *Ledger B*, f. 29.

With this, the master of Mount Vernon made his last acquisition in land on the Potomac.

From 1757 to 1786 Washington added 5601 acres to his estate in seventeen separate purchases. At its peak, the Mount Vernon tract covered 8251 acres. After the single diminution that occurred through transfer of 178 acres to Lund Washington's name,[42] there was, in 1799, a total acreage of 8073.[43] Washington's negotiations had carried the boundaries of his plantation far beyond the original lines in the North and East. Dogue Run furnished a natural western boundary, and on the South more than four miles of Washington's property faced the quiet Potomac.[44]

[42] This was the land in Dogue Run "quarter" purchased from Darrell in 1762. See letter to Bushrod Washington, Oct. 9, 1797, in 36 G. W., 43.

[43] Eugene E. Prussing (*Estate of Washington* . . . 198), gives 8060 as the final acreage and estimates that Washington owned about thirteen square miles in all.

[44] See Washington's 1793 map of his five farms as reproduced in the present volume.

# APPENDIX VI-2

## American Newspapers and Editorial Opinion, 1789–93

"The newspapers," wrote Fisher Ames in an acid mood after the collapse of the Federalists in 1800, "are an overmatch for any government. They will first overawe and then usurp it. This has been done, and the Jacobins owe their triumph to the unceasing use of this engine." [1] In the despair of the hour Ames may have magnified the responsibility of the anti-administration press for the overthrow of President Adams, but he was hitting very near the target of truth. The years between 1789 and 1801 were distinguished, certainly, by a frenzied partisanship of editorial opinion that admits of few parallels in American history. [2] Ever-mounting intensity of party feeling through the decade of the seventeen-nineties fostered a climate ideal for press warfare, and the newspapers made the most of it. Particular gazettes soared in influence and their editors ascended in national importance to heights seldom attained by followers of the profession of journalism. In 1789 there were newspapers which could, with at least a degree of honesty, claim modest adherence to the slogan of political impartiality so often displayed in their mastheads. Within three years, however, the development of a faction hostile to the Federalist administration had compelled even the most circumspect editors to print controversial opinion. The pennant of unanimity was struck down and the garish colors of political allegiance hoisted in its stead. As the decade proceeded, party fever raged and obliterated the careful neutrality of dozens of newspapers and of thousands of citizens who read them. The printer had become an editor and was feeling strength in his new rôle. The choice was his to make. Either he must endorse the policies of Alexander Hamilton and hold his paper fast as an avowed Federalist organ, or he must bend somewhat in the direction of Thomas Jefferson and pay tribute to the philosophy of the Republican party. Tumultuous climaxes came in the Presidential campaigns of 1796 and 1800, but the acrimonious electioneering

[1] Ames to Theodore Dwight, Mch. 19, 1801; 1 *Fisher Ames*, 294.
[2] For summary treatment of the press war in this period, see Frank L. Mott, *American Journalism* (1941), p. 113–34; Willard G. Bleyer, *Main Currents in the History of American Journalism* (1927), p. 100–29; James M. Lee, *History of American Journalism* (1923), p. 100–17; George H. Payne, *History of Journalism in the United States* (1920), p. 153–89. A recent exhaustive study by D. H. Stewart on "Jeffersonian Propaganda . . . 1789–1801," topically arranged, has been reproduced in typescript by University Microfilms, Ann Arbor, Mich.

for Vice President in 1792 gave positive evidence that a battle of editor's ink already was under way just as surely as the war of parties had begun. There had been, in fact, significant divergence of press opinion almost from the first months of government under the Constitution, and before the year 1792 was half spent, Republican journals were decrying on every page the measures of the administration so stoutly defended by the gazettes of Federalist inclination. Late in 1792 came the first point-blank fire of a Republican editor at the figure of President Washington. Mere skirmishing had been replaced by the deliberate cunning of open war in all its brutal aspects. Precisely how this came about, few of Washington's contemporaries could explain with certainty; but it had happened in the years immediately following 1789, and the consequence was dread.

In form and appearance the newspaper of the seventeen-nineties was scarcely distinguishable from the familiar gazette of pre-Revolutionary days.[3] No typographical revolution had accompanied the War. Invariably four pages in length, an issue usually dedicated most of its first and last sides to advertising matter. "Foreign intelligence," generally of English origin and necessarily dependent on ship arrivals, occupied the second page. As headlines in the modern sense were unknown, all overseas items, as well as the domestic news on page three, appeared simply under a caption of place and date—"London, June 10," or "Boston, August 20," for example. This large type indicated that the article below had come, for instance, from a Boston paper of August 20. More often than not, the editor would reproduce literally and without specific citation from the paper of origin, which had been delivered to his shop by fast mail on a basis of mutual exchange. On any page the editor might insert one or more lengthy, ponderous "letters" from his subscribers, or "correspondents," as sometimes he chose to call them, and these contributions consumed a good part of the unsold space in every issue. Frequently political in nature and often fiercely partisan, such letters were either unsigned, vaguely initialed, or given some such classical *nom de plume* as "Brutus," which afforded the author total anonymity and allowed the editor himself from time to time to pronounce a vigorous opinion in disguise. In most cases, these contributions determined the political complexion of the paper, as there existed only the faintest resemblance to the modern editorial strip or column. Bolder printers gradually acquired the habit of inserting, under the paper's "home" caption, a potent paragraph or two on some important question. This was, of course, editorial opinion rather than news, but often the two were recklessly scrambled. This technique of highly colored reporting had precedent in the flaming patriot journals of Boston

---

[3] A careful description of the earlier journalistic techniques is given in Sidney Kobre, *The Development of the Colonial Newspaper* (1944), Chs. XII–XVII.

in the years before the Revolution, and its employment after 1789 separated at once the political editor from less assertive printers content merely to parrot another's sentiments. It is a significant fact that between 1789 and 1801 some 500 newspapers enjoyed existence in the United States.[4] Although most of them were woefully short-lived, their occurrence numerically in so brief a period was in itself remarkable. At the outset perhaps eighty or ninety gazettes were appearing; at the end of the Federalist era some 225 presses were functioning, but only about a tenth of these could boast longevity of twelve years or more. The heavy preponderance at all times was with the weeklies, though the more important political organs sometimes had daily or semi-weekly publication. The great seaboard cities from Portsmouth, N.H., to Savannah continued to exert larger journalistic influence than the towns of the hinterland, but it is noteworthy that already in 1789 the far frontier had a vigorous newspaper at Pittsburgh and another at Lexington, Kentucky. In the northern States a proportion existed of one gazette for 25,000 of population, but the ratio changed to one for roughly 100,000 South of Pennsylvania. Few papers were financially successful and many survived only by utter dependence upon Federal, State or municipal public printing contracts for which, naturally, an editor often found himself at the service of men with political axes to sharpen. The cost of subscription was uniformly high and circulation correspondingly small. The most prosperous paper of the entire decade of the nineties, a semi-weekly at Boston, could claim only 4000 copies at maximum, and a percentage of these were gift or "gratis" subscriptions or otherwise unpaid. The average circulation of the dailies was probably no more than 500. There were files, however, and reading racks in every lodging place and tavern, and the standard editorial practice of exchange and excerpting made it probable that the pungent prose of a particular editor or contributor could be located in one or more sheets of like political inclination if the paper of origin was itself not available. Americans were reading—that was certain—and their attitudes, national or sectional, Federalist or Republican, were being styled and trimmed by the gazettes that came to hand. So manifest was this by late 1793 that Noah Webster did not hesitate to assert in the first issue of his *American Minerva:* "Newspapers are the most eagerly sought after, and the most generally diffused. In no other country on earth, not even in Great Britain, are newspapers so generally circulated among the body of the people as in America." [5]

For those who wished it, the glittering detail of Washington's inauguration was made easily accessible through the numerous well-known news-

[4] This total, and the numerical comparisons which follow, are based on the listings in Clarence S. Brigham, *History and Bibliography of American Newspapers, 1690–1820* (1947), 2 v.

[5] *American Minerva* (New York), Dec. 9, 1793, as given in Mott, *op. cit.*, 158–59.

papers of the great cities in late April and early May, 1789. The most famous sheet in America continued to be Benjamin Edes's *Boston Gazette*, principal instrument of the revolutionary propaganda of Samuel Adams in the seventies. By reason of its uninterrupted existence since 1719, it was the oldest paper in the land. Highly esteemed also for conspicuous gallantry in the crucial years were Isaiah Thomas's *Massachusetts Spy*, now settled at Worcester, Thomas Adams's *Independent Chronicle* of Boston, and William Goddard's important *Maryland Journal* at Baltimore. Pre-revolutionary venerables, honored more for age than for editorial excellence, included the *Pennsylvania Gazette* and the *Pennsylvania Journal* at Philadelphia, the *Maryland Gazette* of Annapolis, the *New-Hampshire Gazette* at Portsmouth, the *Newport Mercury*, the *Providence Gazette*, and in Connecticut, the *Courant* at Hartford, the *Journal* at New Haven and the *Gazette* at New London. Benjamin Russell's *Massachusetts Centinel*, established at Boston in 1784, stood prominently among the latecomers with such dailies as the *Pennsylvania Packet* and Eleazer Oswald's *Independent Gazetteer* of Philadelphia and Francis Childs's *New-York Daily Advertiser*. Other post-war organs which had achieved recognition by 1789 were Thomas Greenleaf's influential *New-York Journal*, the *New-Jersey Journal* at Elizabeth Town, Andrew Brown's *Federal Gazette* at Philadelphia, the *Virginia Independent Chronicle* of Richmond, the *American Mercury* established at Hartford by Joel Barlow in 1784, the *Columbian Herald* and the *City Gazette* at Charleston and, on the frontier, John Scull's *Pittsburg Gazette* and John Bradford's widely diffused *Kentucky Gazette* of Lexington.

In addition to Greenleaf's *Journal* and Childs's *Daily Advertiser*, New York in early 1789 had the tri-weekly *Packet*, the *Morning Post* and the *Daily Gazette*. Significantly, however, the capital city of the new government had no newspaper of pronounced "Federal" views. The *Daily Gazette* had been the first to publish the "Federalist Letters" of Hamilton, Madison and Jay, but little more could be expected from this essentially commercial sheet. Indeed, the *New-York Journal* had been so outspokenly Anti-Federal during the ratification controversy that a mob had stormed Greenleaf's office and wrecked his printing machinery. Federalist organizers, determined that Americans should receive the new government with enthusiasm and endorse its measures without restraint, understood perfectly the myriad uses of a friendly newspaper. Further, no mere mercantile journal would do. What was needed, in effect, was a political gazette to advertise the administration through favorable interpretation of official policy. It is not certain that he was answering the specific call of Federalist agents, but in the early spring of 1789 John Fenno of Boston appeared in New York—his purpose the establishment of a semi-weekly newspaper. Not college trained, but a former writing-master and secretary to General Artemas Ward in 1775, Fenno at 38 had just concluded five years as Benjamin Russell's editorial assistant in the office of the *Massachusetts Centinel*. On April 15, 1789, in sufficient time to report with relish all the minutiae of New York's elaborate preparations for the reception of President Washington, Fenno issued from his shop at 86 William Street the first edition of the *Gazette of the United States*. Readers were struck by the absence of advertising matter, but Fenno explained this innovation on page one in a column-long "Plan" or statement of policy. The new Constitution, Fenno declared, was worthy of every support, for "however various the sentiments respecting the merits of this system, all good men are agreed in the necessity that exists of an efficient federal government." Two years later the editor celebrated the anniversary of the *Gazette of the United States* with an even more vigorous avowal of purpose. His paper had endeavored "to hold up the people's own government in a favorable point of light . . . and so long as the principles of the Constitution are held sacred . . . by every exertion to endear the general government to the people." [6]

To what extent Fenno was encouraged by John Adams and Hamilton, or indeed supported in a material way by the Federalist leaders, cannot be ascertained definitely. It is altogether likely that his shop was promptly favored with much of the "public" piecework or job printing which had begun to flow from government offices. In 1792 his chief rival was to allege that Fenno's contract with the Treasury Department alone assured him annual income of $2500.[7] Certainly his newspaper apprenticeship in Boston had impressed upon him the fact that advertising was imperative to the financial success of any venture into journalism. It is not probable, unless he had iron-clad guarantees, that an experienced printer would launch a semi-weekly newspaper in an unfamiliar city with the bold announcement that advertisements were not welcome. In any event, the *Gazette of the United States* proceeded immediately to its task of glorifying the Federal government. Soon, however, critical readers must have concluded that Fenno's editorial taste was of the poorest. Through the summer and fall of 1789 he served the overrich wine of adulation with the careless hand of an intoxicated host, apparently oblivious to the possibility that some might weary of his lavish fare and others be positively sickened by the indelicacy of the performance. The unparalleled attention paid Washington on his journey from Mount Vernon to the capital was interpreted by Fenno as a sure sign that Americans would never tire of information, however inconsequential, of the daily movements of the President and his circle of official advisers. The editor reported faith-

[6] *Gazette of U. S.* (Philadelphia), Apr. 27, 1791, p. 1.
[7] *National Gazette* (Philadelphia), Aug. 15, 1792, p. 3.

fully and in high detail every "levee" at the President's house, every drawing room party by the President's wife, every "official" entertainment in the city and every visit to the theatre by any "federal" personage. What was more, the *Gazette of the United States* referred always to the President as "His Excellency" and advocated earnestly the adoption by Congress of a formal "style" for all officers of the government. Washington, for example, might better be addressed as "Your Magistracy" or "Your Supremacy," since "Excellency" tended to confuse his function with that of foreign emissaries, and the simple title, "President," left him indistinguishable from Vice President Adams when the latter sat at the head of the Senate.[8] All Federal appointments were listed under the ostentatious caption, "By Authority," and were often praised immoderately.[9] Every act of Congress was reproduced in full text and heralded as a work of political genius,[10] and upon recess it was announced that forthwith "the governmental transactions of the Supreme Executive will receive early and regular insertion." [11] The generous salaries which Congress had allotted its members were strenuously recommended as necessary and fitting.[12] The Constitution was forever revered in the pages of Fenno's *Gazette*, the idea of amendment first dismissed as preposterous [13] and then condemned as ominous.[14] State and local governments were alleged to be guilty of "stretches of power and acts of oppression"; [15] public dissatisfaction with the administration was blasted as the greatest possible curse,[16] and the "propensity to change" looked upon as an insidious evil.[17] Finally, in an effort to justify the uncritical attitude of his paper, the editor denounced as completely erroneous the idea that "reserve and silence" evince public approval—such a notion was "strongly tinctured with the Turkish policy of employing mutes!" [18]

Fenno, however, need not have entertained any fear that his contemporaries of 1789 were lacking in vocal virility. Prominent editors from Portsmouth to Savannah were following his lead, borrowing articles from the "official" *Gazette* at New York, printing one contribution after another sympathetic to the government, inserting their own warm endorsements from time to time, and in every attitude emulating the mode that Fenno had set. By the spring of 1790, as Hamilton's fiscal program was opened to debate in Congress, no question existed that the great newspapers of America were arrayed heavily on the side of the administration. Most influential in New England were such well-accepted sheets as the *New-Hampshire Gazette,* the *Massachu-*

[8] *Gazette of U. S.* (New York), May 16, p. 1, and May 20, 1789, p. 3.
[9] *Ibid.*, Aug. 5, 1789, p. 3.           [10] *Ibid.*, July 8, 1789, p. 2.
[11] *Ibid.*, Sept. 16, 1789, p. 2.        [12] *Ibid.*, Aug. 8, 1789, p. 3.
[13] *Ibid.*, July 11, 1789, p. 2.         [14] *Ibid.*, Aug. 1, 1789, p. 3.
[15] *Ibid.*, Aug. 26, 1789, p. 3.         [16] *Ibid.*, Sept. 2, 1789, p. 3.
[17] *Ibid.*, Oct. 10, 1789, p. 3.         [18] *Ibid.*, Nov. 11, 1789, p. 3.

*setts Centinel*, the *Massachusetts Spy*, the *Providence Gazette*, the *Newport Mercury* and Connecticut's three veteran weeklies at Hartford, New Haven and New London. At Philadelphia the *Gazette* and the *Journal* were thoroughly in line, and approval in Maryland of the *Journal* at Baltimore and the *Gazette* at Annapolis was assured. In the South, favorable sentiment emitted from the offices of the *Virginia Herald* at Fredericksburg, the *North-Carolina Gazette* at New Bern and the *Columbian Herald* and the *State Gazette* at Charleston. Not every one of these, of course, consciously aped the techniques of the *Gazette of the United States*, but all leaned perceptibly to the support of Federal interests in every matter treated. To be sure, an editor of the stamina of Benjamin Russell of the *Massachusetts Centinel* would hardly reduce himself to mere duplication of the copy of a former assistant who had migrated to the capital city—the *Centinel* offered its own incisive argument in the Federal cause. The same may be said, to a lesser degree, of Isaiah Thomas's expertly edited *Massachusetts Spy* and William Goddard's popular *Maryland Journal* of Baltimore. What is significant, all in all, is the abundant fact that the Federal government during Washington's first administration enjoyed not only the larded adulation of Fenno's *Gazette of the United States*, but also the solid endorsement and unqualified esteem of a great majority of the influential newspapers of the land.

Still there was alive a journalistic hostility to the Federal government, and it was present from the start. Fenno's unrestrained flattery, it may be concluded, furnished almost ceaseless irritant to this condition, but by no means had created the opposition. The anti-administration newspapers of 1789 and 1790 were the anti-ratification organs of 1788 and earlier. As Fenno proceeded from one superlative to another in approbation of the new government, New Yorkers of contrary viewpoint were happy to have Thomas Greenleaf's *Journal* and Francis Childs's *Daily Advertiser* as counteractives. In Boston, the renowned *Gazette* of Benjamin Edes remained constant to the anti-centralization policy of its sponsor, Samuel Adams, and the *Independent Chronicle* under the editorship of Thomas Adams began in 1789 a spirited running duel with Russell's *Centinel*. Hartford had an anti-administration journal of some weight in the *American Mercury*, and Eleazer Oswald's daily *Independent Gazetteer* often reflected the tempestuous attitudes of its owner. These, and a few lesser gazettes, represented the artillery of the opposition press at the outset of Washington's first term, but far and away the most devastating was Greenleaf's *New-York Journal*. A friend of Aaron Burr and himself a sachem of Tammany, Greenleaf could take pride that he had been a "patriot" printer in 1774 at the age of nineteen and had in the years after 1785 so successfully managed the *Journal* that he was able to purchase the business in time to oppose the ratification of the Constitution in New York.

Apparently, Greenleaf was fond of experiment and he altered his periodicity often, but always the *Journal* stood against Federalism in editorial policy. Washington had been in office scarcely a month when the scented laudations of the *Gazette of the United States* evoked sharp challenge from Greenleaf. Here began a journalistic feud which was terminated only by the departure of Fenno for Philadelphia, as the seat of government shifted to that city late in 1790. For a year and a half the *New-York Journal* waged relentless and rancorous war against the administration, its architect Hamilton, its symbol John Adams, and its spokesman John Fenno. Answering the proposals of Fenno on titles and "style," Greenleaf would countenance "no serenities, highnesses, nor bashaws." [19] "Will the sound of Majesty," he queried, "discharge our foreign debt? Will it enable the people to pay their taxes?" [20] When Hamilton presented his fiscal program, Greenleaf charged that "vanity and ambition" had tempted the Secretary "to a dangerous originality in finance" [21] which produced, in effect, a masterplan to feather the nests of "our placemen and representatives dressed in purple and fine linen and dining sumptuously." [22] Like a prodigal individual, the *Journal* warned, a prodigal government would encompass its own ruin.[23] The "Spirit of Seventy-six" was vanishing, and Greenleaf prophesied that in ten years men of the stripe of Joseph Galloway and Benedict Arnold would sit in the President's cabinet.[24] Surely, America could not trust the super-aristocrat Hamilton who "seems to insinuate and cast reflections on the virtue of the people," [25] the ingenious "Doctor Slop" who had just foisted "the bastard brat assumption" upon a struggling young nation.[26] The *Journal* scaled new heights of malevolence in the summer of 1790 as the Residence Bill occupied attention in Congress.[27] Hamilton's "balloon of continental certificates and public securities" was lifting the £30,000 Federal Hall from its rightful site in New York and transporting the government to a new capital at Philadelphia.[28] The "spotless Miss Assumption" whom Fenno chose to deify was in actuality "a prude and a prostitute" who had given birth to the illegitimate twins "Patowmacus and Philadelphia." [29] Not even Madison, "our hitherto favorite guardian and deliverer," [30] escaped the venom of Greenleaf's ink. He would be "the most patriotic character we could boast of" if he did not "too often evince a strong aristocratic principle lurking somewhere." [31] Washington himself was slurred indirectly by Greenleaf's criticism of the plan of the Mayor of New York to erect a portrait of the President in City Hall. "Which are the virtues that

[19] *New-York Journal,* June 18, 1789, p. 3.   [20] *Ibid.,* Sept. 10, 1789, p. 2.
[21] *Ibid.,* Mch. 25, 1790, p. 3.   [22] *Ibid.*
[23] *Ibid.,* May 18, 1790, p. 2.   [24] *Ibid.,* June 4, 1790, p. 2.
[25] *Ibid.,* June 8, 1790, p. 2.   [26] *Ibid.,* June 11, 1790, p. 2.
[27] *Ibid.,* June 22, p. 3; July 13, p. 2; July 16, p. 3; July 23, p. 3; July 27, p. 2.
[28] *Ibid.,* June 4, 1790, p. 3.   [29] *Ibid.,* Aug. 31, 1790, p. 3.
[30] *Ibid.,* July 23, 1790, p. 3.   [31] *Ibid.*

render him so respectable?" the *Journal* howled. "Why are they not singled out?" Then, thinly veiled, followed Greenleaf's warning: "The injudicious flattery of the people have often intoxicated their rulers and sanctioned their usurpations." [32] Fenno's *Gazette* was "ornamental and pompous," his contributors like "two asses who lick one another until their skins are quite polished." [33] The State Department was denounced for the size and expense of its diplomatic service: "Has America ever realized any substantial advantage from foreign ministers?" [34] Secretary of War Knox was called to task for his treaty with the Creeks,[35] for his advocacy of a large regular army of "disciplined ruffians." [36] Finally, upbraiding the "partyman" who had emerged in national politics, Greenleaf blamed higher education for the "American nobles" and "learned demagogues" who formulated the policy of the administration: "Too much learning makes these men mad! Guard against them, my countrymen!" [37] In summary, it would appear that Greenleaf's *Journal* sinned more often and more grossly by abuse during the eighteen months of Federal residence in New York than did Fenno's *Gazette* by sycophancy.

As any New Yorker might have predicted, Fenno quit Manhattan in the autumn of 1790 and followed the Federal government to its new seat at Philadelphia. This transfer almost certainly was encouraged by particular supporters of the *Gazette of the United States*; Philadelphia had no paucity of printers at the moment but manifestly there was not an editor among them of really vigorous Federalist sympathies. Quite to the contrary, while no paper in the new capital had disclosed hostility at all comparable to that of Thomas Greenleaf's *New-York Journal,* four organs were being edited by men of acknowledged passive antagonism, at least, to the "aristocratical" philosophy of Hamilton and subsequently to many of the measures of the administration. Eleazer Oswald's *Independent Gazetteer,* a contentious daily, had been the loudest, perhaps, in a battery which included Andrew Brown's badly mislabeled *Federal Gazette*, John Dunlap's *Pennsylvania Packet* and the *General Advertiser* recently established by Franklin's grandson, B. F. Bache. In a rented office on Market Street, Fenno set to work in the first week of November at the familiar task of publicizing the accomplishments of the government, but by the spring of 1791 it must have impressed consistent readers that the editorial decorum of the *Gazette of the United States* was improving sharply. Gone was the overheavy adulation of Fenno's early days in New York. No longer did he report in tiny detail and in "monarchical" language every entertainment at the President's mansion. Acts of Congress

[32] *Ibid.*, July 23, p. 3; August 20, p. 3.
[34] *Ibid.*, Sept. 17, 1790, p. 3.
[36] *Ibid.*, Oct. 1, 1790, p. 3.

[33] *Ibid.*, Aug. 17, 1790, p. 3.
[35] *Ibid.*, Aug. 20, 1790, p. 2.
[37] *Ibid.*, Oct. 20, 1790, p. 3.

and proclamations still were offered in full text but no longer were they captioned "By Authority." It is significant, further, that the *Gazette of the United States* was now devoting occasional space to anti-Hamiltonian sentiments such as the letter of "A Mechanic" which insisted that the "middling and poorer classes" deserved to rule and were equally as able to plan worthwhile economic programs as the "rich and independent." [38] In February Fenno reprinted, with no rebuttal, a piece from Dunlap's paper in strong opposition to the National Bank,[39] and two months later and again in June the editor admitted powerful anti-Bank contributions to his pages.[40] Another interesting divergence was the insertion of a satirical piece out of Bache's *General Advertiser* which ridiculed the craze for "federal beer and federal cakes" and expressed hope that "Reading, Writing, Arithmetic taught on a federal system" would soon be grounded instead upon the principles of "equal liberty." [41] Possibly Fenno had come to realize, or perhaps his mentors had advised him, that it was good journalistic practice to countenance a disparate viewpoint from time to time. At any rate, it is certain that the absence in Philadelphia of so galling an opponent as Greenleaf's *Journal* allowed the *Gazette of the United States* to mellow somewhat in its new surroundings.

Whatever temperance Fenno was displaying, however, brought little satisfaction, if any, to men who could anticipate only the worst in their vision of Hamilton's ascendency in the government. The *Gazette of the United States* remained an "official" organ and did not cease to herald every measure of the administration as magnificently conceived. No proposal for alteration or amendment of the Constitution could expect handsome treatment in Fenno's columns. Hamilton, the *Gazette* now prophesied, would soon rank as "a star of the first magnitude in our political hemisphere," [42] and Vice President Adams continued to receive not simply respect, but abject reverence.[43] Such deferential journalism could not but displease men of the mind of Thomas Jefferson and James Madison as gradually the ground split between "Federalism" and "Republicanism." In the opinion of the Secretary of State, Fenno was fashioning "a paper of pure Toryism," [44] and its influence must be combated like a plague. Since the editor of the *Gazette of the United States* had no potent rival in Philadelphia, it would be necessary to import one. Early in February, 1791, the name of Philip Freneau was recommended to Jefferson by Madison and Henry Lee.[45] Just under forty, Freneau had been Madison's classmate at Princeton, a patriotic poet of some

[38] *Gazette of U. S.* (Philadelphia), Jan. 19, 1791, p. 3.
[39] *Ibid.*, Feb. 5, 1791, p. 3.
[40] *Ibid.*, Apr. 13, p. 3 and June 8, 1791, p. 3.
[41] *Ibid.*, June 1, 1791, p. 3.
[42] *Ibid.*, Jan. 9, 1791, p. 3.
[43] *Ibid.*, Mch. 4, 1791, p. 3.
[44] See 2 *Malone*, 424.                          [45] *Hunt's Madison*, 117 n.

renown in the war years, a planter's secretary in the West Indies, a sea captain and, more recently, an assistant to Francis Childs in the office of the Anti-Federalist *Daily Advertiser* in New York.[46] In the spring of 1790 Freneau began to contribute verses to Childs's paper, and by autumn he had been employed and was exerting an active hand in its management. The pithy insertions of the poet gave the *Daily Advertiser* a more blatantly hostile complexion each month, and by December Freneau was boasting that he was one editor who dealt "neither in court sycophantism nor in sublime dedications." [47] Little doubt existed of Freneau's superior literary abilities—he had been acclaimed "the Peter Pindar of the United States" by no less a journalist than Benjamin Russell of Boston [48]—but could his services be procured? Fenno's *Gazette* was established in the capital city and aimed always at wide circulation—any effective opponent must be of necessity also a "national" paper with its office at Philadelphia. Freneau himself had already formulated definite plans to begin a weekly newspaper in Monmouth County, New Jersey, when Jefferson on February 28, 1791, transmitted to him the offer of a language clerk's position in the Department of State at the annual wage of 250 dollars. The salary was small, the Secretary admitted, but the position "gives so little to do as not to interfere with any other calling the person may choose" and "should anything better turn up within my department that might suit you, I should be very happy to bestow it as well." [49] Freneau exhibited little interest, however, and it took all of Madison's persuasive talents to stir him. Early in May he was scheduled for a visit to Philadelphia to confer with Jefferson, and Madison assured the Secretary in advance that "there is not to be found in the whole catalogue of American printers" a man who could match Freneau's literary skill.[50] When the poet failed to appear, Jefferson concluded correctly that he had paused in New Jersey—perhaps permanently. "I suppose," the Secretary lamented, "he has changed his mind again, for which I am really sorry." [51] Not until late July, some weeks after Jefferson had paid him a personal visit in New York,[52] did Freneau make the decision to transfer to Philadelphia. As it proved, the poet was business-man enough to strike a shrewd bargain. Francis Childs, his employer on the *Daily Advertiser*, agreed to underwrite the entire venture, and Freneau's "national" paper would be printed in the shop of Childs's partner, John Swaine, who had set up in Philadelphia to do contract work for the govern-

---

[46] His career is traced aptly in *Leary, Freneau*. This study, 186–92, and Malone, *op. cit.*, 423–27, treat in detail the negotiations which brought Freneau to Philadelphia and provide a basis for the briefer account given here.

[47] *Daily Advertiser* (New York), Dec. 16, 1790, p. 3.

[48] *Massachusetts Centinel* (Boston), July 18, 1789, p. 3.

[49] 8 *Jefferson*, 133.                              [50] 14 *Madison Papers*, 8, LC.

[51] 4 *Jefferson Papers*, 186, LC.

[52] 6 *Jefferson*, 107. The Secretary was in New York in late May.

ment. Out of this, Freneau would share as a third partner with no capital investment at all.[53] On August 16 Jefferson signed Freneau's commission as "clerk for foreign languages" despite full knowledge that his man was equipped only for French. By late September, the poet was in Philadelphia to take his oath. Meanwhile, the new "national" paper was publicized extensively with advance notices.[54] Madison and Henry Lee sought subscribers in Virginia,[55] and Jefferson lent his wholehearted support.[56] On October 31, 1791, the first issue of the semi-weekly *National Gazette* appeared in Philadelphia. Freneau's dedication, though he may have denied it, was sublime enough, and it conveyed a warning but scantily veiled. His paper would strive to uphold the "great principles upon which the American Revolution was founded, and which alone can preserve the blessings of liberty." [57]

Through the first four months of its publication the *National Gazette,* either by design or by circumstance, showed little partisanship. Why was this? Jefferson's "Republican" party was already taking shape and had absorbed the old Anti-Federalist opposition. The Virginia-New York alliance was a fact; Jefferson and Madison were collaborating with Clinton, and spadework for the election of 1792 had begun. The absence of intense hostility in the columns of the *National Gazette* in its early months may have been the result of specific instructions to Freneau; or perhaps the editor delayed because he sought a reputation of impartiality; or perhaps, simply, it took him some time to warm up. Whatever the reason, the *National Gazette* remained almost neutral until late in February, 1792. A series of intelligent articles by James Madison and Henry Hugh Brackenridge of Pittsburgh lent more to the prestige of the new paper than to its political complexion.[58] Freneau was particularly restrained in his treatment of St. Clair's spectacular failure against the western Indians. Where Bache's *General Advertiser* and *Dunlap's American Daily Advertiser* censured the government severely for its Indian policy,[59] the *National Gazette* was content merely to copy articles both critical and apologetic from other papers.[60] John Fenno, whose effective rebuttal of the charges of Bache and Dunlap put an

[53] The agreement was described ten years later in *City Gazette* (Charleston), Jan. 5, 1801.

[54] Space was purchased in *Freeman's Journal* (Philadelphia), August 24; *Daily Advertiser* (New York), August 25; *Argus* (Boston), September 6; *Maryland Journal* (Baltimore), Sept. 20, 1791.

[55] 6 *Hunt's Madison,* 62 n and 69 n.          [56] 6 *Jefferson,* 106.

[57] *National Gazette* (Philadelphia), Oct. 31, 1791, p. 1.

[58] Brackenridge signed his name. Madison's contributions from Nov. 21, 1791 to Apr. 2, 1792 are in 6 *Hunt's Madison,* 43–105; Brant summarizes them (*op. cit.,* v. 3, p. 346–47).

[59] See *General Advertiser* (Philadelphia), Dec. 14, 1791, p. 3; December 29, p. 3; Jan. 4 and 10, 1792, p. 2 and 3. Dunlap's *Pennsylvania Packet* was now called *Dunlap's American Daily Advertiser;* see issues of Jan. 3, 1792, p. 2; January 4, p. 2; January 6, p. 2; January 10, p. 2; January 17, p. 2; January 29, p. 2.

[60] See *National Gazette* (Philadelphia), Jan. 9, 1792, p. 2–3; January 12, p. 2; January 23, p. 3–4; January 26, p. 3; February 2, p. 1; February 6, p. 3.

end to editorial controversy over the Indian question,[61] had little reason in early February, 1792, to anticipate a challenge from the latecomer Freneau.

Since the transfer of the government to Philadelphia a year and some months before, American readers had enjoyed a period of truce and comparative calm in the war of editorial opinion. Now suddenly peace was ended. Freneau, who had been guilty of hardly a hostile word, loosed without warning a barrage of hypercritical comment late in February, 1792, that surprised Federalist leaders and shook the administration to its foundations. In rapid order and relentlessly through March, April and May, the editor poured weighty, explosive contributions from the pens of "A Farmer," "Brutus," and "Sidney" into the pages of the *National Gazette*. The blatant appeal of "Farmer" to "The Yeomanry of the United States" was sounded on February 23 and lasted until the first week of April. "Though the American Aristocrats have failed . . . to establish titles by distinction of law," this writer cried, "yet the destructive principles of aristocracy are too prevalent amongst us." [62] Between March 15 and April 9 the series by "Brutus" struck savagely at Hamilton's funding system which "like Pandora's box . . . is pregnant with every mischief." [63] The evils of the financial program were manifest.[64] Its victims included "the industrious merchant, the laborious farmer, and generally the poor and middling classes" [65] and in this climate "our political bark seems to be gently gliding down that stream leading from freedom to slavery." [66] The augury of "Brutus" was dark: "The inevitable and fatal consequences of these complicated evils will be . . . an impoverished peasantry on the one hand, and a privileged aristocracy on the other"; [67] but his warning to Federalists rang clear: "Let the Secretary of the Treasury and his adherents beware . . . let them remember, that altho' the republican jealousy of the people may sleep for a time, that it is not extinct." [68] It was this particular series that branded the *National Gazette* as an organ of ultra-Republican propaganda,[69] but the articles by "Sidney" which appeared in subsequent issues were not easily to be dismissed. Ponderously and with infinite precision, "Sidney" examined Hamilton's excise tax and demolished, at least to his own satisfaction, every argument in favor of the Secretary's proposal.[70]

[61] *Gazette of U. S.* (Philadelphia), Feb. 11, 1792, p. 3.
[62] *National Gazette* (Philadelphia), Mch. 1, 1792, p. 4. For this series, see also issues of February 23, p. 4; February 27, p. 2; March 15, p. 2; March 26, p. 4; April 5, p. 1.
[63] *Ibid.*, Mch. 15, 1792, p. 2.          [64] *Ibid.*
[65] *Ibid.*, Mch. 26, 1792, p. 3.
[66] *National Gazette* (Philadelphia), Mch. 26, 1792, p. 3.
[67] *Ibid.*, Apr. 9, 1792, p. 1.          [68] *Ibid.*, Apr. 5, 1792, p. 2.
[69] 2 Malone, 436; Leary, *Freneau,* 199.
[70] *National Gazette* (Philadelphia), Apr. 23, 1792, p. 2-3; April 26, p. 2-3; April 30, p. 2-3; May 3, p. 2-3; May 7, p. 2; May 10, p. 1; May 17, p. 1-2; May 21, p. 1, 4; May 24, p. 1-2. Each of the "Sidney" articles is at least three columns in length, and several cover an entire page and more.

Beyond the devastating artillery of these three contributors, Freneau now called into play from time to time his own cultivated pen for short editorial jabs at Federalist policy and practice. The funding system, he wrote late in February, was responsible for the "thirst for rank and distinction" which afflicted many Americans.[71] By June, the poet-journalist was divining the advent of a "new era" with the November elections, the dawn of a glorious day in which "republicanism flourishes and is again in fashion." [72]

With the coming of spring in 1792 the friends of Federalism could not but recognize the appalling fact that they were confronting a Philadelphia news-paper antagonist of greater potency even than Thomas Greenleaf of New York. What was worse, the defence was unready. John Fenno stood weapon-less as the salvos of "Farmer" and "Brutus" exploded around him. The *Gazette of the United States* had no brace of prolific and perspicacious con-tributors to answer the heavy guns of the *National Gazette*. Three years of experience in journalism, during which time his only close combatant was the vituperative Greenleaf, had failed entirely to instruct Fenno in the art of serious argument. All he could do now was to reply to Freneau in brief editorial salvos more suggestive of retreat than of resistance. Acutely con-scious of his old renown as "court sycophant" and "ministerial puffer," the editor of the *Gazette of the United States* welcomed an article by "Z," arraigning such "prodigiously smart sayings"—"Like common swearing, they give a life and boldness to writing which raise it a mile above the sneaking vulgar style." [73] In this vein Fenno himself commented: "It seems as if sedition had a thousand tongues, and all of brass." [74] "On reading the papers," he lamented as Freneau's first hostile issue appeared, "a stranger would sup-pose that the very worst men in the country had crept in the first offices." [75] Then followed in rhyme three weeks later a reference to the President: "Not George himself escapes the spleen, of canker'd malice and chagrine." [76] When Freneau gave space to the hint of "Valerius" that Vice President Adams might be "the mere creature of party," the *Gazette of the United States* promptly copied the article and accused Freneau of the authorship.[77] "Were it as easy to find competent financiers as it is fault-finders," wrote Fenno in an attempt to shield Hamilton, "no country would perhaps be in a more eligible situation than ours." [78] Through May and June the Federalist editor, in apparent desperation, made bold to strike personally at Freneau, perhaps

[71] *Ibid.*, Feb. 27, 1792, p. 3.   [72] *Ibid.*, May 31, 1792, p. 3.
[73] *Gazette of U. S.* (Philadelphia), Feb. 15, 1792, p. 3.
[74] *Ibid.*, Feb. 22, 1792, p. 3. See also issues of March 21, p. 3; April 4, p. 3; April 11, p. 3.
[75] *Ibid.*, Feb. 25, 1792, p. 3.   [76] *Ibid.*, Mch. 17, 1792, p. 3.
[77] *National Gazette* (Philadelphia), Mch. 29, 1792, p. 3; *Gazette of U. S.*, Mch. 31, 1792, p. 3.
[78] *Ibid.*, Apr. 14, 1792, p. 3; also editorial remarks in issues of April 18, p. 3 and April 21, p. 3

unwisely, and for his trouble received a series of stinging editorial rebukes from the poet.[79] One discourtesy [80] brought from Freneau a characteristic blast: "Mad dogs! Such is the hue and cry raised . . . against every man who writes on the measures of government without dipping his pen in molasses to sweeten every line with panegyrick." [81] Late in June, Fenno categorically charged the *National Gazette* with electioneering for a faction; [82] Freneau replied in silken language that a "faction" did exist and comprised "a very respectable number of the anti-aristocratical and anti-monarchical people of the United States, whom we shall be proud to serve at all times." [83] In the same issue of the *National Gazette*, "W.T." castigated "those monarchical writers on Davila, &c. who are armed with long wigs, long pens and caitiff printers ready to disseminate their poisoned doctrines." [84] This was directly insulting to Adams, whose "Discourses on Davila" had been published in the *Gazette of the United States* a year before. By any standard, Fenno was losing the battle of the press as spring became summer in 1792. A weak effort to defend the National Bank against Freneau's "sophistical absurdities" fell woefully short.[85] Something more would be needed in Fenno's arsenal if the *Gazette of the United States* were to carry on with any effectiveness at all.

Freneau, however, could scarcely expect to proceed unchallenged for long. His newspaper had become so vociferous in so short a time that Federalist leaders were rudely awakened to its menace. In May, Hamilton was communicating to his friend Edward Carrington the suspicion that Jefferson, deliberately and with pernicious intent, caused Freneau to come to Philadelphia.[86] A month later he wrote to Adams: "If you have seen some of the last numbers of the National Gazette, you will have perceived that the plot thickens and that something very like a serious design to subvert the government discloses itself." [87] Early in July Washington himself complained to Jefferson that Freneau's paper was injuring the tranquility of the nation.[88] Indeed, the *National Gazette* appeared more incendiary with each issue. Since 1789 American newspapers generally had been in full sympathy with the objects of the French Revolution; but now Freneau was suggesting that some similar "republican" revolution, or its ideals at least, would prove a healthy

---

[79] For example, see *Gazette of U. S.*, June 9, 1792, p. 3 and June 13, p. 3; compare with *National Gazette*, June 11, p. 3 and June 14, p. 3.
[80] *Gazette of U. S.* (Philadelphia), May 2, 1792, p. 3.
[81] *National Gazette* (Philadelphia), May 10, 1792, p. 3.
[82] *Gazette of U. S.* (Philadelphia), June 20, 1792, p. 3.
[83] *National Gazette* (Philadelphia), June 21, 1792, p. 3.
[84] *Ibid.*, p. 2.
[85] *Gazette of U. S.* (Philadelphia), June 27, 1792, p. 3.
[86] Letter of May 26, 1792, in 9 *A. Hamilton*, 519.
[87] Letter of June 25, 1792, in 8 *John Adams*, 514.
[88] 1 *Jefferson*, 310.

tonic for the citizens of the United States.[89] "Brutus" celebrated the Fourth of July with a remark that "artifice and deception" had accomplished since 1783 "one revolution in favor of the few" and that "another revolution must and will be brought about in favor of the people."[90] This, apparently, was too much—Freneau and his contributors were going too far. On July 7 "Crito" launched the first systematic, heavyweight counter-offensive in the pages of Fenno's *Gazette*.[91] Then, late in the month, a contributor calling himself "T.L." landed a devastating blow: "The editor of the *National Gazette* receives a salary from government . . . is [it] paid him for translations or for publications?"[92] Freneau declared nervously in his next issue that the insinuation of "T.L." was "beneath reply" and asked his readers to judge whether the "small stipend" of a French translator was as likely to influence his "impartial observations" as the "emoluments . . . far more lucrative" which the "vile sycophant" netted from public printing contracts.[93] In this retort Freneau may have been sure of his ground, but at last Fenno had hurt him and he took solace with a remarkable plunge into poetry:

> Since the day we attempted the Nation's Gazette
> Pomposo's dull printer does nothing but fret;
> Now preaching and screeching, then nibbling and scribbling,
> Remarking and barking, repining and whining
> And still in a pet
> From morning till night with the Nation's Gazette.
> One National Paper you think is enough
> To flatter and lie, to pallaver and puff,
> To preach up in favour of monarchs and titles,
> And garters and ribbons, to prey on our vitals;
> Who knows but our Congress will give it in fee
> And make Mr. Fenno the grand patentee![94]

What for months had been a simple frolic for the *National Gazette* became a desperate journalistic fracas with the activation of Fenno's paper in midsummer, 1792. The "T.L." installment on July 25 signalled the adoption of an attitude of aggressive combatancy on the part of the *Gazette of the United States*. The gauntlet was down, and retreat for either Fenno or Freneau was no longer possible. Once so accelerated, belligerent journalism

[89] See *National Gazette* (Philadelphia), June 18, p. 2 and June 21, 1792, p. 3. Freneau also was now printing occasional extracts from Thomas Paine's "Rights of Man."
[90] *National Gazette* (Philadelphia), July 4, 1792, p. 2.
[91] *Gazette of U. S.* (Philadelphia), July 7, 1792, p. 2. The "Crito" articles appeared through July.
[92] *Ibid.*, July 25, 1792, p. 3.
[93] *National Gazette* (Philadelphia), July 28, 1792, p. 3.
[94] *Ibid.*

perpetuated its violent motion from summer to autumn, and beyond. August was the critical month, actually, for then Fenno seized the initiative and drove the editor of the *National Gazette* into a very embarrassing corner. On July 28, "Detector," who qualified himself as "hitherto a silent observor," sounded the cry of battle: "It is high time that the mask were torn from the faces of these professed friends but real enemies of the United States." [95] A second article by "T.L." struck again personally at Freneau in the next issue of the *Gazette of the United States*,[96] and on August 4 Thomas Jefferson himself came under assault. "An American" branded the editor of the *National Gazette* "the faithful and devoted servant of the head of a party, from whose hands he receives the boon." The Secretary of State, this writer charged, had attempted "an experiment somewhat new in the history of political manoeuvres in this country—a newspaper instituted by a public officer, and the editor of it regularly pensioned with the public money in the disposal of that officer." [97] Freneau could not ignore so incisive an allegation. His reputation and Jefferson's political future seemed to hang in jeopardy, and Freneau hastened to the office of the Mayor of Philadelphia, Matthew Clarkson, to swear out an affidavit: The *National Gazette* was at no time "either directed, controlled, or attempted to be influenced in any manner either by the Secretary of State or any of his friends; nor was a line ever directly or indirectly written, dictated or composed for it by that officer. . . . The editor has consulted his own judgment alone in the conducting of it— free, unfettered and uninfluenced." [98] Not a man to turn the other cheek, Freneau lashed back with the insinuation that Hamilton's dexterous hand was behind the "T.L." and "American" articles. "The devil rageth when his time is short . . . The funding system has had its day." [99] To this Fenno did not reply specifically, but "An American" blasted again Freneau's connection with Jefferson as "indelicate and unfit" and suggested that the Secretary of State was "a public officer who has too little scrupled to embarrass and disparage the government of which he is a member—and who has been the prompter, open or secret, of unwarrantable aspersions on men who . . . need never decline a comparison with him." [100] "T.L." appeared again on the same day,[101] and "G" finally came to Freneau's defence with a counter charge that "the immaculate Mr. Fenno" was being subsidized as printer to the Senate and to the Treasury to the amount of $2000 or $2500 annually.[102] Fenno's retort was loud and sure: Was not the New York firm of Childs and

---

[95] *Gazette of U. S.* (Philadelphia), July 28, 1792, p. 3. Cf. *supra,* p. 365.
[96] *Ibid.*, Aug. 1, 1792, p. 1.          [97] *Ibid.*, Aug. 4, 1792, p. 2–3.
[98] Printed in *Gazette of U. S.* (Philadelphia), Aug. 8, 1792, p. 3.
[99] *National Gazette* (Philadelphia), Aug. 8, 1792, p. 3.
[100] *Gazette of U. S.* (Philadelphia), Aug. 11, 1792, p. 2.
[101] *Ibid.*
[102] *National Gazette* (Philadelphia), Aug. 15, 1792, p. 3.

Swaine, at whose Philadelphia office the *National Gazette* was published, also enjoying some of the business of the Treasury Department and, as well, the exclusive patronage of the Department of State and of the House of Representatives? [103] "Fair Play" on the same page questioned bluntly why Freneau had been employed by Jefferson in the first place—had not "Mr. Taylor, an intelligent and respectable man," satisfactorily discharged the duties of translating clerk? [104] "An American" on August 18 chose to defend his anonymity: "He might have good reasons for not discovering himself." [105] In the total, Fenno's exposures through August of 1792 reversed the advantages accrued to Freneau in the spring and spiked or silenced the cannon of the most effective contributors to the *National Gazette*. "Brutus," however, came back briefly on September 1 to hint that Hamilton was writing for Fenno: "It does not appear to me to be a question of federalism or antifederalism— but it is the Treasury of the United States against the people." [106]

Relentlessly through September the two editors pursued their battle in personalities, but it was all anti-climactic. Federalist readers needed little more to be convinced that Jefferson was paying Freneau in public funds to defame the administration. "Catullus" in a sharp series denounced "the institutor and patron of the National Gazette" [107] and prophesied that Jefferson, hitherto "the quiet, modest, retiring philosopher" and "plain simple unambitious republican," would in the future be regarded "the intriguing incendiary, the aspiring turbulent competitor." [108] On the other side, Freneau and his followers were increasingly certain that the pen of Hamilton himself was supplying the *Gazette of the United States* with its explosives.[109] An anonymous writer challenged "American" to explain the action of "the public character who . . . could so far divest himself of gratitude . . . as to erect his little crest against the magnanimous chief who at present is the head of our civil establishment." [110] This was an unmistakable reference to the well-known insubordination of Hamilton as a young colonel on Washington's staff during the war. The critic proceeded to declare that Hamilton had "on many occasions since spoken with levity and depreciation" of the President. On September 22, in a poetic broadside at "a certain high-minded Trio," Freneau set up once more the much-riddled figure of Vice President Adams beside Fenno and Hamilton on the firing line. Distinguished by "breadth of belly" as contrasted with Hamilton's "length of nose," Adams was ridi-

[103] *Gazette of U. S.* (Philadelphia), Aug. 18, 1792, p. 2.
[104] *Ibid.*    [105] *Ibid.*, p. 3.
[106] *National Gazette* (Philadelphia), Sept. 1, 1792, p. 3.
[107] *Gazette of U. S.*, Sept. 15, 1792, p. 2.
[108] *Ibid.*, Sept. 29, 1792, p. 2; see also issues of September 19, p. 2–3, October 17, p. 1, November 24, p. 1, and December 22, p. 1.
[109] See "Mercator" in *National Gazette*, Sept. 8, 1792, p. 3.
[110] *Ibid.*

culed as one who had "scrawl'd some nonsense with his mutton fist" [111]—
an aspersion intended, apparently, for the widely published "Discourses on
Davila" written by the Vice President two years earlier. Indeed, Freneau's
cannon leveled exclusively on Adams as the autumn came in. An elaborate
"Defence of Mr. Jefferson's Political Character," borrowed from *Dunlap's
American Daily Advertiser*, was inaugurated by Freneau late in September
and continued into December,[112] but the editorial emphasis of the *National
Gazette* shifted now to the election of 1792 and focused there as long as a
chance existed that George Clinton might be chosen to replace Adams as
Vice President. Freneau's electioneering began in mid-August and hit a peak
perhaps in late October.[113] He was joined in a progressively vituperative
campaign by the *American Daily Advertiser* and Thomas Greenleaf's *New-
York Journal*. Unqualified endorsement of Washington and immoderate
condemnation of Adams in the same breath lent an uneven tone to the
efforts of the Republican press.[114] This defect Fenno seized and examined
with delight.[115] "Columbus," in Greenleaf's *Journal,* insisted that "the present
worthy chief magistrate is justly entitled to the confidence and esteem of
every American" and then demanded that the voters "lop off every unfruitful
branch, and root out of the soil of freedom all the noxious weeds of aristocracy." [116] Such inconsistencies Fenno took great pains to refute. The
enemies of Adams, he pointed out, declare that "They are for the constitution—they would not mar it—they would not break a twig of the federal
tree." Yet, in favoring the notorious Anti-Federalist Clinton, "they would
choose a man who would have laid the axe to its root." [117]

Once the balloting indicated conclusively that Adams had been approved
for another term as Washington's second-in-command, Freneau swung his
guns away from their battered object and cast his eye about for a fresh
target of journalistic abuse. By mid-December the editor of the *National
Gazette* was training his sights, for the first time now in a clearly personal
fashion, on Washington himself. All else had failed, and the Federalists were
returned to power under the Constitution for another administration. Freneau began now to dedicate space in almost every issue to a form of mockery
intended, without question, to fall at the door of the President rather than
upon the head of either Adams or Hamilton. "Mirabeau," in a piece styled
"Forerunners of Monarchy and Aristocracy in the United States," scorned the
"ceremonial distance between the officers of government and the people" and

[111] *Ibid.,* Sept. 22, 1792, p. 3.
[112] *Ibid.,* Sept. 26, 1792, p. 1; September 29, p. 1; November 18, p. 2; December 12, p. 1.
[113] *Ibid.,* Aug. 15, 1792, p. 2, 3; August 22, p. 2, 3.
[114] *Ibid.,* September 12, p. 4; October 10, p. 2.
[115] *Gazette of U. S.,* November 21, p. 2; November 28, p. 1; December 1, p. 1.
[116] *New-York Journal,* Oct. 3, 1792, reprinted in *National Gazette,* Oct. 10, p. 2.
[117] *Gazette of U. S.,* Dec. 8, 1792, p. 3.

condemned the practice of "keeping the birthdays of servants of the public." [118] Adams at least had made public his "opinions for monarchy," hinted "Fair Play," but were there not others "well known to hold the same principles and views, tho they are careful to deal them out less open-handedly"? [119] "Cornelia" on December 26 agreed with "Mirabeau"—Republicanism had failed to strike the evil at its source: "Witness the Drawing Room!!" [120] Another writer, in an attack on aristocratic titles, suggested that "His Excellency the President" was one of "these diabolical terms." [121] An intense criticism of "those apparent trifles, birthday odes," began on December 19 and was carried with growing zeal into January. Freneau himself was ready with a frontal editorial assault on January 30: "It appears . . . that a new order of citizens has been created . . . consisting only of the officers of the federal government. The privileges of this order . . . consist in sharing exclusively in the profits of the 25,000 dollars a year allowed for the President's table, and in the honor of gazing upon him once a week at his levees." [122] "I tell you," raged "A Farmer" in early February, "that it is dangerous in the extreme to set up any man as an idol . . . witness Cromwell's grip in the name of republicanism!" [123] An unnamed correspondent wrote on March 2: "The President has been pictured as spotless and infallible, as having no likes or dislikes. The glory and achievement of the late revolution have been entirely imputed to him, and were he virtue's self the strains of panegyric could not have been louder in order to complete the shame and disgrace of republican dogmas." [124] A climax to this campaign of exceptional vigor and three months' duration was delivered by "Mirabeau" on March 13, 1793, in a somewhat maudlin appeal to Washington directly: "The splendour of a court suits not the meridian of the United States, and suits not the meridian of your mind." [125]

Did Freneau's preoccupation with Washington in the months immediately preceding the second Federalist inauguration evince the bitterness of frustrated Republicans and mark the opening of a violent era in the war of parties and the battle of newspapers? Or was Freneau, the appointed journalist of Jeffersonianism, presenting a calculated plea to the best instincts of the President to renounce Federalism, as designed by Hamilton, in the years of office before him? Fenno attempted no analysis of the strategy of his opponent. He published a twenty-eight-line ode to Washington on the President's birthday [126] and remarked simply in his issue of March 6: "Re-

[118] *National Gazette*, Dec. 12, 1792, p. 2.
[119] *Ibid.*
[120] *Ibid.*, Dec. 26, 1792, p. 1.
[121] *Ibid.*, p. 4.
[122] *Ibid.*, Jan. 30, 1793, p. 3.
[123] *Ibid.*, Feb. 2, 1793, p. 1.
[124] *Ibid.*, Mch. 2, 1793, p. 3.
[125] *Ibid.*, Mch. 13, 1793, p. 3.
[126] *Gazette of U. S.*, Feb. 23, 1793, p. 3.

spect is the shadow that follows virtue, and where the substance is there will be the shadow." [127] As Washington prepared to take the oath of the Presidency for the second time, one thing was certain: Just as a conflict of political philosophies was under way with no truce in sight, so, too, a contest in political journalism had begun in America with no prospect of peace.

[127] *Ibid.*, Mch. 6, 1793, p. 3.

# SHORT-TITLE INDEX

Identification of all short-titled works appearing in the earlier volumes and used in Volume Six are repeated in this Short-Title Index. Those works not applicable to the present volume were dropped. The same style for citations has been employed throughout the biography. Where the longer, identifying titles are themselves abbreviated, full information is given in the Bibliography of Manuscript and Printed Sources.

*A. Hamilton.* H. C. LODGE, ed. "The Works of Alexander Hamilton." 12 v.
*A.H.R.* American Historical Review.
*Abigail Adams.* STEWART MITCHELL, ed. "New Letters of Abigail Adams, 1788–1801."
*Annals.* "The Debates and Proceedings in the Congress of the United States . . ." compiled by Joseph Gales, Senior. (Usually styled "The Annals of Congress.")
*ASP.* "American State Papers. Documents, Legislative and Executive, of the Congresses of the United States [1st through the 25th Congresses, 1789–1838]." Selected and edited under authority of Congress. 38 v. Washington, 1832–61.
*Baker.* WILLIAM S. BAKER. "Washington After the Revolution, 1784–1799."
*Ballagh, Lee Letters.* J. C. BALLAGH, ed. "The Letters of Richard Henry Lee." 2 v.
*Bancroft, His. Cons.* GEORGE BANCROFT. "History of the Formation of the Constitution of the United States of America." 2 v.
*Bigelow's Franklin.* JOHN BIGELOW, ed. "The Works of Benjamin Franklin." 12 v.
*Bowen.* CLARENCE W. BOWEN, ed. "The History of the Centennial Celebration of the Inauguration of George Washington as First President of the United States."
*Boyd's Boudinot.* GEORGE ADAMS BOYD. "Elias Boudinot, Patriot and Statesman, 1740–1821."
*Brant.* IRVING BRANT. "James Madison." 3 v.
*Brydon, Mother Church.* G. McLAREN BRYDON. "Virginia's Mother Church . . ."
*Burnett.* EDMUND C. BURNETT, ed. "Letters of Members of the Continental Congress." 8 v.
*Butterfield.* LYMAN H. BUTTERFIELD, ed. "Letters of Benjamin Rush." 2 v.
*Chinard.* GILBERT CHINARD, ed. "George Washington as the French Knew Him."
*Conway, Randolph.* MONCURE CONWAY. "Omitted Chapters of History . . . in the Life . . . of Edmund Randolph . . ."
*DAB.* ALLEN JOHNSON and DUMAS MALONE, eds. "Dictionary of American Biography."
*Decatur.* STEPHEN DECATUR, JR. "Private Affairs of George Washington from the Records and Accounts of Tobias Lear, Esquire, his Secretary."
*Diaries.* JOHN C. FITZPATRICK, ed. "The Diaries of George Washington." 4 v.

*DNB.* Dictionary of National Biography.

*EJS.* "Journal of the Executive Proceedings of the Senate of the United States of America." 3 v.

*Elliot's Debates.* JONATHAN ELLIOT. "The Debates in the Several State Conventions on the Adoption of the Federal Constitution . . ." 5 v.

*Emmet Col.* Manuscript Collection of Thomas A. Emmet. NYPL.

*Farrand.* MAX FARRAND, ed. "The Records of the Federal Convention of 1787." 4 v.

*Fisher Ames.* SETH AMES, ed. "Works of Fisher Ames, with a Selection from his Speeches and Correspondence." 2 v.

*Ford.* WORTHINGTON C. FORD, ed. "The Writings of George Washington." 14 v.

*Gates Papers.* Papers of Maj. Gen. Horatio Gates. NYHS.

*Gibbs, Wolcott Papers.* GEORGE GIBBS, ed. "Memoirs of the Administrations of Washington and John Adams, Edited from the Papers of Oliver Wolcott, Secretary of the Treasury." 2 v.

*Greene's Greene.* G. W. GREENE. "The Life of Nathanael Greene." 3 v.

*Griswold.* R. W. GRISWOLD. "The Republican Court, or American Society in the Days of Washington."

*G.W.* JOHN C. FITZPATRICK, ed. "The Writings of George Washington . . ." 39 v.

*G. W. P. Custis.* G. W. P. CUSTIS. "Recollections and Private Memoirs of Washington . . ."

*H.* W. W. HENING, ed. "The [Virginia] Statutes at Large." 13 v.

*Hamilton.* S. M. HAMILTON, ed. "Letters to Washington and Accompanying Papers." 5 v.

*Hamilton's Monroe.* S. M. HAMILTON, ed. "The Writings of James Monroe." 7 v.

*Hamilton Papers.* Papers of Alexander Hamilton. LC.

*Henderson.* ARCHIBALD HENDERSON. "Washington's Southern Tour, 1791."

*Hulbert.* ARCHER BUTLER HULBERT. "Washington and the West . . ."

*Hunt's Madison.* GAILLARD HUNT, ed. "The Writings of James Madison." 9 v.

*Innes Papers.* Papers of Harry Innes. LC.

*Irving.* WASHINGTON IRVING. "Life of George Washington." 5 v.

*JCC.* WORTHINGTON C. FORD [and his successors, eds.] "Journals of the Continental Congress, 1774–1789." 34 v.

*J. C. Hamilton.* JOHN C. HAMILTON. "History of the Republic of the United States of America, as Traced in the Writings of Alexander Hamilton and of his Contemporaries." 7 v.

*Jefferson.* ANDREW A. LIPSCOMB, ed.-in-chief; ALBERT E. BERGH, Man. ed. "The Writings of Thomas Jefferson." 20 v. (This work would have been superseded completely by JULIAN P. BOYD, ed. "The Papers of Thomas Jefferson.")

*Jensen.* MERRILL JENSEN. "The New Nation."

*JHR.* "Journal of the House of Representatives of the United States, Being the First Session of the First Congress: Begun and Held at the City of New York, March 4, 1789." 9 v.

*John Adams.* CHARLES FRANCIS ADAMS, ed. "The Life and Works of John Adams." 10 v.

*John Jay.* H. P. JOHNSTON, ed. "The Correspondence and Public Papers of John Jay . . ." 4 v.

*Jour. H. D. Va.* "Journal of the House of Delegates of Virginia, 1781–1786."

*Jour. Sen. Va.* "Journal of the Senate of the Commonwealth of Virginia; Begun and Held in the City of Richmond on Monday the 17th day of October in the year of our Lord Christ, 1785."

*JS.* "Journal of the First Session of the Senate of the United States of America, Begun and Held at the City of New York, March 4, 1789." 5 v.

*Knox Papers.* Papers of Maj. Gen. Henry Knox. MHS.

*Laws of U. S.* "Laws of the United States of America, From the 4th of March, 1789, to the 4th of March, 1815 . . ." 5 v. (Published by John Bioren and W. John Duane of Philadelphia and R. C. Weightman, Washington, 1815).

*LC.* Library of Congress.

*Leary, Freneau.* LEWIS LEARY. "That Rascal Freneau, A Study in Literary Failure."

*Lee Papers.* "The [Charles] Lee Papers." NYHS Cols., 1871–74. 4 v.

*LOLTW.* LOUIS GOTTSCHALK, ed. "The Letters of Lafayette to Washington, 1777–1799."

*LTW.* JARED SPARKS, ed. "Correspondence of the American Revolution; being Letters of Eminent Men to George Washington . . ." 4 v.

*Maclay.* EDGAR S. MACLAY, ed. "Journal of William Maclay."

*Madison Papers.* Papers of James Madison. LC.

*Malone.* DUMAS MALONE. "Jefferson and His Time." 2 v. to date.

*Matteson.* DAVID M. MATTESON. "Washington and the Constitution."

*McLaughlin.* A. C. MCLAUGHLIN. "The Confederation and the Constitution, 1783–1789."

*MHS.* Massachusetts Historical Society.

*MHSP.* "Massachusetts Historical Society Proceedings."

*Monaghan.* FRANK MONAGHAN. "Notes on the Inaugural Journey and the Inaugural Ceremonies of George Washington as First President of the United States."

*Morgan and Fielding.* JOHN HILL MORGAN and MANTLE FIELDING. "The Life Portraits of Washington and Their Replicas."

*Mrs. Bacon-Foster.* MRS. CORRA BACON-FOSTER. "Early Chapters in the Development of the Patomac Route to the West."

*Mrs. Quincy.* "Memoir of the Life of Eliza Susan Morton Quincy."

*NYHS.* New-York Historical Society.

*Paine Wingate.* CHARLES E. L. WINGATE. "Life and Letters of Paine Wingate." 2 v.

*Papers of G. W.* Papers of George Washington. LC.

*PHS.* Historical Society of Pennsylvania.

*Pickering.* O. PICKERING and C. W. UPHAM. "Life of Timothy Pickering." 4 v.

*Proc. Cin.* JOHN C. DAVES, ed. "Proceedings of the General Society of the Cincinnati."

*Reed.* WILLIAM B. REED, ed. "Life and Correspondence of Joseph Reed."

*Richardson.* JAMES D. RICHARDSON, ed. "A Compilation of the Messages and Papers of the Presidents, 1789–1908." 11 v.

*RIHS.* Rhode Island Historical Society.

*Rowland, Carroll.* KATE MASON ROWLAND. "Life and Correspondence of Charles Carroll of Carrollton." 2 v.

*Rowland, Mason.* KATE MASON ROWLAND. "The Life of George Mason." 2 v.

*Rufus King.* CHARLES R. KING, ed. "The Life and Correspondence of Rufus King." 6 v.

*Smyth's Franklin.* A. H. SMYTH, ed. "The Writings of Benjamin Franklin." 10 v.

*Sparks.* JARED SPARKS, ed. "The Writings of George Washington." 12 v.

*Sparks's Morris.* JARED SPARKS. "The Life of Gouverneur Morris . . ." 3 v.

*Statutes at Large.* RICHARD PETERS, ed. "United States Statutes at Large." 18 v.

*St. Clair Papers.* W. H. SMITH, ed. "The St. Clair Papers." 2 v.

*Steele Papers.* H. M. WAGSTAFF, ed. "Papers of John Steele." 2 v.

*Steiner's McHenry.* B. C. STEINER. "Life and Correspondence of James McHenry."

*T. E. V. Smith.* THOMAS E. V. SMITH. "The City of New York in the Year of Washington's Inauguration, 1789."

*V.* "Virginia Magazine of History and Biography." 60 v. to date.

*VHS.* Virginia Historical Society.

*VSL.* Virginia State Library.

*Washington Papers, Huntington Lib.* Papers of George Washington. Huntington Library, San Marino, Calif.

*Webb.* WORTHINGTON C. FORD, ed. "Correspondence and Journals of Samuel Blachley Webb." 3 v.

*W. W. Henry.* WILLIAM WIRT HENRY. "Patrick Henry; Life, Correspondence and Speeches." 3 v.

# ACKNOWLEDGMENTS

I<small>T IS</small> characteristic of the author that all his works carry a lengthy and varied list of acknowledgments. No service or suggestion, large or small, rendered during his life failed to have his prompt and grateful thanks. This biography, the most extensive of his writings, bears the largest indebtedness to scholars, students, experts in many fields, to family and to friends. Every effort has been made to prepare as complete a listing as possible but it is too much to hope that it will be all-inclusive. Inevitably, there will be omissions. Of those whose favors merit mention not given below, we ask understanding and forbearance; we ask further that they recognize the fact that their kindnesses were gratefully received and that they accept, though unnamed, the warm appreciation that is their due.

First and deepest thanks here, as in all other books from the pen of Douglas Southall Freeman, belong to Mrs. Inez Goddin Freeman, whose first thought and consideration throughout the years was the welfare of the author. She took pains to see that his surroundings were peaceful and beautiful; she recognized the necessity for long, quiet, undisturbed hours in his study; for cheerful companionship when solitude was broken with timely diversion. Her protection, her self-effacement, her unfailing good nature and her confidence combined to fashion the perfect setting for the writer's routine.

To Mr. Raymond B. Fosdick the author wrote, "If you had not urged me to undertake the work, I would not have embarked on it." It is recorded many times in Dr. Freeman's own words that Mr. Fosdick inspired this biography and that his inspiration was unceasingly followed by friendly guidance and encouragement, both spiritual and material.

At every stage of the undertaking, the author's dedicated and indefatigable chief research assistant, Dr. Gertrude R. B. Richards, had a unique place. She was indispensable in collecting materials, in preparing bibliographies, in selecting illustrations, and in verifying references. Dr. Richards examined countless manuscript sources and prepared notes on materials in this country, in Canada, in France and in England—from books or papers that could not be removed from libraries. To her goes credit for much material, both direct and collateral, previously untouched. Incredibly diligent, quick to identify new and important evidence, this valued associate contributed many immensely important items to the definite enrichment of this biography. She was eminently qualified for her assignment as researcher in the primary sources, and her contribution to the fund of rare information is outstanding.

419

Her service to the author in turn served to prove her own scholarly mettle. The careful study she made of contemporary court records and diaries of the Washington era and of Washington's account books yielded much new data and added vastly to the biography. To Dr. Richards the author himself paid high tribute in other volumes; her part in this project is well known to scholars and to the Freeman audience generally.

Thanks are due, most especially, to the officers and Executive Committee of the Carnegie Corporation of New York, who have supported this research from the beginning, not only with financial generosity, but also with friendly understanding. In the author's own words, this grant gave him the "immense satisfaction of being able to pursue all the avenues and to check material in all the repositories where data on the Washington period might be found. The vast potentialities of the project otherwise could not have been realized or even approached." For this magnificent aid to scholarship, particular thanks are in order to Dr. Robert M. Lester, Secretary of the Corporation, to all its officers and trustees.

Additional financial support for the biography was bestowed in more recent years by the John Simon Guggenheim Memorial Foundation and made possible a continued comprehensive research. This generous participation reflects the appreciation and devoted interest of Dr. Henry Allen Moe, Secretary General of that body.

The Johns Hopkins University, during the whole of this enterprise, was custodian and disburser of the funds allocated to it by the Carnegie Corporation and the Guggenheim Foundation toward historical research on the *Washington*—funds used exclusively for expenses of this staff and extended researches. Unfailing courtesy and cooperation on the part of the University officers and co-workers won Dr. Freeman's deepest admiration and appreciation. Mr. P. Stewart Macaulay, Provost, Mr. Henry S. Baker, Treasurer, and the Assistant Treasurer, Mr. John H. Gilliece, went far beyond the discharge of routine duties in the flawless administration of these appropriations. To them and their assistants grateful thanks were repeatedly expressed by the author and his associates. The late President Isaiah Bowman and past President Detlev Bronk also manifested continuing interest.

Dr. Earl G. Swem, that "savant of history" at Williamsburg, read the proofs of earlier volumes and scrutinized them with scholarly care, to the marked benefit of author and book. A multitude of specific queries were handled also in his expert, accurate and prompt manner, to round out the large services for which he was peculiarly qualified.

Mrs. Henrietta Crump Harrison, for many years the author's personal secretary, maintained for him a smoothly functioning office. Her varied and important duties were discharged with calm efficiency, discernment and fine dignity. Hers was a great and important service, loyally and devotedly performed. For the first five years of this undertaking, she had a major part in the transcription and checking of the manuscript and most admirably supervised the work of others.

Mr. John A. Carroll, for several years the full-time researcher for Dr. Freeman in the Library of Congress, early proved his ability by his skill in fulfilling assignments. His scholarly bent was matched by his zeal and earnestness in this work, for which he had a marked affinity. The author found his excellent researches highly gratifying, and to the definite enhancement of this study. He was an indispensable member of the staff during recent months of preparation of Volume Six for publication.

Miss Maud Kay Sites of Washington promptly and efficiently executed many important commissions for the author in the course of his researches and uncovered several items of particular interest and importance.

Mrs. Geneva B. Snelling, the author's librarian, gave wholehearted and loyal support to this enterprise. Her efficiency, her sound sense of values and her resourcefulness were manifest in every phase of her work, especially in the competent handling of bibliographical materials. Special credit is in order for the important contribution she has made toward readying the present volume for the publisher.

Mrs. Floretta S. Watts most admirably transcribed the manuscript and, in the process, made many helpful suggestions and eliminated numerous errors. The accuracy and speed of her work were marked by unfailing good cheer and absolute dependability.

With this book, Mr. Wallace Meyer of Charles Scribner's Sons, has edited fourteen volumes for Dr. Freeman. Over the period of twenty years, their collaboration was one of mutual admiration and respect. To the grateful thanks of the author, long ago expressed and oft repeated, now must be added that of the staff. Mr. Meyer has kept the path open and lightened the way for us all.

The late Mr. Henry Adams of Boston lifted restrictions on his family papers and graciously allowed Dr. Freeman to examine those that related to Washington.

Mr. Alexander W. Armour of Princeton, N. J., gave the writer the photostat of a letter from Washington bearing on his "dental history."

Gen. James A. Anderson, Virginia Highway Commissioner, kindly assisted in the search for information concerning the surveying instruments and books used by Washington.

Dr. Frank Aydelotte of the Institute of Advanced Study at Princeton furnished an item concerning a debt of Lawrence Washington to Brasenose College.

Mrs. Charles Baird of Marshall, Va., and her sister, Mrs. G. H. Diecke of Baltimore, daughters of the late Fairfax Harrison, to whom also a debt is due, pointed the way for the author's location of the portrait of Sally Cary Fairfax reproduced in Volume Two. Their gracious permission for use of reprints from the Belvoir Guest Book also is warmly acknowledged.

Dr. John Bakeless of Seymour, Conn., pointed out countless items of importance and interest. His generous assistance was perennial and productive.

Mr. George A. Ball of Muncie, Ind., made available for inspection the whole of his Washingtoniana and supplied generous information to the writer.

Col. C. Robert Bard in the Office of the Judge Advocate General, Washington, D. C., did research bearing on the court martial proceedings in the case of Gen. Charles Lee.

Mr. E. F. Bartelt of the U. S. Treasury Dept. identified fiscal records kept by Washington during the Revolution.

For use of the important Baylor Papers, privately owned, the author was most grateful.

Mr. Samuel M. Bemiss thoughtfully provided an interesting letter from Edmund Randolph to James Madison.

Dr. L. Minor Blackford of Atlanta kindly lent the author some letters of Washington to Landon Carter of Cleve.

Dr. Wyndham B. Blanton examined the medical evidence in the case of Daniel Parke Custis and diagnosed the probable cause of death.

Dr. Julian P. Boyd, editor of *The Papers of Thomas Jefferson*, now in production, and former Librarian at Princeton University, effected the arrangement for examination of the Lloyd W. Smith Collection, containing the priceless Havemeyer Papers. He also gave timely notice to the author about the forthcoming sale of the Disney Orderly Book, which enabled the Library of Congress to procure that treasure. To these, many other outstanding courtesies were added.

Mr. Lincoln Bryant of Boston sent an important report of the Congressional Committee on cessions of lands in New York and in the West.

Rev. G. MacLaren Brydon graciously and authentically answered queries relating to religion and religious customs in the Episcopal Church of Washington's day.

Dr. Lyman H. Butterfield, Director of the Institute of Early American History and Culture, Williamsburg, Va., forwarded interesting notes on Washington's surrender of his commission and gave the author many other helpful leads.

Dr. Lester J. Cappon of Williamsburg, Va., directed attention to a most interesting article on Washington's weight found in a rare publication; identified Mrs. Campbell's Colonial Coffee House, and rendered other kindnesses.

Professor James R. Case, Bethel, Conn., thoughtfully sent information about the Hempsted Diary.

Mr. Curtis Chappelear, Delaplaine, Va., prepared a plat and explanatory note on Washington's land holdings in Frederick County for which the author expressed warm appreciation.

Col. Bryan Conrad of the Virginia Conservation Commission supplied pertinent information on Washington's route in 1756.

Dr. Roy Bird Cook of Charleston, W. Va., unraveled details of Washington's journey in the Cheat River vicinity and helped clarify other points of the western tour of 1784.

Dr. Howard Corning of Salem, Mass., among other favors, made possible the loan of unpublished Washington letters belonging to Miss Lillian B. Richmond.

Mr. A. L. Crabb sent a fine item on Washington and the Chickasaw Nation.

The late Dr. Jackson Davis seconded Mr. Fosdick in the moral support that encouraged inception of this enterprise, and backed confidence with wise counsel.

Dr. F. M. Dearborn of New York made freely available his fine collections, among them, letters of General Greene, the correspondence of Pulaski, and an extraordinary document, the anonymous spy's report which disclosed Washington's organization of espionage.

Mr. Garrett A. Denise of Freehold, N. J., proficiently conducted the writer over the Monmouth battlefield for a better understanding of that area.

Mr. Willard De Yoe of Hewitt, N. J., helped in many instances to correct error or to establish fact. In particular, he did important service in furnishing information on Pompton and in identifying various sites for the endpaper map of Volume Five.

Mr. G. M. Dillon of Allegheny County, Penn., was instrumental in procuring photostats of a contour map of Braddock, through courtesy of the U. S. Steel Corporation.

Dr. Bernard Drell of the University of Chicago graciously sent a letter of Washington's, uncovered in his research on John Taylor.

Mr. John S. du Mont of Greenfield, Mass., forwarded a copy of the return of killed, wounded and missing at the Battle of the Brandywine, a most useful paper.

Dr. Everett E. Edwards, editor, Agricultural History Society of Washington, D. C., furnished interesting data on agricultural history of Virginia in colonial times.

Mr. H. R. Eubank, Virginia State Chamber of Commerce, examined the manuscript of Volume One in the light of his intimate knowledge of many aspects of the country in which Washington's youth was spent.

Mrs. Charlotte Judd Fairbairn of Charles Town, W. Va., helped greatly on the Washington land titles and sent valued information about the Bullskin tract.

Mr. William S. Febiger of Boston assisted by making accessible the Febiger Papers in microfilm.

Dr. Joseph E. Fields of Joliet, Ill., gave access to his fine Washington materials; provided photostats or transcriptions of original Washington letters and documents. From his unpublished acquisitions came several items of immense interest and importance.

Mr. Eben D. Finney of Baltimore thoughtfully provided a photostat copy of a letter from Governor Stone of Maryland to Washington.

Mr. Otis Fitchett of Caldwell, N. J., never missed an opportunity for passing on some Washington item that might bear fruit. Many helpful and interesting facts were gathered by this loyal friend.

Mr. Percy Scott Flippin of Washington, D. C., most kindly searched the Acts of Parliament for an entry concerning imposition of duty on tobacco.

Mr. Allyn K. Ford of Minneapolis placed at the author's disposal transcripts of important correspondence of Gen. George Weedon, a significant contribution. His collection was rich in documents relating to the Virginia campaign of 1781.

Mr. Henry Needham Flynt of New York furnished transcripts of two items: a letter of Washington to Henry Laurens and a memorandum for the servants prepared by Washington, dated Sept. 11, 1781.

Mr. Charles Edgar Gilliam of Petersburg, Va., made a careful investigation into contemporary evidence on the use of "share" and "plow share."

Mr. C. Fitzhugh Gordon of New York kindly sent a copy of an original letter in his possession written March 28, 1778, by Washington to General Smallwood.

Professor Louis Gottschalk of the University of Chicago helpfully verified items about Washington and Lafayette and forwarded important photostats.

Mrs. E. B. Harold of Charles Town, W. Va., kindly helped with Judge Brooks's Memoirs.

Dr. William H. Higgins, Jr., studied the known symptoms of Washington's illness in 1786 and the treatment administered, at the request of the author, in the interest of making a firm diagnosis.

Mr. H. H. Hill, of Virginia Polytechnic Institute, supplied transcript of a land entry of Washington in 1774.

Mr. Frederic B. M. Hollyday of St. Michaels, Md., rendered timely service in sending a photostatic copy of a letter from Washington to William Tilghman.

Prof. John Newbold Hough of the University of Colorado generously sent an unpublished Washington letter addressed to General Lacey and one of Anthony Wayne to Lacey.

Mr. Arthur E. Howard, Jr., of Hartford, Conn., helpfully supplied a valuable reference on Washington's various routes during the Revolution.

Mrs. Lawrence G. Hoover added information on Washington's land holdings in Montgomery County, Md.

Mr. M. A. deWolfe Howe of Boston made a copy of an original letter in his possession, Washington to Knox, and an interesting note of Washington's.

Gen. Edgar E. Hume of the United States Army directed a search for George Hume's "Field Book."

Mr. Douglas Jerrold of London, England, obtained a copy of the Robert Dinwiddie portrait from the National Gallery there for use in Volume One.

Mr. Stuart Wells Jackson of Gloucester, Va., put at the disposal of the author his full, fine Lafayette collection.

Mr. J. Ambler Johnston conducted the research for information on Washington's surveying instruments and books and thereby performed a most useful task for the author.

Mr. F. B. Kegley of Wytheville aided the author by allowing use of his maps of Washington's tour to the frontier in 1756 and of the frontier forts.

Dr. Bernhard Knollenberg of Chester, Conn., arranged for the author to examine the Wadsworth-Greene Papers given by him to the Yale University Library and suggested other useful references.

Mrs. Katharine McCook Knox of Washington, D. C., is due particular recognition for many kindnesses, chief among them information resulting from her fine study of the Sharples and her careful investigation into the authenticity of the portrait of Tobias Lear reproduced in the present volume.

Professor Laurence LaForge of Cambridge, Mass., furnished useful information about Dorchester Heights and Beacon Hill, as well as data on other topographical features of the Boston area.

Mr. H. T. Louthan of King William County, Va., furnished important information regarding the Custis-Hooe accounts.

Mr. James G. Martin of Norfolk, Va., lent the author a letter from Washington to George Read.

Dr. Walton Martin of New York, through Dr. E. L. Tinker, gave the writer an interesting and little-known bibliographical item.

Mrs. R. Corbin Maupin of Portsmouth, Va., made accessible her useful Lund Washington Papers.

Mr. Earl Chapin May of New York contributed fine information on the Principio Company.

Mr. David J. Mays replied promptly and fully to inquiries concerning Edmund Pendleton and matters pertaining to the defalcation of John Robinson.

Dr. Robert D. Meade of Lynchburg supplied many interesting references, notably some relating to Patrick Henry.

Dr. Thomas W. Murrell, Jr., generously lent the author his original of the "Return of the British Forces in America for October, 1778."

Mr. J. K. Paulding of New York kindly granted permission to consult the 1762 Diary of Washington, deposited by him in the Library of Congress.

Mr. B. D. Peachy of Williamsburg, Va., helped trace ownership of the Sally Cary Fairfax portrait.

Mr. and Mrs. Robert J. H. Powel graciously placed at Dr. Freeman's disposal the important Powel Papers at Mount Vernon, made available for the first time. These documents were exceedingly useful and enlightening. No privilege was more deeply appreciated.

Mrs. James F. Plummer of Mobile, Ala., gave ready access to the valuable Carter Letters in her possession.

Mr. William M. E. Rachal of the University of Virginia thoughtfully sent an interesting transcript of a newspaper record of Washington's weight and that of other officers and pointed out the publication in October, 1857, of two Washington items that otherwise might not have been unearthed in this research.

Mr. William G. Renwick of Weston, Mass., sent a letter written by an aide at Washington's bidding, which concerned a pistol given the General by Braddock.

Dr. Howard C. Rice, Jr., of Princeton University graciously supplied photostats of Washington material in the Bibliothèque Nationale, Paris.

Miss Lillian B. Richmond of Buffalo, N. Y., kindly gave access to a letter of Washington to Mrs. Nathanael Greene.

Dr. Edward M. Riley, Historian of the Independence National Historical Park Project, Philadelphia, carefully answered many queries from the author and supplied many important data. For his continued interest and counsel both author and staff are indebted. Thanks also are in order to Dr. Riley's competent assistant, Mr. James M. Mulcahy.

President David A. Robertson of Goucher College called attention to several unusual Washington items.

The Rev. Stewart Robinson kindly obtained permission from the owner of the Eben. Foote Papers to have them made accessible.

Dr. Francis S. Ronalds of the Morristown National Historical Park repeatedly and most generously supplied microfilms and photostats of Washington letters and other highly significant material, including the manuscript Diary of Sylvanus Seeley. Dr. Ronalds also furnished many data on details of the Army's suffering at Morristown in the winter of 1780 and contributed in countless ways to the fund of fact used by the author, and in the correction of errors. Often consulted, his counsel and his contributions were of immense aid and importance.

Miss Frances Shaw of Delhi, N. Y., graciously granted permission for examination of the Eben. Foote Papers.

Dr. Theodore Sizer of the Yale University Art Gallery generously answered numerous inquiries and forwarded valuable items. He did special service to the author in the matter of illustrations. Thanks of the staff also are voiced for his continued kindness in recent months.

Mr. Edmund L. R. Smith of Lutherville, Md., permitted examination of the several original letters of Washington and other memorabilia in his collection and thereby earned the author's gratitude.

Mrs. Edward Wanton Smith of Philadelphia, through her daughter, Miss Sarah Anne Greene Smith, thoughtfully sent photostats of three unpublished letters of Washington.

Mr. Lloyd W. Smith of Madison, N. J., graciously granted permission for Dr. Freeman to explore to the limit all the resources of his important collection of manuscripts, including the Havemeyer Papers, and thereby illumined a critical period of Washington's life and made possible a great saving of time in the research. His was a treasure house of unsurpassed importance opened to the author.

Mr. Albert Stuart of Montross, Va., supplied a helpful paper concerning the McCarty-Pope affairs.

Rt. Honorable Alberto Tarchiani, Ambassador Extraordinary and Plenipotentiary, Italian Embassy, Washington, helped the author with a doubtful meaning of a phrase of Colonel Bouquet's.

Col. Harrison Tilghman of Easton, Md., was most generous in procuring a photograph of Tench Tilghman.

Dr. Edward L. Tinker of New York supplied information on a medical history of Washington, some important Lafayette references, and rendered other kindnesses.

The late Dr. Francis Whittle Upshur of Richmond was the source of information concerning Washington letters to his great-great-grandfather, Ferdinand Fairfax.

Mr. Charles C. Wall, Resident Superintendent of Mount Vernon, rendered all possible assistance throughout the writing of this biography. His thorough knowledge of Mount Vernon—its people, its buildings, its gardens, its farms

—afforded an added dimension to many aspects of the narrative. Dr. Freeman valued in particular Mr. Wall's excellent description of Mount Vernon during the Revolutionary years. Many factual details were drawn from the rich resources in his custody. The cooperation and generosity of both Superintendent and Board called forth the author's repeated praise. Mr. Wall, as eager to lend as to learn, was indeed a gracious contributor, whose gifts are gratefully acknowledged.

Mr. Nicholas B. Wainwright of the Historical Society of Pennsylvania provided an interesting note on Governor Dinwiddie.

Mr. James B. Warden of Pittsburgh made valiant efforts on behalf of procuring specific Washington manuscript material.

Mr. Melvin J. Weig of the Morristown National Historical Park Project, and specialist in military geography West of the Hudson, made careful researches and compiled the map of the area between Tappan and Elizabeth, used as cover lining for Volume Five.

The Rev. T. Dabney Wellford of Falls Church, Va., made it possible for the author to examine the Landon Carter Diary, a highly useful document.

Dr. C. G. Wilber of New York sent a helpful bulletin containing an article on "The Siege of Yorktown."

Mr. Edward B. Wilcox of Lynn, Mass., pointed out an article of interest in an early magazine publication.

Mrs. H. Blakiston Wilkins of Washington, D. C., generously gave access to the Benjamin Tallmadge Papers in her collection.

The late Mr. G. G. Wolkins of Boston supplied valuable information regarding elevations around Boston and furnished other accurate topographical data.

Dr. Louis B. Wright, while associated with the Huntington Library, submitted valuable materials and many fine sources.

Mr. Walter Muir Whitehill, Director of the Library of the Boston Athenaeum, was most gracious in placing its fine collection of Washington's books at the disposal of the author, in answering queries, in helping obtain illustrative matter, and in the performance of a multitude of other kindnesses.

The late Mr. Edmund Randolph Williams helpfully furnished information pertaining to a subpoena served on Jefferson.

Miss Frances Leigh Williams, Dr. Freeman's valued associate in 1935, helped with the first groundwork of the biography, prior to the author's decision to postpone the project in favor of *Lee's Lieutenants*.

Mr. Alfred Young of Jamaica, N. Y., sent an important unpublished letter, Gen. John Armstrong to Washington, for the author's examination.

To the Libraries, Institutions, Historical Societies and National Park Commissions listed below is due the deepest obligation for tireless and time-consuming service to author and staff:

The American Antiquarian Society at Worcester, Mass., chiefly through its Director, Dr. Clarence S. Brigham, and the Librarian, Dr. Clifford K. Shipton, liberally opened its treasures and gave much valued assistance.

The American Philosophical Society made many fine contributions deserving special mention, notably use of some important Weedon Papers.

The Library of the Boston Athenaeum did repeated favors, besides those specifically conferred by its Director, Mr. Walter Muir Whitehill.

The Boston Public Library was a helpful and responsive repository.

The Chicago Historical Society put within reach many important items and was an additional source for the Weedon Papers.

The Clements Library at Ann Arbor rendered superlative service. The late Dr. Randolph G. Adams and his assistant, Miss Margaret Larson, conscious of the value of their collections, made every possible effort to speed the examination of thousands of letters by removing all restrictions as to the conditions under which the research was done, a contribution as valuable as were the manuscripts themselves.

The Connecticut Historical Society of Hartford gave valued help. Its Director, Mr. Thompson Harlow, and his able staff provided data on Nathanael Greene and on other contemporaries of Washington contained in their collections.

At the Connecticut State Library of Hartford, particular thanks are due Miss Marjory Case for constant and constructive assistance in details concerning the history of their fine collections, particularly those relating to the Trumbull family.

The Duke University Library, through Mrs. Pauline C. Beers, supplied valuable Dismal Swamp Papers in photostat.

The Frick Art Reference Library, New York, at all times rendered gracious and invaluable service to this work. Grateful acknowledgment is especially in order to its Librarian, Mrs. Henry W. Howell, Jr., and her assistant, Miss Mildred Steinbach. The continued cooperation of the Library has made those associated with this work acutely conscious of its excellent services.

The Harvard College Library, exemplary in its treatment of the historical student, proved itself as great in generosity as in scholarship and elicited from the author his highest praise. The Librarian, Dr. K. D. Metcalf, deserves added thanks, and Mr. Robert H. Haynes, who sent rare material from among cherished volumes, did a service that could not have been duplicated in any other library. Mr. William A. Jackson gave continual assistance in providing photocopies of important papers from the Houghton Library also.

The Huntington Library, San Marino, Cal., did conspicuous service in making available all its Washington Papers through microfilms. Its staff gave immediate attention to inquiries and supplied material for several illustrations in this work. During the period of his research professorship there, Dr. Louis B. Wright contributed several important items. Special thanks also are due the present Director, Dr. John E. Pomfret, and to Miss Norma Cuthbert, chief cataloguer of manuscripts, who sent a report on the Fairfax documents.

From the Illinois State Historical Library, Mr. Harry E. Pratt wrote the author about the existence of certain Nathanael Greene letters.

At the John Carter Brown Library, Providence, Mr. Lawrence C. Wroth supplied varied and valuable suggestions as to manuscripts in his collections and elsewhere.

The Library of Congress, principal repository throughout this study, was superlative in service to author and associates. Every member of the incomparable Library staff displayed profound interest and rendered flawless help. Dr. Luther H. Evans, Librarian, and Mr. Verner W. Clapp, Acting Librarian, were exemplary in every way. The former Chief of Manuscripts Division, Dr. St. George Sioussat, and the present Chief, Mr. David C. Mearns, counselled repeatedly, as did the former Assistant Chief, Mr. Leslie W. Dunlap, and Mr. Robert H. Land, present Assistant Chief. Col. Willard Webb, Chief of the Stack and Reader Division, and his Assistant, Mr. Gordon W. Patterson, have been consistently gracious. In the Rare Books Division, Mr. Vincent Eaton made easily accessible whatever his collections held that would be useful, as did Mr. F. R. Goff, the present Chief. Mr. Legare H. B. Obear, Mr. R. L. Henderson and Mr. Bernhard Goldberg of the Loan Division, and Mrs. Emily M. Jahn of the Microfilm Reading Room have taken endless pains to be helpful, as has Mr. Donald H. Mugridge, Fellow in American History; Mr. Hirst D. Milhollen, Curator of Photographs, and the courteous personnel of the Map Division responded often to calls for assistance. The entire staff of the Manuscripts Division merits individual citation: Mrs. Ethel M. Walter, Mrs. Helga Sandburg Goldby, Mrs. Dorothy S. Eaton, Dr. C. Percy Powell, Mr. John J. dePorry, Dr. Elizabeth G. McPherson, Mr. Wilfred S. Langone and Mr. Frank F. White, Jr. In the National Archives, Mrs. Kieran Carroll of the State Department Records Section was most helpful.

From the Maryland Historical Society, Baltimore, the Director, Mr. James W. Foster, forwarded data relating to the Principio Iron Works and to the services of Gen. Otho H. Williams.

The Massachusetts Historical Society through its Director, Mr. Stewart Mitchell, and its Librarian, Mr. Stephen T. Riley, took pains to make investigations and supply interesting details, as well as important illustrative matter which also deserves special notice.

The Monmouth County Historical Association, Freehold, N. J., did notable kindness through the late Miss Laura Flanders, in providing maps, letters and narratives by contemporaries of the Battle of Monmouth.

The Mount Vernon Ladies' Association of the Union put every paper in its excellent collections, so admirably catalogued, at Dr. Freeman's disposal. The archivists, Mr. Worth Bailey, now Director of the Woodlawn Foundation, and Mr. John B. Riggs, whose assistance began in the Library of Congress and crossed the Potomac when he was appointed archivist of Mount Vernon, both fulfilled every need and met every desire of researcher by their accurate knowledge of all that related to Washington. This applies also to Miss Irene Warren, Librarian. The warm friendliness found at Mount Vernon and the perfect cooperation have made a great contribution to this biography. Mr. Charles C. Wall, Resident Superintendent, is given specific notice under his own name.

The National War College Library of Washington provided a military dictionary and other military books of importance relating to the war period.

The New-York Historical Society's part in this work is marked. It is impossible to express adequately appreciation due the staff and, in particular, to Mr. Wayne Andrews and Mr. W. R. Leech for assistance that stopped at nothing in their efforts to provide everything needed, in the shortest possible time.

At the New York Public Library, Mr. Robert W. Hill and Mr. E. B. Morrison helpfully anticipated requests for manuscripts by providing access to pertinent material in their collections.

In the New Jersey State Library, Trenton, nothing of particular importance relating to Washington was found, but the interest of the staff expressed in many valuable suggestions is happily remembered.

The Omaha Public Library, through its Director, Mr. Arthur H. Parsons, Jr., sent an unpublished Washington letter of great interest and information about a Washington Ledger, both on deposit there.

The Pennsylvania Historical Society was responsive and helpful in many ways. Its Director, Mr. R. N. Williams, II, sent various items. The Richard Peters Papers are among the important material made accessible through this repository.

The Princeton University Library made easily accessible all its Washington manuscripts and papers, some of them immensely important. The interest and efficiency of the staff expedited the research. Particular appreciation is due the staff and Dr. Julian P. Boyd, then Librarian, whose fine contribution is separately acknowledged in these pages.

The Rhode Island Historical Society, through its Librarian, Mr. Clifford P. Monshon, and his assistants, gave valuable help by making available letters in the Peck, Bourne and Brown Papers which related to Washington's first administration as President.

From the Rhode Island State Archives came several unpublished Washington letters found among the State Papers there and forwarded by Miss Mary Quinn.

Rutgers University Library is due thanks for two unpublished letters of Washington.

The Smithsonian Institution, Washington, responded graciously to various queries from author and staff.

The University of Richmond lent freely its reference books and added materially to the ease of the research.

The United States Coast and Geodetic Survey promptly and accurately answered several requests for identification of sites and information on sun and tides.

The United States Observatory supplied important astronomical data, specifically, the time of moon rise during the Siege of Yorktown.

The Valley Forge Park Commission deserves marked appreciation. Through the late Gen. Norman Randolph, Executive Secretary, prompt and important information was obtained about Valley Forge. Special thanks are due Mrs. Margaret D. Roshong who clarified, by careful research into the Moore properties, confused data about the Jane Moore House and Moore Hall.

From the Virginia Historical Society the author received consistent help and interest. The late Rev. Clayton Torrence, Director of the Society, and his successors, Col. Catesby ap Catesby Jones and Mr. John M. Jennings, opened their manuscripts at every request of the biographer. Not less valuable were the contributions of Miss Ellen B. Wooldridge, long curator of manuscripts, and a recognized authority on every aspect of Virginia history.

At the Virginia State Library, Dr. William J. Van Schreeven provided every possible facility that would further in any way the problems associated with manuscript researches, relieving the tedium that is associated with deciphering old papers and reducing the time needed under less fortunate conditions. Among his able assistants, the late Mrs. Mary Pollard merits special mention for her knowledge of the resources of the Library and of their value to the biographer. In the Reference and Circulation Section of the General Library Division, Mr. Milton C. Russell gave valued help graciously, as did Mrs. Pinkney A. Smith. The Library rendered a notable service in allowing extended privileges in the use of its volumes.

The University of Virginia Library is due grateful acknowledgment, specifically for the kindness of Mr. Francis Berkeley, Curator of Manuscripts, who sent valuable personal papers to be used in the early chapters of the life of Washington, and gave suggestions as to incidental material, all exceedingly welcome contributions.

From the Wadsworth Athenaeum, Hartford, Conn., came some unlisted but very important letters relating to Washington, Greene and Jere. Wadsworth, discovered in the institution by Mr. C. E. Bulkley, to whom special thanks are due.

From the Yale University Library and Art Gallery also came that model of assistance that marks the ideal repository so dear to the heart of the researcher.

Among the foreign libraries and repositories to which grateful acknowledgment is in order are the following:

At Ottawa, Canada, the late Miss Alice La Mothe, by her tireless research in the Public Archives, and in the Archives de la Province de Quebec in Montreal, brought to light much valuable information on Colonel Bouquet and the French officers who participated in the French and Indian War.

In Paris, M. Olivier, sous-Archiviste of the Archives Nationales, rendered constant and generous service in making available material in every branch of the archives pertaining to the French officers who were in America from 1778 to 1783.

The Public Record Office in London opened its data to this research. The members of its staff gave their time to hunting out tattered fragments of Fairfax Papers and so arranged them as to make the reading of them possible.

At Oxford University, the Brasenose College staff members made accessible the records relating to the Reverend Lawrence Washington.

In Windsor Castle, the late Miss Mary Mackenzie, Curator of the Royal Archives, generously assisted in locating specific data in the Cumberland Papers, which had some bearing on the French and Indian War.

Through the overwhelming generosity of libraries, archives, institutions and individuals, the joy the author found in this long labor was immeasurably increased. Even routine requests were graciously received and expertly handled, almost without exception. To both the man and the book that is a tribute to which Douglas Southall Freeman, in turn, would have paid marked tribute.

SELECT CRITICAL BIBLIOGRAPHY

# GENERAL BIBLIOGRAPHICAL NOTE

## PRINCIPAL MANUSCRIPT SOURCES

In the manuscript sources, this investigation encompassed vast and varied fields. It covered repositories throughout this country and Canada, in France, in England; it included Spain, the British West Indies and even Australia. In the United States, the chief depositories were: the Library of Congress, Mount Vernon, the Henry E. Huntington Library at San Marino, Cal., the Virginia Historical Society, the New-York Historical Society, the New York Public Library, the Massachusetts Historical Society, the William L. Clements Library at the University of Michigan, Harvard College Library, the Library of Princeton University and that at Yale, the Historical Society of Pennsylvania and the Connecticut Historical Society. The more significant archives abroad were the British Museum, the Public Record Office in London, the Library at Windsor Castle, and the Archives Nationales in Paris. Transcripts of many of these foreign manuscripts are in the Library of Congress.

Whereas the accompanying Bibliography is cumulative in that the major, more important sources used in the whole of this work are included, it is selective and not comprehensive. The student who desires more detailed bibliographical information and description would do well, first, to review the Introductions to Volumes One, Three and Five, where stress is laid on the documents as they come to light, and second, to reread the General Bibliography at the end of Volumes Two, Four and Five. In many instances, the author there evaluates given sources as they relate to the persons, events or period enlightened by them. Sources introduced for the first time in the narrative of Volume Six are given somewhat more explanatory treatment in these preliminary remarks. Mention should be made here of the fact that certain single items, even though colorful or important in a particular detail, have received treatment in the footnotes only.

The significant single trove of unpublished material for this biography resides, of course, in the Papers of George Washington—five hundred and more classified, chronologically arranged portfolios in the Division of Manuscripts, Library of Congress. This remarkable collection, estimated conservatively at 75,000 items in 1930, was at that time still in the process of compilation. As had happened with almost every large body of manuscript material for American history, errors were made years ago in the preservation, sorting and binding of the Washington Papers. It became the task of the Library of Congress to gather the documents, correct wherever possible the mistakes of earlier custodians, and arrange the collection conveniently in permanent form. Massive in ambition and monumental in achievement, this undertaking displays for librarians a prime example of what can result from the dedicated perseverance of a group of careful workers under fine supervision. Without such a collection as its tap-root, no large biography of George Washington would have been possible. Furthermore, the use of so vast and diverse a body of material, however well calendared in a card index, would have been infinitely more complicated without the service of a competent guide—a compass, so to speak, for areas of Washington's career hitherto scantily analyzed or wholly neglected. *The Writings of George Washington*, published in thirty-seven volumes by the late John C. Fitzpatrick of the Library of Congress, eminently satisfied this need. Fitzpatrick's exhaustive and meticulous compilation of the written word of Washington, and the accompanying index in two volumes by David C. Matteson, have proven the indispensable roadmarks for the present author's excursion into the Library of Congress manuscripts. It was, in fact, Fitzpatrick's patient labor among these thousands of unexplored documents which gave rise to a conviction on the part of many historical students that the career of Washington should now be considered in the light of all his correspondence and personal records. Meant to be a comprehensive publication rather than an "edition," the *Writings* bring Washington's own works—the letters drafted by him or composed in his autograph—from the obscurity of the original manuscript or Letter-Book copy into the availability of print. For a biography, it remained to match these letters from Washington's pen with those written to him. The letters of his more illustrious contemporaries have, of course, been published in one form or another and are, in the aggregate, complete and textually reliable; also, the myriad of Washingtoniana has produced an occasional offering of *Letters to Washington* such as those of Sparks in 1837 and of S. M. Hamilton in 1898. A glance at the table of contents in any of Fitzpatrick's volumes will suffice, however, to demonstrate that the bulk of Washington's correspondence at every point in his career was with men of less stature than Robert Dinwiddie, Patrick Henry, Lafayette, Hamilton, Jefferson, or Madison. It was, rather, with intimate friends in Virginia before the Revolution, with subordinates of small fame during the War, with old comrades in the period of retirement, with trusted confidants during the Presidential years. The letters of such individuals as Benjamin Lincoln, Tobias Lear and Dr. David Stuart are available nowhere except in manuscript, and the major part of correspondence of this kind has been placed in proper sequence in the Papers of George Washington. Herein lies the dominant value of the collection at the Library of Congress. Some gaps and omissions exist, to be sure, and it has been necessary at times to look elsewhere for an important letter addressed to Washington or even for a whole set of correspondence. The private collection of Lloyd W. Smith at Madison, N. J., for instance, is of inestimable value for the two-hundred-odd Revolutionary documents it contains, as well, amazingly, as for the score of Washington's own letters not unearthed by Fitzpatrick. This collection yielded also two of Washington's account books and a cash ledger which, with the quantity of personal records admirably classified among the Washington Papers at the Library of Congress, fills a particular void and provides the foundation for thorough understanding of Washington's progressively complex private affairs.

For that part of the narrative dealing with Washington's family and ancestral background, it is suggested that the reader consult the Introduction to Volume One and the Bibliographical Note appended to Volume Two, where relevant sources are fully listed and described. The Fairfax Proprietary records, however, are of such exceptional value that they must be mentioned here. It seems proper to give more than summary notice to the principal papers bearing directly on Washington's young manhood as depicted in the first two volumes of this biography and in the opening chapters of Volume Three—specifically, the years from 1732 to 1775. The Papers of Washington begin chronologically with his exercise books and assume marked significance about the time of his brother Lawrence's death in

1752. Washington's travel journals, of course, have been published and are listed in the Bibliography of Printed Sources; but for his earlier years, more can be reconstructed from his accounts than from any other source. George's figures, by and large, hold more of interest than do most of his diaries. This absorbing concern with finances dates from his first earnings at the age of fifteen and a half, when he was paid for making a land survey. Actually, the only extant original records of his boyhood are notations that pertain to money lent or earned by him, or to small sums won or lost at cards. The first of these entry books is a part of the Lloyd W. Smith Collection. Others, the Ledgers, for instance, and the Pocket Day Books, are in the Library of Congress and the Huntington Library. In addition to documents in Washington's own hand, the Wills, Order books and inventories, principally the Court records of Westmoreland County, were immensely useful.

When the period of the French and Indian War was reached, the problem of search for material gave way to that of choice in the mass of data accessible. These extended to transcripts in Canadian archives and papers from the British Museum, notably the excellent manuscripts of Col. Henry Bouquet, the Egerton Papers and, in the London Public Record Office, the Chatham Papers. The Richard Peters Papers in the Historical Society of Pennsylvania also were of high importance. In the Library of Congress, the Halkett Orderly Book, a manuscript record kept by Ensign Daniel Disney, richly fills in details during Braddock's march to Fort DuQuesne. Unpublished letters of Robert Dinwiddie are to be found in the Washington Papers at the Library of Congress and in the Public Record Office, London. The Memorandum of Lord Loudoun at the Huntington Library is important as it bears on that officer's disproved suspicions of Washington as a treasonable figure.

Dating from his marriage in 1759 almost to the day he assumed command of the Army at Cambridge in 1775, Washington's interests were domestic and his activities happily confined to agricultural and family duties. Consequently, the difficult Ledger A, never before analyzed, and other fiscal documents, emerge as the principal evidence for this interim period of fifteen years. This is not to say that letters to Washington found in his Papers are of no import, but simply to point out the fact that his own monetary memoranda better disclose the consuming occupation of his time.

For collateral material of highest importance over the first forty-three years of Washington's life, County Court Records and the Land Office Records in the Virginia State Library provide extensive and diverse information on the social history of the Colony and admirably serve to describe the land system then in effect. Another and even more expository record in this connection is the privately owned manuscript Diary of the great planter, Landon Carter, whose observations emphasize the economic aspects of pre-Revolutionary Virginia society. The picture of Virginia affairs is further enhanced by the Newcastle Papers in the British Museum, and the Custis Papers found chiefly at the Virginia Historical Society and the Historical Society of Pennsylvania.

Beyond Washington's own manuscripts at the Library of Congress, the most fruitful field of investigation for the Revolutionary years remains the voluminous Papers of the Continental Congress deposited in that same institution. They are replete with crucial data which form the basic current of the narrative from 1775 through 1783. Conspicuous among other manuscript sources that contribute to this copious flow of fact are the letters and papers of nine men. They are: Horatio Gates, whose Papers in the New-York Historical Society are more enriched by the letters written to him than by those from his own pen; the wise and loyal Nathanael Greene, whose manuscripts reside in many quarters; Henry Knox, Washington's never-failing friend and father of the American Artillery, whose estimable Papers are in custody of the Massachusetts Historical Society, comprising letters to Washington, to fellow-officers and to Mrs. Knox that have quality and bring interesting light to bear on events and on individuals; Gen. George Weedon, whose letters to John Page in the Chicago Historical Society serve to illuminate some of the most obscure and long-discussed aspects of the Battle of the Brandy-wine and that of Germantown—the same Weedon who was an innkeeper before the war, yet possessed of a mind that expressed itself clearly through a surprisingly large vocabulary; Alexander McDougall, militarily active in the Hudson River area, whose numerous writings in the New-York Historical Society are equally interesting—patriotic McDougall, whose correspondence dealt informatively with the Conway Cabal and made plain his own resentment of it; Joseph Trumbull, with Papers in the Connecticut Historical Society and the Connecticut State Library; Joseph Reed, whose Papers, heavy with well-informed correspondence, are in the New-York Historical Society, and indispensable to the biographer of Washington; Jeremiah Wadsworth, whose Papers are in the keeping of the Connecticut Historical Society, and, lastly, those of Anthony Wayne, interesting and important, housed in the Historical Society of Pennsylvania.

Among the smaller gems, bearing on the period rather than on the person of Washington, is the unpublished material of Tench Tilghman, including his Yorktown Diary. These manuscripts were located in Australia and served richly to enhance his published Memoirs and the beautiful letters to his father that came to an end in 1778. Another excellent contemporary document was the Diary of Dr. Robert Honyman, whose description of the Yorktown defences is especially fine. Honyman was a careful diarist who recorded observations and impressions interestingly and intelligently. To these should be added the Diary of Baron von Closen, Rochambeau's aide during the whole of the French participation, manifestly of military importance, but charming in composition, as well. The Papers of Sir Henry Clinton in the Clements Library at Ann Arbor afford a wealth of unpublished material and comprise the most extensive source of British manuscripts in this country. Their greatest value centers in unparalleled disclosures of British espionage. Also of primary significance is the Diary of William Smith, brilliant lawyer, avowed Loyalist, confidant of Sir Henry Clinton, and the brother of Joshua Hett Smith. This record touches on many topics and contains many items of historical value.

The most important new material of the period from May 1, 1778, to Dec. 23, 1783, comes from the Papers of the Ministry of Marine in the French Archives Nationales, Paris, where new and fascinating memoirs, letters and reports were uncovered. The collections cast welcome light on D'Estaing's movements and activities through a variety of entries—among them the manuscript character sketch of D'Estaing, written anonymously, and used as an Appendix in Volume Five of this work. Included also are letters of DeGrasse and some correspondence of de Ternay.

The years of retirement immediately following the war, with which the present volume opens, are substantial in their yield of manuscript material—but once again the Washington Papers indisputably constitute the richest mine. Here have been found the majority of the letters which came to Mount Vernon from 1784 through 1788. Prime among them are the communications of Henry Knox, Benjamin Lincoln and David Humphreys—old comrades of the Army upon whom Washington depended almost exclusively for accurate news from the North and, after 1786, particularly from New England. Lincoln's letters to Washington confided conditions and affairs in Massachusetts when Daniel Shays was in rebellion. Collateral material of high usefulness has been taken from other letters of Knox in his Papers at the Massachusetts Historical Society. For agricultural affairs and the life at Mount Vernon, utmost detail is available in the folios of Ledger B, Washington's principal account book during this period. With the approach of the Constitutional crisis, the correspondence of Madison and Hamilton, already largely in published form, assumes prominence, but hardly more than that of Edmund Randolph, whose vital letters remain in manuscript among the Washington Papers. The Diary of Robert Lewis, in the Mount Vernon Collection, describes the transfer of the President's family to New York in May, 1789. Something of the difficulty of transition from private to public occupation is exhibited in diversified letters to Washington found in the Thom Collection and in the Powel Papers, both at Mount Vernon. The latter is a new acquisition and deeply interesting.

As one might expect, a somewhat wider range of manuscript matter presented itself once the period of the Presidency, treated in the later chapters of the present volume, had come under consideration. Unlike those of the Continental Congress, the annals of the first Federal administration are almost entirely available in print. Personal writing comprises the bulk of the unpublished material and, of course, Washington's own Papers remain the bedrock of all primary research. Communications to the President were more numerous, perhaps, even than those to the Commander-in-Chief during the Revolutionary years. Were the manuscript letters of one individual to call for special notice, they might be those of Tobias Lear, as interesting evidence of the President's growing reliance on the capacity and judgment of his indefatigable secretary. Scarcely less noteworthy for their pertinence to family and farm business are the long, gracious communications of Dr. David Stuart and the detailed, informative ones of the respective managers of Mount Vernon, Lund Washington and George Augustine Washington. Again, the more important writings of Edmund Randolph, now Attorney General, can be viewed only in the documents that survive in the Washington Papers and in the few miscellaneous pieces scattered through other collections at the Library of Congress. The value of the letters of Knox diminishes somewhat in his function as Secretary of War, but those of Madison and of Hamilton soar in contrast. It may not be amiss to observe that the Papers of Madison and Hamilton, both subjected to lengthy publication, still can be consulted with immense profit at the Library of Congress. No edition of the works of either man is at all exhaustive, and for the study of Washington's first administration these manuscript collections have undergone scrutiny that repaid the author a thousandfold. With Jefferson, on the other hand, the various editions of his writings proved adequate in this research to focus the relationship of the Secretary of State to the President. Moreover, the century-old published works of John Adams were to have been supplemented by a detailed examination of his Papers, for which permission had just been most graciously granted in June, 1953. To a limited extent at least, Washington's rôle in foreign affairs is illuminated by study of the diplomatic dispatches of the Comte de Moustier in the Archives Nationales in Paris, those of Gardoqui in the Archivo

Nacional at Madrid, the Library of Congress photostats of Hammond's reports to the British Foreign Office, and certain unpublished State Department documents in the National Archives at Washington, D. C. Finally, it must be noted that the unprinted literary remains of every public man of any consequence in the years of the first Federal administration have been sought out and searched wherever found. This effort has not been gratifying in its result; little that was new bore directly upon Washington's life. A great deal of opinion and some fabric of fact was recovered from examination of the letters of John Brown in the Harry Innes Papers at the Library of Congress, various documents in the Emmet Collection at the New York Public Library, the writings of Thomas Hartley in the Jasper Yeates Papers at the Historical Society of Pennsylvania, and several references from Clement Biddle's Letter Book in this same depository.

Throughout the entire work, examination of both manuscript and printed sources was limited to the period under study—that is, archives were consulted for a particular phase as the narrative progressed, rather than in wholesale fashion for the entire sweep of Washington's life. This method was adopted as a means of a more intensive combing of the records because it would result in a keener sense of values for the appraisal of new and relevant items that promised to be immense in volume and unequal in quality. For the years covered by this study it is safe to say that the research is conclusive. It is not likely that material of large importance will be unearthed, certainly no data that would alter Douglas Freeman's interpretation of Washington's character and achievements, or markedly affect the author's judgments.

# SELECT CRITICAL BIBLIOGRAPHY
## OF MANUSCRIPT SOURCES

COMPILED BY GERTRUDE R. B. RICHARDS

## IN AMERICAN DEPOSITORIES

ABERCROMBY, JAMES. *Papers*, 1674–1787. All but twenty of these cover the year 1758 when Abercromby succeeded Lord Loudoun in command of the British army in North America. Huntington Library.

ADAMS, JOHN–VAN DER KEMP, ADRIAN. *Correspondence*, 1781–1829. Appraisal of political events, comments on the Revolution, formation of the government, etc. Historical Society of Pennsylvania.

ADAMS, SAMUEL. *Papers*, 1770–81. New York Public Library.

ALEXANDER, WILLIAM, LORD STIRLING. *Journal*, Jan. 1–Apr. 17, 1789. Library of Congress.

ALEXANDER, WILLIAM, LORD STIRLING. *Letters*, 1774–82. Force transcripts, some of which are duplicates of those in the New-York Historical Society; others are copies of lost originals. Library of Congress.

ALEXANDER, WILLIAM, LORD STIRLING. *Papers*, 1718–83. New-York Historical Society.

ALEXANDER, WILLIAM, LORD STIRLING. *Papers*, 1750–83. New York Public Library.

Alexandria (Virginia). *Proceedings of the Trustees*, 1748–67. In custody.

ANDRÉ, JOHN. *Papers*, Sept. 5–25, 1780. Force transcripts of unlocated originals. Library of Congress.

*Anonymous Journal.* An account of the progress of the British fleet up the Hudson. 1775–76. Many non-military comments and details. Library of Congress.

*Anonymous Journal.* "De mes Voyages en Amérique méles d'un Requeil fidelle des différents campagnes que j'y ai faite en des différentes Événments arrivee aux antilles." 1779–82. (Newport and Yorktown are included.) Library of Congress.

ARMAND-TUFFIN, CHARLES, MARQUIS DE LA ROUERIE. *Papers*, 1778–91. Columbia University Library.

ARNOLD, BENEDICT. *Papers*, Sept. 1–23, 1780. Force transcripts, nearly all published. Library of Congress.

BALCH, THOMAS WILLING. *Papers*, 1777–83. Included are several French journals, originals and transcripts. Historical Society of Pennsylvania.

BALDWIN, LOAMMI. *Papers, 1775–77*. Harvard College Library. Other letters are in the *Washington Papers*, Library of Congress, and in the *Papers of the Continental Congress*, National Archives.

BALL, JOSEPH. *Letter-book*, 1744–59. Library of Congress.

BARLOW, JOEL. *Papers*, 1783–1811. New-York Historical Society.

BARLOW, JOEL. *Papers*, 1775–1812. Harvard College Library.

BARLOW, JOEL. *Papers*, 1775–1812. Yale University Library.

BAUMAN, SEBASTIAN. *Military Papers*, 1775–95, relating to his activities as engineer in charge of fortifications along the Hudson and at Yorktown. New-York Historical Society. Other Bauman papers are in the Knox and Steuben Collections.

*Baylor Papers.* Privately owned family papers, some of which cover the military experiences of Gen. George Baylor and John Baylor, serving in the Third Continental Dragoons.

BEELEN-BERTHOLFF, FREDERICK EUGÈNE FRANÇOIS BARON DE. *Letters to Brussels,* on commercial and political affairs in the United States. Historical Society of Pennsylvania.

BEERS, NATHAN. *Journal*, 1777–82, a Force transcript of an unlocated original. Library of Congress.

Belvoir Guest Book. A copy of Thoresby's *Topography . . . of Leedes* (1715), the last pages of which have signatures of guests at Belvoir, on the Potomac, near Mount Vernon. Privately owned.

BLAINE, EPHRAIM. *Papers*, 1766–1805, of incidental importance; *Letter-books*, 1777–83; *Cash-account* as commissary, 1778–80. Historical Society of Pennsylvania.

BLEEKER, ANTHONY LISPENARD. *Letter-book*, 1767–87, containing odd bits of useful information. New-York Historical Society.

BIDDLE, CHARLES. *Papers*, 1763–1829. Correspondence on political and military affairs.

BIDDLE, CHARLES. *Letter-book*, 1789–92.

BIDDLE, CHARLES. *Autobiography*, 1819. Historical Society of Pennsylvania. A printed copy shows variations from the original.

BIDDLE, CLEMENT. *Papers*, 1743–1855. Biddle-Washington correspondence incident to Col. Biddle's activities as commissary general of forage; business relations with Washington during the war and when he assisted in removing Washington's household effects to Philadelphia. Much of the correspondence has been printed.

BIDDLE, CLEMENT. *Letter-book*, relating to trade between United States and England, 1789–92. Historical Society of Pennsylvania.

BOURNE, BENJAMIN. *Letters*, to Jabez Brown and others, on the session of Congress, 1789–92. Rhode Island Historical Society.

BOURNE, SYLVANUS. *Consular letters and reports* from Amsterdam, with comments on British policies, accounts of depredations and letters to other consuls. 1774–1800. Library of Congress.

BRODHEAD, DANIEL. *Military letters*, 1779–81, from the frontiers, and concerned with the Indian depredations. A few are addressed to Washington; others are to General Wayne. Library of Congress.

BURKE, THOMAS. *Papers*, 1744–89, regarding the condition of American troops in 1781; contracts for provisions, etc. Included are letters to General Nathanael Greene, Iredell and Jefferson. University of North Carolina.

BURR, AARON. *Papers*, 1775–1816. Over fifty letters to Washington, Conway, Tilghman and others. Force transcripts of lost originals. American Antiquarian Society.

BYRD, WILLIAM II. *Memorandum-book* of goods imported from England and cash accounts at Westover. Library of Congress.

CADWALLADER, JOHN. *Papers*, 1742–86, chiefly on the campaigns of Trenton and Princeton. Most of this material has been published. Historical Society of Pennsylvania.

CARLETON, SIR GUY. *Papers of the British Headquarters*, 1747–83. Colonial Williamsburg, Inc.

CARTER, DR. JOHN. *Account-book*. Colonial Williamsburg, Inc.

CARTER, LANDON. *Diary*, 1766–67, written on blank pages interleaved in the Virginia Almanac for those years. Clements Library.

CARTER, ROBERT, of Nominy Hall. *Papers*, 1772–93. Plantation records, letter-books, etc. Duke University.

CARTER, ROBERT (KING). *Letters*, 1723–29. Virginia Historical Society transcripts of unlocated originals.

Castellane Papers. *Miscellaneous manuscripts*. Two note-books dealing with the siege of Yorktown; one on the route of the army from Rhode Island to Virginia. Clements Library.

CHALONER and WHITE. *Mercantile Papers*; letters to military leaders, 1777–78. Historical Society of Pennsylvania.

CLEVELAND, REVEREND JOHN. *Diary*, October-December, 1776. Record of his march to join the forces in New York. Library of Congress.

CLINTON, GEORGE and JAMES. *Correspondence* during the Revolution. Library of Congress.

CLINTON, SIR HENRY. *Papers*, 1750–1812. 260 volumes of loose letters, documents, letter-books, warrant-books, ledgers, military intelligence and Clinton's history of the war. Clements Library

*Clinton-Cornwallis Controversy*. Ten volumes and fifty-four pamphlets with Clinton's annotations. Library of Congress.

CLOSEN, JEAN CHRISTOPHE LOUIS FRÉDÉRIC IGNACE, Baron von. *Journal*, 1780–83, with Rochambeau's army. Transcript of the original owned by Baron von Closen Gunderride of Bavaria, by Worthington C. Ford; two volumes with a packet of photographs of illustrations in the original manuscript. Library of Congress.

Continental Congress. *Papers*, 1774–89, recently transferred to the National Archives.

CORBIN, RICHARD. *Letter-book*, 1758–68. Virginia Historical Society.

CROGHAN, GEORGE. *Papers*, 1744–82, in the *Cadwallader Collection*. Historical Society of Pennsylvania.

CUSTIS, COL. JOHN. *Letter-book*, 1717–42. Library of Congress.

CUSTIS, JOHN. *Accounts*, c. 1762–75. These are in bad condition and the dates are not always legible. Washington and Lee University. Virginia Historical Society. Library of Congress.

DABNEY, CHARLES. *Papers*, 2 vols., 1776–82. Virginia Historical Society.

DENEUFVILLE, JOHN and SON, Amsterdam. *Letters and account books*, 1780–85. Of occasional importance as the firm were agents for the United States, 1780–85. New-York Historical Society.

DESTOUCHES, CHARLES RENÉ DOMINIQUE SOCHET, CHEVALIER. *Papers* relating to his services under Ternay and with Rochambeau at Newport and Yorktown. Huntington Library.

*Dismal Swamp Papers*, 1784–85. Duke University Library.

*Dismal Swamp Records and accounts.* Library of Congress.

DUANE, JAMES. *Papers*, 1767–95. New-York Historical Society.

DuSIMITIÈRE, PIERRE EUGÈNE. *Miscellaneous Papers* in four small notebooks, containing also lists of paintings completed, prices of books, etc. Library of Congress.

*Fairfax Grant Papers.* The greater part of this collection is concerned with the controversy between Thomas, Lord Fairfax, and Jost Hite over the boundary between the Fairfax Grant and Virginia. Library of Congress.

*Fairfax Papers.* 1753–1815. Essex Institute, Salem, Mass.
Land grants; Board of Trade papers; correspondence of the Fairfax family; survey warrants, 1722–52; rent rolls of the Northern Neck proprietary. Huntington Library.

FEBIGER, CHRISTIAN. *Papers.* The orderly book for the attack on Stony Point and the letters to Mrs. Febiger there included are most important. Privately owned.

FITCH, JOHN. *Autobiography:* One volume is owned by the Library Company of Philadelphia and the other by the Historical Society of Pennsylvania.

FITCH, JOHN. *Diaries.* Yale University Library.

FITCH, JOHN. *Papers*, 1788–92. Library of Congress.

FOOTE, EBEN. *Papers and letters* relating to supplies of cattle obtained from New England, 1778–81. Privately owned.

FORBES, GENERAL JOHN. *Orderly book.* Library of Congress.

FRANKLIN, BENJAMIN. *Papers*, 1732–90, 76 volumes. American Philosophical Society.

FRANKLIN, BENJAMIN. *Papers*, 1730–90, 14 volumes. Historical Society of Pennsylvania.

FRANKLIN, BENJAMIN. *Papers*, University of Pennsylvania.

FRANKLIN, BENJAMIN. *Papers*, 1747–49. Yale University Library.

FRANKLIN, BENJAMIN. *Correspondence with Congress* while minister to France. Historical Society of Pennsylvania.

GAGE, THOMAS. *Papers*, 1754–83, 180 volumes. Of minor importance after 1776. Clements Library.

GALLATIN, ALBERT. *Papers*, 1780–1848. New-York Historical Society.

GATES, HORATIO. *Papers*, 1750–1825. New-York Historical Society.

GÊNET, EDMOND-CHARLES. *Letters*, 1793–1833. New-York Historical Society.

GERMAIN, LORD GEORGE (later Viscount Sackville). *Papers*, 1683–1785. Clements Library.

GERRY, ELBRIDGE. *Papers*, 1709–1841. Massachusetts Historical Society.

GLOVER, JOHN. *Papers*, 1775–80. Essex Institute, Salem, Mass. Other letters and papers are found in the correspondence of his contemporaries.

GLYN, THOMAS. *Journal*, 1776–77. Princeton University Library.

GREENE, NATHANAEL. *Letters and Papers*, 70 vols. Clements Library.

GREENE, NATHANAEL. *Personal letters* to Griffin Greene. Marietta College. 1742–86.

GREENE, NATHANAEL. *Papers*, 1776–80. American Philosophical Society.

GREENE, NATHANAEL. *Military Papers* in Papers of the Continental Congress. National Archives.

GREENE, NATHANAEL. *Papers and transcripts,* 1775–86, collected by G. W. Greene for publication but never used. Huntington Library.

GREENE, NATHANAEL. *Letters,* 1778–81. Library of Congress.

GREENE, NATHANAEL. *Letters,* 1778–85. Wadsworth Athenaeum, Hartford, Conn.

GREENE, NATHANAEL. *Papers and letters,* 1780–82. Duke University Library.

GREENE, NATHANAEL. *Force Transcripts,* 1780–81; a few of these are not to be found elsewhere. Library of Congress.

HALKETT, FRANCIS. *Orderly book,* 1748–57. Library of Congress.

HAMILTON, ALEXANDER. *Papers,* 84 volumes, 1760–1830. Library of Congress.

HAMILTON, ALEXANDER. *Letters,* 1777–1804. New-York Historical Society.

HANCOCK, JOHN. *Papers,* 1775–93. Massachusetts Historical Society.

HANCOCK, JOHN. *Letter-Book,* when President of the Continental Congress, 1776–77, in *Papers of the Continental Congress,* vol. 58.

HAND, EDWARD. *Papers,* 1776–84. New-York Historical Society.

HARMAR, GEN. JOSIAH. *Military and personal papers,* 1753–1813, covering his command of the first United States troops stationed along the Ohio. Clements Library.

HARMAR, GEN. JOSIAH. *Papers,* 1681–1855. 40 vols. Clements Library.

HARTLEY, DAVID. *Correspondence* while negotiating a treaty of peace for Great Britain with the American commissioners in Paris. Clements Library.

HARTLEY, THOMAS. *Correspondence* with Judge Jasper Yeates, 1789–93. Yeates Papers. Historical Society of Pennsylvania.

*Havemeyer Papers.* Lloyd W. Smith Collection, 1739–49. Also referred to as *Washington Family Papers.*

HAY, UDNY. *Papers and correspondence,* 1776–92. New-York Historical Society.

HENRY, PATRICK. *Letters to Washington* regarding the Conway Cabal, 1778–80. Historical Society of Pennsylvania.

HONYMAN, DR. ROBERT. *Diary,* 1776–82. Library of Congress.

HOPKINSON, FRANCIS. *Papers,* 1775–99. Historical Society of Pennsylvania. Other letters are in the American Philosophical Society collections and in the Library of Congress.

HUGHES, HUGH. *Papers,* 1776–94, regarding army supplies. Library of Congress.

INNES, JUDGE HARRY. *Papers,* 1772–1850, relating to Kentucky's political and economic problems and her struggle for statehood. The collection includes many letters from John Brown, and also Todd Papers. Library of Congress.

IRVINE, WILLIAM. *Military Papers,* 1768–1854. Historical Society of Pennsylvania.

IRVINE, WILLIAM. *Papers,* 1779–80. New-York Historical Society.

JAY, JOHN. *Papers,* 1779–83. New-York Historical Society. Very few of Jay's papers are found in any collection bearing his name but many are scattered through the papers of his contemporaries.

JAY, JOHN. *Letters* covering his mission to Spain, 1779–82. Huntington Library. These are of very little use to the biographer of Washington.

JEFFERSON, THOMAS. The papers of Thomas Jefferson are found in practically every library in the country. These are all being collected and edited under the direction of Dr. Julian P. Boyd at Princeton University, and photocopies placed in the Library of Congress to supplement the large collection of originals there. It seems sufficient to refer any scholar to that collection, which has on each paper the location of the original.

KNOX, HENRY. *Papers, 1750–1825.* Transferred from the New England Historical and Genealogical Society to the Massachusetts Historical Society.

KNOX, HENRY. *Military letters, 1782.* New York Public Library.

KING, RUFUS. *Papers, 1786–1826.* New-York Historical Society.

LAFAYETTE, MARIE JEAN PAUL JOSEPH ROCH YVES GIBERT, MARQUIS DE. *Letters, 1778–1825.* New-York Historical Society.

LAMB, JOHN. *Papers, 1765–1795; letter-book, 1778–80.* New-York Historical Society.

LANGDON, JOHN. *Papers, 1777–78.* Historical Society of Pennsylvania.

LAURENS, HENRY and JOHN. *Letters,* for the most part on foreign affairs, with the fragments of a diary of John Laurens. Library of Congress.

LAURENS, JOHN. *Commonplace book:* observations on the importance of defending South Carolina from the British and on aid rendered by the French fleet in the Delaware and Chesapeake Bays under De Grasse and D'Estaing. Historical Society of Pennsylvania.

LEE, ARTHUR. *Papers, 1766–1823.* American Philosophical Society.

LEE, ARTHUR. *Paris Letter-book* (copy). Virginia Historical Society.

LEE, FRANCIS LIGHTFOOT. *Papers.* Virginia Historical Society.

LEE, HENRY. *Papers.* Virginia Historical Society. The greater part of his letters are in the papers of Washington, Jefferson and Madison.

LEE, RICHARD HENRY. *Papers.* American Philosophical Society.

LEE, RICHARD HENRY. *Papers.* Virginia Historical Society.

LEE, RICHARD HENRY. *Letter-book* in *Papers of the Continental Congress,* vol. 16. National Archives.

LEE, WILLIAM. *Papers and correspondence.* Virginia Historical Society.

LEWIS, ROBERT. *Diary* of his trip to New York with Mrs. Washington, May, 1789. Library of Congress (Toner transcript).

LEWIS, ROBERT. *Diary,* July-September, 1789. Mount Vernon.

LIVINGSTON, ROBERT. *Papers, 1714–1799.* New-York Historical Society.

LIVINGSTON, ROBERT. *Papers.* New York Public Library.

LOUDOUN, JOHN CAMPBELL, 4th Earl of. *Papers, 1510–1777.* Huntington Library.

*Ludwell Papers, 1686–1776.* Virginia Historical Society.

MACLAY, WILLIAM. Journal, with letters included, of the years 1789–93, when he was Senator. Library of Congress. The Journal has been printed but with variations of text.

McDOUGALL, ALEXANDER. *Papers, 1756–95.* New-York Historical Society.

McHENRY, JAMES. *Papers, 1776–1815.* Most of these are on the Revolution and nearly all have been printed. Huntington Library.

McKEAN, THOMAS. *Correspondence, 1759–1847.* Historical Society of Pennsylvania.

MADISON, JAMES. *Papers, 1723–1845.* 105 volumes with many letters from correspondents included. Library of Congress.

MADISON, JAMES. *Correspondence, 1784–1835.* New-York Historical Society.

MARSHALL, CHRISTOPHER. *Diaries, 1773–93.* Nine volumes and a package, extracts from which have been published. Historical Society of Pennsylvania.

MASON, GEORGE. *Papers, 1763–91.* Library of Congress.

MAUDUIT-DU-PLESSIS, THOMAS-ANTOINE, CHEVALIER DE. *Memoirs,* 1778. New-York Historical Society.

MOFFATT, DR. JOHN. *Journal,* 1775–77. Library of Congress. The comments while he was on board a ship before New York are interesting.

MORRIS, ROBERT. *Papers,* 1775–1820. Letters, diaries, financial interests. Library of Congress.

NASH, SOLOMON. *Diary,* 1776–77. New-York Historical Society.

NELSON, WILLIAM and THOMAS. *Letter-book,* 1760–72. Virginia State Library.

NEWTON, DANIEL. *Journal of a trip to New York with Artemas Ward,* 1780–81. New-York Historical Society.

NICHOLAS, GEORGE. *Papers,* 1787–99, largely on affairs in Kentucky. Chicago University Library. Nicholas letters are also in the *Innes Papers,* Library of Congress.

O'BRYEN, RICHARD. *Journal,* 1789–91, on the condition of the prisoners held in the Barbary States. Historical Society of Pennsylvania.

PICKERING, TIMOTHY. *Papers,* 1735–1863. Essex Institute, Salem, Mass.

PICKERING, TIMOTHY. *Papers,* 1759–1829. Massachusetts Historical Society.

PICKERING, TIMOTHY. *Letter-book* about a forage dispute, 1781. *Correspondence* when Quartermaster general, 1777. New-York Historical Society.

PICKERING, TIMOTHY. *Papers,* 1781–1826. Harvard College Library.

PICKERING, TIMOTHY. *Papers,* 1781. Yale University Library.

*Preston Papers* relating to the Virginia frontier, 1757–1891. Virginia Historical Society. Draper Collection, 1730–91. Wisconsin Historical Society.

Principio Papers. *Papers and accounts,* 1768–69. New York Public Library.

Principio Papers. *Papers, letters and accounts,* 1716–60. Maryland Historical Society.

Principio Papers. *Papers* (uncertain dates). Lloyd W. Smith Collection.

Principio Papers. *Cash books, ledgers,* etc., 1724–1803. Historical Society of Pennsylvania.

REED, JOSEPH. *Papers,* 1750–84. New-York Historical Society.

RIEDESEL, FRIEDRICH ADOLPH, BARON VON. *Letters* to Washington and other officers, 1777–82. Library of Congress.

ROCHAMBEAU, JEAN BAPTISTE DONATIEN DE VIMEURE, COMTE DE. *Papers,* 1763–94. Library of Congress.

RODNEY, THOMAS. *Journal,* 1796–97. Historical Society of Pennsylvania.

ROSE, REV. ROBERT. *Diary,* 1746–51. A copy made in 1850 of original later destroyed in the Confederate War. Huntington Library.

RUTHERFORD, JOHN. *Papers,* 1786–1829. New-York Historical Society.

RUTHERFORD, JOHN. *Diary,* 1753–54. Huntington Library.

SCHUYLER, PHILIP. *Papers,* 1773–1813. New York Public Library. Other papers are in the correspondence of Washington, Gates and Duane.

SCHUYLER, PHILIP. *Papers.* New York Public Library.

SCHUYLER, PHILIP. *Letter-book,* 1775–78, with copies of letters and instructions from Washington. New York Public Library.

SCHUYLER, PHILIP. *Letters* of minor importance, 1774–1802. New-York Historical Society.

SEDGWICK, THEODORE. *Papers,* 1770–1813. Massachusetts Historical Society. His letters are also found in the papers of Washington, Greene, Gates and Benjamin Lincoln.

SHELBURNE, SIR WILLIAM PETTY, EARL OF. *Papers*, 1763–82. Clements Library.

SHERMAN, ROGER. *Correspondence with John Adams* on the powers of the executive, 1789. Library of Congress.

SHIPPEN, EDWARD, and EDWARD BURD. *Papers*, 1727–85. Those from 1754–58, dealing with the Indian wars, are of particular importance. Historical Society of Pennsylvania.

SHORT, WILLIAM. *Papers*, 1778–1849. 52 volumes of correspondence much of which is from Spain, France, and the Netherlands. Library of Congress.

SMITH, WILLIAM. *Diary*, 1753–83. New York Public Library.

STEPHEN, ADAM. Autobiographical narrative, parts of which have been published. Library Company of Philadelphia.

STEPHEN, ADAM. *Papers*. Library of Congress. Letters covering the Revolution are transferred to the *Papers of Washington*.

STEWART, WALTER. *Letters and military papers*, 1776–95. New-York Historical Society.

STEUBEN, FRIEDRICH WILHELM, BARON VON. *Military Papers* relating mostly to the Southern Department, 1778–82. New-York Historical Society.

STILES, EZRA. *Papers*, 1744–95. Yale University Library. Other letters are in Library of Congress and National Archives.

STRONG, CALEB. *Papers*, 1785–87, relating to incidents of Shays's Rebellion. Forbes Library, Northampton, Mass.

SULLIVAN, JOHN. *Papers*, 1774–89. New Hampshire Historical Society. (In process of publication.)

TALLMADGE, BENJAMIN. *Papers* (on family and business affairs), 1783–1836. New-York Historical Society.

TALLMADGE, BENJAMIN. *Papers* (two volumes on the Revolution). Litchfield, Conn., Historical Society. Other Tallmadge papers are in the Washington, Greene, Knox and Trumbull papers.

TALLMADGE, BENJAMIN. *Correspondence with William Heath*, 1777–82. Massachusetts Historical Society.

TALLMADGE, BENJAMIN. *Papers*. Yale University Library.

TALLMADGE, BENJAMIN. *Papers*, 1777–82. Clements Library.

TAYLOR, FRANCIS. *Diary*, 1786–99. 13 vols. Virginia State Library.

THOMAS, JOHN. *Papers*. Personal and military correspondence, 1746–91. His letters to his wife are of great value, as he wrote her freely of his campaigns. Massachusetts Historical Society.

THOMSON, CHARLES. *Papers*, 1765–1820, 9 vols. These papers supplement the material in the *Papers of the Continental Congress*. Library of Congress.

TILGHMAN, TENCH. *Papers*, 1785. Maryland Historical Society.

TRUMBULL, BENJAMIN. *Papers*, 1776–86. Yale University Library.

TRUMBULL, JOHN. *Papers*, 1786–1855. Library of Congress.

TRUMBULL, JOHN. *Correspondence*, 1787–1839. New-York Historical Society.

TRUMBULL, JOHN. *Papers*, 1767–83. Yale University Library.

TRUMBULL, JONATHAN. *Papers*, 1767–83. Yale University Library.

TRUMBULL, JONATHAN. *Personal Papers*, 1777–83. Connecticut Historical Society.

TRUMBULL, JONATHAN. *Papers*, 1775–83. Connecticut State Library.

TRUMBULL, JOSEPH. *Papers*, 1760–78. Connecticut Historical Society. Connecticut State Library.

*United States Government,* Department of State: National Archives:
  *Diplomatic Despatches* from the United States Minister to France, 1789–98.
  *Letters* from the United States Minister to Great Britain, 1792–98.
  *Diplomatic Despatches* from the United States Minister to the Netherlands, 1794–98.
  *Diplomatic Despatches* from the United States Minister to Spain, 1792–97.
  *Domestic letters,* 1784–98.
  *Foreign letters,* 1786–90.
  *Miscellaneous letters,* 1789–97.
  *Notes to foreign ministers and consuls in the United States,* 1793–1810.
Virginia Parish Records:
  Abingdon, Gloucester, *Register,* 1678–1761.
  Blissland, New Kent, *Vestry-book,* 1721–86. Virginia State Library.
  Bruton and Middleton, *Register,* 1662–97.
  Charles, York, *Register,* 1648–1800.
  Christ Church, Lancaster, *Vestry-book,* 1739–88.
  Dettingen, Prince William, *Vestry-book,* 1745–1802. Virginia State Library.
  Kingston, Gloucester and Mathews Counties, *Register,* 1756–1820.
    *Vestry-book,* 1679–1796.
  North Farnham, Richmond County, *Register,* 1672–1800.
  Overwharton, Stafford County, *Register,* 1724–1774.
  Petsworth, Gloucester County, *Vestry-book,* 1677–93.
  St. George (Fredericksburg), *Vestry-book,* 1726–45.
    *Records,* 1746–1817. University of Virginia Library.
  St. Mark's, Culpeper, *Vestry-book,* 1730–53.
  St. John's, Richmond City, *Records,* 1730–1860.
  St. Paul's, King George, *Register,* 1716–1793. Virginia State Library.
  St. Peter's, New Kent, *Register,* 1733–(?)
    *Vestry-book,* 1685–1758.
  Truro Parish, Fairfax County, *Register,* in 2 Cockburn Papers, Library of Congress.
    *Vestry-book,* 1742—. Library of Congress.
  Wicomico, Northumberland County, *Vestry-book,* 1703–95.
Virginia State Papers:
  *Council Journals,* 1692–1799; *Minute Books,* 1740–99; *Miscellaneous Papers,* 1698–1799. Virginia State Library.
  *County Records,* Westmoreland, Lancaster, Northumberland, Stafford, King George, Fairfax, Essex, Prince William, Frederick, York. Virginia State Library.
  *Governors' Letter-books.* 1777–99. Virginia State Library.
  *Journal,* Convention of 1788, 2 vols. Virginia State Library.
  *Journals,* House of Burgesses, 1619–1776. Virginia State Library.
  *Journals,* House of Delegates, 1776–99; *Minute Books,* 1777–99. Virginia State Library.
  Land Office: *Patents,* 1623–1774; *Grants,* 1779—; *Surveys.* Northern Neck: *Deeds and Leases,* 1690–1783. Virginia State Library.
  *Miscellaneous,* 1698–1807. Virginia State Library.
  *Miscellaneous,* 1606–1841. Library of Congress.

Virginia transcripts. Virginia State Library:

DeJarnette, *Selections from P.R.O. papers,* 1606–1791.

Eggleston, *Records of Bacon's rebellion,* 1676. Egerton MS. 2395, British Museum.

Sainsbury, *P.R.O. papers,* 1624–1740. 21 vols.

Sparks, Jared: *Selections from Board of Trade Papers,* 1753–56.

Sparks, Jared: *Selections from original papers* in Harvard College Library, 1773–81.

Winder, *Selections from P.R.O. papers,* 1607–76. 2 vols.

WASHINGTON, GEORGE. *Papers* (over 800 volumes). Library of Congress.

WASHINGTON, GEORGE. *Papers.* Huntington Library.

WASHINGTON, GEORGE. *Papers,* 152. *Papers of the Continental Congress,* 11 parts. (As there is scarcely a library without a letter of Washington's, this list includes only the larger collections. Individual letters or important small collections are commented on in the Bibliographical Note.)

WAYNE, ANTHONY. *Papers.* Historical Society of Pennsylvania.

WEEDON, GEORGE. *Instructions,* sent at the time of the siege of Yorktown. 1780. Ann Mary Brown Memorial, Providence.

WEEDON, GEORGE. *Papers,* 1777–86. American Philosophical Society.

WEEDON, GEORGE. *Letters,* 1776–89. Chicago Historical Society.

WILKINSON, JAMES. *Papers and letters.* In vol. 23 of the *Harry Innes Papers,* Library of Congress. Other letters are in the Washington, Greene and Gates *Papers* and in the *Papers of the Continental Congress.*

WILLIAMS, GEN. OTHO H. *Papers,* 1748–94. Maryland Historical Society. Other papers are in the Knox, Gates and Washington collections.

WINGATE, PAINE. *Papers,* 1760–1838. Harvard College Library.

WOLCOTT, OLIVER, JR. *Papers,* 1791–95. Connecticut Historical Society.

WOLCOTT, OLIVER, JR. *Papers,* 1791–95. Library of Congress.

WOLCOTT, OLIVER, JR. *Papers,* 1791–95. Wadsworth Athenaeum.

WOLCOTT, OLIVER, JR. *Papers,* 1791–95. Connecticut State Library.

## IN BRITISH DEPOSITORIES

BRITISH MUSEUM PAPERS:

*Account of battle of Long Island.* Egerton MS., 2135, f. 193 ff.

ARNOLD, BENEDICT. *Letter to Beverley Robinson* and the latter's reply, 1780. Add. MS., 30262.

BRADDOCK, EDWARD. *Letters from America,* 1755. Egerton MS. 2964.

BOUQUET, HENRY. *Papers,* 1754–65. Add. MSS., 21631–60.

BURGOYNE, JOHN. *Letter* (describing the Battle of Bunker Hill). Add. MS. 5847.

*Case of tobacco planters in Virginia,* 1733; Lansdowne MS., 2961.

*Considerations on American trade,* 1739. Lansdowne MS., 3250.

*Cumberland Papers,* 1745–57. Windsor Castle Archives.

*Docket* to Lord Culpeper: Orders and instructions for the better governing of His Majesty's plantation of Virginia, Nov. 23, n.d. Add. MS., 17748.

*French encroachments* in America: 1750–60. Egerton MS., 2694.

HALDIMAN, SIR FREDERICK. *Papers,* 1758–85. (Many of those reprinted have incorrect dates.) Add. MSS., 21661–892.

BRITISH MUSEUM PAPERS: *(cont'd.)*

HARDWICKE, EARLS OF. *Papers, Correspondence.* Add. MSS. 35349–36278.

*Journal:* of operations under Sir William Howe, from the evacuation of Boston until the end of the campaign of 1776. Egerton MS., 2135, f. 7.

*Miscellaneous letters,* relating to America: 1718–96. Those on Revolutionary matters are of importance. Add. MS., 24322.

NEWCASTLE, THOMAS PELHAM HOLLES, DUKE OF. *Newcastle Papers,* 1667–1768. Add. MSS., 32686–33057.

Northern Neck Proprietary: *Original grant* to Lord Hopton *et al.* issued at Saint-Germain-en-Laye, Sept. 18, 1649. Additional Charter 13585.

ORME, ROBERT. *Journal,* 1755. King's MS. 212.

Peace Commission, 1778: *Documents,* 1778. Auckland Papers, Add. MSS., 34415–16. These papers supplement those in P.R.O., O.O.5: 180–81.

Principio Iron Works: *Papers,* 1725–76. Add. MSS. 29600.

*Rainsford Papers:* relating to Hanau and Anspach troops. Add. MS. 23651.

RODNEY, GEORGE BRYDGES. *Letter to George Jackson,* describing his checking the junction of the French and Washington, Oct. 11-Nov. 12, 1780. Add. MS. 9344.

STEPHEN, ADAM. *Letter* (on Braddock's defeat), in *Hardwicke Papers.* Add. MS., 35376.

WASHINGTON, GEORGE. *Letters* to Sir John Sinclair, 1792–97. Add. MS., 5757.

PUBLIC RECORD OFFICE, LONDON.

Collections:

BRADDOCK, EDWARD. *Account of the defeat of.* 98, Chatham Papers.

CORNWALLIS, EDWARD. Correspondence, 1779–80.

Admiralty in-letters:

GRAVES, THOMAS. *Letters,* 1774–77. 485.

CLINTON, SIR HENRY. *Letters intercepted by* (of Washington and of Lafayette, 1781). 1341.

Admiralty out-letters:

*Letter* from Commander of French fleet at Rhode Island, regarding De Grasse's movements.

Admiralty Papers:

DINWIDDIE, ROBERT. *Letters.* 3318.

Colonial Office (C.O.)

BRADDOCK, EDWARD. *Instructions and secret instructions to,* 1754. C.O. 5:6

VAN BRAAM, JACOB. *Memoir.* C.O. 5:16

Carthagena Expedition: *Documents and Letters,* 1740–43. C.O. 5:41–43

*French and Indian War Correspondence,* 1755–56. C.O. 5:46–47

Filius Gallicae: *Letters,* 1756–61. C.O. 5:62

Secretaries of State: *Correspondence,* 1771–81. C.O. 5:138–44

*Burgoyne-Heath Correspondence,* 1777–78. C.O. 5:52

Peace Commission, 1778: *Records.* C.O. 5:276

*Miscellaneous Correspondence,* 1776–81. C.O. 5:1235

*Correspondence,* Virginia. 1689–1783. C.O. 5:1305–53

Governors of Virginia: *Papers,* etc. 1691–1774. C.O. 5:1308–34

Governors of Virginia: *Letters to Board of Trade.* C.O. 5:1316, **1328, 1329**

PUBLIC RECORD OFFICE (*cont'd.*)

PERRY, M. and R. *Petition against Daniel Parke*, 1712. C.O. 5:1316. 321. 324.

Virginia: *Miscellaneous Papers.* C.O. 5:1344

DUNMORE, JOHN MURRAY, EARL OF. *Miscellaneous Papers.* C.O. 5:1355

Virginia: *Executive correspondence*, 1694–1777. C.O. 5:1337–1440; 1444–46

PARKE, DANIEL. *Official Papers*, 1709–10. C.O. 7:1 (Antigua)

CULPEPER, LADY CATHERINE. *Letters*, 1694–95. C.O. 324–26

Privy Council:

DUNBAR, THOMAS. *Appeal vs. Custis*, 1757. P.O. 2:105

War Office Papers:

*Letters to secretaries at war from officers in America.* In-letters, 1–13

*American Letter-books*, 1775–84. Out-letters, 273–75

CANTERBURY. Principal Registry of the Probate, Divorce and Admiralty Division of the High Court of Justice:

JOHN CUSTIS, *Will*, Nov. 14, 1749.

JOHN CUSTIS, *Estate*, 1783.

DANIEL PARKE CUSTIS, *Admonition* (2) 1774.

CLOSE ROLL, 4720, 21 Charles II, 7: no. 10
    4568, 22 Charles II, 17: no. 10

## MAPS

REGIONAL

EVANS, LEWIS. *Middle British Colonies in America:* viz. Virginia, Mariland, Delaware, Pensilvania, New-Jersey, New-York, Connecticut and Rhode Island; of Aquanishuonigy, the Country of the Confederate Indians . . . and of the Lakes Erie, Ontario and Champlain and Part of New France. 1755. Library of Congress.

FISHER, JOSHUA. *A chart of Delaware bay and river,* containing a full and exact description of the shores, creeks, harbours, soundings, shoals, sands, and bearings of the most considerable land marks from the Capes to Philadelphia. 1776. Library of Congress.

Anon: *Campaigns of 1776–77 In New York, New Jersey and Delaware.* 1777. Library of Congress.

ALEXANDER, WILLIAM, LORD STIRLING. *Maps of New York and New Jersey* (made for General Washington in 1777). J. Pierpont Morgan Library.

HILLS, JOHN. *Different Stage Routs* between the Cities of New York, Baltimore, and parts adjacent, to which is added as an Historical Companion, the operations of the British Army from their landing at Elk River in 1777, to their Embarkation at Nevisink in 1778. Published by Savage, 1800, May 1. Library of Congress.

*Maneuvres west of Hudson River between Tappan,* N.Y. and Elizabeth, New Jersey, 1777–81. (After an American Headquarters Map.) New-York Historical Society.

Anon: *Marche de l'armée Francaise de Providence à la rivière du Nord,* 1782. Library of Congress.

STAACK, J. G. *Maryland and Delaware,* 1912 (edition of 1916). Library of Congress.

REGIONAL *(cont'd.)*

*Southeastern New York, New Jersey, eastern Pennsylvania, northeast Delaware, Connecticut, Rhode Island, Massachusetts, southern Vermont, southern New Hampshire.* n.d. Library of Congress.

U. S. Geological Survey: *Pennsylvania, Delaware, New Jersey and Maryland* with the parts adjacent. 1887.

MARYLAND

Chesapeake Bay Area. *Carte de la baie de Chesapeake et de la partie navigable des rivières James, York, Patowmack, Patuxen, Patapsco, North-East, Choptank, et Potomack.* 1778. Paris. Archives Nationales.

MASSACHUSETTS . . . *Boston Area:*

Anon: *Boston Harbor,* Islands, Castle, Forts, Entrances. Feb. 1, 1775. Library of Congress.

Anon: *Plan of attack before Charles Town.* Library of Congress.

*Boston Neck, July 31, 1775.* Plan of General Gage's lines. Historical Society of Pennsylvania.

MONTRESOR, JOHN. Map of Bunker Hill, 1775. Library of Congress.

PAGE, LIEUT. *Boston.* Its environs and harbour, with Rebel works raised against the town in 1775.

*Plan of town and harbor of Boston and the country circumjacent.* July 25, 1775. Library of Congress.

TRUMBULL, JOHN. *Boston* and surrounding Country and posts of American Troops. September, 1775. Library of Congress.

Boston. Batteries, 1775. (Explanation of distances in G. Washington's handwriting is attached.) Library of Congress.

Boston (the South portion), 1775. Library of Congress.

*Boston* with its environs. (Engraved for *Life of Washington* by John Marshall, published in 1806 in Philadelphia.) Library of Congress.

WADSWORTH, ALEXANDER. Boston, including Part of Roxbury, Cambridge, and Charlestown. 1833. Library of Congress.

NEW JERSEY

*Counties:* of Hunterdon, Sussex, Bergen, Essex, Morris, Middlesex, and Somerset, and of Orange and Ulster in New York. n.d. New-York Historical Society.

FADEN, WILLIAM. *Province of New Jersey,* divided into East and West Jerseys, December 1, 1777. Library of Congress.

*Monmouth-Freehold Area:*

*Roads from Sandy Hook to Freehold Court House.* n.d. Clements Library.

Sketch, Different Roads About Freehold in the Jerseys. n.d. Clements Library.

*Road from Freehold to Middletown,* shewing the Skirmish between the Rear of the British Army under the command of his Excellency Genl. Sir Henry Clinton and the advanced Corps of the Rebel Army June 28, 1778. Clements Library.

*Battle of Monmouth,* June 28, 1778. Skirmish of Queen's Rangers with Jersey Militia. Monmouth Historical Society.

*Monmouth-Freehold Area (cont'd.)*:

> *Battle of Monmouth,* June 28, 1778. (With explanations in Sir Henry Clinton's hand.) Clements Library.
> *Battle of Monmouth,* June 28, 1778, showing encampments of Washington, Lee, and the Queen's Rangers near Freehold. Monmouth Historical Society.

*Trenton-Morristown Area:*

> *Road from Morristown towards Springfield.* New-York Historical Society.
> *Road from Springfield to Elizabethtown* (Erskine and DeWitt). New-York Historical Society.
> Map showing Morristown, Pluckemin, Bound Brook, Brunswick (Erskine and DeWitt). New-York Historical Society.

*Trenton-Princeton Area:*

> *Part of New Jersey,* showing Trenton, Princeton, and the American Armies and the British Armies, 1776, Dec. 25–26 to January 1–3. Virginia State Library.
> WILKINSON, JAMES. *The Affair of Princeton,* Jan. 3, 1777. Library of Congress.

*Paulus Hook Area:*

> NICOLE, P. *Paulus Hook and Bergen.* June, 1781. Clements Library.
> HILLS, JOHN. *Plan of Paulus Hook,* showing the Works erected for its defence, July, 1781. Clements Library.

NEW YORK STATE

> SAUTHIER, CHARLES J. *New York State,* 1776. Library of Congress.

*New York City—Long Island Area:*

> RATZER, B. *Plan of the City of New York.* 1766–67. Library of Congress.
> BLASKOWITZ, CHARLES. Plan of the Narrows of Hells gate in the East river near which batteries of cannon and mortars were erected on Long Island with a view to take off the defences and make breaches in the rebel fort on the opposite shore, to facilitate a landing of troops on New York Island. Library of Congress.
> *Map of district from King's Ferry to Sandy Hook and from Staten Island to Lloyd's Neck, L.I.* Clements Library.
> LEWIS, S. *New York and Long Island,* showing forts, and British and American lines, 1776. Library of Congress.
> U. S. Geological Society: *Operations* of His Majesty's Fleet and Army under Command of Vice-Admiral Lord Howe and General Sir William Howe, 1776.
> *Sketch of the position of the Army on Long Island,* upon the morning of the 26th of August, 1776; with the march on the ensuing night and the action of the 27th. Clements Library.
> *The western part of Long Island,* with the engagement of August 27, 1776, between the King's forces and the Americans. Oct. 22, 1776. Clements Library.
> SPROULE, LIEUT. GEORGE. *Plan of the environs of Brooklyn,* showing position of Rebel lines and defences of the 27th of August, 1776. Clements Library.

*New York City—Long Island Area (cont'd)*:

*The Country within twenty-five miles of New York,* September 15, 1776. Library of Congress.

SAUTHIER, CLAUDE J. *Plan of operations, of the King's Army Under General William Howe,* in New York and East New Jersey, against the American Forces commanded by General Washington, Oct. 12-Nov. 28, 1776. Library of Congress.

*Plan of New York,* Long Island, Staten Island, parts of New Jersey; and giving a description of engagement on woody heights of Long Island, August 27, 1775. Library of Congress.

SAUTHIER, CLAUDE. *A Topographical Map of the Northern Part of New York Island,* exhibiting the Plan of Fort Washington, now Fort Knyphausen, with the Rebel lines to the Southward which were forced by the troops under the Command of Rt. Hon. Earl Percy, Nov. 16, 1776. Clements Library.

TAYLOR, GEORGE. *Map of Pass at Jamaica,* surveyed by order of Gen'l. Clinton, Mch., 1782. Clements Library.

*Staten Island Area:*

*The seat of action between the British and American forces:* an authentic plan of Staten Island with the neighbouring counties . . . Aug. 27, 1776. Clements Library.

*New York City:*

Plan of operations of the King's army under command of Gen. Sir William Howe in N.Y. against the American forces commanded by General Washington, 1776. Library of Congress.

Map of *Narrows, Ferry and Defences* on both sides as of October 7, (1776). Library of Congress.

*Hudson River Area:*

KNIGHT, JOHN. *Hudson's River,* showing the position of Fort Montgomery and Fort Clinton with the chevaux-de-frieze, cables, chains &c to obstruct the passage of his majesty's forces up the river, 1777. Library of Congress.

*West Point Area:*

ALEXANDER MACDOUGALL to WASHINGTON, April 25, 1779, enclosing three maps of fortifications along the Hudson. New-York Historical Society.

PENNSYLVANIA

*Map of Rariton River in East Jersey to Elk Head in Maryland,* 1776–77, shewing operations of army. (Drawn by S. Lewis from drawings made by G. Washington.) Library of Congress.

*Western Area:*

Washington's route, on his tour of inspection of frontier forts. British Museum, Add. MS. 15563.

*Plan of Line of March,* of the Detachment from Little Meadows at Fort Duquesne—1755 (Orme). Library of Congress.

458 SELECT CRITICAL BIBLIOGRAPHY

PENNSYLVANIA—*Western Area (cont'd)*:

*Plan of the Disposition of the Advanced* Party, consisting of 400 men at Fort Duquesne 1775 (Orme). Library of Congress.

*Sketch of Ground,* and Disposition of British Troops and Indians at Fort Duquesne, July 9, 1755 (Orme). Library of Congress.

*Plan of Line of March,* with the whole Baggage at Fort Duquesne, 1755 (Orme). Library of Congress.

*Plan of the Field of Battle and Disposition of Troops at Fort Duquesne,* July 9, 1755 (Orme).

*Plan of Encampment,* of the Detachment from Little Meadows at Fort Duquesne, 1755 (Orme). Library of Congress.

McKELLAR, PATRICK. *Map of the Battleground of Braddock's Defeat.* P.R.O. C.O. 5:46, f. 269–70.

*Philadelphia Area:*

*Philadelphia* showing also Kennet, Union, Newton and Chester, 1776. Library of Congress.

SCULL and HEAP. *Plan of Philadelphia* and of environs in 1777 (revised plan of the map of 1770). Library of Congress.

MONTRESOR, JOHN. *Philadelphia,* and its environs shewing the service works constructed . . . under command of Sir William Howe . . . 1777 . . . and attacks on Mud Island. Library of Congress.

Battle lines of Brandywine, September 11, 1777. Chicago Historical Society.

Anon. Battle of Brandywine, 1777. Library of Congress.

BONSALL, SPENCER. (a) *Map of Battleground of Germantown,* 1877. Historical Society of Pennsylvania.

BONSALL, SPENCER. (b) *Map of the environs of Germantown,* 1877. Historical Society of Pennsylvania.

WRIGHT, L. *Itinerary of General Washington,* in Montgomery County, 1777–78. Historical Society of Pennsylvania.

BUTLER, WILLIAM. *Line of march,* between Susquehanna and Delaware Rivers, October 2–16, 1778. Library of Congress.

*Plan de la Retraite de Barrenhill . . . sous le Général de la Fayette,* 27 Mai, 1778. Historical Society of Pennsylvania.

RHODE ISLAND

*Newport Area*

DES BARRES, J.W.F.: Plan of Newport. 1776. Library of Congress.

*Plan de la ville du port et du rade de Newport* . . . 1780. Library of Congress.

*Plan de la position de l'armée Française autour de Newport* . . . 1778. Archives Nationales, Marine.

*Plan de Rhodes Island et position de l'armée Française à Newport.* 1778. Archives Nationales, Marine.

VIRGINIA

*A general map of the known and inhabited parts of Virginia.* 1731. (There is some difference of opinion as to the cartographer of this map. It is identified,

VIRGINIA (cont'd)

however, as the map sent by Governor Gooch to England at the time of the boundary dispute over the Fairfax Grant.) P.R.O.: C.O. 5:1344.

FRY, JOSHUA, and JEFFERSON, PETER. *A Map of the Most Inhabited Part of Virginia,* Containing the Whole Province of Maryland, with Part of Pensilvania, New Jersey, and North Carolina. 1775. Virginia State Library.

*Northern Neck Area*

JEFFERSON, PETER, and BROOKE, ROBERT. *Survey of boundary line of Fairfax Grant,* 1727–31. Virginia Historical Society.

*Coastal Area*

*Map of Portsmouth* . . . showing the works erected in 1781 for defence . . . Library of Congress.

PAGE, CAPT. *Plan of the posts of Gloucester and York,* in the province of Virginia under command of . . . Cornwallis together with the attacks and operations of the American and French forces commanded by general Washington and the comte de Rochambeau. Oct. 17, 1781. Library of Congress.

*Carte de La Partie de La Virginie ou L'Armée Combinée de France & des États-Unis de L'Amérique a fait prisonnière l'Armée Anglaise Comandée par Lord Cornwallis le 19 Oct'bre 1781.* Paris. Archives Nationales.

*Reddition de l'Armee Angloises Commandée par Mylord Comte de Cornwallis aux Armée combinées des États-unis et de France aux ordres des Généraux Washington et de Rochambeau à Yorktown et Glocester dans Virginia le 19 Octobre 1781.* Paris. Archives Nationales.

U. S. Geological Survey. *Battlefield areas of Yorktown,* October, 1781. U. S. Geological Survey Library.

BAUMAN, SEBASTIAN. *Plan of investment of New York and Gloucester,* Oct. 22–28, 1781 (made for General Washington). Library of Congress.

U. S. Department of the Interior. *Yorktown in 1781.* Part of the Master-plan, Colonial National Historical Park Archives, 1941.

*Mount Vernon Area:*

*Plan of the Kitchen Garden of Mount Vernon.* Mount Vernon Ladies' Association.

WASHINGTON, GEORGE. Map of his farm at Mount Vernon, Sept., 1799. Library of Congress.

*Illustrated map of a section of Fairfax County.* Library of Congress.

*Mount Vernon,* and its environs and Washington's neighbours. Library of Congress.

*Map of Mount Vernon Area,* showing roads. Mount Vernon Ladies' Association.

MISCELLANEOUS

BOWEN, EMAN. *Map of Barbadoes,* showing all forts, churches, parishes, parts and chief houses. 1752. Library of Congress.

BOWEN, EMAN. *Map of Antigua,* showing parishes, roads, churches, etc. 1752. Library of Congress.

# SELECTIVE BIBLIOGRAPHY
## OF PRINTED SOURCES

By Geneva B. Snelling

Note

Writings and Biographies of Washington and his Contemporaries
  Writings, Diaries and Letters
  Biographies

Washington and Virginia during his Youth, 1732–1752

Washington and the French and Indian War, 1753–1763

Washington between the Wars, 1763–1775

Washington and the Revolution, 1776–1783

Washington and the Constitution, 1784–1788

Washington and the Presidency, 1789–[1793]

Official and Semiofficial Collections
  Great Britain
  United States
  The States

General References

Travel in America

Washington and the Arts

Maps
  Atlases, Geographies, and Catalogues
  Specific Maps

Newspapers

Periodicals

# NOTE

THE arrangement of the bibliography of printed source material is essentially as planned by Douglas Freeman except for the fact that no references are cited chronologically beyond 1793 where the text of this volume stopped with Freeman's death. Originally intended for the final volume of the biography, two additional sections were to round out the material used: namely, Washington in Retirement, 1798–99; and Portraits, Monuments and Eulogies to Washington. These have now been omitted.

As in all biographical interpretation, the written word of Washington himself is the main stream of this study begun in 1944. John C. Fitzpatrick's edition of the *Writings of Washington* in thirty-nine volumes, including the Index by David M. Matteson, flows like a mighty river through the entire six volumes, evidence of Freeman's esteem for this superb editorial work. Concurrently runs the four-volume edition of Washington's *Diaries,* also by Fitzpatrick. The earlier editions of Washington's *Writings* by Jared Sparks and W. C. Ford were also frequently used. We see Washington and his world through the eyes of his contemporaries in the tributary streams of correspondence, diaries and memoirs. The modern historian is grateful to the facile pens of these men and women of the eighteenth century who thus made their contribution to posterity. Most of the material is available to the student in acceptable printed form, such as Hunt's *Writings of Madison*, Lipscomb and Bergh's *Writings of Jefferson*, Wilson's edition of *William Heath's Memoirs*, Charles Lee's *Papers* published by the New-York Historical Society, William Reed's *Life and Correspondence of Joseph Reed*, the *Papers of Major-General John Sullivan*, the *Letters of Richard Henry Lee* edited by Ballagh, the *Correspondence of Horatio Sharpe*, Brock's *Papers of Robert Dinwiddie*, the *Correspondence and Journals of Samuel Blachley Webb* edited by W. C. Ford, Frederick Mackenzie's *Diary*, Lodge's twelve-volume edition of the *Works of Alexander Hamilton*, the separate editions of the letters of Abigail Adams by Charles F. Adams and Stewart Mitchell, and the Charles F. Adams edition of the *Works of John Adams*, the *Works of Benjamin Franklin* in 12 volumes by Bigelow and Smyth's ten-volume edition, Johnston's *Correspondence and Public Papers of John Jay*, the New-York Historical Society publication of the *Kemble Papers*, the *Diaries* of Archibald Robertson, the *St. Clair Papers*, the *Military Journal* of James Thacher, and the *Warren-Adams Letters*. These works were used extensively in the preparation of several volumes of Washington's biography. For accepted sources in a specific period the reader is directed to the Short Title Index in Volumes Two, Four, Five and Six. The collections, Burnett's *Letters of Members of the Continental Congress*, 8 volumes; Wharton's *Revolutionary Diplomatic Correspondence*, 6 volumes; and Roberts' *March to Quebec* contain significant first-hand accounts.

A new approach to biography was Douglas Freeman's use of letters to Washington. In the Introduction to Volume One he wrote, ". . . nearly as much of the life of a man is set down in the letters addressed to him as in those written by him." Three works were used heavily: Sparks' *Correspondence of the American*

*Revolution; Being Letters of Eminent Men to George Washington . . .* in 4 volumes; S. M. Hamilton's *Letters to Washington* in 5 volumes, and Gottschalk's *Letters of Lafayette to Washington, 1777–99.*

Biographies of Washington and the men around him are almost as numerous as the printed editions of their writings but for various reasons were of limited value in this study. Those used extensively by Freeman are the biographies of Washington by Rupert Hughes (3 volumes), Washington Irving (5 volumes), and John Marshall (5 volumes). Douglas Freeman was well acquainted with Weems' *Life of Washington,* Custis' *Recollections and Private Memoirs of Washington,* and McGuire's *The Religious Opinions and Character of Washington,* which are largely responsible for the creation of the mythical hero. The biographies of Washington's contemporaries used frequently are few in number: G. W. Greene's *Life of Nathanael Greene; Montcalm and Wolf* by Parkman; Sparks' *Life of Gouverneur Morris;* W. W. Henry's *Life, Correspondence and Speeches of Patrick Henry;* Pickering and Upham's *Life of Timothy Pickering;* and Rowland's *Life of George Mason.* Some part of the admirable twenty-volume work, *Dictionary of American Biography,* edited by Allen Johnson and Dumas Malone, was constantly on the author's desk and ranks with Fitzpatrick's *Writings of Washington* in its contribution to the stream of the story.

References used for the periods of Washington's life to 1793 are equally significant in the main current of this work. The never-ending flood of material used by Freeman covers all phases of Washington's life as well as every detail of daily existence from weather conditions, Indian wampum, and music composed by the Colonials to the earliest steamboat, the manufacture of iron, and sophisticated society life surrounding the first President. General works read for background include Gipson's *The British Empire before the American Revolution;* Harrison's *Landmarks of Old Prince William* and *Virginia Land Grants;* Moore's *Diary of the American Revolution from Newspapers and Original Documents;* Force's *American Archives;* Pargellis' *Military Affairs in North America, 1748–1765;* Hugh Jones' *The Present State of Virginia;* Beverley's *History of Virginia;* Conway's *Barons of the Potomack;* Wertenbaker's *Virginia under the Stuarts; The American Revolution* by Trevelyan, *History of the Formation of the Constitution* by Bancroft, and Channing's *History of the United States.*

Material concerning specific campaigns, events, or subjects are cited in this Bibliography in the period of Washington's life where they were most often used. The indispensable references are: Lowdermilk's *History of Cumberland, Maryland;* Flippin's *The Royal Government in Virginia, 1624–1775; The Washington Ancestry* by Hoppin; Pargellis' *Lord Loudoun in North America;* Sargent's *History of an Expedition against Fort Du Quesne in 1755;* Stryker's *Battles of Trenton and Princeton;* Henry P. Johnston's *Campaign of 1776 around New York and Brooklyn;* Bowen's *History of the Centennial Celebration of the Inauguration of George Washington as First President of the United States; The Debates on the Adoption of the Federal Constitution* in five volumes by Elliot; Farrand's *Records of the Federal Convention of 1787;* Chinard's *George Washington as the French Knew Him;* Dawson's André Papers, and Bassett's *The Federalist System.* The reader is reminded that the works mentioned in this note were the ones used most frequently by Freeman. Exclusion of other sources is no attempt at evaluation except as his choice of material might be considered that.

Lest the student wonder about the omission of certain valuable sources, it must be stated at this point that many references relating to the years of Washington's life after 1793 were already on the shelves in the author's study in June, 1953. Material on John Jay, Thomas Pinckney, Genet, American diplomacy and foreign policy in Washington's second administration, and the development of the President's Cabinet was at hand and already entered in the comprehensive bibliography. Volume 8 of Boyd's edition of *The Papers of Thomas Jefferson*, covering the period from February to October, 1785, is now off the press late in 1953. This is one of the many sources Freeman planned to use later. Others are Bemis' *Jay's Treaty* and *Pinckney's Treaty*; the *Diary of Gouverneur Morris* edited by Davenport; *The Mississippi Question, 1795–1803* by Whitaker; Turner's *The Significance of Sections in American History;* J. B. Moore's *American Diplomacy, Its Spirit and Achievements*; and *The Life and Letters of Harrison Gray Otis* by S. E. Morison, to mention a few.

Much use was made of the collections of legislative proceedings and executive documents in printed form. The essential ones were: *Journal of the House of Representatives* and *Journal of the Senate of the United States*; *The American State Papers*; *The Debates and Proceedings in Congress*; Ford's edition of the *Journals of the Continental Congress*; Richardson's *Messages and Papers of the Presidents*; the *United States Statutes at Large*; various state archives, especially those of Pennsylvania, Hening's [*Virginia*] *Statutes at Large*, McIlwaine's *Executive Journals of the Council of Colonial Virginia*; *Journals of the House of Burgesses of Virginia*; and *Calendar of State Papers, Colonial Series*, edited by Sainsbury.

Douglas Freeman was indebted to the publications of certain State historical societies, such as those of Pennsylvania, Connecticut, Massachusetts, New Jersey and New York. *The Proceedings of the American Antiquarian Society* and publications of the Essex Institute of Salem, Mass., also have been valuable.

An element of surprise lies in the part of the bibliography devoted to books on travel. To the student of the twentieth century it is amazing that so many Europeans came to America without benefit of jet planes and travelled the Atlantic Seaboard without diesel engines. Their estimates of Washington and their observations of life in general, and at Mount Vernon in particular, make fascinating reading. Those worth special mention are the anonymous *Journal of a French Traveller in the Colonies, 1765*; Burnaby's *Travels through the Middle Settlements . . .*; *Voyage dans l'Amérique* by Chastellux; *An Englishman in America, 1785 . . .* by Joseph Hadfield; *Brieven en Gedenkschriften . . .* by Hogendorp; *Quebec to Carolina in 1785–1786 . . .* by Robert Hunter; Mereness' *Travels in the American Colonies*; Morrison's *Travels in Virginia in Revolutionary Times*; and Thwaites' *Early Western Travels, 1748–1846.*

Another new avenue of approach used by Freeman was a careful search of contemporary newspapers. From 1781 on they are an increasingly valuable source of first-hand information. The number of papers that were in existence after the Revolution and their growing importance in shaping government policy are a further surprise. Most of them changed their titles frequently and in a few cases their location. These are cited by the name used at the time of Freeman's reference to them. The papers which continued in existence beyond 1793 are indicated thus: 1793 . . . Some of them covered the years of Washington's life and are noteworthy for their longevity. They are: the *Maryland Gazette* of Annapolis, the *Maryland Journal* of Baltimore, the *Boston Gazette*; the *New-York Gazette, and Weekly Mercury*; *Pennsylvania Gazette*; *Pennsylvania Journal*; and *Pennsylvania*

*Packet*, the last three all of Philadelphia; the *Providence Gazette*; and the *Virginia Gazette* of Williamsburg and Richmond. The two principal repositories of eighteenth-century newspapers are the Library of Congress and the American Antiquarian Society at Worcester, Mass. Clarence S. Brigham's excellent two-volume work precludes any further remarks concerning newspapers of the period.

Of passing interest are several books found in libraries of Washington's time, some of them being at Mount Vernon and bearing his autograph. These are listed here:

BLAND, HUMPHREY. *Treatise of Military Discipline*. London, 1727. This was the basic text of the American Army.

FISHER, GEORGE. *The American Instructor: or, Young Man's Best Companion* . . . Philadelphia, 1748.

GORDON, WILLIAM. *The History of the Rise, Progress and Establishment of the Independence of the United States of America*. 4 volumes. First edition London, 1788. Freeman used the third American edition of 1801. Washington granted Gordon access to his public records in 1784. Gordon's stay at Mount Vernon and this resulting history are commented on several times in this volume.

HALE, THOMAS. *A Compleat Body of Husbandry*. London, 1758–1759. On June 12, 1759, Washington ordered this book from Robert Cary & Company in these words: ". . . I desired you would send me . . . the best system now extent of agriculture . . . collected from the papers of Mr. Hale."

LANGLEY, BATTY. *New Principles of Gardening* . . . London, 1728. This was also ordered in 1759.

LEYBOURN, WILLIAM. *The Compleat Surveyor*. London, 1722.

NORDEN, JOHN. *The Surveiors Dialogue, very Profitable for all Men to Peruse, but Especially for all Gentlemen, or any other Farmar, or Husbandman, that shall Either Have Occasion, or be Willing to buy or sell Lands* . . . London, 1610.

SIMES, THOMAS. *A Military Course for the Government and Conduct of a Battalion Designed for their Regulations in Quarter, Camp, or Garrison* . . . London, 1777. This was in the Mount Vernon library and has Washington's autograph on the title page.

[TENNENT, DR. JOHN.] *Every Man his Own Doctor; or, the Poor Planter's Physician*. Williamsburg, 1734. Later editions printed by Benjamin Franklin.

*A View of Great-Britain, During the Administration of Lord North to the Second Session of the Fifteenth Parliament*. In 2 parts. London, 1782. Also at Mount Vernon with Washington's autograph.

Grateful acknowledgment is made to the Reference Department of the Virginia State Library and the following volumes for the help given in preparation and checking of this bibliography: *A Catalog of Books Represented by Library of Congress Printed Cards Issued to July 31, 1942*, of 167 volumes and its Supplement of 42 volumes, printed in 1948; *The Dictionary of American Biography*; *The History and Bibliography of American Newspapers, 1690–1820* by Clarence S. Brigham; and *American Diaries, and Annotated Bibliography of . . . Diaries Written Prior to the Year 1861*, compiled by William Matthews. Also at my elbow have been the bibliographies in Malone's *Jefferson and His Time*, Mays' *Edmund Pendleton* and Hughes' *Life of Washington*.

In listing the printed sources an attempt has been made to conform to Douglas Freeman's statement in the Introduction to Volume One that this shall be a "selected but somewhat extensive bibliography." The following works were selected on the basis of criteria set up by him from a comprehensive and exhaustive bibliography used over the nine years of his study of Washington.

# WRITINGS AND BIOGRAPHIES
## OF WASHINGTON AND HIS CONTEMPORARIES

ANON. *Journal of an Officer of the Naval Army, 1781 and 1782.* Amsterdam, 1783.

ANON. "Substance of Journal Kept at Rochambeau's Headquarters, from Supplement to French Gazette of Nov. 20, 1781." *Pennsylvania Packet,* Feb. 21, 1782.

Also in *Magazine of American History,* vol. 7, 1881; pp. 224–226.

ADAMS, ABIGAIL. *New Letters of . . . , 1788–1801.* Edited by Stewart Mitchell. Boston, 1947.

ADAMS, JOHN. *The Works of . . . , Second President of the United States: with a Life of the Author, Notes and Illustrations by his grandson Charles Francis Adams.* 10 vols. Boston, 1850–1856.

ADAMS, JOHN and ABIGAIL. *Familiar Letters of John Adams and his Wife Abigail during the Revolution.* Edited by Charles Francis Adams. New York, 1876.

AMES, FISHER. *Works of . . . with a Selection from his Speeches and Correspondence.* Edited by Seth Ames. 2 vols. Boston, 1854.

ANDRÉ, JOHN. *Journal. Operations of the British Army under Lieutenant Generals Sir William Howe and Sir Henry Clinton, July, 1777 to November, 1778 . . .* Tarrytown, 1930.

ANDRÉ, JOHN. *Journal.* Edited by Henry Cabot Lodge. 2 vols. Boston, 1903.

ANGELL, ISRAEL. *Diary of Colonel . . . 1778–1781.* Edited by Edward Field. Providence, 1899.

BALDWIN, JEDUTHAN. *The Revolutionary Journal of Colonel . . . , 1775–1778.* Edited by Thomas Williams Baldwin. Bangor, 1906.

BANGS, ISAAC. *Journal of Lieutenant . . . , April 1 to July 29, 1776.* Edited by Edward Bangs. Cambridge, 1890. Extracts in *New Jersey Historical Society Proceedings,* ser. 2, vol. 8, 1856–1859; pp. 120–125.

BARKER, JOHN. *The British in Boston, Being the Diary of Lieutenant . . .* Edited by Elizabeth E. Dana. Cambridge, 1924.

BAURMEISTER, MAJOR. "Letters of . . . during the Philadelphia Campaign 1777–78." Translated by B. A. Uhlendorf and E. Vosper. *Pennsylvania Magazine of History and Biography,* vol. 59, 1934; pp. 392–419. *Ibid.,* vol. 60, 1935; pp. 34–52, 161–183.

BEDINGER, HENRY. "Journal, 1775–1776." In Dandridge, Danske, *Historic Sheperdstown.* See Washington and the Revolution, *infra.*

BELKNAP, JEREMY. "Journal of a Tour to the Camps around Boston, October, 1775." *Massachusetts Historical Society Proceedings,* ser. 1, vol. 4, 1858–1860; pp. 77–86.

BIXBY, SAMUEL. "Diary, May 5, 1775–Jan. 3, 1776." *Massachusetts Historical Society Proceedings,* ser. 1, vol. 14, 1875–1876; pp. 285–298.

BLAIR, JOHN. "Private Diary, Jan.–Dec., 1751." *William and Mary Quarterly,* ser. 1, vol. 7, 1898–1899, pp. 133–153. *Ibid.,* ser. 1, vol. 8, 1899–1900, pp. 1–17.

BLANCHARD, CLAUDE. *The Journal of . . ., Commissary of the French Auxiliary Army, 1780–1783.* Translated by William Duane, edited by Thomas Balch. Albany, 1876.

BLAND, THEODORICK, JR. *The Bland Papers, Being a Selection of the Manuscripts of . . .* Edited by Charles Campbell. 2 vols. Petersburg, Va., 1843.

BOUDINOT, ELIAS. *Journal of Historical Recollections of American Events during the Revolutionary War.* Philadelphia, 1894.

BOURG, CROMOT DU. "Diary of a French Officer (Presumed to be that of Baron Cromot du Bourg, Aide to Rochambeau)." *Magazine of American History,* vol. 4, 1880; pp. 205–214, 293–308, 376–385, 441–449. *Ibid.,* vol. 7, 1881; pp. 283–295.

BROWN, MRS. CHARLOTTE. "Military Journal, Nov., 1754–Aug., 1756." *Virginia Magazine of History and Biography,* vol. 32, 1924; pp. 305–320.

BURNETT, EDMUND C., ed. *Letters of the Members of the Continental Congress. Aug. 29, 1774–July 25, 1789.* 8 vols. Washington, 1921–1936.

BUTLER, RICHARD. "Military Journal, Sept.–Oct., 1781." *Virginia Historical Magazine,* vol. 8, 1864; pp. 102–112.

BYRD, WILLIAM. *The Writings of "Colonel . . ., of Westover in Virginia, esq."* Edited by John Spencer Bassett. New York, 1901.

BYRD, WILLIAM. *Another Secret Diary of . . . of Westover, 1739–1741, with Letters and Literary Exercises, 1696–1726.* Edited by Maude H. Woodfin. Richmond, 1942.

CARTER, ROBERT. *Letters of . . ., 1720–1727; the Commercial Interests of a Virginia Gentleman.* Edited by Louis B. Wright. San Marino, Calif., 1940.

CARTER, WILLIAM. *A Genuine Detail of the Several Engagements, Positions, and Movements of the Armies during 1775–76 with an Account of the Blockade of Boston and a Plan of the Works on Bunker Hill . . .* In a Series of Letters to a Friend. London, 1784.

CHILTON, JOHN. "Military Journal, January–September, 1777." *Tyler's Quarterly Historical and Genealogical Magazine,* vol. 12, 1931; pp. 283–289.

CLAP, CALEB. "Diary of Ensign . . ." *Historical Magazine,* ser. 3, vol. 3, 1874–1875; pp. 133–137, 247–251.

CLARENDON, EARL OF, EDWARD HYDE. *The Life of . . . in Which Is Included a Continuation of his History of the Grand Rebellion. Written by Himself.* 2 vols. Oxford, 1857.

CLARK, JOSEPH. "Military Journal, May 1777–Nov. 1778." *New Jersey Historical Society Proceedings,* ser. 1, vol. 7, 1853–1855; pp. 93–110.

CLINTON, GEORGE. *Public Papers of . . .* Compiled by Hugh Hastings. 10 vols. Albany, 1904.

COBB., LT. COL. DAVID. "Diary of . . . during the Yorktown Campaign." *Massachusetts Historical Society Proceedings,* vol. 19, 1881–1882; pp. 67–72.

COOPER, SAMUEL. "Diary, April 19, 1775–May, 1776." *American Historical Review,* vol. 6, 1900–1901; pp. 303–341.

CORNWALLIS, MARQUESS, CHARLES. *Correspondence of . . .* Edited by Charles Ross. 3 vols. London, 1859.

CRESSWELL, NICHOLAS. *Journal, 1774–1777.* New York, 1924.

DAYTON, ELIAS. "Papers of . . ." *New Jersey Historical Society Proceedings,* ser. 1, vol. 9, 1864; pp. 175–194.

DEANE, SILAS. *Papers.* Edited by Charles Isham. 5 vols. New-York Historical Society Collections, vols. 19, 20, 21, 22, 23. New York, 1887–1890.

DEARBORN, HENRY. *Revolutionary War Journals of . . ., 1775–1783.* Edited by Lloyd A. Brown and Howard Peckham. Chicago, 1939. Extracts in *Massachusetts Historical Society Proceedings,* ser. 2, vol. 2, 1885–1886; pp. 275–305. *Ibid.,* ser. 2, vol. 3, 1886–1887; pp. 102–133. Also in Roberts, *March to Quebec,* pp. 129–168, cited *infra,* Washington and the Revolution.

DENNY, EBENEZER. *Military Journal of . . ., an Officer in the Revolutionary and Indian Wars.* Edited by William Denny. Philadelphia, 1859. Also in *Pennsylvania Historical Society Memoirs,* vol. 7, 1860; pp. 205–492.

DEUX-PONTS, COMTE WILLIAM DE. *My Campaigns in America; A Journal Kept by . . ., 1780–1781.* Translated by Samuel Abbott Green. Boston, 1868.

DINWIDDIE, ROBERT. *The Official Papers of . . .* Edited by Robert A. Brock. 2 vols. Virginia Historical Society Collections, vols. 3 and 4, new series. Richmond, 1883.

DUMAS, COMTE DE, MATHIEU. *Memoirs of his Own Time . . .* 2 vols. London, 1839.

DUROI, AUGUST WILHELM. *Journal of . . . Lieutenant and Adjutant in the Service of the Duke of Brunswick, 1776–1779.* Translated by Charlotte Epping. New York, 1911.

EVELYN, JOHN. *The Diary of . . .* Edited by William Bray. 2 vols. Washington, 1901.

EVELYN, W. GLANVILLE. *Memoir and Letters of . . .* Edited by G. D. Scull. Oxford, 1879.

EVELYN FAMILY. *The Evelyns in America; Compiled from Family Papers and Other Sources.* Edited by G. D. Scull. Oxford, 1881.

EWING, GEORGE. *George Ewing, Gentleman, a Soldier of Valley Forge.* Edited by Thomas Ewing. Yonkers, 1928.

FAIRFAX FAMILY. *The Fairfax Correspondence. Memoirs of the Reign of Charles the First.* Edited by George W. Johnson and Robert Bell. 4 vols. London, 1848–1849.

FELTMAN, WILLIAM. *The Journal of Lieut. . . ., of the First Pennsylvania Regiment, 1781–1782.* Philadelphia, 1853. Also in *Pennsylvania Archives,* ser. 2, vol. 11, 1895; pp. 709–762. *Pennsylvania Historical Society Collections,* vol. 1, 1853; pp. 303–348.

FERSEN, HANS AXEL DE. "Letters of . . ., Aide-de-camp to Rochambeau, to his Father in Sweden." *Magazine of American History,* pt. 2, vol. 3, 1879; pp. 437–448.

FISHER, ELIJAH. "Military Diary, May 1775–Feb. 1785." In Godfrey, Carlos E., *The Commander-in-Chief's Guard.* See infra, Washington and the Revolution.

FITHIAN, PHILIP VICKERS. *Journal and Letters I.* Edited by J. R. Williams. Princeton, 1904. Also edited by Hunter D. Farish, Williamsburg, 1943.

FITHIAN, PHILIP VICKERS. *Journal and Letters II.* Edited by R. G. Albion and L. Dodson. Princeton, 1934.

FORBES, JOHN. *Writings of General . . . Relating to his Service in North America.* Edited and compiled by Alfred P. James. Menasha, Wis., 1938.

FRANKLIN, BENJAMIN. *Autobiography of . . .* Compiled and edited by John Bigelow. New York and London, 1909.

FRANKLIN, BENJAMIN. *The Works of* . . . Edited by John Bigelow. 12 vols. Federal edition. New York, 1904.

FRANKLIN, BENJAMIN. *The Writings of* . . . Edited by Albert H. Smyth. 10 vols. New York, 1907.

GAGE, THOMAS. *The Correspondence of General* . . . Compiled and edited by Clarence E. Carter. 2 vols. New Haven, 1931.

GALLATIN, GASPARD DE. *Journal of the Siege of Yorktown* . . . *Operated by the General Staff of the French Army, as Recorded in the Hand of* . . . Washington, 1931.

GEORGE III. *The Correspondence of George the Third from 1760 to December, 1783*. Edited by Sir John Fortescue. Printed from the original papers in the Royal Archives at Windsor Castle. 6 vols. London, 1928.

GIST, CHRISTOPHER. *Journals*. Edited by W. M. Darlington. Pittsburgh, 1893. Extracts in *Massachusetts Historical Society Collections*, ser. 3, vol. 5, 1836; pp. 101–108.

GRAVES, THOMAS. *The Graves Papers and Other Documents Relating to the Naval Operations of the Yorktown Campaign, July to October, 1781*. Edited by French E. Chadwick. New York, 1916.

GRAYDON, ALEXANDER. *Memoirs of His Own Time by* . . . Edited by J. S. Littell. Philadelphia, 1846.

GREEN, ASHBEL. *The Life of* . . . , *Begun to be Written by Himself* . . . Edited by Joseph Jones. New York, 1849.

HAMILTON, ALEXANDER. *Works of* . . . Edited by Henry Cabot Lodge. 12 vols. Federal edition. New York, 1904.

HAMILTON, STANISLAUS MURRAY, ed. *Letters to Washington and Accompanying Papers*. 5 vols. Boston and New York, 1898–1902.

HARROWER, JOHN. *Diary of* . . . , *1773–1776*. New York, 1900. Also in *American Historical Review*, vol. 6, 1900–1901; pp. 65–107.

HAWS, SAMUEL. "Journal, April, 1775–February, 1776." In *The Military Journals of Two Private Soldiers, 1758–1775*, compiled by Abraham Tomlinson, pp. 49–90. See *infra* in this section.

HEATH, WILLIAM. *The Heath Papers, Parts I, II, III*. Massachusetts Historical Society Collections, ser. 5, vol. 4, pp. 1–285; *ibid.*, ser. 7, vols. 4 and 5. Boston, 1878–1905.

HEATH, WILLIAM. *Heath's Memoirs of the American War*. Edited by Rufus R. Wilson. New York, 1904.

HILTZHEIMER, JACOB. *Extracts from the Diary of* . . . , *1765–1798*. Edited by Jacob C. Parsons. Philadelphia, 1893.

HOOD, SIR SAMUEL. *Letters Written by* . . . *in 1781–1783*. Edited by David Hanay. (n.p.) 1895.

HOW, DAVID. *Diary of* . . . Edited by G. W. Chase and H. B. Dawson. Morrisania, N. Y., 1865

HOWE, WILLIAM. *Narrative of Lieutenant General Sir* . . . , *in a Committee of the House of Commons, on the 29th of April, 1779, Relative to his Conduct, during his Late Command of the King's Troops in North America: to which are Added some Observations upon a Pamphlet Entitled Letters to a Nobleman*. London, 1781.

HUNTINGTON, EBENEZER. *Letters Written by* . . . *during the American Revolution*. Compiled by C. F. Hartman. New York, 1915.

HUNTINGTON, JOSHUA and JEDEDIAH. *The Huntington Papers—Correspondence of the Brothers . . . , 1771–1783.* Connecticut Historical Society Collections, vol. 20. Hartford, 1923.

JAY, JOHN. *The Correspondence and Public Papers of* . . . Edited by Henry P. Johnston. 4 vols. New York, 1890–1893.

JEFFERSON, THOMAS. *The Writings of* . . . Edited by Paul L. Ford. 10 vols. New York, 1892–1899.

JEFFERSON, THOMAS. *The Writings of* . . . Edited by Andrew A. Lipscomb and Albert E. Bergh. 20 vols. Memorial edition. Washington, 1904.

JONES, JOSEPH. *Letters of . . . of Virginia, 1777–1787.* Edited by Worthington C. Ford. Washington, 1889.

KEMBLE, STEPHEN. *The Kemble Papers.* 2 vols. New York Historical Society Collections, vols. 16 and 17. New York, 1883–1884.

KING, RUFUS. *The Life and Correspondence of* . . . Edited by Charles R. King. 6 vols. New York, 1894–1900.

KRAFFT, JOHN CHARLES VON. "Hessian Military Journal, May, 1776–January, 1784." *New-York Historical Society Collections,* vol. 15, 1882; pp. 1–200.

LAFAYETTE, MARQUIS DE. *Memoirs, Correspondence, and Manuscripts, Published by his Family.* 4 vols. Paris, 1837.

LAFAYETTE, MARQUIS DE. *The Letters of Lafayette to Washington, 1777–1799.* Edited by Louis Gottschalk. New York, 1944.

LAURENS, JOHN. *The Army Correspondence of Colonel . . . in the Years 1777–1778, now first Printed from Original Letters to his Father . . . ; with a Memoir by William Gilmore Simms.* New York, 1867.

LAUZUN, DUC DE. *Memoirs of the . . . (Armand Louis de Gontaut, duc de Biron) 1747–1783.* Translated by E. Jules Méras. New York, 1912.

LEAR, TOBIAS. "Diary of . . ." In *The Writings of Washington,* edited by Sparks, vol. 10, p. 463. See *infra,* this section.

LEE, CHARLES. *The Lee Papers, 1754–1811.* 4 vols. New-York Historical Society Collections, vols. 4, 5, 6, 7. New York, 1871–1874.

LEE, HENRY. *Memoirs of the War in the Southern Department of the United States.* New York, 1869.

LEE, RICHARD HENRY. *Letters of* . . . Edited by James C. Ballagh. 2 vols. New York, 1911–1914.

LEWIS, COL. CHARLES. "Journal of . . . " *West Virginia Historical Magazine,* vol. 4, 1904; pp. 109–116. Also in *Virginia Historical Society Collections,* vol. 11, 1891; pp. 203–218.

MACKENZIE, FREDERICK. *Diary of . . .* 2 vols. Cambridge, Mass., 1930.

MACLAY, WILLIAM. *Journal of* . . . Edited by Edgar S. Maclay. New York, 1890.

MADISON, JAMES. *Writings of* . . . Edited by Gaillard Hunt. 9 vols. New York, 1900–1910.

MARSHALL, CHRISTOPHER. *Extracts from the Diary of* . . . Edited by William Duane. Albany, 1877.

[MARTIN, JOSEPH PLUM]. *A Narrative of Some of the Adventures, Dangers, and Sufferings of a Revolutionary Soldier . . . Written by Himself.* Hallowell, Maine, 1830.

McCLELLAN, JOSEPH. "Journal, August, 1780–April, 1782." *Pennsylvania Archives,* ser. 2, vol. 11, 1880; pp. 601–614, 659–706, 709–762.

McCURTIN, DANIEL. "Journal of the Times at the Siege of Boston since our Arrival at Cambridge, Near Boston, August 9, 1775." In *Papers Relating Chiefly to the Maryland Line*, edited by Thomas Balch. See Washington and the Revolution, *infra*.

McMICHAEL, JAMES. "Journal, May, 1776–May, 1778." *Pennsylvania Magazine of History and Biography*, vol. 16, 1892; pp. 129–159. *Pennsylvania Archives*, ser. 2, vol. 15, 1893; pp. 195–218.

MENONVILLE, M. DE. "Military Journal, October, 1781." *Magazine of American History*, vol. 4, 1880; pp. 449–452.

MONROE, JAMES. *Writings of* . . . Edited by Stanislaus M. Hamilton. 7 vols. New York, 1898–1903.

MONTRESOR, JOHN. *The Montresor Journals*. Edited by G. D. Scull. New-York Historical Society Collections, vol. 14. New York, 1882.

MOREAU, JACOB NICOLAS. *Mémoire Contenant le Précis des Faits, Avec Leurs Pièces Justificatives, pour Servir de Réponse aux Observations envoyées par les Ministres d'Angleterre, dans les Cours de l'Europe*. Paris, 1756.

MORGAN, DANIEL. *Cowpens Papers, Being Correspondence of General* . . . Compiled by Theodorus B. Myers. Charleston, S. C., 1881.

MORRIS, GOUVERNEUR. *The Diary and Letters of* . . . Edited by Anne C. Morris. 2 vols. New York, 1888.

NASH, SOLOMON. *Journal of* . . . Edited by Charles I. Bushnell. New York, 1861.

NEW YORK MORAVIAN CONGREGATION. "Congregational Journal." *Pennsylvania Magazine of History and Biography*, vol. 1, 1877; pp. 133–148, 250–262.

NICHOLAS, EDWARD. *The Nicholas Papers. Correspondence of Sir* . . . Edited by George F. Warner. 4 vols. London, 1886–1920.

*The Operations of the French Fleet under the Count de Grasse in 1781–1782 as Described in Two Contemporaneous Journals*. New York, 1864.

ORME, ROBERT. "Military Journal, February–July, 1755." In Sargent, Winthrop. *The History of an Expedition against Fort du Quesne in 1755*. See Washington and the French and Indian War, *infra*.

PAINE, THOMAS. *The Writings of* . . . Edited by Moncure D. Conway. 4 vols. New York, 1894–1896.

PATTISON, JAMES. *Official Letters of Major General* . . . , *Commander of Artillery*. New-York Historical Society Collections, vol. 8. New York, 1876.

PERCY, LORD HUGH. *Letters of Hugh, Earl Percy from Boston and New York, 1774–1776*. Edited by Charles K. Bolton. Boston, 1902.

PITT, WILLIAM, EARL OF CHATHAM. *Correspondence of* . . . *When Secretary of State, with Colonial Governors and Military and Naval Commissioners in America*. Edited by Gertrude S. Kimball. 2 vols. New York, 1906.

PONTGIBAUD, CHEVALIER DE. *The Chevalier de Pontgibaud, a French Volunteer of the War of Independence*. Translated and edited by Robert B. Douglas. Paris, 1898.

POWELL, LEVEN. *Colonel* . . . Edited by Robert C. Powell. Alexandria, 1877.

PRICE, EZEKIEL. "Private Diary, May 23, 1775–August 17, 1776." *Massachusetts Historical Society Proceedings*, ser. 1, vol. 7, 1863–1864; pp. 185–262.

QUINCY, ELIZA SUSAN MORTON. *Memoir of the Life of* . . . Boston, 1861.

REED, JOSEPH. *The Life and Correspondence of* . . . Edited by William B. Reed. 2 vols. Philadelphia, 1847.

RICHARDS, SAMUEL. *Diary of . . . , Captain of Connecticut Line, War of the Revolution, 1775–1781.* Philadelphia, 1909.

ROBERTSON, ARCHIBALD. *. . . His Diaries and Sketches in America, 1762–1780.* Edited by H. M. Lydenberg. New York, 1930.

ROCHAMBEAU, COMTE DE. *Mémoires Militaires, Historiques et Politiques de . . . , Ancien Maréchal de France.* 2 vols. Paris, 1809.

RODNEY, ADMIRAL LORD GEORGE. *The Life and Correspondence of . . .* Edited by Godfrey B. Mundy. 2 vols. London, 1830.

RODNEY, THOMAS. *Diary of Captain . . . December, 1776–January, 1777.* Edited by Caesar A. Rodney. Wilmington, 1888.

ROWE, JOHN. *Letters and Diary of . . .* Edited by Anne R. Cunningham. Boston, 1903.

RUSH, BENJAMIN. *Letters of . . .* Edited by Lyman H. Butterfield. 2 vols. Princeton, 1951.

RUSH, BENJAMIN. *The Autobiography of . . . , His "Travels Through Life" together with his Commonplace Book for 1789–1813.* Edited by George W. Corner. Princeton, 1948.

SERLE, AMBROSE. *The American Journal of . . .* Edited by Edward H. Tatum. San Marino, Calif., 1940.

SHARPE, HORATIO. *Correspondence of . . .* 4 vols. Archives of Maryland, vols. 6, 9, 14, 31. Baltimore, 1888–1895.

SHAW, MAJOR SAMUEL. *The Journals of . . . with a Life of the Author by Josiah Quincy.* Boston, 1847.

SHIRLEY, WILLIAM. *Correspondence of . . . , Governor of Massachusetts and Military Commander in America, 1731–1760.* Edited by Charles H. Lincoln. 2 vols. New York, 1912.

SMITH, SERGT. JOHN. "Military Journal, Sept. 4–Dec. 31, 1776." *Mississippi Valley Historical Review,* vol. 20, 1933–1934; pp. 247–270.

SMITH, WILLIAM LOUGHTON. "Diary, August, 1790 to May, 1791." *Massachusetts Historical Society Proceedings,* vol. 51, 1917–1918; pp. 20–76.

SPARKS, JARED (comp.). *Correspondence of the American Revolution, being Letters of Eminent Men to Washington, 1775–1789.* 4 vols. Boston, 1853.

SPOTSWOOD, ALEXANDER. *The Official Letters of . . .* Edited by Robert A. Brock. Virginia Historical Society Collections, new series, vols. 1 and 2. Richmond, 1833.

ST. CLAIR, ARTHUR. *The . . . Papers. The Life and Public Services of . . . with his Correspondence and Other Papers.* Edited by William H. Smith. 2 vols. Cincinnati, 1882.

STEELE, JOHN. *Papers of . . .* Edited by H. M. Wagstaff. 2 vols. Raleigh, 1924.

STEPHEN, ADAM. "Col. Stevens' [sic] Life Written by Himself for B. Rush, 1775." *Pennsylvania Magazine of History and Biography,* vol. 23, 1899; pp. 43–50.

STEUBEN, FREDERICK WILLIAM VON. *Personal Relics of . . . together with the Revolutionary Papers of William North, Aide-de-Camp to . . .* Sold by order of the present owner, William M. Austin. American Art Association Catalogue. New York, 1929.

STILES, EZRA. *The Literary Diary of . . .* Edited by Franklin B. Dexter. 3 vols. New York, 1901.

STOBO, ROBERT. *Memoirs of Major . . . , of the Virginia Regiment . . .* Pittsburgh, 1854.

SULLIVAN, JOHN. *Letters and Papers of Major-General . . .* Edited by Otis G. Hammond. 3 vols. New Hampshire Historical Society Collections, vols. 13, 14, 15. Concord, N. H., 1930–1939.

TALLMADGE, BENJAMIN. *Memoir of Colonel . . .* Edited by Henry P. Johnston. New York, 1904.

THACHER, JAMES. *Military Journal During the American Revolutionary War.* Boston, 1823.

TILDEN, JOHN BELL. "Extracts from the Journal of . . ." *Pennsylvania Magazine of History and Biography,* vol. 19, 1895; pp. 51–63, 208–233.

TILGHMAN, TENCH. *Memoir of Lt. Col. Tench Tilghman.* Compiled by Samuel Alexander Harrison. Albany, 1876.

TOMLINSON, ABRAHAM (comp.). *The Military Journals of Two Private Soldiers.* Poughkeepsie, 1855.

TRUMBULL, REV. BENJAMIN. "Military Journal, July, 1776–November, 1777." *Connecticut Historical Society Collections,* vol. 7, 1899; pp. 137–218.

TRUMBULL, JOHN. *Autobiography, Reminiscences and Letters from 1756 to 1841.* New York, 1841.

TUDOR, DEACON JOHN. *Diary.* Edited by William Tudor. Boston, 1896.

VAN CORTLANDT, PHILIP. "Autobiography." *Magazine of American History,* part 1, vol. 2, 1878; pp. 278–298.

WALDO, DR. ALBIGENCE. "Surgeon's Military Journal, Nov. 10, 1777–Jan. 8, 1778." *Historical Magazine,* vol. 5, 1861; pp. 129–134. Also in *Pennsylvania Magazine of History and Biography,* vol. 21, 1897; pp. 299–323.

WALPOLE, HORACE. *Memoirs of the Reign of King George the Second.* Edited by Lord Holland. 3 vols. London, 1847.

*The Warren-Adams Letters, Being Chiefly a Correspondence among John Adams, Samuel Adams, and James Warren.* 2 vols. Boston, 1917.

WASHINGTON, GEORGE. *The Writings of . . .* Edited by John C. Fitzpatrick. 39 vols. Bicentennial edition. Washington, 1931–1944.

WASHINGTON, GEORGE. *The Writings of . . .* Edited by Worthington C. Ford. 14 vols. New York, 1889–1893.

WASHINGTON, GEORGE. *The Writings of . . .* Edited by Jared Sparks. 12 vols. Boston, 1834–1837.

WASHINGTON, GEORGE. *The Diaries of . . .* Edited by John C. Fitzpatrick. 4 vols. Boston and New York, 1925.

WASHINGTON, GEORGE. *. . .'s Rules of Civility and Decent Behavior in Company and Conversation.* Edited by Charles Moore. Boston, 1926.

WASHINGTON, GEORGE. *Journal of my Journey over the Mountains . . . while Surveying for Lord Thomas Fairfax, . . . , in 1747–1748.* Edited by Joseph M. Toner. Albany, 1892.

WASHINGTON, GEORGE. *Daily Journal of Major . . . in 1751–1752, Kept While on a Tour from Virginia to the Island of Barbadoes, with his Invalid Brother, Maj. Lawrence Washington.* Edited by Joseph M. Toner. Albany, 1892.

WASHINGTON, GEORGE. *Journal of Colonel . . . , Commanding a Detachment of Virginia Troops, Sent by Robert Dinwiddie, Lieutenant-Governor of Virginia, across the Alleghany Mountains, in 1754, to Build Forts at the Head of the Ohio . . .* Edited by Joseph M. Toner. Albany, 1893.

WASHINGTON, GEORGE. . . .'s *Accounts of Expenses while Commander-in-Chief of the Continental Army, 1775–1783, Reproduced in Facsimile.* Edited by John C. Fitzpatrick. Boston and New York, 1917.

WASHINGTON, GEORGE. *Monuments of Washington's Patriotism: Containing . . . his Publick Accounts Kept During the Revolutionary War and . . . Documents Connected with his Command and Civil Administration; . . . Farewell Address to the People of the United States, together with an Eulogium on the Character of Washington, by Major W. Jackson.* Washington, 1838.

*Correspondence of General Washington and DeGrasse August 17–November 4, 1781.* Edited by the Institut Français de Washington. Washington, 1931.

*Washington and the West; Being George Washington's Diary of September, 1784, Kept during his Journey into the Ohio Basin in the Interest of a Commercial Union between the Great Lakes and the Potomac River . . .* Edited by Archer B. Hulbert. New York, 1905.

*Letters from George Washington to Tobias Lear.* Introduction and notes by William H. Samson. Rochester, N. Y., 1905.

WATSON, ELKANAH. *Men and Times of the Revolution; or Memoirs of . . . , Including Journals of Travels in Europe and America from 1777 to 1842.* Edited by Winslow C. Watson. New York, 1856.

WEBB, SAMUEL BLACHLEY. *Correspondence and Journals of . . .* Edited by Worthington C. Ford. 3 vols. New York, 1893.

WIEDERHOLD, ANDREAS. "Military Journal, Nov., 1776." *Pennsylvania Magazine of History and Biography,* vol. 23, 1899; pp. 95–97.

WILD, EBENEZER. "Journal of . . ." *Massachusetts Historical Society Proceedings,* ser. 2, vol. 6, 1890–1891; pp. 78–160.

WILKINSON, JAMES. *Memoirs of My Own Times.* 3 vols. Philadelphia, 1816.

WOLCOTT, OLIVER. *Memoirs of the Administrations of Washington and John Adams, Edited from the Papers of . . . , Secretary of the Treasury.* Edited by George Gibbs. 2 vols. New York, 1846.

## WRITINGS AND BIOGRAPHIES
## OF WASHINGTON AND HIS CONTEMPORARIES

### BIOGRAPHIES

ALDEN, JOHN RICHARD. *General Charles Lee, Traitor or Patriot?* Baton Rouge, La., 1951.

ALDEN, JOHN RICHARD. *John Stuart and the Southern Colonial Frontier, a Study of Indian Relations, War, Trade and Land Problems in the Southern Wilderness, 1751–1775.* Ann Arbor, 1944.

AUSTIN, JAMES T. *The Life of Elbridge Gerry.* 2 vols. Boston, 1828–1829.

BAILEY, KENNETH P. *Thomas Cresap, Maryland Frontiersman.* Boston, 1944.

BOYD, GEORGE ADAMS. *Elias Boudinot, Patriot and Statesman, 1740–1821.* Princeton, 1952.

BRANT, IRVING. *James Madison.* 3 vols. New York, 1941.

CARSON, GEORGE BARR, JR. *The Chevalier de Chastellux, Soldier and Philosophe.* Chicago, 1944.

CARY, WILSON MILES. *Sally Cary; a Long Hidden Romance of Washington's Life.* New York, 1916.

COFFIN, CHARLES. *The Life and Services of Major General John Thomas.* New York, 1844.

COLEMAN, MARY HALDANE. *St. George Tucker.* Richmond, 1938.

CONWAY, MONCURE DANIEL. *Omitted Chapters of History Disclosed in the Life and Papers of Edmund Randolph, Governor of Virginia; First Attorney-General United States, Secretary of State.* New York, 1888.

CUSTIS, GEORGE WASHINGTON PARKE. *Recollections and Private Memoirs of Washington, by his Adopted Son, . . . , with a Memoir of the Author, by His Daugher; . . .* Philadelphia, 1861.

DELAPLAINE, EDWARD SCHLEY. *Life of Thomas Johnson.* New York, 1927.

*Dictionary of American Biography.* Edited by Allen Johnson and Dumas Malone. 22 vols. New York, 1928–1936.

*Dictionary of National Biography.* Edited by Leslie Stephen and Sidney Lee. 66 vols. London, 1885–1901.

DODSON, LEONIDAS. *Alexander Spotswood, Governor of Colonial Virginia.* Philadelphia, 1932.

DRAKE, FRANCIS S. *Life and Correspondence of Henry Knox.* Boston, 1873.

FAUNTLEROY, JULIET (comp.). *Colonel Moore Fauntleroy, his Ancestors and Descendants.* 2 vols. Altavista, Va., 1936.

FLIPPIN, PERCY SCOTT. *William Gooch, Successful Royal Governor of Virginia.* Williamsburg, 1924.

FORD, EMILY ELLSWORTH FOWLER. *Notes on the Life of Noah Webster.* Edited by Emily Ellsworth Ford Skeel. 2 vols. New York, 1912.

FORD, WORTHINGTON CHAUNCEY. *The Washington Family.* Reprint from vol. 14 of the *Writings of George Washington.* New York, 1893.

GRAHAM, JAMES. *Life of General Daniel Morgan of the Virginia Line . . .* New York, 1859.

GREENE, GEORGE WASHINGTON. *The Life of Major-General Nathanael Greene.* 3 vols. New York, 1867–1871.

HALL, CHARLES S. *Life and Letters of Samuel Holden Parsons.* Binghamton, N. Y., 1905.

HAMILTON, JOHN C. *History of the Republic of the United States of America, as Traced in the Writings of Alexander Hamilton and of His Contemporaries.* 7 vols. Philadelphia, 1868.

HART, CHARLES HENRY, and BIDDLE, EDWARD. *Memoirs of the Life and Works of Jean Antoine Houdon, the Sculptor of Voltaire and of Washington.* Philadelphia, 1911.

HENRY, WILLIAM WIRT. *Patrick Henry; Life, Correspondence and Speeches.* 3 vols. New York, 1891.

HILL, HELEN DAY. *George Mason, Constitutionalist.* Cambridge, 1938.

HORNER, FREDERICK. *The History of the Blair, Bannister, and Braxton Families before and after the Revolution.* Philadelphia, 1898.

HUGHES, RUPERT. *George Washington.* 3 vols. New York, 1926–1930.

HUMPHREYS, FRANK LANDON. *The Life and Times of David Humphreys.* 2 vols. New York, 1917.

HUNT, LOUISA LIVINGSTON, ed. *Biographical Notes Concerning General Richard Montgomery.* Poughkeepsie, 1876.

IRVING, WASHINGTON. *The Life of George Washington.* 5 vols. Putnam, N. Y., 1856–1859.

KAPP, FRIEDRICH. *The Life of John Kalb.* New York, 1884.

KAPP, FRIEDRICH. *The Life of Frederick William von Steuben.* 2 vols. New York, 1859.

KOONTZ, LOUIS KNOTT. *Robert Dinwiddie.* Glendale, Calif., 1941.

LEAKE, ISAAC Q. *Memoir of the Life and Times of General John Lamb . . .* Albany, 1850.

LEARY, LEWIS. *That Rascal Freneau, A Study in Literary Failure.* Brunswick, N. J., 1941.

LODGE, HENRY CABOT. *George Washington.* 2 vols. Boston, 1889.

LUSHINGTON, STEPHEN. *The Life and Services of General Lord Harris.* London, 1811.

MALONE, DUMAS. *Jefferson and His Time.* 2 vols. to date. Boston, 1948–1951.

MARSHALL, JOHN. *The Life of George Washington, Commander in Chief of the American Forces . . . and First President of the United States . . .* 5 vols. London, 1804.

MARTYN, CHARLES. *The Life of Artemas Ward, The First Commander-in-Chief of the American Revolution.* New York, 1921.

MAYS, DAVID JOHN. *Edmund Pendleton, 1721–1803.* 2 vols. Cambridge, Mass., 1952.

MCREE, GRIFFITH JOHN. *Life and Correspondence of James Iredell.* 2 vols. New York, 1857–1858.

PALMER, JOHN MCA. *General von Steuben.* New Haven, 1937.

PARKMAN, FRANCIS. *Montcalm and Wolfe.* 2 vols. Boston, 1884.

PARTRIDGE, BELLAMY. *Sir Billy Howe.* London, 1932.

PICKERING, OCTAVIUS, and UPHAM, CHARLES W. *The Life of Timothy Pickering.* 4 vols. Boston, 1867–1873.

RAINIER, G. S. "A Detail of Particular Services Performed in America during the Years 1776, 1777, 1778 and 1779 by Commodore Sir George Collier, Commander-in-Chief on the American Station." *Naval Chronicle for 1814,* vol. 32; pp. 267–272. London, 1814.

ROWLAND, KATE MASON. *Life and Correspondence of Charles Carroll of Carrollton.* 2 vols. New York, 1898.

ROWLAND, KATE MASON. *The Life of George Mason.* 2 vols. New York, 1892.

SABINE, LORENZO. *Biographical Sketches of Loyalists of the American Revolution . . .* 2 vols. Boston, 1864.

SARGENT, WINTHROP. *Life of John André.* New York, 1871.

SELLERS, CHARLES COLEMAN. *Charles Willson Peale.* 2 vols. Philadelphia, 1947.

SPARKS, JARED. *The Life and Treason of Benedict Arnold.* New York, 1844.

SPARKS, JARED. *The Life of Gouverneur Morris with Selections from His Correspondence.* 3 vols. Boston, 1832.

STEINER, BERNARD C. *The Life and Correspondence of James McHenry.* Cleveland, 1907.

STILLÉ, CHARLES J. *Major-General Wayne and the Pennsylvania Line in the Continental Army.* Philadelphia, 1893.

STONE, EDWIN M. *The Life and Recollections of John Howland.* Providence, R. I., 1857.

TURNER, ELLA MAY. *James Rumsey, Pioneer in Steam Navigation*. Scottdale, Pa., 1930.

WARFEL, HARRY F. *Noah Webster, Schoolmaster to America*. New York, 1936.

WEEMS, MASON LOCKE. *The Life of George Washington; with Curious Anecdotes . . .* Philadelphia, 1918.

WESTCOTT, THOMPSON. *The Life of John Fitch, Inventor of the Steamboat*. Philadelphia, 1857.

WHARTON, ANNE H. *Martha Washington*. New York, 1897.

WINGATE, CHARLES EDGAR LEWIS. *Life and Letters of Paine Wingate*. 2 vols. Medford, Mass., 1930.

WIRT, WILLIAM. *Sketches of the Life and Character of Patrick Henry*. Philadelphia, 1817.

*The Washingtoniana: Containing a Biographical Sketch of the Late Gen. George Washington, with Various Outlines of his Character, from the Pens of Different Eminent Writers, both in Europe and America; and an Account of the Various Funeral Honors Devoted to his Memory. To which are annexed his will and schedule of his property . . .* Baltimore, 1800.

*The Washingtoniana: Containing a Sketch of the Life and Death of the Late Gen. George Washington; with a Collection of Elegant Eulogies, Orations, Poems &c, Sacred to his Memory. Also, an appendix, comprising all his most valuable public papers, and his last will and testament.* Lancaster, 1802.

## WASHINGTON AND VIRGINIA
## DURING HIS YOUTH, 1732–1752

AMBLER, CHARLES HENRY. *George Washington and the West*. Chapel Hill, N. C., 1936.

ANDREWS, CHARLES M. *The Colonial Period of American History: The Settlements*. 3 vols. New Haven, 1934.

ARMES, ETHEL. *Stratford Hall, The Great House of the Lees*. Richmond, 1936.

BAILEY, KENNETH P. *The Ohio Company of Virginia and the Westward Movement, 1748–1792; a Chapter in the History of the Colonial Frontier*. Glendale, Calif., 1939.

BALCH, THOMAS. *Letters and Papers Relating Chiefly to the Provincial History of Pennsylvania, with Some Notices of the Writers*. Philadelphia, 1855.

BALLAGH, JAMES CURTIS. *A History of Slavery in Virginia*. Baltimore, 1902.

BALLAGH, JAMES CURTIS. *White Servitude in the Colony of Virginia*. Baltimore, 1895.

BARTON, ROBERT THOMAS, ed. *Virginia Colonial Decisions; the Reports by Sir John Randolph and by Edward Barradall of the Decisions of the General Court, 1728–1741*. 2 vols. Boston, 1909.

BASSETT, JOHN SPENCER. "The Relation between the Virginia Planter and the London Merchant." *American Historical Association Annual Report*, vol. 1, 1901; pp. 551–575.

BEAUCHAMP, WILLIAM MARTIN. *Wampum and Shell Articles Used by the New York Indians*. Albany, 1901.

BEER, GEORGE LOUIS. *British Colonial Policy, 1754–1765 . . .* New York, 1907.

BEVERLEY, ROBERT. *The History of Virginia, in Four Parts*. Richmond, 1855.

BLANTON, WYNDHAM B. *Medicine in Virginia in the Eighteenth Century.* Richmond, 1931.

BRUCE, PHILIP ALEXANDER. *Institutional History of Virginia in the Seventeeth Century.* 2 vols. New York, 1910.

BRYDON, GEORGE MACLAREN. *Virginia's Mother Church and the Political Conditions under Which it Grew.* 2 vols. Richmond, 1947–1952.

BUCK, SOLON J., and BUCK, ELIZABETH HAWTHORN. *The Planting of Civilization in Western Pennsylvania.* Pittsburgh, 1939.

BURTON, L. W. *Annals of Henrico Parish . . . History of St. John's P. E. Church . . . A Complete Roster of the Vestries from 1741 to 1904 . . .* Edited and compiled by Josiah Staunton Moore. Richmond, 1904.

CHAMBERLAYNE, C. G., ed. *Bristol Parish Vestry Book and Register.* Richmond, 1898.

CHAMBERLAYNE, C. G., ed. *St. Paul's Parish Vestry Book.* Richmond, 1940.

CHAMBERLAYNE, C. G., ed. *St. Peter's Parish Vestry Book and Register.* Richmond, 1937.

CHAMBERLAYNE, C. G., ed. *Stratton Major Parish Vestry Book.* Richmond, 1931.

CLARENDON, EARL OF, EDWARD HYDE. *The History of the Rebellion and Civil Wars in England.* 6 vols. Oxford, 1827.

CONWAY, MONCURE DANIEL. *Barons of the Potomack and the Rappahannock.* New York, 1892.

CULPEPER, LORD THOMAS. "Report on Virginia in 1683." *Virginia Magazine of History and Biography,* vol. 3, 1895–1896; pp. 225–238.

DUANE, WILLIAM. *A Military Dictionary, or Explanation of the Several Systems of Discipline of Different Kinds of Troops . . .* Philadelphia, 1810.

EUBANK, HENRY RAGLAND. *Touring Historyland; the Authentic Guide Book of Historic Northern Neck of Virginia, the Land of George Washington and Robert E. Lee.* Colonial Beach, Va., 1934.

EVANS, LEWIS. *Geographical, Historical, Political, Philosophical and Mechanical Essays.* Edited by Lawrence Henry Gipson. Philadelphia, 1938.

FLIPPIN, PERCY SCOTT. *The Financial Administration of the Colony of Virginia.* Johns Hopkins Univ. Studies in Historical and Political Science, ser. 33, no. 2. Baltimore, 1915.

FLIPPIN, PERCY SCOTT. *The Royal Government in Virginia, 1624–1775.* New York, 1919.

GIPSON, LAWRENCE HENRY. *Lewis Evans; to which is added Evans' A Brief Account of Pennsylvania . . .* Philadelphia, 1939.

GLENN, THOMAS ALLEN. *Some Colonial Mansions and Those Who Lived in Them . . .* Philadelphia, 1899.

GOODWIN, RUTHERFOORD. *The William Parks Paper Mill at Williamsburg . . .* Lexington, Va., 1939.

GREEN, BENNETT WOOD. *Word-Book of Virginia Folk Speech.* Richmond, 1899.

GREENE, EVARTS BOUTELL, and HARRINGTON, VIRGINIA D. *American Population before the Federal Census of 1790.* New York, 1932.

GROOME, HARRY CONNELLY. *Fauquier during the Proprietorship . . .* Richmond, 1927.

GROOME, HARRY CONNELLY. "Northern Neck Lands." *Fauquier Historical Society, Bulletin* No. 1. Warrenton, 1921.

HARRISON, FAIRFAX. *Landmarks of Old Prince William.* 2 vols. Richmond, 1924.

HARRISON, FAIRFAX. *The Proprietors of the Northern Neck.* Richmond, 1926.

HARRISON, FAIRFAX. *Virginia Land Grants, a Study of Conveyancing in Relation to Colonial Politics.* Richmond, 1925.

HARTWELL, BLAIR, and CHILTON. *The Present State of Virginia, and the College. To which is added, the Charter for Erecting the said College, granted by their late Majesties King William and Queen Mary* . . . Edited by Hunter Dickinson Farish. Williamsburg, 1940.

HAYDEN, HORACE EDWIN. *Virginia Genealogies.* Washington, 1931.

HODGE, FREDERICK WEBB, ed. *Handbook of American Indians North of Mexico.* 2 vols. Washington, 1905.

HOPPIN, CHARLES ARTHUR. *The Washington Ancestry and Records of the McClain, Johnson, and Forty Other Colonial American Families.* 3 vols. Greenfield, Ohio, 1932.

HOWE, HENRY. *Historical Collections of Virginia . . . Relating to its History and Antiquities* . . . Charleston, S. C., 1856.

*Indian Treaties printed by Benjamin Franklin, 1736–1762.* Introduction by Carl Van Doren and notes by Julian P. Boyd. Philadelphia, 1938.

"Instructions to Lord Thomas Culpeper." *Virginia Magazine of History and Biography,* vol. 27, 1919; pp. 59–61, 326–335.

JACOBSEN, GERTRUDE ANN. *William Blathwayt, a Late Seventeenth Century English Administrator.* New Haven and London, 1932.

JAMES EDWARD WILSON, ed. *The Lower Norfolk County Virginia Antiquary.* 5 vols. Baltimore, 1895–1906.

JONES, HUGH. *The Present State of Virginia.* New York, 1865.

KEGLEY, FREDERICK B. *Virginia Frontier, 1740–1783.* Roanoke, 1938.

KERCHEVAL, SAMUEL. *A History of the Valley of Virginia.* Strasburg, Va., 1925.

LEDUC, GILBERT. *Washington and the Murder of Jumonville.* Boston, 1943.

LEE, EDMUND JENNINGS. *Lee of Virginia, 1642–1892. Biographical and Genealogical Sketches of the Descendants of Col. Richard Lee.* Philadelphia, 1895.

LEWIS, THOMAS. *The Fairfax Line. Journal of 1746.* Newmarket, Va., 1925.

MAY, EARL CHAPIN. *Principio to Wheeling, 1715–1945, a Pageant of Iron and Steel.* New York, 1945.

M'GUIRE, EDWARD CHARLES. *The Religious Opinions and Character of Washington.* New York, 1836.

MEADE, WILLIAM. *Old Churches, Ministers and Families of Virginia.* 2 vols. Philadelphia, 1857.

NEILL, EDWARD DUFFIELD. *Virginia Carolorum.* Albany, 1886.

NORRIS, J. E., ed. *History of the Lower Shenandoah Valley, Counties of Frederick, Berkeley, Jefferson and Clarke* . . . Chicago, 1890.

O'BRIEN, MICHAEL JOSEPH. *The McCarthys in Early American History.* New York, 1921.

OSGOOD, HERBERT LEVI. *The American Colonies in the Seventeenth Century.* 3 vols. New York and London, 1904–07.

PERRY, WILLIAM STEVENS, ed. *Historical Collections Relating to the American Colonial Church.* 5 vols. Hartford, 1870–1878.

*Prince William [County, Va.] The Story of its People and its Places.* American Guide Series. Richmond, 1941.

RIPLEY, WILLIAM ZEBINA. *The Financial History of Virginia, 1609–1776.* New York, 1893.

SLAUGHTER, PHILIP. *The History of Truro Parish in Virginia*. Philadelphia, 1908.

SNOWDEN, WILLIAM H. *Some Old Historic Landmarks of Virginia and Maryland Described in a Hand-book for the Tourist* . . . Philadelphia, 1894.

STANARD, WILLIAM GLOVER (comp.). *The Colonial Virginia Register. A List of Governors, Councillors and Other Higher Officials, and also of Members of the House of Burgesses, and the Revolutionary Conventions of the Colony of Virginia*. Albany, N. Y., 1902.

SUTHERLAND, STELLA HELEN. *Population Distribution in Colonial America*. New York, 1936.

TYLER, LYON G. *History of Hampton and Elizabeth City County, Virginia*. Hampton, Va., 1922.

TYLER, LYON G. *Williamsburg, the Colonial Capital*. Richmond, 1907.

WASHINGTON, ELLA BASSETT. "The Mother of Washington." *Century Magazine*, vol. 43, 1902; pp. 830–842.

WERTENBAKER, THOMAS JEFFERSON. *The Planters of Colonial Virginia*. Princeton, 1922.

WERTENBAKER, THOMAS JEFFERSON. *Virginia under the Stuarts, 1607–1688*. Princeton, 1914.

WILLIS, BYRD CHARLES. *The Willis Family*. Richmond, 1909.

WISE, JENNINGS CROPPER. *Ye Kingdome of Accawmacke; or, The Eastern Shore of Virginia in the Seventeenth Century*. Richmond, 1911.

WRIGHT, LOUIS B. *The First Gentlemen of Virginia, Intellectual Qualities of the Early Colonial Ruling Class*. San Marino, Calif., 1940.

## WASHINGTON AND THE FRENCH AND INDIAN WAR, 1753–1763

(Note: Entries relating to the war are included to the date of the Peace of Paris, but references relating directly to Washington after his retirement from the army are entered in the next section, Washington Between the Wars.)

[Anon.] *Relation de la Victoire Remportée par les François, sur un Corps de Troupes Angloises, Commandé par le Général Braddock, près l'Ohio dans l'Amérique Septentrionale, 1755*. Boston, 1939.

ALBERT, GEORGE DALLAS. *Frontier Forts of Western Pennsylvania*. Report of the Commission to Locate the Site of the Frontier Forts of Pennsylvania. Edited by Thomas L. Montgomery. 2 vols. Harrisburg, 1896–1916.

BAKER-CROTHERS, HAYES. *Virginia and the French and Indian War*. Chicago, 1928.

BALCH, THOMAS WILLING. *The Philadelphia Assemblies*. Philadelphia, 1916.

BEAUCHAMP, WILLIAM MARTIN. *A History of the New York Iroquois, now Commonly Called the Six Nations*. Albany, 1905.

BEER, GEORGE L. *British Colonial Policy, 1754–1765*. New York, 1933.

BELCHER, HENRY. *The First American Civil War, 1755–1778* . . . 2 vols. London, 1911.

BLAIR, EMMA HELEN. *The Indian Tribes of the Upper Mississippi Valley* . . . 2 vols. Cleveland, 1911.

CAMPBELL, CHARLES. *History of the Colony and Ancient Dominion of Virginia*. Philadelphia, 1860.

COURVILLE, LOUIS DE. *Mémoires sur le Canada depuis 1749 jusqua 1760.* Quebec, 1838.

DULANY, DANIEL. "Military and Political Affairs in the Middle Colonies in 1755." *Pennsylvania Magazine of History and Biography,* vol. 3, 1879; pp. 11–31.

FISHER, GEORGE H. "Brigadier General Bouquet." *Pennsylvania Magazine of History and Biography,* vol. 3, 1879; pp. 121–143.

FORBES, THOMAS. "A Journal Descriptive of Some French Forts." In *Christopher Gist's Journals.* See Writings of Washington and his Contemporaries, *supra.* Also in *Maryland Historical Magazine,* vol. 4, 1909; pp. 272–275.

FORTESCUE, SIR JOHN WILLIAM. *A History of the British Army.* 13 vols. London, 1899–1930.

HULBERT, ARCHER BUTLER. *Washington's Road (Nemacolin's Path), the First Chapter of the Old French War.* Cleveland, 1903.

HUTTON, EDWARD. *Colonel Henry Bouquet, 60th Royal Americans, 1756–1765.* Winchester, Eng., 1911.

KOONTZ, LOUIS KNOTT. *The Virginia Frontier, 1754–1763.* Baltimore, 1925.

LOWDERMILK, WILLIAM HARRISON. *History of Cumberland, (Maryland) from the Time of the Indian Town, Caiuctucuc, in 1728, up to the Present Day, Embracing an Account of Washington's First Campaign, and Battle of Fort Necessity, . . .* Washington, 1878.

MARGRY, PIERRE. *Découvertes et etablissements des français dans l'ouest et dans le sud de l'Amérique Septentrionale (1614–1754) . . .* 6 vols. Paris, 1876–1886.

MARTIN, JAMES, ed. *A New and Comprehensive Gazetteer of Virginia to 1758.* Charlottesville, 1835.

McGRADY, EDWARD. *The History of South Carolina under the Proprietary Government, 1670–1719.* New York, 1897.

MORGAN, LEWIS HENRY. *League of the Ho-de-no-sau-nee, or Iroquois.* Rochester and New York, 1851.

NEILL, EDWARD DUFFIELD. *The Fairfaxes of England and America in the Seventeenth and Eighteenth Centuries, Including Letters from and to Hon. William Fairfax, President of Council of Virginia, and his Sons Col. George William Fairfax and Rev. Bryan, Eighth Lord Fairfax, the Neighbors and Friends of George Washington.* Albany, 1868.

OSGOOD, HERBERT LEVI. *The American Colonies in the Eighteenth Century.* 4 vols. New York, 1924.

PARGELLIS, STANLEY McCRORY. *Lord Loudoun in North America.* New Haven and London, 1933.

PARGELLIS, STANLEY McCRORY, ed. *Military Affairs in North America, 1748–1765.* New York and London, 1936.

PARKMAN, FRANCIS. *The Conspiracy of Pontiac and the Indian War after the Conquest of Canada.* 2 vols. Boston, 1874.

PRITTS, JOSEPH. *Mirror of Olden Time Border Life . . .* Abingdon, Va., 1849.

SARGENT, WINTHROP. *The History of an Expedition against Fort Du Quesne in 1755.* Philadelphia, 1855.

SAVILLE, MAX. *The Diplomatic History of the Canadian Boundary, 1749–1763.* New Haven, 1940.

SIPE, CHESTER HALE. *Fort Ligonier and its Times . . .* Harrisburg, 1932.

# WASHINGTON BETWEEN THE WARS,
## 1763–1775

ABERNETHY, THOMAS PERKINS. *Western Lands and the American Revolution.* New York, 1937.

ALVORD, C. W. *The Mississippi Valley in British Politics.* 2 vols. Cleveland, 1917.

BURNETT, EDMUND CODY. *The Continental Congress.* New York, 1941.

CHAMPION, RICHARD. *American Correspondence of a Bristol Merchant, 1766–1776.* Berkeley, Calif., 1934.

CONWAY, MONCURE DANIEL, ed. *George Washington and Mount Vernon, a Collection of Washington's Unpublished Agricultural and Personal Letters.* Brooklyn, 1889.

COOK, ROY BIRD. *Washington's Western Lands.* Strasburg, Va., 1930.

EDGAR, LADY MATILDA. *A Colonial Governor in Maryland, Horatio Sharpe and his Times, 1753–1773.* London, 1912.

EDWARDS, EVERETT E. *George Washington and Agriculture.* Washington, 1931.

FARRAND, MAX. "The Taxation of Tea, 1767–73." *American Historical Review,* vol. 3, 1897; pp. 266–269.

FLIPPIN, PERCY S. *The Royal Government in Virginia, 1624–1775.* New York, 1919.

FORD, WORTHINGTON CHAUNCEY. *George Washington as an Employer of Labour.* Brooklyn, 1889.

GRAY, ARTHUR P. "Washington's Burgess Route." *Virginia Magazine of History and Biography,* vol. 46, 1938; pp. 299–315.

HAWORTH, PAUL LELAND. *George Washington, Country Gentleman.* Indianapolis, 1925.

HINKHOUSE, FRED J. *Preliminaries of the American Revolution as Seen in the English Press.* New York, 1926.

LINGLEY, CHARLES R. *The Transition in Virginia from Colony to Commonwealth.* New York, 1910.

LOSSING, BENSON J. *Mount Vernon and its Associations.* Cincinnati, 1886.

MASON, FRANCES NORTON, ed. *John Norton and Sons, Merchants of London and Virginia, being the Papers from their Counting House for the Years 1750 to 1795.* Richmond, 1937.

NETTELS, CURTIS P. *The Roots of American Civilization.* New York, 1938.

POWELL, MARY G. *The History of Old Alexandria, Virginia, from July 13, 1749 to May 24, 1861.* Richmond, 1928.

THWAITES, REUBEN GOLD, and KELLOGG, LOUISE PHELPS [eds.]. *Documentary History of Dunmore's War. . . .* Madison, Wis., 1905.

TURNER, FREDERICK J. *The Frontier in American History.* New York, 1920.

WALL, CHARLES C. "Notes on the Early History of Mount Vernon." *William and Mary Quarterly,* ser. 3, vol. 2, 1945; pp. 173–190.

WILLIAMS, SAMUEL C. *Dawn of Tennessee Valley and Tennessee History.* Johnson City, Tenn., 1937.

WILSTACH, PAUL. *Mount Vernon. Washington's Home and the Nation's Shrine.* Indianapolis, 1930.

## WASHINGTON AND THE REVOLUTION,
### 1775–1783

Anon. [An Officer of the Army, Capt. Hall] *The History of the Civil War in America. Comprehending the Campaigns of 1775, 1776, and 1777.* London, 1780.

ABBATT, WILLIAM. *The Crisis of the Revolution, Being the Story of Arnold and André* . . . New York, 1899.

ABBOTT, WILBUR C. *New York in the American Revolution.* New York, 1929.

"The Allies Before Yorktown. News From the Front." *Magazine of American History,* vol. 7, 1881; pp. 445–453.

"American Scenic and Historic Preservation Society. 19th and 20th Annual Reports to the Legislature of the State of New York." Albany, 1914. Pamphlets.

AMORY, THOMAS COFFIN. *Old Cambridge and New.* Boston, 1871.

ANDERSON, TROYER STEELE. *The Command of the Howe Brothers during the American Revolution.* London, 1936.

BAKER, WILLIAM SPOHN. *Itinerary of General Washington from June 15, 1775 to December 23, 1783.* Philadelphia, 1892.

BALCH, THOMAS WILLING. *Papers Relating Chiefly to the Maryland Line during the Revolution.* Philadelphia, 1857.

BARCK, OSCAR T. *New York City during the War for Independence.* New York, 1931.

BEAN, THOMAS W. *Washington at Valley Forge One Hundred Years Ago* . . . Norristown, Pa., 1876.

BECKER, CARL L. *The Declaration of Independence: a Study in the History of Political Ideals.* New York, 1945.

"Bibliography of the Virginia Campaign and Siege of Yorktown in 1781." Colonial National Historical Park. Yorktown, 1941. Pamphlet.

BILL, ALFRED HOYT. *The Campaign of Princeton, 1776–1777.* Princeton, 1948.

BOLTON, CHARLES KNOWLES. *The Private Soldier under Washington.* New York, 1902.

BOYD, JULIAN P. *The Declaration of Independence: the Evolution of the Text as Shown in Facsimiles of Various Drafts by its Author, Thomas Jefferson.* Princeton, 1945.

BRADDOCK, EDWARD. *Orderly Books, from Feb. 26 to June 17, 1755.* Cumberland, Md., 1878. Also in Lowdermilk, *The History of Cumberland, Maryland* . . . See Washington and the French and Indian War, supra.

BURNETT, EDMUND C. *The Continental Congress.* New York, 1942.

CHINARD, GILBERT, ed. and trans. *George Washington as the French Knew Him; a Collection of Texts* . . . Princeton, 1940.

DANDRIDGE, DANSKE. *Historic Shepherdstown.* Charlottesville, 1910.

DAWSON, HENRY BARTON. *The Assault on Stony Point, by General Anthony Wayne, July 16, 1779.* Morrisania, N. Y., 1863.

DAWSON, HENRY BARTON, ed. *New York City during the American Revolution, being a Collection of Original Papers from the MSS in the Possession of the Mercantile Library Association.* New York, 1861.

DAWSON, HENRY BARTON, ed. *Papers Concerning the Capture and Detention of Major John André.* The Gazette Series, vol. 1. Yonkers, 1866.

DAWSON, HENRY BARTON, ed. *Record of the Trial of Joshua Hett Smith for Alleged Complicity in the Treason of Benedict Arnold, 1780.* Morrisania, N. Y., 1866.

DELANCEY, EDWARD F. "Mount Washington and its Capture, Nov. 16, 1776." *Magazine of American History,* pt. 1, vol. 1, 1877; pp. 65–90.

DONIOL, HENRI. *Histoire de la Participation de la France à l'Établissement des États-Unis d'Amérique: Correspondance Diplomatique et Documents.* 5 vols. Paris, 1886–1892.

DRAPER, LYMAN COPELAND. *King's Mountain and its Heroes: History of the Battle of King's Mountain, October 7, 1780, and the Events Which Led to It.* Cincinnati, 1881.

FIELD, THOMAS W. *The Battle of Long Island with Preceding and Subsequent Events.* Long Island Historical Society, Memoirs, vol. 2. Brooklyn, 1869.

FORCE, PETER. *American Archives of a Collection of Authentick Records, State Papers . . . and Letters and other Notices of Publick Affairs, the whole Forming a Documentary History of the Origin and Progress of the North American Colonies.* 9 vols. Washington, 1837–1853.

FORD, WORTHINGTON CHAUNCEY, ed. *Defences of Philadelphia, 1777.* Brooklyn, 1897.

FORD, PAUL LEICESTER. *Orderly Books of the Revolution.* Brooklyn, 1891.

FRENCH, ALLEN. *The First Year of the American Revolution.* Boston, 1934.

FROTHINGHAM, RICHARD. *History of the Siege of Boston, and of the Battles of Lexington, Concord, and Bunker Hill.* Boston, 1849.

FUTHEY, J. SMITH. "The Massacre of Paoli." *Pennsylvania Magazine of History and Biography,* vol. 1, 1877; pp. 285–319.

GODFREY, CARLOS EMMOR. *The Commander-in-Chief's Guard, Revolutionary War.* Washington, 1904.

GOTTSCHALK, LOUIS. *Lafayette and the Close of the American Revolution.* Chicago, 1942.

GOTTSCHALK, LOUIS. *Lafayette Joins the American Army.* Chicago, 1937.

HARRELL, I. S. *Loyalism in Virginia.* Durham, 1926.

HART, ALBERT BUSHNELL, ed. *Varick Court of Inquiry to Investigate the Implication of Colonel Varick with the Arnold Treason.* Boston, 1907.

HATCH, LOUIS CLINTON. *The Administration of the American Revolutionary Army.* New York, 1904.

HEITMAN, FRANCIS B. *Historical Register of Officers of the Continental Army During the War of the Revolution; April, 1775 to December, 1783.* Washington, 1914.

HENKELS, STAN V., compiler, for Thomas Birch. "Catalogue No. 663. An Extraordinary Collection of Washington's Letters, Relics, Revolutionay Documents and the Rarest Works on American History . . . offered for sale in 1891." Philadelphia, 1891. Pamphlet.

HENKELS, STAN V., compiler, for Thomas Birch. "Catalogue No. 683. Revolutionary Manuscripts and Portraits . . . to be sold April 5th and 6th, 1892." Philadelphia, 1892. Pamphlet.

HOLMES, ASHER. "Letter on the Battle of Germantown, 1777." *New Jersey Historical Society Proceedings,* new series, vol. 7, 1922–1923; pp. 34–35.

HOWARD, GEORGE ELLIOTT. *Preliminaries of the Revolution, 1763–1775.* American Nation Series, vol. 8. New York, 1905.

Howe, Sir William. *Orderly Book of General Sir William Howe at Charlestown, Boston, and Halifax, June 17, 1775 to May 26, 1776.* Edited by Benjamin F. Stevens. London, 1890.

Jackson, Joseph. "Washington in Philadelphia." *Pennsylvania Magazine of History and Biography,* vol. 56, 1932; pp. 110–155.

James, W. M. *The British Navy in Adversity.* London, 1926.

Jameson, J. Franklin. *The American Revolution Considered as a Social Movement.* Princeton, 1926.

Jensen, Merrill. *The Articles of Confederation. An Interpretation of the Social-Constitutional History of the American Revolution, 1774–1781.* Madison, Wis., 1940.

Johnston, Henry Phelps. *The Battle of Harlem Heights, September 16, 1776.* New York, 1897.

Johnston, Henry Phelps. *The Campaign of 1776 around New York and Brooklyn.* Long Island Historical Society, Memoirs, vol. 3. Brooklyn, 1878.

Johnston, Henry Phelps. "The Evacuation of New York by the British, 1783." *Harper's Magazine,* vol. 67, 1883; pp. 909–923.

Johnston, Henry Phelps. *The Storming of Stony Point on the Hudson.* New York, 1900.

Johnston, Henry Phelps. *The Yorktown Campaign and Surrender of Cornwallis, 1781.* New York, 1881.

Jones, Thomas. *History of New York during the Revolutionary War and of the Leading Events in the Other Colonies at that Period.* Edited by Edward Floyd DeLancey, 2 vols. New York, 1879.

Kite, Elizabeth S. "General Duportail at Valley Forge." *Pennsylvania Magazine of History and Biography,* vol. 56, 1932; pp. 341–354.

Knollenberg, Bernhard. *Washington and the Revolution, a Reappraisal; Gates, Conway, and the Continental Congress.* New York, 1940.

Landers, Howard Lee. *The Battle of Camden, South Carolina.* Washington, 1929.

Landers, Howard Lee. *The Virginia Campaign and the Blockade and Siege of Yorktown, 1781 . . .* Washington, 1931.

Lasseray, André. *Les Français Sous les Treize Étoiles (1775–1783).* Paris, 1935.

"Henry Lee's Report on the Powles Operations." In Moore, *Diary of the American Revolution . . .* vol. 2, p. 207. See this section, *infra.*

Lewis, Virgil A. *History of the Battle of Point Pleasant.* Charleston, W. Va., 1909.

Lossing, Benson J. *The Pictorial Field Book of the Revolution.* 2 vols. New York, 1851–1852.

[Mauduit, Israel]. *Observations upon the Conduct of William Howe at White Plains.* London, 1779.

Mayo, Katherine. *General Washington's Dilemma.* New York, 1938.

Miller, John C. *Triumph of Freedom, 1775–1783.* Boston, 1948.

*Minutes of a Court of Inquiry upon the Case of Major John André, with Accompanying Documents, Published in 1780 by Order of Congress, with an Additional Appendix.* Albany, 1865.

Montgomery, Thomas. "The Battle of Monmouth, Described by Dr. James McHenry, Secretary to General Washington." *Magazine of American History,* vol. 3, 1879; pp. 355–363.

MOORE, FRANK (comp.). *Diary of the American Revolution from Newspapers and Original Documents.* 2 vols. New York, 1860.

MOORE, GEORGE H. *The Treason of Charles Lee, Major General.* New York, 1860.

"Mount Vernon Ladies' Association. General Washington's Swords and Campaign Equipment, an Illustrated Catalogue of Military Memorabilia in the Mount Vernon Collection." Washington, D. C., 1944. Pamphlet.

NEVINS, ALLAN. *The American States During and After the Revolution, 1775-1789.* New York, 1924.

PAINE, THOMAS. *The American Crisis.* Philadelphia, 1776.

PAULLIN, CHARLES OSCAR. *The Navy of the American Revolution* . . . Chicago, 1906.

PENNYPACKER, MORTON. *General Washington's Spies on Long Island and in New York.* Brooklyn, 1939.

ROBERTS, KENNETH, ed. *March to Quebec; Journals of the Members of Arnold's Expedition.* New York, 1938.

SCHLESINGER, ARTHUR MEIER. *The Colonial Merchants and the American Revolution, 1763-1776.* New York, 1939.

SEYBOLT, ROBERT F., ed. "A Contemporary British Account of General Sir William Howe's Military Operations in 1777." *American Antiquarian Society Proceedings,* vol. 40, 1930; pp. 69-92.

"The Siege of Boston. Letters." *Massachusetts Historical Society Proceedings,* ser. 1, vol. 14, 1875-1876; pp. 275-298.

SMITH, JOSHUA HETT. *An Authentic Narrative of the Causes Which led to the Death of Major André* . . . London, 1808.

SMITH, JUSTIN H. *Our Struggle for the Fourteenth Colony: Canada and the American Revolution.* 2 vols. New York, 1907.

STEVENS, BENJAMIN FRANKLIN (comp.). *B. F. Stevens' Facsimiles of Manuscripts in European Archives Relating to America, 1773-1783.* London, 1889-1895.

STEVENS, BENJAMIN FRANKLIN, ed and coll. *The Campaign in Virginia, 1781* . . . *The Clinton-Cornwallis Controversy, with* . . . *Manuscript Notes by Sir Henry Clinton.* 2 vols. London, 1888.

STEVENS, JOHN AUSTIN. "The Allies at Yorktown." *Magazine of American History,* vol. 6, 1881; pp. 1-53.

STEVENS, JOHN AUSTIN. "Bauman's Map of the Siege of Yorktown." *Magazine of American History,* vol. 6, 1881; pp. 54-55.

STOKES, I. N. PHELPS. *The Iconography of Manhattan Island.* 6 vols. New York, 1915-1928.

STRYKER, WILLIAM SCUDDER. *The Battle of Monmouth.* Edited by William Starr Myers. Princeton University, 1927.

STRYKER, WILLIAM SCUDDER. *The Battles of Trenton and Princeton.* Boston and New York, 1898.

STRYKER, WILLIAM SCUDDER. *The Forts on the Delaware in the Revolutionary War.* Trenton, 1901.

TARLETON, [BANASTRE]. *A History of the Campaigns of 1780 and 1781 in the Southern Provinces of North America.* London, 1787.

TAYLOR, FRANK H. *Valley Forge, a Chronicle of American Heroism.* Valley Forge Park Commission. Philadelphia, 1905.

TOWER, CHARLEMAGNE, JR. *The Marquis de Lafayette in the American Revolution;* . . . 2 vols. Philadelphia, 1895.

TREVELYAN, GEORGE OTTO. *The American Revolution.* 4 vols. New York, 1905.

TRUMBULL, JONATHAN, JR. "Minutes of Occurrences Respecting the Siege and Capture of York in Virginia . . ." *Massachusetts Historical Society Proceedings,* ser. 1, vol. 14, 1875–76; pp. 331–338.

VAN DOREN, CARL C. *The Secret History of the American Revolution.* New York, 1941.

VAN TYNE, CLAUDE H. *The Loyalists in the American Revolution.* New York, 1902.

WARD, ARTEMAS. "Orderly Book, Apr. 20–Sept. 26, 1775." *Massachusetts Historical Society Proceedings,* ser. 1, vol. 15, 1876–77; pp. 75–160.

WARREN, MERCY. *History of the Rise, Progress and Termination of the American War.* 3 vols. Boston, 1805.

WEIG, MELVIN J., and CRAIG, VERA B. "Morristown, A Military Capital of the American Revolution." Washington, 1950. Pamphlet.

WERTENBAKER, THOMAS JEFFERSON. "The Battle of Princeton." An article in *The Princton Battle Monument.* Princeton, 1922.

WHARTON, FRANCIS, ed. *The Revolutionary Diplomatic Correspondence of the United States.* 6 vols. Washington, 1889.

WILLARD, MARGARET WHEELER. *Letters on the American Revolution, 1774–1776.* Boston, 1925.

WILLIAMS, CATHERINE R. ARNOLD. *Biography of Revolutionary Heroes; Containing the Life of Brigadier Gen. William Barton and also of Captain Stephen Olney.* Providence, R. I., 1839.

WOODHULL, ALFRED A. *The Battle of Princeton, a Preliminary Study.* Princeton, 1913.

WOODMAN, HENRY. *The History of Valley Forge.* . . . Oaks, Penn., 1922.

## WASHINGTON AND THE CONSTITUTION,
### 1784–1788

AMES, HERMAN V. "Proposed Amendments to the Constitution during the First Century of its History." *American Historical Association Annual Report,* vol. 2, 1896; pp. 3–422.

ANDERSON, FRANK M. "Contemporary Opinion of Virginia and Kentucky Resolutions." *American Historical Review,* vol. 5, 1899–1900; pp. 45–63, 225–252.

BACON-FOSTER, MRS. CORRA. *Early Chapters in the Development of the Potomac Route to the West.* Records of Columbia Historical Society, vol. 15. Washington, 1912.

BAILEY, KENNETH P. *The Ohio Company of Virginia and the Westward Movement, 1748–1792* . . . Glendale, Calif., 1939.

BAKER, WILLIAM SPOHN. *Washington after the Revolution, 1784–1799.* Philadelphia, 1898.

BANCROFT, GEORGE. *History of the Formation of the Constitution of the United States of America.* 2 vols. New York, 1903.

BURKE, AEDANUS. "Considerations on the Society or Order of the Cincinnati . . ." Philadelphia, 1783. Pamphlet.

CABELL, WILLIAM. "Letter to James Higginbotham." *William and Mary Quarterly*, ser. 2, vol. 9, 1929; pp. 124–125.

DAVES, JOHN C., ed. "Proceedings of the General Society of the Cincinnati . . ." vol. 1, 1784. Baltimore, 1925. Pamphlet.

*Debates and Other Proceedings of the Convention of Virginia, Convened at Richmond, on Monday the 2d day of June, 1788, for the Purpose of Deliberating on the Constitution Recommended by the Grand Federal Convention . . .* Petersburg, 1788–1789. Reprint of 1828.

DUNBAR, LOUISE BURNHAM. *A Study of Monarchical Tendencies in United States from 1776 to 1801.* University of Illinois Studies in Social Sciences, vol. 10. Urbana, Ill., 1923.

ELLIOT, JONATHAN. *The Debates in the Several State Conventions on the Adoption of the Federal Constitution, as Recommended by the General Convention at Philadelphia in 1787. Together with the Journal of the Federal Convention . . .* 5 vols. Philadelphia, 1907.

FARRAND, MAX, ed. *The Records of the Federal Convention of 1787.* 4 vols. New Haven, 1937.

FISKE, JOHN *The Critical Period of American History, 1783–1789.* Boston and New York, 1888.

HULBERT, ARCHER B. *The Great American Canals.* Cleveland, 1904.

HUME, EDGAR E. "Early Opposition to the Cincinnati." *Americana*, vol. 30, 1936; pp. 597–638.

JENSEN, MERRILL. *The Articles of Confederation . . . 1774–1781.* Madison, Wis., 1940.

JENSEN, MERRILL. *The New Nation, a History of the United States during the Confederation, 1781–1789.* New York, 1950.

"Letter of Dr. James Craik to George Washington, Oct. 2, 1784." *American Historical Review*, vol. 28, 1923; pp. 705–722. See also Grace Nute, ed. *Washington and the Potomac,* in this section, *infra.*

MATTESON, DAVID MAYDOLE. *Washington and the Constitution.* Washington, 1931.

McHENRY, JAMES. "Papers of Dr. . . . on the Federal Convention of 1787." *American Historical Review*, vol. 11, 1906; pp. 595–624.

McLAUGHLIN, ANDREW CUNNINGHAM. *The Confederation and the Constitution, 1783–1789.* New York, 1905.

McLAUGHLIN, ANDREW CUNNINGHAM. *A Constitutional History of the United States.* New York and London, 1935.

MINER, CLARENCE E. *The Ratification of the Federal Constitution by the State of New York.* New York, 1921.

MINOT, G. R. *The History of the Insurrections in Massachusetts in the Year 1786 and the Rebellion Consequent Thereon.* Boston, 1810.

MIRABEAU, COUNT DE. *Considerations on the Order of Cincinnatus . . .* Translated from French. London, 1785.

"Mount Vernon Ladies' Association of the Union. Annual Report, 1950." Washington, D. C. Pamphlet.

NOBLE, JOHN. "A Few Notes on the Shays Rebellion." *American Antiquarian Society Proceedings*, new series, vol. 15, 1902–1903; pp. 200–232.

NUTE, GRACE L., ed. *Washington and the Potomac.* New York, 1923. Also in *American Historical Review*, vol. 28, 1923; pp. 497–519, 705–722.

PICKELL, JOHN. *A New Chapter in the Early Life of Washington in Connection with the Narrative History of the Potomac Company.* New York, 1856.

RUMSEY, JAMES. *A Short Treatise on the Application of Steam . . . to Propel Boats or Vessels of any Burthen against Rapid Currents with Great Velocity.* Philadelphia, 1788.

SANDERLIN, WALTER S. "The Great National Project; a History of the Chesapeake and Ohio Canal." *The Johns Hopkins Univ. Studies in Historical and Political Science*, ser. 64, no. 1; pp. 1–316. Baltimore, 1946.

SCHUYLER, R. L. *The Constitution of the United States: An Historical Survey of its Formation.* New York, 1923.

SPAULDING, ERNEST WILDER. *His Excellency George Clinton, Critic of the Constitution.* New York, 1938.

VAN DOREN, CARL. *The Great Rehearsal, the Story of the Making and Ratifying of the Constitution of the United States.* New York, 1948.

WARD, GEORGE WASHINGTON. "Early Development of the Chesapeake and Ohio Canal Project." *The Johns Hopkins Univ. Studies in Historical and Political Science*, ser. 17, nos. 9, 10, 11. Baltimore, 1899.

## WASHINGTON AND THE PRESIDENCY,
### 1789–[1793]

ASHMEAD, HENRY GRAHAM. "The Chester [Penn.] Washington Knew." Chester, Penn., 1916. Pamphlet.

BAILEY, THOMAS A. *A Diplomatic History of the American People.* New York, 1940.

BASSETT, JOHN SPENCER. *The Federalist System, 1789–1801.* New York and London, 1906.

BEARD, CHARLES A. *The American Party Battle.* New York, 1928.

BEMIS, SAMUEL F., ed. "Thomas Jefferson" in *American Secretaries of State and their Diplomacy.* vol. 1. New York, 1927.

BEMIS, SAMUEL F. *A Diplomatic History of the United States.* New York, 1950.

BEMIS, SAMUEL F. "The London Mission of Thomas Pinckney, 1792–1796." *American Historical Review*, vol. 28, 1923; pp. 228–247.

BOWEN, CLARENCE WINTHROP, ed. *The History of the Centennial Celebration of the Inauguration of George Washington as First President of the United States.* New York, 1892.

BOWEN, CLARENCE WINTHROP. "The Inauguration of Washington." *Century Magazine*, vol. 37, 1888–1889; pp. 803–833.

BOWERS, CLAUDE G. *Jefferson and Hamilton; the Struggle for Democracy in America.* Boston and New York, 1925.

BURT, NATHANIEL. "Address of George Washington, February 12, 1875, on the Washington Mansion in Philadelphia." Philadelphia, 1875. Pamphlet.

COGSWELL, JAMES L. "Washington's Reception as President at New York." *Historical Magazine*, vol. 4, 1860; p. 244.

*Columbia Historical Society Records.* Vol. 2, 1899; vol. 11, 1908; vol. 13, 1910; vol. 17, 1914; vol. 22, 1919. Washington, D. C.

DECATUR, STEPHEN, JR. *Private Affairs of George Washington from the Records and Accounts of Tobias Lear, Esquire, his Secretary.* Boston, 1933.

DEWEY, DAVIS R. *Financial History of the United States.* New York and London, 1936.

FORD, WORTHINGTON CHAUNCEY, ed. *The United States and Spain in 1790.* Brooklyn, 1890.

FORMAN, SAMUEL E. "The Political Activities of Philip Freneau." *The Johns Hopkins Univ. Studies in Historical and Political Science,* ser. 20, nos. 9–10. Baltimore, 1902.

FRASER, CHARLES. *Reminiscences of Charleston, Lately Published in the Charleston Courier* . . . Charleston, 1854.

GRAHAM, GERALD S. *Sea Power and British North America, 1783–1820.* Cambridge, 1941.

GRISWOLD, R. W. *The Republican Court, or American Society in the Days of Washington.* New York, 1854.

HARRISON, CONSTANCE CARY. "Washington in New York in 1789." *Century Magazine,* vol. 37, 1888–1889; pp. 850–865.

HART, JAMES. *The American Presidency in Action, 1789.* New York, 1948.

HAZEN, CHARLES D. *Contemporary American Opinion of the French Revolution.* Baltimore, 1897.

HENDERSON, ARCHIBALD. *Washington's Southern Tour, 1791.* Boston and New York, 1923.

HENKELS, STAN V. *A Description of a Collection of Washington Letters, Correctly Copied with Valuable Historical Notes, also Important Letters to General Washington . . . with Engraved Portraits . . . acquired by Mr. G. A. Ball . . . from an English Admirer of our Great General . . .* Philadelphia, 1926.

HINSDALE, MARY L. *A History of the President's Cabinet.* Ann Arbor, Mich., 1911.

HUNT, GAILLARD. *Calendar of Applications and Recommendations for Office during the Presidency of George Washington.* Washington, 1901.

HUNT, GAILLARD. *The Department of State of the United States: its History and Functions.* Washington, 1893.

IRWIN, RAY W. *Diplomatic Relations of the United States and the Barbary Powers.* Chapel Hill, N. C., 1931.

KITE, ELIZABETH S. *L'Enfant and Washington, 1791–1792.* Baltimore, 1929.

LEARNED, HENRY BARRETT. *The President's Cabinet: Studies in the Origin, Formation and Structure of an American Institution.* New Haven, London, Oxford, 1912.

MERRIAM, C. EDWARD. *History of American Political Theories.* New York and London, 1920.

MONAGHAN, FRANK. *Notes on the Inaugural Journey and the Inaugural Ceremonies of George Washington as First President of the United States.* New York, 1939.

MORRIS, MISS H. "Extracts from letter of . . . , daughter of Robert Morris, to John F. Watson concerning General and Mrs. Washington after the inauguration in 1789." *Historical Magazine,* ser. 1, vol. 8, 1864; pp. 90–101.

"Mount Vernon Ladies' Association of the Union. Annual Report, 1952." Washington, D. C. Pamphlet.

SALMON, LUCY MAYNARD. *History of the Appointing Power of the President.* New York and London, 1886.

SMITH, THOMAS E. V. *The City of New York in the Year of Washington's Inauguration, 1789.* New York, 1889.

STRYKER, WILLIAM SCUDDER. "Washington's Reception by the People of New Jersey in 1789." Trenton, N. J., 1882. Pamphlet.

TAUSSIG, FRANK W. *The Tariff History of the United States.* New York and London, 1931.

THOMAS, CHARLES MARION. *American Neutrality in 1793; a Study in Cabinet Government.* New York, 1931.

TREAT, PAYSON J. *The National Land System, 1785–1820.* New York, 1910.

TURNER, FREDERICK J., ed. *Correspondence of the French Ministers to the United States, 1791–1797.* American Historical Association Annual Reports, 1896, 1897, 1903, 1912, 1913. Washington.

TURNER, FREDERICK J. "The Diplomatic Contest for the Mississippi Valley." *Atlantic Monthly,* vol. 93, 1904; pp. 676–691, 807–817.

TURNER, FREDERICK J. "The Policy of France Toward the Mississippi Valley in the Period of Washington and Adams." *American Historical Review,* vol. 10, 1905; pp. 249–279.

WHARTON, ANNE H. "Washington's New York Residence in 1789." *Lippincott's Monthly Magazine,* vol. 43, 1889; pp. 741–745.

WHITAKER, ARTHUR P. *The Spanish-American Frontier: 1783–1795.* Boston and New York, 1927.

WILLIUS, F. A., and KEYS, T. E. "The Medical History of George Washington." *Staff Meetings of the Mayo Clinic,* vol. 17, 1942; pp. 92–96, 107–112, 116–121.

## OFFICIAL AND SEMIOFFICIAL COLLECTIONS

### GREAT BRITAIN

*Acts of the Privy Council. Colonial Series.* 6 vols. London, 1908–1911.

*British Statutes at Large from Magna Carta to . . . 1806.* Edited by Danby Pickering et al. 46 vols. Cambridge, 1762–1807.

*Calendar of British State Papers, Domestic Series.*
   1625–1638. Edited by J. Bruce. In progress. London, 1858 . . .
   1649–1650. Edited by M. A. E. Green. 13 vols. London, 1875–1876.
   1660–1661. Edited by M A. E. Green. In progress. London, 1860 . . .

*Calendar of State Papers, Colonial Series, America and West Indies, 1574–1732.* Edited by William N. Sainsbury, et al. 34 vols. London, 1860–1932.

*Calendar of Treasury Books [1660–1745].* Edited by William A. Shaw. 23 vols. London, 1897 . . .

*Historical Collections of Private Passages of State, Weighty Matters in Law, Remarkable Proceedings . . . Beginning . . . 1618 and ending . . . 1648.* Edited by John Rushworth. 8 vols. London, 1721–1722.

"Historical Manuscripts Commission. Report on American Manuscripts in the Royal Institution of Great Britain." 11th and 12th reports. London and Dublin, 1904–1906. Pamphlets.

*Journals of the Comissioners for Trade and Plantations, 1704 . . .* 14 vols. London, 1920.

SAINSBURY, WILLIAM N. "The British Public Record Office and the Materials in it for Early American History." *American Antiquarian Society Proceedings,* new series, vol. 8, 1893; pp. 376–389.

### UNITED STATES

*American State Papers, Documents, Legislative and Executive of the Congresses of the United States.* Edited by Walter Lowrie and Matthew Clarke. 38 vols. Washington, 1832–1861.

*A Compilation of the Messages and Papers of the Presidents, 1789–1908.* Edited by James D. Richardson. 11 vols. Washington, 1908.

*The Debates and Proceedings in the Congress of the United States.* Compiled by Joseph Gales. 42 vols. Washington, 1834–1856.

*Diplomatic Correspondence of the United States, 1783–1789.* 3 vols. Washington, 1837.

*Documentary History of the Constitution of the United States of America, 1787–1870.* 5 vols. Washington, 1894–1905.

*Journals of the Continental Congress, 1774–1789.* Edited by Worthington Chauncey Ford and successors. 34 vols. Washington, 1904–1937.

*Journals of the Continental Congress, 1774–1783.* Edited by Gaillard Hunt. 25 vols. Washington, 1904–1922.

*Journal of the House of Representatives of the United States, Being the First Session of the First Congress: Begun and Held at the City of New York, March 4, 1789 [to March 2, 1793].* 9 vols. Washington, 1826.

*Journal of the Executive Proceedings of the Senate of the United States of America.* 3 vols. Washington, 1828.

*Journal of the First Session of the Senate of the United States of America, Begun and Held at the City of New York, March 4, 1789 [to March 2, 1793].* 5 vols. Washington, 1820.

*Laws of the United States of America, from the 4th of March, 1789, to the 4th of March, 1815 . . .* 5 vols. Washington, 1815.

*United States Statutes at Large.* Edited by Richard Peters. 18 vols. Boston, 1845.

### STATE COLLECTIONS
#### Maryland

*Archives of Maryland.* Publications of the Maryland Historical Society. 65 vols. to date. Baltimore, 1883.

#### Massachusetts

*The Journals of Each Provincial Congress of Massachusetts in 1774 and 1775, and of the Committee of Safety, with an appendix, Containing the Proceedings of the County Conventions—Narratives of the Events of the Nineteenth of April, 1775—Papers relating to Ticonderoga and Crown Point, and other Documents . . .* Boston, 1838.

#### New Hampshire

*Provincial and State Papers.* Published by authority of the Legislature of New Hampshire. 34 vols. Concord, N. H., 1867–.

#### New Jersey

*New Jersey Archives. Documents Relating to the Colonial, Revolutionary and Post Revolutionary History of the State of New Jersey.* 47 vols. to date. Newark, 1880–.

### New York

*Documents Relative to the Colonial History of the State of New York.* Edited by Edmund Bailey O'Callaghan. First series, vols. I–XI. Albany, 1853–1861.

### North Carolina

*The Colonial Records of North Carolina.* Collected and edited by William L. Saunders. 10 vols. Raleigh, 1886–1890.

### Pennsylvania

*Pennsylvania Archives.* 9 series. Philadelphia, 1852–1856; Harrisburg, 1874–.
*Pennsylvania Colonial Records. 1683–1790.* Edited by Samuel Hazard, 16 vols. Philadelphia and Harrisburg, 1851–1853.
*Minutes of the Supreme Executive Council of Pennsylvania. Colonial Records of Pennsylvania.* 16 vols. Harrisburg, 1838–1853.

### Virginia

*Acts of the States of Virginia, Maryland, and Pennsylvania, and of the Congress of the United States, in Relation to the Chesapeake & Ohio Company; with the Proceedings of the Convention which Led to the Formation of the Said Company. Also, the Acts and Resolutions of the States of Virginia and Maryland concerning the Potomac Company* . . . Washington, 1828.
*Calendar of Virginia State Papers.* Edited by W. P. Palmer, 11 vols. Richmond, 1875–1893.
*Executive Journals of the Council of Colonial Virginia.* Edited by H. R. McIlwaine and W. L. Hall. 5 vols. Richmond, 1925–1945.
*Journals of the House of Burgesses of Virginia.* Edited by John Pendleton Kennedy and H. R. McIlwaine. 13 vols. Richmond, Va., 1905–1915.
*Journal of the House of Delegates of Virginia, 1781–1786.* Richmond, 1828. Reprint.
*Journal of the House of Delegates of the Commonwealth of Virginia* . . . *1786–1790.* Richmond, 1828. Reprint.
*Journal of the Senate of the Commonwealth of Virginia; Begun and Held in the City of Richmond on Monday the 17th day of October in the year of our Lord Christ, 1785.* Richmond, 1827.
*Legislative Journals of the Council of Colonial Virginia.* Edited by H. R. McIlwaine. 3 vols. Richmond, 1918–1919.
*Minutes of the Council and General Court of Colonial Virginia, 1622–1632, 1670–1676, with notes . . . from Original Council and General Court Records, into 1683* . . . Edited by H. R. McIlwaine. Richmond, 1924.
*Official Letters of the Governors of the State of Virginia.* Edited by H. R. McIlwaine. 3 vols. Richmond, 1927–1929.
*The Statutes at Large; Being a Collection of all the Laws of Virginia from the First Session of the Legislature, in the Year 1619.* Edited by William Waller Hening. 13 vols. Richmond, 1810–1823.

## GENERAL REFERENCES

BANCROFT, GEORGE. *History of the United States.* 10 vols. Boston, 1852–1878.

BOLTON, ROBERT. *History of Westchester County . . .* 2 vols. New York, 1848.

BRIGHAM, CLARENCE S. *History and Bibliography of American Newspapers, 1690–1820.* 2 vols. Worcester, Mass., 1947.

BURK, JOHN DALY. *The History of Virginia, from its First Settlement to the Commencement of the Revolution.* 3 vols. Petersburg, Va., 1822.

CARMAN, HARRY J., and SYRETT, HAROLD C. *A History of the American People.* 2 vols. New York, 1952.

*A Century of Population Growth from the First Census of the United States to the Twelfth, 1790–1900.* Bureau of the Census, Dept. of Commerce and Labor. Washington, 1909.

CHANNING, EDWARD. *A History of the United States.* 6 vols. New York, 1920–1925.

CHRISTIAN, WILLIAM ASBURY. *Richmond, Her Past and Present.* Richmond, 1912.

CRAVEN, AVERY O. *Soil Exhaustion as a Factor in the Agricultural History of Virginia and Maryland, 1606–1900.* Urbana, Ill., 1926.

FLICK, ALEXANDER C., ed. *History of the State of New York.* 10 vols. New York, 1933–1937.

GANOE, WILLIAM A. *History of the United States Army.* New York, 1942.

GIPSON, LAWRENCE HENRY. *The British Empire before the American Revolution.* 7 vols. New York, 1936–1949.

HOPKINS, ALFRED F. "Weapons and Equipment of the Early American Soldiers." *National Park Service.* Popular Study Series, History No. 2. Washington, 1947. Pamphlet.

HUNTER, DARD. *Papermaking; the History and Technique of an Ancient Craft.* New York, 1943.

MATTHEWS, WILLIAM (comp.). *American Diaries, An Annotated Bibliography of American Diaries Written Prior to the Year 1861.* Berkeley, Calif., 1945.

McMASTER, JOHN BACH. *A History of the People of the United States, from the Revolution to the Civil War.* 8 vols. New York, 1883–1913.

MORGAN, GEORGE. *The City of Firsts, Being a Complete History of the City of Philadelphia from its Founding, in 1682, to the Present Time.* Philadelphia, 1926.

MULLER, JOHN. *Treatise of Artillery.* London, 1780.

OBERHOLTZER, ELLIS PAXSON. *Philadelphia: a History of the City and its People, a Record of 225 Years.* 4 vols. Philadelphia, 1912.

OSGOOD, HERBERT L. *The American Colonies in the Eighteenth Century.* 4 vols. New York, 1924–1925.

RUSH, RICHARD. *Occasional Productions, Political, Diplomatic, and Miscellaneous.* Edited by his executors. Philadelphia, 1860.

SAWYER, CHARLES W. *Firearms in American History.* 2 vols. Boston, 1910.

SCHARF, J. THOMAS. *The Chronicles of Baltimore.* Baltimore, 1874.

SCHARF, J. THOMAS and WESTCOTT, THOMPSON. *History of Philadelphia, 1609–1884.* 3 vols. Philadelphia, 1884.

SCHLESINGER, A. M. and Fox, D. R., eds. *A History of American Life.* 13 vols. New York, 1927–1948.

SCHOULER, JAMES. *History of the United States of America under the Constitution.* 7 vols. New York, 1908.

STILLWELL, MARGARET BINGHAM. "Checklist of Eulogies and Funeral Orations on the Death of George Washington." *New York Public Library Bulletin,* May, 1916; pp. 403–450.

SWEM, EARL GREGG, comp. *Virginia Historical Index.* 2 vols. Roanoke, Va., 1934–1936.

WAYLAND, JOHN W. *The German Element in the Shenandoah Valley of Virginia.* Charlottesville, 1907.

WARD, A. W., ed. *The Cambridge Modern History.* 13 vols. Cambridge, Eng., 1902–1912.

WATSON, JOHN FANNING. *Annals of Philadelphia to which is Added an Appendix Containing . . . Researches and Reminiscences of Old New York City.* Philadelphia, 1830

WERTENBAKER, THOMAS JEFFERSON. *The Old South.* New York, 1942.

WILSON, JAMES GRANT, ed. *The Memorial History of the City of New York.* 4 vols. New York, 1892–1893.

WINSOR, JUSTIN, ed. *The Memorial History of Boston, Including Suffolk County, Mass., 1630–1880.* 4 vols. Boston, 1880–1881.

WINSOR, JUSTIN, ed. *Narrative and Critical History of America.* 8 vols. Boston and New York, 1884–1889.

## TRAVEL IN AMERICA

Anon. "Journal of a French Traveller in the Colonies, 1765." *American Historical Review,* vol. 26, 1921; pp. 726–747. *Ibid.,* vol. 27, 1921; pp. 70–89.

ANBUREY, THOMAS. *Travels through the Interior Parts of North America.* 2 vols. London, 1791.

AYERS, ELISHA. *A Journal of Travel in Different Parts of the United States . . .* Preston, Conn., 1847.

BRISSOT DE WARVILLE, JACQUES PIERRE. *New Travels in the United States of America.* London, 1792.

BURNABY, ANDREW. *Travels through the Middle Settlements in North America, in the Years 1759 and 1760.* London, 1775.

CARVER, JONATHAN. *Three Years Travels through the Interior Parts of North America . . .* Philadelphia, 1813.

CASTIGLIONI, LUIGI. *Viaggio negli Stati Uniti dell' America Settentrionale . . . 1785, 1786, e 1787.* 2 vols. Milan, 1790.

CHASTELLUX, FRANÇOIS JEAN, MARQUIS DE. *Voyages dans l'Amérique septentrionale dans les années 1780, 1781 & 1782.* 2 vols. Paris, 1788–1791.

GORDON, LORD ADAM. "Travels in America and the West Indies." In Mereness, *Travels in the American Colonies.* See infra, this section.

HADFIELD, JOSEPH. *An Englishman in America, 1785, Being the Diary of Joseph Hadfield.* Edited by Douglas S. Robertson. Toronto, 1933.

HOGENDORP, GIJSBERT KAREL VAN. *Brieven en Gedenkschriften van Gijsbert Karel van Hogendorp.* 7 vols. The Hague, 1866–1903.

HUNTER, ROBERT, JR. *Quebec to Carolina in 1785–1786, Being the Travel Diary and Observations of Robert Hunter, Jr., a Young Merchant of London.* Edited by Louis B. Wright and Marion Tinling. San Marino, Calif., 1943.

LEDERER, JOHANN. *Book of Travels.* Edited by Louis P. Henninghausen. Baltimore, 1889.

MAY, JOHN. *Journal and Letters of Colonel John May, of Boston, Relative to Two Journeys to the Ohio Country in 1788 and '89.* Cincinnati, 1873.

MERENESS, NEWTON D. *Travels in the American Colonies.* New York, 1916.

MICHEL, FRANCIS LOUIS. "Report of the Journey of Francis Louis Michel from Berne, Switzerland, to Virginia, Oct. 2, 1701–Dec. 1, 1702." Translated by W. J. Hinke, *Virginia Magazine of History and Biography,* vol. 24, 1916; pp. 113–141, 275–303.

MONAGHAN, FRANK. *French Travellers in the U.S., 1765–1932.* New York, 1933.

MORRISON, A. J., ed. *Travels in Virginia in Revolutionary Times.* Lynchburg, Va., 1922.

"Observations in Several Voyages and Travels in America." *William and Mary Quarterly,* ser. 1, vol. 15, 1907; pp. 143–159, 215–225.

ROBIN, CLAUDE C., ABBÉ. *Nouveau Voyage dans l'Amérique Septentrionale en l'Année, 1781; et Campagne de l'Armée de M. le Comte de Rochambeau.* Philadelphie et Paris, 1782.

SCHOEPF, JOHANN DAVID. *Travels in the Confederation (1783–1784).* Translated and edited by Alfred J. Morrison. 2 vols. Philadelphia, 1911.

SMYTH, JOHN FERDINAND DALZIEL. *A Tour in the United States.* 2 vols. London, 1784.

THWAITES, REUBEN GOLD, ed. *Early Western Travels, 1748–1846.* 32 vols. Cleveland, 1904–1907.

WALKER, THOMAS. *Journal of an Exploration in the Spring of the Year, 1750.* Boston, 1888.

## WASHINGTON AND THE ARTS

BRYAN, WILLIAM ALFRED. *George Washington in American Literature, 1775–1865.* New York, 1952.

EISEN, GUSTAV. *Portraits of Washington.* 3 vols. New York, 1932.

FORD, PAUL LEICESTER. *Washington and the Theater.* New York, 1899.

KIMBALL, FISKE. "Joseph Wright and His Portraits of Washington." *Antiques,* vol. 15, 1929; pp. 377–382.

KNOX, KATHARINE McCOOK. *The Sharples, Their Portraits of George Washington and his Contemporaries.* New Haven, 1930.

MORGAN, JOHN HILL. *Paintings by John Trumbull at Yale University of Historic Scenes and Personages Prominent in the American Revolution.* New Haven, 1926.

MORGAN, JOHN HILL, and FIELDING, MANTLE. *The Life Portraits of Washington and Their Replicas.* Philadelphia, 1931.

PENNIMAN, JAMES HOSMER. "George Washington, as Man of Letters." n.p., 1918. Pamphlet.

## MAPS

### ATLASES, GEOGRAPHIES, AND CATALOGUES

[Anon.] *The American Atlas.* J. Reid, publisher. New York, 1796.

[Anon.] *Atlas of Battles of the American Revolution.* London, 1770–1793.

ADAMS, JAMES TRUSLOW, ed. *Atlas of American History.* New York, 1943.

ADAMS, RANDOLPH G. *British Headquarters Maps and Sketches Used by Sir Henry Clinton while in Command of the British Forces Operating in North America during the War for Independence, 1775–1782* . . . Documents now preserved in the William L. Clements Library at the University of Michigan. Ann Arbor, 1928.

CARRINGTON, HENRY BEEBEE. *Battle Maps and Charts of the American Revolution.* New York, 1881.

EATON, DAVID WOLFE. *Historical Atlas of Westmoreland County, Virginia.* Richmond, 1942.

FADEN, WILLIAM. *Catalogue of a Curious and Valuable Collection of Original Maps and Plans of Military Positions Held in the Old French and Revolutionary Wars* . . . Compiled by E. E. Hale. Boston, 1862.

FADEN, WILLIAM, ed. *The North American Atlas.* London, 1777.

HULBERT, ARCHER BUTLER, ed. *The Crown Collection of Photographs of American Maps.* 5 vols. Cleveland, 1904–1908.

*A List of Maps of America in the Library of Congress* . . . Washington, 1901.

LORD, C. L. and E. H. *Historical Atlas of the United States.* New York, 1944.

MARTIN, LAWRENCE, ed. *The George Washington Atlas.* Washington, 1932.

MORSE, [JEDEDIAH]. *The American Universal Geography.* Boston, 1796.

PAULLIN, CHARLES O. *Atlas of the Historical Geography of the United States.* Washington and New York, 1932.

POWNALL, THOMAS. *A Topographical Description of the Dominions of the United States of America.* Edited by Lois Mulkearn. Pittsburgh, 1949.

### SPECIFIC MAPS

REGIONAL:

EVANS, LEWIS. "Analyses of the Map of the Middle Colonies." Gipson, Lawrence Henry. *Lewis Evans* . . . p. 171. See Washington and Virginia During his Youth, *supra.*

HULBERT, ARCHER BUTLER. *Braddock's Road and Three Relative Papers.* Cleveland, 1903.

MARSHALL, JOHN. *The Life of George Washington.* See the Writings of Washington and his Contemporaries, *supra.*

"The Colonies of Virginia and Maryland." Oldmixon, John. *The British Empire in America.* 2 vols. London, 1741. Vol. 1, p. 209.

"A Map of the Travels of George Washington." *National Geographic Society.* Engraved and printed by Redfield-Downey-Odell Co. New York, 1931.

"Early Unpublished Maps of the Mississippi and Great Lakes." Parkman, Francis. *France and England in North America.* Boston, 1879. Pp. 449–458.

WINSOR, JUSTIN. *The Mississippi Basin. The Struggle in America Between England and France, 1697–1763.* Boston and New York, 1895.

MASSACHUSETTS:

"Map of Boston with its Environs." Gordon, William. *The History of the Rise, Progress and Establishment of the Independence of the United States* . . . Vol. 2. See Bibliographical Note, *supra*.

"Environs of Boston, June, 1775." *The Remembrancer*. 3rd edition. London, for J. Almon, 1775.

"New and Correct Plan of the Town of Boston." *Gentlemen's Magazine,* August, 1775.

NEW JERSEY:

"Battle of Trenton, Dec. 26, 1776, by Three Hessian Officers." Stryker, William S. *The Battles of Trenton and Princeton*. See Washington and the Revolution, *supra*.

"Plan of Operations of General Washington Against the King's Troops in New Jersey from 26 Dec., 1776 to 3d Jan., 1777." Faden, William. *The North American Atlas*. London, 1777.

"Battle of Princeton." Bill, Alfred Hoyt. *The Campaign of Princeton, 1776–1777*. P. 102. See Washington and the Revolution, *supra*.

"Battle of Princeton." Wertenbaker, Thomas Jefferson. "The Battle of Princeton" in *The Princeton Battle Monument*. P. 75. See Washington and the Revolution, *supra*.

"Battle of Princeton." Woodhull, Alfred A. *The Battle of Princeton, a Preliminary Study*. See Washington and the Revolution, *supra*.

NEW YORK:

STOKES, I. N. *The Iconography of Manhattan Island*. See Washington and the Revolution, *supra*.

"Battle of White Plains." Rösch, John. *Historic White Plains*. White Plains, 1939.

"Stony Point." Johnston, Henry Phelps. *The Storming of Stony Point on the Hudson*. See Washington and the Revolution, *supra*.

PENNSYLVANIA:

"The Colony of Pennsylvania." *Pennsylvania Archives*. Series 1, 2, and 3. Edited by Samuel Hazard and W. H. Egle. See Official and Semiofficial Collections, *supra*.

"Map of Youghiogheny and Monongahela Rivers." *Christopher Gist's Journals*. Edited by W. M. Darlington. See Writings of Washington and His Contemporaries, *supra*.

"Map of the Monongahela River." Hulbert, Archer Butler, ed. *Washington and the West*. See Writings of Washington and His Contemporaries, *supra*.

VIRGINIA:

ROBINSON, MORGAN P. *Virginia Counties, Those Resulting from Virginia Legislation*. Richmond, 1916.

SWEM, EARL G., comp. "Maps Relating to Virginia in the Virginia State Library with the 17th and 18th Century Atlas Maps in the Library of Congress." *Virginia State Library Bulletin,* vol. 7, Richmond, 1914; pp. 33–263.

VIRGINIA: (cont'd.)

GRAY, ARTHUR P. "Washington's Burgess Route." *Virginia Magazine of History and Biography*. See Washington Between the Wars, *supra*.

"Courses of the Rappahannock and Potomac Rivers." Winsor, Justin, ed. *Narrative and Critical History of America*. Vol. 5, p. 276. See General References, *supra*.

"The Campaign of the Marquis de Lafayette and Lord Cornwallis in Virginia, in 1781." Tower, Charlemagne. *The Marquis de Lafayette in the American Revolution*. Vol. 2, p. 288. See Washington and the Revolution, *supra*.

"Plan of the Siege of York Town in Virginia." Stevens, John Austin. "The Allies at Yorktown." *Magazine of American History*, vol. 6, 1881; p. 8.

*Washington's Map of Mt. Vernon, in Facsimile from Original in Huntington Library*. Introduction by Lawrence Martin. Chicago, 1932.

## NEWSPAPERS

### CONNECTICUT

Hartford
*American Mercury*, 1784–1793 . . .
*Connecticut Courant*, 1764–1793 . . .

New Haven
*Connecticut Journal*, 1767–1793 . . .
*New-Haven Gazette*, 1784–1786.

New London
*Connecticut Gazette*, 1763–1793 . . .

### DELAWARE

Wilmington
*Delaware Gazette*, 1785–1793 . . .

### DISTRICT OF COLUMBIA

Georgetown
*Times, and Patowmack Packet*, 1789–1791.

### GEORGIA

Augusta
*Augusta Chronicle*, 1789–1793 . . .
Savannah
*Georgia Gazette*, 1763–1776, 1788–1793 . . .
*Royal Georgia Gazette*, 1779–1782.

### KENTUCKY

Lexington
*Kentucky Gazette*, 1787–1793 . . .

### MARYLAND

Annapolis
*Maryland Gazette*, 1724–1734, 1745–1793 . . .

Baltimore
*Maryland Gazette,* 1778–1779, 1783–1792.
*Maryland Journal,* 1773–1793 . . .

MASSACHUSETTS

Boston
*Boston Evening-Post,* 1781–1784.
*Boston Gazette,* 1719–1793 . . .
*Continental Journal,* 1776–1787.
*Herald of Freedom,* 1788–1791.
*Independent Chronicle,* 1776–1793 . . .
*Independent Ledger,* 1778–1786.
*Massachusetts Centinel,* 1784–1790.
*Massachusetts Gazette,* 1785–1788.
*Massachusetts Spy,* 1770–1775.
Cambridge
*New-England Chronicle,* 1775–1776.
Newburyport
*Essex Journal,* 1784–1793 . . .
Salem
*Salem Gazette,* 1781–1785.
*Salem Mercury,* 1786–1789.
Worcester
*Thomas's Massachusetts Spy,* 1775–1793 . . .

NEW HAMPSHIRE

Portsmouth
*New-Hampshire Gazette,* 1756–1793 . . .
*New-Hampshire Spy,* 1786–1793.

NEW JERSEY

Chatham
*New-Jersey Journal,* 1779–1783.
Elizabethtown
*New-Jersey Journal,* 1786–1793 . . .
Trenton
*New-Jersey Gazette,* 1778–1786.

NEW YORK

Albany
*Albany Register,* 1788–1793 . . .
Fishkill
*New-York Packet,* 1777–1783.
New York
*Daily Advertiser,* 1785–1793 . . .
*Gazette of the United States,* 1789–1790. Moved to Philadelphia in October, 1790.
*New-York Daily Gazette,* 1788–1793 . . .
*New-York Gazette, and Weekly Mercury,* 1768–1783.
*New-York Journal,* 1766–1776, 1784–1793.

*New-York Mercury*, 1752–1768, 1779–1783.
*Royal American Gazette*, 1777–1783, Alexander and James Robertson.
*Royal Gazette*, 1777–1783, Rivington.

### NORTH CAROLINA

New Bern
  *North-Carolina Gazette*, 1768–1778, 1786–1793 . . .

### PENNSYLVANIA

Philadelphia
  *Dunlap's American Daily Advertiser*, 1791–1793 . . .
  *Federal Gazette*, 1788–1793.
  *Freeman's Journal*, 1781–1792.
  *Gazette of the United States*, 1790–1793 . . . John Fenno moved this paper
    from New York in 1790.
  *General Advertiser*, 1790–1793 . . .
  *Independent Gazetteer*, 1782–1793 . . .
  *National Gazette*, 1791–1793. Freneau's Anti-Federalist views were voiced here.
  *Pennsylvania Evening Post*, 1775–1784.
  *Pennsylvania Gazette*, 1728–1793 . . .
  *Pennsylvania Herald, and General Advertiser*, 1786–1788.
  *Pennsylvania Journal*, 1742–1793.
  *Pennsylvania Mercury*, 1784–1792.
  *Pennsylvania Packet*, 1771–1790.
Pittsburgh
  *Pittsburgh Gazette*, 1786–1793 . . .

### RHODE ISLAND

Newport
  *Newport Mercury*, 1758–1793 . . .
Providence
  *American Journal*, 1779–1781.
  *Providence Gazette*, 1762–1793 . . .
  *United States Chronicle*, 1784–1793 . . .

### SOUTH CAROLINA

Charleston
  *City Gazette*, 1787–1793 . . .
  *Columbian Herald*, 1784–1793 . . .
  *South Carolina Gazette*, 1732–1775.
  *State Gazette of South-Carolina*, 1785–1793.

### VIRGINIA

Alexandria
  *Virginia Journal*, 1784–1789.
  *Virginia Gazette*, 1789–1793.
Fredericksburg
  *Virginia Herald*, 1787–1793 . . .
Petersburg
  *Virginia Gazette, and Petersburg Intelligencer*, 1786–1793 . . .

Richmond
*Virginia Gazette,* 1780–1781.
*Virginia Gazette, and General Advertiser,* 1790–1793 . . .
*Virginia Gazette and Independent Chronicle,* 1783–1789.
*Virginia Gazette, and Public Advertiser,* 1789–1793.
*Virginia Gazette, and Weekly Advertiser,* 1781–1793 . . .
*Virginia Gazette, or, the American Advertiser,* 1781–1786.
*Virginia Independent Chronicle,* 1786–1790.
Williamsburg
*Virginia Gazette,* 1736–1750, William Parks
                    1751–1761, William Hunter
                    1761–1765, Joseph Royle & Co.
                    1766–1774, Alexander Purdie and John Dixon
                    1775–1778, John Dixon and William Hunter
                    1766–1776, William Rind, John Pinkney
*Virginia Gazette,* 1775–1780, Alexander Purdie, John Clarkson and Augustine Davis

GREAT BRITAIN

London
*London Chronicle,* 1757–1793 . . .
*London Gazette,* 1665–1793 . . .

## PERIODICALS

*American Antiquarian Society Proceedings.* Worcester, Mass., 1812–1933.
*American Historical Association. Annual Reports.* Washington, 1890 . . .
*American Historical Review.* New York, 1895 . . .
*The Annual Register, or a View of the History, Politics, and Literature for the Year 1780.* Edited by J. Dodsley. London, 1753–1872.
*Century Magazine.* New York, 1870–1930.
*Columbian Magazine, or Monthly Miscellany.* Philadelphia, 1786–1790.
*Connecticut Historical Society Collections.* Hartford, 1860 . . .
*DeBow's Review. Agricultural, Commercial, Industrial Progress and Resources.* Edited by J. D. B. DeBow. New Orleans, 1846–1880.
*Gentleman's Magazine.* London, 1731–1907.
*The Historical Magazine.* Boston and Morrisania, New York, 1857–1875.
*Historical Register* . . . Edited by W. H. Egle. Harrisburg, Pa., 1883–1884.
*The London Magazine, or Gentleman's Monthly Intelligence.* London, 1732.
*Long Island Historical Society. Memoirs.* Brooklyn, N. Y., 1867–1889.
*Magazine of American History.* Chicago, 1877–1893.
*Maryland Historical Magazine.* Maryland Historical Society. Baltimore, 1906 . . .
*Massachusetts Historical Society Collections.* Boston, 1792 . . .
*Massachusetts Historical Society Proceedings.* Boston, 1791 . . .
*Mount Vernon Ladies' Association of the Union.* Annual Reports. Washington, D. C., 1858 . .
*New England Historical and Genealogical Register.* Boston, 1847 . . .
*New Jersey Historical Society Collections.* Newark, 1846 . . .
*New Jersey Historical Society Proceedings.* Newark, 1847 . . .

*New-York Historical Society Collections.* New York, 1811–1859.

*Niles' Weekly Register.* Baltimore, 1811–1849.

*Pennsylvania Historical Society Collections.* Philadelphia, 1851–1853.

*Pennsylvania Historical Society. Memoirs.* Philadelphia, 1826–1895.

*Pennsylvania Magazine of History and Biography.* Historical Society of Pennsylvania. Philadelphia, 1877 . . .

*Register of Pennsylvania.* Edited by Samuel Hazard. Philadelphia, 1828–1835.

*The Remembrancer; or Impartial Repository of Public Events.* Edited by John Almon. London, 1775–1784.

*Southern Literary Messenger.* Richmond, 1834–1864.

*Tyler's Quarterly Historical and Genealogical Magazine.* Richmond, 1920 . . .

*The Virginia Almanac for the Year of our Lord God 1756, Being Bisextile or Leap Year.* Williamsburg, 1756.

*Virginia Historical Magazine.* Richmond, 1891–1892.

*Virginia Historical Register, and Literary Companion.* Richmond, 1848–1853.

*Virginia Historical Society Collections.* Richmond, 1833–1892.

*Virginia Law Journal.* Richmond, 1877 . . .

*Virginia Magazine of History and Biography.* Richmond, 1893 . . .

*The West Virginia Historical Magazine Quarterly.* Charleston, West Virginia, 1901 . . .

*Western Pennsylvania Historical Magazine.* Pittsburgh, 1918 . . .

*William and Mary College Quarterly Historical Magazine,* Williamsburg, 1892 . . .

# INDEX

*Compiled by Donald M. Allen*